SIMON DE CRAMAUD AND THE GREAT SCHISM

Simon de Cramaud
and the
Great Schism

HOWARD KAMINSKY

Rutgers University Press

New Brunswick

New Jersey

Library of Congress Cataloging in Publication Data

Kaminsky, Howard, 1924–
Simon de Cramaud and the Great Schism

Includes index.
1. Cramaud, Simon de, ca. 1345–1423.
2. Schism, The Great Western, 1378–1417.
3. Catholic Church—France—History.
4. France—Church history—Middle Ages, 987–1515.
I. Title.
BX4705.C7815K35   282'.09'023   81-17764
ISBN 0-8135-0949-1   AACR2

Contents

Preface

I FIRST met Simon de Cramaud more than fifteen years ago in the *Libri de Schismate* of the Vatican Archive, when I was looking for something else. It turned out that volume after volume of that seductive collection carried references, in the text or marginalia, to a personage called "the patriarch," who was obviously one of the enemies of Pope Benedict XIII and who seemed important enough to make me wonder why I had never heard of him. A few hours with Noël Valois's *La France et le Grand Schisme d'Occident* remedied my ignorance and at the same time evoked a certain sympathy for Simon de Cramaud, patriarch of Alexandria, whose leading role in the French union program was noted in some detail but whose character and accomplishments seemed to share in the distaste that Valois obviously felt for the French subtraction of obedience as well as in his contempt for what he regarded as its failure. Both Simon and his program were awarded more substance in Johannes Haller's *Papsttum und Kirchenreform*—but again with a tone of hostility and scorn, this time because of Simon's lack of interest in anything resembling a political ideal; Haller's enthusiasm went rather to the ardent Gallican Pierre Leroy and the inflexible papalist Benedict XIII. Having myself arrived at a time of life when the successes of calculating egoism seemed more interesting than idealism in any of its political forms, I dug in, so to speak, began to put my mind in resonance with Simon's, and tried to look at the Great Schism and the councils that ended it from his point of view. As yet I had no particular intention of writing anything. That came in due time—not "as I sat musing amidst the ruins of the Capitol," but as I was sitting in the penumbras of the Bibliothèque Nationale, transcribing one of the manuscript copies of the patriarch's major treatise, *De substraccione obediencie*, in order to study it. That was a good while ago, but I still remember a colleague passing my desk, looking at my half-filled notebook, and asking in tones of *num* whether I was making an edition. "Of course not," I replied, and then began to contemplate just that. A few years later I realized that there would be a monograph in my future as well.

If the reader feels at this point that he is being told more than he needs to know, he is asked to consider the above fragment of autobiography as merely the most economical way of explaining how an apparently peculiar approach to the history of the Great Schism was forced upon the author by his originally unfocused study of the primary sources. For it turned out that Simon's treatise could only be understood in the light of Brian Tierney's *Foundations of the Conciliar Theory*, and this understanding has revealed the depth and substance of the French program that the treatise justified. The "way of abdication," or *via cessionis*, and the subtraction of obedience that implemented it, appear, not as failed experiments that at best cleared the way to conciliarism, but rather as manifestations of the identical corporatist ecclesiology that animated the councils of Pisa and Constance. At the same time, the political history of the French program can only be reconstructed as a story whose hero is Simon de Cramaud, and when we work out in detail the sequence of events in which he moved from the presidency of the First Paris Council in February 1395 to the presidency of the Council of Pisa in 1409, we see that the latter council was not the successor to the French program but rather its consummation. All of which, finally, requires an equally detailed study of Simon himself—his life, career, affinities, desires, achievements—for without an understanding of his mentality as revealed in these dimensions of his behavior, the canonist, publicist, politician, statesman, diplomat, and lifelong client of the duke of Berry can only be treated as a sort of black box about which we know everything except how things were brought together inside. The reconstruction of a mentality in these terms has nothing to do with "psychohistory" but is rather the creation of a minimal persona whose cognitive utility is nothing more than its capacity to integrate the diverse actions of the subject it represents. Simon the whole person is forever beyond our reach.

My edition of Simon's treatise is being published by the Medieval Academy of America. This monograph, while related to it genetically, is an independent essay in the interpretation of the Great Schism and its resolution. It is not a history of the Schism, or of the general councils, or of the French polity in the reign of Charles VI—all subjects that urgently demand monographic treatment in their own right—and this disclaimer will explain why in these matters much is omitted and much is taken at second hand. It is really Simon's story, along with the thesis that this is in fact the big story of how the Schism was ended; there is also a more adventurous thesis, that the structure of public action in that period and the ideas relevant to it are to be understood as individuals' play in the game of Estate, which was different from the games that make up our own world of social and personal meanings.

The Social Science Research Council, the American Council of Learned

Societies, the John Simon Guggenheim Memorial Foundation, the University of Washington, and Florida International University have all been involved in the material support of my work. The Bibliothèque Nationale, the Archives Nationales, the Bibliotheca Apostolica Vaticana, and the Archivio Segreto Vaticano, I thank for providing their services free to a foreign scholar. M. François Villard, director of the Archives départementales de la Vienne in Poitiers, I thank for the same reason and also for the very kind and helpful interest he has taken in my work. I also owe much to Fredric Cheyette, who initiated me into the scholarly mysteries of Paris when we were both on leave there. Hartmut Hoffmann's contributions to this book have been so numerous and important that I am ashamed to list them; a few are duly identified in the notes to Chapter III. Also for Chapter III, I wish to acknowledge the use of my article, "The Early Career of Simon de Cramaud" which appeared in *Speculum* 49 (1974):499–534. Finally, I also wish to thank The Bibliothèque Nationale for the use of the photograph appearing on this book's jacket.

Abbreviations

ADV	Archives départementales de la Vienne (Poitiers)
AHP	*Archives historiques du Poitou*
ALKG	*Archiv für Literatur- und Kirchengeschichte des Mittelalters*, 5, 6, 7 (Berlin, 1889, 1892, 1900)
Ampl. coll.	*Veterum scriptorum et monumentorum amplissima collectio*, ed. E. Martène & U. Durand, 7 (Paris, 1724)
AN	Archives Nationales, Paris
ASV	Archivio Segreto Vaticano
Auber	Abbé Auber, "Recherches sur la vie de Simon de Cramaud, cardinal, Évêque de Poitiers," *MSAO*, 7 (1840)
BdeC	Bourgeois de Chastenet, *Nouvelle histoire du Concile de Constance* (Paris, 1718), *Preuves*
BN	Bibliothèque Nationale, Paris
Bouvet, *Somnium*	*L'apparicion Maistre Jehan de Meun et le Somnium super materia scismatis d'Honoré Bonet*, ed. Ivor Arnold (Paris, 1926)
BSAO	*Bulletin de la Société des antiquaires de l'ouest*
Buisson	L. Buisson, *Potestas und Caritas. Die päpstliche Gewalt im Spätmittelalter* (Cologne, 1958)
Bulaeus	C. E. Du Boulay (Bulaeus), *Historia universitatis parisiensis*, 4, 5, 6 (Paris, 1668, 1670, 1673)
CUP	*Chartularium universitatis Parisiensis*, ed. H. Denifle & E. Chatelain, 3 (Paris, 1894)
Douët-d'Arcq	L. Douët-d'Arcq, *Choix de pièces inédites relatives au règne de Charles VI*, 2 vols. (Paris, 1863, 1864)
DRTA	*Deutsche Reichstagsakten*, ed. J. Weizsäcker, 3, 6 (Berlin, 1877, 1886)

DSO   Simon de Cramaud, *De substraccione obediencie*, ed. H. Kaminsky (Cambridge, Mass., in press)

Église   E. Delaruelle, et al., *L'Église au temps du Grand Schisme et de la crise conciliaire*, 1 vol. in 2, *Histoire de l'Église*, 14 (1962)

Ehrle, *Alpartil*   F. Ehrle, ed., *Martin de Alpartils Chronica actitatorum temporibus domini Benedicti XIII*, 1 (Paderborn, 1906)

Favier, *Finances*   Jean Favier, *Les finances pontificales à l'époque du Grand Schisme d'Occident, 1378–1409* (Paris, 1966)

GDGSO   *Genèse et débuts du Grand Schisme d'Occident.* Colloques internationaux du Centre national de la recherche scientifique, no. 586 (Paris, 1980)

Gerson, *Oeuvres*   Jean Gerson, *Oeuvres complètes*, ed. P. Glorieux, 6, *L'oeuvre ecclésiologique* (Paris, 1965)

Haller, *PKR*   Johannes Haller, *Papsttum und Kirchenreform*, 1 (Berlin, 1903)

Kaminsky, "Cession"   Howard Kaminsky, "Cession, Subtraction, Deposition: Simon de Cramaud's Formulation of the French Solution to the Schism," *Studia Gratiana*, 15 (1972)

Kaminsky, "Early Career"   Idem, "The Early Career of Simon de Cramaud," *Speculum*, 49 (1974)

Kaminsky, "Politics"   Idem, "The Politics of France's Subtraction of Obedience from Pope Benedict XIII, 27 July 1398," *Proceedings of the American Philosophical Society*, 115 (1971)

Lehoux   Françoise Lehoux, *Jean de France, duc de Berri, sa vie, son action politique (1340–1416)*, 4 vols. (Paris, 1966, 1966, 1968, 1968)

Mager, *Entstehung*   Wolfgang Mager, *Zur Entstehung des modernen Staatsbegriffs, Akademie der Wissenschaften und der Literatur in Mainz, Abhandlungen,* no. 9 (1968)

Mansi   J. D. Mansi, ed., *Sacrorum conciliorum nova et amplissima collectio*, 22, 26, 27 (Venice, 1784)

Mollat, *Popes at Avignon*   Guillaume Mollat, *The Popes at Avignon,*

1305–1378, trans. J. Love (London, 1963) from the 9th French ed., *Les papes d'Avignon* (Paris, 1949)

MSAO — *Mémoires de la Société des antiquaires de l'ouest*

Nordberg — Michael Nordberg, *Les ducs et la royauté: Études sur la rivalité des ducs d'Orléans et de Bourgogne 1392–1407* (Uppsala, 1964)

Ordonnances — *Ordonnances des rois de France de la troisième race*, ed. D. F. Secousse, 6, 7, 8, 9 (Paris, 1745, 1749, 1750, 1755)

Palmer, *EFC* — J. J. N. Palmer, *England, France and Christendom, 1377–1399* (London, 1972)

Perroy, *L'Angleterre* — Édouard Perroy, *L'Angleterre et le Grand Schisme d'Occident*, 1 (Paris, 1933)

Polemik — Franz Bliemetzrieder, *Literarische Polemik zu Beginn des Grossen abendländischen Schismas* (Vienna, 1910)

Post, *Studies* — Gaines Post, *Studies in Medieval Legal Thought* (Princeton, 1964)

Renouard, *Avignon Papacy* — Yves Renouard, *The Avignon Papacy 1305–1403*, trans. D. Bethell (London, 1970) from *La Papauté à Avignon* (Paris, 1954)

RSD — *Chronique du religieux de Saint-Denys contenant le règne de Charles VI.*, ed. L. Bellaguet, vols. 1–6 (Paris, 1839, 1840, 1841, 1842, 1844, 1852)

Swanson — R. N. Swanson, *Universities, Academics and the Great Schism* (Cambridge 1979)

Thes. nov. — *Thesaurus novus anecdotorum*, ed. E. Martène & U. Durand, 2 (Paris, 1717)

Tierney, *Foundations* — Brian Tierney, *Foundations of the Conciliar Theory* (Cambridge, 1955)

Ullmann, *Origins* — Walter Ullmann, *The Origins of the Great Schism* (London, 1948)

Valois — Noël Valois, *La France et le Grand Schisme d'Occident*, 4 vols. (Paris, 1896, 1896, 1901, 1902)

SIMON DE CRAMAUD AND THE GREAT SCHISM

CHAPTER ONE

The Great Schism in the Western Church and the Age of Schism in Europe

ON 13 SEPTEMBER 1376* Pope Gregory XI, sixth in a line of French popes who had ruled the universal church from Avignon, left that city for Rome, taking with him seventeen of the twenty-three cardinals and many functionaries of the papal government. On 27 March 1378 he died there, and on 8 April the predominantly French College of Cardinals, importuned and threatened by the Romans, elected an Italian to replace him: Bartolomeo Prignano, archbishop of Bari and longtime official of the papal Curia, who took the name of Urban VI. A month later the cardinals had been convinced by Urban's hostile, domineering, and intemperate behavior that they had made a mistake; they began to desert him and by the end of June all the French cardinals were gathered along with other papal officials in Anagni, where on 9 August they formally declared that Urban's election had been invalid because of intimidation. On 20 September at Fondi they went further, with the tacit support of three Italian cardinals who had joined them, and elected a new pope, Cardinal Robert of Geneva, who became Clement VII. Supported by King Charles of France and his brother Duke Louis of Anjou, Clement eventually won the allegiance of Scotland, the Spanish realms, Queen Joanna of Naples, and other powers in the French orbit; but he failed to win wider recognition nor could his few allies in Italy overcome the hostility of most of their countrymen. He had to return to Avignon, 20 June 1379, with the hope that his own propaganda and French diplomacy might make him universal. But the rest of Europe with very few exceptions continued to recognize Urban, who stayed in Italy. The Great Schism in the Western church had begun.[1]

A Clementist contemporary who read the chronicles of papal history

---

Dating: The French reckoned the year from Easter to Easter; thus, for example, "1391" began on Easter Sunday 26 March 1391 and ran to 13 April 1392 (the day before Easter of that year). At the same time, 1 January was considered New Year's Day for all other purposes. The papacy began the year on Christmas Day (25 December). It will be noted that the French system (*mos gallicus*) sometimes makes it difficult to fix a year in modern style. All dates in this work have been put into the modern style.

1. Valois, 1:8–303; *Église:* 3–44.

I

counted twenty-one previous schisms but concluded that "there never was a case like this one."[2] For both popes had been elected by the same College of Cardinals, whose assertion that the first election was invalid because of intimidation could be judged only by their own testimony to that effect, which however seemed to many to be vitiated by the evidence of their behavior in recognizing Urban for over a month after the election.[3] Noël Valois, who has provided the most complete and exact canvass of the facts, concluded that "the solution escapes the judgement of history," and many other historians have agreed with him,[4] while those who have not prove him right anyway by arguments that fail to end the debate.[5] The solution escapes not only the judgement of history but that of religion, for the Roman Catholic church has never officially declared which side was schismatic, in spite of its evident belief in the sole legitimacy of the Urbanist line.[6] Indeed, twenty years after 1378, argu-

---

2. *Super scismatibus*, ASV, *Arm. 54*, t. 22, fols. 10r–19v; fol. 11v: "XXII^m. scisma fuit presens, maius et melius coloratum aliquo alio. . . . Item nota quod similis casus nunquam fuit isti." Here and throughout, all translations into English have been made by me unless otherwise noted. Cf. similar remarks by Raymond Bernard, 21 August 1383, in *Thes. nov.*, 2:1125.

3. The case against the cardinals' testimony is put best by Ullmann, *Origins*, esp. Chs. 3–5; all contemporary polemics made the point; see, e.g., Simon de Cramaud's observations, App. II, Pt. II, "Theses," and the texts noted later in this chapter.

4. Valois, 1:82; cf., e.g., *Église*: 7 f., and Guillaume Mollat in *The Cambridge Medieval History*, 7 (Cambridge, 1932):291, with a bibliographical note. While most non-French (and some French) historians have judged Urban VI legitimately elected (see the following note), there are signs of a modern swing to skepticism if not Clementism: e.g., in Olderico Přerovský, *L'Elezione di Urbano VI e l'insorgere dello scisma d'occidente, Miscellanea della Società Romana di storia patria*, 22 (Rome, 1960); K. A. Fink, "Zur Beurteilung des grossen abendländischen Schismas," *Zeitschrift für Kirchengeschichte*, 73 (1962):338; August Franzen, ed., *Das Konzil von Konstanz* (Freiburg, 1964): 5–7; Richard Trexler, "Rome on the Eve of the Great Schism," *Speculum*, 42 (1967):489–509. Some recent work indeed reacts against this new tendency: W. Brandmüller, "Zur Frage nach der Gültigkeit der Wahl Urbans VI.," *Annuarium historiae conciliorum*, 6 (1974):78–120 (Urban's election was valid—contrary to Přerovský—but Clement's may have been too: "Das Schisma-Problem ist also nach wie vor offen"); Marc Dykmans, "La troisième élection du pape Urbain VI," *Archivum historiae pontificiae*, 15 (1977):217–264. The issues are discussed later in this chapter.

5. Valois, 1:4–7, reviews the conflicting opinions; cf. Alexander Flick, *The Decline of the Medieval Church*, 1 (London, 1930):263. Ullmann, *Origins*, explicitly rejects Valois's indeterminacy (p. 170) and argues the Urbanist case; a new preface in the otherwise unchanged 1972 reprint reaffirms his view but accepts the thesis of the other side as well: Urban was indeed "megalomaniac and insane." Some Urbanist scholars (E. Pasztor, R. Bautier) represented in *GDGSO* vindicate Urban's sanity and stress his extreme devotion to religious and institutional reforms that the cardinals simply could not accept.

6. The Italianized papacy since the Schism has reused "Clement VII" and "Benedict XIII," but there has been no explicit decision. See Valois, 1:4; Flick, *Decline of the Medieval Church*: 263, Denis Bethell, "Appendix," in Renouard, *Avignon Papacy*: 135.

ing for a program of ending the Schism by disregarding the question of legitimacy, Simon de Cramaud would observe that a solution was both impossible and undesirable, and in any case far less important than the obvious fact that *both* contenders were guilty of making the Schism by their contention. Even St. Peter, Cramaud wrote, would have to have his papacy taken away from him if that were the only way to end a schism like the present one.[7] This sort of commonsense thinking applied to an issue that popes and papalists preferred to envelop in mystique seems to have appealed to several political leaders in the 1390s—John of Gaunt, for example, who thought that neither contender was a true pope and that both should give way to a new one, and Coluccio Salutati, who did not doubt that Urban had been elected under duress ("otherwise so many French cardinals would hardly have voted for an Italian") but noted that the cardinals had spoiled their case by not complaining until after Urban had begun to castigate them and "show himself to be their superior."[8] But the same could have been said even in 1378 when the issues of fact and law were no different from those perceived in the 1390s, and if Europe's powers responded to the events of 1378 by choosing sides, thereby making the Schism Great, it was not because the case for either contender was so overwhelming as to compel adherence. The Schism was created by acts of the will—not, of course, a will to rend the seamless garment of Jesus Christ, but a will to pursue one's own interests and sympathies even though doing so meant destroying the unity of the church. The judgement attributed to King Richard II in 1394, speaking of the cardinals, could apply just as well to the secular decision makers: "They should certainly have suffered every evil rather than cause such a scandal."[9]

The mentality making for schism was of course complex. One sees its obvious aspect at the surface of practical politics. The political community of France, for example, drew many benefits from having a French papacy in Avignon controlling the French church, and the Schism itself allowed Duke Louis of Anjou to hope for an Italian kingdom as reward

---

7. See App. II, Pt. II, "Schism and Heresy," and Pt. III, at the very end.

8. For Gaunt's dictum see below; Salutati's letter to Margrave Jobst of Moravia, 20 August 1397, *Thes. nov.*, 2:1156.

9. See also Michel de Boüard, "L'empereur Robert et le Grand Schisme d'Occident," *Mélanges d'archéologie et d'histoire*, 48 (1931):215: "Crise d'origine politique, le Schisme eut de nombreuses et profondes conséquences politiques; trop nombreux étaient les souverains, voire les aventuriers dont l'affaiblissement du pouvoir temporel et spirituel de l'Église faisait le jeu, pour que certains ne fussent tentés, sinon de refuser toute collaboration à la solution de la crise, du moins de proposer des remèdes dont le premier effet fût de leur procurer à eux-mêmes quelque avantage." His *La France et l'Italie au temps du grand Schisme d'Occident: Les origines des guerres d'Italie* (Paris, 1936) develops this thesis; but cf. *Église*: 27 n. 1. For Richard's view see Bouvet, *Somnium*: 89.

for conquering the Urbanists of Italy.[10] England at last had a pope who did not support her French enemy and perhaps, as some remarked, would have given her allegiance to whichever contender the French had rejected.[11] The Western Electors of the Empire were Urbanist for similar reasons, and one can understand why France's allies in Spain and Scotland sooner or later supported Clement. But such calculations only raise the deeper question of how Europe had come to the point of allowing immediate political interests to determine allegiance and in many cases conviction in so crucial a matter as papal legitimacy, which involved not only the sacredness of the church but also, in the minds of some, the validity of sacraments, the legitimacy of titles to benefices, and the chances of salvation.[12] The point becomes still clearer when we note the failure of those who urged at the beginning that the inchoate schism be nipped in the bud by a general council of the universal church, held to

---

10. For the significance of the Avignon papacy in French public life, see below, at nn. 51, 80. The association of the Schism with French efforts to conquer parts of Italy is treated by Valois, *passim*; E. Jarry, "*La voie de fait* et l'alliance franco-milanaise, 1386–1395," *Bibliothèque de l'École des Chartes*, 53 (1892):213–253, 505–570; Boüard, *France et l'Italie*.

11. Valois, 3:76 n. 3; the passage quoted here as anonymous was written by Simon de Cramaud, ca. 1400.

12. While the common people were probably unaffected by the Schism (see Jean Favier in *GDGSO*: 15 f.), the educated might well feel concern. Some theologians indeed identified the sacred entity of the church with the pope: "The pope, not the church, is the successor of Christ"; "The church has legitimacy from the pope"; "The pope *is* the church." See Michael Wilks, *The Problem of Sovereignty in the Later Middle Ages* (Cambridge, 1963): 31–33 and index, s.v. "pope"; Bernard Guillemain, *La cour pontificale d'Avignon 1309–1376* (1962; repr. Paris, 1966): 90 f.; *Église*: 513–516. That obedience to the pope was prerequisite to salvation had been stated in the famous *Unam Sanctam* of 1302 and was asserted by some canonists; John Wyclif rejected it in principle and noted how the Schism had reduced all such papalist tenets to absurdity—J. Loserth, ed., *Tractatus de potestate pape* (London, 1907): 247 f.: "Cum ex famosis principiis legistarum oportet facere sub pena peccati mortalis quicquid papa mandaverit, oportet credere ut fidem, quicquid in excommunicacione et infidelitate papa decreverit. . . . Sentencia autem catholica . . . stat in isto, quod nec . . . Urbano nec Roberto tenetur fidelis credere, nec est de substancia fidei explicite credere alterum eorum esse papam." But there must have been others who, like Salutati, believed that the schismatic side lacked sacerdotal jurisdiction and went on to deny the validity of its sacraments and ordinations (*Thes. nov.*, 2:1160 f.); Jean Gerson found it necessary to refute these ideas (*De modo se habendi tempore schismatis*, Gerson, *Oeuvres*, 6:29–34). Simon de Cramaud at first expressed a more limited concern, no doubt shared by many, about the legitimacy of benefice titles conferred by a pope who might later be judged schismatic; he cited the drastic severity practiced by Alexander III and other victors in past schisms—see his letter to the archbishop of Canterbury, *Thes. nov.*, 2:1232; also App. II, Pt. III. Later, in 1406, he raised the more radical set of doubts (BdeC: 120 f.). Since there were plenty of grounds for doubt about both sides, some felt that nothing done during the Schism

be the "ordinary"—that is, legally normal—remedy in a case of the sort.[13] For the council they had in mind was a "way of justice" (*via iusticie*) that would have judged one claimant to be rightful pope, the other one and his adherents to be schismatics, and this mode of solution was rejected by all decisive voices then and always. When, much later, the councils of Pisa and Constance did end the Schism, it was not by deciding between the rival papacies but by terminating all of them,[14] in accord with the political imperatives laid out in the 1390s as seen above. The Schism began as one thing, it was resolved as another, and that transformation is the main subject of its history. The problem here is usually overlooked by historians whose interest lies in the ideas of conciliarism: they treat the making of the Schism as a calamity; ask which side was right; go on to disapprove of the subsequent decade or so as a period of feckless inaction; regard the attempted solutions of 1395–1408 as failures expressing a yearning for unity; and seize on fifteenth-century conciliarism as the saving solution born of theological or canonistic ingenuity. Calamity, however, is only the negative aspect perceived by disapproval; the Schism also had a positive aspect as a construction created by treating the church as an object of political interest—and this style of thought not only made the Schism but developed it and then, after the pattern of political interests had shifted, decreed its end by means of a policy that sacrificed the papal interest in legitimacy to the political prerequisite of non-judgement.

While the application of political interest to the papacy was a commonplace of medieval history and indeed the cause of many of the previous schisms, the later Middle Ages brought a new dimension to the old story. Earlier schisms had been struggles for control of the papacy; the Great Schism originated in the collaboration of all parties to divide

---

was any good—Bouvet, *Somnium*: 109: "Querunt jam layci an crisma quod conficitur isto tempore sit salutiferum, utrum congrue hodie baptizetur, utrum ad sacros promoti per illum et per istum recipiant potestatem."

13. Michael Seidlmayer, *Die Anfänge des grossen abendländischen Schismas* (Münster, 1940): 121 ff., with full references to the older literature, of which the most important item is Franz Bliemetzrieder, *Das Generalkonzil im grossen abendländischen Schisma* (Paderborn, 1904): 1–103. That a general council was considered the "ordinary" remedy (in the legal sense of the word) is clear from the sources—e.g., Simon de Cramaud, App. II, Pt. I, and in his glosses on the "Fundamenta vie iusticie," AN, J 518, fol. 339v: "viam concilii dumtaxat ordinariam reputo." Tierney, *Foundations*, shows how this general consensus was formed.

14. The discrepancy between the conciliarisms of 1378 ff. and 1398 ff. is noted by F. Ehrle, *ALKG*, 6:139; Haller, *PKR*: 199 f., 306 f., 314, 331; Bliemetzrieder, *Generalkonzil*: vi, vii; Valois, 4:494 ff.; Seidlmayer, *Anfänge*: 193; Swanson: 49. See also Ch. VII, below.

the papacy in two, and for at least a decade and a half the aspects of consolidation and stabilization on both sides were far more prominent than either political or military actions by one side against the other. This readiness of Europe to settle down with two papacies for an indefinite period shows that the spiritual dimension of the papacy as the vicariate of Christ was not uppermost in men's consideration of the problem, for the papacy in this sense could not be thought of as divisible. Papal governance of the church, on the other hand, was readily divisible in its institutional structures, and it was precisely the extraordinary elaboration of these structures achieved in the previous century and a half that caused Europe's secular and ecclesiastical leaders to see the reality of the papacy above all in its objectified forms. That was why, as Salutati observed in 1397, "everyone seemed ready to believe in the pope from whom he would get more profit and 'honor,'"[15] a point made often enough in the course of the Schism.[16] A number of writers went further and observed that if the Great Schism was deeper and more stubborn than previous ones, it was because in earlier times the popes had not acquired the power to levy revenues from the clergy and control appointments to all major (and many minor) benefices; hence, it was argued, the papacy itself was coveted as it would not have been earlier, and hence the upper clergy everywhere identified their interests with those of the popes who had given them their benefices.[17] As far as matters like these were concerned, it was more important that one's own pope be recognized as rightly exercising papal powers in one's own land than that the world know which of the two contenders was the true vicar of Christ.

The tendency to see the realities of the ecclesiastical institution in

---

15. Letter to Jobst of Moravia, *Thes. nov.*, 2:1158.

16. Cf. Cramaud's letter to the archbishop of Canterbury in 1401 (*Thes. nov.*, 2:1241): "Et multi sunt reges et praelati qui altero istorum obedire se dicunt, si ad nutum ipsorum de spiritualibus disponant. Tunc enim et non aliter obediunt." For an example see Seidlmayer, *Anfänge*: 315–317, the text of the king of Castile's demands for a drastic reduction of papal power to collate and collect, as the price of the king's recognition of Clement VII in 1381.

17. John Wyclif, e.g., in his *De pontificum Romanorum schismate* in *Select English Works of John Wyclif*, ed. Thomas Arnold, 3 (Oxford, 1871):242 (I modernize the forms): "It seemeth that dissension of this popehood is for covetise of worship [i.e., honor] and winning of this world. . . . For if the pope hold cleanly that that Christ gave to Peter, he should have goods of virtues and travail with poverty, and none of this worldly glory. . . . But who would then strive thus for the pope's office?" Pierre Plaoul said much the same before the Parlement of Paris, 7 September 1406 (AN, X 1A 4787, fol. 425v): "Ecclesia lamentabiliter dissipatur, cuius dissipacionis medium est pinguedo temporalitatis, que si non esset non essent qui pugnarent pro ea. Et istud est quod facit scisma." See Haller, *PKR*: 357 ff. For loyalty to the pope as giver of benefices, see Simon de Cramaud's treatise, App. II, Pt. II.

each territory as more interesting than abstract questions about papal legitimacy corresponded to certain late-medieval modes of thought about public affairs.[18] One of them, much studied in recent years, was the use of Romano-canonical legal concepts to grasp the supra-personal reality of communities and offices in church and state—or rather, to create this reality. As far as the church was concerned, the way had been prepared by the twelfth century, when "the church" had come to be thought of for practical purposes less as "the ensemble of the faithful under the working of Christ" than as "a great apparatus of grace to which the faithful must submit in order to receive the working of Christ."[19] The apparatus was in general the clerical institution headed by the papacy; but in particular it consisted of all the local churches, each of which had its properties, jurisdictions, and other rights vested in those holding offices within it. The thirteenth-century canonists, especially Innocent IV and Hostiensis, worked to create the legal concepts to represent these realities.[20] Each diocesan church was treated as a corporation in the legal sense, with the bishop as head and the canons as members; and on this basis the lawyers discussed such practical problems as how decisions for the whole were to be made by bishop and canons together, just how and to what effect the bishop represented his church, and how the often-conflicting interests within the church were to be resolved. The key concept was the welfare of the church-corporation, its "status" or estate, which represented not only the corporation's proper functioning and the stability of its property, powers, and revenues, but also its structures of order and regulation that secured these things.[21] The church's estate was its supreme interest—its "public utility" or "common good"—to which the individual interests or "private utility" of both head and members had to be subordinate as the part to the whole.[22] We shall see the dynamics of this distinction at work in Simon de Cramaud's doctrine later on; here we note that while older spiritual concepts of the church

---

18. See, e.g., *Église*: 899.

19. Yves Congar, "L'ecclésiologie de S. Bernard," *Analecta sacri ordinis cisterciensis*, 9 (1953):179.

20. The following discussion is based in good part on Tierney, *Foundations*: 106–153, with some simplification and differences of pointing.

21. Yves Congar, "Status ecclesiae," *Studia Gratiana*, 15 (1972):21 f., notes the twelfth-century shift (I would say extension) of the meaning of *status* from health and stability to *règlement*, hierarchical order, public powers. Cf. Michael Wilks, "Corporation and Representation in the *Defensor Pacis*," ibid.: 253 ff.; and Post, *Studies, passim*, for discussion of the many important meanings of the concept of *status*.

22. Post, *Studies, passim*; but cf. Mager, *Entstehung*: 13–16, for the difference between medieval and modern notions of the "public." That "utilitas publica debet preferri private" was a commonplace of legal writers. There is more on this below; and cf. App. II, Pt. III, "Reply to 'It Is not Allowed,'" no. 9.

did not disappear after the twelfth century, they were pushed into the background of public thought by legal concepts designed to secure the "status" of each corporate church in relation to the rights of its head and members. The bishop inevitably came to be regarded less as the husband or personification of his church than as its president or "procurator"—its agent. Inasmuch as the whole church was thought of in similar terms, its head, the pope, was correspondingly reduced to the procurator of "the general status of the universal church." Canonists discussed the ways in which his ordinary powers could be rationally defined; they preferred not to dwell on his power to rise above such limitations; and the legal mind was led into thinking of the pope, too, as merely the president of a corporation, with his individual rights, including his title to office, subordinate to the public utility. One could go on to talk of bureaucratization, routinization, and *Entzauberung*, but the point is already clear: the choice offered in 1378 to all the decision makers of Europe—to help make the Schism or not—may have been difficult, but it was not particularly awesome, and political interest prevailed in almost every case.[23]

The second mode of thought involved in the Schism ran counter to the first, with which it nevertheless combined; it consisted in the apprehension of all possessed things, no matter how diverse, in terms of the homogeneous category of property right. In France, even public offices were so treated, in spite of the Roman-law distinction between *res publica* and *res privata* that all in principle acknowledged; individuals often sold their offices to others. A royal ordinance of 24 January 1387 prohibited such private sale of major offices but explicitly allowed it for petty ones, and an ordinance of 4 January 1408 shows that in fact even major offices like those of *bailli* and royal attorney were being bought and sold among individuals. In the sixteenth century the crown itself would sell such offices openly and regularly.[24] Lawsuits in our period often resulted from conflicts over personal title to offices—that is, over property right in them—and references to the principle of non-vendibility usually appear as mere random throw-ins on either side. Thus, for example, Gontier Col, when sued in 1417 over a royal secretaryship,

---

23. The advocates of a general council in 1378 ff. evidently thought that restoring the unity of the papacy was the supreme good; see n. 13 above. Valois, 1:239, 302 f., rightly emphasizes the factor of sincere conviction in many choices of allegiance, but one may doubt his premise that interest and conviction are mutually exclusive explanations; in any case he is not talking about the primary choice, between ending the Schism and making it.

24. Bernard Guenée, *Tribunaux et gens de justice dans le bailliage de Sens à la fin du moyen âge* (Paris, 1963): 170–175, a corrective of R. Mousnier, *La vénalité des offices sous Henri IV et Louis XIII* (Rouen, 1945), in regard to the late-medieval period.

defended his title on several grounds, but also alleged that his rival had bought the office, "which was forbidden," and that in any case the one who had sold it had never really held it. The other party replied with a charge that Col himself had bought and sold the office many times.[25] A similar reification affected church benefices—not that these were bought and sold privately, but rather, that the litigation over property right in them, which occupied an unbelievable amount of clerical time, induced a way of thinking in which "a prebend was only the right to take that prebend's revenues and emoluments" and in which "spiritual" referred to the portion of a bishop's revenues that derived from ecclesiastical jurisdiction, tithes, and the like, in contrast to the temporal revenues from landlordship and other secular rights.[26] No one denied that there was indeed such a thing as a prebend apart from its revenues, but the operational definition focused on these because they were what interested the clerical careerists. We shall see a similar reification of "obedience" as something to be "subtracted" from a pope: it designated very concretely the objects of the particular powers and revenue rights that the pope possessed.

So it was with the papal office itself. The question of who was the true pope was conceived of as the question of which contender had the right to the papacy—or rather *in* the papacy, *habere ius in papatu*, this being understood as a special case of *ius in re*, the formula for a real benefice right.[27] But this right was treated as simply an individual's property right in a thing, as the formula implies.[28] Thus even a theologian, perhaps Jean Gerson, could write in 1391: "While the office of the papacy is a dignity concerning the common good, nevertheless as far as

25. AN, X 1A 4791, fols. 229rv, 240v–241r. Cf. the exchange in 1426 between Jean de Cramaud and the bishop of Poitiers, the former claiming that he had sold the captaincy of the Albigeois for 2,000 francs to help out his late uncle Simon, the latter primly countering that Simon would not have wanted such an office to be sold: "Il n'est a presumer qu'il eust voulu offices estre vendues, et maxime de judicature" (AN, X 1A 9198, fols. 179v, 185v; cf. below, Chs. III, IX).

26. AN, X 1A, 35, fol. 169r: Simon de Cramaud's argument in 1387, with a reference to an earlier *arrêt* in which Parlement had agreed that "prebenda nichil aliud erat quam fructuum et emolumentorum ipsius prebende percepcio." See also Haller's discussion of the reification of church offices, *PKR*: 184, with a quotation from the *Speculum aureum*: "Nomina quasi ad sola temporalia commoda translata videntur et non officia, sed beneficia nuncupantur." For the material sense of "spiritual," see AN, X 1A 4789, fol. 55r, a plea in 1411 by Simon de Cramaud, archbishop of Rheims: "Defend l'opposant et dict qu'il est archevesque . . . et pair de France, . . . et non obstant celle noblesse n'a pas de temporel iii mille et de spirituel ii mille [francs]."

27. Examples of such formulations can be found in Simon's treatise, App. II, *passim*, and in the texts cited just below.

28. Carl Gross, *Das Recht an der Pfründe* (Graz, 1887): 172–187.

the person of the pope is concerned it is a private good."[29] It is instructive
to see this sort of thinking at work in the very beginning of the Schism
in a discussion between Cardinal Pierre Flandrin and Pedro Tenorio,
archbishop of Toledo, over the validity of Urban VI's election; for the
discussion turned on the technical legal problem of the conditions under
which acquisition of property right in a benefice (*proprietas, ius in re*) was
distinguishable from acquisition of possession of it (*possessio*).[30] But as far
as property was concerned, even mere possession created a sort of substance, and in another passage Flandrin referred to the fact that Urban
VI "possessed the papal estate [*statum papalem*] de facto" and urged him
"to lay down the papal estate."[31] Thus the papal status or estate, unlike
the vicariate of Christ, could be possessed de facto by someone who may
not have possessed it *de jure* and so would not have been the true pope.
Urban's partisans were not begging the question, therefore, in arguing
that "justice required" that Urban or his successor be restored to "the
possession of the papacy of which he had been despoiled."[32] This legal
style of thought made it possible to conceive of a divided papacy, for
while there could not be two vicars of Christ, two heads of Christ's
body, there could quite well be two or even more men who each possessed papal estate, in the sense of actually wielding papal powers,
exacting revenues, and enjoying obedience. Simon de Cramaud worked
routinely with this sense of "papacy" as material and hence divisible. In
1414, for example, he refuted the argument that Gregory XII could not
renounce his papacy without incurring mortal sin: "Where is the papacy
that he cannot renounce without mortal sin? I see only Carlo de Malatesta and a few others!"[33] Or again, he charged that Benedict XIII wanted
only "to keep that part of the papacy which he possesses."[34] Simon of

---

29. Gerson, *Oeuvres*, 6:10 f. Cf. the subtractionist treatise of 1399 written by the
canonist Bernard Alamant, bishop of Condom, ASV, *Arm.* 54, t. 26, fol. 59r: "Licet iste
pontificatus sit officium publicum, . . . tamen quod Silvester ille presideat, hoc sibi dat
ius assumpcionis illius privatum personaliter sibi quesitum et sibi proprium, et tale ius
personale et sibi privatum dicuntur habere clerici in titulis beneficiorum"; and fol. 61r:
"quamvis dicatur nobis quod ille vel iste ius vel non ius habeant in pontificatu Romano,
vel dicatur quod ambo ius habent vel quod neuter: illa iura privata privatim non
inquirimus."
    30. Tenorio's letter to Flandrin, *Thes. nov.*, 2:1105; Flandrin's reply, *Polemik*: 81 f.
    31. *Polemik*: 60, 62.
    32. E.g., in the first letter of the University of Oxford to the king of England, 1396
(Bulaeus, 4:776 f.): "Iustitia exigente ut . . . Urbanus VI qui de possessione papatus
fuerat spoliatus, sit in suo successore . . . restitutus."
    33. "Ubi est ergo papatus, quem iste non posset dimittere sine mortali peccato, non
video, nisi Karolum de Malatestis . . . et paucos alios"—Simon's glosses on a letter of
Cardinal John Dominici, 1414, ed. H. Finke, *Acta Concilii Constanciensis*, 1 (Münster,
1896):285.
    34. Simon's treatise, App. II, Pt. III, "Reply to 'It Is not Allowed,'" no. 7.

course knew that "papacy" also meant something more abstract than concrete obediences and powers and was in this sense indivisible, but the material sense was the working one. So it was in most minds in political society, and this explains much. The structure of the Schism from beginning to end as a reduction and indeed disintegration of the papacy can be understood in large part as the work of a mentality that already conceived of church and papacy in reified terms.

The nature and import of this mentality were well understood at the time by religious spirits who were revolted by the identification of "the church" with this-worldly estate. We may single out the Czech theologian Matthew of Janov (d. 1393), who responded to the Great Schism by noting that there neither was nor could be any schism in "the congregation of the holy men and women of God, living in and moved by the spirit and life of Jesus Christ."[35] From about 1200 on, however—in a vaguely Joachite periodization that Matthew shared with others who had studied in Paris—this true spiritual church had been progressively overwhelmed by the institutional establishment "abounding in riches and glory," enjoying "the greatest peace of this world," and ruled by a papacy that sapped the local life of the church by its financial aggrandizement, its usurpation of rights of appointment to benefices, and its grants of privileges that undermined episcopal authority. Thus "the great Antichrist had extended his swollen body throughout the church."[36] Henceforth the simple faith of Christ had been pushed aside by "Greek rules, Aristotelic justice, Platonic sanctity, and gentile rites and honor"; it had also been overlaid by an endless multiplicity of cults, beliefs, rituals, and religious orders.[37] These growths within the church were intimately related to the increasing complexity of the society in which the church was established, and Matthew did not see the matter otherwise: "Every division or diversity which even in the slightest point damages the union of Christ's family or the similarity in it of each to each—even diversity in external goods and way of life—is directly contrary to the working of the Holy Spirit." The origin of the Great Schism could be fixed accordingly: "The workings of men which have destroyed unity and caused schism in the body began in externals, in the division of goods, and then proceeded within to the division of minds and spirits."[38] It was only by virtue of this division that the Great Schism had

---

35. Matthiae de Janov, *Regulae veteris et novi testamenti*, ed. V. Kybal, 2 (Innsbruck, 1909):158. See in general Howard Kaminsky, *A History of the Hussite Revolution* (Berkeley, 1967): 14–23.

36. Matthiae de Janov, *Regulae*, 1 (1908):178 f.; 4 (1913):133. See below, Ch. VII, at n. 44, for a Parisian use of the same periodization.

37. Matthiae de Janov, *Regulae*, 1:209 f.

38. Ibid., 2:175, 187 f.

taken shape as a political construction of hostile realms and peoples: "All
are divided from each other, dispersed and torn apart, through their
kings and for the sake of their kings; they regard other Christians as
aliens to be fought and killed."[39] My explanation of how Europe's Christians had come to the point of sacrificing church unity to their several
this-worldly interests aimed to show how the Schism had been possible;
Matthew's explanation includes mine but goes deeper, to suggest that
the Schism was indeed inevitable, inasmuch as the objectification of the
church in societal structures had subjected it to all the dissensions,
diversities, and contradictions of a complex, pluralistic society oriented
to mastery and enjoyment of this world. Europe had reached a point at
which church unity was no longer possible.

On this reading of history, the Great Schism appears not as an episode
but as the end of one era and the start of another. Whatever the cardinals of 1378 may have desired, the Schism they occasioned "began the
destruction of the medieval papacy"; for it caused, allowed, or provoked
important changes that were not reversed by the restoration of a more or
less united papacy in 1417. Papal prestige was diminished; the European
churches were further territorialized as clerical estates of their respective
polities—a situation expressed more and more clearly in the theory and
practice of Gallicanism and its analogues—and it was during the Schism
that Hussite Bohemia began its secession from the Roman system. Furthermore, in a change closely related to all the others, the reduction of
papal power during the Schism and in the general councils that ended it
entailed a great reduction of papal revenues. While these were not
"almost annihilated" as Martin V would claim, they did remain at only
one-third of what they had been in the Avignon period.[40] And the reunited papacy, strongly Italianized in composition and interests, came
under repeated attack from the Europe it claimed to direct; the contradictions manifested at the Council of Pavia-Siena (1423–1424) exploded
at the Council of Basel (1431–1449), where they led to a new schism
and a new counter-pope, Felix V (1439–1449). The papal victory over
Basel did not restore the status quo ante and did not recover Hussite
Bohemia, nor did the papacy itself ever adjust to the new realities. The
final secession of most of northern Europe from the Roman obedience,

---

39. Ibid., 2:192.

40. For the comparison with Avignon see Peter Partner, "Papal Financial Policy in
the Renaissance and Counter-Reformation," *Past and Present*, no. 88 (August 1980):20,
citing J. Haller, *Concilium Basiliense*, 1 (Basel, 1896):168. For Martin V's claim, in a
letter of 10 March 1419, see F. Ehrle, *Historia bibliothecae romanorum pontificum*, 1 (Rome,
1890):670. See in general *Église*: 203 ff., 295–447; Favier, *Finances*: 689; G. Holmes,
Europe: Hierarchy and Revolt (London, 1975): 174.

beginning in 1517, was only another stage in the schismatic process, and not the last one.

Perspectives of this sort suggest the wider frame of reference in which the Great Schism's constructive dimensions can be represented along with its disintegrative tendencies as special cases of a historical dialectic at work in other spheres of public life as well, and over a vastly longer period than that of the Schism. The "perpetuall and restlesse desire of Power after power, that ceaseth onely in Death," which Thomas Hobbes saw as "a generall inclination of all mankind," was more likely the special dynamic of the aristocratic Western European society that had incorporated war into its higher culture and its fundamental structures of public order.[41] From at least the twelfth century on, the development of that order appears in a double aspect as both the self-aggrandizement of kings and princes, and the struggle of nobles, corporations, estates, and regions to preserve their rights in the face of central power's integrating action. The result of such processes was a rhythm of alternations as a prince's thrust to increase his power was supported by some estates but sooner or later evoked resistance and counter-thrust from others, either within the political community of the whole or by regional groupings of estates against the claims of central power.[42] "Counter-thrust" is a negative definition, as are revolt, rebellion, revolution, separatism, regionalism, particularism; more specific terms are apt to be pejorative: subversion, treason, heresy, terrorism, crime, schism. What our political vocabulary lacks is a set of terms that would do justice to the constructive dimension of these movements, which in most countries frustrated tendencies to absolutism and imposed the more effective integrating structures of the political dialectic. For both princes and estates were dedicated to the security of property rights, which required effective central government as well as the recognition that the "estate" of the propertied orders was itself a property right, not to be liquidated

---

41. *Hobbes's Leviathan* (Oxford, 1909): 75. Cf. C. B. Macpherson, *The Political Theory of Possessive Individualism* (Oxford, 1962): 19–59; I think the features he attributes to the "possessive market society" of seventeenth-century England appear already in the later Middle Ages. Cf. V. G. Kiernan's remarks about the Western European state as a warlordship and by-product of war, in "State and Nation in Western Europe," *Past and Present*, no. 31 (July 1965):31.

42. The dualist structures of "Old Europe," from the twelfth to the eighteenth century, have been defined in a number of contexts by Dietrich Gerhard; see, e.g., his "Periodization in European History," *American Historical Review*, 61 (1956):900–913. Also Otto Brunner, "Inneres Gefüge des Abendlandes," *Historia Mundi*, 6 (Bern, 1958):319 ff.; Otto Hintze, "Typologie der ständischen Verfassungen des Abendlandes," *Historische Zeitschrift*, 141 (1930):229–248; É. Lousse, *La société d'ancien régime*, I (Louvain, 1943). These are only pioneering examples; they do not, however, stress the diachronic pattern discussed here.

from above. Princes and estates often worked in harmony but often did not, and the long view of history shows incessant alternations between the two moments, along with an inexorable growth of the integrating action of government resulting as much from episodes of conflict as from periods of overt collaboration. Whatever the positive law of the central state may have decreed, "feuds," "private" wars, local resistance, and more or less massive rebellions always remained possible in the society of Old Europe and always retained a claim to legality.[43]

Returning to our theme, we can note that the rhythm of thrust and counter-thrust has sometimes been European in extent and that the four-teenth century was such a time. Its first decades saw a widespread reac-tion against strong monarchy: in the England of Edward II (1307–1327), in France from the last year of Philip IV (d. 1314), in Bohemia with the extinction of the native dynasty and the consequent baronial resurgence (1310), in a number of German principalities where estates reacted against earlier princely aggrandizement.[44] To this list we must add the French reduction of the papacy in reaction to the extreme pretensions of the thirteenth century manifested in the pontificate of Boniface VIII (d. 1303); the result was a line of southern-French popes who resided in Avignon, appointed an overwhelming majority of French cardinals, and were responsive to the wishes of the royal house of France. The middle of the century saw similar parallels in a temporary balance of forces under princes who were strong and popular but whose increased power was based on collaboration with their upper estates, rather than on overt attempts to diminish the estates' rights. Such princes were Edward III in England (1327–1377), Charles V in France (1364–1380), Henry II in Castile (1369–1379), Casimir the Great in Poland (1333–1370), Louis the Great in Hungary (1342–1382), and Charles IV in Bohemia and the Empire (1346–1378). Again we must add the papacy, whose increase in power took place within the framework of the Avignon system, involv-ing a collaborative relationship between pope and cardinals, and an intensified subjugation of territorial churches on the basis of collabora-tion and profit sharing between the papacy and the secular princes.[45] It is striking that in all these cases including the papacy the terminal dates fall within a short span of years around 1375, after which a good deal of European political history consists of various modes of reaction led by

---

43. Otto Brunner, *Land und Herrschaft*, 4th ed. (Vienna, 1959), *passim*.

44. For the German case, Hans Spangenberg, *Vom Lehnstaat zum Ständestaat* (Munich, 1912): 38–93.

45. I cite only a few authorities. Haller, *PKR*: 116–118; Mollat, *Popes at Avignon*: 305–310; Ullmann, *Origins*: 6 f.; W. A. Pantin in C. Lawrence, ed., *The English Church and the Papacy in the Middle Ages* (London, 1965): 164 f., 188; Geoffrey Barraclough, *Papal Provisions* (Oxford, 1935): 62.

the uppermost estates of princes, barons, and cardinals, but often involving lower orders as well. Again a mere list will serve to declare the
thesis: the conflicts in England from the last years of Edward III on,
culminating in the struggles of the magnates against Richard II and the
Lancastrian usurpation of the crown; the exploitation of the French
monarchy by the Valois dukes, who first used the crown's power to
enhance their own appanages, then fell into civil wars that temporarily
ruined the monarchy; the wars between the Bohemian barons and King
Wenceslas IV, the Hussite movement towards a territorial church, and
later the revolutionary resistance of the Bohemian Hussite estates and
commons to Wenceslas's heir King Sigismund of Hungary and the
Empire; the opposition of the West German princes to the same Wenceslas and their effort to depose him in 1400; the turbulence of Castile
under Henry III and the chaos following his death in 1406. Perhaps the
consolidation of the mosaic of city-states in northern Italy would fit into
the picture as the positive aspect of chaos. The chronicle of revolt must
certainly include as well the popular risings of "the revolutionary years"
1378–1382: a half-dozen big ones, like the Ciompi in Florence (1378),
the English rising of 1381, the several revolts in Ghent and Bruges
(1380, 1381), the "Harelle" in Rouen and the "Maillotins" in Paris
(1382), as well as many more of lesser éclat.[46] The popular revolution of
the Taborites (1419 ff.) was even more profound.

It was precisely in this period of general reaction that the Great
Schism broke out, took on its structure, and began the sequence of crises
in the church already noted. Nor can the Great Schism be denied the
positive dimension that one recognizes in the secular reactions, although
the usual story of irresponsible cardinals selfishly plunging the whole
church into disaster does make an image of respectability seem unduly
difficult. One obtains it nevertheless by beginning with the obvious
perception that the outbreak of the Schism can be seen as either an
Italian revolt against a French papacy or a French revolt against an
Italian one (that is, it was both) and that the latter included the cardinals' self-assertion against a tyrannical pope, one who behaved as their
master, not their chief. The picture takes shape when we consider just
what France was in the late-medieval world: not one country among
others but *the* nation par excellence, the pioneer and model in many
forms of public life and culture, the dominant power whose strength,
expansion, interests, and policies focused the activity of others. In respect to the papacy, "French" princes, warriors, and churchmen were
competing with those of the Empire as representatives of Europe by the

---

46. M. Mollat & P. Wolff, *Ongles bleus, Jacques et Ciompi: Les révolutions populaires en Europe aux XIVe et XVe siècles* (Paris, 1970): 139 ff.

end of the eleventh century; from the thirteenth century on, France replaced the Empire. The European commitment implied by the papacy's aspiration to effective rule over the European churches proceeded in uneasy conjunction with the Italian orientation towards Rome and the papal states; but both lines led to French influence on the papacy, sometimes, as under Alexander III and Innocent IV, French protection of the papacy, and French penetration of the Curia. It was indeed the all-out struggle of the papacy against the Italian power of the Hohenstaufen, begun by Innocent IV, that brought France into the papacy and into Italy itself. The new era began with the advent of the French pope Urban IV (1261) and his appointment of French cardinals; then in 1264, on commission from Urban, Charles of Anjou, brother of King Louis IX, invaded Italy with French men and resources, crushed the Hohenstaufen, made himself king of South Italy and Sicily, and extended his power over Rome and the papacy, the latter coming under strong French influence exercised from both Paris and Naples. It is here that we find the roots of the Avignon papacy of the next century and the Schism that was a struggle over it; we also find the manifestations of the issue of substance that would later become more clear: a French papacy oriented primarily to governance of the European church in collaboration with Europe's secular powers, or a papacy controlled by the great Roman families, absorbed in Italian issues first of all, and taking up the Roman claims of universal supremacy asserted by the Italian popes of the previous two centuries.

The issue crystallized in the pontificate of Boniface VIII (1294–1303), whose espousal of the most extreme high-papalist principles went hand in hand with his use of papal power and resources to build up an Italian principality for his family, the Gaetani. His broader policy, focused on the recovery of Sicily from its Aragonese rulers, was certainly not anti-French, but it required the French kings to pursue interests remote from those which Philip IV at least regarded as the immediate objects of expansionist desire: the struggle over Flanders, the war with Edward I over claims in Aquitaine, and the encroachment on the western borders of the Empire. Boniface also had the misfortune to rule at a time when the kings of France and other countries were extending their sovereignty over the estates of their realms, including the clergy, who increasingly looked to the king for protection of their property and had therefore to reconcile themselves to paying him taxes and accepting royal jurisdiction in property cases. An extension of royal lordship over the clergy was ipso facto a reduction of papal lordship, and the contest was unequal enough to make the outcome foreseeable. To cite only one example: when the bishop of Poitiers was harassed by royal officials and faced with opposition from the clergy and laity of his diocese, he turned to the crown and got royal orders commanding the officials to stop their own activity and suppress that of others; when he turned to the pope, however, he could get only the "spiritual sword"—permission to excommunicate his enemies.[47] When Boniface VIII set himself to prohibit royal taxation of the clergy without papal consent, and a few years later to denounce royal criminal jurisdiction over the clergy, in both cases basing his decrees on far-ranging assertions of papal supremacy in the old style, he found that only a portion of the French clergy would support him. King Philip IV could fight back with much clerical support and general support from the lay estates. Boniface VIII was cited to Paris on an array of charges touching even the legitimacy of his papacy; he was arrested abortively at his own residence of Anagni; and only his death soon after saved him from worse. His defeat ended the Roman attempt to combine effective lordship over the European churches with the abstract ideal of absolute papal sovereignty.

The papacy now fell under irresistible French influence, and after the short pontificate of Benedict XI, the papal office passed, in 1305, to the Gascon Bertrand de Got—Clement V. He never went to Italy but settled in Avignon, which became the seat of the papacy under the next six popes, all coming from the south of France. A new era of papal government began in which the popes rose to unprecedented heights of power over the finances and personnel of the European church, most of whose major benefices and many of whose minor ones were now filled by papal appointment.[48] At the same time, the Avignon popes found it necessary to be obliging to the princes of France, especially in matters of appointment to benefices and in grants of church revenues. Papal "foreign policy" also served French interests in a number of ways.[49] But the popes extended a comparable pattern of collaboration to other European princes, who supported papal control over their clergies because they received a share of the profits and were able to get their candidates for benefices taken care of. Except for the conflict between John XXII and the Emperor Louis of Bavaria, which characteristically centered on competing rights in Italy and which did not have a dramatic denouement, the claims to world supremacy were neglected in favor of a more politic flexibility that made possible the advances just noted. It is all the more significant that this extraordinary European development of the papacy

47. The texts in L. Redet, ed., *Cartulaire de l'évêché de Poitiers ou Grand-Gauthier*, *AHP*, 10 (Poitiers, 1881): 62–64, 121–124, 157.

48. Mollat, *Popes at Avignon*: 335–337; Barraclough, *Papal Provisions*: 19; Renouard, *Avignon Papacy*: 97–100; Guillemain, *Cour pontificale*: 104–106.

49. Mollat, *Popes at Avignon*: 249–251; Giovanni Tabacco, *La casa di Francia nell'azione politica di papa Giovanni XXII* (Rome, 1953), *passim*; Carl Kehrmann, *Frankreichs innere Kirchenpolitik . . . 1378–1409* (Jena, 1890): 76 f.

in fact involved the latter's thoroughgoing conversion into a French establishment. Clement V had been elected by a college that included thirteen Italian cardinals and two French, but at the time of his death there were eight Italians and sixteen French; during the whole Avignon period of about seventy years before the Schism, there were 111 French cardinals appointed as against 14 Italians and 9 from all other parts of Europe. Among the French there was a preponderance of men from the south (95 out of the 111), reflecting both the nepotist and regionalist policies of the popes, all southerners.[50] Still more significant was the fact that the whole papal apparatus of government became part of the system of opportunities in which the clerical careerists of French political society pursued their ambitions, moving smoothly from ducal to royal to papal service, or back and forth, with high promotion granted regularly to clients of the Valois. Two of the Avignon popes had indeed begun their careers in the royal service.[51] At Avignon, moreover, which was comfortable, relatively secure, and well located for dealings with Europe at large, the expansion of papal power led to the enormous elaboration of the bureaucracy of papal government; the city became the home of a whole society—brilliant, luxurious, cosmopolitan, but also French.

At the heart of this society were the cardinals, who shared in papal government. Theoretically as absolute as ever, the Avignon popes actually ruled as chiefs of a corps; they respected the cardinals' privileges and constantly amplified them.[52] The canonist Cardinal Jean Lemoine had declared that the papal fullness of power resided not in the pope alone but in the corporate entity of pope and cardinals together,[53] and while his formula was not embodied in permanent structures of constitutional law, it did define the way of thinking at the core of Avignon practice. The cardinals had a definite share of papal revenues, elaborate sumptuary privileges, enormous wealth derived from enormous numbers of benefices, key roles in papal government, and a customary right to be con-

---

50. Guillemain, Cour pontificale: 183–192.

51. Ibid.: 122–125, 192–211, 454 (70 percent of all identified officials of the Curia were French).

52. Ibid.: 181 f.; Mollat, Popes at Avignon: 305–310; Église: 903–906, 512 f. For canonistic exaltations of the status of the cardinalate, see Tierney, Foundations, index, s.v. "cardinals." The best systematic study of the rise of the cardinalate in fact and idea is offered by Martin Souchon, Die Papstwahlen von Bonifaz VIII bis Urban VI und die Entstehung des Schismas, 1378 (Braunschweig, 1888) and idem, Die Papstwahlen in der Zeit des grossen Schismas: Entwicklung und Verfassungskämpfe des Kardinalates von 1378–1417, 2 vols. (Braunschweig, 1898–1899). Bernard Guillemain, "Cardinaux et société curiale aux origines de la double élection de 1378," GDGSO: 21 ff., summarizes the most recent literature.

53. Tierney, Foundations: 180–190; cf. p. 151: Hostiensis had previously expressed the same view.

sulted on all major decisions including new appointments to their ranks. Many cardinals were of noble birth; many were men of learning; almost all were of proven social and political ability. This extraordinary princely estate was a major construction of the Avignon papacy, whose prestige and power were greatly enhanced thereby; it is all the more noteworthy that the cardinalate was so overwhelmingly French and so closely tied to the structures of French political society.

Yet the last two popes of this happy line, Urban V and Gregory XI, decided to move the papacy to Rome—in both cases against the strong opposition of the Valois and of the cardinalate. It was not a whimsical decision, for the Avignon popes had regularly devoted much energy and vast sums of money to the pacification of the papal states and of Rome, evidently with the intention that some day the popes might return to the city and people whose bishops they were. One can only guess at other motives—a desire to escape French pressures, fear of disaffection on the part of the English, Germans, and Italians, a realistic sense that the papacy could preserve its integrity only when the popes were resident princes of a substantial territorial state.[54] On the other hand there were good reasons not to go, as Urban V found out after he left Avignon in 1367; the papal states and the city of Rome were neither congenial nor even safe, and by 1370 Urban was back on the banks of the Rhone. His successor could himself have drawn the obvious lesson, which Froissart's hindsight put into the mouth of Duke Louis of Anjou:

Holy Father, you are going to a land where the people have little liking for you, . . . and what you are doing may throw the church into great tribulation. For if you die there, as your physicians tell me is rather likely, the insolent and treacherous Romans will dominate all the cardinals and force a pope to be made at their pleasure.[55]

And yet Gregory, chronically ill as he was, left Avignon on 13 September 1376 with a cadre of officials and most of the cardinals; they arrived

---

54. According to Renouard, *Avignon Papacy*: 37 ff., the first two Avignon popes, Clement V and John XXII, intended to reside in Italy; Avignon was thought of as the normal papal residence only in the next three pontificates, 1334–1362; then Urban V and Gregory XI, neither of whom had come to the papacy by the normal *cursus honorum*, returned to the idea of a move to Rome. The question of why, especially in the case of Gregory XI, has been the subject of a scholarly debate which Renouard calls "pointless" —"Who knows the secrets of hearts?" (p. 65). Mollat, *Popes at Avignon*, regards the return as a moral obligation which only the turbulence of Italy prevented the popes from discharging; when the popes felt able to return, they did (pp. 154–171). The biassed but knowledgeable Boniface Ferrer, writing in 1411 (*Thes. nov.*, 2:1450), said a major cause of Gregory XI's move, as the pope himself "had said to many," was "that he could neither endure the raging importunities nor satiate the endless appetite of the French, nor grant their improper requests." Cf. the similar explanation in *ALKG*, 7:86.

55. Quoted in *Église*: 5.

in Rome 13 January 1377. One wonders what the pope expected—if indeed he was not just a sick man seizing his last chance to act. Since he could hardly have looked forward to the Italianization of the papacy that eventually ensued, he might have hoped that the advantages of the Avignon system with its specific traits could be kept, the disadvantages eliminated by the move to Rome and effective lordship over the papal states. Such a papacy would still have had a strong French component, with more representation of Italy and other nations; it might have developed the combination of grandeur, power, and flexibility that would have prevented not only schism but even the secession of Hussite Bohemia and the Protestant north. Or if not this, then perhaps some other project of comparable scope, similarly based on the idea of preserving the positive features of the papacy's French period.

But Louis of Anjou had been right; Gregory XI led his cardinals into a nightmare of horror.[56] The papal states were mutinous, the papal armies unreliable, and the Romans ready for anything to get back the papacy from the hated French. Florence, at war with the papacy since 1375, fed subversion and rebellion everywhere, not least by maintaining a regular network of spies, agitators, and conspirators in Rome, where they stimulated anti-French passion, threatening violence or even death to all Frenchmen including the French cardinals. The Roman nobility on whom the papacy counted were powerless; the Roman magistrates both allowed and cultivated the atmosphere of violence; and it is possible that some of the Italian personnel of the papal court, which included four Italian cardinals, were involved in the plotting.[57] We are told that Gregory realized he had made a mistake, but by this time he had moved into his final illness, in early 1378, and could do nothing to prevent a forced election other than authorize the cardinals to elect without regard for the canonical forms, and order the castellan of the papal fortress, the Castel Sant'Angelo, not to deliver its keys to anyone without an order from the cardinals who had remained in Avignon. Gregory died on 27 March 1378.

The cardinals were now told more than once by various Romans including the magistrates that if they did not elect a Roman their lives would be unsafe. Measures were also taken to prevent the cardinals from

---

56. The following account is based on Valois, 1:8–55, and on Richard Trexler, "Rome on the Eve of the Great Schism," *Speculum*, 42 (1967):489–509. Both support the cardinals' thesis of intimidation; Trexler gives the evidence for the work of Florence's agents.

57. Trexler: 504. Flandrin's treatise of 1378/1379 argues that the French cardinals could not speak openly in the conclave to repudiate their election of Urban "because there were many Italians in the conclave, the *familiares* of the Italian cardinals" (*Polemik*: 41).

leaving the city; their noble allies were expelled, and crowds of armed men from the countryside came in to increase the tension. As for the conclave which the cardinals entered on 7 April, Valois's account—a masterpiece of terror containing, however, nothing but facts—will convince those at least who understand how fear can be generated by threats, noise, and the systematic disruption of routine.[58] The conclave was not properly walled up; there were irregular entries of Roman officials bearing threats; there was the din of Roman soldiers on the floor below and the smoke of their fires; there was the clamor of the mob in the square outside and the endless clang of church bells sounding like tocsins through the night. Again and again the cardinals heard the people shouting, "Romano lo volemo!" "Romano lo volemo o italiano!" "Romano lo volemo, se non che tutti li occideremo!" ("We want a Roman, a Roman or an Italian, a Roman or we'll kill them all!") These were not the sounds of drunken high spirits or Latin temperament, as would be alleged by Urban VI and his apologists up to the present,[59] but the culmination of months of tension and deadly menace. One must suppose that under these conditions the politicking customary before and during a conclave did not have the free play it would have enjoyed back in Avignon (where there were, moreover, six more cardinals) or in some quiet place outside Rome. A Limousin faction built up by the appointments of three of the last four popes, who had come from that region, counted seven of the cardinals in Rome; five others, including the Aragonese Pedro de Luna, formed a "French" (i.e., northern French) group; there were four Italians. An abundance of accounts and depositions generated by the controversies of the Schism show that, under the conditions just described, the inability of any faction to muster the required two-thirds majority had led to sentiment even before the conclave in favor of a candidate from outside the college and that the one appealing to most was Bartolomeo Prignano, archbishop of Bari and papal vice-chancellor, whose long service in the papal government commended him as a friend of the French. His moral probity perhaps seemed to promise decent behavior as pope, while the fact that he was not Roman but Neapolitan meant that his election would not seem too obvious a victory for the Romans. He was elected amidst some tumult in the morning of 8 April, then re-elected during a calmer spell that evening. The next day the cardinals again came together, deliberated, and formally notified

---

58. I know of no one who has directly impugned Valois's account, although Ullmann seems to ignore it. Přerovský, Elezione: 40, says that "Valois's work still remains the fundamental one" and that Ullmann's account is "too decisive." Seidlmayer, Anfänge, a work not used by Ullmann, offers much the same picture as Valois of the strengths and weaknesses of each side's case.

59. Ullmann, Origins: 39, 77 f.

Prignano of his election; he consented, took the name of Urban VI, and was enthroned, "adored," and proclaimed as pope to the people, who accepted him. All the legal forms were now fulfilled, and the coronation took place on Easter Sunday, 18 April.

The cardinals served the new pope in the normal ways, assisted at his coronation and consistories, asked and received the usual favors from him, and proclaimed his election to the princes of Europe and to their six colleagues back in Avignon. It could be argued then and since that this behavior constituted the "convalidation" of an admittedly irregular election, and while the cardinals would later claim that all such acts had been performed out of a continuing fear, there is little evidence that such was the case.[60] Without pretending to address the basic issue of Urban's legitimacy, we may suppose that the cardinals' dominant emotion in April after the election was not fear but dismay, as the new pope daily gave them new reasons to believe that they had created a monster.[61] Cancelling Gregory XI's still outstanding grants of expectancies, Urban declared his intention of ending the abuses of pluralism and absenteeism, beginning with the cardinals—whose great wealth came in large part from multiple benefices. He also demanded that they lead a sober life, stripped of pomp and luxury, that they live in Rome and devote their extra funds to the upkeep of their titular churches. His devotion to the ideals of religious reform was no doubt as sincere as the cardinals' contrary conviction that their courtly life-style was both appropriate and useful to the church as it actually was. Since, however, he made his points in coarsely abusive language, frequently losing his temper and meeting opposition by flat assertions of his papal omnipotence, the

---

60. The cardinals' acceptance of the new pope was a feature of Urbanist polemic (e.g., the *Factum Urbani* quoted by Ullmann, *Origins*: 22–25), which was refuted in point of fact and canon law by Flandrin (*Polemik*: 10, 38–61) on the grounds that the state of fear continued after the election and that in any case no non-electoral acts could make or remake an election. Archbishop Pedro Tenorio of Toledo, neutral at the time, responded with a distinction: a party's subsequent consent to an election "validates it if it was valid to begin with, in the sense that he renounces his right of impugning it, not that he gives it legality" (*Thes. nov.*, 2:1107). In this sense the cardinals' behavior after the election could be taken as "convalidation," a view that has been revived by Seidlmayer (*Anfänge*) and Přerovský (*Elezione*: 41) and which is distinct from the commonplace observation then and now (e.g., Valois, 1:63–67) that this behavior weakened the cardinals' credibility (and see ibid.: 66 for the lack of evidence of fear).

61. Ullmann, *Origins*: 44–50, 165–169, 174. Much of what follows is based on several of the essays in *GDGSO*: Bernard Guillemain, "Cardinaux et société curiale" (pp. 19–30); Edith Pasztor, "La Curia Romana all'inizio dello Scisma d'Occidente" (pp. 31–43; esp. for Urban's ideas of reform and the cardinals' own ideas); Henri Bresc, "La genèse du Schisme: les partis cardinalices et leurs ambitions dynastiques" (pp. 45–57; on the French-Limousin interplay); Daniel Williman, "The Camerary and the Schism" (pp. 65–71).

cardinals could only conclude that Urban intended to liquidate the whole structure of papal governance in its Avignon form. There would be no more mutual respect, no more co-governance of pope and college; the new papacy, fixed in Rome, would be absolutist and Italian, while they would figure only as anachronisms to be first repressed, then gradually replaced. Cardinal Robert of Geneva, the head by kinship and nobility of the "French" faction, put the pope on notice that the new line was unacceptable: "Holy Father, you have not treated the cardinals with the honor you should show them, as your predecessors did, but you are diminishing our honor. I tell you the truth, the cardinals will endeavor to diminish your honor too." The veteran Valois client Cardinal Jean de La Grange, who had been away from Rome at the time of the election and returned on 25 April to be horrified by what his pusillanimous colleagues had done, replied to one of Urban's charges of malfeasance by saying that "the little archbishop of Bari" was a liar.[62] At the same time the apostolic camerary (camerarius), Pierre de Cros, a Limousin and indeed brother of the cardinal "of Limoges," used his wide-ranging powers of fiscal control to hire troops and prepare Anagni for the cardinals' eventual withdrawal there. As the single most important papal official, whose powers did not lapse during a papal vacancy, he could do what the individual cardinals could not; he had never fully recognized Urban in any case, and now he seems to have joined with La Grange to create a French-Limousin entente capable of remedying the disease in the papacy.[63] For the cardinals could now suspect what later events would indeed show, that Urban was mentally unbalanced, and they could reasonably suppose that they might have realized this before the election if they had been given enough time to study the record.[64]

---

62. Ullmann, Origins: 47 f.

63. Bresc, "Genèse du Schisme," emphasizes the role of La Grange; Williman, "Camerary and the Schism," that of Pierre de Cros; I put the two together.

64. See Ullmann, Origins: 168, for Urban's later savagery. In his reply to Pedro Tenorio, Cardinal Pierre Flandrin wrote that as soon as Urban accepted his election "he miraculously lost whatever good mores he had had" (Polemik: 76) and in his treatise characterized the election as defective because Urban was "notoriously lacking in all the things required in a good shepherd" (p. 32). But, Flandrin pointed out, canon law provided that a papal election could not be invalidated by exceptions based on such alleged defects in the elect; therefore he did not push this line of argument (pp. 25, 27, 32). On the other hand Urban's defects did make a case ex post for the cardinals' claim that their election had been made under duress, and such is the argument of Přerovský, Elezione. Urban's behavior to the cardinals after his election showed "uno squilibrio mentale"; "la sua incapacità, . . . che poteva assumere in costei circostanze anche degli aspetti patologici della mancanza di equilibrio" (pp. 87, 188). But Urban's record in his previous career, which Přerovský studies in detail, had already given evidence of ominous traits—"carrarere scontroso, autoritario, intransigente ed ostinato nell'esigere il suo diritto" (p. 63)—and the cardinals chose him without sufficient knowledge of the man or a

If the elections of 8 April had indeed not been "canonical," the cardinals' immediate obligation was to fulfill the provisions of the canon *Si quis pecunia* (*Decretum,* 79. di., c. 9), which said that if a man had secured the papacy by simony or violence, without a canonical election, the cardinals should take steps to remove him and make a true election, withdrawing if necessary to a safe place outside Rome.[65] At the beginning of May the French cardinals (we now include the Limousins and Pedro de Luna) began to leave Rome for Anagni along with other members of the papal court, including Pierre de Cros, who brought the whole financial office and papal treasure with him. It was he who on 8 May sent a messenger to Charles V of France to inform Paris of the true circumstances of Urban's election and who on 20 July made the first official declaration that the election had been invalid.[66] The cardinals sent their own messengers as well and asked for royal support, at the same time inviting the Italian cardinals to join them in resolving the problem posed by Urban's lack of right to the papacy. On 2 August a public statement of the case for regarding the election as invalid was joined with a request that Urban give up his office; here too the cardinals acted under the presidency of the camerary inasmuch as they themselves did not have legal power during a vacancy to do anything but meet to make an election.[67] On 9 August Urban was declared a non-pope and anathematized. By this time only one cardinal remained true to him: the aged and ailing Pietro Tebaldeschi. The other three Italians left him about the end of July, motivated by the same interests and perceptions that moved the French but less ready to follow the warlike way of defiance. They proposed instead that a general council of the whole church be convened to determine the problem of Urban's legitimacy.[68] Against this and other calls for a council, the French cardinals opposed a flat refusal

---

due study of the facts about him. Flandrin makes this point too (*Polemik*: 31): while the cardinals were legally allowed to take a long time in electing, "they were deprived of this benefit by the Romans, when the cardinals were coerced to elect right away (*statim*) and without deliberation."

65. See Williman, "Camerary and the Schism": 69.

66. Valois, 1:92; Williman, "Camerary and the Schism": 68, 70 f. (the text of 20 July).

67. Valois, 1:88–97, for the flow of events; Williman, "Camerary and the Schism": 68, for the role of Pierre de Cros.

68. For the events, see Valois, 1:74–80. Seidlmayer, *Anfänge*: 179 f., observes in this connection that the Italian cardinals were "die eigentliche Urheber der Konzilspropaganda" (but cf. ibid.: 134 f., a report by Alfonso of Jaén that Pedro de Luna had at first held that Urban was to be obeyed until a general council should decide against him). Bliemetzrieder, *Generalknozil*: 3 f., 19, discusses the nature of the council envisaged by the Italians: either a "general council" of all the bishops, or a "particular" one of representatives of the units of the church, with one-third each from Italy, France, and the rest of Europe.

backed up by canonistic treatises proving that the cardinals had the right to declare an election invalid, that they were the only ones with such a right, that canon law did not provide for a council except on papal summons and under papal presidency, and that history showed that no schism had ever been settled by such a council.[69] Had they wanted above all to prevent schism, or if they would have been content with a conciliar annulment of Urban's election, they could have found the appropriate arguments. But as Ullmann has shown, their action was per se an assertion that the government of the church should be an oligarchy rather than an untrammeled monarchy; and this issue, which would not have been determined in their favor by a council relying on existing canon law,[70] could be kept central only by their persistence in the unilateral action that had brought it to the fore. Their appeal was therefore not to a general council but to King Charles V, who together with his brother Duke Louis of Anjou supported the cardinals after the acts of August with money and arrangements for troops to protect them.[71] As it happened, they already had a company of more or less French mercenaries at their disposal, along with the support of Queen Joanna of Naples and the count of Fondi, to which last place they moved and where they were joined by the three Italians in mid-September. There, on 20 September, the French cardinals with the tacit agreement of the Italians elected Cardinal Robert of Geneva as pope. He took the name of Clement VII and was crowned on 31 October.

A curious formula written by Clement VII in May of 1380 to refute the idea of a legal solution by way of a council stated that "the duration of the crisis means that the nomination of Urban, the declaration [of his non-papality] at Anagni, and the election of Clement have to be regarded as simultaneous."[72] In other words the issue could not be analyzed

---

69. The first major treatise was written by Pierre Flandrin, cardinal deacon of Sant'Eustachio, in 1378/1379 (text in *Polemik*: 3–71); it proves the invalidity of Urban's election and the competence of the cardinals to establish and declare this fact. In the second half of 1379, Pierre Ameilh, cardinal "of Embrun" created by Clement VII, wrote a treatise specifically against a general council (*Polemik*: 91–111).

70. Souchon, *Zeit des grossen Schismas*, 1:61, 162; cf. 185 f. Also Ullmann, *Origins*: 4, 172–187; *Église*: 904. Cf. Pasztor, "Curia Romana": 33.

71. Valois, 1:96–112, 143–158.

72. Harry Bresslau, "Aus der ersten Zeit des grossen abendländischen Schismas," *Abhandlungen der preussischen Akademie der Wissenschaften,* Phil.-Hist. Klasse (Berlin, 1919), no. 6:24 f.: "Tota questio videtur stare in hoc, utrum secunda instruccio cardinalium infringat primam vel reddat eam dubiam. Duracio periculi facit nominacionem Urbani et declaracionem Anania et eleccionem Clementis censeri simul factas." Bresslau identifies the whole text (pp. 21–25) as a "Selbstkonsultation" in Clement's own hand, and dates it in May 1380 on internal evidence (pp. 26–30). It contradicts Clement's earlier policy, stated on 14 November 1378, which recognized the validity of Urban's provisions made before the cardinals' declaration of 9 August: see Pasztor, "Curia Romana": 40 f.

in terms of a sequence of acts subject to legal judgements step by step, but only in terms of the coexistence of two mutually exclusive claims. This is the formula for war in the legal sense of a judgement by battle, and one guesses that the cardinals had this in mind when they went to Anagni: French and pro-French power would drive Urban out and install Clement, with Europe as a whole falling in line. More than a century of French expansionism and preeminence must have made the prospect seem not only possible but realistic.[73] It was only because this did not happen that Clement turned out to be the pope only of France and her allies, residing in Avignon after he had failed to get Rome and had been forced to leave Naples in May of 1379. Meanwhile he had struck a bargain with Louis of Anjou, 17 April 1379, by which the latter would conquer the papal states for Clement and would receive for his own a kingdom of Adria carved out of them as a vassal state of the Holy See.[74] The failure of this project did not deter Clement from promoting similar ones in the future, and what we see as the stagnancy or indeed the consolidation of the Schism appeared to him from first to last as a temporary standoff whose only possible solution could be by the "way of force," the *via facti,* Avignon's triumph by force of French arms.[75]

In this sense the structure of the Great Schism from beginning to end was determined by the government of France. While there is no reason to believe the claim of Urban's propaganda that Charles V had "persuaded the cardinals by threats and promises to elect Robert and make him antipope,"[76] neither would the cardinals have proceeded with their action unless they had been confident of Valois support;[77] and it was no doubt this that two of them had in mind in 1398 when they observed

---

73. Apart from the implications of the cardinals' actions in 1378, there is the later testimony of Ameil du Breuil, archbishop of Tours, in his ballot against subtraction of obedience at the Third Paris Council in 1398: "Si dicatur quod pars nostra debet incipere et ita alii principes subsequenter facient, respondent quod similis racio fuit inicium et causa principalis scismatis in ecclesia" (AN, J 518, fol. 437r; ASV, *Arm.* 54, t. 46, fol. 4r). The author of the "Heidelberg Postil" similarly supposed that France's original intention had been to restore the happy days of the Avignon papacy, when popes recognized by all of Europe exalted France to the detriment of the Empire and other states; the point of Clement's papacy was to bring everyone into his obedience (*DRTA,* 6:402). Valois, 4:53, remarks in this connection that "la France a toujours eu l'ambition de répandre ses idées au dehors."

74. Valois, 1:145–158.

75. The *via facti* was advocated by Clement VII down to the day of his death (Valois, 2:427); see *passim* below. Bouvet, *Somnium* (of 1394): 102, has him telling the king of France: "dudum de mente plurium assistentium quondam domino nostro Clementi sentivi eos opinari quod vos procederetis per arma, . . . sicut . . . vestri . . . predecessores . . . adduxerunt dejectos ad sedem in Roma."

76. Valois, 1:142.

77. See Johannes Haller's remarks, *Historische Zeitschrift,* 163 (1941):596.

that Charles V "was the beginning and foundation of our obedience; he made it."[78] That the French clergy fell in line was a matter of submission to the crown and a desire for benefices;[79] it is more interesting to see that there was practically no opposition from even the semi-autonomous southern-French princes not directly related to the Valois and that sooner or later France's allies recognized Clement too. It has been argued above that the renewed Avignon papacy created in 1378 by the cardinals and by France represented the old Avignon principle of a Europeanized papacy, both in its non-Italian composition and in the modes of papal government and papal action in dealing with the territorial churches. Similarly the new Avignon papacy, like the old one, sought to establish its lordship in Italy by force of arms. Now, however, the Avignon cause depended on French imperialism and in particular on the ambitions of certain dukes—Louis of Anjou, then his son Louis II, later on Charles V's younger son Louis of Orléans—who wanted to achieve royal status by ruling Italian realms. The same sort of modified continuity appears in Clement's dependence on Valois favor and his servitude not only to the king and dukes but even to their clients—"Servant of the Servants of the Princes of France," in Nicholas de Clamanges's complaint.[80] Benefices went regularly to the nominees of the princes; aids from the French church were granted year after year to fill out the royal budget; and of course the Schism itself made papal "foreign policy" identical to that of Paris with only one or two notable exceptions. This situation may have been at the root of Clement's notorious simony, merely one element of an increased fiscalism that made up for the expenses of Schism policy, the loss of Urbanist revenues, and a loss of some customary revenues even from the part of Europe which recognized him.[81] In a more subtle

---

78. *ALKG*, 6:268.

79. Simon de Cramaud in his refutation of the Toulouse letter, 1402, wrote (AN, J 518, fol. 527v): "O si in principio scismatis huius, reges Francie et Castelle omnium sibi subditorum requisivissent consilium, utrum esset Bertholomeo obediendum, testis est deus, qualem oppinionum diversitatem reperiissent"; and fol. 528v: "O rex inclitissime! Si omnes illi qui in regno vestro, Castelle, et Aragonie et alibi in terris obediencie nostre nunquam in consciencia crediderunt Clementi vel Benedicto, eciam signati incederent, flebilem forsan multitudinem videritis. Et si illi qui istos ambos de libro vivencium deleri optarent . . . distingui possent, . . . maiorem forsan multo copiam sic opinancium videritis"; and fol. 552r: "In regnis Francie, Castelle, et Aragonie, et aliis terris in quibus habuit dominus Clemens obedienciam, credebatur a multis quod eius eleccio canonica non fuisset, sed lex et ordinacio regum compulit eos suum captivare intellectum in obsequium Cristi" (cf. 2 Cor. 10:5). (Bonn University S 594, ii, fols. 55v, 56v, collated.) For the rest, no one not recognizing Clement could have gotten or indeed kept a major benefice in France.

80. Haller, *PKR*: 206 ff.

81. At the Paris Council of 1406 the dean of Rheims, Guillaume Fillastre, praised Benedict XIII for having put an end to the simony practiced by Clement VII, when "les

way it may have had something to do with his style of luxury, extravagance, and easy-going morality that perhaps surpassed even the Avignon of Clement VI. One critic indeed gives details of homosexual parties where Clement VII and his companions, to whom he had given high benefices, enjoyed the society of handsome boys—"we all know what sort of squires and servitors he had"—one of whom, the squire of the archbishop of Rouen, had his eyebrows shaved. The boys wore the stylish jackets of the time, barely long enough to reach the buttocks, but Clement said even these were too long. The same source tells us, no doubt with exaggeration, that in the whole realm of France, church benefices were held by prelates who had started out as lubricious and unlearned boys in the papal entourage. The author of De ruina ecclesie, probably Nicholas de Clamanges, makes an identical remark: "Clement granted almost all the vacant bishoprics and other high dignities to handsome and elegant youths, whom he loved most of all to associate with."[82] While his homosexual disposition was an accident, his flagrant self-indulgence may not have been. Perhaps it reflected a loss of inner strength by a pope who saw the slough into which his papacy was sinking as his total dependence on France was consolidated by French military failure and inaction into a permanent fact of life. And Clement lived long enough to see the still more distasteful reverse side of that

---

prelatures et grands benefices estoient à cely qui plus en donnoit: et aucunes fois avenoit que quand deux en donnoient un mesme prix, tous deux le perdoient, et venoit un tiers qui mettoit dessus et l'emportoit" (BdeC: 129). Favier, Finances: 687–689, calculates that from the outbreak of the Schism to the subtraction of obedience (1378–1398), the Avignon papacy enjoyed yearly revenues averaging about 180,000 florins, in contrast to ca. 300,000 florins in the pontificate of Gregory XI. Favier notes that given the reduced size of the Avignon obedience after 1378, the reduction was proportional. But the Curia's expenses were not reduced, and there were financial concessions to secular princes (e.g., the king of Castile got tenths from the Castilian clergy, who in recompense were not required to pay procurations to the pope—Favier, Finances: 235; cf. Haller, PKR: 207, for a suggestion that Castile's exemptions went even further), as well as extraordinary expenses due to the Schism. These losses were made up by an increased fiscalism "reaching the extreme limit of exploitation of the clergy" (Favier, Finances: 695). The brunt was borne by the clergy of France.

82. ALKG, 7:75 f.; Nicholas de Clamanges, De ruina ecclesie, ch. 27, quoted in Bulaeus, 4:703. The short jackets were the end result of a long evolution of fashion that had seen tunics climbing at the papal court even before the Schism, from the calf to the knee and higher, a movement that, fortunately for Clement VII, his predecessors had been unable to stop—Norman Zacour, "Papal Regulation of Cardinals' Households in the Fourteenth Century," Speculum, 50 (1975):443. Matthew of Janov, contemporary to Clement, tells us of the same stimulating fashions in Bohemia—Regulae, 4:226 f. Women promoted their breasts, and men wore short jackets and tight trousers designed to emphasize the genitals and the buttocks, across which the fabric was stretched so tight that it sometimes split when a man knelt or bowed.

fact, when the French government controlled by the dukes of Berry and Burgundy decided to give up the expansionist ambitions implied by Avignon's claims and therefore to give up the Avignon papacy as well.

The story of how France ended the Schism is the subject of the pages that follow, but there is room here for a few observations about it in the light of what has been said about the structure of the Schism and the Age of Schism in which it took shape. The action of the cardinals in 1378, the political interests determining the choice of allegiance by this or that prince, the intensified territorialization of the churches at the expense of papal power, the anti-papalist sentiments of the territorial clergies as expressed in ideologies like Gallicanism and in programs of reform—all of these were reactions against papal centralization or papal absolutism; all of them can be brought down to the crude issue of how the revenues from ecclesiastical property and offices should be divided. The French program for ending the Schism did not address itself to these matters, although it certainly involved them. The program presupposed the reduction of the papacy to an object of secular interest, to the status of presidency of a corporation, to a complex of property rights. On these bases it was argued that the question of legitimacy raised in 1378 was not capable of solution; that anyway neither side would accept a solution that made it the schismatic one; that while the "status of the universal church" certainly required a head, it did not specifically require this one or that; that the papal contenders had only property rights to allege; and therefore the Schism had to be ended by terminating both papacies without judgement. This was a reasonable and rather modest solution, although it took longer to implement than had been foreseen; what it achieved, however, was only the formal restoration of papal unity. The issues involved in the outbreak and consolidation of the Schism were pushed only as ancillaries to the instruments of the basic program. In this way, Gallicanism was involved in the French subtraction of obedience in 1398; constitutional changes in the papacy and reforms of abuses were involved in the councils of Pisa and Constance; and increased princely control over the territorial churches figured in the concordats of princes with Pope Martin V, chosen at the Council of Constance. In the end, however, the deeper issues of the Schism were not satisfactorily resolved, and it is significant that the Hussite revolution in Bohemia worked out a whole complex of them in the framework of reformation, sectarianism, and secession from the Roman system. No wonder, then, that the crisis of papal authority continued so long after Constance and that in the long run it issued in a permanent state of multiple schism in Western Christendom. One can only speculate whether a different outcome would have resulted if the French crown had fulfilled its earlier promise of European hegemony, had conquered

Italy for Clement VII, and had imposed Avignonism anew on the European churches. Any such development was precluded by the fact that the Great Schism in the church was part of an Age of Schism in Europe, when grand enterprises by central governments were hardly conceivable and if attempted usually proved abortive.

CHAPTER TWO

The Valois Turn toward Union, 1392–1394

WHILE the Great Schism lasted a long time—from 1378 to 1409—the enterprise of its beginnings was over rather soon. This was the joint effort of Clement VII and Louis of Anjou to subject Naples, Rome, and the papal states to Clement's obedience; begun in 1379, it ended in 1384 with the death of Louis in the midst of inconclusive military campaigns. Similar schemes were revived up through 1393 with a succession of Valois princes as their central characters— Louis II of Anjou, Charles VI, Louis of Orléans, even the duke of Bourbon—but little came of any of them and nothing came of most. Without supposing that the men (and one woman, Marie of Anjou) were anything but earnest, one still has the impression of a sort of charade played over and over because that was what the Avignon-Paris Schism program called for and there was no way to stop. More exactly, there was a way, but it required a depth and breadth and consistency of effort that must have made another stab at Italy seem relatively attractive, no matter how dubious its chances. For if the Valois rulers were to base their policy on a recognition that Europe would not follow France, that French princes could not conquer Italy, and that Clement could not be imposed on Italy or Europe by force, it would be necessary to reverse the policies which aimed at these ends, find some respectable way to give up the Avignon enterprise, and persuade the rest of Europe to join France in working out a formula by which France could do all this without incurring the disgrace of having been schismatic. When indeed the French government did commit itself to this way of union, in 1394, it was after two years of backing and filling, with fifteen more years to follow before the policy attained its goal. The alacrity with which Europe's rulers made the Schism was matched by their reluctance to give it up. Contemporaries noted both dispositions and explained them by reference to national hatreds, selfish sloth, and a cold-blooded desire to get and keep a larger share of church revenues;[1] to these no doubt valid reasons we may add the more general explanation outlined in the preceding chapter,

---

1. Bouvet, *Somnium*: 91, 95.

that the Schism was the creation of a certain sort of mentality in a time when Europe was experiencing both centrifugal reaction in many political contexts and the pluralism generated by an increasingly complex civilization.

That the Schism was ended nevertheless can hardly be explained by supposing that people were sick of it,[2] or by imputing to everyone a "thirst for union" detectable in various writings of piety or public relations,[3] and still less by pointing to the happy advent of the conciliar theory, "which made possible a resolution of the Schism."[4] Indeed one of the more fascinating possibilities in that time of rank mutations was that the Schism might pass into normality, become permanent, or even continue growing into a Europe of multiple papacies.[5] If this did not happen, it was because the government of France—or more particularly, the dukes of Berry and Burgundy—determined to switch from supporting Avignon to working for union. This "volte-face in French policy" was, in the words of a recent writer on the subject, "arguably the most important single development in international relations in the 1390s . . . the essential condition for all the subsequent attempts to heal the Schism by the concerted action of England and France and other powers."[6] One can put it still more strongly: the French policy in question was the *only* significant agent of union activity; and while it certainly presupposed a general sense that union was desirable, this sense was so basic, hence non-specific, that it could never of itself generate concrete political action. That the French push, moreover, was sustained (with one brief diversion) for fifteen years and worked out with patience, flexibility, and the massive application of wealth and power in the face of at-first-inexpugnable resistance, in a period when France was sliding into chaos: this attests one of the most remarkable political enterprises of late-medieval history.

It began when on 5 August 1392 King Charles VI was struck by a mental disorder that would condemn him to spend the rest of his long life alternating between actual lunacy and spells of increasingly imbecilic clarity; it ended the period of his direct rule, which he had begun in 1388 at the age of twenty. At that time he had dismissed his uncles, the

---

2. Valois, 2:391, attributes the French turn away from Avignon to "le mécontentement, la lassitude, le dépit."

3. *Église*: 76; Tierney, *Foundations*: 239.

4. Francis Oakley, *The Political Thought of Pierre d'Ailly* (New Haven, Conn., 1964): 3 f.

5. For examples of sentiment in favor of multiple papacies, see Hartmut Boockmann, "Zur politischen Geschichte des Konstanzer Konzils," *Zeitschrift für Kirchengeschichte*, 85 (1974):45 f. Other examples are given by the works cited below, Ch. VIII, n. 91.

6. Palmer, *EFC*: 194.

dukes of Berry and Burgundy, from his court; now it was their turn to come back and resume control of the government, which, as their earlier period of control had made clear, they regarded as a family enterprise that ought to work for the benefit of the family's chiefs, themselves. Both continually tapped the royal treasury for cash and taxation rights; they put through royal decisions in their favor, got lucrative royal offices, and in general made the French crown serve their own interests as princes of very large appanages organized as increasingly autonomous states.[7] The duke of Burgundy, Philip the Bold, was intelligent, far-sighted, judicious, and effective in his works. The duke of Berry, Jean, was inferior to his brother in all these respects but had the strength of his limitations: a peasant's sort of petty, stubborn devotion to *things*, except that—as he was successively son, brother, and uncle of the kings of France—the things of his devotion ranged from bits of land and water mills to jewels, paintings, and palaces, and further, to grants of hundreds of thousands of francs from the royal fisc and the right to own or ravage whole provinces.[8] Françoise Lehoux, his recent biographer, has taught us to see the perversely attractive traits of a character whose defects have been singled out by historians for easy condemnation; but even more, she has shown how powerful and important was the role played by this duke in public affairs, which have generally been presented as controlled by Burgundy alone.[9] At the same time, however, her stress on Berry's caution; on his refusal "ever to throw himself unreservedly into any enterprise"; and indeed on his motto, The Time Will Come (*Le temps viendra*),[10] does not prepare us to find that precisely in the matter of union policy Berry did commit himself unreservedly, consistently, and radically—more so than his brother of Burgundy and even after the latter's death in 1404, when Berry's other interests and the

7. Nordberg offers the only systematic study of appanage policy in the Paris action of the dukes; unfortunately he deals only with Orléans and Burgundy. Richard Vaughan, *Philip the Bold* (Cambridge, Mass., 1962): 39–58, makes the point for Burgundy; Berry's policies have to be inferred from René Lacour, *Le gouvernement de l'apanage de Jean, duc de Berry 1360–1416* (Paris, 1934), and Lehoux, 2. Brief but important statements are made by Édouard Perroy, "Feudalism or Principalities in Fifteenth Century France," *Bulletin of the Institute of Historical Research*, 20 (1947):183–185.

8. Lehoux, *passim*, for Berry's greed, and 1:xlvii–l for his character; cf. 3:421.

9. Some examples: Édouard Perroy, *The Hundred Years War*, trans. W. Wells (London, 1959): 187–191 ("the government of the uncles, or rather of Philip"); A. Coville in *The Cambridge Medieval History*, 7 (Cambridge, 1932):372; Palmer, *EFC*: 3, 68; Vaughan, *Philip the Bold*: 40–44. Cf. Lehoux, 2:348: in the years after the king's attack of insanity, "it was Berry who governed in the name of the king"; unlike Burgundy and Orléans he left the affairs of his appanage and his other interests to lieutenants in order to spend most of his time on the affairs of the crown.

10. Lehoux, 1:1.

new political situation might have dictated a switch back to support of the Schism.[11] One supposes that here as elsewhere the duke's action was normally based on counsel provided by his officials and clients, who might well have shaped Berry's thinking about even rather high levels in the calculus of means and ends. Nor is there any reason not to suppose this in the case of Burgundy too. These considerations can help explain why the dukes' return to power in August of 1392 was also the beginning of a union policy so remarkable in its depth and persistence.

For it is clear that in this matter each of the dukes acted in rapport with his chief ecclesiastical client. Burgundy's was Jean Canart, bishop of Arras, who was also his chancellor and "the linch-pin" of the Burgundian state.[12] We shall see him beside the duke in the latter's conversations about union with Cardinal Pedro de Luna, the future Benedict XIII; we shall also see him prominent in the First Paris Council, of February 1395, and in the ducal embassy which went to Avignon to impose the decision of that council on Benedict XIII.[13] In 1398 we shall see him as a leader of those French prelates who sought to make subtraction of obedience the occasion for a permanent emancipation of the Gallican church from fiscal and administrative servitude to the papacy,[14] and his doctrinaire passion suggests the conviction of a cleric rather than the policy of a duke; one guesses that Burgundy's own Gallican dicta reflected Canart's sentiment.[15] It is hard to imagine that Canart did not have something to do with Burgundy's original decision to seek union.

As for Berry, the corresponding surmise is far stronger, since not only was he quite incapable of originating the grand design himself and sticking to it, but his chief ecclesiastical client was Simon de Cramaud, the leader and theoretician of the whole union movement. His early career (treated separately in the following chapter) had been that of a Berry client, serving the duke directly as an official and then more generally as the duke's man on the royal council. His royal offices, his high position in the church—patriarch of Alexandria with the administration of the see of Carcassonne—and his remarkable success in getting lands, revenues, and "estate" for himself and his family were all due in

---

11. Thus on 1 December 1405 Berry allied himself with Louis of Orléans against Philip's son John the Fearless (Lehoux, 3:62) and subsequently stood with the Armagnacs against Burgundy, but he did not range himself with the Orléanist and southern-French policy of supporting Benedict XIII.

12. Vaughan, *Philip the Bold*: 141.

13. Below, at n. 80; and see Ch. IV below.

14. Below, Ch. VII, and App. I.

15. Thus in his own vote for subtraction in 1398, Burgundy remarked that it would bring great honor to the king, by "restoring the church of his realm to its ancient liberties and franchises" (Douët-d'Arcq, 1:146).

the first place to the duke's support; and as high as Simon soared, he could not leave his clientship behind.[16] But if Simon certainly began his organization of the union program in response to Berry's wishes, he probably played a role in shaping these wishes; and in any case there are certain features of the union program that we shall see—a brutality of form and content calculated to make negotiation with Pope Benedict XIII impossible—which cannot be explained in terms of ducal interest or political realism but only as the creation of a man whose whole future depended on total victory. Like the lawyers of the last Capetians a century earlier, Simon and his fellow careerists served the crown and their patrons with the primary aim of profiting from their official functions in order to acquire baronial "estate"; the enterprises they carried out were apt to be ones that they themselves had proposed, and if they pursued them with ruthless persistence it was because their own destinies depended on the success or failure of their policies.[17]

Let us now return to the dukes and their political interests and ask why these included putting an end to the Schism. Rather than attempting a direct answer, we can begin by observing that apart from the issue of papal legitimacy, which was taken as the primary factor by few outside the papal apparatus, the point of the Schism as far as the Valois were concerned was French expansionism in general, a French program of Italian conquest in particular. By the 1390s, with their brother of Anjou dead, this program had nothing to attract Berry or Burgundy, both of whom had magnificent appanages and other dominions, more than enough to satisfy their sense of princely estate and to occupy all their efforts of statesmanship, administration, and lordship. At the same time, they looked to the French crown for various benefits: offices, money, and abdications of crown rights in their appanages. Other members of the family with greater ambitions or fewer possessions might hope to win a royal crown in Italy,[18] and Berry and Burgundy might go along with the scheme for one reason or another, looking out for themselves in any case; but they would not be enthusiastic about an action that diverted revenues away from themselves and threatened their other interests as well. They must have drawn particularly pungent lessons from their last experience with the *via facti,* when in 1390/1391 Charles

---

16. Of the many indications that Simon always remained Berry's client, *stricto sensu,* the most revealing is his adherence to Louis of Orléans on 11 December 1405, right after Berry's alliance with Louis (Valois, 3:426 n. 4).

17. Franklin Pegues, *The Lawyers of the Last Capetians* (Princeton, N.J., 1962): 131, 223–228.

18. Thus Louis II of Anjou inherited his father's claim to the kingdom of Naples; Louis of Orléans's marriage to Valentina Visconti, a daughter of Gian-Galeazzo of Milan, drew him into the latter's expansionist schemes in north Italy.

VI had mobilized the whole available strength of the realm for a great expedition intended to set Clement VII in St. Peter's, Louis II of Anjou in Naples, the king's brother Louis in a kingdom to be carved out of the papal states, and Charles himself, perhaps, on the throne of the Holy Roman Empire.[19] Enormous amounts of wealth and military force were brought together; Berry and Burgundy were of course due to take part; Clement VII rushed to make preparations for the move—and then, at the end of February 1391, the whole thing was called off, probably because King Richard II of England had threatened a full-scale renewal of the war in France if Charles were to go ahead with his plan.[20] While peace per se was nobody's chief desire, a succession of bungled war games whose expense and danger were compounded by their futility was even less attractive; and this was what the Schism had come to mean.

The association of *via facti* with renewal of the English war was significant. It is of course known that after the French reconquests of 1369–1375, peace negotiations were begun (at Bruges, 1375–1377) that continued off and on through the 1380s and into the 1390s. Palmer has pointed to the usually overlooked fact that these negotiations were extremely important to both sides, for the "stalemate" after 1375 was a drain on the English treasury that brought no compensating glory and little profit, while France saw large regions ravaged by "English" troops and chronic turbulence in all the western areas of French interest: Castile, Brittany, Flanders—the last particularly important to Burgundy, who had become its count in 1384.[21] The English pursuit of peace by the government of Richard II in 1383–1386 was so assiduous that Palmer has called it "appeasement"; and while the duke of Gloucester succeeded in promoting war for a few years after that, the peace negotiations were taken up again from 1389 on. As for France, her desire for peace with England was strong, but Charles VI seemed to think that this matter could be separated from the Schism and the *via facti*. The abortion of 1391 proved otherwise, and the lesson was spelled out by Richard's uncle John of Gaunt, duke of Lancaster, in conversation with a French writer, Honoré Bouvet, in the spring of 1392:

When there is peace between the kings of England and France, then we will quickly have a single pope, but not before. The one in Rome is not the pope but neither was Clement rightly elected; both should resign and another one be set up. At the same time the King of England will never agree that

19. Palmer, *EFC*: 143; also, in more detail, idem, "English Foreign Policy 1388–1399," in *The Reign of Richard II,* ed. F. Du Boulay & C. Barron (London, 1971): 86–100.

20. Palmer (as in n. 19); also Valois, 2:179–188, with, however, attention to other probable causes as well.

21. Palmer, *EFC*: 1–25.

Clement remain pope if the one in Rome is condemned; for he would not let himself be marked by such a stain.[22]

Other evidence supports Bouvet's: while Gaunt told Cardinal Pedro de Luna that peace between France and England would bring peace in the church more or less inevitably by forcing the Avignon cardinals to end the Schism (or be exterminated),[23] this partisan formulation, due no doubt to the circumstances of the conversation, was replaced on other occasions by support for double abdication as Bouvet indicates: "both should resign."[24] Similar views were expressed a bit later by Richard II talking to Simon de Cramaud, who wrote: "I heard it from the lips of . . . King Richard of England that he sensed his realm so disposed that as long as there was war between us and them, his people would not be willing to take up any good means of concord in the matter of the church."[25] To sum up: there were two possible constructions of French foreign policy, one of them, associated with Clement VII, Charles VI, and the latter's brother Louis (duke of Orléans since 4 June 1392), emphasizing expansion into Italy, ending the Schism by the *via facti,* and keeping the English question simmering peacefully on a back burner; the other, forced on France by Richard II and accepted by the dukes of Berry and Burgundy, put peace with England in the first place and thereby involved a reduction of Italian commitments and a non-victorious end to the Schism by the only acceptable means thereto, the *via cessionis,* which required *both* papacies to be terminated without judgement between them.

This last point, a non-juridical solution to the Schism, was of the essence. John of Gaunt had spelled it out as early as 1392;[26] and explicit evidence no less than common sense tells us that the princes of all sides

---

22. Bouvet, *Somnium*: 92—the author, writing in August/September 1394, represents Lancaster as recalling what he had said to Bouvet in 1392. For the name of the author see Gilbert Ouy, "Honoré Bouvet (appelé à tort Bonet), prieur de Selonnet," *Romania,* 80 (1959):255–259.

23. *RSD,* 2:80.

24. Thus Bouvet, *Somnium*: 92, represents Lancaster as believing in 1394 that "because of the division among kings and realms, both papacies have to be quashed." Simon de Cramaud wrote to the archbishop of Canterbury ca. 1401 that he heard from "many worthy of belief" that the late duke of Lancaster "always praised and approved" the *via cessionis* (*Thes. nov.,* 2:1245).

25. Valois, 3:76, where the passage is quoted as anonymous; the author was in fact Simon de Cramaud.

26. The *idea* of even a coerced abdication as a possible or desirable solution had emerged much earlier, e.g., at a meeting of the University of Paris on 8 January 1379, at which "many said that it would be better to force both contenders to renounce the papacy and for the university to be neutral" than to come out for one or the other (Valois, 1:122; Bulaeus, 4:565; *CUP,* 3: no. 1616; and see Swanson: 45). For the suggestion of England's primacy in cessionist *policy,* see J. J. N. Palmer, "England and the Great Western Schism, 1388–1399," *English Historical Review,* 83 (1968):522.

could hardly have been expected to work together for a solution that
would have condemned some of them to go down in history as schismatics.[27] The French dukes may have been told this by their councillors,
but they would not have needed much telling. We may also impute to
the dukes an attitude presupposed by the non-juridical solution, namely,
that the world could get along without ever knowing which papacy had
been the true one; here, as noted in the previous chapter, we see one
aspect of the reduction of the papacy to its institutional entity. But the
via cessionis had less evident dimensions, discernible as fact or probability
by practitioners of *Realpolitik* but perhaps unpleasant enough to be left
murky by princes who liked to think of their public actions as so many
displays of their magnificence. Each papacy in the Schism was a complex
of interests and symbols that meant everything to the two popes and a
great deal to their cardinals, officials, and clerical supporters; neither
pope would be likely to resign freely and thereby admit that everything
he had stood for was inconsequential. They would have to be pressed to
resign, forced to resign, or in the end deposed—all of which would have
to be carried out as a massive, sustained sequence of escalations, requiring tactical planning, political and personal manipulations, the spending
of much money, and the use of power to punish and reward. Last but
not least, the whole effort would require the construction of theory to
make it appear rightful and rational. Little if any of this fell within the
ducal purview; most of it was to be the work of Simon de Cramaud and
others, from the University of Paris and the College of Cardinals, whom
we shall see working with him.

We can reasonably imagine that the dukes of Berry and Burgundy
functioned here as patrons from above, as power bases from below, with
the politicians doing the actual work and creating their own tactics and
even their long-range plans. This structure of political action has not
been appreciated because historians have conventionally assigned the key
role in unionism to the University of Paris, whose arts and theology

---

27. Martin Souchon, *Die Papstwahlen in der Zeit des grossen Schismas: Entwicklung und
Verfassungskämpfe des Kardinalates von 1378–1417*, 1 (Braunschweig, 1898):217,
takes notice of this point, which is attested by many sources. Thus in a letter commend-
ing the *via cessionis* to the kings of the Avignon obedience, 12 July 1395, the dukes of
Berry, Burgundy, and Orléans declared that Charles VI and the leading men of his realm
"ne consentiroyent que leur honneur feust mis en main d'arbitres," who might judge
them to have been schismatic (Lehoux, 2:340). A draft of a letter from Charles VI to the
king of the Romans, Wenceslas IV of Bohemia, 1397, suggests the same consideration
to the other side: "Credo quod vestra serenitas non libenter audiret sentenciam per quam
in effectu appareret felicis memorie dominum Karolum, patrem vestrum, malam in facto
ecclesie opinionem tenuisse" (AN, J 518, fol. 290r). See also Pedro Tenorio's statement
below, Ch. V, at n. 34.

faculties had indeed been hotbeds of unionist sentiment even in the days when *via facti* reigned supreme. The sentiment continued, but it had to be used by the politicians; the academy had to be politicized, coordinated, and managed; the ideas of its leaders had to be shaped and pointed to fit into the political enterprise that would replace speculative purity as the ground of theory. None of this happened overnight or without effort, and this is the point of the foregoing remarks: if the return of the dukes in August 1392 meant the beginning of the end for Avignon, it was indeed only that—the point of departure for a complex political construction to be planned and carried through by political agents who could not move faster than the medium would allow. The reality of the *via cessionis* would take years to work out.

The Valois family itself could be led by its elders without too much trouble at this time. King Charles VI does to be sure appear in the official and narrative sources of the time as though he actually made decisions and took action during his periods of lucidity—the spells of insanity were alluded to as "the king's absence"[28]—and modern historians often write the same way;[29] but the contrary is suggested by the course of events and explicitly stated in one or two sources: when sane, Charles could understand what was said to him and say yes in reply, but he did not impose his will.[30] "The king" was in fact the royal council dominated in these years by the power of Berry and Burgundy working through their clients.[31] Louis of Orléans, the king's brother, would eventually challenge the Berry-Burgundy bloc, but in 1392 he was only twenty years old and followed his uncles' lead. He did, however, have his own interests. His relatively small appanage made him depend on the crown for regular grants of money, a relationship that on the one hand led him to build up a power of his own by patronage of the career officials in the royal government, on the other hand made him susceptible to the temptations of Italian adventure—the more so because of the Milanese con-

---

28. E. Jarry, *La vie politique de Louis de France, duc d'Orléans, 1372–1407* (Paris, 1889): 96.

29. To give only a recent example, Palmer, *EFC*, constantly constructs his narrative on the assumption that there was a Charles VI who directed events even after August 1392; the assumption is never proven and often patently wrong (e.g., p. 196), and events requiring explanation in terms of ducal interests and power are set forth simply as Charles's own decisions. One does, to be sure, have the impression that the periods of royal sanity in the early years of the king's illness saw him more lively than he would later be, but nothing suggests that he could even then play a role of his own (for a contrary opinion see Nordberg: 64, with no proof). Haller, *PKR*: 263, puts it so: "'The king' meant the diverse and often conflicting forces that then made up the government."

30. For examples of the king's incompetence when sane, see Valois, 3:169 f., 338.

31. Perroy, "Feudalism or Principalities": 184; Noël Valois, *Le conseil du roi aux XIVe, XVe, et XVIe siècles* (Paris, 1888): 74, 80, 98.

nections of his wife, Valentina Visconti.[32] Since his uncles could hardly deny him his share of what was after all a family business, they lent themselves to the Italian opening, despite its anti-unionist implications, but they did so in a way that guaranteed failure. Anjou's old project of a kingdom of Adria was revived on Orléans's behalf and proposed to Clement VII in the spring of 1393,[33] but with no Paris commitment to foot the bill. The pope, therefore, still laboring under debts incurred in support of Louis of Anjou a decade earlier, also no doubt mindful of the abortive royal expedition of 1390/1391, and fresh from similarly disappointing and expensive experiences with the duke of Bourbon in 1392/1393,[34] refused to get involved with Orléans under these conditions and repeated the refusal a year later in 1394.[35] The net effect, however, was to slow down the movement towards cessionism, for the Paris-Avignon relationship based on negotiations over the *via facti* gave a continued dimension of reality to the basic principle of Clement VII's papacy. As long as this was the case, a policy implementing the *via cessionis* could hardly emerge.

The prime obstacle to such a policy was Clement himself and the extraordinarily intimate bond between his papacy and the Valois. He was of course dependent on them, but dependency has many modes and is in any case a two-way relationship; the Valois had their own pope, but their possession would be valuable only insofar as they treated him with at least the forms of respect and much of the substance, so that his papacy could remain credible. Clement understood this perfectly, for his situation was only quantitatively different from that of his Avignon predecessors before the Schism, who also had to oblige the Valois, who also saw themselves forced to bear the overwhelming burden of financing military action in Italy, and who set an example for their successor by increasing the power of their government over the territorial churches in order to raise the money their policy required. The big difference was that the French church, which had provided 44 percent of the money received from the collectories by the *camera apostolica* in the time of Innocent VI (1353–1362), now provided pretty much all of it—with Aragon contributing about 10 percent after 1387.[36] Since the rationale and vital principle of Clement's papacy lay in the *via facti*, which concretely meant French enterprises to conquer Italy, also the justification of these enterprises by Clement's title and their financing by his trea-

---

32. Jarry, *Vie politique*: 96 f.; Lehoux, 2:293; Nordberg: 4–60.
33. Valois, 2:193–198.
34. Favier, *Finances*: 627 f.
35. Ibid.: 631 f.
36. Ibid.: 580, 475.

sury, we can see his papacy in this light as a machine to collect French ecclesiastical revenues, concentrate them, and turn them over to the Valois. Thus, for example, Duke Louis of Anjou was granted the revenues of four collectories in 1379, and in 1382 he was given all the net revenues of the papacy for three years, which worked out to 240,000 francs a year.* All in all, over an eight-year period, Clement spent a million florins on Angevin expeditions.[37] There were other outpourings too in other manifestations of the *via facti*. Quite apart from this, Clement's papacy functioned similarly when he regularly sanctioned royal taxation of the French clergy—the revenues from which came to be regarded as essential to the French crown[38]—and put much of the French church at the disposal of the king and dukes by giving them rights to appoint and by himself appointing their nominees.[39] It was all very comfortable most of the time; and in the case of the duke of Berry, the Avignon connection was a source not only of profit but of pleasure. He visited the papal court frequently, sure always of finding an agreeable reception, and seems to have developed a genuine liking for Clement as a person. By 1392 he could see that the party had to end, but he was glad to find reasons to go slowly "and meanwhile defend the truth."[40]

Monetary units: Late-medieval Europe continued to use the Carolingian system of pounds-shillings-pence, in France livres-sous-deniers, with only the last unit (penny/denier/denarius) existing as an actual silver coin; twelve of these made up a shilling, and twenty shillings made up a pound. The actual values depended on the weight and fineness of the penny; in late-medieval France the most frequently used unit, the *livre tournois*, was worth four-fifths of the *livre parisis*. The *franc* was originally a gold coin weighing 3.885 grams, but after 1385 it was no longer minted and it became money of account, worth a *livre tournois*. The *écu* was a gold coin weighing about 4 grams. The Avignon papacy's money of account was the *florin*, worth one *livre tournois* after 31 May 1393, 18s. 8d. *tournois* before.

37. Ibid.: 403 f., 627.

38. The pope gave the crown a share in papally levied tenths and also authorized the clergy to grant aids (*gabelles*) directly to the crown (Valois, 3:143 f.; Favier, *Finances*: 208–211, 225). In 1398 Berry said, "Without the aids the realm might go under" (Douët-d'Arcq, 1:148; see below, Ch. VII).

39. Papal appointment of royal nominees was a common Avignon practice; see Mollat, *Popes at Avignon*: 338 f. See below, Ch. III, for examples of Clement's doing this for Berry and the king as simple routine. Papal grants of power to appoint could be extremely valuable; thus in a letter dated 7 November 1389 (but "expedita" 6 November 1391), Clement VII gave Berry the right to nominate to sixty canonries in the episcopal and collegiate churches of France, both within and outside of his appanage (ASV, *Reg. aven.* 263, fols. 554v–555v sqq.). Another example: Charles VI appointed Pierre d'Ailly to canonries in Rouen and elsewhere on the basis of authority granted by the pope (ASV, *Reg. sup.* 78, fol. 53r; the text, 1 April 1391, mentions the prior appointments).

40. Bouvet, *Somnium*: 97 f., presents Berry as recognizing 'that detractors said he defended Clement because of "carnal affection and temporal love"; he conceded that he "loved him tenderly." See Valois, 2:413 f. See below, n. 43.

All of this explains why the French government's move towards a policy of union took so long to complete even after the political desirability of union had been perceived by the royal uncles in 1392. Historians usually write that Burgundy wanted to move briskly but that Berry frustrated him as long as Clement VII was alive,[41] so that only the pope's death on 16 September 1394 made possible the ducal unity that would lead to immediate political action. In fact, Burgundy's unionism was not so urgent as to make him oppose objectively anti-unionist policies, like Orléans's Italian project of 1393/1394;[42] and Berry's Clementism did not prevent him from going along with or even fostering certain manifestations of unionism on the part of the University of Paris. It is safer to stick to the rather general surmise that the two dukes worked together on the basis of a well-founded sense that their common interests and brotherly affection outweighed any differences of opinion about a matter that to them at least was not crucial. Furthermore, Berry's well-attested devotion to Clement's cause may have expressed recognition of a fact that could hardly have escaped the notice of his brother as well, namely, that the integration of the French church into the French polity under the government of the Avignon papacy, a process that Clement VII's pontificate furthered but had not begun, was a massive reality that had to be considered in any action committing France to abandon Avignon. The fact may well have been appreciated in terms of cases of interest and practical advantage rather than by means of rational analysis, but it would not have been ignored. The best way to do it justice was to proceed slowly and tentatively, allowing reality to work its way into the politics of union at each step.[43]

To talk of reality in human affairs is to talk of mental structures, ranging from the implicit principles of behavior to the velleities of sentiment and on to the systematic ratiocination expressed in formal arguments and treatises. While one cannot know these structures in their multitude, variety, and instability in any given situation, the

---

41. E.g., Vaughan, *Philip the Bold*: 46; Haller, *PKR*: 212; see the references in Valois, 2:393, and cf. 2:413.

42. It is remarkable that Bouvet, *Somnium*: 100, does *not* present the figure of Burgundy as having been active for union up to August 1394, but rather the reverse: Burgundy is made to confess: "Venacio nobis *hactenus* placuit; gaudebamus mimos et ystriones audire, . . . sed ex quo *nunc* videmus . . . [etc.]."

43. Ibid.: 98: Berry refutes charges that he has opposed union; he wants it very much, "but we are seeking ways to it with our lord the king and his sound council, and we are studying the situation and events until the occasion and means shall present themselves to the king. For while so great a matter asks for speed, it must nevertheless be taken up with careful deliberation, lest confusion ensue where unity is hoped for, and so that due honor be preserved in what is promulgated. And meanwhile defend the truth that was once approved!"

history of public action can define significant public opinion as the relevant mentality of those who act in this or that case. Let us note at once that as far as France's Schism policy was concerned, the relevant public opinion was that of the secular magnates, the upper clergy, and the universities, above all the University of Paris; furthermore the political community which eventually agreed that the Avignon papacy had to be given up was that of the north of France, the *lingua gallicana*,[44] focused in Paris. Conventional use of the word *French* often conceals the extremely important political differences between north and south: the Avignon papacy had always been a southern construction; it enjoyed the support of Languedocian (and Spanish) princes and prelates well after the north had abandoned it; and the regional patterns of university recruitment in that period made the University of Toulouse a kind of intellectual center of the south, opposed to Paris and loyal to Avignon.[45] Leaving aside the question of how strongly or honestly the northern clergy believed in the legitimacy of the Avignon line in the Schism, we can point to much evidence that professors at the University of Paris and prelates who in most cases were its alumni had a well-developed belief that the Avignon papacy as a whole had reduced the "Gallican" church to a servitude far worse than that of other territorial churches.[46] While *Gallican* in this usage meant French, it was in fact the collectories of the north that provided most of Avignon's revenues from France, so that Clement VII's

---

44. See below, Ch. VII. For "lingua gallicana" as meaning the north, see, e.g., *Ordonnances*, 7:557: "tam in Gallica quam Occitana Linguis" (4 April 1393). A similar formula appears in reference to collecting aids in BN, *ms. fr.* 20, 886, no. 33: "tam in lingua gallicana quam occitana."

45. For the preponderantly southern (i.e., from south of the line between the French and Occitan languages) personnel of the Avignon papacy before the Schism, see Bernard Guillemain, *La cour pontificale d'Avignon 1309–1376* (1962; repr. Paris 1966): 150 (the popes were all southerners), 187 (95 out of 111 French cardinals were southerners), 476–480 (predominance of southerners among officials generally); see also the maps showing all this: nos. 1, 5, 7. Cf. Renouard, *Avignon Papacy*: 87 f. Jacques Verger, "Le recrutement géographique des universités françaises au début du XVe siècle," *Mélanges d'archéologie et d'histoire*, 82 (1970):855–902, shows that the great majority of students went to the university of their region (p. 893 ff.) and observes that the University of Toulouse was "the intellectual capital of the whole southwest of France" (p. 898 f.). For the role of Toulouse as supporter of Benedict XIII against Paris, see below, Chs. VII, VIII.

46. Haller, *PKR*: 208, and *passim*, touches on several aspects of this idea, which figures in the general ideology of the Gallican Liberties. A number of statements at the Third Paris Council mentioned the special servitude of the Gallican church: Gilles Deschamps (BdeC:46); Pierre Leroy (AN J 518, fol. 427v: "L'eglise de France est et a este en greigneur subieccion et servitute que nulle autre"); Nicholas de Bosc (fol. 426v); the abbot of Jumièges (fol. 430r); the bishop of Chartres (fol. 395r). Similar statements were made on other occasions, e.g., by Jean Petit in 1406 (Valois, 3:436). Deschamps, Leroy, and Petit were or had been masters at the University of Paris.

unprecedented fiscalism necessitated by his support of the Angevin *via facti* was also an unprecedented milking of the north by the south.[47] Tenths of clerical revenues were collected regularly for the pope's benefit; all major benefices were reserved to papal provision and hence subjected to annates or *servicia communia*; episcopal and archidiaconal procuration fees from churches subject to visitation were reserved for the pope; caritative subsidies were demanded of new prelates as a kind of price for their appointment; the principle was asserted and often enforced that the *servicia* of new bishops and abbots had to be paid in full and at once, instead of in sometimes endless installments.[48] There was much grumbling about all this, but a modern taxpayer will hardly be impressed by the economics of the complaints and will note in any case that there was no shortage of candidates for the allegedly ruined prelacies;[49] the main thing is that the sense of resentment could be converted into a Gallican program of anti-papalism when conditions called for it.

These appeared after the death of Louis of Anjou in 1384, the end of Clement VII's big chance to fulfill the raison d'être of his pontificate and the beginning of the first period of Berry-Burgundy control of the royal government. The Angevin enterprise had required the fiscal impositions noted above, and the pope's debts required that they be continued, with two subsidies imposed in the same year (10 April and 17 December 1384), much to the discontent of the clergy and with protests from the University of Paris.[50] But the *via facti* had no charm for Paris at this time; Burgundy was intent on extending his power in the Low Countries, and Berry was especially keen to take Provence away from the child Louis II of Anjou and add it to the crown, in which endeavor he was frustrated by Clement VII's refusal to go along.[51] The time had come to bring the papacy into line with reality, and two ordinances, 3 and 6 October 1385, now for the first time took "the liberty and franchise" of the Gallican church under the protection of royal law.[52] The first declared that the royal power would henceforth not back the papal collectors in exacting subsidies. The second was more diffuse: (1) it instituted royal commissioners to seize portions of the revenues from cardinals' benefices in

47. Favier, *Finances*: 474–476, 695, for the north's contribution and Clement's fiscalism.

48. Ibid.: 124, 206, 235, 369 f.

49. But cf. ibid.: 393–396, where Favier refutes Jean Petit's exaggerations about several points of papal fiscalism, but nevertheless writes, "C'est l'ensemble de la charge fiscale qui était insupportable."

50. Ibid.: 222 f.

51. Valois, 2:94–112.

52. *Ordonnances,* 7:131 f., 133–137 (the quoted phrase on p. 136).

order to provide for the upkeep of the churches neglected by their absentee commendatories; (2) it decreed that the papal collectors would not be allowed to seize the movable property (*spolia*) of dead prelates and abbots, but that this property was to be put in the king's hand so that those with a claim to it might sue to recover in the royal courts; (3) it complained about the papal reservation of a year's assessed revenues (annates) from all vacant benefices, not just those vacant *in curia* or traditionally in the pope's gift; (4) it prohibited the collectors from taking such annates from vacant benefices in the gift of the king or other lay lords. It was appropriately the first president of the Parlement of Paris, the layman Arnaud de Corbie, who was chosen to go to Avignon at the end of November to tell the pope what had been done; the chronicler of St. Denis writes that the pope promised to abide by the new rules. Since Valois did not know of any other papal response, he assumed that this apparently monumental novelty was only a passing unpleasantness due to pique over the Provence affair and that the evidence of continued concern for its enforcement could be interpreted as showing its ineffectiveness.[53] It was one of his few big mistakes, as we see from a text discovered after his time.

It is a memorandum by Pierre Gérard, bishop of Le Puy, whom the pope sent to Paris after the ordinances had been in force for several months, in order to get the royal government to modify them.[54] We learn from it first of all that a number of other issues were on the table: there were royal complaints about the tenths and subsidies levied by the pope, about his reservation of procuration fees, and about the collectors' practice of insisting on the full assessed value of annates and *servicia* even though in most cases this was much higher than the real value.[55] The papal legate had his own complaints about pretty much everything in

---

53. Valois, 2:391f. Haller, *PKR*: 211, goes astray by assuming that the careful Valois must have known all the extant sources; it is a reasonable enough assumption for the BN and AN but not for the ASV (see n. 54). The account by the chronicler of St. Denis (*RSD*, 1:400) is cited by Valois (2:391 f.) and quoted by E. Léonard, "Négociations entre Clément VII et Charles VI au sujet des charges de l'Église de France et de l'ordonnance royale du 6 octobre 1385," *Revue historique de droit français et étranger*, 4th series, 2 (1923).

54. The text, ASV, *Instr. misc.*, no. 4283, is presented by Léonard, "Négociations": 272–286.

55. Annates, collected from lesser benefices, were assessed as one year's net revenue; *servicia*, from the major benefices, were supposed to be one-third of a year's gross revenue—see Favier, *Finances*: 341. But the assessments of the values of benefices had been fixed in the past and no longer corresponded to real values, which were lower; see Jean Favier, "Temporels ecclésiastiques et taxation fiscale," *Journal des Savants* (1964):102–127 (esp. 106 ff.).

the ordinances, as well as a general complaint showing how the crown's
action had mobilized the clergy's resentment into a political reality:

Because of this ordinance the rights of the apostolic *camera* have been more or
less annihilated. For, detestably, those who are obligated to the *camera*
and are quite capable of paying have become utterly disobedient; they care
nothing about sentences pronounced against them or about papal proceedings,
but commonly say that the king has prohibited them from paying anything
to the pope's agents.

The royal response, apparently worked out by the councillors and members of Parlement who were negotiating with Gérard, reflects the ideology of Gallican Liberty cultivated in the University of Paris:

The king will issue letters declaring that it was not his intention in the new
ordinance to interfere in any way with the old rights (*jura antiqua*) of
our lord the pope or of his apostolic *camera, viz.* in regard to *servicia communia,*
arrears of tenths imposed in the past, and other moneys that the *camera*
has of old been accustomed to get from the benefices of the realm.

Royal action had destroyed the papalist elaboration of the pope's plenitude of power; royal action would now replace it with a papal power cut
back to the good old days and exercised by grace of the crown. The
difference between the two would fall under the crown's jurisdiction.

Thus Gérard got very little: perhaps a two-year grace period for the
extended scope of annates, a confirmation of the ordinance's non-appli-
cation in Languedoc, and an abandonment of the protest about papal
arrogation of procurations (in exchange for the pope's exemption therefrom of procurations due to archdeacons in the royal service). As for
tenths and subsidies, we are told only that agreement had been reached
—presumably to exempt the clergy of the north, for these did not have
to pay when Clement imposed a rash of subsidies in the years 1389–1392
—they fell on Aragon, Castile, and Languedoc.[56] Otherwise the crown
stood pat on the ordinance, took the necessary steps in the future to keep
it in force, eventually extended it to Languedoc (26 April 1392), and,
through Parlement, regularly took cognizance of cases involving *spolia*
and the related matter of repair costs to churches; "the ordinance was
executed punctually."[57] One would like to know more—Who planned
this Gallican construction? To what end?—and one cannot help wonder-
ing if it was somehow related to the markedly Gallican struggle of the
Paris university masters against the tyranny of Jean Blanchard, the chancellor appointed by Clement VII, in just these years of 1385 and 1386;

----

56. Favier, *Finances*: 223–225; but Favier does not cite Léonard's document ("Négociations") or refer to the negotiations of 1385–1386.
57. Guillaume Mollat in F. Lot & R. Fawtier, eds., *Histoire des institutions françaises
au moyen âge,* 3(Paris, 1962):442 f.; Favier, *Finances*: 259 f.; Valois, 2:392 n. 4.

but there are few grounds for even guesses.[58] The important thing was the construction itself, which brought together a number of factors that would eventually form the presuppositions of union policy: the government's assumption of direct lordship over the clergy in certain areas, the clergy's understanding that a French papacy was in the first place a papacy that exploited the French church, the university's doctrine of Gallican Liberty as an alternate system to high papalism. The community of action created by the government in 1385 to curtail Clement's power would be reactivated ten years later to demand abdication of his successor.

Here, as always in history, the clear lines constructed by analysis are blurred in the course of events, probably because we have so little evidence for the programmatic thinking of the principals, and certainly because of the play of accidents. At one extreme we have the clarity of Haller's formula: "The day that France was convinced that the disadvantageous consequences of the Schism outweighed the advantages afforded by the half-papacy in Avignon—on that day the fate of the Avignon contender was sealed"[59]—a simple statement requiring volumes of explication. At the other extreme there is the positivist account by Valois, a masterpiece of erudition that epigones must use but cannot imitate, which however achieves its precision by contenting itself with explanations that are casual and often trivial. We shall have to find our way between abstraction and detail, taking as guide the big fact that when the news of the death of Clement VII (16 September 1394) reached Paris (22 September), the royal council and the dukes of Berry and Burgundy reacted instantaneously with a program of action designed to terminate the Avignon papacy and to impose a similar end on the Roman line. The unanimity, decisiveness, and commitment revealed on that occasion must have been grounded deep in the structures and forces of policy during the previous years; that they did not manifest themselves earlier must have been due in good part to Clement himself,

---

58. The Léonard text ("Négociations") says nothing about any role of the dukes or their agents in the ordinances or the negotiations. The duke of Berry was not in Paris when the measures were taken and perhaps not when the negotiations took place (his itinerary in Lehoux, 3:468 f.); his client Simon de Cramaud, however, was in Paris, perhaps uninterruptedly, from ca. 30 August to 17 November (AN, X 1A 1472, fol. 377r; X 1A 1473, fol. 192v). Simon appears in Avignon on 21 December 1385 (ASV, *Oblig. et sol.* 43, fol. 106v) and had no doubt arrived earlier—perhaps at the time when Arnaud de Corbie came to present the ordinances to Clement. But the data do not allow more than conjecture. See Swanson: 75 for a possible revival of unionism by the university right after this episode, and see Alan Bernstein, *Pierre d'Ailly and the Blanchard Affair* (Leiden, 1978), *passim* and esp. pp. 180 ff.

59. Haller, *PKR*: 212.

that is to the loyalties and interests that he could activate on his be-half.[60] Our scheme is thus the following: the dukes' return to power after August 1392 meant that the French government would seek to end the Schism by the *via cessionis*, but the manifestations of this new decision and its emergence as actual policy were frustrated by Pope Clement VII and his agents. What we will look for in this period, 1392–1394, are the elements that would figure in the structure of policy after it, on both sides, Paris and Avignon.

We are best informed about one of these elements, the mobilization of the University of Paris. Sometime in early 1391, when Charles VI was still intent on his Italian expedition, he had ordered the university to cease the agitation for union that it had recently taken up.[61] The profes-sors of canon law advised obedience, and the university as a whole seems not to have acted otherwise; but at least one theologian—perhaps Jean Gerson—wrote a treatise asserting the university's obligation to pursue union no matter what and concluding that the canonists' Christian faith would be open to suspicion if they persisted in their attitude.[62] He also spelled out the possible ways of ending the Schism. Arbitration (the *via compromissi*) would not be good, but a general council to decide between the contenders would be "the most just and reasonable way" according to the university's views at the beginning of the Schism; the *via cessionis* was put last but was highly praised and well fortified by what would become the standard arguments: even a true pope must resign if church union cannot be obtained otherwise; everyone is obliged to give up his prop-erty if necessary for the common good; and "while the office of the papacy is a dignity concerning the common good, nevertheless as far as the person of the pope is concerned it is a private good."[63] A typical Gersonian touch, significant for our understanding of exactly what "the university" was, appears in several passages exalting the theologians of the University of Paris, both professors and graduates, and claiming for them the right to determine all matters of faith as an obligatory guide to the actual definitions pronounced by the prelates.[64] One may judge these

---

60. Apart from Clement's ties to the Valois, there is the fact that by this time a large number of the benefices in the French church had been filled by him, including most of the bishoprics, and the legitimacy of his appointees' titles depended on his own. See, for example, Simon de Cramaud, App. II, Pt. III, "Reply to 'It Is not Allowed,'" no. 6; also Jean de Lacoste at the Third Paris Council, 30 May 1398: "Et miror de multis qui magis titubant circa titulum domini nostri pape quam circa titulum suum, cum resoluto iure domini nostri non videam ius eorum posse stare"—ASV, *Arm.* 54, t. 21, fol. 218r.

61. Valois, 2:394–397; cf. John Morrall, *Gerson and the Great Schism* (Manchester, 1960): 30–32. Cf. Swanson: 76–89 on the events discussed in the following pages.

62. Gerson, *Oeuvres,* 6:1–18; cf. *CUP,* 3:595 f.

63. Gerson, *Oeuvres,* 6:10 f.

64. Ibid.:7, 14.

views as either ludicrous or pathetic; they were in any case anachronistic by Gerson's time, when

a debilitated and watered-down theology had often ceased to draw from the sources, no longer read the fathers and great theologians of the past, but rested content with convenient promptuaries and with the patristic excerpts in Gratian's *Decretum*—a theology that did not solve the new ecclesiastico-political problems according to its own specifically competent criteria but, in degrading dependence on canon law, looked for appropriate passages in the canonistic sources.[65]

In fact, quite apart from the issues raised by the quoted passage—or perhaps not quite—the professors and graduates in theology did not have the same access to power and political office enjoyed by the canonists; and when they did enter public life, their opportunistic ways and "assentatory" behavior were no different from anyone else's.[66] Gerson, who preserved some purity by foregoing direct influence on public action, pronounced positions that we can take as those of a kind of ideal University of Paris. Thus we may note his strong but vain and unwelcome insistence that the king should concern himself with church union, in his sermon of 6 January 1391 preached to the king,[67] and his much more definite arguments two years later, December 1392, when the government was receptive to such advice. On this latter occasion, in the disputations preliminary to his getting the master's degree in theology, Gerson rejected a judiciary general council, advocated the *via cessionis,* and produced all the arguments therefor with refutations of all possible objections. The pope, he held, was obliged to resign if that was necessary for union.[68] One guesses that the disputation was not just a scholastic exercise but a serious expression of what Gerson and other theologians were ready to advocate.

As for the royal government, it had already begun to create the forms that would give unionism its public entity: there had been a demarche to Avignon in October, probably in connection with the efforts of Peter of Mondovi, prior of the Carthusians of Asti, to bring the two popes into contact;[69] and when Peter went on to Paris in December 1392, his

---

65. Ehrle, *Alpartil*: 462.

66. See, e.g., Haller, *PKR*: 322–326, for sharp remarks about the opportunism of leading French prelates and professors, including the theologians Pierre d'Ailly, Pierre Plaoul, and Guillaume Fillastre. The university readily condemned such behavior in others; in its letter of 23 October 1394 to Benedict XIII (*RSD,* 2:208), it warned him lest he be persuaded by the curialists to hang on to his papacy: "Accedent aulici omnes, presentis assentatores potencie. . . ."

67. Morrall, *Gerson*: 30 f.

68. Ibid.: 34–38.

69. Valois, 2:398–401.

message from Pope Boniface IX was received graciously by "the king."[70] Soon after, the Paris theologian Gilles Deschamps spoke for the university in the royal presence; his thesis was the absolute imperative of pursuing union: anyone qualified to act who did not do so was in mortal sin; and—a significant point—if either of the two popes opposed the cause of union, he should be expelled from his see.[71] Meanwhile there were religious processions for union in which the king, princes, and prelates took part and—no doubt in resonance with all this—a series of similar public actions in Avignon.[72] If we bear in mind the statement about union made by John of Gaunt in the spring of 1392, the strongly cessionist thesis of Gerson's disputation in December, and the cessionist shape that unionism would assume in the future, we can surmise that the royal government directed by the uncles was building up to a union policy that would be a form of the *via cessionis,* requiring the liquidation of the Avignon papacy.

No such policy was in fact promulgated in 1393, for reasons that can only be guessed on the basis of the obvious consideration, that—in Haller's terms—the disadvantages of Avignon did not yet outweigh its advantages. Palmer has argued that France's union policy was a simple function of her negotiations for peace with England and that in the first half of 1393 these "had made insufficient progress to allow any positive action to be taken to terminate the Schism."[73] Perhaps "require" would be better than "allow." In any case, as we have seen, the *via facti* in the shape of an expedition by Louis of Orléans to conquer Rome and become king of Adria was still kept alive in talks between Paris and Avignon, even if both sides seemed unduly nonchalant; and the ducal uncles, who had been living happily and profitably with the Schism for a decade and a half, might well see in it no great loss for themselves during the immediate future. Gerson and Deschamps of course presented union as the supreme, absolute, overriding urgency, but no policy was that urgent to a Valois duke, particularly if he had reasons to procrastinate. Clement VII indeed made it his business to provide such reasons as soon as he realized the danger in the unionist public relations generated in Paris in the latter part of 1392. In February of 1393, "when he heard that the *via cessionis* was being freely propounded at the University of Paris," he sent the Carmelite Jean Golein to Paris to make propaganda against that *via* and in favor of the *via facti.*[74] Then in March he sent

---

70. Valois, 2:402; *RSD,* 2:54–56, writes that on this occasion "all the princes of the lilies joined in the king's favorable disposition, for they all wished to end the Schism— except for the duke of Berry."

71. Valois, 2:404.

72. Valois, 2:403.

73. Palmer, *EFC:* 195.

74. *RSD,* 2:58–60.

a much more important figure, Cardinal Pedro de Luna, the future Benedict XIII.

Pedro's behavior during his mission, which lasted until early September 1394, became a subject of controversy as soon as he was elected pope, and the modern literature still reflects these ancient quarrels. On the one hand the main public point of his mission was to represent the Avignon interest in the peace negotiations between the royal uncles on both sides: Berry, Burgundy, Lancaster, and Gloucester. He made it his business to be present at Leulingham in the spring of 1393, and on 28 May he had the French dukes get him an audience with the English ones, whom he tried to convince that Clement's election in 1378 had been legitimate; he also asked that arrangements be made for him to argue Clement's case in England. A year later he repeated the effort. But the English dukes were not convinced, and although something was said about getting permission for Pedro to go to England, in fact he never was able to.[75] If his efforts had any result at all, it was to prompt the English to reassert their fidelity to the Roman contender and even try—no doubt pro forma—to include the matter in the negotiations.[76] In any case it is clear enough that Pedro was pushing hard-line Avignonism, what was called the *via reduccionis*: union to come from the other side's conversion. Some reports about his activity in Paris during these years confirm the picture: he allegedly responded with harsh criticism when the University of Paris expounded its union program to him in August 1393, and he was allegedly among those working to prevent the royal government from giving its favor to the university's efforts in 1394.[77]

On the other hand, however, there is a great deal of testimony to the effect that Pedro in Paris was speaking the language of union and specifically praising the *via cessionis*. All of this testimony dates from a

---

75. Valois, 2:322 f. In early 1395 the author (no doubt Simon de Cramaud) of the instructions for the royal embassy to Avignon observed that Pedro had been at Boulogne twice in two years "before the uncles of the king of England and other great lords of his council, and he sent and wrote many times to England . . . in order to get a hearing to show the sound justice of our holy father Clement's cause. But a number of days were set, there were delays, and in the end he could neither get a hearing nor even be received" (*Ampl. coll.*, 7:455). There are various reports of what Lancaster said: Pedro could cross the channel but it would do no good (*RSD*, 2:80); "the clergy and people of England held as an article of faith that Urban's election had been canonical" (Simon de Cramaud, quoted as anonymous by Valois, 4:520); "the English would give a hearing to the justice of our side if the French would give a hearing to theirs" (Pierre Ravat's "Allegations," ASV, *Arm.* 54, t. 22, fol. 136v; Benedict must have told him this—he writes, "Item audivi quod dux Lencastrie expresse dixit domino nostro pape tunc legato . . ."). See n. 115 below.

76. Valois, 2:323; also the items quoted in n. 75.

77. Valois, 2:422; *RSD*, 2:80, 130–134, 182.

time when Pedro had become Benedict XIII and had set himself in
opposition to the *via cessionis*; the recollections of his different discourse
in 1393/1394, as Haller has argued, were obviously intended to embar-
rass him.[78] So, for example, two of his cardinals wrote in 1398: "When he
was a legate in France he said to the dukes of Burgundy and Lancaster,
and to a large number of members of the University of Paris, that the
way of abdication by both contenders was the better, shorter, and more
expedient way, and he urged these lords to do what they could to
promote it; this is known from the two dukes themselves."[79] Indeed the
duke of Burgundy did recall in 1395 that Pedro had said to him in the
bishop of Paris's chamber that "he saw no other way but that of cession"
and in 1398 recalled the same episode by saying that Pedro "had himself broached the *via cessionis* to him." Benedict's claim was that the
duke had been misled by his chancellor Jean Canart, who had served as
interpreter,[80] and it is easy to imagine how this might have happened; for
if Benedict's own union proposals (which we shall study in later chapters) included the possibility of abdication, they also included much else
and in particular a discussion of legitimacy, whereas the Paris *via cessionis*
came down to a double abdication without such a discussion. "Cession"
could have been used in one sense by Benedict and understood in another by Canart, in good faith or bad on either side or both.

Simon de Cramaud's testimony may give the answer. In 1406 he
recalled how he had rejoiced in the news of Benedict's election—"I
would have voted for him myself!"—because, he said, he had been taken
in by the holy devotion to union that Pedro had shown in Paris: "He
played the little lamb of God, he seemed to be a regular marvel, but it
was just hypocrisy!"[81] This is rather general, but in 1400 Simon wrote:
"As God is my witness, he told me—in Clement's lifetime, in the
bishop of Paris's chamber—that he wouldn't want to hold the papacy for
even one day if the good of union required him to give it up."[82] This must

---

78. Haller, *PKR*: 524–535, a review of most of the evidence.

79. *ALKG*, 6:258 f.; the authors were probably Pierre de Thury and Jean de Lagrange.

80. AN, J 518, fols. 143v, 144v: during his discussions with the duke in Avignon,
10 June 1395, Benedict recalled the devotion to union that he had expressed in conversation with Burgundy in the castle of La Trémoille; Burgundy perhaps pointedly replied
that there had been *three* conversations, the two others in the reception room (*camera
paramenti*) and chapel of the bishop of Paris, with Jean Canart present as interpreter, and
it was *then* that Pedro de Luna had praised cession. The 1398 statement appears in
Burgundy's vote for subtraction (Douët-d'Arcq, 1:144). Benedict's suggestion that Canart had distorted the statements he was interpreting (BdeC: 114) is accepted by Haller,
PKR: 533. See also nn. 112, 115, below.

81. BdeC: 216.

82. Glosses on Salva's "Allegations," BN, *ms. lat.* 1475, fol. 51r: "Nunc iste qui ante
dicebat quod pro bono unionis nollet tenere papatum per unum diem, et testis est michi

have been at the time recalled by Burgundy, and the report was most likely exact; for while Benedict XIII would always deny that he had committed himself to the *via cessionis* in his legatine conversations with Burgundy,[83] he frequently said more or less what Simon reported. The "if" was of course a big one, and in Benedict's thinking it was always associated with a determination of legitimacy.[84]

We will come back to Pedro's unionism in a moment; meanwhile we can suppose that at least part of the reason for the lack of official efforts for union in 1393 was the activity deployed on several fronts by Clement's agents, Jean Golein and Pedro de Luna, who variously made propaganda against the *via cessionis*; extolled the *via facti*; pursued the *via reduccionis*; won over Burgundy, the court clergy, and the university unionists by speaking their language; and—quite possibly—won over Berry by giving or promising him material favors.[85] In doing all this they could hardly have imagined that Paris might be turned back to the good old days of *via facti,* only that the crown's leaning toward the *via cessionis* might be kept within the limits of a policy that Clement could live with. For they must have known that the die had been cast. Sometime in October "the king" wrote letters to the bishops of the realm—or at least to one of them, Bernard Alamant, bishop of Condom, who gives us the information—in which it was said that the king was much concerned to bring union to the church and that he intended to move rapidly toward that end.[86] Alamant received such a letter on 5 November 1393 and by 18 November had produced a treatise in support of the

---

deus, tempore Clementis in camera episcopi Parisiensis ipse dixit michi, nunc . . . vult . . . retinere partem papatus."

83. Commenting on the assertion that Pedro de Luna had spoken for cession in Paris and had compacted with Burgundy to that effect (see n. 115 below), Pierre Ravat wrote (ASV, *Arm.* 54, t. 27, fol. 185r): "Audivi . . . dominum nostrum . . . frequenter hec que sibi imponuntur hic negantem constanter."

84. Right after his election Benedict XIII notified Charles VI that "he would rather spend his life as a hermit or monk than be the occasion for prolonging the Schism" (*RSD,* 2:206). A few weeks later, in an audience granted to envoys of the University of Paris, "he took off his cloak and told them that he was just as ready to resign the papacy" (ibid.). In his treatise of 1396/1397 Simon de Cramaud referred to reports that Benedict "has publicly said that if he could only meet with his adversary, he would make peace in the church even if he himself had to remain a poor priest without a benefice" (App. II, Pt. II). Thus Benedict envisaged a possible cession but *not* the *via cessionis,* which would have excluded the kind of meeting he insisted on, in which the question of legitimacy would have been discussed and resolved. See below, Ch. VIII.

85. Valois, 2:419–424; *RSD,* 2:182–184; cf. Bulaeus, 4:685 f.

86. Valois, 2:405 f. Alamant noted that he had received his letter on 5 November (BN, *ms. lat.* 14,643, fol. 38v), and that it conveyed "the royal intention to unite the church" (fol. 198v); in another context, a letter of 26 March 1394 to Clement VII, he referred to the letter with the phrase "ad ecclesie unionem ad quam multum intendebat, prout michi scripserat" (fol. 222v). For Alamant's career, see below, Ch. V, n. 64.

royal desire, which he sent to the king and other notables in Paris.[87] Inept at getting to a point and incapable of sticking to one, he could not have made much of a splash with his all-but-unreadable work—except among the Avignon apologists later on, who reacted very strongly to his arguments against the original legitimacy of Clement VII.[88] He did, however, include some information of interest here, to the effect that the royal project involved a double abdication, and it was the royal council which would work out that plan.[89] Thus it would seem that underneath the apparent immobilism of 1393 something was in fact going on: the royal council was favorably considering a double abdication and had circulated letters to this effect among the bishops, presumably in order to evoke their political support. Since we know this only because one bishop happened to write about it, we can guess that other such practical steps were being taken more or less quietly at the same time. Still undecided however—and this was the area in which Clement's envoys could work —was the nature of the new policy: would it be gracious, sluggish, and flabby, or would it be imposed by force and carried through with power?

The former alternative would have been in the ducal style. The latter required the kind of *Realpolitik* described above, which combined a number of elements: an imperial sense of royal power cultivated in court circles at the time, an egoistic ruthlessness characteristic of the careerists who ran the political machines, and the academic radicalism of an abstract style of thought harnessed to professorial savagery. One can point

---

87. Valois, 2:406, for the recipients, the surviving mss., and printed excerpts.

88. The text of the treatise in the Bibliotheca Apostolica Vaticana, *Barb. lat.* 872, has enormous glosses by Pierre Ravat refuting the passages in Alamant's Pt. XI which argue that the canonical provisions for papal elections exclude the kind of objection raised by the cardinals in 1378. The glosses were written after January 1397 (fol. 77v). At the Third Paris Council of May/July 1398, another papal spokesman, Jean de Lacoste, referred to Bernard Alamant as one "who in his treatise seems to say that our lord [Benedict] is not the pope" (BdeC: 20).

89. Bib. Apost. Vat., *Barb. lat.* 872, fol. 83v: (Addressing the king) "sanctissimus conceptus vester eo fit factibilior et honorabilior et tucior quo [*ms.*: que] . . . utrique capiti concertancium minor subest racio resistendi. Is enim penes quem non sunt claves cum tota parte sua tenetur cedere, veritati acquiescere, et Cristo incorporari, ut dictum est. Is autem penes quem sunt claves, antequam tantum bonum obmitteretur, pro recolleccione, cura, et pastu ovium infirmarum humiliter se deberet exhiberi [*sic!*] cessurum oneri et honori, eciam cum effectu, per talem cessionem dispersa congregans." While this speaks only of the king's *conceptus*, an earlier exhortation that the royal council take cognizance of the Schism suggests Alamant's recognition of the council's de facto supremacy: (fol. 82r) "Penes quam partem sit culpa scismatis, et qualiter huic gravi et periculose materie sit utilius [et] celerius occurrendum, ponderet et deliberet providum et deo amabile consilium regium." Both passages show Alamant still thinking in terms of the problem of legitimacy in contrast to the strictly political *via cessionis* that was winning favor in Paris.

to several antecedents of this sort of structure, but the consummated archetype and probable model was the action of Philip IV's government against Pope Boniface VIII, a connection that struck contemporaries as it does us.

> Whenever a pope does anything against the French or the house of France— whether rightly or wrongly it doesn't matter, just so it doesn't please them—he all of a sudden stops being pope: they immediately start bringing accusations against him, they subtract obedience, they call him a heretic and schismatic, they make themselves his superiors and judges. . . . Consider what they did to Pope Boniface VIII![90]

This comes from a time after the French had done all those things to Benedict XIII, but one can usefully bear it in mind as defining the entelechy whose beginnings were the object of decision making in the last year of Clement VII. It can be related to what we know of the university's line of thought at that time. Master John of Moravia, a student in the theology faculty, attracted attention by preaching that both popes should be killed.[91] Jean Gerson's disputation of December 1392 in favor of the *via cessionis* argued that a pope who refused to resign for the common good was guilty of mortal sin and that the supreme good of church union made it unnecessary to worry about even the gravest consequences of the *via cessionis*—that the church might not have a legitimate pope and that no one would know which clerical ordinations were valid.[92] Pierre d'Ailly, Gilles Deschamps, Nicholas de Clamanges— these luminaries of arts and theology were willing to declare that a pope who refused to enter a suitable *via* of union should be driven out of office and killed.[93] Those high in the Paris government who wanted to put teeth in the new policy of *via cessionis* had only to look across the river for all the fangs they could use. At the same time, however, a government policy functioning in the real world of interest and power could not take shape in any simple way as the instrument of academic radicalism; the ideas of the academy had to be translated into politically viable pro- grams, and the spokesmen of the academy could take part in this process only if they became politicians. The royal government needed the uni- versity as a source of theory and authority, but it had to be a usable university, one that played ball and knew the score. It would take time and work to obtain this result, and in the process almost all of the unionist notables we have named would drop out and become papal

---

90. Boniface Ferrer writing in 1411 (*Thes. nov.*, 2:1449).
91. Simon de Cramaud mentions this in his treatise, App. II, Pt. II, "Schism and Heresy," and in a gloss of ca. 1400 (quoted by Valois, 4:521).
92. Morrall, *Gerson*: 34–38, with Morrall's Catholic objections on p. 38.
93. See the passage quoted below at n. 106.

agents or—as in the case of Gerson—ineffective natterers;[94] but there were
new leaders ready to take over who could be counted on to do neither
more nor less than what the government expected of them.

It remains to trace the steps in which the *clercs* and *politiques* consummated their marriage. In January 1394 a university delegation went
before the king, recently emerged from a spell of lunacy, to tell him that
he had to work for union; the official reply came from the duke of Berry,
"Pope Clement's principal champion," who to everyone's alleged surprise
said the following: "We believe that this most abominable Schism has
flourished to the point of being a shame to my lord the king and the
royal family. Everyone is sick of it. Try to find some way of ending it to
the honor of the realm, and if this way seems good to the royal council
we will certainly execute it with diligence."[95] The episode must have been
staged to create an image of wholesome solemnity, since the way of
honor had long been found; the royal council had long been aware of it
and had in fact approved it; while if the "abominable Schism" continued
to flourish, it was because the French government had deliberately not
taken decisive action to end it. What was needed now was the kind of
practical collaboration provided for on 28 January, when the royal chancellor and certain royal councillors were appointed to work with the
university "in thinking out the ways, means, and forms of expeditiously
arriving at the concord of union."[96] The university for its part contributed
to the grand image by ostentatiously basing its findings on a sort of
plebiscite of all its members, who were invited to deposit their opinions
in a chest set up for the purpose in the cloister of the Mathurin convent;
we are told that 10,000 were put in, a figure hard to believe even when
we allow for multiple voting.[97] In any case the opinions were read some-

---

94. The phrase is mine; for the substance see, e.g., Haller, *PKR*: 323; Morrall,
Gerson: 40–43, 56, 65–68, and *passim*; Bernhard Bess, *Johannes Gerson und die kirchen-
politischen Parteien Frankreichs vor dem Konzil zu Pisa* (Marburg, 1890): 22: "Gerson was
much too idealistic to have been able to work successfully in an area where it was always
political interests that decided."

95. *RSD,* 2:96–98.

96. The information comes from the university's letter of 6 June 1394 (Bulaeus,
4:687; *CUP*, 3, no. 1676; Valois, 2:407). The guess in *CUP* that Simon de Cramaud
was one of the councillors appointed is offered without supporting evidence; I note that
although he was in Paris as of 2 January 1394 (AN, X 1A 1477, fol. 397r), he must
have left for Avignon soon after, for he appears there on 28 January (AN, JJ 147, fol.
4v), the day when the appointments were made. See n. 113 below.

97. Valois, 2:407 f.; *RSD*, 2:100. Gerson's *De subtractione schismatis* [*sic pro* "obedientiae"] *Oeuvres*, 6:23, argues that the issue of subtraction should be determined by the
theology faculty in live discussion, not just by ballots (*schedulae*); he observes, no doubt
with the February 1394 voting in mind: "It can happen that one man will deposit a
hundred *schedulae* for his opinion, just as some have in fact done."

time in February and digested into a comprehensive memorandum for the use of the deputies chosen by the university on 26 February to enter into conference with the government's representatives.[98]

The latter had meanwhile received new instructions, *not* to collaborate with the university deputies but only to listen to their ideas.[99] Evidently "the king" had decided not to press for union after all, at least not in the form of a grand public action based on the university's "ways." The university and its sympathizer who wrote the official royal chronicle had no doubt that the royal switch was due to the machinations of yet another of Pope Clement's envoys, the apostolic camerary and archbishop of Narbonne, François de Conzié, sent from Avignon in March to counter the new union movement. He and his staff, we are told, gave rich gifts to members of the royal court to get them to change the dukes' minds, and they were helped in all this by Pedro de Luna.[100] The gift takers—who in this construction must have included the major clients like Simon de Cramaud—shared the blame with Clement's curialists, who had a vested interest in the Schism ("they get great offices and fat benefices now that the church is in turmoil, which they rightly believe they could never get in a whole and united church").[101] One supposes that a more tactless statement would have put the finger on the dukes themselves, or at least on the duke of Berry, as direct recipients of papal bribes.[102] Furthermore, to pick up part of an explanation offered by Palmer, the Anglo-French negotiations, which had been expected to issue in a definitive peace treaty, bogged down in June because one basic point of the settlement, the transfer of Aquitaine to John of Gaunt as a French fief, was prevented by the Gascon revolt which began on 6 April:

---

98. *CUP*, 3:611–615.

99. The letter of 6 June (*CUP*, 3:618) describes the new instructions and the repeated rebuffs that the university representatives experienced—evidently during February, when the king was on pilgrimage to Mont Saint Michel ("regia vestra majestas hinc aberat"). In a sermon of 19 April 1394 Gerson complained of this (ibid.:616f.) See Valois, 2:412.

100. *RSD*, 2:130–132: Conzié and his staff "non sine donis uberioribus aulicos et servientes regios induxerunt ut persuaderent dominis ne aliquid contra ipsum [*scil.*, Clement VII] universitas attemptaret. Cardinalis de Luna adjutorio et consilio . . . utebantur." See also Valois, 2:425 f.; but cf. n. 115 below.

101. *CUP*, 3:622 f. (the university's letter of 6 June).

102. The university proclaimed that it was *not* putting the blame on the royal council as a body: "nec suspicetur quispiam nos propter regium vestrum consilium hec dicere" (*CUP*, 3:623), which the editors annotate as a covert reference to the duke of Berry. *RSD*, 2:132–134, has no such hesitation in naming Berry as collaborating directly with the papal agents ("Duce Biturie, cardinali de Luna, et camere papalis familiaribus obviantibus . . ."), and Bouvet, *Somnium*: 98, has the figure of Berry refer to his bad reputation among the unionists: "Ve etiam eis qui nobis detrahunt quod impediverimus unitatem"—this was written August/September 1394.

now, as in 1393, there was nothing to *force* the dukes to escalate their
unionism into action.[103] Far better to avoid a break, keep talking about
Adria, profit from Clement's generosity, and meanwhile urge him non-
publicly to accept cession.

So it was that the university felt obliged to proceed on its own. The
canvass of opinion in February had produced arguments and practical
suggestions for three "ways": a general council, arbitration, and cession.
Now Pierre d'Ailly and Gilles Deschamps were commissioned to put
this program into publishable form, the actual text to be composed by
the university's star rhetor Nicholas of Clamanges; it was approved by
the university on 6 June.[104] One notes at once that although the traditional
order of these by-now-familiar ways was as listed just above, and this
had also been the order of presentation in the February memorandum,
the letter of 6 June put cession first and praised it the most, "chiefly
because it avoided scandal and preserved intact the honor of the princes
and realms of each side." Both arbitration and the general council lacked
this merit, for they aimed at judging which pope was the true one.[105] One
sees the university here taking another step into the service of the crown,
breaking with its older conciliar tradition and also going counter to the
pope's sentiments which favored, if worst came to worst, at least a "way
of judgement" (*via iusticie*) that would allow the Avignon claim to legitimacy to be considered. But by this time the university's frustrations
and humiliations had dissolved its last ties of respect for its papacy, and
the letter of 6 June culminated in a paragraph of unique ferocity:

There is one more thing which we boldly assert, . . . namely that if one or
both of the rivals should obstinately refuse to enter upon one of these three
ways, and offer no suitable alternative, we deem that he should be judged a
pertinacious schismatic and consequently a heretic, no pastor of Christ's

---

103. Palmer, *EFC*: 195 f., where, however, the vicissitudes of France's union policy
are made to be nothing but reflections of the changing fortunes of the peace negotiations. This seems unlikely, not least because, while the royal policy turned against
collaboration with the university sometime in February, the Gascon revolt which doomed
the peace negotiations did not begin until 6 April 1394 and did not have its effect until
June—idem, *EFC*: 158; also idem, "The Anglo-French Peace Negotiations," *Transactions
of the Royal Historical Society*, 5th series, 16 (1966):89–94. Palmer's conjecture also fails
to account convincingly for the lack of a decisive step towards unionism in the first part
of 1393, when peace seemed close, and for the explosive emergence of a drive for union
right after the death of Clement VII, when there was no change in relations with
England (cf. *EFC*: 196).

104. The text in Bulaeus, 4:687–696; abridged in *CUP*, 3:617–624; see Valois,
2:413.

105. The *via compromissi* involved choosing "solemnes viros . . . tanquam in plenarios
diffinitores controversie"—i.e., to judge the case; the *via concilii generalis* also provided
that the council would deal with issues "que . . . decerni aut diffiniri contingerent"
(*CUP*, 3:619 f.).

flock but rather its disperser and tyrant. His orders should henceforth not be obeyed, and he should not be allowed to retain any administration of government or the use of the church's patrimony. He himself should be driven out of Jesus Christ's sheepfold as a savage wolf rather than a sheep or a shepherd, the harshest punishments for schismatics should be inflicted upon him, and his portion should be not in the land of the living but with those worst of schismatics, Dathan and Abiram.[106]

We learn from Numbers 16 that Dathan and Abiram had tried to lead a people's revolution against the Moses-Aaron priestly establishment; they and their cohorts were swallowed up by the earth. France never got around to advocating just that in her later struggle to enforce cession on her pope, but she came close to it, and the quoted paragraph in fact previews the course of escalated sanctions that would be applied to Benedict XIII. Had the government continued on the path marked out in January 1394 and worked out an effective union policy in conjunction with the university, this is what would have resulted. Perhaps her leaders were still not ready to go this far against Clement VII.

Berry indeed seems to have experienced a revulsion against even the talk of such things, and when the university asked him to secure a royal audience at which the letter of 6 June might be presented, he lost his temper, threatened to have the university's leaders drowned if they refused to stop, and declared that he would make it his business always to prevent them from having an audience before the king.[107] We are told that in carrying out this threat he was joined by Pedro de Luna and the members of the Conzié mission but that they were prevailed upon by others, apparently supported by the duke of Burgundy, to relent; thus an audience was finally arranged for 30 June.[108] It was an impressive occasion, the king on his throne, the royal brother, uncles, and other kinsmen standing by, with a large attendance of prelates including Simon de Cramaud, patriarch of Alexandria. The letter of 6 June was read out—the king enduring this with what the chronicler calls a serene countenance—and the king ordered the written text to be translated into French for careful consideration, with discussion to take place at a set date later on. But once again, we read, the efforts of Pedro de Luna and other papal partisans caused this favorable disposition of "the king" to be changed. No further audience was granted, and when the university's

---

106. *CUP*, 3:621; Valois, 2:417.
107. *RSD*, 2:132.
108. Ibid.; this is the main item of evidence for the historiographic tradition that makes the duke of Burgundy at this time a proponent of a strong union policy in alliance with the university. It is not much, particularly since the author of the chronicle was pro-university, pro-union, and fundamentally pro-Burgundy (see Nordberg: 1, and *passim*; Jarry, *Vie politique:* vii).

delegates approached the chancellor on 10 August, he told them that "the king had changed his mind about pushing this matter," and the university was commanded "by royal authority" not to push it either. When the delegates tried to get the chancellor to moderate these orders, he told them that he could not, the royal decree had been the work of the duke of Berry, and they would have to talk to him when he returned to Paris.[109] The university could only protest by suspending its classes; meanwhile, on 17 July, it had sent letters to Clement VII and the cardinals in which it reviewed the vicissitudes of its union activity, blamed its reverses on "a hostile man" (probably François de Conzié), and told the pope in blunt terms that it was his duty to bring about union, presumably by one of the three ways in the 6 June letter, a copy of which the king had forwarded to Avignon.[110]

Although this high-level standoff persisted until the death of Clement, 16 September, the impression it gives—an impression conveying the view of the university leaders and the chronicler of St. Denis, our major sources—is deceptive. The university's image of how matters should have proceeded was illustrated by a drawing on the manuscript of the 6 June letter that it handed to the king on 30 June: the king was shown sitting on his throne with the clergy of the realm standing around him; he said to them, "Pray ye for the things that are for the peace of Jerusalem: and abundance for them that love thee," and they responded, "Let peace be in thy strength" (Ps. 121:6–7). The picture in its context represented something like Gerson's model of public action in the matter of union: the theologians should determine what was right; the prelates should pronounce it; the king should execute it. One notes that John Wyclif, another theology professor, cultivated similar ideals.[111] The structure of politics is of course more complicated than that. The sequence of university actions and statements had not led to the results intended by their authors, but they *had* constituted the public entity of the movement for union, an object that could be seen, with the resulting images now lodged in the mentalities of all members of the political community. A reality had thus been created that the government could use in its own way; this, presumably, was what the government wanted, not learned advice on a matter whose understanding required only normal common sense.

As for the government's way of proceeding, it took the form of quiet communication with Clement VII, demanding that he accept the *via*

---

109. *RSD*, 2:182–184; Valois, 2:417 f.

110. *CUP*, 3:631–633.

111. For the picture see *RSD*, 2:134 (the copy has not survived). Cf. A Pollard & C. Sayle, eds., *Iohannis Wyclif, Tractatus de officio regis* (London, 1887): 48 f.

cessionis and threatening that if he did not, France's "obedience" might be subtracted. In other words, he would be deprived of his revenues from the French church and his control of appointments to benefices. The duke of Burgundy said as much to Clement's legate in Paris, Cardinal Pedro de Luna: "If Clement refuses to abdicate, the obedience and administration of the church of France may well be subtracted from him." (To which Pedro: "Alas my lord, for God's sake don't say that and don't go to such an extreme.")[112] The threat must certainly have been brought to Clement's attention; and it would seem that the duke of Berry also required the pope to accept cession, even while blocking the university's initiatives in this direction. For Simon de Cramaud later recalled (in 1406): "I knew Clement and while he had not sworn to abdicate [scil., as Benedict XIII had], I think that if he had lived one year longer we would now have peace in the church. I can say with certainty that he charged me in writing to tell my lord of Berry that he was fully prepared to renounce the papacy for the good of church union."[113] There are also less specific sources for this action of Paris upon Avignon in the last year or so of Clement's reign,[114] and the fact can be inferred from the elaborate "little lamb of God" routine that Pedro de Luna performed during his Paris mission. Whether he was really fervent or

---

112. Burgundy recalled this conversation in audience with Benedict on 10 June 1395 (see above, n. 80): AN, J 518, fols. 143v, 144v; see Valois, 2:424. According to Jean Petit's version in 1406 of the Avignon audience (BdeC: 113 f.), Burgundy recalled that it was *Benedict* who had proposed "that the two contenders be summoned and if they didn't proceed [to union], obedience should be subtracted from them." There is a similar statement in the University of Paris's appeal of January 1407 (*Thes. nov.*, 2:1297). This seems like the kind of distortion one would expect after more than ten years of incessant propaganda.

113. BdeC: 216. Cf. Simon's recollection in his speech of 22 May 1398 at the Third Paris Council (*Ampl. coll.*, 7:713): "Deinde . . . rex . . . ante mortem . . . Clementis . . . voluit quod videretur via, . . . et fuerunt ordinati certi tam de universitate, quam de consilio suo, et reperierunt certas vias, et specialiter viam cessionis, et ordinavit quod . . . Clemens summaretur, qui tamen fuit morte praeventus"; and cf. the subtraction ordinance of 27 July 1398, which Simon helped draft, for a similar reference: "tunc . . . excitavimus Clementem" (in *Ordonnances*, 8:259).

114. E.g., the royal government's sending the pope the university declaration of 6 June 1394 (above, at n. 110). A memorandum by a cardinal ca. 1397 notes that Clement finally saw that no one would get justice for him, and therefore "voto se astrinxit unire quanto cicius ecclesiam per viam cessionis utriusque, et hoc aliquibus ex dominis cardinalibus et prelatis et domine matri ecclesie declaravit paulo ante mortem" (AN, J 518, fol. 171v; *Ampl. coll.*, 7:549). (Valois, 2:428 n. 1, quotes this from another manuscript which reads "matri sue" instead of our "matri ecclesie.") Haller, *PKR*: 213 f., does not believe it; but it and Simon's testimony just quoted do seem to go together as items of Clement's public relations, and they suggest strong French pressure on the pope.

just running for the office that he later got,[115] his holy union talk must have been intended to resonate with sentiment in the political community. Furthermore, although Clement certainly never intended to abdicate, he was forced in the end to give up the immobilism he personally favored. We know that he appointed a committee of cardinals to propose ways of union and that there was some literary activity in this sense at his court. The result was a recommendation not of the *via cessionis* but of one or another form of the *via convencionis*—both popes to meet and discuss their respective claims—with elements of the *via compromissi*—deputies of each pope would meet, discuss, and then impose a solution as they saw fit.[116] While these ways had little to recommend them in the eyes of anyone but a pope determined to hang on—hence their eventual espousal by Benedict XIII—they can be taken as signs of Clement's recognition that he had to produce something to satisfy Paris's demand for action. His cardinals indeed made themselves agents of this pressure, meeting independently sometime in August and telling Clement that he

---

115. Cardinal Leonardo di Giffone wrote in 1398 that when Benedict XIII had been a legate in France, he said to the duke of Burgundy and the University of Paris "that it was not possible to unite the church unless both contenders abdicated"; this got back to Avignon, Clement was warned, and he therefore sent François de Conzié to Paris as his new legate, to counter Pedro de Luna (in Ehrle, *Alpartil*: 411). Other cardinals similarly hostile to Benedict wrote in the same year that Pedro and Burgundy had secretly compacted for the *via cessionis* and that Clement knew there was a secret but could never find out what it was (ASV, *Arm.* 54, t. 27, fol. 185r; cited in *CUP*, 3:602). Benedict's supporters had their own version of all this: Pedro de Luna had persuaded the English "que se juntassen con el para que entendiessen la justicia que el papa Clemente tenia en el pontificado," but his enemies among the cardinals told Clement "que el cardenal de Aragon [scil., Pedro] tratava que ambos pontifices renunciassen a su elecion y que tenia fin de ser eligido en su lugar" and thereby had his English mission blocked (Jeronimo Zurita, quoted in Haller, *PKR*: 534). These reports do not really conflict with each other, and we may note in this connection another statement from Benedict's circle, in 1399 (*ALKG*, 7:75 f.), to the effect that if Pedro de Luna had advocated cession in Paris, it was because Clement VII's simony, homosexuality, and other vices made him unsuitable, not because Pedro wanted to terminate the Avignon papacy—once he himself became pope, indeed, the *via cessionis* was no longer in order.

116. Pierre Ravat mentions the "cardinales . . . deputati ad videndum de viis unionis ecclesie," who came up with the "via convencionis aliquorum deputandorum per utramque partem" (ASV, *Arm.* 54, t. 27, fol. 185r; cf. the account in *ALKG*, 6:259). An anonymous little treatise about ways of union seems to come out of this situation at the end of Clement's pontificate. It rejects the way "according to God"—evidently the *via cessionis*—because "per paucos qui essent in tali statu amplectaretur via ista," and it also rejects the way of the world—apparently the *via facti*—because it is evil. The only ways "according to both God and the world" that the author regards as feasible are mediation by agreeable men or a *via compromissi* similar to the *via convencionis* favored by the cardinals: each side would choose six representatives; the twelve would meet with full power to end the Schism as they saw fit. The text in ASV, *Arm.* 54, t. 22, fol. 150rv.

would have to follow one of the three ways set forth in the University of Paris program.[117] Pedro de Luna acted in the same sense when he returned to Avignon from Paris at the beginning of September 1394: declaring his disgust with Clement's failure to do anything, he started packing to go home to Aragon, and the pope could dissuade him only by promising to accept one or another way of union and by offering the *via convencionis*.[118]

Where all of this would have led if Clement had in fact lived one year longer is something to speculate about as a way of considering factors that must have been in play but for which we have little or no direct evidence. Simon de Cramaud offers one example: he took part as royal councillor in most of the major episodes covered above, but his role as Berry's client and counselor did not at this time produce a residue of evidence for our information—except for his own passing reference quoted above, which shows him corresponding with Clement, close to Berry, and serving as a link between the two.[119] What sort of advice was he feeding his patron during the two years we have covered? Was there any sort of collaboration between him, a former professor of canon law at the University of Paris, and the theologians who generated the academy's crescendo of unionism? Was he indeed among the "*aulici*" whom the chronicler of St. Denis blamed for persuading the dukes to rebuff the university's demands for a hard line against Clement?[120] Although he was in Paris most of the time, we do find him in Avignon on 28 January

117. Valois, 2:427.

118. This according to the statements of cardinals hostile to Benedict XIII: quoted in Valois, 2:424 n. 3; another text in ASV, *Arm.* 54, t. 27, fol. 185r. Pierre Ravat's comment, cited above, n. 116, was that the *via convencionis* offered at this time was not a meeting of the two popes but rather of deputies. His comment also confirms the exceptional position Pedro de Luna had earned as, among other things, *the* union man in the college: "hoc scio, quod illo mane quo mortuus d. Clemens sancte memorie—immo credo eciam hora mortis, missi fuerunt aliqui cardinales ad dominum nostrum [scil., (the former) Pedro de Luna], qui fuerunt deputati ad videndum de viis unionis ecclesie, ut facerent sibi relacionem."

119. See Ch. III below, for the course of Simon's career up to this point, including his unsuccessful attempt to become a cardinal. This disappointment of 1391, along with the ruthless vigor of his unionist leadership after the death of Clement VII, suggests that he would not have been hostile to the university's agitation in the intervening period covered here; but there is no evidence of his views.

120. See n. 100 above; the men who could persuade the dukes could only have been the latter's top counselors, and there would not have been more than a few of these. Is there any evidence that Simon received the rich gifts mentioned? I can offer only one possible item: when he had been given the bishopric of Carcassonne in 1391, he asked for the privilege of collating to eight lesser benefices ordinarily in the bishop's gift; this was granted in a papal letter dated 20 November 1391 but not issued ("*expedita*") until 19 May 1394, which would have been on time for the bribery (ASV, *Reg. aven.* 269, fol. 593v).

1394 (in connection with a purchase of property from Marie of Anjou).[121] Had Berry sent him, perhaps, to tell Clement of the incipient alliance that month between crown and academy, and was this what prompted Clement to send François de Conzié to Paris? Playing with these questions we find no answer, but we are struck by that very fact: the canonist and Berry client who emerged immediately after Clement's death as an extremely prominent figure—the chief of the coalition between crown, clergy, and university—played no such role before; he seems rather to have functioned as an important Berry agent in the political pattern we have reconstructed, in which the crown's rejection of an alliance with the unionist theologians was coupled with strong but quiet pressure exerted on Clement and the cardinals.

We have seen that this pressure included a threat to subtract obedience, and here too a certain degree of hypothetical thinking can be useful. A sort of subtraction had already taken shape in 1385, and it had created the form of the crown's "protection" of the upper clergy against papal exactions; it was presumably with this relationship in mind that the bishops were solicited to support the crown's switch from Avignonism to cessionism in 1393 (we have noted the case of Bernard Alamant). Let us add to this the commonsense probability that a number of the older and more influential prelates must have sensed that their careers had topped out under the current dispensation, so that they would have felt little enthusiasm for Avignon's future under an aging pope who had shot his bolt of *via facti* and had nothing much to hope for. Factors of this sort are not attested in chronicles and public declarations, but one guesses that they underlay some of the data of papal finance which Favier has put together. Thus we note that immediate and total payments of *servicia communia* by the prelates crashed to a spectacular low in 1392 and did not rise much in the next two years.[122] Although Favier does not distinguish the period 1392–1394 as one about which questions should be asked, his data sometimes confirm our picture and never contradict it.[123] The economic viability of the Avignon papacy depended on the clergy's routine assumption that they had to pay and on the royal government's collaboration with the collectors and others; once it was generally recognized that the crown was going to push for union by the *via cessionis,* papal credit crumbled. The next step would have been the

---

121. AN, JJ 147, fol. 4v; in *AHP*, 24 (1893):185–190.

122. Favier, *Finances*: 371—two graphs which seem to show the changes noted, although one would have preferred a table of dated items; cf. pp. 372–374 for additional data to this effect.

123. E.g., ibid.: 564–570, a discussion of loans to the pope by cardinals, bishops, curialists, and princes: not a single example given falls in the period from August 1392 to September 1394.

formal mobilization of the clergy by the crown to impose cession on the pope; this was not done under Clement VII but was begun immediately after his death, with a progressive implementation of precisely the violently radical program laid out in the theologians' Dathan-Abiram paragraph quoted above. As perplexing and ambiguous as the events of 1392–1394 may seem, they obviously created solid foundations for the action to come.

CHAPTER THREE

The Rise of Simon de Cramaud

THE MAN whose public action we have glimpsed in the Valois turn toward unionism and who is the central figure in the pages that follow, had been prepared for his role by a certain kind of education and a certain kind of early career, both working on and with a certain kind of human material. While not much can be said about the last of these beyond what is obviously inferable, and while the first becomes known only through consideration of Simon's writings, the early career can be traced in some detail. Appreciating its formative importance, however, as something more than just background, requires a sense of the particular political society in which it was pursued. Here our modern categories of cognition are often inept, inasmuch as late-medieval society was not just a stage leading up to our own but also a structure very different from our own, requiring different conceptualizations. We still think disjunctively, in nineteenth-century style, of politics as the realm of the state and society as the realm of its members' private activity; and we accordingly distinguish sharply between the public and the private spheres of life. But in the late Middle Ages and to a considerable extent during the whole period of Old Europe that it began, the only truly private life was that of the man or woman who owned no property and belonged to no community or corporate body; the others held whatever property was theirs by virtue of some sort of privilege, even if only so vicarious or general a one as a town's charter of laws, and this status involved them in relationships and responsibilities that we would call public. Furthermore, the various late-medieval terms for property (like *suum, bona, res propria, quod habet*; less often *proprietas*) covered more than "property" does today, for they included not only material things constituting the objects of ownership, like money, land, or houses, but also non-material things like jurisdictions, exemptions, lordships, monopolies, even public offices, as we have seen. Furthermore, the property rights in question were themselves held as property, so that even material things like rent money were tied into a web of rights that gave them a sort of personality. The game of public life under these conditions was different from what it is today, and those who were trained as its players were correspondingly different in their mentalities and values.

Our nineteenth-century disjunctions must therefore be replaced by concepts representing property in its undifferentiated complexity, as well as the continuum of interests—at once "public" and "private," "social" and "political"—that it engendered. The key term would be the one used at the time, *estate*—or in Latin, *status*—which signified the condition or relative societal standing that someone or some collectivity enjoyed as a result of his or its property. But inasmuch as someone's estate was also his property, it therefore shared in the basic presumption of rightfulness attaching to property-as-rights; in this respect, estate was not like modern status or prestige or social position, for late-medieval estate had a legal, public quality that modern property and its immediate effects do not. Thus, for example, a modern government would not openly give money to a rich and prominent man for the express purpose of helping him continue to be rich and prominent, but that was what the French crown did when—to take one case from many—it granted Duke Louis of Bourbon 1,000 francs a month "for his estate." It was what Pope Benedict XIII did when he granted 1,000 francs a year from church revenues to the (Franciscan!) son of the count of Foix in order "to sustain his estate."[1] It is inconceivable today that a widow who remarried beneath her social standing, or before her period of mourning was over, could be held to have forfeited her share of her late husband's property (her "dower"), on the grounds that she had sunk in estate and honor; but so it was argued in 1423, allegedly according to the custom of Poitou, for "the purpose of a dower is to maintain estate and honor."[2] Or consider the case of the guileless Abbot Henri who in 1398 argued for the *via cessionis* by declaring that if the union of the church depended on *his* resigning his abbacy, "I would do so at once, upon my soul!—with a moderate estate secured to me from the abbey's property, so that I would not be impoverished and a beggar!"[3] We see a world where honor had public, societal status; where social mobility was not well conceptualized; and where the underlying premise that the social hierarchy should be stable gave a presumption of public value to the actual "estate" of every individual and collectivity. Christian doctrine itself was adjusted

---

1. Douët-d'Arcq, 1:48, and Favier, *Finances*: 319, respectively.

2. AN, X 1A 9197, fol. 217v: "Dit que par la coustume de Poictou, dame qui se desemparage ou se marie infra tempus luctus pert son douaire. . . ." "Et toutesvoies, douaire est pour conserver estat et honneur; ainsi in faciendo contrariam se doit perdre."

3. AN, J 518, fol. 417r: "Se il ne tenoit a autre chose que sainte eglise ne deust estre briefment en vraie unite et estre bien pourveue de bon pastre, que de renuncier a m'abbaye, je renuncerois incontinent, sur l'ame de moy, pourveu mon estat moyen des biens dicelle, que je ne fusse mendiz et en povrete." Cf. Simon de Cramaud's remark in his treatise (*DSO,* at n. 400) that "loss of estate" (*amissio status*) was not a valid objection to the program of abdication by both popes because they would be well compensated therefor—"fiet eis bona recompensacio status."

accordingly, so that it, too, approved the pursuit of wealth—to the
extent required by one's estate.[4]

In fact, of course, ambitious types went after as much wealth as they
could, just as they do today. The difference would lie in the kinds of
riches preferred; the acceptable ways of getting them; the relation among
money, property, and honor as goals of ambition; and the responsibilities consequent on success. It is in these areas that the rise of someone
like Simon de Cramaud can be made to yield specifically late-medieval
meanings which in turn allow inferences about his mentality. We will
see him here as a player in the game of "estate"; we will infer something
of the nature and rules of the game from the way he played it; and we
will go on to assume that neither the game nor his mode of play would
change when he moved onto the new field represented by the French
crown's push to end the Schism.

If one stands today in Cramaud, a dozen or so peasant houses on a hill
overlooking the river Graine, about twenty miles west of Limoges, one
sees nothing to suggest a medieval lordship—no castle, although local
tradition still says there had been one,[5] no ruins of one, not even an
obvious place for it. One does, however, see the massive walls and
towers of the castle of Rochechouart on a hill a mile or so away, and off
on another hill the former parish church of Biennac, where the Cramauds had worshipped. The view in the fourteenth century would not
have been much different, except that Rouchechouart Castle would have
been still higher (the donjon has since been amputated), and one would
have seen in Cramaud the seigneurial residence for which Simon's father

---

4. This point was made by Aquinas and a number of others, e.g., Nicholas of Lyra,
quoted in Howard Kaminsky, *A History of the Hussite Revolution* (Berkeley, 1967): 217 n.
228. For the general idea of estate see, e.g., F. M. Powicke, "Reflections on the
Medieval State," *Transactions of the Royal Historical Society,* 4th series, 19 (1936):9 ff.,
who defines *status* in its late-medieval sense as "that which gives validity to a thing, so
that it is more than fleeting or capricious" and observes, "When the word is used by
itself it is charged with the significance of our word 'condition', with a sense of value."
Note also Max Weber's by-now-classic definition: "In contrast to the purely economically
determined 'class situation' we wish to designate as 'status situation' every typical component of the life fate of men that is determined by a specific, positive or negative, social
estimation of *honor*," from *Wirtschaft und Gesellschaft,* trans. in H. Gerth & C. Wright
Mills, eds., *From Max Weber* (New York, 1958): 186 f. Cf. Guy Fourquin, *Les soulève-
ments populaires au moyen âge* (Paris, 1972): 54 ff.

5. The tradition is that the castle in Cramaud (commune of Rochechouart) was
demolished to provide stones to build the church of Biennac; the stones were drawn by
two white oxen without a driver. It is recorded in O. Marquet, "Monographie de
Biénac," *Bulletin de la Société les amis des sciences et des arts de Rochechouart,* 6 (Rochechouart,
1896); peasants in nearby Cramaux (commune of Chailhac) told it to me without
prompting in April 1973.

Pierre did homage to the viscount of Rochechouart in 1326: "his house of Cramaud with the revenue rights that he has over the manses of Volonzac, Le Rore, and Biennac."[6] Even if we allow for the Cramaud acquisitions of *rentes*, tithes, and pieces of land that may not have been held as fiefs, the family property seems to have been quite modest,[7] and it is hard to imagine the house as anything more than a *maison forte*. Rochechouart, the seat of a viscounty and of the local castellany—a Poitevin feudal enclave within Limousin—was evidently the only center of military power and high justice. The Cramauds were only one of about a half-dozen major families subject to the viscounts in a radius of about five miles around the castle, all of whom appear in the Rochechouart archives, avowing their fiefs, witnessing transactions within the viscount's family, and registering their own acquisitions of feudal lands and revenues.[8] Perhaps another sign of subordination is the appearance

---

6. BN, *ms. fr.* 31,959, fol. 86r: "Pierre de Cramau damoiseau avoua tenir en fief des hoirs de feu Messire Simon, Vicomte de Rochechouart, son habergement de Cramau avec les redevances qu'il avoit sur les mas de Volonzac, du Rore, et de Biénac." The original document of 14 March 1326 was in the Rochechouart archives, which are said to have been largely destroyed in the Revolution. Here and in what follows I use the more or less paraphrastic copies made by Dom Villevieille in the decades just before the end: ibid. 31,959 and 31,960; the texts are printed, inaccurately, in *Histoire de la maison de Rochechouart* by Le Général Comte de Rochechouart, 2 (Paris, 1859):277 ff. Since Ville-vieille's copies include even the pettiest items, one can suppose that he covered the whole archival collection—see Henry Passier & Alphonse Passier, *Trésor généalogique de Dom Villevieille*, 1 (Paris, 1875):i–xvi. In these copies, the family name is normally spelled Cramau.

7. The only Cramaud acquisitions documented in the Rochechouart archives seem to have been properties held ultimately from the viscounts. Thus the first Cramaud appear-ance is in a document of 23 November 1302 (BN, *ms. fr.* 31,959, fol. 82v): "Jean Tricondel clerc de Bienac vend a Guy de Cramau une rente de 8 septiers de seigle et 10s. sur la grande dixme de la paroisse de Bienac en la partie mouvante du fief d'Aimery vicomte de Rouchechouart." Other properties were acquired in similar circumstances: *rentes* on the *mas* of Linhon by Guy de Cramaud, 24 April 1310 (fol. 84v); *rentes* on part of the wheat tithes of Biennac and Rouchechouart by Pierre and Guy de Cramaud, 1 December 1311 (fol. 85r); rights in the wine tithe of Biennac by another Guy de Cramaud, 1 May 1346 (fol. 89v). See also the list of properties below, at n. 15. These are not big properties, and there is no reason to assume that Cramaud acquisitions outside the Rochechouart fief, if any, were bigger. Moreover, some of the items above were acquired by another branch of the family than Simon's.

8. For the local situation see Marquet, "Monographie de Biénac": 65, 95 f. Some Rochechouart documents bring it home. Thus on 18 December 1304 Viscount Aimery permitted Pierre le Prévôt to construct a rabbit warren in his manse, with the attested consent of eight "nobles de sa châtellenie de Rochechouart," including Pierre de Cra-maud, knight (BN, *ms. fr.* 31,959, fol. 82v); and on 21 May 1305 the brothers Pierre and Guy de Cramaud were among six witnesses to a property exchange within the Rochechouart family (fol. 83v). The two also appear on 2 June 1305 in more important company as executors of the will of Viscount Aimery (fol. 83v).

among the Cramauds of several Rochechouart Christian names: Aimery, Simon, Guy.

It is suggestive that while one finds no evidence of the fourteenth-century Cramauds, before Simon's rise, elsewhere than in the Rouche-chouart archives, the thirteenth-century picture is quite different. The Cramauds are absent from these archives—although their local peer-families are not—but we do find other evidence, indicating a certain substance. In 1244 the Cramaud brothers Joubert and Pierre had a house in Cramaud important enough that they could get a privilege from the bishop of Limoges to set up a domestic chapel.[9] Also in the 1240s, a Guillaume de Cramaud was a canon of Rheims cathedral—a sign of high family status—and while he might have come from a different Cramaud (there was a village of similar name in the Rheims diocese), a tie to the south appears in his endowment of masses in Rheims in honor of St. Martial, patron saint of Limoges and of the Rochechouarts, whose battle cry was "Sainct Marcial!" When Simon became archbishop of Rheims in 1409, he found Guillaume's name in the cathedral martyrol-ogy and claimed him for a kinsman,[10] on what other evidence we do not

---

9. The Latin text of 8 April 1244 in a vidimus of 9 March 1254 by the bishop's official is published from the ms. "pouillé" of Nadaud by Marquet, "Monographie de Biénac": 66–68. Joubert is a *miles,* Pierre a *domicellus.* See H. Beauchet-Filleau, et al., *Dictionnaire historique et généalogique des familles du Poitou,* 2d ed., 2 (Poitiers, 1895):729 f., for one or two other thirteenth-century Cramauds, one of them (Hélie) a knight.

10. Pierre Varin, ed., *Archives législatives de la ville de Reims,* 2, *Statuts,* 1 (Paris, 1844):108, prints the text of a Rheims necrology datable to mid-1414 which gives details about Simon's endowment of masses in the cathedral and adds the explanation: "Et fuit idem dominus archiepiscopus motus ad faciendum fieri servitium suum predic-tum in crastinum Conceptionis B. Marie, quia magister Guillelmus de Cramaudo olim tempore Innocentii IV, jam sunt fere CC anni, de hospitio et genere predicti domini archiepiscopi oriundus, dedit de suo ut festum Conceptionis in ecclesia remensi solem-nizaretur, sicut scriptum invenitur in martyrologio ecclesie; quam fundationem, et solemnitatem B. Martialis, etiam per predictum magistrum Guillelmum fundatam, idem archiepiscopus, Domino adjuvante, augmentare intendit." Although the spelling of Guillaume's family name here is the same as Simon's, Varin's index—*Archives . . . de Reims, Table générale des matières* (Paris, 1853)—gives the forms "Cramans" and "Cramant" for a village and parish in the diocese, and for the names of Guillaume and others presumably from there. Internal *u* and *n* are of course often indistinguishable in manuscripts of the period, while the final consonants would have been at the mercy of the scribe; French texts of the time normally spell Simon's name Cramaut or Cramault. There are many questions here that would have to be run down by special study. As for St. Martial, see Rochechouart, *Rochechouart,* 1 (1859):5, for the family battle cry, which presumably attests a tie to the abbey of St. Martial in Limoges. St. Martial was also one of the two saints whose feast days the thirteenth-century Cramauds had to observe in the church of Biennac rather than in their domestic chapel (the document cited in n. 9 above). The cult of this third-century saint, first bishop of Limoges, radiated to the south; it would hardly have affected a Rheims canon unless he had personal ties to the region. Did these in fact involve Simon's family, and had Simon known of Guillaume before seeing his name in the martyrology?

know. All of which is important here only as emphasizing the relative unimportance of the family in our period: no evidence of a domestic chapel, no records other than those of local subordination, no extra-local family ties—indeed the reverse, for early in the fourteenth century the local Cramauds split into two branches and divided Cramaud itself.[11] The data are sparse, but the picture they suggest fits in perfectly with the generalizations of social history about the late-medieval noblesse and its unstable fortunes.[12]

Simon's father Pierre, a squire, married Marthe de Sardène from Solignac, and they had three sons, of whom Simon, born about 1345,[13] was the second. A third, Aimery, vanishes after 1370, and the first,

---

11. The split seems to go back to the two brothers Pierre and Guy (n. 8 above), each of whom founded a line with the respective Christian names appearing in subsequent generations. There were two formulas of Cramaud homage to the Rochechouarts. Compare that by Simon's father Pierre (n. 6 above) with that by the "noble homme Jean de Cramaud damoiseau de Bienac" on 27 June 1410 (BN, *ms. fr.* 31,960, fol. 97r): Jean, son of Guy, "avoua tenir en fief . . . son habergement de Cramau qui fut aux Chabardit, l'habergement de Cramau qui fut a feu Pierre de Grane, chevalier, le mas et le moulin de Champanhas, etc." These Cramaud properties had thus been acquired from others. Is all this related to the fact that there are two villages of the name in the region, Cramaux and Cramaud (n. 5 above)?

12. Most of what is here said about the Cramauds in Limousin can be taken as an illustration of Edouard Perroy's "Social Mobility among the French *Noblesse* in the Later Middle Ages," *Past and Present*, no. 21 (1962):25–38; note particularly his remarks, based on data from Forez, about the extremely modest revenues of the lesser families below the level of castleholders and about the high rate—50 percent a century—at which families disappeared from the noblesse because of economic adversity, subdivision of property among too many children, or actual dying out. Cf. L. Genicot, *L'économie rurale Namuroise au bas moyen âge*, 2 (Louvain, 1960), Chs. 3–5.

13. Maurice Ardant, "Simon de Cramaud, patriarche d'Alexandrie," *Bulletin de la Société archéologique et historique du Limousin*, 14 (1864):103–105, publishes a note written in a missal donated by Simon to the cathedral of Limoges, 26 December 1405: "Reverendus in Christo pater dominus Symon de Cramaudo, loco juxta Rupem Cavardi [Rochechouart], ex nobilibus patre Petro de Cramaudo et matre Martha de Sardena ville Solempniaci [Solignac], diocesis Lemovicensis, genitus, dedit istud missale." For an almost identical note see Varin, *Archives législatives*, 2, *Statuts*, 1:107. The names of the father, mother, and brothers also appear in the document cited below, n. 15. See also the biographical note by Paul Guérin, *Recueil des documents concernant le Poitou . . . . , 5, AHP*, 21 (Poitiers, 1891):319 n. 1. And Auber: 249–380; he drew on the data in older works: Pierre Frizon, *Gallia purpurata* (Paris, 1638): 468 f.; P. Anselme, *Histoire généalogique et chronologique de la maison royale de France*, 3d ed., 2 (Paris, 1726):43 f.; *Gallia christiana*, 2:1194–1196; he also used the transcripts of D. Fontenau, for which see *Tables des manuscrits de D. Fontenau conservés à la Bibliothèque de Poitiers*, 1 (Poitiers and Paris, 1839). The modern encyclopedia articles offer only abridgements of the data in Auber and Valois: L. Salembier, in the *Dictionnaire de théologie catholique*, 3 (Paris, 1907):2022–2026; Guillaume Mollat, "Cramaud (Simon de)," *Dictionnaire d'histoire et de géographie ecclésiastique*, 13 (Paris, 1956):1012 f. I agree with Auber's conjectured date of birth (p. 251), which gives Simon the usual age of about thirty at the time of his doctorate (below).

Pierre, inherited the family fief sometime before that date. He either inherited or created a position high in the Rochechouart connection, for he fought in the Battle of Poitiers in 1356, carrying the banner of Rochechouart,[14] and he subsequently became captain of Rochechouart Castle. As such, he made what must have been the worst miscalculation of his life. The region had passed into English lordship as a result of the Treaty of Brétigny in 1360, and Viscount Louis de Rochechouart at first accepted this situation but then began to hope for a Valois reconquest, on one occasion going to Paris to plot with King Charles V to that end. Pierre de Cramaud informed the Black Prince of this, and Louis was imprisoned for a time after his return. But the Valois reconquest in fact began in 1369, and in 1370 Louis was able to bring Pierre to feudal justice, forcing him to buy his lord's pardon by ceding a number of Cramaud acquisitions: half of the tithes of St. Pierre of Vayres, a share of the bourg of St. Laurent, half of the wine tithes of Biennac.[15] The old tie was thereby restored, with Pierre once more on the side of his lord,[16] but he could hardly have looked forward to a good future under the Rochechouart aegis. Indeed even the other branch of the family suffered a loss of grace in these years and had to yield some of its properties to the viscount and his new captain, Guillaume de Prunh.[17] Painfully accumulated acquisitions had been lost; the ravages of war had probably reduced

---

14. See below, quotation at n. 26.

15. BN, *ms. fr.* 31,959, fol. 94r; for Louis's policies see Rochechouart, *Rochechouart,* 1:135 ff.; Lehoux, 1:214; Guérin in *AHP,* 21:30 n. 1. The record of the pardon transaction was written on 20 February 1370; the father, Pierre, is referred to as dead, but the mother, Marthe, is noted as consenting, along with son Pierre's wife Almodie de Coux. The brothers Simon and Aimery, named in that order, are declared to have no rights in the surrendered properties; they must have been acquisitions, not heritages (see n. 65 below).

16. BN, *ms. fr.* 31,959, fol. 94v: on 14 December 1370 Pierre de Cramaud, *chevalier,* and Jean de Cramaud, *écuyer,* appear among the witnesses on Louis's side against a Rochechouart bastard who had gone English.

17. Sometime in the early 1370s Guy de Cramaud, *miles,* and his son Jean (and Jean's wife) brought a suit in Parlement complaining of *ordinaciones et gravamina* done against them by Guillaume de Prunh, *scutifer* and seneschal of the viscount of Rochechouart. On 22 October 1373 they withdrew the suit in order to settle out of court (AN, X 1C 28B, no. 156), and on 24 April 1374 they agreed to fine with the viscount for their "mépris" in order to negotiate with him (no. 157). On 13 May 1375 the viscount gave up certain claims on the Prunhs on condition that Guillaume cede to him "the rights he had acquired" from Guy and Jean de Cramaud in the village of Champagnac, Biennac parish (BN, *ms. fr.* 31,959, fol. 95r), and on 17 May Guillaume was made captain of Rochechouart Castle (ibid.). It had been hardly a century since the ministerial Jean de Prunh, a Rochechouart *prévôt,* had been freed of all *tailles et servitudes* and admitted by Viscount Aimery to hold his lands *en fief de chevalier* (ibid., fol. 80r; May 1283). In 1346 the viscount had recognized the name Puyjoyeux for the seat of a subsequent Jean de Prunh (the place is very close to Cramaud). But our Guillaume de Prunh, married about 1360, had a son Jean who at some point—presumably after the

the value of what was left;[18] and the Cramauds seemed doomed to insignificance or extinction.

If this did not happen, it was because of the new horizons opened by the reconquest of Limousin and Poitou, in which Pierre fought under the royal constable Bertrand du Guesclin and the marshal Louis de Sancerre, both of these working under the duke of Berry, to whose appanage the provinces had been restored. The Cramaud home base was not given up, but neither was it extended;[19] and Pierre seems to have sought his advantage in service to the duke, who for his part may well have welcomed the adherence of a feudatory of one of the great barons who opposed the duke's arrogation of quasi-royal sovereignty in his appanage.[20] At the same time, the Cramauds' greatest asset was not Pierre but Simon, about whose earlier education we know nothing,[21] but who in these years was studying law at the University of Orléans—the normal way for a younger son of the upper classes to qualify himself for a career in the church, the secular government, or both. The duke was in great need of such men to staff the large governmental apparatus of his appanage,[22] and he was prepared to use his extremely powerful patronage in Avignon to get benefices to support them.[23] Simon in fact had student

---

events of 1373–77—married a Cramaud daughter: Joseph Nadaud, *Nobiliaire du diocèse et de la généralité de Limoges*, 3 (Limoges, 1880):393. This and perhaps other alliances seem to have brought the families together to the benefit of both branches of the Cramauds in the years after Simon's rise. In a letter of 19 February 1399 Simon appears as the tutor of the children of a Guillaume de Prunh (AN, X 1A 46, fols. 24v–25r), and in his will he mentions land acquired from Guillaume [AN, X 1A 8604, fol. 91(bis)v]. An *arrêt* of 24 November 1408 shows a Pierre de Cramaud as lord of Puyjoyeux and married to a daughter of the important lord of Mirepoix (AN, X 1A 56, fol. 199r; cf. fol. 87v).

18. See below, n. 28; cf. Perroy, "Social Mobility": 28.

19. Our Cramauds do not appear at all in the Rochechouart documents after 1370, presumably because they had ceased to make local acquisitions. While there are no subsequent records of homages for their old property either, the family's continued presence there is implied by the fact that when Simon endowed a commemorative chapel in Biennac for himself and his parents in 1406, he entrusted the presentation of the chaplains to future lords of Cramaud (below, Ch. IX, n. 78). In 1423 Jean de Cramaud was still called "dominus dicti loci de Cramaudo" (AN, X 1A 9195, fol. 175v). It is strange that the other branch of the family is absent from the sources relating to Simon.

20. René Lacour, *Une incursion anglaise en Poitou en Novembre 1412* (Poitiers, 1934): 6 f.; cf. idem, *Le gouvernement de l'apanage de Jean, duc de Berry 1360–1416* (Paris, 1934): 322 ff. See below for Pierre's service to the duke.

21. In *Gallia christiana*, 2:1194, Simon is said to have been a monk at St. Lucien of Beauvais, "ubi visuntur ejus insignia," but there is no other evidence for this, and he is never referred to as an ex-monk or dispensed monk, not even in his papal provisions.

22. Lacour, *Gouvernement*, Chs. 3–6.

23. Since the papal registers of supplications for 1367–1378 are lost, it cannot be shown that the duke supplicated for Simon, but otherwise there are many records of Berry's *rotuli* and supplications, some of them explicitly for students: ASV, *Reg. sup.* 48, fol. 326r (1378/1379); 52, fol. 5rv (1378/1379)—both for students in Paris; AN, X 1C 113, no. 5 (a document of 14 December 1416)—for a student in Orléans.

benefices while at Orléans, and after getting his doctorate in laws he received two really big ones, a canonry in Rheims, 25 April 1375, and a canonry in Orléans with the office of *scholasticus*, on 15 June 1375. Both were papal provisions of the best sort, made *motu proprio* and with *anteferri* clauses, not mere expectancies.[24] Furthermore, although the Orléans benefice carried the obligation of residence, so that one thinks of Simon as intending to stay there to profess law, he soon moved to Paris, where he was "doctorized" as a regent master in the faculty of canon law and, at the same time, by 1376, got the office of *maître des requêtes* of the *hôtel du roi*.[25] While there is no direct evidence that this shower of good fortune was managed by the duke of Berry, everything that we do know points this way: the ducal recruitment of clients, his use of them to represent him in the royal government, and the lifetime association of Simon with the duke, the first evidence for which comes a few years later. In any case, Simon's rise began a new chapter in the history of his family.

There is, however, another version of all this, presented in 1426 to the Parlement of Poitiers by Jean Jouvenel, lawyer for Simon's nephew Jean, against whom Simon's successor as bishop of Poitiers was trying to establish rights of devolution in certain properties that Simon had given to Pierre or bequeathed to Jean and which the bishop claimed had been

---

24. The Rheims canonry: ASV, *Reg. aven.* 198, fols. 188v–189r; the Orléans one in *Reg. aven.* 199, fol. 180rv; cf. ASV, *Reg. sup.* 54, fol. 204v (1379: "providemus Symoni de Cramaudo, licenciato in legibus Aurelianensi rigorose. . . ."). But that he got his degree in 1375 is already implied by the provision to the Orléans canonry, for a condition was that he resign his *prestimonia* and other benefices held in Spain, as well as his chapel of St. Thomas of Thury, in the diocese of Meaux, which was in fact granted out on the same day (ASV, *Reg. aven.* 196, fol. 225rv). A *prestimonium* was a benefice carrying no ecclesiastical title or obligation, especially current in Spain, and used typically to support students: see Charles Ducange, *Glossarium*, s.v., and Gaetano Romano, *Dizionario di erudizione storico-ecclesiastica*, 55 (Venice, 1852):186. For the first three items in this note, and other data, see K. Eubel, *Hierarchia catholica medii aevi*, 2d ed., 1 (Münster, 1913):77, and *CUP*, 3:241, and nos. 1431, 1624. I have checked them in the manuscripts but have not been able to find important new evidence at this point, nor any at all before 1375.

25. In the benefice roll submitted to Clement VII by the University of Paris between 14 November 1378 and 28 October 1379, Simon is described as "doctor decretorum Parisius regens": ASV, *Reg. sup.* 54, fol. 204v; cf. *CUP*, 3:241. For doctorization see below, n. 26. He appears as *maître des requêtes*—for the first time as far as I know—at the end of a royal letter of 29 May 1377, ed. P. Guérin, *AHP*, 21:30; also in *Ordonnances*, 6:266. The older tradition that he entered the royal service under Charles VI (e.g., Valois, 3:33 f.) is wrong; see below, n. 41. Simon first appears as attending the council of Parlement on 20 December 1376 (AN, X 1A 1470, fol. 281v), and afterwards he attends frequently, probably as *maître des requêtes*—see Édouard Maugis, *Histoire du Parlement de Paris*, 3 (Paris, 1916):ix–x.

bought with episcopal funds. One of Jouvenel's arguments was a family history that he had no doubt received from his client:

He said that the defendant's grandfather was a very noble lord, who had three sons: Pierre, the defendant's father, the late cardinal [i.e., Simon], and Aimery. Pierre carried the banner of Rochechouart at the Battle of Poitiers; he served in the wars with the late Guesclin and the late Sancerre, constables of France; he served my lord of Berry and profited greatly. He supported the late M. Simon his brother in the schools, and caused him to have the prebend and office of *scholasticus* of Orléans. Simon, in his time, committed many youthful follies, and Pierre bailed him out at his own expense. He provided Simon with estate, had him given the prebend of Coutances and other notable benefices. He said that Pierre had caused Simon to have an audience in Avignon before the pope. Pierre was there, and Simon gave a notable legal dissertation. All of this cost Pierre a good deal, as did Simon's doctorization in Paris. And it was by Pierre's efforts that Simon became *maître des requêtes* of the *hôtel du roi*.[26]

While this passage seems to have furnished the older works of erudition with most of the few biographical data they give for Simon, and while the actual events it relates stand up to verification by other sources,[27] its construction was obviously determined by the lawyer's design, to show that whatever Simon had done for Pierre was no more than what the latter had coming. The bishop's lawyer refuted it briskly:

As for M. Pierre de Cramaud's having been a great lord and having done many good things for the late cardinal, etc.—he said that the region had been destroyed by the war, so that Pierre and his son had no more than 50 or 60 livres of revenue. . . . He said that the late cardinal had advanced MM.

---

26. The entries in the case from 22 April 1426 to 25 February 1427 may be found in AN, X 1A 9198, fols. 150v–151r, 163v, 179rv, 184v–185v, 187r, 241v, 249rv. The translated passage (on fol. 179r) is quoted by A. Bossuat, "Une relation inédite de l'ambassade française au pape Benoît XIII en 1407," *Le moyen âge*, 55 (1949):81 n. 14. Rather than quote it again here, I note the phrases requiring explanation: "Pierre . . . servi feu Mons. de Berry et proufita moult. Il tint aux escoles feu M. Simon . . . Lequel . . . Simon en son temps fist des jeunesses moult, dont Pierre le releva. . . . Dit que Pierre lui fist avoir ambaxade en Avignon devers le pape, . . . Simon y fist notable repeticion; ouquel fait Pierre fist grant frait, et aussi pour sa doctorisacion a Paris. Simon fut au pourchaz de Pierre Maistre des Requestes." For "jeunesses" see, e.g., AN, X 1A 4790, fol. 313r: "jouer et suir femmes et . . . boir, et . . . autres jeunesses." For "repeticion" see P. Fournier, in *Histoire littéraire de la France*, 37 (Paris, 1938):161. Since Simon already had his degree, "doctorisacion" would have meant reception as regent master by the Paris law faculty, perhaps with papal intervention; for an analogous case see J.-M. Vidal, *Bullaire de l'inquisition française au XIVe siècle* (Paris, 1913): 306 f. As for "au pourchaz de," I have chosen the most general translation.

27. It was evidently used by Frizon and Anselme (above, n. 13). Insofar as the data can be checked, other sources confirm them: e.g., the genealogy is confirmed by the document cited above, n. 15; Pierre's army service, by that cited below, n. 30; Simon's Orléans benefice, above, n. 24.

Pierre and Jean, and if Pierre had great authority, it was by virtue of the cardinal's efforts, not the reverse; and it was through his personal qualities of intellect and competence that the cardinal had become *maître des requêtes* and had advanced in honors, estate, benefices, and profits.[28]

Here too, of course, we have a lawyer's construction, but one that seems probable. We have noted the paltry status of the Cramauds before 1370 and the family disaster caused by Pierre at that time. It may be added that in all the vast number of surviving accounts and receipts for wages paid by the royal war treasurers, there is not a single mention of a Cramaud until 1380, after Simon's rise, when Pierre appears as a knight and the head of a band of nine squires "of his chamber," part of a company of seven such bands led by Aimery de Rochechouart (not Pierre's feudal lord, by the way, but the head of a different branch of the family and at that time royal seneschal of Limousin). Subsequently both Pierre and Jean appear in these accounts, Jean with some frequency;[29] had Pierre had enough substance to field a band before 1380, some receipts of his service would have survived, for there were many campaigns in those years. Furthermore, it was common for more or less important partisans of the Valois to be rewarded with grants of confiscated enemy

---

28. AN, X 1A 9198, fol. 185rv: "Et quant a ce que M. Pierre de Cramaut fut grant seigneur et fist moult de biens au feu cardinal, etc.—dit que le pays estoit destruit por la guerre, et ne avoient Pierre et son filz plus de 50 ou 60 livres de revenue. . . . Dit que feu le cardinal avanca lesdits MM. Pierre et Jehan, et se Pierre eut grant autorite, ce fut par moien dudit cardinal, nec e converso; aincois par le sens et souffisance de sa personne le cardinal avoit este maistre des requestes et avancie en honneurs, estaz, benefices, et proufiz."

29. For the nature of these documents and their relation to the hiring and mustering of soldiers, see Philippe Contamine, *Guerre, état et société à la fin du moyen âge* (Paris, 1972): 80, 90, 143, and *passim*; note that the name of the "chef de montre" was always recorded, the names of his followers not always. The receipts and accounts surviving in the BN in various *fonds* have been exploited comprehensively in the index volumes for noble families in the *Salle des manuscrits*, a chronological *fichier* of the *pièces originales* (in the BN stacks), and—inter alia—a manuscript "Dictionnaire alphabétique et chronologique de la noblesse," by Charles-Joseph Bévy (AN, AB XIX). I have searched all and found no Cramaud before 1378–1381. Nor is there any in BN, *ms. fr.* 32,510, an extract from a register of the *Chambre des comptes* covering army musters from 1217 on. The first mention of Pierre, with the details I have given, is in an account for 11 December 1380, BN, *nouv. acq. fr.* 7414, fol. 284v. The next is for 1381–1383, *nouv. acq. fr.* 20,528, with the same details of service. After that, Jean de Cramaud appears each year from 1386 to 1389, serving under Louis de Sancerre and others: BN, *ms. fr.* 32,510, fols. 289r, 301v, 303r, 314r; *pièces orig.* 925, no. 20,431, items 2–4; G. Demay, *Inventaire des sceaux de la collection Clairambault*, 1 (Paris, 1885): no. 2948; Bévy, "Dictionnaire," s.v. Pierre also appears, 1 September 1388, at the head of nine squires (BN, *ms. fr.* 32,510, fol. 303r). Note also that Pierre's first mentions are evidently in the Limousin context, under Aimery; subsequently he and Jean are received at Poitiers and elsewhere.

property, grants which were often recorded in the royal registers. Pierre got no such grant until 1378—the lands, in Limousin, were those of the notorious Mérigot de Marchez—and then only up to the value of 100 livres revenue.[30] Finally, in regard to Pierre's alleged service to the duke of Berry, the latter's *hôtel* accounts from 1 June 1370 to the end of 1378 do not mention his name, as they would have if Pierre's service had been more than just that of a knight in the army.[31] What, then, is left of Jean's family history? If we allow Pierre only what we have no reason to deny him, we can imagine him advancing some money to his younger brother, drawing Berry's attention to him, and later listening to Simon demonstrate his learning in Avignon. Otherwise, the high favor enjoyed by Simon must have come from a much higher personage, and no one but Berry could have played that role. Simon de Cramaud was not the lucky son of a great family, and his most important heritage was simply his noble blood; for the rest, "his personal qualities of intellect and competence" had justified the favor he received.

Soon after Simon had established himself in Paris, the event occurred that would eventually dominate his destinies. We have seen how the Great Schism began and how entirely dependent the cardinals were on French support. This was in fact given to them in practical ways, but when King Charles V convoked a council of prelates and professors to consider the matter, 11 September 1378, and give him formal counsel, the majority expressed strong doubts about the cardinals' enterprise and advised inaction and further study.[32] Even after the election of Clement VII on 20 September, Charles V at first reserved his decision; but his brother, Duke Louis of Anjou, gave Clement abundant support, and when an assembly of selected prelates, meeting under royal guidance at Vincennes on 16 November, declared for Clement, Charles ordered that he be recognized throughout France.[33] It is not known whether Simon de Cramaud played any role in the action thus far; he was, however, among

---

30. AN, JJ 113, no. 321 (16 October 1378). The grant refers to the great losses Pierre has suffered in the king's wars, serving under the constable and marshal of France, and gives him Mérigot's lands and rights, as stated, with the usual reservation of the king's right to revoke the grant if the original owner returned to obedience. Mérigot's execution in 1391 took care of that. For him see J. Glénisson & J. Day, eds., *Textes et documents d'histoire du moyen âge, XIVe–XVe siècles,* 1 (Paris, 1970):125–143; P. Contamine, *Azincourt* (Paris, 1964): 71–84.

31. AN, KK 251, KK 252.

32. Valois, 1:103 f. A report of the council's proceedings is published by Michael Seidlmayer, *Die Anfänge des grossen abendländischen Schismas* (Münster, 1940): 303–307, and in *Polemik*: 1–3 (the two together form the full text).

33. Valois, 1:113–115.

the University of Paris's doctors of canon law who declared for Clement sometime between January and May of 1379; he was present at a council of the clergy at Vincennes, 7 May 1379, which supported the royal policy; and on 25/26 May he was one of the deputies announcing the university's decision for Clement.[34] This opened the way for the university to present benefice rolls to the new pope, with Simon serving as the law faculty's envoy and being awarded a canonry in the Paris cathedral; his name also appeared on another roll that year, requesting a canonry in the cathedral of Bayeux.[35] About twenty years later, when wholly committed to the program of terminating both papacies without a judgement of which was rightful, Simon would expatiate on how impossible it was to decide this question and would recall that many who doubted the validity of Clement's election nevertheless recognized him as pope in simple obedience to the royal command;[36] this would have applied all the more to Simon, a high royal official and councillor.[37] Such influences need not have excluded a subjective sincerity; the decisive fact, however, was that once the king had recognized Clement, no one who did not could have hoped to get a benefice in France. A believer in "putting one's intellect in captivity" in order to obey the king, Simon was also a collector of benefices; and in one of his arguments for the via cessionis, he confessed that he personally would resist even a general council's decision against the legitimacy of the Avignon line, for that would subject his own benefice titles to cancellation.[38] One sees something of what made the Schism "great."

The next major event that shaped Simon's future was the death of Charles V on 16 September 1380 and the succession of the twelve-year-old Charles VI. The late king had provided for such a minority by naming Duke Louis of Anjou as regent, but the two other royal brothers, Berry and Burgundy, and the royal brother-in-law of Bourbon insisted on sharing power and its emoluments. The young Charles was accordingly declared of age and crowned on 4 November; the regency

---

34. *CUP*, 3, nos. 1619, 1621, 1626.

35. ASV, *Reg. sup.* 54, fol. 204v; *CUP*, 3:241. The provision was to a canonry with revenues to come either from a prebend in the cathedral or from a parish church in Paris. For the Bayeux provision, ibid.: no. 1431.

36. See above, Ch. I, n. 79.

37. It is not clear exactly when Simon received the title of royal councillor, still less when he began sitting regularly in the council; the first indication I know is the phrase, "regis Francie consiliarius" in a supplication to Clement VII sometime in 1379 (ASV, *Reg. sup.* 54, fol. 187v). A royal letter of 9 August 1383 (below, n. 46) calls him "dilectum et fidelem consiliarium nostrum." See also the references for the composition of the council in 1380–1388 in Noël Valois, *Le conseil du roi au XIVe, XVe, et XVIe siècles* (Paris, 1888): 88 ff.

38. App. II, Pt. III, "Reply to 'It Is not Allowed,'" no. 6. One of Simon's references to the captive intellect is quoted above, Ch. I, n. 79.

was terminated; and the monarchy which Charles V had tried to develop as the crown's government of France was replaced by a "polyarchy" of four dukes using royal power for a France that consisted above all of themselves and their respective interests. The officials who had run the government under the late king were pushed into the background, and the dukes set up a permanent council of twelve as the instrument of their joint control.[39] Berry's client Pierre de Thury, a former judge in Parlement and now to become bishop of Maillezais and a royal *maître des requêtes*, would be his chief agent on the council.[40] Simon de Cramaud, whose career would have a course similar to Thury's on the Berry road of advancement, had his appointment as *maître des requêtes* renewed and continued to attend meetings of Parlement's council until at least 23 February 1381,[41] but he was then moved into the duke's direct service.

One of the first acts of the ducal junta had been to make Berry royal lieutenant in Languedoc, an exceptionally lucrative office for someone as greedy as he, but also a politically interesting one, inasmuch as the duke's brother-in-law, Count Jean II of Armagnac, was locked in family conflict with Count Gaston Phoebus of Foix for dominance in the southern provinces. It was here that Berry moved by mid-1381, taking Simon with him. On 12 August we see Simon as a member of the duke's council, although still keeping his royal office, and in the ducal entourage in Carcassonne, where he was given the profitable sinecure of "conservator of the Jews' privileges" in Languedoc.[42] He now became one of

---

39. Valois, *Conseil*: 73–86, 91ff.; Lehoux, 2:11–22 (for "polyarchy" see p. 21).

40. Sometime in 1377 Berry supplicated Gregory XI to grant the archbishopric of Vienne to Pierre de Thury; Gregory replied, 20 December 1377, that it had already been granted to another but he would keep Thury in mind—Guillaume Mollat, ed., *Lettres secrètes et curiales du pape Grégoire XI* (Paris, 1955): no. 2106. One of the benefice rolls submitted to Clement VII by the duke of Berry, approved with the date of 25 November 1378, has Pierre de Thury, councillor of the king and of the duke, in first place (ASV, *Reg. sup.* 46, fol. 111r). A councillor in Parlement since 23 August 1376, Thury appears in 1378 as one of the judges of Parlement sent to hold Berry's Grands Jours of Poitou and being suitably rewarded (Berry's household accounts, AN, KK 252, fols. 167v, 173v, 180v). Subsequently he became bishop of Maillezais (2 May 1382) and royal *maître des requêtes*, then became Berry's chancellor sometime after July 1383. It was in 1382 that he was appointed to the royal council of twelve (Valois, *Conseil*: 85 f.; Lehoux, 2:73 n. 6, 150 n. 7).

41. François Blanchard, *Les généalogies des maistres des requestes ordinaires de l'hostel du roy* (Paris, 1670): 51, gives a now-lost royal letter of 21 December 1380, appointing Simon as *maître des requêtes*; it was not the first appointment (above, n. 25). His presence in the council of Parlement on 23 February 1381 is noted in AN, X 1A 1471, fol. 528r—the last time until 12 November 1383 (AN, X 1A 1472, fols. 1r, 156r).

42. C. Devic & J. Vaissette, *Histoire générale de Languedoc*, new ed., 9 (Toulouse, 1886): 899; cf. BN, *ms. Baluze* 379, fols. 308r–309r: Simon is addressed by Berry as "nostre amé et feal conseiller, le maistre des requestes de l'hostel de mon . . . seigneur." Cf. Lehoux, 2:16–18.

the duke's chief all-purpose agents, used first of all from 21 September on in negotiations with Gaston Phoebus, who was working with the Languedocian estates to become their captain. By the end of 1381 the two principals had come to terms and Languedoc had submitted.[43] Berry had evidently decided to use Simon for still more important functions, for on 30 May 1382 he increased his client's estate by having him made bishop of Agen;[44] and a year later, 28 April 1383, when renewed English military activity called the duke to the north, he left Simon behind as his chief lieutenant in Languedoc and head of the ducal council there, to exercise the duke's powers with the counsel of the seneschal of Beaucaire. His work in this capacity provoked resistance, and several years later he was awarded 700 francs in damages for "defamatory" letters issued against him by the consul and commune of Carcassonne; one supposes he had just been trying to gratify his patron's desires.[45] The duke must have been pleased, for Simon's career kept moving. On 7 August the pope transferred him from Agen to Béziers, and the commission over the Jews could be given up.[46] While we know little of his actual work in this period—he did help manage a meeting of the Languedoc estates, July to September 1383, in Lyons[47]—the bare data alone leave no doubt of his importance.

They also suggest that Simon was moving through a decisive stage of the careerist game. The see of Agen was remote from his field of work, but Béziers was in the heart of it, an excellent base for a man who was going to settle in as a high ducal official in Languedoc.[48] The past two

---

43. Lehoux, 2:28–51; Devic & Vaissette, *Languedoc*, 9:905 n. 2; 10 (Toulouse, 1885):1654 f.

44. Eubel, *Hierarchia*, 1:77; ASV, *Reg. aven.* 228, fols. 46r–47v. Berry was in Avignon on the day the bishopric was granted: Lehoux, 2:64. The bishop of Agen mentioned by S. Baluze, *Vitae paparum avenionensium*, ed. Guillaume Mollat, 2 (Paris, 1928):611, as an envoy of Louis of Anjou in Avignon, February 1382, was Simon's predecessor; *Gallia christiana*, 2:926, identifies him as Simon, and Auber: 254 f. follows this account, which includes related information that seriously confuses Simon's biography.

45. For the lieutenancy see Devic & Vaissette, *Languedoc*, 10:1659 f.; cf. 9:913 n. 6 and Lehoux, 2:77 n. 2, 78, 95 n. 5; BN, *ms. Baluze* 379, fols. 309v–310v. For the Carcassonne affair see Devic & Vaissette, *Languedoc*, 10:1796–1799.

46. Eubel, *Hierarchia*, 1:138, on 17 August Simon promised to pay his *servicia*: ASV, *Oblig. et sol.* 43, fol. 91r. Devic & Vaissette, *Languedoc*, 10:1675, gives the royal letter of 9 August 1383, noting Simon's resignation as commissioner of the Jews.

47. Lehoux, 2:97 ff.; Devic & Vaissette, *Languedoc*, 9:914.

48. One guesses that the location was what counted, since there is no reason to think that Béziers was a richer see. Eubel, *Hierarchia*, gives Agen's rating at 1,500 florins, but in fact Simon's *servicia communia* for the see amounted to 2,440 florins, while for Béziers he had to pay only 2,000: ASV, *Oblig. et sol.* 43, fols. 84r, 91r; also Hermannus Hoberg, *Taxae pro communibus servitiis ex libris obligationum ab an. 1295 usque ad an. 1455*, *Studi e testi*, 144 (1949), s.v. In principle equal to a third of the respective annual gross

years could have led to such a profitable dead end, and Simon's career
might well have been cut short on the gallows when the day of reckoning
came, or even on a burning pyre, like that of Jean de Bétizac,
another ducal extortioner. But Berry had decided otherwise (one guesses
that Simon's ambition may have been a factor), and when the duke
returned to Paris in the middle of October, after the English threat had
been ended, he summoned Simon to join him there and resume his
functions in the royal government, where we find Simon sitting in the
royal council and in Parlement from November on.[49] Meanwhile the duke
had left to negotiate with the English, returning at the beginning of
February 1384; when the ducal party then left for Bourges at the end of
March, Simon was in it.[50] After a tour in Languedoc in April and May,
they returned to Paris by July; Berry himself left in August, but Simon
remained, working in the royal government through the autumn.[51] He
drops out of our sight from 18 November 1384 until the beginning of
March 1385, by which time Berry was back in Paris with a new assignment for him: to go as the clerical member of an embassy to Hungary
headed by a top man in the Berry apparatus, Jean de la Personne,
viscount of Acy. Their mission was to make a proxy marriage between
Marie of Hungary and Count Louis of Valois, the king's brother; it was a

---

values, these figures were actually unrelated to current realities. For general statements
about the drastic effects of war and other calamities on Agen and Béziers, see H. Denifle,
La désolation des églises, monastères et hôpitaux en France pendant la Guerre de Cent Ans, 2
(Paris, 1899):644 ff., and *passim*. Jean Favier, "Temporels ecclésiastiques et taxation
fiscale," *Journal des savants* (1964): 109 f., notes that in our period the see of Béziers
yielded only a third of what its rating presupposed. Cf. also Favier, *Finances, passim*, for
the problem of ratings and values, and p. 368 for Simon's payments.

49. AN, X 1A 1472, fols. 1r, 156r (12 and 13 November 1383); AN, JJ 123,
fol. 144r (November 1383); AN, X 1A 1472, fol. 162v (14 January 1384). Cf. Berry's
movements according to Lehoux's itinerary: Lehoux, 3:464 ff.; also Lehoux, 2:85 ff.

50. Berry's last attested presence in Paris was on 19 March 1384; on 27 March he
appears in Bourges. Simon was at a meeting of the council of Parlement on 13 February
(AN, X 1A 1472, fol. 165v), the last meeting he attended until July. According to
Gallia christiana, 6:353, the Gaignières collection in the BN includes receipts from
Simon, bishop of Béziers and royal councillor, for money received "ut in Occitaniam
proficeretur," the receipts made on 9 March 1383 and 2 March 1384. Since Simon was
not yet bishop of Béziers in March 1383, the dates must be understood as *more gallico* and
changed to 1384 and 1385, respectively; see also below, n. 53. On 29 March 1384
Simon witnessed the signing, in Bourges, of the marriage contract between Marie de
Berry and Guy de Châtillon (Lehoux, 2:103).

51. For his presence in the council in Parlement: AN, X 1A 1472, fols. 180rv,
181v, 182rv, 184r, 351r (16 and 22 July; 20, 26, 29 August; 1 and 9 September; 18
November). AN, J 276, no. 24, shows him in the royal council on 7 July; see also AN,
JJ 126, fol. 10v. For his presence in the duke's council in Paris in July, see Devic &
Vaissette, *Languedoc*, 9:922.

Berry project inasmuch as the duke hoped that Marie's dynastic claim to
Provence might help the French crown take that territory away from
Louis II of Anjou and his mother the duchess.[52] Simon's last attested
presence in Paris was on 4 March; he must have left soon after for the
south, en route to Hungary via Venice, and by the beginning of July
France knew that the mission had been successful.[53] Meanwhile the
ambassadors had left for home, passing through Venice in July and
Avignon in mid-August, to be greeted and rewarded by Berry. By the
end of August Simon was back in Paris.[54] None too soon, for Sigismund
of Luxemburg, refusing to accept the loss of the Hungarian kingdom
that his family had long earmarked for him, appeared in Buda at the end
of September, with an army, to claim Marie's hand; this turned out to
be a real marriage, consummated forthwith.[55] It was one of the decisive
events of European politics, but from what would have been Simon's
point of view at the time, the important thing was the magnificent trip

52. According to Jean de Cramaud's account of Simon's career, in 1426 (AN, X 1A
9198, fol. 179r), Simon "fut evesque d'Agen, puis de Beziers; fut ambaxeur pour le
mariage que on cuida faire de la Royne de Ungarie a feu Monseigneur d'Orleans." See E.
Jarry, *La vie politique de Louis de France, duc d'Orléans, 1372–1407* (Paris, 1889): 22 f.
The prime source is Froissart, *Chroniques de J. Froissart,* ed. Gaston Raynaud, 9 (Paris,
1899):222, where the context dates the mission in 1385, and it is said that the bishop of
Maillezais went along with Jean de la Personne. Since news of the marriage reached
France by 6 July (below), this would have been Pierre de Thury (Raynaud's note, p. lvi),
before his elevation to the cardinalate on 12 July 1385. But his presence in Avignon on
13 June is attested by the *Journal de Jean le Fèvre,* ed. H. Moranvillé (Paris, 1887): 121,
and the same source also mentions (p. 187) that one of the ambassadors to Hungary had
been "l'evesque de Besers" (i.e., Béziers)—hence, Simon. Since, as will be seen, Simon
was Pierre de Thury's immediate successor as chancellor to the duke of Berry, Froissart's
confusion of episcopal identities (not uncommon in the sources of the time) can be
accounted for. For Personne and Berry's ulterior motives see Lehoux, 2:228; Valois, 2:99
ff., 3:8.

53. Simon's departure from Paris can be associated with his receipt of 2 March 1385
for travel money: above, n. 50, and in Demay, *Clairambault,* 1: no. 996. He was in the
council of Parlement on 4 March, but not again until 30 August 1385 (AN, X 1A
1472, fols. 361r, 377r). For Venice's decision to provide transport to Zengg in Croatia
for the French ambassadors, see W. Gusztáv, ed., *Monumenta Hungariae historica,* series
4, 3 (Budapest, 1876): no. 313. On 27 June Venice was informed that the marriage
had been made (ibid.: no. 320), and Jean le Fèvre in Avignon wrote *ad* 6 July (Moranvillé, *Journal de Jean le Fèvre*: 139), "Ce jour vindrent nouvelles du mariage accordé entre
messire Loys conte de Valois et la fille heritiere de Hongrie."

54. Gusztáv, *Monumenta Hungariae historica*: no. 323, a deliberation of the Venetian
senate mentioning the arrival of the French ambassadors on their way home, 10 July
1385 (also in Jarry, *Vie politique*: 390); for Simon in Paris see above, n. 53. The passage
through Avignon is my inference from the source published by Valois, 2:105 n.—
assuming that the French and Hungarian envoys returned together.

55. The news reached Avignon 18 October 1385 (Moranvillé, *Journal de Jean le Fèvre*:
187).

(including a tour of the Palazzo Ducale in Venice),[56] with the cash windfalls that ambassadors usually enjoyed and the enhancement of status due to having been a royal ambassador.

If we look back at this kaleidoscopic record of service to the duke, we recognize the way in which a great far-flung conglomerate enterprise selects its top men: transfers from one job to another, movement from place to place, the testing of competence to meet all sorts of demands and of ambition to rise to all required heights. Simon had evidently passed the tests, for the duke now selected him as his next chancellor, to replace Pierre de Thury, whom Berry had decided to have moved up into the cardinalate (the pope made the appointment on 12 July 1385). Thury continued for a time to do chancellor's work for the duke, until Simon could take over, probably after mid-November when he moved from Paris, presumably to join the duke in Languedoc and to exchange the now-inappropriate see of Béziers for that of Poitiers, 24 November.[57] On 21 December he was in Avignon to arrange payment of his *servicia*.[58] Already a wealthy man, as we shall see, he could now look forward to much more. Poitiers was rated by the Apostolic Camera at 2,800 florins (800 more than Béziers), in principle a third of its actual gross value, which would thus have come to about 7,880 livres tournois; but war and other factors had cut this at least in half.[59] The ducal chancellorship

56. An inference, as Simon would have wished, from this passage in a work written ca. 1400 (BN, *ms. lat.* 1475, fol. 47r): "Fredericus imperator, ut recuperaret filium suum quem Veneti tenebant captivum, rediit ad obedienciam Alexandri tercii . . . , sicut ad perpetuam rei memoriam in domo communi Venetorum notabilissime pictum reperies, si ibidem vadas." One can see it today, but in a later painting.

57. Eubel, *Hierarchia,* 1:399. Neither Lacour, *Gouvernement,* nor Lehoux fixes the term of Simon's chancellorship correctly. The first I know of his holding the office is an entry *ad* 12 February 1386 in Moranvillé, *Journal de Jean le Fèvre:* 237, "l'evesque de Poitiers chancelier de monsegneur de Berri." Cardinal Pierre de Thury had continued to function as Berry's chancellor in Languedoc while the duke was in the north (see Lehoux, 2:177 n. 2, 161 n. 7, 166 n. 6). At the Sixth Paris Council, on 27 November 1406, Simon said that he had been the duke of Berry's chancellor "par l'espace de x. ans" (BdeC:123; BN, *ms. fr.* 23,428, fol. 17v, compared), but he must have been thinking of his whole stretch in Berry's direct service, 1381–1391, for he held the office of chancellor only six years. After his promotion to patriarch of Alexandria, he turned it over to Ithier de Martreuil, whom I first find mentioned in that capacity on 25 September 1391 (ASV, *Reg. sup.* 78, fol. 137rv).

58. Hoberg, *Taxae,* and ASV, *Oblig. et sol.* 43, fol. 106v. Favier, *Finances:* 368, says Simon paid promptly, but in fact 1,100 florins were still owing to the College of Cardinals on 6 April 1391, when his successor had to promise to pay them (*Oblig. et sol.* 43, fol. 140r). See also Favier, *Finances:* 343—arrangements to pay *servicia* had to be made in person at Avignon, unless there were weighty reasons for an exception.

59. For the rating see Hoberg, *Taxae,* and for the rest, including the ratios between livres and florins, see Favier, *Finances:* 36, 341. See also his "Temporels ecclésiastiques": 106 ff., on the problems of using such figures. On p. 115 he notes that about 1420 the

carried a pension and wages totalling perhaps 3,000 livres,[60] and Simon had other revenues, from benefices and royal offices. Let us say, *faute de mieux*, that his net revenues were several thousand livres a year, apart from cash bonuses and valuable gifts from the duke. His New Year's present for 1386, for example, was a clasp with three rubies, an emerald, and three pearls, costing 150 francs—not less than the gift for the count of Trastamara, and probably substantially more than the revenues from the original Cramaud properties in Limousin.[61] But money is not everything; there is power and there is prestige. Simon never settled in at either Agen or Béziers, but he did at Poitiers, despite his frequent absences on ducal business; and his bishopric gave him a great deal of local importance, particularly since it resonated with his position in the

---

papal assessment of Poitiers was reduced by half, to 1,400 florins, which would imply a gross value of almost 4,000 livres. More data could be given, but they all come down to someone's guess, rarely if ever based on account books and often expressing mere desire. Thus when Simon de Cramaud sued his predecessor in 1416 for 500 francs (= livres) as about seventy days worth of Poitiers revenues (below, Ch. IX, n. 41), which would imply a yearly figure of 2,600 (presumably net, according to the context), he may have been just seeing how much he could get. Or did he have in mind the revenues of those particular seventy days, rather than a fraction of a year? A plea of 1430 claimed the see was worth only 1,620 livres, presumably net—here the interest would have been in a low figure (Collection Le Nain, *Table des matières*, vol. 37, s.v. "Poitiers"). Perhaps the papal reassessment of 1420 would represent a reasonable value.

60. Since Berry's *hôtel* accounts for the period of Simon's chancellorship do not survive, the salary or "pension" can only be estimated. The accounts show that Simon's predecessors got 80 francs a year as clothing gifts plus 2 to 4 francs per diem on the duke's business (AN, KK 251, fols. 21v, 22r, 67r, 104v; KK 252, fols. 120r, 141v), while his successor Ithier had a per diem of 8 francs (AN, KK 253, fols. 6v, 7r, for 1397/1398; BN, *ms. fr.* 6744, fol. 7v, for 1402). As for the pension, Lacour, *Gouvernement:* 161, notes that the chancellor Pierre de Giac got 1,000 livres a year (1375) besides his per diem; and in 1413 the chancellor Guillaume Boisratier, archbishop of Bourges, received the same amount plus 8 francs per diem (the document ibid., *Pièces justificatives*: 11). Simon's gifts, pension, and wages would hardly have been less. To a 1,000-livre pension we can thus add a maximum of 2,920 francs as wages (365 multiplied by 8). While we cannot say how close to the maximum Simon claimed, his successor Ithier claimed 1,456 livres for six months, which comes very close indeed (BN, *ms. fr.* 6744, fol. 7v). When in 1426 the bishop of Poitiers claimed in his lawsuit against Jean de Cramaud that Simon had gotten 500 livres a year from the duke during his chancellorship (AN, X 1A 9198, fol. 185v), we must note that his argument called for a low figure. Jean de Cramaud's lawyer, with the opposite interest, claimed that Simon had gotten more from the chancellorship than from his bishopric (fol. 179r); and whatever one may say about the latter's value (n. 59 above), it was hardly less than four times the bishop's figure. All things considered, the pension and wages must have come to at least 3,000 livres.

61. A fragment of Berry's accounts for 1385/1386 (BN, *ms. fr.* 10,369, fol. 54v) records his payment to a goldsmith for jewelry that the duke had ordered for New Year's presents.

innermost circle of Berry henchmen, a group appearing—at least in the admittedly oblique light of the registers of Parlement—to have worked as a kind of gang, using the ducal authority to grab properties and revenues at every opportunity.[62] Simon could now become one of the gang, and we shall see that he did. If, then, we have appreciated him so far as a youngish man on the make, climbing to the top, we must now view him as being there.

Eventually he would resume his climb, for the top was not flat. Meanwhile, however, he must have seen that while his estate was high, it was also rather top-heavy, consisting as it did chiefly of cash and offices. He needed to support it by building an infrastructure of property and to consolidate it by investment in his family. Here it may be useful to lay stress on the obvious, the peculiar importance of family and real property in that age, before the emergence of capitalist industry, of stable institutions of finance, and of the modern state. It was an age, moreover, when economic, political, and social pressures had disintegrated every bundle of land, lordship, jurisdiction, and service into fragmented property rights that formed a web of local interrelations among families and corporations, and when claims at law turned not on questions of clear title but on seizin and novelty.[63] In a modern capitalist society, with titles clear, property truly private and fully protected by the public order and written law of the state, a newly rich man can put his money into investments that carry no local involvements and do not depend for their security on his own power. In Simon's time, such a man could acquire substance only by buying real property, chiefly land; and here he would have to face the fact that, even in the fourteenth century,

---

62. The above-cited works of Lacour and Lehoux study the duke's government of his appanage, his private life, and the sequence of his own high-level public acts; what is needed is a study of the structure and function of his machine and the behavior of the men who made it up. Morinot de Tourzel, for example, the duke's cupbearer, appears remarkably often in the registers of Parlement, and the cases are always good reading. In addition to the material at n. 94–96, below, one can cite the cases in AN, X 1A 50, fols. 91r–93r; X 1A 1476, fols. 113v–115r; X 1A 4791, fols. 293r, 295v; they show Morinot getting a grant of a castle that had not in fact been confiscated, getting a *rente* of 2,000 livres as his reward for a confiscation that went to pay off the duke's debts, and having a jewel merchant imprisoned in order to extort a ruby from him for the duke. The acts themselves are less important than the style of action, which helps us to understand Simon's.

63. Fredric Cheyette, "Custom, Case Law, and Mediaeval 'Constitutionalism': A Re-Examination," *Political Science Quarterly*, 78 (1963):362 ff. Marc Bloch, *Feudal Society*, trans. L. Manyon (London, 1961): 199–210, and *passim*. Jacques Poumarède, *Les successions dans le sud-ouest de la France au moyen âge* (Paris, 1972): 186 ("Les ayants droit sur une même terre sont parfois si nombreux que le procès verbal de l'aveu renonce à les énumérer tous").

when sales were legal and frequent, any attempt to put together a massive agglomeration of properties—to insert oneself into the local web—was apt to be challenged by kinsmen or other right-holders with an interest in some aspect of the property that was sold.[64]

The only sound basis for holding property against such threats was as a "heritage," that is, as vested in the prime durative entity of the time, the family, which had the great power to make heritages out of "acquisitions" by the succession of its generations.[65] Moreover, the "estate" based on such a family position had a solidity that even the highest position in public life did not, for the latter depended on favor, patronage, and hence on the uncertainties of political life. These could be very drastic, and the victims of change were precisely the careerists, who could be stripped of everything from one day to the next and even pay with their lives for having served the wrong side. The destinies of dozens of members of political society were totally transformed by accidents in high places: the death of Charles V in 1380, the sudden madness of Charles VI in 1392, the death of Philip of Burgundy in 1404, the murder of Louis of Orléans in 1407—each one a turning point for men like Simon. If public life was symbolized by Fortune and her wheel, it was because of the literal impossibility of making oneself immune from such casual vicissitudes; so while the careerist rode the wheel as hard as he could to get all possible profit from its revolution in his favor, he could not suppose that his "estate" might rest safely on the rim. If his natural recourse was to use his success to advance his family, it was for the reasons set forth above and on the basis of a conceptualization corresponding thereto, one centered in the concept of "estate," which homogenized all his interests as indiscriminately his. A modern disjunction between private interests and public offices, each sphere having its own goals, possibilities, and norms, would have been anachronistic and therefore useless; nor would it have occurred to him in the first place. If Simon's efforts now turned to the advancement of his family, it was not

---

64. Thus at every stage in his career, Simon had to engage in numerous lawsuits—many dozens in all—to secure his properties and rights, both personal and official. One notes also the extremely complicated formulas used in the effort to make a property transfer final and trouble-free, e.g., AN, X 1C 53, no. 21, the transfer of Niort property to Jean de Cramaud.

65. J. C. Holt, "Politics and Property in Early Medieval England," *Past and Present*, no. 57 (1972):12ff., has a discussion of the practical distinction between acquisitions and heritages that is relevant to our context too; see also Ralph Giesey, "National Stability and the Hereditary Transmission of Political and Economic Power," a published typescript of a report to the Fourteenth International Congress of Historical Studies, San Francisco, 1975. The church was another durative entity that could be used to consolidate estate; we shall see Simon's use of it later on, in his commemorative foundations.

merely because of his feelings as brother and uncle; it was the next stage in his own career.

Simon had indeed made the decisive move in 1383 while bishop of Béziers, when he arranged the marriage of his nephew Jean. Since it was Simon who had negotiated and signed the contract (Jean himself was off on a fashionable Prussian tour with the Teutonic Knights),[66] financed the marriage, and then directed the family effort to exploit it, he would also have been the one to choose the bride: Orable de Montléon, recently widowed daughter of one of Simon's fellow powers in the Berry apparatus, Renaud de Montléon, the duke's *maître d'hôtel*. It was an important Poitevin family whose history for the previous hundred years, however, reads like a textbook case of the crisis of the late-medieval feudality.[67] Their chief lordships had long been alienated. The barony of Montmorillon had been sold to King Philip III in 1281; the castle of Montléon had been sold to the bishop of Poitiers in 1295; annuities (*rentes*) had been sold on a number of their lands; family divisions had diminished their estates; the ravages of war had dilapidated them; and we may as well complete the picture by thinking of the Black Death and the price scissors. At the same time, there was a fight to survive: some of the annuities and alienations may have been economically sound; marriages and purchases brought new estates into the heritage; and service to the Valois—especially by Renaud, one of the first Poitevin lords to declare for the dynasty in 1369—brought rewards in the shape of offices, cash, and grants of property confiscated from the enemy. It could have meant prosperity, had Renaud not had the bad luck to be captured by the English at least once, in the fight for Limoges, 19 September 1370, and to be charged with a ransom of 3,650 livres—a very large sum but typical for the time, when many a noble family was literally ruined by a ransom debt.[68] In one of his captivities, Renaud ceded his main Poitevin

---

66. AN, X 1A 4788, fol. 380v (10 December 1409): "Lui estoit en Prusse; . . . son oncle estoit lors evesque de Besiers, si fit tant que Hoirable fu femme de lui."

67. Except as otherwise noted, the following information is drawn from André Du Chesne, *Histoire généalogique de la maison des Chasteigners* (Paris, 1634): 231–245; also Guérin's long note in *AHP*, 19 (1888):354 n. 1. Cf. Lacour, *Gouvernement*: 144 f.; Lehoux, 1:215. For the beginnings of the family and its implantation in Poitou in the twelfth century, see Charles Tranchant, "Le chateau de Touffou et ses seigneurs," *BSAO*, 3d series, 3 (1913–1915):183 ff.

68. Du Chesne, *Chasteigners*, gives the figure without indicating his source and refers to two captures by the English. For the excessive size and disastrous effects of ransom debts, see M. H. Keen, *The Laws of War in the Late Middle Ages* (London, 1965): 158 f.; P. S. Lewis, *Later Medieval France* (London, 1968): 211 f.; Contamine, *Guerre*: 195 n. 68. For Reynaud's capture see Lehoux, 1:314 n. 5.

seat, Touffou, to the English supporter Jean d'Angle; Renaud later claimed it was done under threat of death, but perhaps it was to discharge his debt.[69] A gift of 400 livres from the duke of Berry contributed to this purpose on 29 June 1371,[70] and by the end of the year Renaud was free. A year later Charles V restored Touffou to him as a heritage.[71] Most of his ransom debt remained (or was perhaps reincurred with the restoration of Touffou), to burden him the rest of his life; for with estates producing hardly more than 600 or 700 livres a year,[72] he could raise cash chiefly by selling annuities (the normal rate was 10 percent),[73] each of which diminished his future income, so that by the time of his death his net revenues were less than 200 livres.[74] Destiny had delivered him to Simon de Cramaud, a member of the "patriciat politique" whose large sums of cash amassed by service allowed them "to insinuate themselves

---

69. The details appear in two royal grants, the restoration of Touffou to Renaud by Charles V, 10 November 1372 (Du Chesne, *Chasteigners*, "Preuves": 113–115) and the confirmation by Charles VI of Jean de Cramaud's proprietorship of Touffou, 14 January 1388 (AN, JJ 132, fol. 45rv). The latter gives the value of Touffou at the time as "up to 300 livres tournois of *rente*," which would correspond to a capital value of about 3,000 livres tournois (n. 73 below). The claim that the cession was under threat of death appears in the former grant; it would have come from Renaud himself, to be incorporated without question in the royal letters. One need not believe it, and it is already reduced to a "comme l'en dit" in the confirmation of 1388. Its point was to make the cession legally invalid.

70. AN, KK 251, fol. 69v: "pour aidier a paier la raencon."

71. Above, n. 69. The king could have claimed the castle as the confiscated property of a traitor and then merely granted it as such—an acquisition—to Renaud. Instead he restored it as a heritage, together with a new grant "if necessary."

72. These are not hard figures. They come from the later pleas in the Touffou case, when the Cramauds claimed that the total worth of Renaud's property apart from Touffou and Chincé (worth 20 livres tournois) was 400–500 livres tournois a year (AN, X 1A 9191, fol. 124v); add to this the 300 livres tournois for Touffou. On another occasion they claimed that Renaud's Angevin lands in Mirebeau castellany were worth 300 livres tournois a year, which would also give a global revenue of about 700 or 800 livres (AN, X 1A 9199, fol. 189v). Since it was in the Cramauds' interest to make the figures high, we deduct a few hundred livres to arrive at an order of magnitude.

73. In about 1400 the Poitevin Huet le Brun sold a *rente* of 100 livres tournois for 1,000 livres tournois (AN, X 1A 9190, fol. 173r). In pleas before Parlement in 1415 Simon de Cramaud, claiming that he had fulfilled an obligation to convert a lump sum into *rentes* for the Collège de Reims in Paris, said that his acquisition of 200 (alias 100) livres of *rentes* was equivalent to a credit of 2,000 (alias 1,000) livres of the lump sum (AN, X 1A 4790, fols. 292rv, 301v).

74. Thus Renaud II alleged in 1430 (AN, X 1A 9199 fol. 315r): "Le tout de la succession, deductis les charges, ne valoit 140 *l.* de rente." His interest lay in giving a low figure. Renaud I's sale of annuities because of his ransom debt is explicitly cited in one case by his son (in 1430; AN, X 1A 9199, fol. 224v): "Dit que ledit defunct fu mis a rencon des Anglois, et lui convint vendre 40 livres de rente audit [Jehan] de Londres" —for which, see below.

into the fissures opened up by the disintegrating fortunes of those nobles who still knew only one trade, that of arms."[75] The situation was the more attractive because Renaud had no son to succeed to his estate, only two daughters.

The marriage contract signed in 1383 promised Orable a dowry of 100 livres of *rente*, but she would get it only after her father's death, when she and Jean would inherit the Angevin properties of Villiers and La Grimaudière and others necessary to yield the full income; meanwhile Renaud would possess these properties in the name of the couple and collect the revenues. All that Orable was to get immediately was a *rente* of 10 livres, secured by her and Jean's possession of Chincé, in Poitou. Renaud also promised to secure the approval of his wife and other daughter and to accept a penalty of 4,000 livres in case of his nonfulfillment of the contract, half to go to the couple, half to the crown. Orable, as usual in such cases, renounced all claims as heiress.[76] The Cramauds for their part offered cash—a dower from Jean and a gift from Simon (who no doubt also paid the dower)—and the marriage took place in 1384. But at the time of Renaud's death in 1385, none of the terms had been fulfilled; nor did his heirs allow the couple to take over Villiers and La Grimaudière; nor had Renaud's wife, Orable de Preuilly, ever approved the contract, no doubt because the income it promised her daughter Orable was about twice what was due to her as heiress and would have impoverished both the other daughter Beatrice and a third offspring to come—for Orable *mère* was pregnant. Disaster came when she gave birth to a son, Renaud II, who as male enjoyed the right of primogeniture: an equal or better share of the properties, according to local custom, and sole proprietorship of the main family seat of Touffou.[77]

---

75. Guy Fourquin, *Les campagnes de la région parisienne à la fin du moyan âge* (Paris, 1964): 339 f.

76. For this and the following see Guérin, *AHP*, 21:323 n. 1; cf. 340 n. 1; he uses AN, X 1C 55, no. 27. The picture can be made more exact by comparing the pleas in the case of Renaud II versus Jean de Cramaud and Orable, as summarized in an *arrêt* of 13 April 1429 (AN, X 1A 9191, fols. 121r–125r). Renaud's argument emphasized (fol. 121r) that his father had consented to the marriage "instante et suggerente Simone de Cramaudo, Pictavensi episcopo, . . . tunc magne auctoritatis" and had promised Villiers and La Grimaudière "instigante dicto Simone de Cramaudo." In their pleas, the Cramauds noted that Simon had not been bishop of Poitiers but of Béziers at the time (AN, X 1A 4788, fol. 381v). That the marriage took place in 1384 can be inferred from the *arrêt* (AN, X 1A, 9191, fol. 123r), although the date is given mistakenly as 1404; cf. the parallel mistake of 1407 for 1387 on fol. 124r. For the penalty clause see fols. 121v, 123r.

77. AN, X 1A 9191, fol. 123v: "Johannes de Cramaudo dictam Aurabliam bene et decenter dotaverat, dictusque Simon de Cramaudo dicti matrimonii contemplacione magnas pecuniarum summas dicte Aurablie donaverat." That the contract was made

It was a disaster because the Cramaud plan, fairly evident from the peculiarities of the marriage contract whose non-fulfillment must have been counted upon, and still more evident from the subsequent course of events, was to install Jean in Touffou and thus move the Cramauds into the Montléon position in Poitou. In 1383 this could have been envisaged as a painless and even wholesome operation; after the birth of Renaud II it could be carried out only by coercing the widow and disinheriting the orphan.

But Simon's resources were equal to the task. In addition to his wealth and his high position in the Berry apparatus, he now had the great advantage of being bishop of Poitiers and thereby not only a major lord in the region but also the overlord of Touffou, which was a fief held of the bishop's lordship of Chauvigny. All of these capacities came into play. First he acquired claims on Touffou. During Renaud I's lifetime, Simon had bought a *rente* from him of 20 livres on Touffou and had given it to Jean. Renaud's wife, Orable de Preuilly, also had a *rente* on Touffou, of 15 livres, and this was acquired from her by Jean's father Pierre, no doubt with Simon's money. Finally, the collegiate church of St. Jean de Ménigoute had a *rente* of 20 livres on Touffou,[78] which Simon induced the canons to sell to Pierre by using his episcopal and feudal power to seize the canons' property of La Galicherie (a fief of Touffou) after the death of Renaud I and by seeing to it that the canons were not

---

before the birth of Renaud II is stated on fol. 122v; the year of birth was 1383 (AN, X 1A 4788, fol. 399r—against the Cramaud claim that it was ca. 1380, fol. 381v). That Orable's dowry was excessive was charged by Renaud II (AN, X 1A 9191, fol. 122v; cf. X 1A 9199, fol. 315r) and more or less admitted by the Cramauds, who claimed that an extra-large dowry was permissible (AN, X 1A 4788, fol. 382r). Renaud II's rights are set forth in AN, X 1A 9191, fol. 121rv; the Cramauds did not reject these rights in principle but, rather, insofar as Renaud asserted that Touffou was the main family seat. In fact Renaud II's claim was moderate; cf. the statement in an unrelated case of 27 January 1390 (AN, X 1A 1475, fol. 28v): "par la coustume de Poitou les puisnez tous ensemble ne doivent avoir que un quart de l'eritage." For the rest, Renaud I's death is dated in AN, X 1A 9191, fol. 123v, as "1385 vel circa"; Renaud II's age at the time is given as two on fol. 121r; Orable *mère*'s opposition is asserted in Renaud II's plea (fol. 121r) and also by the Cramauds (fol. 123v).

78. The acquisition of *rentes* is set forth several times, e.g., in AN, X 1C 55, no. 27. Additional details are in AN, X 1A 4788, fol. 381r; X 1A 9199, fol. 189v. The *rente* held by the canons of Ménigoute had originated in a sale by Renaud I of 40 livres *rente* to Jean de Londres in order to help pay the ransom debt (AN, X 1A 9199, fol. 224v); 20 livres were subsequently redeemed, but the remaining obligations were not met, and a total of 150 livres arrears accumulated (Guérin, *AHP*, 19:356 n.). Jean de Londres remitted 50 livres of this in exchange for La Galicherie, held as a fief of Touffou, 6 November 1375, and then gave this fief and the 20 livres *rente* to the chapter of Ménigoute (AN, X 1A 1475, fol. 16v—where it is erroneously given as 10 livres; AN, X 1A 4788, fol. 381r).

received in homage for it, either by Orable de Preuilly (whom Simon had recognized as mistress of Touffou) or by Jean de Cramaud (who said, "Talk to my uncle the bishop") or by Simon's seneschal. This last, accosted by the canons in church, quoted Isaiah 56:7, "Mine house shall be called a house of prayer," and refused to consider their complaint. In their suit before Parlement, the canons noted that the reason for all this was that Simon wanted to get their *rente* for Jean, and so indeed it happened.[79] Thus Jean now had a total of 55 livres of *rente* on Touffou, plus the claims for Orable's dowry and the arrears thereof, plus the right to invoke the 4,000 livres penalty clause. In order to get himself into Touffou he had the royal government appoint him captain of the castle, on the plea that it was a frontier fortress.[80] Perhaps he also alleged the need to defend the interests of Renaud II against another claimant, Jean Ysoré.[81] Orable de Preuilly was induced to honor the appointment.

According to the later statement of her son, Orable de Preuilly was now urged to pay a visit to Jean's father and mother, in Simon's bourg of Chauvigny, and on her return found herself locked out of Touffou.[82] Be that as it may, she was certainly subjected to the enormous pressure of the Cramaud financial demands, which were brought against her in an action before the Parlement of Paris, and she may have been subjected

---

79. For the canons' pleas, 30 December 1389: AN, X 1A 1475, fols. 16v, 17r, 19r; also the *arrêt* of 7 January 1390, fol. 120r. Cf. AN, X 1A 49, fol. 59rv; *AHP*, 21:310 n. 1, 341. In the pleas in AN, X 1A 4788, fol. 381r, the Cramauds say the canons sold the *rente* to them because the canons "were unable to hold it."

80. Parlement's summary of Renaud II's version (AN, X 1A 9191, fol. 121v): "[Johannes] de Cramaudo, dictum castrum maliciose occupare cupiens, colore quesito contra veritatem quod dictum castrum erat in fronteria inimicorum, . . . a . . . genitore nostro [i.e., Charles VI] literas impetraverat, per quas . . . genitor noster ipsum Johannem de Cramaudo dicti castri de Touffou capitaneum constituerat et ordinaverat; quibus literis dicte Aurablie . . . presentatis per eundem de Cramaudo, asserto quod dictum officium capitaneatus ad tuicionem et conservacionem jurium dicti actoris solum et duntaxat habere desiderabat, . . . ipsa Aurablia . . . eundem de Cramaudo in possessionem dicti officii capitaneatus . . . poni mandaverat." The frontier status was alleged in order to give the king a right to impose a captain; cf. Contamine, *Guerre*: 230 f.

81. So he said in 1409 (AN, X 1A 4788, fol. 382r): "Pour ce que Messr. Jean Ysore voloit soy bouter et tenir de fait Toufo, fu avisie qu'il estoit bon qu'il y eust capitaine, et pour ce s'i bouta." It is characteristic of the legal argumentation of the time that, just a moment before, the Cramauds' lawyer had alleged, inter alia, that "Touffou had not belonged to Renaud but to Ysoré." The Ysoré claim went back to an occupation of Touffou by Philippe Ysoré, married to a Montléon daughter, early in the fourteenth century (Du Chesne, *Chasteigners*: 236)—perhaps another unpaid dowry. Jean Ysoré still asserted the claim but waived it at the time of Renaud I's transfer of Touffou to Jean d'Angle, Ysoré's brother-in-law (*AHP*, 19:313); he was finally bought out by the Cramauds (below, n. 89).

82. AN, X 1A 9191, fol. 121v.

to actual intimidation by Jean, Simon, and the latter's vassals and retainers.[83] By now, indeed, Simon was a man of such "great authority and power" in Poitou as to be irresistible.[84] Therefore the Montléon kinsmen, realizing that if events took their course the whole family might be ruined, intervened to persuade Orable de Preuilly to accept an accord that would take the case out of Parlement (deactivating the penalty clause).[85] This was done in the episcopal palace of Poitiers before the seneschal of Poitiers Renaud de Vivonne (another important Berry official), who on 1 March 1387 appointed Léonnet de Montléon as the four-year-old Renaud II's guardian to make the accord, which the whole family testified would be to the orphan's benefit. On the next day the accord was made, on terms proposed by Jean and Simon. The dowry of 110 livres *rente,* the other *rentes* of 55 livres, all arrears and penalties—all were discharged by the cession of Touffou Castle, its appurtenances, and Chincé to Jean and his wife, to pass as heritage to their children or to be divided as their respective heritages if they were childless. Léonnet did what he had to and soon after went to Paris, where Simon allegedly wined him and dined him and dazzled him with the majesty of Parlement; but in any case, Simon had him give power of attorney to Jean Rabateau, Berry's permanent agent in that court. Rabateau then registered the accord in Parlement, 3 August 1387.[86] The final conse-

---

83. Ibid., fol. 123v, for the suit before Parlement, and fol. 121v, according to Renaud II: "Et eo quod ipsa Aurablia alienacioni dicti castri consensum prebere noluerat, dicti Simon de Cramaudo et Johannes de Cramaudo eius nepos, aliique plures dicti Simonis tunc episcopi Pictavensis subiecti et vassalli, minis et terroribus vehementibus ipsam Aurabliam terruerant, adeo quod ipsa dictis Simoni et Johanni de Cramaudo quidquid voluerant facere toleraverat, nullum tamen expressum consensum prebuerat."

84. Above, n. 76, and similarly, AN, X 1A 9191, fol. 126v: "mediante . . . Simone de Cramaudo, . . . pro tunc [i.e., 1387] magne auctoritatis et potencie."

85. The role of the kinsmen appears in the Cramaud arguments, AN, X 1A 9191, fol. 123v: "Aurablia . . . et Beatrix . . . pluresque ex propinquioribus dictorum liberorum parentibus et amicis, processus et discordia vitare pro commodo ipsorum liberorum [volentes]." Also: "parentibus et amicis . . . instantibus et judicialiter requirentibus," and: "attentis obligacionibus supradictis, ipsis liberis insupportabilibus." It is also evident in the instrument of the accord, AN, X 1C 55, no. 27: the accord was made "pour eschiver plaiz, debaz, coustes, missions, et despenses, . . . par le conseil et advis de plusieurs parens et amis d'une partie et d'autre." Eleven of the Montléon kin are listed, and eight appear as witnesses.

86. Renaud II later claimed that Léonnet had not duly looked out for his ward's rights (AN, X 1A 9191, fol. 122r); the Cramaud point was that the accord was necessary and that while Orable could have made it herself, Léonnet was appointed "ad maiorem cautelam" on the insistence of the kin (n. 85). One of the original copies of the accord, a huge parchment sheet, is no. 27 of AN, X 1C 55; the registration in Parlement is noted on the back. Items nos. 28 and 29 are the procuratories of Léonnet and Beatrice, 20 July 1387 and 13 June 1387. For Simon's presence in Paris in July, see *Ordonnances,* 7:170–172, and *Table des manuscrits de D. Fontenau,* 1:311 (24 July); he was there with the duke, for whose presence see Lehoux, 3:471. Renaud II later charged (AN, X 1A

cration was procured by Simon himself: a royal letter of 14 January 1388, witnessed by Berry, in which Charles VI renounced any claims he might have on Touffou and confirmed it to Jean and Orable in full proprietorship.[87]

That Touffou eventually returned to the Montléons in 1429 was due to such accidents as the death of Simon, the failure of Jean and Orable to have children, and the political necessities of the future Charles VII in Poitou. At the end of 1387, however, the prospect was as bright as could be. The Cramauds were now a major power in Poitou, their local position backed up by access to royal, ducal, and ecclesiastical revenues, so that Simon's money could be used to restore and improve what Renaud I had allowed to decay.[88] The ruined castle was repaired—at a cost of 4,000 livres, the Cramauds later claimed; the competing claim of Jean Ysoré was bought out, 12 March 1388; a number of *rentes* in money, grain, and wine were redeemed; adjacent properties were acquired.[89] Simon, Pierre, and Jean had meanwhile made an agreement to

---

4788, fol. 398v): "Et se l'accort fu passe ceans [scil., in Parlement], dit que Leonnet de Montleon vint a Paris et ly fit bonne chiere l'arcevesque de Reims [scil., Simon], puiz le fit adiorner ceans dont fu esbahy, et puiz lui fit laisser un procureur pour ratifier, accorder, etc." For Rabateau see Lehoux, 3:29.

87. *AHP*, 21:339–345 (AN, JJ 132, no. 81, fol. 45r).

88. Guy Bois, "Noblesse et crise des revenus seigneuriaux en France aux XIVe et XVe siècles," in *La noblesse au moyen âge*, Philippe Contamine, ed. (Paris, 1976): 219–233, shows how the nobility of our period, unable to maintain their social hegemony from the diminishing revenues of their estates, sought a remedy in war and the access to royal tax revenues that military service and office holding provided. Our story of the Montléons and Cramauds fits exactly into this framework, while showing how complex the process could be. Here a noble family with inadequate access to royal moneys was superseded in its territorial seigneury by another noble family that could draw on not only royal but also ecclesiastical revenues.

89. These details come from pleas in the lawsuits consequent on Renaud II's efforts to get Touffou back—see Ch. IX below. The Cramaud story (AN, X 1A 9191, fol. 124r): "Quia tempore dicti accordi dictum fortalicium de Touffou erat valde ruinosum et quasi inhabitabile, dicti defensores plures magnas reparaciones utiles et necessarias usque ad valorem quater mille librarum tur. ascendentes in dicto fortalicio fecerant . . . et deinde plures terras et possessiones circumcirca dictum fortalicium, que non erant de dicta terra tempore dicti accordi, acquisierant, dictamque terram de Touffou pluribus magnis reddituum vini, bladi, et argenti annuis oneribus exoneraverant. Praeterea Johannes Ysore miles, dicens et asserens . . . dictum fortalicium . . . ad ipsum iure hereditario spectare, die xiiª marcii A.D. 1387 [= 1388] ipsum fortalicium . . . dicto de Cramaudo vendiderat." The redeemed *rentes* are detailed in AN, X 1A 9199, fol. 189v (4 August 1429). A parchment record in ADV, G 207, tells us of one example of Cramaud investment in Touffou, ca. 1389, when Simon and Pierre bought the lordship of Jardres from Denis Gisler; it was a dependency of Touffou. In 1435, Jean de Cramaud's heirs gave it to the chapter of Poitiers in lieu of a 50-livre *rente* Jean had bequeathed for daily masses on behalf of his soul; in 1467 the chapter claimed it was worth only 25 livres; its cost in 1389 must have been at least 300 livres, perhaps 500.

pursue the family partnership with Simon's money, which would be used to buy properties in the name of the others, himself to have the usufruct during his lifetime.[90] "The Cramauds," it was later said, "never bought a thing that was not paid for with Simon's money."[91] The plan can be seen at work on 2 July 1386, when Jean acquired the *terre de Niort* for 1,300 gold francs supplied by Simon, who would have the usufruct. This was in fact a package of properties in and around Niort, including houses, mills, fisheries, lands, revenue rights, and a whole village; it had belonged to Geoffroi de Kérimel (below).[92] One sees how men with Simon's cash and connections could rise amidst the same turmoil in which others were sinking. Another important acquisition under the plan was the lordship of Chapelle-Bellouin, which Simon bought in Pierre's name from Catherine de Maille, but also used himself.[93]

He bought property in his own name too, including two pieces that had been acquired by perhaps the most voracious land-grabber in the Berry gang, Morinot de Tourzel, cupbearer to the duke. One was the Poitevin lands of Kérimel, confiscated because he had followed his lord, Duke Jean of Brittany, in siding with the English. Morinot had received the lands from the duke of Berry, and in 1386 he sold them to Simon, with Berry's approval and a confirmation by the king.[94] They included a house in Niort. Another item was more problematical but also more important to Simon: the Paris house of Jean Chauchat, a receiver general of royal revenues in Languedoc, whose misfortune it had been to die with some of his routine debts to the treasury unpaid, thus giving Berry

---

90. In Simon's will of 11 March 1422 he refers to these arrangements: "Temporibus retroactis quamplures acquisiciones nonnullarum terrarum et possessionum de meis pecuniis nomine quondam domini Petri de Cramaudo fratris mei primogeniti, et domini Johannis de Cramaudo filii sui, nepotis mei, et eciam meo simplici nomine feci" [AN, X 1A 8604, fol. 91(bis)r].

91. According to the plea of the bishop of Poitiers in 1426, AN, X 1A 9198, fol. 185v: "onques ne acheterent riens que ce ne feust des deniers de feu le cardinal."

92. AN, X 1C 53, nos. 20, 21; cf. *AHP*, 21:340 n. 1. The usufruct provision reads (no. 21): "Desquelz heritages et possessions . . . Reverent pere en dieu Monsieur Simon de Cramaut, evesque de Poitiers, aura . . . sa vie durant seulement, les usfruis, . . . du consentement . . . dudit achateur . . . avecques ledit . . . evesque."

93. *AHP*, 21:340 n. 1; cf. the pleas cited above, n. 26. In a plea of 31 March 1422 (AN, X 1A 9197, fol. 66r) we read that opponents in a benefice case were cited before Simon, as bishop, at Chapelle-Bellouin.

94. AN, JJ 132, no. 56, fols. 33v–34v. The confiscation had occurred in 1379, and although Kérimel returned to Valois allegiance along with Jean of Brittany in 1381 and had the various confiscations of his lands cancelled by royal order (AN, JJ 119, no. 356, fol. 212v), in fact he did not get his property back. See Guérin in *AHP*, 21:315–321. These Niort properties may have been the same as those bought by Jean and Simon at this time (above); in that case Simon's purchase of them from Morinot would have represented only the neutralization of a possible challenge.

a pretext to seize much of his property as security.[95] Foreseeing just such a grab, Jean had prudently asked Morinot to be executor of his will, promising him in payment a bequest of the Paris house, which title Morinot then sold to Simon for the huge sum of 4,000 francs, with a 500-franc sales tax to make it official. The legalities were fragile, but Simon was poised to exploit them; and immediately on Jean's death he had his own men and horses move into the house. The widow was frightened into renouncing her claim to the estate by being told of Jean's debts to the crown, which his heirs would have to pay. She was also assured that she would be compensated if she went to Bourges (the capital of Berry). As soon as she got there she was arrested and kept in prison for eighteen months, while Simon established his title of real possession. By the time the Chauchats could sue for recovery, it was too late for anything but the sort of protracted, open-ended lawsuits that for Simon were simply a mode of holding property; the house remained his.[96] So did most of his other acquisitions, including a cluster of more than a half-dozen properties and lordships that he put together in Anjou, in Loudunois.[97] This region had indeed become another center of Cramaud importance with Jean's marriage; for Orable's first husband had been lord of Mons, and as guardian of her children Jean could wield their rights, the necessary privileges having been secured from Duchess Marie

---

95. AN, JJ 132, fol. 172rv, a royal confirmation of Berry's seizure of the Chauchat holdings in Auvergne, 12 June 1388, with a gift of them to Morinot de Tourzel, up to the value of 3,000 gold francs. For other details see Simon's plea of 25 April 1391 (AN, X 1A 1475, fol. 234r), which gives Chauchat's debt to the crown as 4,000 lions. According to the allegations of Chauchat's widow in a later case (the *jugé* of 24 November 1408 in AN, X 1A 56, fols. 301v–302v), the duke of Berry had caused Chauchat's Paris property to be put into the royal hand on the pretext of the debt and had had moneys therefrom paid to himself, by ducal letters of 27 May 1388, while the duke's secretary had gotten possession of the rest pending settlement of the debt, although he in fact treated it as his own. Cf. Lehoux, 2:252 n. 3, for an entirely ducal picture of the affair.

96. According to Chauchat's widow and sister (AN, X 1A 1475, fol. 234v), his legacy to Morinot was "a la charge de ce qui estoit deu au roy," and, "se Chauchat lui avoit laissie, c'estoit pour ce qu'il s'estoit chargie seul et pour le tout du fait de son execucion, dont il ne fist onques riens." For the other details see the pleas of both parties (fols. 234r–235r) and the comprehensive review in the *arrêt* of 1 July 1391 (AN, X 1A 38, fols. 233v–234v). The case went on for years (AN, X 1A 39, fol. 10rv; X 1A 40, fols. 147r–148v; X 1A 42, fols. 145v–146r).

97. The best piece was perhaps the castle and castellany of Rocherigaut, which Simon bought from Duchess Marie of Anjou on 28 January 1394, along with the lordship of Ranton, for 400 gold écus; the royal confirmation of December 1394 is in *AHP*, 24:185–190. Some of the others were Nouzilly, bought on 12 April 1397 (ibid.: 420 n.), Bour (AN, X 1A 51, fol. 122v), Chapelle-Bellouin (*AHP*, 21:340 n. 1), Tilly (*AHP*, 24:423–426), and Pouant [Jean Besly, *Evesques de Poictiers* (Paris, 1647): 200–202].

of Anjou thanks to Simon's position as Berry's chancellor.[98] All in all, the
Cramauds had come a long way from Rochechouart, as we can also see
from Jean's military service: in 1386 he led a band of eleven squires, in
1387 a band of eighteen; the former band included some Montléon kin;
the latter, after the Touffou affair, did not.[99] We are not surprised to find
him enhancing his estate by serving in North Africa under the duke of
Bourbon in 1390 and later enjoying the title of royal chamberlain, or
even captain of Albigeois.[100]

Simon could hardly have won the extraordinary successes of his career
and his family planning if he had possessed nothing more than the
egoism, ambition, ruthlessness, and lust for worldly things that the successes imply. These traits must have been harnessed by a mind capable
of grasping the essence of particulars and at the same time putting
these together, by techniques of abstraction and synthesis, into large-
scale speculative constructions pointing to their author's goals. To balance the picture, however, we must also put in the external virtues
required by the game of "estate" and the inner ones that were the
condition of success in a political system of clients and patrons. High
estate was grounded in wealth but had to be manifested in behavior. Its
possessor was supposed to act *comme il faut* and do something more
besides; he should appear conventionally decent, liberal, and generous.
As for clientage, it called for personal acceptability, reliability, loyalty,
and competence in pursuit of the patron's goals. While we have not had
occasion to notice such virtues in Simon's acquisition of Touffou and his
Paris house, we do find them when we study his public function as
bishop of Poitiers. If we do not see them here accompanied by holiness,
we are not surprised; rare at all times, such a combination was all but
non-existent in Simon's age and place.

The contemporary ideal of a good bishop is nowhere better expressed
than in this image of self-praise constructed in 1416 by the archbishop
of Toulouse, referring to his earlier tenure of Albi:

He had governed well without exacting fees on his seal, without demanding a
caritative subsidy, and had prosecuted the rights of the bishopric. He

---

98. Moranvillé, *Journal de Jean le Fèvre*: 237: "Lundi xiie jour [of February 1386]
sellées III lettres pour messire J. de Cramauld neveu de l'evesque de Poitiers chancelier
de monsegneur de Berri." The grants were a privilege to the inhabitants of Mons, a
release to Jean, as guardian, of Huet's revenues, and a permission to exercise a purchase
option (*rachat*) on an Odart kinsman's lands.

99. BN, *pièces orig.* 925, no. 20,431, items 2, 4.

100. A royal letter of 26 January 1400 (AN, X 1A 47, fol. 6rv) refers to Jean as
cambellanus noster; on 1 May 1400 he was among 179 knights receiving the king's livery:
Douët-d'Arcq, 1:165. The captaincy of Albigeois is mentioned in AN, X 1A 9198, fol.
179v (1426). For the rest see Guérin in *AHP,* 21:341 f.

had supported orphans, widows, and the needy; he had distributed goods to the poor—not to his own relatives, even though he was noble on both sides. He had acquitted the poor of their debts. He had supported his clergy and ruled mildly, not burdening them or the people. As soon as he had become bishop he spent more than a thousand livres to repair the hall of the episcopal palace; then he gave fine jewels to the church, had the portal rebuilt, and made several repairs. He had served God well and had devotedly resided in his see and preached and taught, for he is a man of great learning, and he did very well. *Omnia bene fecit.*[101]

The Christian virtue of charity here seems to be more of a traditional adornment than an essential principle, and it rests uneasily amidst considerations of estate, administrative responsibility, zealous prosecution of property rights, and worldly munificence. It is missing altogether in another definition of episcopal merit that we can infer from Élie de Lestrange's charge that Pierre d'Ailly, his predecessor in Le Puy, had been a bad bishop. For while Pierre "had had three years' revenues from the see, he did nothing good there but only levied as much as he could through his deputies. . . . He never spent more than twenty-and-a-half sous on repairs, nor did he serve in the church, nor did he reside there, nor did he prosecute the rights of the church."[102]

Returning now to Simon as bishop of Poitiers, we must note that his position as chancellor of the duke of Berry required him to spend a good deal of time away from his see; moreover, we have just met two widows and one orphan who could not have regarded him as a protector; and he may well have used episcopal revenues to help his family—he was noble on both sides. But by and large he did what he was supposed to do, and perhaps more. Poitiers was the center of the new Cramaud family position, and we have already seen how closely linked this was with Simon's episcopacy. Later on, after moving to another see, he would nevertheless keep himself involved in the affairs of Poitiers, which he singled out for special benefactions and chose as the place for his tomb. Eventually he would return as bishop.[103] His idea of his own estate could hardly have been kept separate from his sense of what was due to the episcopacy, and he served both at once.

Thus, for example, we see him attending to the episcopal bourg of Chauvigny by trying to consolidate the bishop's jurisdiction there and by starting a new portal. He further "prosecuted the rights of the

---

101. AN, X 1A 4791, fol. 42r (20 February 1416).

102. Valois, 3:131 n. 1.

103. See below, at n. 130, and see Ch. IX below. Robert Favreau, *La ville de Poitiers à la fin du moyen âge, MSAO*, 4th series, 15 (Poitiers, 1978):231 ff., notes the extraordinary involvement of Simon and succeeding bishops of Poitiers in political affairs that took them away from their see, and their consequent use of vicars-general. See below for the trouble this caused Simon.

church" in a large number of lawsuits, vindicating episcopal rights of presentation to canonries; rights of visitation and procuration over St. Jean de Ménigoute; rights of jurisdiction over the border village of Yseure, which the duke of Touraine was trying to take over; and much more.[104] Nor, after his first tenure of Poitiers, did his successor bring him to court on charges of having neglected repairs—one of the more common types of lawsuit at the time.[105] Nor do we find complaints about his having exacted money. Quite the contrary—his financial administration of the see was so negligent that many years later he was still trying to make his former vicar-general Raymond Arnaud produce a clear statement of income and expenses. He tried in vain, for when the experts of the *Chambre des comptes* examined the accounts, they found them so amateurish as to defy comprehension by anyone but their creator.[106] If we ask why a man of Simon's shrewdness appointed this sort of a vicar-general in the first place, we can either suspect some sort of complicity or else put it down to his frequent absences.

His most important single action as bishop during this tenure of the see presents a similarly ambiguous picture, in which indubitable service to the episcopal estate involved disservice as well, because Simon was also serving himself. The Poitiers cathedral chapter, like many others, had received papal privileges confirming its independent status vis-à-vis the bishop. In 1307, Pope Clement V had exempted it from the bishop's jurisdiction and confirmed its liberties, which included the right to 600 francs a year from the bishop's judicial revenues. Henceforth the chapter demanded that each new bishop swear an oath including, along with the usual promise to preserve the church's rights and recover alienated prop-

---

104. Simon pursued a long-term controversy between the bishops of Poitiers and Louis d'Harcourt, viscount of Chatellerault, over the division of judicial rights in Chauvigny (AN, X 1C 55, no. 31; 6 August 1387) and sought, unsuccessfully, to solve the issue by acquiring all of them (AN, X 1A 9198, fol. 185v). For the Chauvigny portal see fol. 179r. For the rest see, e.g., AN, X 1A 35, fols. 168r–169v (an episcopal right of presentation); AN, X 1A 1475, fols. 72r, 76r, 79r, and AN, X 1A 38, fol. 136rv (the bishop's visitation rights over St. Jean de Ménigoute; Simon won, in an interlocutory decree that became permanent: AN, X 1A 4784, fols. 217v, 219r); AN, X 1A 1475, fol. 81r, and AN, X 1A 4784, fol. 384r (the rights over Yseure). The list could be made very much longer. For some of his other episcopal acts, including the reception of homages, see *Tables des manuscripts de D. Fontenau*, 1:311; Auber: 256 ff.

105. He boasted of this later, when sued by his successor to Carcassonne (AN, X 1A 4790, fol. 173r; 11 December 1414), saying that he was "valiant, sage, and prudent, and has therefore held a number of bishoprics in the realm and has kept them in excellent repair, so that he has never before been sued for repairs." For a modern judgement in the same sense, see Robert Favreau, "L'entretien du temporel episcopale: L'exemple de Poitiers au XVe siècle," *BSAO*, 4th series, 9 (1967):446.

106. AN, X 1A 45, fol. 7rv (20 December 1397); X 1A 46, fols. 16r–17v (8 January 1399); Favreau, *Ville de Poitiers*: 233 n. 596.

erty, a promise "to observe punctually and fully the Clementine privilege and the composition it mentions." The bishops allegedly swore as required, but since they then tried to avoid paying the 600 francs, the papal privilege generated contention and lawsuits for the next three-quarters of a century. It would seem that Simon had grasped the problem from the first and had seen the way to a solution that would benefit all parties while bringing profit and honor to himself as well. He began it during his installation on 24 February 1387, in the presence of the duke of Berry and the major episcopal vassals, as well as other prominent persons. As the barons were carrying him to the door of the church, the canons emerged with their "Red Book" containing their text of the oath and asked him to swear it, but he refused, swearing fully only to the usual obligations. As for the rest, he said, "I swear to the Clementine privilege only insofar as I am legally bound to swear it." The canons let him into the church anyway (did they know his plan?), and when he reached the main altar they duly asked him to repeat the oath; he replied, "I swear in the manner and form in which I swore when entering the church." After the ceremony, he had the ducal secretary and public notary Gontier Col see to the preparation of an official instrument recording the whole business.[107] Soon after, he began the complicated negotiations that would dissolve the issue once and for all.[108] His plan was to establish a yearly revenue for the chapter that would equal its claims, and he did so by giving up some episcopal rights and buying out the *capiceriatus* (*chevecerie*) of the church, a sinecure with only the nominal obligation of keeping candles lit. Its revenues were joined to the chapter's mensa as of 27 May 1389, and the arrangement was approved by Pope Clement VII on 22 April 1389.

---

107. An original copy of the instrument survives in ADV, G 1, no. 16; cf. the various texts in the chapter's "Red Book" (ADV, G 182); one of them (fol. 33v) describes the sequence of acts making up the installation ceremony. The account by the Abbé Auber, "Histoire de la cathédrale de Poitiers (4e partie)," *MSAO*, 16 (1849):65 ff., covers the events and the historical background, but it is unreliable in details.

108. For the general pattern see Guillaume Mollat, "Conflits entre archidiacres et évêques aux XIVe et XVe siècles," *Revue historique de droit français et étranger*, 4th series, 35 (1957):549–560; also idem, in *Histoire des institutions françaises au moyen âge*, ed. Ferdinand Lot & Robert Fawtier, 3 (Paris, 1962):342 ff. My brief summary of the matter below is taken chiefly from Clement VII's bull of 22 April 1389, ed. L. Redet, *Cartulaire de l'évêché de Poitiers ou Grand-Gauthier*, AHP, 10 (1881):197–205; also Clement's confirmation of Simon's foundation, 25 April 1390 (ASV, *Reg. aven.* 263, fols. 562r–563v), which quotes in full a public letter on the subject by Simon, 1 February 1390. Also a letter by the Dauphin Charles, dated Poitiers, 9 June 1419, which reviews the terms of the foundation from Simon's point of view (see below, n. 111). A surviving inscription originally above Simon's tomb includes a summary of his settlement; it is published in the Abbé Auber's "Cathédrale de Poitiers": 162. For the early history of the controversy see *AHP*, 10, no. 72.

So far so good. One question arises, however, when we learn that the very large sums of money needed to finance this solution came from selling off timber rights in a forest belonging to the see; we can only wonder if the net result was profitable enough to Simon and his successors to justify this sort of dipping into capital.[109] A more serious question is raised by Simon's subsequent action; for instead of stopping with this resolution of the matter, he used it to get Clement's approval to re-obligate the bishop's judicial revenues to the extent of 100 livres a year to pay the canons for four yearly masses in the cathedral. The beneficiaries were to be Simon, his parents, the duke of Berry, and Clement VII. The pope agreed, 25 April 1390.[110] Since Simon's successors as bishops of Poitiers saw no reason why they should pay for his masses, the new controversy replaced the old in massive litigation in both Avignon and Paris; the bishops always lost.[111] The terms of the re-obligation show that Simon had foreseen these troubles, and it is hard to avoid the obvious conclusion, that his act of statesmanship was not conceived of as what we would call public service but was, rather, a move in the game of "estate." The resolution of the original conflict was a grand public action that brought Simon honor; his yearly revenues were perhaps increased; his family's name would henceforth be linked to those of the duke and the pope. Honor and piety, externalized as pomp and ceremony, went to

---

109. On 20 December 1429 the bishop of Poitiers's lawyer (Jouvenel) defended episcopal rights over the forest of Mareuil against the chapter's claim to hold a one-third share *indivisa* by noting that one precedent for joint ownership alleged by the chapter had been a special case. There had been a 500-livre charge on the episcopal judicial revenues (his "seal"), and the then-bishop decided to acquit the charge by selling wood from the forest, the chapter getting one-third of the price (AN, X 1A 9199, fol. 212v). This must refer to the matter at hand (the bishops' original obligation of 600 livres was liquidated as one of 500 livres, the remaining 100 still due to the chapter for Simon's foundation, as below), and it fits in with what the lawyer Letur said on behalf of the bishop in 1426, arguing (against Jean de Cramaud) that Simon's action of 1389 had indeed been meritorious but also profitable to himself (AN, X 1A 9198, fol. 185v): "A ce qu'il acquita la crosse au eveschie envers chapitre de Poictiers, il en prist voirement la cure, il y estoit tenu, mais ce fut par l'union de la chevecerie qu'il porchaca et les bulles, et ne fut point a sa charge, mais lui valu depuiz chascun an les 500 livres."

110. The copy of the papal letter in the register (above, n. 108) was dated 7. Kal. May (25 April), "anno duodecimo" (1390); then the last word was crossed out and "terciodecimo" (1391) was written in the margin. But by 25 April 1391, Simon was already patriarch of Alexandria, whereas the papal letter addresses him as bishop of Poitiers. The confusion may have come from Simon's own letter, incorporated in the papal one; it was dated ("in our castle of Chauvigny") 1 February 1390. Perhaps the papal scribe assumed this was French usage and changed the papal date accordingly.

111. BN, *ms. lat.* 18,377, pp. 207–209, 217, 213–223; *Tables des manuscripts de D. Fontenau,* 1:319. Foreseeing all this, Simon had stipulated in the foundation that the bishop could keep 50 of the 100 livres unless he refused to pay; then he would be liable for the whole sum.

magnify estate, and it remains for the modern mind to ask questions about self-interest and public benefit. Or perhaps not to ask them, but simply to note that Simon's pursuit of his own aims within the public world of his time necessarily produced by-products of benefit to others. If, finally, we ask how good a bishop he was, we can best avoid an anachronistic answer by noting the remarkable fact that the cartulary of the Poitiers bishopric (the "Grand Gauthier") was neglected after 1310 by all the bishops except Simon, whose twenty entries from 1387 to 1421 virtually took it over; there was only one entry after his, in 1506.[112]

Still in his forties, evidently energetic, endowed with intellectual powers and resources of character that had not yet been fully exploited, Simon did not intend to stop his climb. Had he done so, slacking off and thus indicating that the limit of his usefulness had been reached, he would probably have lost what he had; for then the Berry influence would flow less powerfully, challengers would appear, lawsuits would go sour, and the Poitevin web of estates would snap back into its original shape, tossing out the Cramaud intruders. The normal thing was to keep moving, and it was Berry's policy to get his men placed as high as possible. Two previous chancellors had become cardinals, Guy de Malesset and Pierre de Thury, and one, Pierre de Giac, had become chancellor of France. Now it was Simon's turn. Unfortunately the political situation in France had just changed for what most historians call the better. In November of 1388 Charles VI, prompted by his brother Louis and his father's old officials, declared himself of age and took over the government of the realm; among his first acts was telling his ducal uncles that their presence at court could be dispensed with. The old officials, called "marmosets" by their enemies, emerged from the wings to help direct the royal government, often enough toward their own advantage. From then until August 1392, when the first attack of insanity hit the king and brought them back, the dukes were unable to have everything their own way. For Simon de Cramaud, used to frequent trips to Paris and elsewhere in the duke's service, the new situation must have seemed dangerously stagnant.[113] All his hopes now focused on a promotion that

---

112. Redet, *Cartulaire*.

113. Simon's itinerary in this period is instructive, particularly since we have the attendance lists of the council of Parlement, which Simon seems normally to have sat in on when he was in town. In 1388 he was in Paris through January and into February (AN, X 1A 1474, fols. 177r, 179v; J 187A, no. 30; *Ordonnances*, 7:763) and again in May and June (Lehoux, 2:221 n. 1; AN, X 1A 1474, fols. 192r, 193r). These presences accord fully with the duke of Berry's itinerary (Lehoux, 3:472 ff.). In the period after the king's assumption of power, Simon was in Paris on 16 December 1388 (AN, X 1474, fol. 338v), then in 1389 on 30 June, 31 July, and 4 September (fols. 356r, 358v,

would lift him up and out, into the higher reaches of the ecclesiastical hierarchy as archbishop of Sens, replacing the incumbent Guy de Roye, who was due to be moved to Rheims in early July 1390.[114]

Simon had begun well before to press Berry to get him the post, and Berry obliged by asking Pope Clement VII—all three were on very good terms.[115] The appointment was made,[116] and the news came to Simon by special messenger about mid-July; sending the messenger back richly rewarded to pay the *servicia* and get the letters of provision,[117] Simon began to prepare for his move and to have himself "served" as archbishop. Too soon, for Charles VI had his own candidate for Sens, Guillaume de Dormans, bishop of Meaux, while one of the royal *maîtres des requêtes,*

362r)—the last two occasions evidently in the company of the duke, who on 1 September had to resign his lieutenancy of Languedoc (Lehoux, 2:256; cf. 3:474). After that, I find Simon in Paris only twice, 29 April 1390 (AN, X 1A 1475, fol. 128v) and October 1390 (see below), until October 1392 (St. Denis), after the king's insanity. From then on the frequency of his presences in the council of Parlement becomes even greater than in the old days. Note that Berry was not in Paris at all, according to Lehoux's itinerary, during 1390 and 1391.

114. Eubel, *Hierarchia,* 1, s.v. "Remensis." The date of the transfer in the papal letter of provision is 27 May 1390, but this was a predating (below, n. 116). An archbishop of Sens was in Avignon on 2 July 1390, when he lent his name to a *rotulus* (ASV, *Reg. sup.* 77, fol. 110r); this must still have been Guy.

115. For Berry and Clement see, e.g., Lehoux, 2:313 f. Simon's favor with the pope is attested by the plea of the bishop of Poitiers in 1426 (AN, X 1A 9198, fol. 185v): "Le [i.e., Simon] fist pape Clement evesque d'Avignon ex benivolencia, et que bien le cognoissoit et amoit." For the requests, see below.

116. Eubel, *Hierarchia,* 1:399 n. 6. Clement's letter was dated 27 May 1390 (ASV, *Reg. aven.* 262, fols. 360v–361r). A letter of the same date transferred Bishop Jean of Castres to Poitiers (ibid., fols. 363v–364v), and a letter dated 26 June 1390 provided for Jean's swearing of his oath for Poitiers (ASV, *Reg. aven.* 263, fol. 434v). Since Simon only received news of Clement's action, which had not yet been embodied in letters of provision, about mid-July (see below), the papal letter of provision must have been written after the date it bears.

117. The story that follows is taken from H. Duplès-Agier, ed., *Registre criminel du Châtelet de Paris,* 1 (Paris, 1861):516–556—the interrogation of the royal dispatch rider Pierre Le Breton, begun on 9 September 1390. He said that he had begun his mission (see below) about six weeks before, hence in the last days of July. A witness later testified that he had seen Le Breton in Poitiers about three weeks before 15 August (pp. 549 f.)—hence about 25 July—and that Le Breton had arrived the day before. I follow this evidence in my dating of the episodes below. Le Breton gave three versions of what happened, as noted below; they begin on pp. 516, 520, 524. The discrepancies do not affect the dating. I infer from the context that Simon had received news of his appointment only a short time before Le Breton's mission. The messenger whom he sent back to Avignon to get the actual letters (p. 532) must also have taken the money for Simon's *servicia,* for these were both pledged and paid on 20 July (Favier, *Finances:* 346, citing ASV, *Intr. ex.* 366, fols. 38v, 39v). In this case, evidently, obligation by proxy was accepted, no doubt because accompanied by payment.

Pierre Fresnel, counted on getting Meaux for himself. The two procured letters from the king to both Simon and Berry, instructing the former not to press the duke or the pope on his behalf, the latter not to press the pope. But the letters did not arrive in Poitiers until about 24 July; and when the dispatch rider, Pierre Le Breton, learned that Simon had already been named, he decided not to deliver his letters. Dormans and Fresnel did not accept defeat but prepared what may have been a frame-up. Pierre Le Breton was arrested, held in the Châtelet, and questioned from 9 September on. First he said the letters had been stolen from him; then he said that they had not but that he had not thought it in order to deliver them after Simon had been made archbishop. At this point Le Bègue de Villaines, a marmoset and royal councillor, intervened to insist on the king's behalf that the "true" story be elicited. Le Breton was tortured and promptly confessed that on his arrival in Poitiers Simon had offered him 100 francs not to deliver his letters. This story was evidently used to bring accusations against Simon, for in September/October 1390 he had to come to court—at Compiègne, then in Paris—in order to deny them.[118] It was good for him that later Le Breton himself repudiated his latest confessions, saying that if tortured again he would confess anything, even that he had betrayed the whole realm of France, but that in fact his second story was the true one. We can only guess that perhaps it was: what he had said under torture did indeed make him guilty of some degree of treason, but on the other hand the story he stuck to was most disagreeable to those in power, who might well have made a deal with him if he had agreed to testify "right." In any case, it is clear that the affair involved a contest between the king's clients on the one side, the duke's on the other, and that Le Breton's interrogation was only one move in the game. It was evidently pushed only far enough to cause Simon to lose Sens to Guillaume,[119] not to the point of attainting him of a crime that if proven could have caused his ruin. As for the pope, he presumably felt that he had to please the king before he could please the duke.

But in a few months he could please Berry too, and on 17 March

---

118. We read in Duplès-Agier, *Registre criminel*, 1:528, of "les excusacions proposées par messire Symon de Cramaut, evesque de Poitiers et chancellier de mons. le duc de Berry, contre les confessions ou accusacions faites par ledit chevaucheur contre ledit mons. l'evesque," 13 October 1390 and thereafter.

119. Guillaume's provision to Sens was dated 17 October 1390 (Eubel, *Hierarchia*, 1, s.v. "Sens"); a papal letter of the same date restored bishop Jean to his see of Castres, which was vacated by moving his replacement, Pierre Aimery, up to the archbishopric of Bourges (ASV, *Reg. aven.* 262, fols. 374r–376v). Presumably the basic decision was made in Paris after Le Breton's hearing before the chancellor of France, 13 October (Duplès-Agier, *Registre criminel*, 1:528 ff.).

1391 he named Simon patriarch of Alexandria—an archiepiscopal rank —with the administration of the see of Avignon. Simon was in Avignon with the duke at the time[120] and probably stayed on, for we find him there on 26 April, 13 June, and thereafter on various dates until at least the end of April 1392.[121] Apart from some politico-diplomatic service in the wars with Raymond de Turenne, his work for the pope is unknown, and we can only infer from his presence at the Curia and his holding the see of Avignon that, with the ducal government left behind and the royal government practically inaccessible, the papal government was to be the theater of his ambition.[122] At this stage he could not have aspired to anything less than the cardinalate. Two decades later, old curial hands still commented on the fact that Simon had been one of only two non-cardinals of archiepiscopal rank who insisted on their ancient prerogative of having their trains carried behind them not only in the streets of Avignon but even within the papal court.[123] Another report

---

120. Eubel, *Hierarchia*, 1:82, 124; ASV, *Reg. aven.* 265, fols. 206v–207v. For the duke in Avignon see Lehoux, 3:475. For Simon see ASV, *Intr. et exit.* 367, fol. 22r, 20 March 1391: receipt of a subsidy "a domino Symone olim Pictavensi, nunc Avinionensi episcopo." Although the entries show many prelates hit by this emergency subsidy— "pro expellendo societates gencium armorum de comitatu Venayssini" (cf. Valois, 2:342 ff.)—only some bishops are represented. Inasmuch as a normal collection from a bishop would have been made by the regional collector and accounted for in a special register (*collectoria*), the above receipt from Simon may be taken as indicating his presence in Avignon; cf. Favier, *Finances*: 78 f.

121. On 26 April 1391 Simon arranged payment of his *servicia* for Avignon (ASV, *Oblig. et sol.* 43, fol. 140v). On 13 June he supplicated for his chaplain Pierre Granassi (ASV, *Reg. sup.* 78, fol. 125v); he composed *rotuli* on 26 August (correct "Iherosolimitanum" to Alexandrinum), 28 October, 9 December (ibid., fols. 133v, 168r; *Reg. sup.* 79, fol. 9r). ASV, *Intr. et exit.* 367, fol. 170v, has this entry for 7 July 1391: "*Guerra*: . . . fuerunt soluti domino Iohanni Cardinali de Murolio pro tradendo gentibus armorum que sunt ante Anconam, per manus domini Symonis Patriarche Alexandrini . . . M. flor." and fol. 199r has this one for 18 September 1391: "*Guerra*: . . . equitatori qui mittitur cum . . . Patriarcha Alexandrino ad . . . missos per regem . . . , V. flor." (Valois, 2:346, misconstrues this.) On 26 November 1391 Simon paid part of his *servicia* (ASV, *Intr. et exit.* 369, fol. 6r). On 24 April 1392 he paid another part (ibid., fol. 22r); on the same day he received payment for a loan he had made to the Camera (fol. 95v), and a payment was also made (ibid.) "domino Patriarche qui fuit missus duabus vicibus per dominum nostrum papam ad . . . missos per regem Francie pro tractatu pacis cum . . . Raymundo de Turenna; pro expensis . . . , 300 scut. auri." An entry ibid., fol. 100v, for 6 May 1392 seems to imply that Simon was still in the papal service: "Aymerico Dassier domicello qui nunc est cum domino episcopo Carcassonensi [scil., Simon]." All but the first three of these items were provided by Hartmut Hoffmann, Göttingen.

122. For the special relationship between the Curia and the see of Avignon, see Favier, *Finances*: 310–312.

123. *Gesta Benedicti XIII.*, in L. Muratori, ed., *Rerum Italicarum scriptores* 3(2), (Milan, 1734):805–808.

informs us that when at the papal court on 15 May 1406, Simon sat, at a papal high mass, right in the midst of the cardinals, ahead of the sub-episcopal ones, and wore clothes just like theirs, omitting only the pearls on the shoes.[124] Everything we know about the man and his career indeed gives substance to the statement made later by one of Benedict XIII's familiars, Martin de Alpartil, to explain why Simon led France's union policy against Benedict: the latter, while still Cardinal Pedro de Luna, had blocked the duke of Berry's "most urgent" efforts to have Clement VII make Simon a cardinal; therefore, Martin says, Simon hated Benedict.[125] Simon indeed could hardly have been aiming at anything less than the cardinalate, and we have seen that Berry was in the habit of pressing the pope on behalf of his protégés. But this time he failed. Why? Quite likely because there was indeed opposition from within the Sacred College—for in such matters Clement usually obliged the duke. Why the opposition? Here the guesses become less probable: perhaps the parvenu's pushiness betrayed by the episodes noted above made Simon seem uncongenial; or perhaps Pedro de Luna, an Aragonese papalist with his own ambitions for the future, did not like the prospect of yet another Valois client in the college. As for when the decision was made, we can only note that on 19 September 1391 Simon was shifted from Avignon to Carcassonne; soon thereafter he began a lawsuit against his predecessor for the costs of repairs that had been neglected and pursued the lawsuit over papal opposition.[126]

---

124. Ehrle, *Alpartil*: 162.

125. Ibid.: 16 f., 118.

126. For the shift to Carcassonne see Eubel, *Hierarchia*, 1:166; ASV, *Reg. aven.* 265, fols. 184v–185r. Simon began his lawsuit by having the previous bishop (Pierre de St. Martial, now archbishop of Toulouse) cited before royal judges in Carcassonne; then the two agreed to submit to the arbitration of the papal *camerarius*. After about a year of no action, Simon withdrew from the arbitration and brought his suit before the Parlement of Paris, alleging that at least 20,000 francs were needed for due repairs; an *arrêt* was issued 16 July 1393 noting that experts had assessed the actual costs at 9,328 livres, 18s. 6d. (AN, X 1A 40, fols. 260r–262r); cf. M. Boulet, ed., *Questiones Johannis Galli* (Paris, 1944): 371 f. But on 2 May 1392 Pope Clement VII had granted a privilege to Pierre that he might not be forced to respond to Simon's lawsuit (ASV, *Reg. aven.* 269, fol. 563v; I have this item from Hartmut Hoffmann). In fact the case was pursued, as noted (see also AN, X 1A 40, fol. 96r; X 1A 41, fol. 2v), until the parties agreed to settle out of court (AN, X 1A 41, fol. 65v, a letter of 8 August 1394). That all this implies a certain estrangement between Simon and the Curia is only a possible guess, perhaps confirmed by another item (ASV, *Reg. aven.* 269, fol. 593rv; I have it from Hartmut Hoffmann), a privilege from Clement granting Simon's supplication that he be allowed to provide to eight lesser benefices in the ordinary gift of the bishops of Carcassonne; for while it was dated 20 November 1391, it was not "*expeditum*" until 19 May 1394 ("Dat. Avin. XII. kl. Dec. anno quartodecimo, Exp. XIIII. kl. Iunii anno sextodecimo"; cf. p. 63 above).

Simon was rescued from this dead end on 5 August 1392 when King Charles VI was struck by insanity and the ducal uncles could once again direct the royal government. On 9 October, Simon was at St. Denis for the translation of St. Louis's relics;[127] on 12 November he was on hand for the opening of Parlement,[128] and there are frequent attestations of his presence in Paris during the next years.[129] At the same time, we must suppose that he moved about on his own and the duke's business. He must have spent time in Poitou, where he could maintain an official presence by virtue of a papal privilege "to reform what had to be reformed" in the church of Poitiers;[130] and we see him in Avignon in early 1394, where, *inter alia,* he bought the castle and castellany of Rocherigaut in Loudunois from the Duchess Marie of Anjou. He would indeed keep on buying properties in this region and elsewhere during the 1390s.[131] Otherwise, in defect of information about what he actually did, we may perhaps best think of him now as simply a leading figure in the royal government, one of Berry's most important clients on the royal council. The only way he could reach a higher position, though not necessarily a more powerful one, was by promotion in the church, a˙path that had been blocked. If we postulate such ambition on his part, and it would be the opposite postulate that would have to be proven, we must assume that he could not have looked forward with pleasure to a continuation of Clement VII's papacy, or indeed to that of a successor coming from the ranks of those cardinals who had frustrated him in 1391. That the duke of Berry was moving somewhat fitfully to a similar position; and that from 1392 on, the issue of church union was coming more and more into prominence both in Paris and Avignon; and that even Clement VII now found it advisable to write Simon de Cramaud that he should inform the duke of Berry of Clement's readiness to resign the papacy if necessary—this whole development of "public opinion" and royal policy considered in the preceding chapter—was the framework which included

---

127. *RSD*, 2:34.

128. AN, X 1A 1477, fol. 1r.

129. Ibid., fols. 186r, 14r, 189r (13 November, 3 December, 18 December 1392); fols. 191v–198r, *passim* (January–March 1393); fols. 208r–214v, *passim* (June–August 1393); fols. 394v, 397r (22 November 1393, 2 January 1394); etc.

130. ASV, *Reg. aven.* 270, fol. 626v, a rubric dated only "anni quarti decimi" (i.e., 20 September 1391 to 20 September 1392): "Symoni Patriarche Alexandrino reformandi reformanda in ecclesia Pictavensi datur facultas"; the text is lost. (Provided by Hartmut Hoffmann.)

131. See n. 97 above for Rocherigaut, Ranton, and Nouzilly; lands and *rentes* in Morry were bought on 13 May 1392 (AN, X 1C 70B, no. 226); one-third of Brigneuil in Limousin was bought for 1,500 livres on 16 May 1398 (AN, X 1A 50, fols. 169r–171v; cf. X 1A 46, fol. 73v). Several other purchases known but not datable must have fallen in this period too.

Simon's own position. It was not a mere coincidence. What we have examined for Simon in detail can be summed up by saying that the Great Schism meant, for practical purposes, the pontificate of Clement VII and that this had been enormously advantageous to him, but he had exhausted its advantages. The same would apply, mutatis mutandis, to many others in France, particularly now that the king's incapacity had practically ended the prospect of conquering Italy—the original Schism policy of Paris and Avignon.

   The last years of Clement VII had seen the Valois dukes turning toward unionism and the *via cessionis*. They had also seen the emergence of precisely the high prelate, politician, Berry client, and royal councillor whose talents and interests fitted him for leadership of the new policy. Clement's death on 16 September 1394 crystallized these elements into a new political structure destined to last for many years.

CHAPTER FOUR

The First Paris Council
and the *Via Cessionis*

FRANCE'S union policy, which ran for fifteen years from the death of Clement VII on 16 September 1394 to the Council of Pisa 25 March to 7 August 1409, can be understood from first to last as a fight between two champions, Simon de Cramaud and Benedict XIII. The arena was Western Europe; the duel involved battalions of princes, prelates, cardinals, and professors on both sides; but the sustained thrusts of will and intellect that created the story came from the two political chiefs. Each side had its principles and ideas which touched vital issues of religion, church, and polity, but the battle of ideas was a mode and sometimes only an instrument of the political struggle whose essential structures of mind and heart lay well below the level of formal ratiocination. The substance of the struggle itself must of course be defined in terms of interests and powers, and in these terms there was a big difference between the antagonists. Benedict was the embodiment of centuries of papal tradition, the focus of both religious and secular loyalties, and the dominating force of his side; Simon was the political agent of the Valois dukes and only therefore capable of playing his other roles: mobilizer of the Gallican church, theoretician of the coercive *via cessionis*, statesman and diplomat of European range. Benedict was in his way a grand and tragic figure, Simon a glorified hatchet man. But in the battle that joined them, they were equivalents, like two otherwise disparate players in a game of chess, creating their antagonistic constructions with the same repertory of means.

Benedict's aim was to make all Europe recognize that he and his fellow cardinals of 1378 had been right, that the Avignon line in the Schism was legitimate, and that he, its current embodiment, was the true pope and hence indispensable—as vicar of Christ and as monarch in matters of church and faith—to any valid solution of the Schism. Simon wanted a concert of European princes to compel both popes to habilitate each other's side and then abdicate without any discussion of legitimacy; a new pope could then be chosen by some agency of the now-united church. The contradiction between these goals was clear from the first, so that the dealings between Paris and Avignon from 1394 on were always contests despite certain forms of collaboration imposed by the traditions of harmony and the residues of respect. As for the forms of action in the contest, they were determined on each side by the nature of the play. Since it was Paris that pressed for union, the initiative came from her, and Benedict was pushed into the weak position of a refuser. Moreover, since the unstable structures of political life at that time did not allow long-term calculations of means and ends, each move in the game tended to take the form of a paradigm of its side's ultimate goal, with Simon creating anticipatory realities of collaboration among the secular powers; transfer of control over the French church from pope to bishops and king; and insulting, domineering approaches to Benedict that treated him as a favorer of schism. Benedict for his part insisted on expressing papalist sovereignty in his every action, even when tactical flexibility might have been more productive. It was characteristic of Old Europe, in any case, that it saw public life as exhibition, with calculation and manipulation kept hidden. Public action, in short, was creation of public entity. Here the useful analogy would be not a chess game or some direct contest of strength against strength, but rather a theatrical production, actually two competing ones, each putting on a succession of dances whose patterns and rhythms might make the political community move to the same music and in the same steps. Such works of art were the reality that our sources tell us about and that must be reconstructed as the object of historical study—only then can we, if we wish, raise the further questions of underlying interest, intention, and theoretical principle on the part of this or that leader.

The sources themselves are embedded in works of art, for while there are many documents, treatises, letters, and the like which survive more or less haphazardly, most of what we know comes from massive collections prepared by men committed to one side or the other.[1] If the

---

1. The most important is the *Libri de Schismate* now in the Vatican Archive, for which see Michael Seidlmayer, "Die spanischen 'Libri de Schismate' des Vatikanischen Archivs," *Gesammelte Aufsätze zur Kulturgeschichte Spaniens*, 8 (Münster, 1940):199–262; also idem, *Die Anfänge des grossen abendländischen Schismas* (Münster, 1940): 195–228, where the work is characterized as "the great documentary working tool" which Cardinal Martin de Salva put together, chiefly in the 1390s, as an aid in Benedict's struggle. In fact, Pierre Ravat did much of the work, wrote many of the texts and marginalia, and seems, to judge from the latter, to have kept his own collection within the larger framework. The Vatican Library manuscript *Barb. lat.* 872 was part of Ravat's set, as were perhaps some of the "Tractatus de Schismate" originally in Benedict's court but now in the Paris BN (*DSO*, introduction, *ad* ms. *C*). The original order of both Salva's and Ravat's collections has been hopelessly mixed up by subsequent bookmakers but could be restored by reference to an original table of contents of the *Libri* (published by Seidlmayer, as above) and to the abundant cross-references in Ravat's marginalia. Other important but less extensive collections are the two Jumièges codices now in Rouen (nos. 1355, 1356) and BN *ms. lat.* 14,644, put together by Simon Plumetôt; also AN, J 518, for which see below.

collections consist of authentic texts that pose no big problem for historical criticism, nevertheless, much art is apt to lie underneath the authen-
ticity, especially in the collection that will concern us here, codex J 518
of the Paris Archives Nationales. This is a handsomely decorated, large
vellum book prepared ca. 1402, almost certainly on order from Simon
de Cramaud, including a number of his works along with many other
items documenting his and the crown's union policy from 1394 on.
Among the most valuable of these are copies of a series of "instruments"
prepared for the most part by the royal secretary and Berry client Gontier Col, containing narratives and texts of the royal actions from 22
September 1394 to 10 July 1395: the deliberations in the royal council
after the death of Clement VII, the First Paris Council, the tactical
program devised by the crown for dealing with Benedict, and the royal
embassy to Avignon which brought the royal thrust home to the pope
and cardinals. Although portions of these instruments survive in the
chronicle of the Monk of St. Denis, who presumably drew on the origi-
nals, the full texts survive only in J 518, which here and probably
elsewhere can be considered as a copy of Simon de Cramaud's own
working collection; we know he had one with him for reference during
his public appearances,[2] and it was most likely among the books he lost
on one of his trips to Rome.[3] At least one of the instruments was written
by Gontier Col at Simon's command, perhaps others too,[4] and it is
certain that they give us information he wanted on the record, in the

---

2. In his speech of 30 May 1398 at the Third Paris Council, Simon cited a number of
documents (or acts recorded in documents), all of which form part of codex J 518: the
conclave oath, the decision of the First Paris Council, the opinions of the cardinals for
cession in June 1395, the record of the ducal embassy to Avignon that year, and
Benedict's bulls rejecting cession in June and July 1395 and prohibiting the cardinals
from formally adhering to it (BdeC: 21). At Pisa he mentioned having with him at least
two of these documents: the conclave oath and Benedict's bull of 20 June 1395 rejecting
cession; he also had an instrument of a papal statement to that effect—Johannes Vincke,
"Acta Concilii Pisani," *Römische Quartalschrift*, 46 (1938):220 f.
    3. In a lawsuit of 1417 Simon's lawyer mentioned that his client "avoit perdu livres,
vaisselle, et tous ses meubles a la prise de la cite de Rome" (AN, X 1A 4791, fol. 216v;
Valois, 4:213 n. 2). In another lawsuit Renaud de Montléon's lawyer alleged that Simon
"maiorem . . . partem bonorum suorum mobilium ut puta libros, vestes, vasa argentea,
et alia quamplurima bona mobilia in quodam suo viagio Rome perdiderat" (AN, X 1A
9191, fol. 127v; an *arrêt* of 13 April 1429). Simon was in Rome in 1407 (16 July to
mid-August) and 1413 (from January on to at least 13 April, when he was made a
cardinal); the "prise" in question would most likely have been that by Ladislas of Naples,
8 June 1413.
    4. See n. 83 below; cf., as an example of the same sort of official care to obtain a
record, the duke of Berry's command that the Monk of St. Denis describe the ceremonies
at the peace negotiations of May 1393: "quas et dux Biturie michi jussit scriptis re-
digere" (*RSD*, 2:76).

form that he wished. It might be in order to think of J 518 as itself Simon's "White Book" of 1402, containing copies of similarly intended texts of 1394/1395—except that the analogy skips over the enormous differences due to the printing press and other media of preservation and publicity. An official "instrument" in Simon's time was not merely a record for practical purposes, one publication among others, but also one of the modes of being of the action it recorded—publicity in the most concrete sense of the word. For after the action had been choreographed and produced, it lived only in memory; and the public memory existed not as miscellaneous recollections nor as spontaneous recordings but as a version preserved in more or less official notarized instruments which could be later produced and read out at their possessor's will.[5] We shall see further on how artful and indeed fraudulent the Paris version of the First Paris Council appears when confronted by fragments of an Avignon version, but we shall also see how in this and other cases Simon de Cramaud used the official Paris version again and again to create the image he wanted, so that by, say, 1398, the First Paris Council was what he said it had been. To escape his reach we must use J 518 creatively, putting as much art into its interpretation as went into its composition.[6]

It was probably in late 1396 or early 1397 that Gontier Col was commissioned to compose the account which tells of the Paris reaction to the death of Clement VII some years earlier.[7] Relying no doubt on

---

5. Cf. the formula used in acts creating public notaries: "Ne contractuum memoria deperiret, inventum est tabellionatus officium, quo contractus legitimi ad cautelam presencium et memoriam futurorum manu publica notarentur" (e.g., ASV, *Reg. aven.* 305, fols. 196v–198v; August 1399). The same applied to public transactions in a time when there was no printing to publish the record definitively. Note that Gontier Col is described indifferently as royal secretary and public notary. Cf. the extraordinarily revealing remarks of Jean Petit in 1406 about the already obscure facts of 1398 (BdeC: 228): "Un moult grand et suffisant clerc . . . me disoit qu'à la sustraxion autrefois faitte, toutes les difficultés . . . furent encore mieux touchées et avisées, que l'on n'a fait maintenant. J'en ay tout un grand livre que l'en m'a presté; mais je n'ai point encore eu loisir de le veoir."

6. The narrative that follows is an attempt at such interpretation, with no effort to record all the details as Valois has done; his account (3:3–67) here as elsewhere is in this sense imperishable.

7. This is part of a historical introduction to Col's account of the ducal embassy to Avignon, May–July 1395; he went along as royal secretary (the whole account is in AN, J 518, fols. 119r–167v; *Ampl. coll.*, 7:479–528). The historical introduction would have been added after Col had written up his diary of the embassy, hence after 10 July 1395 and probably still later, for on fol. 130v there is a reference to Pierre Blau as "at present" a cardinal—he was elevated 24 December 1395. If the text in J 518 copied an integral exemplar, the latter would have been composed, most likely, in the context of the crisis of the *via cessionis* in late 1396 and early 1397 (see Ch. V below). The point here is that

memoranda, he wrote that, when the news reached Paris on 22 September, the royal council at once met to consider what the king should do and that the advice adopted almost unanimously (with a slight demurrer from the Orléanist client Pierre Fresnel, bishop of Meaux) was Simon de Cramaud's proposal that "the king" write at once to tell the Avignon cardinals to hold off a new election until a plan to use the opportunity might be devised, "for if there were an election one would have to deal with two contenders rather than only one." Burgundy was out of town; Berry was ill in his Paris palace; but Simon's plan was also his patron's; for Berry had been informed of Clement's death, perhaps by his chief client in the Sacred College, Pierre de Thury,[8] and had held his own council, which had come up with just this plan. The following day the University of Paris sent delegates to the king to suggest the same thing, also that a national council of clergy, barons, and nobles be summoned to advise on ways to union, that the way to pursue be the *via cessionis,* and that royal letters be sent to the Roman contender and the princes of his obedience. We are told that the delegates were "well satisfied" with the government's answer and that the university now resumed the classes it had suspended in August. The constellation of unionist forces demanded in vain by the university ever since January 1394 had thus come into being, and to complete the picture we need only imagine the comings and goings and conversations in which the alliance was worked out. Even the harsh line earlier advocated by the university now made its appearance, for Simon's formulation of the royal request that the cardinals not elect was backed up by a threat: "if you wish to have the obedience and credence of us and our realm." The clarity of this picture may be deceptive, but its main lines seem true.

When we ask exactly what intention lay behind the royal request, we are best informed by the cardinals themselves: anticipating pressure from Paris, they hurried to make their election; and when the royal courier arrived, they refused to hear his message even though their conclave had not yet been locked—for, as we are told and could anyway guess, they had a good idea of what the message would be.[9] Evidently

---

there is no reason to regard Col's record of the events consequent on the death of Clement as a "procès-verbal" (Valois's term, 3:3); rather, they should be regarded as a set of memoranda and documents, quite possibly given to him with propagandistic intent by Simon de Cramaud, the hero of the story.

8. Thury had sent his own courier to Paris with the news and a letter to the king (AN, J 518, fol. 119v); one assumes that the courier stopped off at Berry's Hôtel de Nesle.

9. The Spaniard Boniface Ferrer, head of the Carthusian order, writing in 1411 of the French insistence on having a French pope, noted (*Thes. nov.,* 2:1461) that "for this reason it was said among the cardinals after the death of Clement VII, . . . 'Unless we

they feared that Paris would lead them into union negotiations under conditions not to their advantage, perhaps under a shadow pope whom they would be told to elect for the single purpose of habilitating the other side and then resigning—simultaneously with the Roman contender *en principe*, but who could be sure of what the latter would do and of what might happen to the Avignon cardinals in the end?[10] Since, however, they could hardly buck Paris on the big issue and had in fact previously told Clement that, in a showdown, they would choose Paris over him,[11] they prefaced their election with an oath that all swore:

Each and all of us, cardinals of the holy Roman church, . . . swears to work . . . for union of the church, . . . and each of us will pursue to the extent of his ability all useful and apt ways for the utility and union of the church, without tricks or excuses or delays, and he will do so even if elected pope; these ways extend even to his having to abdicate if that should seem advisable to a majority of the present or future cardinals for the sake of the church's welfare and union.[12]

There followed a day of discussions, and then, on 28 September, Cardinal Pedro de Luna was elected pope, taking the name Benedict XIII. He was probably the best of the cardinals in point of intellect and character; he was one of the eight surviving *cardinales antiqui,* the veterans of 1378 and the only cardinals whose title one could be sure about; and he had the reputation which we have seen him cultivating of being *the* proponent of unionism in a college otherwise torpid in this regard.

There are many statements to the effect that Paris—Simon de Cramaud, the university, perhaps others—greeted the election with enthusiasm.[13] One wonders. Politicians are often stupid about policy but rarely about persons, and it is hard to imagine someone like Simon de Cra-

---

hurry up and elect, there'll be more pressure on us from France than there was in Rome [in 1378].'" Boniface wrote that the instigators of this pressure were Jean de Lagrange and Pierre de Thury, the latter wishing to be the new pope. We read in *RSD,* 2:198, that "it is a likely guess that the cardinals had a good idea of the royal command in the letter, and that they unanimously decided not to open it in order that they not seem to take the command lightly."

10. If, as Boniface Ferrer and others in Benedict's circle suggested (n. 9 above; *ALKG,* 7:74 f.), Thury might have been Paris's candidate for the papacy, one can understand the cardinals' apprehensions. The Valois client par excellence, he could certainly not be depended on to protect the interests of the cardinalate.

11. *ALKG,* 7:74; *RSD,* 2:186. Both these sources, although opposed to each other in sympathy, blame this action of the cardinals for the chagrin that caused Clement's death.

12. The text in AN, J 518, fol. 136r; see Valois, 3:14; cf., Martin Souchon, *Die Papstwahlen in der Zeit des grossen Schismas: Entwicklung und Verfassungskämpfe des Kardinalates von 1378–1417,* I (Braunschweig, 1898):212 ff.

13. Valois, 2:423; 3:22–27.

maud being unduly impressed by the unionist pieties of a papal legate who had sought for two years to preach Avignon's legitimacy to the English; nor would he have mistaken the significance of the fact that Benedict XIII was no servile French client of the Valois but an Aragonese nobleman of high degree who, unlike his colleagues, could and did think of other things than the revenues of his French benefices.[14] There was also the fact that Benedict was elected almost unanimously by a predominantly French college that would quite soon and almost unanimously turn against him at the Valois' behest; that they elected him in the face of Valois disapproval may have been due to their understanding of his potential for recalcitrance, which in the long run could guarantee a tolerable *via cessionis* and in the short run would certainly enhance the value of the cardinals as allies against him. The conclave oath would work to this effect, and one sees its programmatic implications most clearly in a false version of it that soon circulated in Paris—perhaps the work of cardinals like Pierre de Thury and Jean de Lagrange who kept in · constant contact with the capital. This version had the new pope promising to pursue whatever ways of union "seemed opportune to a majority of the cardinals with the counsel [*or* council] of the king of France, . . . including free renunciation of the papacy . . . as soon as this should seem expedient to them."[15] It was known that Benedict had sworn the conclave oath once again after he had been elected pope, and he at once generated a lot of union talk to show that his pious disposition had not been changed by his elevation; the effect of all this in Paris may have been to reinforce the scenario implied by the false oath. It is worth noting, however, that the University of Paris's several expressions of joy over the advent of so holy and unionist a pope were, in context, preludes to very blunt warnings—to Benedict lest he be seduced by his courtiers, to the king of Aragon that he urge Benedict to pursue union and thereby forestall a possible change of the papal heart, "should he become prey to unbridled cupidity and her colleague, *dominandi libido*."[16]

The first messages from Avignon came from the new pope and some

---

14. See below at n. 102, 103.

15. The text is printed from a Cambrai manuscript in Kervyn de Lettenhove, ed., *Oeuvres de Froissart*, 15 (Brussels, 1871):382 f.—also, thence, in Lehoux, 2:324 n. 6. Pierre Ravat, writing ca. 1399, noted that the false text was sent to Paris "per aliquos, non tamen per dominos [cardinales]" in response to a request for a copy of the oath (*ALKG*, 5:405); he must have meant that it was not sent by the cardinals as a college. Whoever did send it must have been someone with an interest in seeing its scenario become reality. See n. 61 below.

16. Bulaeus, 4:721 f.; and see above, Ch. II, n. 66. Cf. the harsh and threatening letter sent to the cardinals by King Juan of Aragon, 22 September 1394, warning them that if they did not act to end the Schism, the kings would do so, and telling them that if they hypocritically claimed not to know how, they should consult the kings and princes of their party—in S. Puig y Puig, *Pedro de Luna* (Barcelona, 1920): 448 f.

cardinals immediately after the election; they sought to show that all had been for the best. The coronation followed, on 11 October, and one week later Benedict chose his envoys—Gilles Bellemère, bishop of Avignon, and the canonist Pierre Blau—to bring official notification of his accession and to begin the long-awaited collaboration in formulating a policy for union. But the confidential instructions of these envoys[17] show how remote their mission was from anything that might correspond to the Paris program. They were to use all the resources of "sweet and pleasant words" to win over the dukes of Burgundy, Berry, Orléans, and Bourbon, without whom they were to attempt nothing, and whom they were to convince of Benedict's esteem for them and the king, his confidence in their devotion to church union, and his "total disposition to please them and the king." The last would be proved by promises of lavish papal favors "to preserve, exalt, and amplify" the dukes' and king's estate. The royal council was to be told, if this seemed advisable, that Benedict's election had been necessary, for "without a true pope the unity of the church could not be attained"; if indeed union were to be achieved in some way that would allow a new pope to be elected by a majority of "pseudo-cardinals," the result would be "something far worse than schism, namely to adore an idol on earth," and "the world would be set in permanent error." Benedict's desire for union was to be presented forcefully, but in these terms: he was totally devoted to union "by ways and means both reasonable and possible for him," and he would accept and pursue any way offered by Paris "as far as he can do so with God and a clear conscience." One can admire the pope's hard core of commitment to the holy grandeur of his office even as one realizes from the above instructions that Benedict was actually proposing nothing more or less than the old and changeless Avignon program of the *via reduccionis* (in a version henceforth to be called a *via iusticie*) with the usual opening towards *via facti*: the true pope's legitimacy had to be recognized, and if the Valois wanted to conquer Italy and thus "exalt" their estate, the pope would gladly sanction that.[18] As for the *via cessionis*, Benedict did not dare to attack it openly now, but he evidently regarded its Paris form, predicated on the premise that the world did *not* have to know who had been the true pope, as unacceptable. Again, let us note the rectitude of this view, especially when advanced by a pope who believed that what he and the others had done in 1378 had been right and that he, unlike his predecessor, was a worthy representative of the legitimacy of his cause.[19] Let us recognize also the tragedy of his situation: his legatine mission in Paris must have taught him that if the dukes

---

17. *ALKG*, 6:153–157.
18. So Benedict would suggest to the dukes in July 1395 (Valois, 3:61).
19. See, e.g., *ALKG*, 7:75 f.; cf. Swanson: 117.

could be induced to refrain from coercing their pope, it was because they did not want to get rough with Clement VII; he himself could hardly hope to enjoy a similar grace, and yet he had no moral choice but to stake everything on just such a hope.

His envoys were received graciously enough by "the king" and the royal council about the middle of November, and they presented their master's formal request that the government complete its investigation of ways to union and send Benedict a high-ranking, fully empowered, and fully instructed embassy to inform the pope of the ways that were deemed suitable.[20] "The king" promised to do just that, indeed to send the royal kinsmen as ambassadors, but the embassy could not be constituted until the duke of Burgundy should have returned to court. In fact a delay was essential, for if Benedict was pressing for an essentially ceremonial embassy that would offer him a bouquet of "ways" to choose from, the Paris unionists had not deviated from their original program, the *via cessionis,* and it was certainly clear to them now that Benedict would not accept this non-juridical *via* unless Paris could force him to do so; time was needed to mobilize the force. In the event, the crown decided to use a device of the sort suggested by the university on 23 September: to summon a national council of the upper clergy to meet as an estate of the realm, under royal authority, and give "the king" its counsel. While presenting this move publicly as a response to the pope's requests for advice about ways—"Considering these requests the king's council advised that the weight of the matter required him to summon the prelates of his realm"[21]—the government was in fact planning an anti-papal move of extraordinary import. The prelates, abbots, and canons of the "Gallican church" would meet as an estate under their secular lord the king; would consider and vote on a religious issue; and the king, accepting this counsel, would thereby soak up the religious potency of the French church to validate his union program against the pope's. This was the view of a University of Paris canonist writing at this time, who argued that even though a general council of the church would have been the normal authority to put the popes on notice of their

---

20. Valois, 3:22 ff. We read in *RSD,* 2:218, that the envoys asked the king to choose one best way, with the counsel of the clergy and the university; this is no doubt a distortion to validate ex post the work of the First Paris Council.

21. AN, J 518, fol. 130v. Simon de Cramaud would repeatedly say that the First Paris Council was in effect authorized by Benedict's request for counsel from the king— see his treatise, App. II, Pt. II, "Benedict Must Obey a Council of His Obedience," and his glosses on the Toulouse letter of 1402 (AN, J 518, fols. 509v, 510r—quoted in part, as anonymous, by Valois, 3:32 n. 4); also below, at n. 34. In Benedict's circle, the council was regarded quite simply as a machination by his enemies, including above all the cardinals whom his reforms of curial vices had antagonized (*ALKG,* 5:404).

obligation to resign, it could be done by the prelates and the doctors of theology and law, but that if these were afraid, "let the notice (*monitio*) be given by the temporal princes on the basis of a mandate from the prelates, universities, and other ecclesiastics."[22] One thinks of the picture that the University of Paris had caused to be drawn on the presentation copy of its letter of 6 June 1394—the king enthroned, the clergy around him, their prayers resonating with his strength to create power for the good of the faith—except that what was then an academic dream would now come true in the reverse sense: it was not the clerics using secular power but the opposite.

The theoretical implications of this novelty were spelled out only later when conflict sharpened the issues and called for formulations of them, but these statements are as relevant to the First Paris Council as to its successors, and it will be illuminating to draw them in here. Perhaps the most striking was Simon de Cramaud's comment at the Paris Council of 1406, replying to Guillaume Fillastre's argument that the king of France's power was only that of the secular sword and that he was not competent to take cognizance of Benedict XIII's alleged heresy. Simon objected:

The dean [scil., Fillastre] has said, "It is amazing, the patriarch would make the king judge of the crime of heresy; but the king has no such power." Sire, he knows better than that. Does he call this assembly the Châtelet, or Parlement? Sire, you have more bishops and archbishops than do the kings of Castile, Aragon, Navarre, England, etc. In your realm and in Dauphiné you have 110. This assembly could therefore indeed have cognizance of heresy if it should come to that.[23]

To this we can add a number of statements by Simon and others which show that they thought of the Paris councils of the clergy essentially as amplified meetings of the royal council;[24] the only difference was that, as Simon put it, the clerical assemblies presided over by the king had a spiritual authority and could act as a spiritual court, while other royal courts (the Châtelet, Parlement) wielded only the secular sword. It was

---

22. The text in Swanson: 92 n. 15.

23. BdeC: 215 (BN, *ms. fr.* 23,428, fol. 68r, compared), responding to Guillaume Fillastre's mention of the Châtelet and Parlement (in a somewhat different context—BdeC: 139, cf. 174); cf. BdeC: 201–204 (Fillastre's arguments for dualism of powers). Arguments similar to Simon's were offered in 1406 by Pierre Plaoul (BdeC: 192 f.).

24. Simon's glosses on the Toulouse letter, addressed to the king, refer to the Third Paris Council as "curia vestra" (AN, J 518, fol. 504r); the chapter of Narbonne's ballot at that council referred to it as "consilium regium" (fol. 473v), and a royal letter of 1410 (AN, X 1C 100B, no. 194) refers to it as "nostre grant conseil." In 1406 Jean Jouvenel referred to the current Paris Council as the "counseil general du roy de France" (BdeC: 233). See also the discussion of procedures at the Paris Councils, below.

not, however, just a matter of judicial action but also of policy decisions and statutes; all these were in principle identical. This was the political reality of the "Gallican church" as a corporate entity under the king, whose lordship here was derived from a number of sources, including his temporal lordship over the prelates, the legal obligation attested in his coronation oath to preserve the church of his realm in its liberties, his quality as "rex christianissimus" with its historical sense of a mission to protect the papacy and thereby the church as a whole.[25]

To Benedict XIII and his supporters, however, all this was a subversive confection. Without necessarily denying the king's capacity to summon the clergy for temporal action like raising a tax (although even this was supposed to be by papal permission), they insisted that the only spiritually competent meetings of the clergy were its own synods summoned and presided over by its own bishops and archbishops, and each was competent only within the geographical limits of its president's authority.[26] In this sense there was no Gallican church, for there was no instance between the archbishops and the pope; Benedict XIII did not like even the term *Gallican,* and Boniface Ferrer wrote amusingly of the

─────────────

25. The letters of 30 May 1396 by which the king summoned the prelates to the Second Paris Council commanded attendance "sur la feaulté, en quoy vous estes tenus à nous et à la corona de France" (*ALKG,* 6:207); the letters for the Third Paris Council had a similar formula, "sur la foy, que vous nous devez et estes tenus a nous" (*ALKG,* 6:275). The coronation oath was referred to by Gilles Deschamps at the Third Paris Council in these terms (BdeC: 38): "Quod autem pertinet ad regem providere ecclesiae sui regni, propter libertates et franchisias conservandas, clarum est per juramentum quod praestat rex in sui coronatione." At the council of 1406 Simon de Cramaud linked the oath with the structure of the council itself (BdeC: 217): "le serment . . . que vous fites à vostre coronation, que au fait de l'Église, vous procederiés par le Conseil de vos Prelats." For the actual oath, which referred simply to securing the church of the realm in its privileges, law, rights, and defense, see Percy Schramm, *Der König von Frankreich,* 2d ed., 1 (Darmstadt, 1960):198; cf. Pierre Bertrand's "Apparatus" on the *Prohemium* of the *Liber Sextus,* ca. 1335 (BN, *ms. lat.* 4085, fol. 4r): "Rex eciam Francie in coronacione sua promittit se servaturum ecclesiis regni sui privilegium canonicum, in quo includitur quod servetur iurisdiccio ecclesie." For the development towards the interpretations we have noted, see V. Martin, *Les origines du Gallicanisme,* 1 (Paris, 1939):86; also Buisson: 270–347. The *topoi* of "rex christianissimus" and the traditional role of the French kings in protecting the true pope in case of schism—these were used to incite "the king" to act for church union (e.g., by Bouvet, *Somnium:* 101; Gilles Deschamps ca. January 1395, ASV, *Arm.* 54, t. 21, fol. 56r; idem on 24 May 1395, AN, J 518, fol. 128v) but also and more often by Benedict's spokesmen as a reason for the king to stay loyal to Avignon (e.g., Élie de Lestrange in 1396, *ALKG,* 6:237). See App. II for the argument and Simon's rejection of it.

26. Thus Élie de Lestrange at the Second Paris Council, June/July 1396 (*ALKG,* 6:235 f.): "Et si dicatur, quod ideo vocantur prelati, quibus disponendi de factis ecclesie est attributa potestas, habet verum circa que ipsorum tangunt dumtaxat provincias vel dioceses, non alias."

"ecclesia Gallicantina."[27] The juristic point was best put by Benedict's supporter Élie de Lestrange, bishop of Le Puy, in 1396 and then in 1400:

What is called the Gallican church is not a *collegium*, constituting a *universitas* or any other *corpus*; even if all the prelates and clergy of the realm were to meet together, they would be only a gathering of individuals, not a corporation. For a body cannot exist without a head, . . . and since all the clergy within the boundaries of France do not as such have any head as Frenchmen or within France . . . distinct from the common head of all churches, which is the Roman church and its pope, . . . it is impossible that they should make up a *corpus*; and therefore they cannot make statutes.[28]

This was the legal theory of the papalist *libertas ecclesie* of the past two or three centuries. But prior to that, as Simon de Cramaud noted in the case of Clovis, kings had routinely summoned meetings of the territorial clergy, had appointed their presidents, and had taken action in matters of faith concerning the whole church.[29] By the fourteenth century there was nothing odd about meetings of the clerical estate under royal lordship for secular purposes. Furthermore there was no lack of theory by this time to create the conceptual reality of the Gallican sort of structure: Marsilius of Padua's *Defensor pacis* was well known in Paris;[30] John Wyclif had constructed a massive ecclesiology in which the king was "priest and pontiff" of his realm, the *ecclesia Anglicana*;[31] John Hus and his

---

27. Benedict XIII, arguing in 1411 against the author of a cessionist treatise, mentioned the scandal, etc., caused by the resignation of Pope Celestine V and the election of Boniface VIII, "quod . . . experta fuit ecclesia, specialiter *ut eius utar vocabulo*, gallicana" (*ALKG*, 7:548; my emphasis). For Ferrer's little joke see *Thes. nov.*, 2:1505, 1511, 1520, 1524.

28. *Allegaciones . . . Helie de Lestrangiis*, BN, *ms. lat.* 1475, fol. 62v (quoted in Latin in Kaminsky, "Politics": 379); see also *ALKG*, 6:235 f.

29. Glosses against the Toulouse letter, AN, J 518, fol. 508v: "De Clodoveo legimus, quod iussu eius consilium prelatorum huius regni fuit congregatum, in quo Melanus episcopus Redonensis, eius precepto, presidebat; et statuerunt canones qui universam ecclesiam astringunt, et in corpore canonum sunt redacti" (Bonn University ms. S 594, ii, fol. 46r, collated). Pierre aux Boeufs used this example at the Paris Council of 1406 (BdeC: 102).

30. Pope Gregory XI launched an investigation in 1375 to find out who was responsible for a French translation of the *Defensor pacis* circulating in Paris (*CUP*, 3:223–227); the translation may have been made many years before. For this and the circulation of the Latin text, see Albert Menut, ed., *Maistre Nicole Oresme: Le libre de politiques d'Aristote*, *Transactions of the American Philosophical Society*, 60 (6) (Philadelphia, 1970):7–9; Jean-Pierre Royer, *L'Église et le royaume de France au XIVe siècle* (Paris, 1969): 37 ff., 57 ff. (for the use of the *Defensor pacis* in the *Somnium viridarii* and the *Songe du vergier*).

31. H. Kaminsky, "Wyclifism as Ideology of Revolution," *Church History*, 32 (1963): 57–74; A. Pollard & C. Sayle, ed., *Iohannis Wyclif, Tractatus de officio regis* (London, 1887): 152: "ad regem, qui debet esse sacerdos et pontifex regni sui."

fellows in Bohemia were preparing to produce the Wyclifite scenario as a political reality.[32] The reality had indeed come into being in England before the Wyclifism that conceptualized it; the king as lord of the church interposed his authority to frustrate papal fiscal exactions and collationary powers to a considerable extent—as the French enviously noted.[33] The First Paris Council would not go so far, but its successors would; meanwhile the spectacle of its public entity would finally transform the *via cessionis* into a structure of public law, the solemn and official program of the politico-ecclesiastical community mobilized under its head, the king.

Since we have no direct evidence for the details of planning, we have to rely on more or less obvious inference. The decision to convoke the council of prelates on 2 February 1395 must have been made long before; one guesses that the arrival of Burgundy in Paris on 16 December had to be waited for but that the preliminary plans had already emerged from consultations among Berry, Simon, and the university leaders in the weeks after the royal audience at which Benedict's envoys had presented the pope's message. A royal letter was sent to Avignon to announce that the assembly was to meet in response to the papal envoys' request that the king come up with union ways; the account in J 518 comments: "It is said that the pope found this agreeable."[34] Before the council began, its members elected Simon de Cramaud as president— unanimously but also in response to the crown's wish;[35] he ran things with a very firm hand, assisted by the university speakers Gilles Deschamps and Pierre Leroy, and with Burgundy's chancellor Jean Canart playing a leading role. We can assume that these men formed the group that did the preliminary planning and that it was this coalition of Berry, Burgundy, and the university which was responsible for the character of the council as a production, managing proceedings and manipulating members to keep everything in line with the political scenario. The university's role in this drama was quite important, but it was not what its former leaders had had in mind back in the first part of the year, when they had formulated three acceptable ways and left the choice to others.

---

32. H. Kaminsky, *A History of the Hussite Revolution* (Berkeley, 1967): 35–96; Hus called King Wenceslas IV "the first prelate" of the Bohemian clergy (p. 94).

33. Haller, *PKR*: 375–479, 543–552.

34. AN, J 518, fol. 130v: "Et dit on qu'il ot agreable."

35. *RSD*, 2:224: "Omnes prelati . . . consensu unanimi . . . dominum patriarcham Alexandrinum, Simonem Cramaudi vocatum, elegerunt, qui pro congregandis consiliis, audiendis racionibus hinc et inde, determinandisque conclusionibus auctoritate presideret." Simon himself wrote (AN, J 518, fol. 509v): "Rex . . . fecit prelatos . . . Parisius convocari, et ipsis ibidem congregatis ordinavit inter ipsos unum prelatum presidentem."

It was now necessary to push the letter of 6 June 1394 into the background; drop its two judicial ways (*compromissum* and *concilium generale*), which involved the "absolutely inexpedient" discussion of legitimacy; make sure that only the *via cessionis* would enjoy the university's sponsorship; and adapt the coercive proposals accordingly so that they would apply not to a pope who refused the three ways and failed to offer a fourth but simply to a pope who refused the *via cessionis*.[36] With Pierre d'Ailly and Nicholas de Clamanges already finding their way into papal favor and with Gerson holding himself aloof from any form of *via cessionis* not based on the free and simultaneous abdication of both popes, opposition to the new university leadership of Deschamps and Leroy, both of whom were ready to collaborate fully with Simon de Cramaud, was disorganized enough to be readily mastered. We hear complaints later on of the fraud and coercion used from this time on in order to obtain a "university" opinion conformable to the government's program, and common sense suggests that they were more or less true.[37] In any case, the University of Paris would henceforth be ready to act as Simon wished. The pope's November message had made clear his insistence on a "way of judgement" and his consequent opposition to the Paris concep-

36. All this is inferred from the upshot, the university's position at the First Paris Council. It instructed its speaker to mention the three ways of 6 June 1394 but to insist that the king now choose one definite way; the speaker was then "to come down to the *via cessionis* in particular, praising it with all the arguments in the original letter and adding other arguments"—which occupy the rest of the instructions (Bulaeus, 4:737–739). A number of passages in hostile writings refer to the contradiction between the university's original letter and its commitment henceforth to the single way of cession, e.g., Gerson, *Oeuvres*, 6:27 f. At the end of the university's instructions, after the definition of cession as obligatory ("quilibet eorum . . . tenetur renunciare papatui"—Bulaeus, 4:739), there is a passage referring in veiled but unmistakable terms to the sanctions set forth in the 6 June letter: "explicet proponens modos in Epistola tactos," adding that the university is ready "to explicate these modes when the time and place are opportune" (ibid.). An anonymous treatise very similar in language and content to these instructions argues, "quod regi consuli debeat, ut . . . ista via [cessionis] sit aliis pretermissis prosequenda" (*Motiva pro via cessionis*, ASV, *Arm.* 54, t. 21, fol. 47r), and it goes on to urge that if all else fails, the one or both refusing cession should be treated as schismatic and that a general council of princes and prelates should proceed "ad alia . . . remedia opportuna, pro nunc silencio committenda." See also n. 63 below.

37. Complaints about the suppression of free discussion at the University of Paris were made at the Third Paris Council by Pierre Ravat (see Valois, 3:153 f., 162 f.), and in his ballot on that occasion Ameilh du Breuil, archbishop of Tours, openly said that "many things had been done in the university in the past three years without common consent, without formal procedures, and without freedom of counsel and of deliberation" (AN, J 518, fol. 438v; ASV, *Arm.* 54, t. 46, fol. 6r). For the rest, see Valois, 3:25 f.; Gerson, *Oeuvres*, 6:24; Gilbert Ouy, "Gerson et l'Angleterre," *Humanism in France* (Manchester, 1970): 52; cf. John Morrall, *Gerson and the Great Schism* (Manchester, 1960): 40.

tion of the way of cession. His envoys to the Paris Council would promise that he indeed had a *via* of his own—"a good and speedy one, which would please the king and everyone"—but that he would only reveal it to the high embassy that the crown would send to Avignon.[38] It was to forestall any such papal initiative that the Paris cessionists determined to produce a council that would vote overwhelmingly to present Benedict not with a selection of ways for his choice but with an ultimatum backed up by the power of the French political community. It remained only to devise the mechanisms by which Simon's junta could manage the coming council to this effect.

The problem of how to program the First Paris Council was pre-shaped by the decision—or perhaps just the unthinking assumption—that the council would be essentially an amplification of the *concilium regis* rather than a more or less autonomous synod of the clergy. It would be summoned by royal letters sent individually to the bishops, abbots, and perhaps others who would attend. Its opening mass of the Holy Spirit would be sung in the Sainte Chapelle of the royal palace; its meetings would be in the palace; its president would be the government's man Simon de Cramaud—suited to the role but not determined thereto by his exceptional rank as patriarch of Alexandria.[39] All members would swear an oath, administered by Simon, that they would give loyal counsel to the king as to which way of union he should adopt and advise the pope to adopt.[40] The procedures of deliberation and voting would be determined by Simon, who did so in a manner that excluded anything like an open, spontaneous debate and atomized the prelates into vote units, each giving his own "counsel" publicly and in turn, as the roll was called by the president.[41] Even the official formulas tell us that the prelates' so-called deliberations proceeded on the basis of a preliminary layout of the issues and arguments that had been worked up before the council met and which was now presented to them.[42] Benedict's envoy Gilles Bellemère described how this was done:

The president of the council Simon de Cramaud, . . . immoderately fixed on the *via cessionis,* got his way by ordaining that the matter be discussed in the presence of the prelates and a great many of lesser rank summoned to

---

38. Se we are told in the instructions of the ducal embassy, *Ampl. coll.* 7:438; and see below.

39. All this from *RSD,* 2:218–220, who draws from the instrument in AN, J 518, fol. 98rv, printed in *Ampl. coll.,* 7:458 f.

40. *Ampl. coll.,* 7:462; also Simon's glosses on the Toulouse letter, AN, J 518, fol. 509v.

41. *Ampl. coll.,* 7:462.

42. This is Simon's account cited below, n. 80; for the passage referred to here, see below at n. 75.

the council by the king. And only two ways were presented, the *via cessionis* and a *via compromissi* which included cession. For the president appointed certain ones to argue for one way and certain ones to argue for the other, but all those whom he appointed on either side turned out to be in favor of the *via cessionis*.[43]

He also charged that Simon conducted the subsequent discussions in an unfair way, giving the floor to those agreeing with him and taking it away from those who did not.[44] Bellemère's colleague Pierre Blau said the same thing: "There were very many of the prelates and from the university who condemned the *via cessionis*, but the presidents refused to hear them"; and a year or so later Élie de Lestrange cited his own experience at the council in the same sense.[45] In 1396 Pierre d'Ailly called for "a true account and a calm consideration of the deliberations in the First Paris Council," and he remarked: "It is not inadvertently that I say 'a *true* account.'"[46]

What these complaints tell us is that the council was planned, plotted, and choreographed with much care and that the effort paid off. The enterprise of planning the spectacle, moreover, was the matrix in which the whole ideology of the *via cessionis* and its implied escalations—subtraction of obedience, coercion, eventual deposition—was worked out by Simon de Cramaud, Pierre Leroy, and Gilles Deschamps. The surviving sources are scanty but surprisingly adequate as documents of a body of thought that would soon explode into whole codices of verbosity; and

---

43. E. Baluze & G. Mansi, eds., *Miscellanea novo ordine digesta*, 2 (Lucca, 1761):591: "et jam praelati ibidem existentes ante dictorum nuntiorum adventum, multa concilia tenuerant; et fuit deputatus pro concilio praesidens D. Simon Cramandi [*sic*], Patriarcha Alexandrinus, administrator Ecclesiae Carcassonensis, praedictam viam cessionis utrinque affectans prae caeteris ultra modum, qui ut perveniret ad intentum suum, ordinavit ut materia disceptaretur in praesentia Praelatorum et aliorum quamplurimorum gradus inferioris, de mandato Regis ad concilium hujusmodi vocatorum, et de omnibus viis reduxerunt consilium ad duas, videlicet ad viam cessionis utriusque et ad viam compromissi, cessionem hujusmodi concludentis; et deputavit certos ad sustinendam unam viam, et certos ad aliam viam sustentandam. Sed de omnibus per eum pro una vel altera parte deputatis, constabat ei quod ad viam cessionis utriusque inclinati erant."

44. Ibid.: "in emissione votorum pro affectione sua deponentibus optatam audientiam praebuit, et aliorum sapientium audientiam interrupit."

45. Blau: "Quamplures eciam fuerunt, tam de prelatis quam de universitate, qui illam dampnaverunt viam, sed presidentes illos recusabant audire. Et hoc vidit et audivit qui hoc scripsit" (ASV, Arm. 54, t. 20, fol. 184r). Lestrange: "Et fuerunt multi clerici . . . qui . . . conati fuerunt hoc [scil., the case against obligatory cession] iuridice ostendere nec potuerunt audiri, ut . . . michi constat" (*ALKG*, 6:234 f.).

46. The text in Ehrle, *Alpartil*: 478. Yet d'Ailly seems to have been part of the machine, as a programmed opposition (see below); perhaps his later alliance with Benedict and the consequent ambiguity of his position in Paris were responsible for both the critical sense and the cautious form of his 1396 dictum.

these ideas, created as a political act, were functional components of a complex policy of publicity and manipulation. The whole enterprise was devised (the First Paris Council was indeed a novelty)[47] according to the principles regulating counsel in the *concilium regis* when an especially weighty or difficult matter came up. Simon de Cramaud had several occasions in later years to mention these principles: "It was customary in France that when some matter was discussed before the king, he would assign some men of his choice to support one side and others to support the contrary."[48] The debate would proceed on alternate days, or at least in a pattern of alternation between the sides, until the matter was fully "opened."[49] Such a debate could be very lively—indeed it was supposed to be—for while the assigned speakers were not held personally responsible for the views they propounded, they must have been selected in most cases because of their known commitment to the side they would represent.[50] At the same time, the debate was held to very strict rules inasmuch as it dealt with a definite question whose presuppositions might not be challenged and whose limits might not be infringed; nor were the speakers supposed to introduce their own views as such in their arguments.[51] It was such a formal discussion that Simon and the rest envisaged for the First Paris Council; what they had to do in the weeks

---

47. As Valois observes, 3:27 f.

48. A statement of 1407 quoted by A. Bossuat, "Une relation inédite de l'ambassade française au pape Benoît XIII en 1407," *Le moyen âge,* 55 (1949):99.

49. The subtraction ordinance of 27 July 1398, probably drafted by Simon (see Haller, *PKR:* 238 f.), refers to this method of taking counsel: "And wishing to open the matter before the members of the [Third Paris] Council, so that afterwards each one might better counsel us, . . . we . . . deputed certain ones to defend the affirmative, . . . and others the negative. And so on alternate days in our council, in the manner and form by which audiences are given in our curia, . . . all the reasons and arguments were fully opened by those we had deputed, and fully discussed, in the council" (*Ordonnances,* 8:266). Cf. Simon's similar remarks defending this procedure at the Paris Council of 1406, BdeC: 176, 290.

50. So it was at all the Paris councils for which we have the details (in 1396, 1398, 1406): all the speakers were in fact partisans of the side they were assigned to speak for. But *RSD,* 2:526, tells of a debate in which the subtractionists Jean Canart and Pierre Plaoul were assigned with others to support "the pope's side"; cf., however, the discussion of this below, Ch. V.

51. Thus at the Third Paris Council, where the issue was whether to execute the *via cessionis* by subtraction of obedience, even the papal spokesmen had to accept the value and official status of the *via cessionis,* which none of them thought good; the subtractionist Gilles Deschamps could therefore score a small point against his opponents who had refuted subtraction without suggesting other ways to implement cession: "sic secundum eos, via [cessionis] bona est, sed sine exequutione" (BdeC: 37). And Simon de Cramaud criticized Pierre Ravat, bishop of St. Pons, for overtly expressing his opinion: "quamquam nunc dicam, non dicam pro mea opinione, ut fecit D. S. Pontii, sed requisitus dicam, cum tempus affuerit" (BdeC: 22). Deschamps in fact did express one view in his commissioned speech in 1398, another—his own—in his ballot (see below, Ch. VII).

before was formulate the question to be put and develop the prefabricated debate whose upshot would be a strong vote for what they wanted. The kind of thinking called for was not speculative inquiry into the true and the just, which might lead anywhere, but invention of reasons to validate the decision already imposed by policy.

We know next to nothing of the politicking involved in all this—conceivably because there was no real opposition in the royal council—and if it had been up to Simon, we would have known as little about how the "deliberations" were prepared, for the only instrument in J 518 that summarizes the play of ideas at the council does so rather schematically and with a certain retrospective loftiness that tends to create Simon's desired image of quasi unanimity.[52] Again it is Gilles Bellemère who reveals the seamy side of the business, in his account of how Simon presented the council's deliberations to the king, 18 February:

> When the patriarch finally got a majority vote as he wished, he asked the king for a public audience, where he reported the council's work as he saw fit. He said that just about all, with few exceptions, had concluded for the *via cessionis,* and that the few had not directly contradicted this but had made some other points which were not worth very much. Even though in fact many prelates had contradicted this *via* and had advanced effective arguments, the patriarch presented, amplified, and dwelt upon the arguments of his own side, totally suppressing those of the other.[53]

One can appreciate in this light the silence of the official sources about the play of ideas in the preparatory period, about which we are told only that "the king" commanded that "before the assigned date (of the council, 2 February) the matter should be considered at a number of meetings, where indeed it was discussed notably, at length, and with great maturity, touching on all the union ways that could be thought of, with their respective arguments, also the doubts and the solutions of these"; the participants were various prelates, royal councillors, and academics, with the royal chancellor sometimes present, and notaries on hand.[54]

---

52. This is the long French "Instruction" for the ducal embassy (AN, J 518, fols. 83r–98r; in *Ampl. coll.,* 7:437–458); its author could hardly have been anyone but Simon, for it agrees closely with the Latin draft of instructions, presented at the council and corresponding closely to Simon's views, which was obviously his work in his capacity as president empowered to formulate the council's conclusions; see n. 35, 80.

53. Baluze & Mansi, *Miscellanea,* 2:591: "Demum votis pro majori parte ad ejus voluntatem obtentis, publicaque a Rege audientia impetrata, idem Patriarcha prout sibi placuit de dicto consilio relationem fecit, referendo quod quasi omnes, paucis exceptis, concluserant pro via cessionis utriusque, et quod illi pauci non contradixerant de directo, sed posuerant se in aliis, quae non multum valebant; licet multi Praelati contradixissent illi viae, et motiva ad hoc probabilia induxissent, ipseque Patriarcha motiva suae partis induxit et dilatavit, fimbrias ampliando, et motiva partis alterius totaliter subticendo."

54. *RSD,* 2:226–228, the text (with some mistakes) of an instrument in AN, J 518, fol. 131r (see n. 80 below); cf. the parallel report in another J 518 instrument, fol. 98v, printed in *Ampl. coll.,* 7:459.

Fortunately someone took notes of some of these speeches—by Simon, Deschamps, and Leroy—and we have a more substantial record of a speech by Pierre d'Ailly on the other side; these items allow us to see something of how the council's consent would be engineered.

The political issues in play during the preparatory period were crystallized in the question of exactly what the prelates would be asked to vote on. Pierre d'Ailly, the king's almoner, member of the royal council, and chancellor of the University of Paris, had been sent by the king to Avignon in late October as a first envoy to the new pope; there, he had been attracted to Benedict, perhaps by force of the pope's qualities but also by grants of benefices and, probably, promises of future preferment.[55] Returning to Paris in time to take part in the preparatory meetings, d'Ailly played the role of opponent—how sincerely we do not know—to the program of Simon's group. His speech urged that the issue to be put to the council should be twofold: "Whether the king should come down to some particular way for peace in the church and induce the pope to accept it, and if so which way should be advised?"[56] He based his argument on the fact that the university letter of 6 June 1394, which he had helped compose, had validated three ways and left other possibilities open; thus all that could be asked of Benedict was that he pursue some suitable way, and "thank God he has already said that he would pursue a reasonable way." On this basis d'Ailly could present the considerations of expediency, decency, honor, and tactics that made it advisable for the king to leave the choice of way to the pope. This was of course what Benedict wanted. Pierre d'Ailly then went on to argue that *if* one way were to be adopted as royal policy, it should be the *via compromissi,* the

---

55. Valois, 3:25–27. A doctor of theology (since 1381) whose excellence transcended the political context in which he made his career, d'Ailly was also a careerist, practicing habits of calculation that determined his position in the conflicts of the time; he enjoyed royal favor and had the usual multiple benefices. Benedict XIII would make him bishop of Le Puy in 1395, then of Cambrai in 1397; the Pisan pope John XXIII would make him a cardinal in 1411. Boniface Ferrer draws a sharp picture of the deformation of character that was the price at which so splendid a career was bought by the son of a Compiègne bourgeois so lowly that the aristocratic canons of Cambrai "would have relegated him to a place among their sheep dogs": "With his every word and movement carefully watched by his many rivals and enemies looking for even the slightest pretext to get rid of him, . . . such a man would never even in his most secret moments say or write or express fairly what he really thought" (*Thes. nov.,* 2:1464 f.). This is the d'Ailly we are concerned with here, not the splendid political theorist of voluntarism whom Francis Oakley has illuminated in *The Political Thought of Pierre d'Ailly* (New Haven, Conn., 1964).

56. The text in Ehrle, *Alpartil:* 471–474. It begins so: "Queritur in hoc consilio regis proxime congregando. . . ."—thus dating itself and the other speeches in the same debate before the formal opening of the First Paris Council on 2 February. The same dating is implied in Deschamps's contrary speech, n. 59 below.

way of arbitration, according to which each pope would constitute arbiters who would then have the power to end the Schism as they saw fit, possibly by imposing abdication on both contenders. (This may have been the *"via compromissi"* which included cession," in Bellemère's report quoted above.) The Avignon arbiters would include the *cardinales antiqui,* whose presence would guarantee at least in a formal sense the continuity of the legitimate line; this was one of Benedict's points, as we have seen.[57] But d'Ailly did not mention Benedict's other interest in this *via,* namely, that the arbiters would consider the issue of legitimacy; this had been allowed for in the university's letter of 6 June, but by the end of 1394 the unionist coalition in Paris regarded a judicial procedure as "absolutely inexpedient" because it would guarantee failure.[58]

This speech was refuted point for point by the theologian Gilles Deschamps, who zeroed in on d'Ailly's proposed question for the council and insisted that it would be inept not to pose the main issue as one of substance: "which is the more expedient way?" This after all was required by the nature of counsel, and it would be hard in good faith to assemble the prelates otherwise.[59] The university's letter of 6 June had merely defined three "licit" ways; but licit and expedient were not the same thing, and the question was which way was the expedient one *now.*[60] He offered a number of arguments against letting the pope choose first, noting, inter alia, that the conclave oath—which everyone including d'Ailly knew only in the false version[61]—obliged the pope to follow the

---

57. Above, at n. 17.
58. Below, at n. 63.
59. The text in ASV, *Arm.* 54, t. 21, fols. 55r–56v, the "cedula Magistri Egidii de Campis," beginning "Primo videtur notandum qualiter questio sub forma posita per Elemosinarium [scil. the royal almoner, d'Ailly] pertinens est, an scilicet aliqua via in speciali sit per regem pape consulenda, et si sic, que est illa? Nec tamen eidem impertinens materie videtur inquirere que via sit expediencior, cuius tamen contrarium dominus E. pretendebat—quoniam in materia consilii cadit tota expedientis discussio. Secundo, . . . quoniam alias forsan cum difficultate prelati poterunt tam sincere congregari."
60. Ibid., fol. 55r: "nec repugnat hoc epistole universitatis, quia solum intendit quod per quamlibet viam licite potest scisma terminari, sed non dixit quamlibet pro nunc expedientibus [*sic*]."
61. D'Ailly (Ehrle, *Alpartil*: 471): "iuramentum pape, ubi consensus cardinalium preponitur consilio regis." Deschamps (ASV, *Arm.* 54, t. 21, fol. 55v): "in iuramento continetur quod papa illud faciet quod maior pars cardinalium de consilio regis videret expedire." Simon de Cramaud (fol. 61r): "item debet cedere cedula, si videatur regi et consilio melius expedire, quia videtur iurasse." By mid-January the leaders must have had doubts about this text (or must have decided that its use for propaganda had to give way to a policy that would meet the facts), for at that time, "the king" sent a copy of it to Benedict and asked if it were correct (Valois, 3:30 n. 3; *Ampl. coll.,* 7:447). Although Benedict's negative reply, dated 3 February, did not arrive in time to be used in the preparations for the First Paris Council, the existing doubt was perhaps responsible for the very restricted use of what would have been an unbeatable argument.

way that "the cardinals with the king's counsel should judge to be expedient." Furthermore, he asked why, if the pope had a *via* of his own, as his envoys had just declared, he had not revealed it to "this council"—presumably the *concilium regis.*[62] For the rest, Deschamps refuted the *via compromissi,* partly because this way in its proper sense was intended to provide "a discussion of the rights of both sides, and this discussion seems absolutely inexpedient—it would be long, extremely difficult, and unlikely to achieve the effect we desire." Insofar as it would likely result in cession anyway, it was superfluous.[63] He then turned to the matter of substance, declared that the *via cessionis* was the more expedient way, and referred to Simon de Cramaud's arguments to this effect. D'Ailly himself had conceded that abdication would be excellent and that the pope was perhaps even obliged to it by divine law, to end the Schism, but it would have to be "a voluntary and caritative" action, not one to which he was exhorted by the king.[64] Deschamps simply asked why, if cession was so good, the king should not counsel the pope to pursue it.

Pierre Leroy, abbot of St. Michel, also refuted d'Ailly, but with the ponderous apparatus of a star canonist. Leroy's special contribution was a long refutation of the *via concilii generalis,* a corollary refutation of the *via compromissi,* and a demonstration that therefore, and also for positive reasons, "the *via cessionis* was the only adequate way."[65] In any case, no way should be considered "by which it might happen that Boniface would remain as pope."[66] Since the pope was obligated to work for the end of the Schism, and since cession was the only way thereto, he was obligated to pursue the *via cessionis.*[67] This obligatory character of cession,

---

62. Deschamps (ASV, *Arm.* 54, t. 21, fol. 55v): "Item quia si hoc honorem pape reputamus, quod ipse ex se viam specialem aperiat, cur si quam habet, ut dicitur, illam non fecit *huic consilio* intimari?" If the emphasized words referred to a current First Paris Council, we would have to redate the speech and its fellows accordingly, but they could have referred to the extended *concilium regis* of the preliminary debates, or perhaps to the imminent First Paris Council.

63. Ibid., fol. 56r: "vel hoc [scil., the *via compromissi*] intelligitur ad finem discussionis iurium utriusque partis, et hec discussio videtur absolute inexpediens, quia longa, difficillima, et effectus quem querimus non indubia promotrix, eciam si fiat per consilium generale. Si vero viam illam expedienciorem dicat ad inveniendum modum expedienciorem pro unione, et melius . . . secundum eum non est nisi cessio: sequitur quod ad vitandum circularitatem et prolixitatem sanxius, virtuosius, et honestius est, ut illam se ipsi faciant."

64. Ehrle, *Alpartil:* 472.

65. The "cedula Abbatis Sancti Michaelis," in ASV, *Arm.* 54, t. 21, fols. 57r—59r.

66. Ibid., fol. 58v: "non debet queri aliqua via per quam posset contingere quod Bonifacius remaneret papa, tum propter exempli perniciem, tum propter regis, cleri, populi, et universitatis honorem."

67. Leroy here presented his argument as a further development contracting the program of the university's letter of 6 June, which was presupposed. Ibid.: "ita relin-

fortified by a fairly massive dossier of canons and auxiliary arguments from Roman law, would turn out to be extremely important as the justification for presenting this *via* to Benedict as an ultimatum and later for imposing sanctions on the recalcitrant pope; and one supposes that Leroy therefore took pains to establish it now, even though it went beyond the program of the First Paris Council.

The same can be said for Simon de Cramaud's speech, at any rate the one of which we have a record.[68] It differs from those of his allies by neither refuting d'Ailly nor trying to validate the contraction of the university's original three ways into only one; but like Leroy's it addresses itself to the obligatory and coercive aspects of the *via cessionis*. In this respect the two canonists differed from the theologian Deschamps, who simply presented that *via* as the more expedient one. The record also gives the impression of a *better* speech, and it may be worth noting here that Simon's future works, which we have directly from his dictation, give the same impression of tight clarity—easy reading in fact, as his writings were only one mode of expression of a mind accustomed to speaking to the point in meetings of councils. Pierre Leroy, in contrast, seems to have been fundamentally academic (he was called the greatest canonist in the realm),[69] and his major treatise is constipated and obese, in the academic style of the time.[70] It is also noteworthy that Simon's speech in these meetings of early 1395 contains on one page the gist of what he would later develop in extensive treatises.

The speech begins with a citation of Simon's basic canon, *Si duo forte contra fas* (*Decretum*, 79. di., c. 8), which states that if, irregularly, two men have been elected pope, neither should remain, but a new pope should be elected.[71] Agreeing of course that the Avignon popes had *not* been elected irregularly, Simon nevertheless pointed out that most of Christendom thought otherwise. Hence there was doubt, that is, the Schism, and this could only be removed by a double abdication, which

---

quitur quod de tribus viis advisatis [in the letter], sola illa cessionis est sufficiens ad presentis scismatis cessacionem omnimodam. Et per consequens papa ad ipsam tenetur parere." Cf. fol. 59r: "Quia tamen universitas scripsit istam viam [cessionis] tanquam sufficientem, . . . pono . . . quod ubi alia via non posset haberi conveniencior quam ista, deberemus cicius ad istam condescendere quam sic in scismate remanere."

68. ASV, *Arm.* 54, t. 21, fol. 61rv: "Ista sunt tacta per Patriarcham" (for the text see *DSO*). There had been at least one other speech, referred to by Deschamps (fol. 56r—"patet per raciones alias factas per dominum patriarcham") and also by Pierre d'Ailly in an unrecorded statement (again Deschamps, ibid.—"dominus [Elemosinarius] ad quandam racionem d. patriarche . . . respondebat"—we have neither the *racio* nor the response). Our text of Simon's speech refers to Deschamps's (below) and is thus not the one Deschamps had in mind.

69. By Guillaume Fillastre in 1406 (BdeC: 199).

70. For Leroy's *Factum* see below, Ch. V.

71. See below, Ch. VI, for a translation of the text.

was also called for by "the *duty* of charity": compassion for the souls imperilled by the Schism. Furthermore, "a bishop is *compelled* to resign when his subjects are obstinate against him," according to the canons; "and the reason is that public utility is preferred to private." This also applies to the bishop of Rome, for "even though he is not subject to positive law he has the precept of divine law, namely to abide by his own legislation." "And if he should not do this, it would seem necessary to proceed against him; since he has no superior, this would have to be by force, as against one who had usurped the papacy." For "to keep the papacy wrongly is equivalent to getting it wrongly." Since "the Lord has entrusted the protection of the church to the catholic princes, they would be the ones to compel such a pope"; and in the present case this applied particularly to the king of France, inasmuch as Benedict was bound by the conclave oath "to resign if it should seem expedient to the king and the [royal] council." Gilles Deschamps had expressed the view in his speech that "it would not be expedient at this time to discuss compelling the pope to accept a particular way,"[72] but Simon politely disagreed: "Even though we should not insist on discussing the *mode* of compulsion, as Master Gilles has argued, the matter requires us to counsel the king about this publicly, and requires the king to intimate it to the pope." He concluded: "It seems then that our lord (the pope) must resign and we for our part must counsel this, chiefly because the *via cessionis* is the more effective and suitable way, as clearly shown by the arguments presented by the university and the other speakers." One sees how the alliance worked: the spokesman of power took from the politicized academy its prestigious determination that the *via cessionis* was the best and obligatory way; he put this into his own construction which dropped all qualifications, explorations, and superfluities in order to create the image of public action imposing cession on the pope by force. In 1409 the Council of Pisa would depose both popes; Simon had already prepared for this in 1395.

Although the First Paris Council was formally opened on 2 February with a mass of the Holy Spirit and the administering of oaths, it had really begun with the preliminaries just reviewed, which, like the council, were actions within the framework of an extended royal council. One imagines that the preliminary meetings were attended by many prelates who arrived before opening day and that the atmosphere of officially approved cessionism impressed them duly. The culminating preliminary was a public audience of the University of Paris before the king, at

---

72. ASV, *Arm.* 54, t. 21, fol. 55r: "videtur notandum quod discussiones de compulsione domini pape ad aliquam viam determinatam pro nunc non expediunt." The "pro nunc" meant just that; Deschamps went on to observe "quod compulsio locum haberet contra quemque qui debitum nollet adimplere."

which the university's chancellor Pierre d'Ailly resumed the famous letter of 6 June, including its praise of the *via cessionis* as the best way;[73] this, too, must have been designed to form opinion. It was perhaps then that Simon de Cramaud was chosen president.[74] The formal opening consisted of the mass of the Holy Spirit and the administering of the oath, but the next day re-established the pattern of continuity as "the matters previously debated, pronounced, and treated were presented to the prelates so that each might deliberate with greater clarity."[75] This seems to have been done through a reprise of the preliminary debate, presented as *via compromissi* versus *via cessionis,* but with ultimate cession included in the *compromissum.*[76] This is what Gilles Bellemère has told us, and his

---

73. *RSD,* 2:224—on 1 February, before the beginning of the council, the university received an audience it had requested, at which Pierre d'Ailly spoke: "Et cum vias et motiva epistole universitatis venerande serietenus recitasset, concludit in finalibus, quod via cessionis erat . . . a cunctis fidelibus tanquam brevior, lucidior et expediencior eligenda." This is confirmed, but at a different date, by Gilles Bellemère's account in Baluze & Mansi, *Miscellanea,* 2:591: on 4 February the university had a meeting, decided that cession was the best way, asked for an audience with the crown, and Pierre d'Ailly proclaimed this decision before the king and council. There is no way to decide which date is correct; in any case the important thing is that according to both accounts d'Ailly spoke for the university (no doubt as chancellor) and for the *via cessionis*—in contrast to the ostensible thrust of his speech in the preliminary debate as described above. Ehrle, *Alpartil:* 469 f., supposed, on the basis of this speech, that the *RSD* account gave a distorted summary of d'Ailly's views, but he was apparently unaware of Bellemère's corroboration. I assume that d'Ailly played each role as it was assigned him.

74. *RSD,* 2:224, describes Simon's election, then continues with d'Ailly's speeches to the king, which were made "before Simon ordered the council to begin."

75. AN, J 518, fol. 131r; *RSD,* 2:228.

76. The only substantial information we have about the actual discussions at the council comes from the instructions for the ducal embassy (see n. 52 above), whose author, probably Simon, summarizes the arguments for and against each *via* as they were set forth at the council. A good deal of this obviously came directly from the preliminary debate; perhaps all of it did—we do not have the full texts of the debate. Proof would require too much space, but a few examples will make the point. Compare the instructions, *Ampl. coll.,* 7:441, with Pierre Leroy's speech, ASV, *Arm.* 54, t. 21, fol. 58r: "Outre par la sentence du concile qui seroit donnee pour l'un d'eux, il n'auroit pas droit acquis en la dignite de pape s'il n'y avoit droit paravant"; "Sentencia sive diffinicio consilii generalis non auferret ius pape nec de novo ius in papatu tribueret alias non habenti." Compare Deschamps's argument quoted above, n. 63, with *Ampl. coll.,* 7:443: "Si le compromis enclouoit en soy la voye de cession, . . . si seroit un circuit superflus de faire compromis, . . . et est a presumer que chacune des parties, si le failloit faire, aimeroit mieux . . . de sa franche volonte" (cf. the original, AN, J 518, fol. 97r). And Pierre d'Ailly's incidental arguments against a decision for cession—the king would be said to doubt Benedict's legitimacy; Benedict would be said to doubt it; the king did not proceed thus against Clement his kinsman and fellow Frenchman; we will end up with an Italian pope—all these appear as points brought up at the council (Ehrle, *Alpartil:* 472 f.; *Ampl. coll.,* 7:454 f.). One guesses that the so-called deliberations of the council were in fact the staged debate reported by Bellemère and alluded to by Simon (above, n. 43, 75).

report, though partisan, was probably correct; one can imagine the effect of Pierre d'Ailly's advocacy of the *via compromissi* (which indeed included cession) coming after his presentation of the university's cessionist letter of 6 June and in a discourse in which he himself declared that the best way would be for both popes freely to abdicate and that they were obliged to do so by divine law. We know that the university instructed its speaker at the council to argue only for cession and to present the "generality" of the 6 June letter as passé; it was now necessary that one definite way be chosen—advised by the council and adopted by the king.[77] Opinions presented by the Celestines and Carthusians were also for cession, the Carthusians presenting a refreshingly religious argument that reads well after the political calculations of the secular leadership.[78] Thus there could hardly have been any room left for serious opposition based on the view that the king should *not* choose one way but should, rather, leave the choice to the pope. For one thing, the three main ways had been "opened" over a half year ago by the university's letter, and there would be no point in calling a council for that; for another, as Deschamps had pointed out, the prelates who had assembled and sworn to counsel the king were obligated thereby to tell him what they thought best.[79] One would like to know more of just how such reasons were brought home to the council's members, but the result seems clear: the prelates had been brought onto a stage where a full-scale spectacle was already in progress, with everyone singing and dancing the song of cession; the pressure was overwhelming for them to normalize themselves and join the chorus.

At some point in the proceedings, Simon de Cramaud prepared and perhaps read out his own lengthy opinion, resuming the history of the affair since Benedict's request for counsel from the king, presenting all the significant arguments of himself and his allies in favor of choosing one way, against the ways of a general council and arbitration, and for the *via cessionis*. He then proceeded, in line with his opinion at the preliminary meetings, to work out the uses of power. Cession, he proposed, should be presented by the royal ambassadors to the pope with a

---

77. The text in Bulaeus, 4:737–739.

78. *Ampl. coll.*, 7:462; AN, J 518, fols. 115v–118r (the Carthusian opinion).

79. Deschamps's *cedula*, ASV, Arm. 54, t. 21, fol. 55r, had argued that to refrain from choosing one way (out of the university's original three) would be wrong, "quia hoc esset infringere legem consilii, que ad apparens melius constringit." Cf. the instructions in *Ampl. coll.*, 7:444: "Il a semblé que ceux qui ont esté mandez par le roy pour cette cause, et qui ont fait serment de le loyaument conseiller, luy doient conseiller la voye qui leur semble la meilleure." It goes on, "Et outre, le roy pour néant auroit mandé ses prelats, se il ne scavoit leurs advis de la meilleure voye, mesmement que il y a plus de demy an que par l'epitre . . . baillée par l'université de Paris, les voyes ont este ouvertes."

statement that it was in fact the only way deemed acceptable by the king, and if Benedict rejected it he should be told, "semper cum reverencia et honore," that the king was going to pursue it anyway. There followed rather detailed specifications about getting the collaboration of the princes of the other side, presenting cession to the Roman pope and if necessary imposing it on him, and arranging the actual double abdication. The text as a whole was conceived as a possible draft of instructions to the royal embassy and advice to the king.[80] There seems to have been some discussion of it, perhaps in the unfair way described by Gilles Bellemère, and the result was that most of the prelates accepted it, others preferring a more polite and deferential approach to the pope. By this time, evidently, even Benedict's supporters had given up any hope of blocking the Paris drive to cessionism, but—interestingly—they chose not to stand fast as an opposition. Their spokesman Élie de Lestrange, at that time bishop of Saintes, seems to have put aside his own convictions in order to avoid an open break between Paris and Avignon.[81] The

---

80. It was incorporated into an official instrument of the council headed "Secuntur illa que pro instruccionibus dominorum ducum et aliorum consiliariorum suorum quos rex intendit mittere Avinionem erga dominum papam et dominos cardinales conclusa et deliberata fuerunt"—the text in AN, J 518, fols. 131r–133v, 125r–127r (the order was mixed up); also in part in *RSD*, 2:226–244. After a brief résumé of the background to the council, Simon's opinion proper begins: "Oppinio modica loquentis fuit. . . ." Right after it there is a note, evidently by the secretary Gontier Col (fol. 125r): "Et in congregacione prelatorum fuit facta post discussionem plenissimam materie quedam cedula que supradicta continebat in effectu, per magistrum Johannem Canardi, episcopum Attrebatensem, . . . quem secuti fuerunt fere quatuor partes prelatorum et aliorum in congregacione prelatorum existencium, ut apparet per tenorem instrumenti super hoc." This instrument appears on fols. 98r–102r (printed *Ampl. coll.*, 7:458–465) and includes the abridged text of Simon's opinion. Another copy of the full text of this opinion exists in ASV, *Arm.* 54, t. 21, fols. 51r–54r, entitled "Opus unius magni prelati cui plus quam tres partes prelatorum et aliorum vocatorum adheserunt"; at "prelati" there is a note by Martin de Salva: "creditur quod patriarcha."

81. His *cedula* is at the end of the first of the instruments cited above in n. 80 (AN, J 518, fols. 126v–127r; another copy, fols. 100v–101r, is in the instrument containing the abridged text of Simon's opinion), with a prefatory note: "Et aliqui episcopi qui venerant de Avinione videbantur magis inclinati ad complacendum pape, quorum unus eciam ut securior haberetur conclusio consilii eciam posuit opinionem suam in scriptis et illum eciam sunt secuti alii." Col's note at the end reads: "Et hanc cedulam manu propria episcopi Xantonensis scriptam tradidit idem episcopus in consilio . . . XVta die Februarii. . . . Et collacio eiusdem cedule facta per me Gontier." The *cedula* begins: "Ad principale quesitum quo queritur quid regi principi et domino nostro consulo per eum domino nostro pape consulendum pro breviori, honestiori, ac faciliori modo unionis habende in universali dei ecclesia, Deus cuius causa agitur iudicet scribentem si aliter loquatur quam credat et senciat negocio de quo agitur profuturum." I translate the last part so: "May God judge the writer if he speak otherwise than he thinks and feels may be serviceable to the business at hand"; and I suppose the phrasing was intended to indicate a disjunction of the absolutely right and the practically useful in the given political situation.

proposal that he drafted differed, he wrote with exaggeration, hardly at all from Simon's but urged only that the royal embassy allow Benedict to present his way first and in private; and only then, if his way turned out to be neither cession nor something "feasible and good," should the embassy gently try to bring him around, discretely asking the cardinals to use their influence if that should prove necessary. But if possible, the pope should be followed in a matter of this sort. This text was submitted on 15 February and read out to the council along with an abridged version of Simon's text prepared by Jean Canart, bishop of Arras and chancellor of Burgundy. The prelates were now asked to vote—in effect for one or the other; eighty-seven voted for Simon's text, twenty for Lestrange's, and two bishops (one guesses Benedict's envoy Bellemère was one) were unsatisfied with either.[82]

It remained only for Simon to bring the prelates before the king and the royal dukes on 18 February and in solemn audience relate the results of the council.[83] We have seen Bellemère's comments about how he did this. Bellemère was probably correct; for Simon subsequently always made a point of referring to the vote at the First Paris Council as virtually unanimous, with "few if any exceptions" (Pierre Ravat later glossed this comment in his copy of Simon's treatise with the remark: "The bishop of Le Puy [scil., Élie de Lestrange] should be heard about that").[84] We have seen something of how this triumph was achieved, and we can infer some of the rest from the remarkable lack of oppositional literature in the surviving sources (in contrast to the case for subsequent Paris councils) and from the lack of any record of debates at the council itself. The prefabricated opening debate seems not to have been recorded; the subsequent discussion seems to have been deliberately kept abortive by Simon; and by the time voting was in order, the question before the house was already contracted as the cessionists wished, to presuppose that just one way would be recommended: "What do you advise the king to counsel the pope as the shorter, more reputable, and easier way of having union?"[85] Given the massive public relations for the *via cessionis,* the answer was not in doubt.

---

82. The instrument in AN, J 518, fol. 100v, gives these figures; see *Ampl. coll.,* 7:463.

83. AN, J 518, fol. 101rv. Gontier Col adds a concluding note: "Qua relacione sic facta, ante et post ac pluries predictus dominus patriarcha de omnibus predictis dum modo predicto fierent et dicerentur, peciit a nobis notariis predictis fieri publicum instrumentum unum vel plura ad opus ipsius et omnium quorum interest vel interesse poterit in futurum. Et eciam . . . rex peciit sibi fieri de huiusmodi relacione publicum instrumentum."

84. ASV, *Arm.* 54, t. 26, fol. 95v: "audiatur dominus Aniciensis episcopus super hoc" (written 1397/1398; Lestrange was by this time bishop of Le Puy).

85. Lestrange's formulation, n. 81 above.

Still, we may ask why at least Benedict's supporters did not openly urge the way he favored, a variety of the *via compromissi*. Perhaps because Pierre d'Ailly had more or less sterilized that way by his mode of advocating it; more likely, because Benedict himself did not want the issue to be forced at that time and in that place. Avignon, not Paris, was where such matters should be decided.[86] We have seen that Benedict's envoys in November had asked for a high-ranking embassy capable of making commitments on behalf of "the king" and that his envoys to the Paris Council had promised a papal *via* to be revealed only to that embassy, only in Avignon. A similar intention lay behind Benedict's response in another matter: sometime about mid-January "the king" wrote to ask him for a true copy of the conclave oath, since there was talk that the version circulating in Paris was false; Benedict replied that this version was indeed false but that he would reveal the true text only to the royal embassy in Avignon.[87] The obvious inference is that the pope was well aware of how things were being run in Paris; that he realized that as long as he was being dealt with by Simon de Cramaud, working in a royal council that accepted his leadership in this matter, there was no hope for a policy that would meet the pope's requirements; and that the only hope lay in direct dealings with the dukes, pried loose from the Paris matrix. Perhaps he also recalled that Simon had his own reasons for hostility.[88] Hence, the supreme importance, from his point of view, of avoiding a showdown at the First Paris Council.

His envoys had arrived in Paris during the preliminary meetings at the end of January,[89] with instructions to urge that "the king" not delay longer in dispatching his embassy and to remonstrate gently that it would be wrong for "the king" to fix on one definite way before consulting the pope and the cardinals—Avignon evidently knew that "some were machinating" to this effect.[90] Helpless to do more than watch the

---

86. "Ista negotia non erant Parisius terminanda sed hic"—this was Benedict's view according to Pierre Ravat (*ALKG*, 5:405).

87. AN, J 518, fol. 124r; *Ampl. coll.*, 7:447.

88. See above, Ch. III, at n. 125, and cf. the remark of Pierre Blau (ASV, *Arm.* 54, t. 20, fol. 183v): "multi fuerunt inter illos [scil., in the First Paris Council] qui voluntarie et contra omnem racionem ad illam opinionem [scil., the *via cessionis*] moti sunt, ex causis pro nunc tacendis."

89. The instructions of the ducal embassy say: "Environ la journée assignée aux prélats pour venir devers le roy, qui fust à la Chandeleur [2 February], nostre saint pere envoya derechef ses messages pardevers le roy" (*Ampl. coll.*, 7:438). Bellemère wrote (Baluze & Mansi, *Miscellanea*, 2:591): "et jam praelati ibidem existentes ante dictorum nuntiorum adventum multa concilia tenuerant." The bulls constituting the papal envoys were dated 12 January 1395; if they had left about then, they could have been in Paris by the end of the month; see Valois, 3:31.

90. The instructions for Benedict's envoys, *ALKG*, 6:160–162.

machine roll on in the First Paris Council, no doubt drawing a hard lesson from the vote that gave a mere twenty to their ally Élie de Lestrange, the envoys could only address themselves directly to the dukes, especially Burgundy, from whom they claimed to have received a satisfactory reply; it is Gilles Bellemère who tells us:

The envoys said to the dukes, especially Burgundy, that they should take care that no certain and definite way be chosen at Paris or conveyed by the royal embassy to our lord the pope. They said that if such were done they believed that our lord would not accept the way chosen or offered, above all if it should be the way on which the university had decided. . . . The duke of Burgundy and several other princes replied that there was no need to worry, for no certain way would be chosen at Paris, but that they would deal and deliberate with our lord about this.

But, as Bellemère continues, "It was brought about by who knows whom that men committed to the *via cessionis* were the ones chosen to draw up the instructions for the royal ambassadors and to go with them, assist them, and counsel them."[91] Was Burgundy deliberately deceiving the papal envoys? Or was the government's response less clear than the envoys recalled?[92] In any case, it was not Burgundy who was directly behind the big cessionist push but, rather, Berry, whose client Simon de Cramaud was the organizer and machinator and who himself would play the obviously leading role later on when the ducal embassy was in Avignon.[93] Simon could hardly have forged the cessionist alliance or have carried through the sustained effort that led to the triumph of 18 February if Berry had not radiated his power in that sense, nor indeed would Simon then have wished to. It would of course have been equally impossible for this effort to have been made without the support of Burgundy, whose chancellor Jean Canart stood with Simon in the council. The instructions for the ambassadors could only have been what they in fact were: Simon's proposal read out at the council and approved by the vote of eighty-seven to twenty-two.

The text of the instructions is a French translation of Simon's proposal, amplified by a more elaborate summary of the debates at the

---

91. Baluze & Mansi, *Miscellanea*, 2:591.

92. While Bellemère said the response was made by Burgundy and several other princes, the account in Benedict's *Informacio seriosa* of 1399 has it that "the king answered and agreed, with the dukes and other councillors present and agreeing." But Pierre Ravat wrote in the margin: "Was it the king or the chancellor who replied?" and Martin de Salva wrote his answer: "I think it was the chancellor, according to the envoys' report." All this in *ALKG*, 5:404 f. Perhaps the content of the response was recalled with similar imprecision.

93. Apart from the facts which show Berry's leadership, there is his own statement in 1399 that "the whole business with the pope had been committed to him from the first, and only accessorily to Burgundy and Orléans" (*ALKG*, 7:93).

council and with a number of more or less occasional points added; there is virtually no difference in the substance.[94] Here, as always, we must regard Simon as the exponent of a policy approved by his superiors, whose thinking, however, he undoubtedly influenced. When we read the record of the embassy's transactions in Avignon, we are also struck by the way in which the dukes, with Berry in the lead, not only adhered to the instructions but guided their adherence by repeated conferences with what the embassy's secretary Gontier Col referred to as "the king's council"—the large number of ducal clients and royal councillors who were taken along.[95] It was in effect the Paris government transported to the banks of the Rhone, and one notes Benedict's futile efforts to break through this front by direct conversations with the dukes.

Equally striking is the strategic foundation of the instructions which regulated the whole approach to the pope: Benedict was required to give his unconditional assent to a *via cessionis* whose only condition was that the other contender had to resign also; it would be up to the king of France to obtain this condition by direct dealing with the princes of the other obedience, and it would be up to the secular powers of both sides to program and protect the actual process of the double renunciation, which the Paris formulation of the *via cessionis* laid out in some detail.[96] It was a scenario that assigned the two popes the roles of puppets whose every move was prescribed by the agents of secular government. This was Simon de Cramaud's way of thinking, determined no doubt by the ruthless habits of his successful careerism, by the often-unrealistic ideas about the world generated in princely courts and capitals, perhaps too by a desire to exalt himself and humble Benedict, but also by a well-founded sense—to be validated by the abortive papal negotiations of

---

94. See n. 52 above; cf. Valois, 3:41 n. 6.

95. For their names see Valois, 3:45. Col's usage varies: "fust tenu le conseil auquel furent noz troiz seigneurs ensemble, touz ceulx du conseil, et ceulx de l'universite" (AN, J 518, fol. 146v); "firent . . . les ducs assembler tous ceulz du conseil du roy" (fol. 142v; also fols. 138v, 136v); "puis nosseigneurs et le conseil se retrairent a part" (fol. 138r).

96. *Ampl. coll.*, 7:449 ff.: "In the meetings held about this matter at the king's command, clerics, theologians, and canonists discussed how according to divine and canon law the way of renunciation could be reasonably executed by the help of the kings, princes, and lords of both sides." "After the kings and great lords of our side shall have consented to the way of renunciation, the latter should be made known to the kings, princes, and great lords of the other side and the cities of Italy, to induce them . . . to get the intruder in Rome and his anticardinals to consent." "The king [of France] could write to the intruder and some of the anticardinals." Simon's original formulation was more explicit: if Benedict accepted cession, he and the king could spread the news to the rulers of the Avignon side, but it would be these "and not lord Benedict who would inform the rulers of the other side" (*RSD*, 2:240), "nor is the *via cessionis* to be made known to the intruder before telling it to the princes of his obedience" (ibid.).

1408—that only failure could come from leaving any part of the *via cessionis* to the initiative of two men whose raison d'être was their respective conviction of legitimacy. Paris could hardly have been unaware of Benedict's thinking in this matter, for his acts had already made clear what he would later tell the dukes and what indeed he would never change in the rest of his life: he would rather die than accept a *via* which sacrificed the "justice" of his cause.[97] A clever negotiator could perhaps have led him to change his mind, but more likely not; and in any case, Simon and his associates seem to have regarded coercion not as the last resort but more likely as the first.

The embassy was constituted soon after the end of the First Paris Council on 18 February, and the official instructions were composed after that; but the actual departure for Avignon did not begin until the latter part of April, and the three dukes did not enter Avignon until 22 May. If the delay had any particular cause, it may have been the crown's preoccupation in this period with the task of turning Richard II of England away from his proposed marriage with Yolanda of Aragon and to a marriage and alliance with the royal house of France in the person of Isabelle, the king's six-year-old daughter.[98] Here, as on other occasions before and after, the rather murky political program of cessionism— joint action by the secular powers of both sides—was probably an extrapolation from the sense of entente with King Richard II, the Urbanist prince par excellence from the French point of view. This in turn was one reason why the Paris form of the *via cessionis* could seem implausible and therefore threatening to Benedict and many others. Unimpressed by English hopes, they saw the *via cessionis* as little more than giving Paris a free hand to take the papacy on an undefined course through uncharted and hostile waters; for it would take years before the Roman contender and his other princes came to regard the idea of abdication with anything but scorn. The embassy could indeed show little evidence of interest from the other side. It took along the text of two letters from Boniface IX to Charles VI in 1392/1393, which expressed merely the Roman's desire for union on his terms; for the rest, as the instructions hopefully continue, "if there are any noteworthy letters sent by any of the kings or princes of the intruder's obedience, let them be taken along." There were none. Other documents taken included the Univer-

---

97. Valois, 3:63, collects the reports of these statements, all of course by Benedict's enemies but still plausible. In his reply to the Toulouse letter of 1402, Simon de Cramaud wrote (AN, J 518, fol. 540r) that Benedict had had his confessor say publicly, in Avignon, that he would rather be torn limb from limb (*membratim delaniari*) than accept the Paris *via cessionis*.

98. Valois, 3:46, and Lehoux, 2:329, for the embassy's movements; Palmer, *EFC*: 166 ff., 180 ff., for the marriage projects.

sity of Paris's letter of 6 June 1394, its letter to Clement VII of 17 August 1394, Benedict's bulls declaring his intention of discussing the conclave oath and other matters of union with the ambassadors, and an instrument recording the course and results of the First Paris Council.[99]

Benedict meanwhile had not been inactive, for he was as familiar with Paris's thinking as Paris was with his. He needed above all the support of his cardinals, both because this was necessary in any such weighty matter which touched their status as well as the estate of the church and because the conclave oath had cast them as the arbiters of his future. He therefore appointed a committee of eight cardinals, including his closest associate the cardinal of Pamplona, Martin de Salva, but also Pierre de Thury and Jean de Lagrange, the two leading Valois clients in the college.[100] Moved by their own status interests or by some sort of pressure from the pope, all gave first place to a way that Benedict himself thought sound: a preliminary meeting between the popes and their colleges, or between plenipotentiaries of each papacy, to discuss the issue of legitimacy; if no agreement were reached on this, then the plenipotentiaries (constituted now if not already before) would impose whatever solution seemed to them best, including perhaps the *via cessionis*—this according to all but two, Martin de Salva and Guy de Malesset. Almost all the committeemen assigned important roles to the princes of France, in some cases seeming to presuppose that even the other side would be happy to accept Valois direction of the enterprise; and a number of the opinions included the provision that any program chosen should explicitly refer to the agreement of the king and princes as a sine qua non. Thury and Lagrange went even further, the former urging that the pope and cardinals state in advance that they would follow whatever way seemed best to the king and dukes, Lagrange saying the same but adding a frank explanation:

This way we will gratify the king, the dukes, and the realm, recognizing the benefits we have received, and we will put our persons and estate securely beyond all perils. Critics of us and our estate will be silenced, the hatreds of clergy and people will stop, and we will no doubt be making a virtue of necessity, which is a very prudent thing to do. Whatever happens then, the king, the dukes, the whole realm, and the king's allies will certainly stand by us, so that during the period in which union of the church is being pursued

---

99. These documents are listed as a kit at the end of the official instructions for the embassy, *Ampl. coll.*, 7:457 f. They in fact appear in AN, J 518, fols. 1r–10v, 13r–28v (the university's letters); 98r–102r (the instrument of the council); 106r–108r (Boniface IX's letters to Charles VI); 121v–124v (Benedict's bulls). No letters from other princes are there.

100. What follows is based on Ehrle's analysis and the texts he published in *Alpartil*: 451–461; cf. Valois, 3:43 f.

we will have all the prerogatives and advantages that the king and dukes can give us.[101]

This passage is the key to the behavior of all the cardinals except Pamplona, at this point and later, even the cardinals who would be created by Benedict from the ranks of his most ardent supporters. All would desert him when forced to choose between him and the Valois. Boniface Ferrer, head of the Carthusian order, would note this in 1411, in lines of biting contempt whose evident malice does not make them less true. Cardinal Nicholas Brancacci had, Ferrer said, admitted it to him: "There are no greater traitors in the world than we cardinals, because we denied our lord so as not to lose our benefices in France." Pierre Blau, whom we have met as Benedict's envoy to Paris and who was soon after elevated to the college as cardinal of Sant'Angelo, in which capacity he deserted Benedict to take part in the Council of Pisa, allegedly said at that time: "If Benedict had put me in safe possession of 3,000 francs of revenue a year, or even of 2,000, outside the realm of France, I'd never have left him." To keep their benefices and keep drawing their revenues, Ferrer said, the cardinals "would commit all the evils imaginable in this world"; "they would even adore idols," for "they have as much of Christ's faith as the amount of revenues from their benefices, and no more."[102] Even cardinal Leonardo di Giffoni, who had spurned rewards, endured imprisonment, and risked death at the beginning of the Schism because he believed in the papacy of Clement VII, had become thoroughly Avignonized by 1395: asked by Benedict to write on the best *via*, he came up with a hard-hitting treatise against the *via cessionis*, only to join his fellows in embracing that *via* a few months later, when required by the dukes to choose between them and his pope.[103] Thus while Benedict could face the French embassy with his cardinals' support for a *via convencionis* that would be a *via iusticie*, the support was there only so long as it was not put to the test.

The test began on 28 May, after several days of more or less ceremonial preliminaries notable chiefly for the pope's reluctance to allow the royal notaries to make a true copy of the conclave oath; eventually he

---

101. In Ehrle, *Alpartil*: 458.

102. *Thes. nov.*, 2:1491 (Brancacci); 2:1465 (Blau); 2:1454, 1474; Ferrer points to the wordly ways by which the cardinals had gotten their rank: "by the powerful requests of princes, or by fear or favor of nation and fatherland, or by kinship, or carnal friendship, or by fraud, . . . or by first getting themselves the titles of councillor, president, or chancellor of some prince" (2:1498).

103. Clément Schmitt, "La position du cardinal Léonard de Giffoni, O. F. M. dans le conflit du Grand Schisme d'Occident," *Archivum Franciscanum Historicum*, 50 (1957): 273–331; 51 (1958):25–72, 410–472 (see esp. 50:296 ff.; 51:26 ff.). The text of the treatise is excerpted in 50:303–331.

gave in. When it came down to presenting concrete plans, Benedict went first and gave his *via convencionis*: both popes and their colleges to meet in a place near France and under the protection of the king of France, where "they would deal with the way of obtaining peace in the holy church and would hear the arguments of the one and the other side." He could not dispense with this last point, Benedict said, "for it was necessary to have the consent of both parties."[104] On 1 June Gilles Deschamps gave the embassy's response (here, as previously, the prescriptions of the official instructions were followed to the letter), which boiled down to an explanation of how and why the First Paris Council had rejected five ways after careful consideration and had settled on the *via cessionis* as the only acceptable one. Although Benedict's way had not been among the five, Deschamps made it so by a tendentiously false definition of the rejected *via compromissi*.[105] The pope's reply, after some recriminations about being coerced, was to ask for a written text of the *via cessionis* which would include both its argumentation and provisions for execution. The instructions as well as other instruments brought by the embassy covered both matters in detail, but there was no provision for the negotiations about them that Benedict was obviously trying to provoke; hence after a brief huddle with "their council," the dukes refused, saying that no text was necessary, for the *via cessionis* could be adequately understood in two words. Thus Benedict was not to negotiate or discuss but only submit; he put the point himself by replying that he had his office from God and might not be coerced by men.

That afternoon the dukes summoned the cardinals to attend them in Villeneuve, across the river in France, where Berry asked them for their personal opinions about the best way. They replied after a conference that it was getting late and they did not want to weary the dukes— tomorrow would be a better time. But Berry said he was not tired and he wanted them to answer now. Every one of them then said in turn that

---

104. In Gontier Col's report of the embassy's transactions, AN, J 518, fols. 136v–137r: "et oissent les raisons et couleurs de l'une et de l'autre partie qui sont de necessite a oir premierement, et [*Benedict*] tient que ainsi se doit il faire, ne autrement ne se peut faire bonnement; car il fault de necessite avoir le consentement des parties." Col's report is the basis for what follows.

105. According to the instructions the *via compromissi* was "que les deux parties du consentement de leurs colleges se soumissent en arbitrage ou ordonnance d'aucunes bonnes personnes qu'ils eliroient"—these could even impose abdication (*Ampl. coll.*, 7:442; cf. d'Ailly's speech—at n. 57 above—from which the gist of this definition seems derived). The instructions do not mention the *via convencionis* as one of those discussed at the council. Deschamps, however, said on 1 June that the *via compromissi* discussed and rejected by the Paris Council was "d'assembler ensemble en lieu seur soubs la proteccion du roy les deux parties pour traictier illec entre eulx de voie convenable pour avoir union; et contient en soy ceste voie la voie de compromis" (AN, J 518, fol. 137v).

cession was best—except for admirable Pamplona, who first pointed out how irregular it was for the cardinals to act as individuals with the dukes rather than as a college with the pope, then went on to state that since Benedict was the true pope it was the duty of Catholics to support him. Hence the true and just way of union would be to expel the intruder from Rome; as for cession, "justice does not call for someone to renounce his good rights," and such a way would be shameful to Avignon believers dead and alive, including the royal house of France. The pope's *via convencionis* moreover was a quicker and easier way to come to union than the *via cessionis*—a conclusion that in context suggests a military dimension of the pope's way that was presumably in Benedict's mind as well as Martin de Salva's: "Why," a contemporary asked, "has the pope offered a *via* which obviously will not be accepted by the intruder?"[106] In any case, Salva's forthright statement points up the submissiveness of the others; henceforth the cardinals' role as a group would be played within the Paris scenario. Let us note, by the way, that while Salva's independence may have been reinforced by the fact that most of his benefices, including the bishopric of Pamplona, lay in Navarre, it was actually a personal trait; even before he had been made cardinal, he had had the courage to stand up to Urban VI in 1378 on two occasions, telling that pope to his face that he was no pope and should step down.[107]

The remainder of the embassy saw the cardinals acting on the dukes' side, detached from their legitimate head. On 1 July they confronted the pope with their declaration that they adhered to the *via cessionis,* and they requested the pope to do so as well, an action that put him under the formal obligation of fulfilling his conclave oath. While he forbade them to sign the written text of this declaration, and they obeyed, the import of their action was nevertheless clear.[108] At the same time, Benedict

---

106. Salva's statement is summarized by Col in AN, J 518, fol. 141rv, along with those of the other cardinals (fols. 138v–142r); the Latin instrument prepared at the time (fols. 102r–106r; in *Ampl. coll.,* 7:466–472) gives essentially the same text with some variations. There is much evidence that a solution of the Schism by force was regarded as the right way by men close to Benedict, e.g., Sancho Muler, who at the Third Paris Council carefully refused to join in the usual condemnation of the *via facti* (ASV, *Arm.* 54, t. 21, fol. 244r), and Pierre Ravat, who rejected Simon de Cramaud's condemnation of that *via* with the marginal comment: "Licet papa pro nunc illam non prosequatur, dic michi quare ergo iura . . . de principibus contra scismaticos sunt introducta?" (*Arm.* 54, t. 26, fol. 111r). See also Valois, 3:371, 385, 407. Hence the point of the question put in the anonymous "Impugnaciones . . . circa viam iusticie," ASV, *Arm.* 54, t. 27, fol. 119r: Why has the pope offered a way "de qua prima facie presumitur quod non acceptabitur per intrusum?"

107. José Goñi Gaztambide, *Los obispos de Pamplona del Siglo XIV* (Pamplona, 1962): 311–316, and *passim.*

108. Valois, 3:60–62.

did all that he could within the narrow limits allowed by his principles to impress the dukes with his sense of right and to extend his own proposed *via* so that it would make some contact with cession: on 20 June he amplified the *via convencionis* to include the *via compromissi* through delegates; on 28 June he added that he would do everything necessary according to the duty of his office and the obligations imposed by the conclave oath; on 5 July he emphasized his fidelity to that oath.[109] Cession was thus brought in by reference to the oath. Benedict himself, however, did not repeat the promise to abdicate but instead kept mentioning the key phrase "*per vias iuridicas,*" which he understood as signifying the opposite of the *via cessionis* that Paris had presented to him.[110] We may note too that his advisers would show endless ingenuity in proving that the conclave oath did not necessarily bind the pope to resign.[111] Some of these advisers now, to be sure, urged Benedict to make a clear offer of cession, perhaps in the context of a general council of the

---

109. The three responses are transcribed in Col's record, AN, J 518, fols. 149r–150v ("Cum dudum," 20 June); 156r ("Quamvis nuper," 28 June); 163v–164r (Quoniam sicut ad nostrum," 5 July). For printed texts see Valois, 3:57 n. 3; 59 n. 3; 62 n. 2. The bulls are also reproduced elsewhere in AN, J 518, fols. 111r–115v, with critical glosses and comments by an exponent of the Paris program—one supposes, Simon de Cramaud.

110. Thus in "Cum dudum" Benedict wrote (AN, J 518, fol. 149v): "At nos attendentes quod dicta via cessionis pro sedandis scismatibus nec a iure statuta nec a sanctis patribus fuerat hactenus in dei ecclesia casu simili practicata—quinymo, ut in gestis Romanorum pontificum et alibi legitur, ut non conveniens aliquando repulsa—ne in acceptacione vie huiusmodi . . . quicquam . . . improvide . . . attemptaretur quod posset non solum in . . . dampnum ecclesie, . . . contemptum clavium et censure, ac libertatis ecclesiastice lesionem, sed eciam in scandalum prelatorum et . . . omnium qui veritati et iusticie partis nostre adheserunt . . . ignominiam redundare . . . [etc.]." He went on to declare that his whole desire was to obtain union "per viam seu vias racionabiles, iuridicas, et salubres animabus" (fol. 150r) and that if the discussions and arbiters of his *via convencionis et compromissi* should fail to lead to agreement, he would then "aperire seu aperiendas recipere et prosequi cum effectu viam seu vias racionabiles, honestas, et iuridicas" (fol. 150v). At this last point the critical commentator, probably Simon, noted: "Excludit cessionem quia prius dixit hanc non esse a iure statutam" (fol. 112v). The second bull also talks of "juridical ways" (fol. 156r), but refers to the pope's obligation to seek union by virtue of his office "et alias in quantum virtute cuiusdam cedule facte in conclavi teneamur." Here the commentator wrote: "Illa verba . . . non includunt viam cessionis ut patet evidenter, quoniam illam viam in responsione precedenti . . . papa multipliciter impugnat" (fol. 113r); also: "Papa vult prosequi vias per ipsum apertas . . . non . . . extendendo responsionem ultimam ad novam viam, maxime cessionis" (fol. 113v).

111. E.g., the text in Bulaeus, 4:749; Pierre Ravat's "Allegations" of 1395 on the *cedula conclavis* (ASV, Arm. 54, t. 22, fols. 132r–143r); there were many others, all drawing on the rich store of canonistic doctrine about oaths—which lawyers naturally tended to analyze in order to dissolve absolute obligations. See Valois, 3:51; Swanson: 98 f., 102 f.

Avignon obedience; but their counsel did not prevail,[112] so that Benedict's position appeared all too honestly as a flat repudiation of the royal way. It was perhaps as a corollary to this strategy that he combined his "juridical" proposals with efforts to get the dukes back to the good old notions of *via facti*. He complained that they were behaving differently to him than they had to Clement; he insisted on private conferences with each of them; he promised them great things (which Cardinal Giffoni told them meant lordship over the papal states—but they would have to conquer them first).[113]

In vain. The instructions of the embassy had foresightedly prohibited the dukes from making any supplications to Benedict for themselves or others—including indeed any request "touching the liberties, franchises, and rights" of the Gallican churches—until the union negotiations had been successfully concluded. The *via facti* had also been carefully refuted in advance.[114] In the end, the dukes left Avignon 10 July with no agreement whatever between them and the pope; what they had achieved, and it was perhaps the only positive outcome foreseen or desired, was to attach the cardinals solidly to the crown's policy,[115] thus laying the foundations for action against Benedict as not only one who refused to unite the church but also a perjuror who denied his own oath. The dukes probably promised that the cardinals would be consulted in the event of such action, which would of course affect their interests.[116] For the

112. Pierre Ravat's glosses of ca. 1400 on the *Factum* of the subtracting cardinals (for which see Valois, 3:193 n. 1), ASV, *Arm.* 54, t. 27, fol. 205r: "Loquitur textus . . . de cessione, circa quam dixi alias mentem meam, . . . postea coram papa, . . . et sepe in consiliis, . . . sed ultimate eciam pape. . . . Et utinam dominus noster multis et michi credidisset, et apercius loqutus fuisset illam offerendo vel consilium congregando, etc. Sed hiis non obstantibus, dato quod male—salva sanctitate sua—fecerit aliter non respondendo per prius . . . [etc.]." Cf. *ALKG,* 7:165, 195, 201, for evidence that Ravat, Élie de Lestrange, and others had advised a council of the obedience as early as 1395.

113. AN, J 518, fol. 142v sqq.: Benedict had private conversations with each of the dukes, 9–10 June, who met afterwards to tell each other what the pope had said. He had spoken to Burgundy of his affection for the house of France, had complained of the harsh and disrespectful way the dukes had demanded cession of him—"and that if he had been of the realm of France they would not have proceeded against him so." Also that ugly words had been used of him and his fellow Aragonese (fol. 143v). See Valois, 3:61, 64. Benedict's *Informatio seriosa* of 1399 claims that those antagonized by Benedict's reforms spread false stories in France to the effect that the pope "despised the French nation and would move the Curia to Italy" (*ALKG,* 5:404).

114. *Ampl. coll.,* 7:439, 446 f., 457.

115. This appears even more explicitly in the account incorporated into the pro-Benedict *Informatio seriosa* of 1399 and thence in the *acta* of Benedict's Council of Perpignan, *ALKG,* 5:408 ff., e.g., p. 416: the dukes requested "consilium et auxilium" from the cardinals, who in turn asked the dukes to take them "under special protection." These were the technical terms of lordship.

116. So stated by 'Cardinal Guy de Malesset in 1400 (*Thes. nov.,* 2:1230).

initial action could only be subtraction of obedience, long in the air and now threatened explicitly by the dukes, particularly Berry, who exclaimed after the third papal response on 8 July: "Holy Father, do you want to have any power in France?"[117]

117. "Pater sancte, vultis aliquid mandare in Franciam?"—in Bellemère's report (Baluze & Mansi, *Miscellanea,* 2:594), which goes on to say that it was commonly believed at the papal court and among the people "that unless the pope gave in totally to the will of the dukes, the king would subtract the revenues and obedience of the realm from him, and that all the curialists of French nationality and with benefices in France would fall into the king's and dukes' displeasure and would be in danger of losing their estate." Similar reports were made by the Datini correspondents in Avignon; see the citations in Lehoux, 2:334 n. 1, 335 n. 4; cf. the additional evidence cited by Schmitt, "Giffoni," 51 (1958): 415 n. 1.

From Cession to Subtraction, 1395–1397

"SUBTRACTION of obedience" sounds rather odd to a modern ear, and one's immediate reaction is to ask why the simple word *disobedience* should not have been used instead, particularly when it was a matter of challenging a public authority like the papacy. The answer would be that *disobedience* carries the double sense of inner disposition and external action, with the latter apt to be a sign of the former; and very few thought this way about subtraction of obedience in our context. When we first encounter the term in the mouths of the Valois dukes, talking to or about the Avignon pope, whom they accepted as legitimate, it is as part of a threat that unless the pope conforms to France's union policy he will be deprived of his revenues from the French church and his power to appoint to French benefices;[1] this action would soon be called, variously, *partial subtraction* or *subtraction of partial* (or particular) *obedience*. *Obedience* here meant not the act of obeying in relation to the subject's inner virtue of obedience, but the act of obeying in relation to the material things and the particular rights over which papal authority claimed the right to dispose. It was also used very commonly to designate the objects and rights themselves within this same context.[2] The tendency to reification manifest here has already been noted as a late-medieval characteristic, and we can guess that it corresponded to the realities of Old Europe, when governmental rights and powers were still

---

1. See above, Ch. II, at n. 112; Ch. IV, n. 117.

2. In the debates at the Third Paris Council of 1398, there was only one reference to obedience as a subjective virtue, by Benedict's apologist Sancho Muler, who argued that distinctions between partial and total subtraction, also between subtraction of obedience from the pope and subtraction from a king, had to do only with external acts ("loquendo de . . . mandato cui obeditur"). Otherwise, "loquendo de obediencia, ut est virtus ex qua obeditur," "non est nisi una virtus obediencie in uno homine," so that anyone "mortaliter" disobedient to even one precept stifles that virtue and can obey other precepts only from fear, cupidity, or custom (ASV, *Arm.* 54, t. 21, fols. 246v–247r). The argument was theological (Thomist in fact) and quite unrelated to the discourse common to the other polemicists, chiefly canonists, on either side. For *obedience* in its objective and often reified sense, see below, Ch. VI, n. 29.

associated with property rights and had not yet become public abstractions. One might, therefore, subtract obedience from the pope in this or that matter without thereby denying his papal estate or his quality as vicar of Christ.

That obedience might indeed be subtracted in precisely the two matters in question proceeded from an additional determination, namely, the episcopalist ecclesiology that had emerged in thirteenth-century France as the "Gallican" reaction to the aggrandizement of papal power at the expense of the bishops.[3] In papalist thought, Christ had established authority in the church in the person of Peter, whose successors were the popes, so that the other bishops held their official powers through papal mediation and subject to papal pleasure. The thesis of Gallicanism was that Christ had given authority to all the apostles, whose successors were the bishops, and since these held their rights and powers from Christ's institution, the pope might not remove or diminish them. If, then, the popes of the past century had taken over fiscal and collationary rights in the French church, this was a usurpation that could be legitimately cut back. A corollary would be that the bishops of, say, France had the legal capacity to act independently vis-à-vis the pope. Born in the thirteenth-century struggle in the church at large and in the University of Paris over papal privileges to the mendicants, crystallized in the struggle between Philip IV and Boniface VIII, developed in its political dimensions as the fourteenth-century church was more and more tightly integrated into the French body politic under the crown—the tradition of Gallican Liberty was cultivated without interruption in the University of Paris, where a century later the manuscripts of the earlier struggles were still being studied.[4] The tradition could now

---

3. For what follows see K. Schleyer, *Die Anfänge des Gallikanismus im 13. Jahrhundert* (Berlin, 1937), and above all Yves Congar, "Aspects ecclésiologiques de la querelle entre mendiants et séculiers dans la seconde moitié du XIIIe siècle et le début du XIVe," *Archives d'histoire doctrinale et littéraire du moyen âge,* 28 (1961):35–151. For the fourteenth century: Guillaume Mollat, "Les origines du Gallicanisme parlementaire aux XIVe et XVe siècles," *Revue d'histoire ecclésiastique,* 43 (1948):90–147; Jean-Pierre Royer, *L'Église et le royaume de France au XIVe siècle* (Paris, 1969), esp. 227 ff.

4. The continuing interest in the literature of Philip IV's quarrel with Boniface VIII is attested by the manuscript traditions of the treatises; see, e.g., Norma Erickson, "A Dispute between a Priest and a Knight," *Proceedings of the American Philosophical Society,* 111 (1967):288 f. The quarrel became more Gallican in retrospect than it had in fact been; when in February 1399 a Paris council of prelates abolished debts to the Camera they decreed "that henceforth the churches of the realm would remain in the pristine liberty they had enjoyed before Boniface VIII" (*ALKG,* 7:42 f.); see also below, Ch. VI, n. 1. For the University of Paris's tradition of Gallican interest, see Haller, *PKR:* 368 ff.; V. Martin, *Les origines du Gallicanisme,* 1 (Paris, 1939):243 ff.; *RSD,* 2:10–16. Guillaume de Saint-Amour's anti-mendicant work of 1256, *De periculis novissimorum*

emerge to figure in the French government's program of ending the Schism in opposition to the papacy. Subtraction of particular obedience was, in fact, Gallicanism applied to the Schism, and its association with the *via cessionis,* which was intrinsically anti-papalist itself, can be understood as the natural extension of a single line of thought.

Politics, however, does not proceed by natural extensions of ideas. Quite apart from the fact that threats of subtraction, or even the reality, were hardly apt to bring Benedict XIII to his knees ("St. Peter," he remarked, "was no less pope because he did not have obedience in the kingdom of France"),[5] there was the still more important consideration that the *via cessionis* was conceived as a European program of action for the secular powers of both obediences. Even if Benedict had accepted that *via* when it was offered him by the dukes, it would still have been necessary to bring the other Clementist princes into line and—a far harder task—to get the Urbanist princes to join in. Benedict's refusal made the work of diplomacy more urgent but not much more difficult than it already was, particularly since his rival Boniface IX was equally recalcitrant. While continued talk of union and cession was always required, it now had to be supplemented by new tones of coercion that might in time build up a European readiness to get rid of both popes; this work of publicity could only be accomplished by propaganda and diplomacy, both pursued together systematically, unremittingly, and over a long pull. While the principles of Gallican Liberty, alias partial subtraction, were too French in context and concern to serve this purpose, the general idea of subtraction perfectly formulated the subversive and anti-papalist lines of policy that could be developed into a theory to justify the final solution: deposing the two contenders. So it happened that partial subtraction was first accompanied and then rivalled by something else: "total subtraction" from a pope whose perpetuation of the Schism made him a schismatic, hence a heretic, hence incapable of exercising *any* papal functions, regardless of how legitimate his election had been.

By the end of 1408 this set of ideas had been accepted by enough of European public opinion to be decisive; to cite an odd and therefore

---

temporum, was still alive at the university in the late fourteenth century, when the Czech student Matthew of Janov found it there—H. Kaminsky, *A History of the Hussite Revolution* (Berkeley, 1967): 14—and when Jean Gerson declared (in 1402) that he had read it, along with all the other texts discussed in the *Roman de la rose*—in Eric Hicks, ed., *Le débat sur "le Roman de la rose"* (Paris, 1977): 172. Gallican constructions in another work by Saint-Amour were taken over by Pierre d'Ailly in a speech of 1386: see Alan Bernstein, *Pierre d'Ailly and the Blanchard Affair* (Leiden, 1978): 160.

5. In Ehrle, *Alpartil:* 368 (a recollection at Pisa, 1409, by Cardinal Nicholas Brancacci).

significant case, Abbot Ludolf of Sagan, writing in Silesia, could note as a matter of course that "now the universal church of both obediences deems it necessary to subtract itself from the obedience of both Gregory [XII] and Pedro de Luna."[6] The Council of Pisa proved him right, and Simon de Cramaud presiding at the session which declared both popes deposed could reflect that he too had been right when he had laid the foundations of total subtraction, coercion, and deposition as far back as the First Paris Council of February 1395 and then pursued this line as politician, diplomat, and theoretician in the following years. Without necessarily claiming that he was a genius in any of these fields of work, we must insist on at least his superior skill in all of them; otherwise we will fail to appreciate how much vision, art, and strength of character lay behind the Europeanization of the French program that he effected in the years 1395–1398. For details we still consult the work of Valois; but when we look for the story of success moving purposefully from beginning through middle to end, we turn to the political action of Simon de Cramaud. If there is one theme unifying the whole, it is Simon's drive for total subtraction as the ineluctable complement of cession and the essential preliminary to deposition.

Much of the story in these years turns on the Anglo-French peace negotiations (which issued eventually in a long truce and a marriage alliance); the dukes had not left for Avignon until these had been launched, and they had to cut short their stay and return to Paris when an English embassy arrived there in July to present conditions for peace so extravagant as to require the dukes' immediate decision.[7] Most of August was taken up with this matter, which included the question of English collaboration in pursuing the *via cessionis*. It was therefore Simon de Cramaud who headed a French embassy including both prominent lay personages and university spokesmen and charged with the task of presenting the *via cessionis* to King Richard II and the English political community.[8] Only when all this had been arranged did Jean Canart

---

6. Franz Bliemetzrieder, ed., "Abt Ludolfs von Sagan Traktat 'Soliloquium scismatis,'" *Studien und Mitteilungen aus dem Benediktiner- und dem Cistercienser Orden*, 26 (1905):477.

7. On 8 July the dukes told the pope that the king had urgently recalled them (AN, J 518, fol. 167v); cf. *RSD*, 2:322, for the haste of the return trip, presumably due to the English question. Cf. Valois, 3:64; also Palmer, *EFC*: 169–171, for the English envoys' demands.

8. Richard II's safe-conduct for Simon and his team was granted on 25 August, hence before the University of Paris's request for embassies on 25 and 31 August (below)—see F. Ehrle in *ALKG*, 6:201; Perroy, *L'Angleterre*: 366; Valois, 3:75 f. The text shows Simon's status as head of the embassy: "Rex . . . suscepit in salvum . . . conductum suum . . . Patriarcham Alexandriae, cum quater-viginti equitibus in comitiva sua"—report in Thomas Rymer, *Foedera*, 7 (London, 1709):808.

formally present the royal council with a report of the ducal embassy to
Avignon (24 August); he was followed the next day by the University of
Paris proposing new initiatives to "the king." These amounted to making partial subtraction the official policy of the crown, in the manner
that had now become normal: first let "the king" summon a council of
princes, prelates, abbots, and professors of the realm, the agenda to
include removal of two "impediments" to union—the pope's power to
collate to French benefices and to levy money from the French clergy;
then the university would make "some great and weighty proposals" at
the council about these and perhaps other issues. Meanwhile let embassies be sent to the powers of both obediences to propagate the *via
cessionis*; let the king protect advocates of the *via* from papal reprisals;
let enemies of cession be coerced into silence.

The Gallican premises of all this are evident enough; they are spelled
out in the written memorandum which the university laid before the
royal council on 31 August: removal of the "impediments" was "not a
withdrawal from due obedience to the pope but rather a return to
common law."[9] This last term, *ius commune*, could carry a heavy ideological charge inasmuch as it was both vague and equivocal (*ius* includes
several meanings distinct in English: law, rights, even justice). It was
indeed so used in lawsuits as a cheap way of casting doubt on particular
laws that seemed to favor one's opponent.[10] In our context it implied that
the papal powers which the Gallicans objected to were based on the
papal self-aggrandizement of the past century by means of decretals in
which the popes gave privileges to themselves, overriding the "old" or
"common" law that safeguarded the rights of the local churches.[11] Ideas of
this sort were held by many in the University of Paris and also by a good
number of its alumni who filled the prelacies of France; in due course
they would appear within the program of royal policy and, at and after
the Council of Constance, would come into their own as demands that
the restored papacy had to accept. Meanwhile, however, they were politically premature for reasons touched on above and obvious enough as
soon as one starts thinking in terms of strategy, tactics, diplomacy,
and public opinion. To have embarked on a doctrinaire adventure of a
specifically French sort, unrelated to the immediate task of creating a
European entity for the policy of cession, would have been useless and

---

9. Valois, 3:74; Swanson: 94 ff. For the Latin text see *Thes. nov.*, 2:1135 f.

10. Bernard Guenée, *Tribunaux et gens de justice dans le bailliage de Senlis à la fin du
moyen âge* (Paris, 1963): 90: "le droit commun n'est pas une preuve, c'est un effet
oratoire."

11. App. II, Pt. III, at end; cf. *DSO*, n. 428.

probably disadvantageous—and nowhere more so than in the crucial negotiations with the English.

Here, as often elsewhere in our story, we can only regret that the University of Paris in this period has not been given the sociological, prosopographical, and statistical study that would allow us to understand the play of interests and powers that determined its action. Were its proposals of 25 and 31 August just the maverick self-indulgence of its Gallican doctrinaires, expressing the Gallican self-image of the corporation? The question arises when we note that about this same time, "the university," or at least a significant section of it, deliberately floated a project for what would later become known as "total subtraction." This was a set of nine questions sent to the pope which suggested (they were questions only in rhetorical form) that if he continued to refuse to accept cession, he would be a schismatic, a heretic, and a perjurer; that he had no power to command the cardinals' obedience in anti-cessionism or to condemn his other opponents in this matter; that he could be judged and deposed by a council of his obedience; and that appeals against his acts could be lodged with a future general council of the universal church.[12] Apparently more extreme than the official proposals of 25 and 31 August, the Nine Questions were in fact more practical: they fitted in perfectly with the need for a European rather than a Gallican mode of coercion; they defined in advance the only possible program for the coalition of secular powers necessary to implement the *via cessionis*; and they foreshadowed the major treatise that Simon de Cramaud would write a year and a half later to validate just this program—which turned out to be the one that ended the Schism.

Finally, in this same busy week, the university produced its official determination for the *via cessionis* in a public letter "to all Christians" issued on 26 August 1395. We recall that its letter of 6 June 1394 had defined three ways to union but that at the First Paris Council the university had been political enough to apply this letter in an exclusively cessionist sense; then, during the Avignon embassy, its spokesmen had been told by the dukes to drop the other two ways (general council and arbitration) altogether.[13] Now it did so. The letter of 26 August[14] gave all possible arguments of theology and common sense (but not of canon

---

12. Valois, 3:71 f.; the text in Bulaeus, 4:753 f. Haller, *PKR*: 222, adds that six theses corresponding to the Nine Questions were nailed to the door of the papal palace in Avignon.

13. Valois, 3:69 f.; *RSD*, 2:312–314.

14. Valois, 3:70 n. 3, for the mss.; cf. Swanson: 95 (with an unexplained date of 25 August). I use the text in AN, J 518, fols. 29r–37v.

law!) to show that cession was not only best but uniquely obligatory,
indeed demanded by so wide a consensus of all the faithful as virtually to
give it the sanction of the Holy Spirit and the authority of a general
council.[15] Emphasis was put on the big political issue: "This way preserves
intact the honor of each obedience more than other ways which involve a
discussion of rights; for here the good repute of the realms, princes, and
peoples adhering to the one or the other remains unimpaired, without
any mark ever of error or infamy."[16] As for the two contenders, their
honor would also be preserved by their holy action of self-denial, in
which indeed they would be following the evangelical model of Christ,
whom they in particular were required to imitate. The tone was lofty,
perhaps indeed too much so, inasmuch as all discussion of the practicalities of executing cession (the *practica cessionis*) was eschewed;[17] and one can
be sure that the letter was conceived with great restraint as an instrument of European propaganda. The real sentiments of the university
were expressed in the other documents we have considered, reflecting its
conviction that voluntary cession could never be expected from Benedict
XIII—the university's envoys on the ducal embassy had of course given a
full report of how the pope had not only rejected the French program in
which the university had collaborated but insulted the "daughter of
Zion" by refusing to grant its spokesmen an audience in full consistory.[18]

The next move lay with the government: to establish the paradigm of
inter-obedience royal action for union on the basis of the *via cessionis,*
hence of the Paris letter of 26 August. It was one of the tasks of Simon
de Cramaud's embassy to England, which unfortunately had the additional duty of presenting Richard II with France's rejection of his new
peace conditions; it was at this point that the goal of formal peace was
practically given up in favor of a long truce bolstered by a marriage
alliance, which then became the subject of a new series of negotiations.[19]
Since the projected unionist drama could hardly be played on the now-
naked stage, Richard II did not allow the Paris professors who had come

---

15. AN, J 518, fol. 37r: "Sonat vox omnium fidelium . . . cessionem clamancium
. . . (f. 37v) quos sacrato instigante spiritu sic unanimiter loqui credendum est." "Ymo
consensus iste et universalis acclamacio fidelium pro via ista videtur equiparari consilio
quodammodo generali."

16. AN, J 518, fol. 32v: "Hec via magis salvat inviolatum honorem utriusque
obediencie . . . quam alie qualescunque iusticie discussive. Hic enim decus regnorum,
principum, et populorum alterutrum tenencium illesum permanet absque ulla unquam
nota erroris aut infamie."

17. See Simon's remarks, App. II, Pt. III, "Reply to 'It Is not Allowed,'" no. 5.

18. These complaints appear in the *gravamina* preceding the university's first appeal,
21 March 1396 (below) (Bulaeus, 4:801, 803); also in the appeal itself, ibid.: 818,
which uses the phrase "daughter of Zion" for the university.

19. Palmer, *EFC*: 171; Valois, 3:75 f.; Perroy, *L'Angleterre*: 365 f.

with the embassy to discuss their arguments with their Oxford counterparts; nor was Pierre Leroy allowed to present the gist of a massive
Factum he had brought along, crammed with canonistic dossiers for
cession, for its implementation by royal action, and against the other
competing ways.[20] Richard simply said that Oxford's professors were in
vacation, that he would pass the new Paris letter on to them, but that
his realm was not disposed to consider a change of policy so long as there
was no peace with France.[21] This was not so much a rejection as a
promise, which would in due course be kept; meanwhile Simon's mission had at least taken the indispensable first step of creating a European
dimension for cessionism simply by talking about it, however abortively, at the highest public level.

In any case, the rhythm of Anglo-French rapprochement had been
maintained and it continued to move, bringing a major settlement in
March of 1396: a twenty-eight-year truce (sealed on 9 March) and Richard's marriage by proxy to Charles VI's six-year-old daughter Isabelle,
celebrated by Simon de Cramaud on 12 March. It was during this stage
of the negotiations that Richard finally sent the Oxford professors the

---

20. The text of the *Factum* in Bulaeus, 4:755–772, with a title taken from the ms.
including the phrase "coram Rege Angliae, Anno 1395." Ehrle, *ALKG*, 6:201; Valois,
3:76; Perroy, *L'Angleterre*: 366; and others have supposed that this work was brought by
Leroy to England and then left there with the king to be forwarded to Oxford. There is
no evidence for the last point, and it is important to know that the Oxford letter of 17
March 1396 (see below) replies uniquely to the University of Paris letter of 26 August
1395, which is also the only text mentioned as submitted by the French in ambassador
Scrope's credential of 1 July 1396, printed in Perroy, *L'Angleterre*: 377 n. 2. In fact,
although the *Factum* was most probably written ca. August 1395, after the return of the
ducal embassy from Avignon (see the references to Benedict's responses, Bulaeus, 4:763)
and was evidently addressed to a king (e.g., p. 772: "ut ministerio vestro . . . Ecclesia
pacem consequatur"), this king certainly belonged to the Avignon obedience and was
most likely the king of France (e.g., p. 757, on the duty of princes to keep peace in the
church, "quod maxime in illis procedit, quorum praedecessores hoc facere consueverunt";
also p. 757': "non sufficit convertere ad obedientiam nostram . . ."; on p. 771 the
Urbanist pope is referred to as "adversarius"). The work also contains little notes by the
author to himself (p. 756: "et potest dilatari materia"; p. 760: "Et dilata materiam").
These and other indications, like the inclusion of several arguments made originally at
the First Paris Council by Leroy and others, suggest that the *Factum* was a sort of
enormous memorandum of all the arguments for cession and its implementation by the
kings; that Leroy compiled it originally as the basis of a speech he would make to the
French royal council at the end of August 1395, when that body was dealing with the
matter; and that while he probably took it to England as material for a speech that he
hoped to deliver, he would scarcely have left it there in its raw form. Thus, and this is
the point of the present note, the English in general, Oxford in particular, had no
canonistic justification of the French program at this time; when Richard II led his realm
into the *via cessionis* a year later (below), it was on the basis of his will alone.

21. Above, Ch. II, at n. 25; Perroy, *L'Angleterre*: 366.

Paris letter of 26 August and required their response, which was produced in haste by 17 March.[22] Its tone of hard-core Urbanism, the Schism
seen as nothing but the schismatic refusal of Avignon to submit to the
true pope in Rome, contrasted sharply with the Paris implication of a
dispute between two sides equal in subjective rectitude, to say nothing
of the realistic attitudes of John of Gaunt and indeed Richard II. In any
case, Oxford rejected the *via cessionis* as unwholesome in principle, since
the true pope should not have to give up his rights, and impossible in
practice without coercion by the secular arm and even subtraction of
obedience, neither of which could be admitted against the true pope. (It
is odd that the Paris *practica* of early 1395, which would have gone some
way towards forestalling the Oxford complaints about the inefficacy of
"nuda cessio," had not been made available.) The only sort of cession
Oxford approved would be Benedict's abdication and submission to
Boniface IX, who could then call a general council to clean up the residues of Schism. At the end, in fact, Oxford came out for a general council of this sort as the best way to union (and reform of the church).

At the same time, the English university could hardly defy its king,
who at a later date would indeed find ways to make it more agreeable to
his plans.[23] In the present case, Richard may have been satisfied with an
overall recalcitrance that enhanced his own bargaining position vis-à-vis
France but which on one point yielded to give him what he wanted, in a
remarkably complaisant passage that has usually been overlooked:

Finally, in order that this way [of a general council] or any other one discussed
speculatively among the learned [*inter litteratos viros*] may be put successfully into practice, there first has to be negotiation among the parties, and we
counsel this before anything else, so that it may be clearly seen which way
of peace the parties would decide to accept. And if they should consent to any
way whatever, that is all right with us as long as the unity of the church
be wholesomely reconstituted thereby.[24]

---

22. The text of the letter in Bulaeus, 4:776–785; more correctly edited by Gilbert
Ouy, "Gerson et l'Angleterre," *Humanism in France,* ed. A. Levi (Manchester, 1970):
56–73. See Valois, 3:77 f., 102 f., 108 f.; Perroy, *L'Angleterre:* 368–370; Palmer, *EFC:*
171–177; Swanson: 109–113. The letter excuses its defects by references to the short
time allowed for its composition (Ouy, "Gerson et l'Angleterre": 73—"brevitas indulti
nobis temporis")—hence my inference that Richard had waited several months before
seizing the Oxonians of the Paris letter.

23. Two recent articles by Margaret Harvey show how markedly, if reluctantly,
Oxford moved from its 1396 position when the king required more reasonable counsel in
1399: Oxford now agreed that voluntary cession was acceptable and that a general
council could be held even against the will of Boniface IX; had Richard not been deposed
soon after, Oxford would no doubt have bent still further. See "The Letters of the
University of Oxford on Withdrawal of Obedience from Pope Boniface IX," *Studies in
Church History,* 11 (1975):187–198; "The Letter of Oxford University on the Schism, 5
February 1399," *Annuarium historiae conciliorum,* 6 (1974):121–134.

24. Ouy, "Gerson et l'Angleterre": 72.

Since the "parties" (*partes*) were evidently the two popes, this was still remote from the Paris program of enforced cession; in fact it came close to Benedict XIII's *via convencionis*; but it left the room needed for the royal diplomacy that Richard was preparing to practice.

While the English envoys who brought this letter to Charles VI at Compiègne in the beginning of July refused to stay and debate with the French intellectuals—including Jean Gerson—who had come for the purpose, the political progress continued. Richard II met with Burgundy at Calais in August and agreed to send a mission to both popes declaring his full agreement with the policy of his new father-in-law and demanding that both popes accept the *via cessionis* by 22 July 1397.[25] Then at the end of October 1396 Richard and Charles met personally at Calais; there were conferences between Richard and the French uncles; on 4 November Richard married Isabelle in person; and on 5 November there was a comprehensive treaty providing for a peace conference between the two countries by 1 April 1397 with steps meanwhile to pursue the *via cessionis*. A joint embassy would be constituted in Paris by 16 February 1397 and would go to the popes to demand that they resign and "a third person" be elected by 29 September (later changed to 2 February 1398); there was probably talk about what to do if the popes refused, with subtraction of obedience at least mentioned as a conceivable sanction; furthermore the two kings would try to get Wenceslas IV of Bohemia and the Empire to join the unionist push, while Charles would bring in his ally Henry III of Castile.[26] All of these efforts were

---

25. *RSD*, 2:432, 448; Ouy, "Gerson et l'Angleterre": 50; Perroy, *L'Angleterre*: 378 f.

26. The text of the agreements of 5 November in Perroy, *L'Angleterre*: 414 f.; cf. Valois, 3:109; *RSD* 2:450–472, offers a memorable description of the Calais meetings. The French later claimed that the pact of 5 November included a promise that "in case the two papal contenders did not make peace in the church within the set term, the two kings would deny them all obedience in their realms" (a French memorandum of August 1398, in Valois, 3:119 n. 4, and in Perroy, *L'Angleterre*: 417); this is not in the text cited above but was allegedly in an original indenture (now apparently lost): "et aussi en fu faite une charte partie entre eulx deux." Perroy, *L'Angleterre*: 380, and Palmer, *EFC*: 177, believe that such a promise was indeed made. Harvey, "Letters of the University of Oxford": 189 f., argues persuasively that it was not, and I would add that Simon de Cramaud's treatise, begun about this time, includes an argument that France could and should begin subtraction alone if necessary. At the same time, it is hard to believe that the French in 1398 would have merely fabricated an earlier English commitment to subtract, and I suppose that the matter was discussed in the meetings leading to the agreements of November 1396, that promising statements may well have been made, and that these were not pinned down. Finally, while J. J. N. Palmer, "English Foreign Policy 1388–1399," in *The Reign of Richard II*, ed. F. Du Boulay & C. Barron (London, 1971): 103, alleges that the Calais agreements included an Anglo-French military expedition to north Italy for the spring of 1397, presumably in order to implement the *via cessionis*, he cites no direct evidence, only a few vague allusions, and in idem, *EFC*: 176 f., mentions the "projected Italian expedition" only as an "excuse" cited by the French crown later on for postponement of a peace conference.

made, except for the peace conference;[27] and although the popes remained obdurate, the net effect of such massive international diplomacy must have been substantial in the sense frequently noted above, that such actions were essentially theater, producing a public reality that had not existed before.

There were indeed many such efforts of diplomacy in these years, with batteries of royal councillors and Paris professors travelling all the roads of Europe seeking declarations in favor of cession and sometimes getting them, although never with the coercive and indeed deadly point that Paris, at least, knew to lie under the rose.[28] The payoff would come ten years later. One such embassy, however, was immediately important in its own terms; this was the one which Simon de Cramaud led to Spain on 20 March 1396.[29] Spending April in Aragon, early May in Navarre, the French scored a few insignificant successes before moving on to their real goal, Castile, where they spent four months negotiating a renewal of the Franco-Castilian alliance and the adherence of the young king Henry III to the French policy of *via cessionis*.[30] A year before, Henry had complained that he was being left out of the unionist negotiations in Avignon; now he received a full report along with texts of the *via cessionis* and its *practica* as developed in Paris[31]—also, of course, the flatter-

27. Palmer, *EFC*: 177.

28. Valois, 3:75–84; his negative estimate of the success of the whole diplomatic effort seems to me shortsighted. Cf., e.g., the text of the letter of 12 May 1396 sent by the University of Vienna to that of Paris, in Franz Bliemetzrieder, ed., "Antwort der Universität in Wien an diejenige zu Paris, 12. Mai 1396," *Studien* . . . [as above, n. 6], 24 (1903):100–105: the Viennese declared that they knew of "no more apt way than cession" but that for tactical and psychological reasons it would be better to ask their pope first rather than just present him with the other side's program; if, however, he refused, then the University of Vienna favored discussions "in ordinem ad viam cessionis" and continued coordination of its efforts with Paris. The most important Viennese convert to the French program was Henry of Langenstein; see Swanson: 107 f.

29. Valois, 3:83 f., 109 f., 123; Georges Daumet, *Étude sur l'alliance de la France et de la Castille* (Paris, 1898): 64, 201 (the text of Charles VI's letter constituting the embassy on 15 February). See Jesús María Arraiza, "Simón de Cramaud, su embajada a Navarra, y su tratado . . . ," *Príncipe de Viana*, 18 (1957):497–516, esp. 502 n. 18, for the action of the Navarrese preliminary envoys in Paris, where Simon advanced them 800 francs, to be repaid by their king.

30. The itinerary is established by José Goñi Gaztambide, "La embajada de Simón de Cramaud a Castilla en 1396," *Hispania Sacra*, 15 (1962):165–176 (but he wrongly says that Pierre d'Ailly was along). While there is no mention of Schism policy in Charles VI's letters constituting the embassy or in Henry III's constitution of his own ambassadors in reply, 20 September 1396 (text in Daumet, *France et . . . Castille*: 203 f.), that was in fact the issue that occupied the two parties; the renewal of the alliance may indeed have been only a pretext, since Henry III had already sworn adherence to it on attaining his majority, 16 January 1394 (ibid.: 62).

31. For Henry's complaint to the cardinals 30 July 1395, see *Thes. nov.*, 2:1136 f. His response to the embassy shows he was now fully informed: *Ampl. coll.*, 7:553 (cf. Valois, 3:66 n.); the Castilian text in Gaztambide, "Simón de Cramaud": 170–172.

ing attention of an embassy that included Colard de Calleville (a royal chamberlain), the now-prestigious theologian Gilles Deschamps (a royal councillor), and the obligatory squad of Paris professors, to say nothing of Simon himself.[32]

At the same time, Benedict XIII's envoys were on hand to solicit the king's adherence to their master's program, no doubt the same one announced to the Valois dukes a year before: a meeting between the two popes and colleges to discuss the question of legitimacy (Benedict's key point, a *via iusticie*); then if no agreement were reached, Benedict's promise not to leave the meeting before he had found a way to end the Schism.[33] A child could see the vanity of such a program, and it appeared nakedly enough to King Henry's veteran councillor Pedro Tenorio, archbishop of Toledo, who would later (10 June 1397) write a very frank letter to Cardinal Martin de Salva pointing out the utter impossibility of a *via iusticie* ("Who would want to be judged to have been schismatic for the past twenty years?") and the unique acceptability of the "sanctissima" *via cessionis*. Here and elsewhere, the letter shows that Simon's embassy had fully convinced the Castilians,[34] perhaps in ordinary conversations, perhaps too at the Segovia Cortes of August 1396, where Simon and Gilles Deschamps argued at length for cession in the presence of the papal envoys and of lay and clerical notables of the realm.[35] At the same time, Henry—or more likely Tenorio—deemed it politic to "combine the pope's way with that of the king of France" by first giving the popes and their colleges a chance to meet and discuss legitimacy—for no more

---

32. Colard de Calleville was currently a *bailli*; in 1398 he would be named French governor of Genoa, and his close relatives were prominent in the service of Louis of Orléans (Nordberg: 41). Deschamps had been a member of the royal council for at least a year (Valois, 3:45 n. 1).

33. The papal plan presented to the Valois dukes a year before was communicated to Henry of Castile by Simon's embassy; Benedict's own envoys to Castile at this time had come to request that Henry send an embassy to Avignon to hear the pope's intentions (Henry's statement to this effect in Gaztambide, "Simón de Cramaud": 170), but they must also have brought some information about what those intentions were. In any case, the pope's plan had not changed, and on 10 June 1397 Pedro Tenorio could remark (see the next note) that Benedict's plan recently brought to him by the bishop of Cuenca was hardly different from the responses to the dukes two years earlier. See also Valois, 3:97, for "*via iusticie.*"

34. The letter (dated "die dominica in Albis," i.e., Pentecost, evidently of 1397) was written in reply to Martin de Salva's complaint that Simon de Cramaud had fooled the Castilians into accepting an impractical French plan; it is edited by Gaztambide, "Simón de Cramaud": 169–176. It includes the Castilian text of Henry's plan (below). Tenorio must also have been the author of Henry III's letter to Martin of Aragon, 10 September 1397, which similarly defends cession against Martin's and Benedict's *via iusticie*; the text in Luis Suarez Fernandez, *Castilla, el Cisma y la crisis conciliar (1378–1440)* (Madrid, 1960): 213–223.

35. See App. II, Pt. II, "Benedict Must Obey a Council of His Obedience."

than thirty days—with the provision that, if a single pope emerged from these discussions, he might *not* be "the intruder" (i.e., the Urbanist contender) and that if no agreement were reached in this period, both popes would have to resign on the thirty-first day.[36] The Castilian addition was obviously only pro forma, as Tenorio more or less admitted when remarking that if thirty days seemed too short a time for such discussions, three years would also be too short.[37] In any case, Henry III was now fully in the French enterprise, even obligating himself at Simon's and Colard's insistence to a definite timetable of action: his envoys would present his plan to the pope in November but would move on to spend January in Paris; should they fail to do so, Henry would simply follow the Paris plan as then developed by the king of France and his council.[38] Meanwhile Simon and Colard pledged to keep Henry's plan secret until the end of January.[39] The timetable was presumably intended to fit in with the plan for Anglo-French unionist diplomacy noted above, which was formally adopted on 5 November 1396 but must have been envisaged far enough in advance so that Simon would have known about it at least before his departure from Spain in mid-September. At any rate, Castile would indeed join in the projected embassy.

It is instructive to see that Castile's adherence to the *via cessionis* involved the same sort of reduction of papal powers that was manifested in the French ideas of subtraction. On 24 September, four days after naming his ambassadors to Avignon and Paris, Henry III issued a "pragmatic sanction" prohibiting foreigners from drawing the revenues of Castilian benefices, a measure aimed above all at the Avignon cardinals.[40] We recall that Castile's original decision for Avignon in 1381 had been accompanied by a number of such nativist or territorialist demands as well as others designed more simply to reduce the pope's share of Castilian church revenues in favor of the crown's; thus the king had received permanent enjoyment of clerical tenths, and papal procurations were not to be levied on Castilian prelates.[41] England, in the other obedience, was

---

36. See above, n. 31, for the texts.
37. Gaztambide, "Simón de Cramaud": 174 f.
38. Ibid.: 171 f.
39. Ibid.; cf. Valois, 3:110 n. 1.
40. Gaztambide, "Simón de Cramaud": 166. Haller, evidently unaware of Henry III's action in 1396, nevertheless records evidence (*PKR*: 207 n. 1) of the continuing effectiveness of the pragmatic sanction in 1399 (*ALKG,* 6:299) and 1415 (BdeC: 467). Tenorio's letter of 10 June 1397 responds to complaints about the measure and holds forth the possibility of modifications; the complaints had referred to an ordinance "facta . . . contra omnes . . . cardinales" (in Gaztambide, "Simón de Cramaud": 169).
41. See above, Ch. I, n. 81; for the demands of 1381 see the text in Michael Seidlmayer, *Die Anfänge des grossen abendländischen Schismas* (Münster, 1940): 315–317.

the prime case of reduction of papal powers during the Schism, from first to last;[42] but similar things were happening everywhere, and if eventually all of Europe embraced the cessionist solution in its ultimate anti-papalist form—subtraction of obedience, deposition—it was probably because of these structural changes in the European status of the papacy and the ways of thought that went with them. Benedict XIII recognized these profundities of cessionism at once, and that, rather than mere self-interest, was why he said he would rather be skinned alive than accept the *via cessionis* in its Paris form;[43] the same may have been more or less true of his successive Urbanist rivals.

Events in Paris had meanwhile not stopped during Simon de Cramaud's long absence in Spain. It was indeed on 21 March 1396, the very day after he had left, that the university escalated its own policy of defiance, foreshadowed in the Nine Questions of the previous August, by making a formal appeal from Benedict XIII to a future pope.[44] The past half-year had given it reasons to do so: the Nine Questions had prompted an outpouring of papalist refutations in which the university was threatened with reprisals of every sort, including the penalties for lèse majesté, schism, and heresy;[45] Benedict had reportedly begun procedures that could implement these threats by action against the academy and its members;[46] he had also begun a massive diplomatic campaign of

---

42. Haller, *PKR*: 375–465; more recent accounts are not better: Perroy, *L'Angleterre, passim; Église*: 379–396.

43. Valois, 3:63. For the Paris form see, e.g., a treatise of late 1395, ASV, *Arm. 54*, t. 36, fol. 6r, refuting the "via cessionis utriusque sine aliqua cognicione veritatis vel diligencia circa illam, ut petitur." See n. 45 below.

44. Valois, 3:86 f.; the text of the original redaction in Bulaeus, 4:799–820; the abridged and perhaps official form is in AN, J 518, fols. 191r–200r.

45. Valois, 3:72–74; the list of refutations which he gives can be extended, e.g., by the treatise in ASV, *Arm. 54*, t.36, fols. 5r–35v, attributed by the table of contents [ed. Michael Seidlmayer, "Die spanischen 'Libri di Schismate' des Vatikanischen Archivs," *Gesammelte Aufsätze zur Kulturgeschichte Spaniens,* 8 (Münster, 1940): 238] to a certain Guillermus Benedicti. He rather sarcastically propounds the question, inter alia, "Utrum dominus noster papa . . . possit dici . . . scismaticus . . . quia expressius universitati Parisiensi vel alteri nec publicavit nec predixit mentem suam ad requestam et iuxta velle eorum" (fol. 12r). He rejects the whole basis of the French program by affirmatively answering the question, "Utrum procurans vel consulens quod veritas papatus seu scismatis non videatur de iure seu eciam agnoscatur, quod [*sic*] favorem impendat ipso facto scismati, et sic incidat in penam fautorie scismaticorum" (fol. 24v). Also: "isti [scil., the university professors] declarando et publicando papam hereticum vel scismaticum hostili animo animati sunt, et sic clare apparet ipsos crimen lese magestatis commisisse," especially "quia hoc fecerunt in publico in sermonibus publicis et commovebant . . . populum contra dominum nostrum" (fol. 17r). He goes on at great length to detail the penalties with evident relish.

46. The text in AN, J 518, fol. 195r, refers to Benedict's threats "coram multis et magnis" against the university and its members and adherents, namely, to proceed "ad

his own in both obediences, intended to secure support for his own *via iusticie* or at least to counter the French work for cession.[47] It is noteworthy that the university did *not* appeal to a general council, as suggested in its Nine Questions, for this way and every other judicial way were now categorically rejected in favor of a *via cessionis* whose likely consequences were made explicit: coercion and even deposition.[48] Benedict's rejection of that *via* in fact and principle had, it was said, made him objectively a "favorer" of schism; his subsequent actions had proven his "obstinacy" and "incorrigibility" as a schismatic; and if the resonance of these technical terms did not suffice to indicate his consequent heresy, the university spelled it out in still another standard locution: schism and heresy were like the little foxes whose tails were tied together.[49]

The matter was put even more clearly when the appeal was repeated, 3 August 1396, in response to Benedict's declaration of 30 May that it was null:

If he has not accepted the holy way [of cession] . . . but has tried to destroy it, should he not be considered obstinate? . . . Is he not to be deemed a favorer of schism? And if he defends his line obstinately, is he not suspect of

---

privacionem privilegiorum actuum et graduum scolasticorum, beneficiorum ecclesiasticorum amocionem, inhabilitaciones personarum, declaraciones scismatice vel heretice pravitatis, excommunicaciones suspensiones interdicciones ceterasque censuras et penas ecclesiasticas." It goes on to say that the university has heard that Benedict has deputed commissioners "qui suos iam processus inceperunt." See Swanson: 105.

47. Valois, 3:88–104.

48. The refutation of the *via concilii generalis* (as a way of judgement) is in the Bulaeus text (4:813 f.); it is followed by a refutation of even a council that would *not* judge; see also p. 809 ("ad cedendum compellendus") and AN, J 518, fol. 195v, where deposition is suggested in a pun: "non orietur habundancia pacis donec auferatur luna."

49. Referring to the dukes' requests and Benedict's refusals during the embassy of 1395, the appeal asserted: "Hec quaterna admonicio dictorum ambaxiatorum et vie cessionis refutacio nedum fautoriam scismatis sed eciam suspicionem, nedum suspicionem sed pertinaciam, nedum pertinaciam sed incorrigibilitatem in auribus quorumcunque fidelium censetur resonare" (AN, J 518, fol. 194v). And Bulaeus, 4:817: "Quare [*Bulaeus*: quanquam] ergo dominus . . . non admoneri possit super Schismate vel haeresi quae caudas habent adinvicem alligatas, verum etiam accusari si pertinax est et incorrigibilis. Et idem de quibuscunque criminibus tendentibus ad depositionem." The terms *fautoria, pertinacia,* etc., were canonistic designations of qualities relevant to a judgement of heresy; similarly the "tails tied together" (Judg. 15:4; cf. Song of Sol. 2:15) applied to the unity underlying diverse heresies, e.g., in a decree of the Fourth Lateran Council of 1215 (Mansi, 22:986): "Excommunicamus . . . universos hereticos . . . facies quidem habentes diversas, sed caudas ad invicem colligatas." See H. Grundmann, "Der Typus des Ketzers in mittelalterlicher Anschauung," *Kultur- und Universalgeschichte* (Walter Goetz Festschrift; Leipzig, 1927): 100. The university here implied but evidently did not wish to specify the formal equivalence of the schismatic with the heretic, something later spelled out canonistically by Simon de Cramaud; see App. II, Pt. II, "Schism and Heresy."

heresy? And if the church is scandalized by this, can it not withdraw from him, can he not be accused and even ejected or deposed from his see? Many popes have in fact been ejected from their see by the secular arm![50]

This was the language of total subtraction, and while one can only guess about the background of the appeal, the government's grand design was certainly served thereby. We may also guess that a government decision perhaps in February 1396 to convoke another council of the French clergy for 16 April was linked with the university's decision to lodge its appeal.[51] The government's decision was, however, cancelled; still another pure guess would be that it was because the crystallization of the English alliance in March, and the perhaps consequent delay and prolongation of the mission to Spain, would occupy the dukes of Berry and Burgundy and keep Simon de Cramaud away from the scene. But by 31 May the government switched again, summoning a Second Paris Council to meet on 15 August "to give counsel in the matter of church union." While it is hard to imagine who made this decision and why, it may be that here, too, the requirements of French diplomacy were decisive; for if Benedict XIII was to be requested once more to accept the *via cessionis*—and such was to be one aim of the Anglo-French entente—a decision of the Gallican church to that effect would have been useful. At any rate, this was the function actually served by the Second Paris Council.

But it is only because a brief account of the Second Paris Council happened to be copied into the *Libri de Schismate* that we can construct its history. The narrative sources overlook it; contemporary references to it are brief and rare; Simon de Cramaud totally ignored it in his several later statements of the sequence of events in the development of the French program.[52] Such neglect was hardly accidental and can therefore be instructive—in the first place, about the sort of thing likely to happen when major councils and debates were staged without clear direction from a properly led government (neither Berry nor Burgundy was in Paris) and without manipulative leadership from prelate-politicians (Si-

---

50. Bulaeus, 4:823.

51. For the decision and its inferable date, see Ehrle, *ALKG*, 6:203; the university appeal of 21 March must have come after at least several weeks of discussions and preparations—thus, e.g., the *procuratorium* for those formally registering the appeal with public notaries was issued on 12 March (AN, J 518, fol. 196v). When we recall that the crown constituted the embassy to Castile on 15 February (n. 29 above), we naturally imagine that the embassy, the decision to summon a council, and the university's appeal were all parts of a comprehensive political program.

52. For the text of the account—the source for all otherwise not annotated information given below—see *ALKG*, 6:206–224; cf. Ehrle's remarks (ibid.: 193 ff.) for the scanty sources and resulting scholarly confusion; cf. Simon's treatise, App. II below, and his refutation in 1402 of the Toulouse letter (AN, J 518, fols. 509v–510r) for silence about the Second Paris Council where the context might have called for mention of it.

mon de Cramaud was still in Spain; Jean Canart was no doubt with his master Burgundy at Calais, treating with Richard II).[53] One has the impression indeed that the royal council had no idea what it wanted the prelates to do when they assembled in Paris around mid-August—they were reduced to meeting by themselves on 16 August and electing their own spokesman, Bishop Bernard Alamant of Condom, who would lead them the next day to the royal residence of St. Paul and tell the king that they were there, "ready to do what he wished." Four days later, the royal chancellor Arnaud de Corbie assured them that they would indeed meet in proper form: in the royal palace, with the services of a royal secretary, and with two bishops commissioned by the crown to present the agenda. Neither of these two was a significant figure in unionist politics: Ithier de Martreuil of Poitiers was Berry's chancellor but also Benedict's appointee in his see, and his later views on subtraction seem to have been waffling; Jean Dodieu of Senlis was simply a veteran royal councillor.[54] Far from relishing such lack of guidance, the prelates recognized its disadvantages and perhaps dangers well enough to request that the king or at least the chancellor preside over their meetings; they were told that both had other things to do. As it happened, however, the chancellor did preside the next day, to further develop the council's machinery: the chancellor of the duke of Orléans was added to the panel presenting the agenda, and a set of two presidents and two sub-presidents were elected by the prelates. On 23 August there were preliminary formalities—a mass of the Holy Spirit, checking of attendance, swearing of the oath to give true counsel and keep it secret; then on 25 August Jean Dodieu recapitulated the public action since the election of Benedict XIII, and Pierre Leroy, just returned from an embassy to Central Europe and the Western princes of the Empire, reported on what had been achieved in the way of declarations for cession. At the end of the meeting, however, it was announced that the duke of Orléans would preside henceforth, as he did beginning the next day, sitting on a chair above the seats of the elected presidents.

Orléans began the actual proceedings on 26 August with an official stipulation that the *via cessionis* itself was royal policy and hence not to be debated but that the prelates were to deliberate "on the way to be followed in executing that *via.*" He then presented Bernard Alamant, who put the official questions on behalf of the crown:

---

53. Valois, 3:104 f.; Lehoux, 3:480.
54. For Ithier see the discussion of the Third Paris Council, Ch. VII below; for Jean Dodieu see Valois, 3:45, and cf. his ballot at the Third Paris Council (AN, J 518, fol. 407v)—he voted the government's line of total subtraction, but only as permissible, and only until Benedict should accept the *via cessionis*—compared to other votes, his seems unenthusiastic.

Whether in view of . . . our lord the pope's contumacy, . . . obedience should
be subtracted from him in regard to collations of benefices, exactions of
procurations and of other revenues of the Apostolic Camera, so that agreement
to the *via cessionis* might be more quickly obtained from him and that
union might be achieved in the church of God. Or indeed, should all obedience
be totally denied to him for these reasons and for obtaining so great a good?[55]

Alamant then went on to argue that partial obedience should indeed be
subtracted and that total might be. The former thesis was what the
University of Paris was pushing for, and its delegates began their arguments on 28 August; but Louis of Orléans intervened with an order
that "the matter was to be opened up" by a formal debate, a series of
speeches in which the university's spokesmen would alternate with the
pope's. It has been supposed by Ehrle, Valois, and others following
them that this action by Orléans was a partisan effort to protect the
pope's interests by making sure that each speech for subtraction would
be countered by one against it;[56] in fact, as we have seen,[57] the "opening" of
problems by contradictory debate was a normal procedure in the royal
council, and the form at least had been used in the First Paris Council.
While Orléans later supported the pope against his uncles, probably in
1397 and certainly from 1398 on, and began his actively anti-Burgun-
dian policy in the latter part of 1398,[58] there is no reason to think that in

55. The text is given in what seems to be a quotation with some paraphrase,
by Élie de Lestrange (ASV, *Arm.* 54, t. 24, fol. 252r—see n. 59 below): "Utrum
attenta diuturnitate presentis scismatis, domini nostri pape contumacia, malis scandalis
et periculis et contra fidem exinde secutis, . . . esset domino nostro subtrahenda
obediencia in collacionibus beneficiorum, exaccionibus procuracionum, et aliorum pro-
ventuum camere apostolice pro celerius exigenda via cessionis, quam supponebat indubie
meliorem, breviorem . . . [etc.], ad consequendam unionem in ecclesia dei; quinymo, et
an totaliter ob predicta et ad tantum bonum consequendum esset sibi omnis obediencia
deneganda." He identifies it as the official formulation presented by Alamant "ut dicitur
de iussu domini nostri regis" (fol. 260r). The much briefer summary in *ALKG,* 6:219,
accords with this.

56. Ehrle, *ALKG,* 6:205; Valois, 3:105 f.

57. Above, Ch. IV, at n. 48 ff.

58. E. Jarry, *La vie politique de Louis de France, duc d'Orléans, 1372–1407* (Paris,
1889): 133, 162, attributes Louis's conformity to his uncles' policies during the Avignon
embassy of 1395 to a combination of his youth (he was born 13 March 1372) and loyalty
to the crown. Palmer, *EFC:* 223, attributes a generally anti-cessionist tendency to Louis
during the 1390s but dates the beginning of his emergence as "a major disruptive force"
only from about the end of 1396 (after the defeat of the crusade at Nicopolis on 25
September). Nordberg: 110 refutes the view that there was a conflict between Orléans
and Burgundy as early as 1395, and on p. 232, referring to the treaty of 25 October
1396 with Genoa, he writes: "A cette époque les relations étaient toujours bonnes entre
Louis d'Orléans et Philippe de Bourgogne." For the change ca. 1398, see Nordberg:
233; Palmer, *EFC:* 223; Jean Schoos, *Der Machtkampf zwischen Burgund und Orléans*
(Luxembourg, 1956): 122 (cf. 108). It is not a matter for precise dating, and while
Louis's policies in favor of Benedict XIII and against the duke of Burgundy came to fit
together, their respective motives and origins were probably unrelated.

1396 he had cast either die. He had not rocked the boat in Avignon the year before, and even in 1398 he would formally accept his uncles' policy of total subtraction once the crown had officially decided on it. The point here is negative: unless we assume that Orléans must have been working in the pope's interest, we can find nothing in the manner of his presidency at the Second Paris Council to suggest manipulation, only an ordinary desire to get through the due forms as neatly as possible. To what end, we shall see later on.

As grateful as we must be to the anonymous participant who composed the report referred to above, we must also observe that he was a lazy man who excused himself from giving more than the barest gist of the speeches by observing that "the full texts can be obtained from those who spoke." It is mere luck that one such text does survive—the pro-papal "Allegations" of Élie de Lestrange, bishop of Saintes[59]—and that it tells us something of what the other side said, information that can be eked out by a few other bits of evidence. The important thing is that for reasons either of ineptitude, Gallicanism, or maybe both, the cessionist forces chose to push partial subtraction rather than total, although as argued above it was the latter which the current stage of French policy required. Bernard Alamant's formulation of the issue and the manner of his own determination of it have already been noted; insofar as he produced any argument for total subtraction, it was the rather modest point that, while the pope's whole Petrine office consisted in "feeding the sheep committed to him by Christ," he was killing them instead.[60] The university's chief spokesman, the theologian Pierre Plaoul, seems to have found nothing better to offer than something like *epieikeia,* or equity, that "pseudo-legal, meta-juristic panacea"[61] which could justify partial subtraction, total, or anything else. According to the no-doubt-colored report of Élie de Lestrange, Plaoul argued thus:

Although subtraction of obedience may seem contrary to the rights written down in laws and canons, nevertheless natural reason dictates that this cause of God not be subject to laws or canons or any other rights contained in writing or otherwise handed down but rather that these be entirely spurned and

---

59. The "Allegaciones episcopi Aniciensis, olim Xanctonensis" survive in the *Libri de Schismate,* ASV, *Arm.* 54, t. 24, fols. 252r–263v. Cf. *ALKG,* 6:222, for a bare reference to their presentation as a speech.

60. *ALKG,* 6:219, a very bare mention which can be supplemented by comparison with Alamant's commentary on the "Disputacio inter clericum et militem" (Biblioteca Apostolica Vaticana, *ms. Borghes.* 29, fols. 30r–31r), esp. 30r: suggesting how the "Knight's" case could be strengthened, Alamant wrote, "Non . . . est concedendum quod Petrus commissarius . . . possit omnia que dominus committens potest; ut patet quia eius commissio est ad certum, puta pastum ovium Cristi et non plus"—this becomes the basic point of his whole commentary. See M. Maccarone, *Vicarius Christi* (Rome, 1952): 231 f., for discussion of this passage.

61. Ullmann, *Origins*: 199.

this distressing case resolved no matter how, the faster the better, with all laws and rights put aside.[62]

More specifically, Plaoul argued that the "law of authority" could, and in the present case should, be superseded by the "law of necessity" and the "law of charity."[63] Easily refuted, these arbitrary bits of applied theology serve at least to point up the lack of any *canonistic* argument for total subtraction. Bernard Alamant mentioned totalism only as a possibility and did so "without allegations," although his degree was in law;[64] the great canonist Pierre Leroy seems never to have produced a totalist treatise and spoke now only for partial subtraction, perhaps because Gallicanism was the cause closest to his heart.[65] A few remarks in ballots later cast at the Third Paris Council by participants in the Second confirm that it was "particular subtraction which the university concluded in the previous council," and one such participant stated his understanding that the issue actually proposed for discussion at that time was indeed partial subtraction, not total.[66] One can only wonder

---

62. "Allegaciones," ASV, *Arm*. 54, t. 24, fol. 252r: "Licet substraccio obediencie videatur iuribus scriptis legum et canonum contrariari, attamen hanc causam dei (ut dicebant) non debere subesse legibus, canonibus, ac aliis quibuscunque iuribus scriptis vel qualitercunque traditis, dictabat naturalis racio—sed illis spretis omnino, casum hunc flebilem quoquomodo finiendum, et quanto celerius tanto melius, legibus et iuribus omnibus sequestratis."

63. Ibid.: fols. 261r–263r, e.g., in Lestrange's refutation, fol. 262v: "Etsi essent leges, ille . . . quas ipse nominat caritatis, necessitatis, et artis, adhuc subessent legi—vel saltim essent inferiores illa—quam vocat auctoritatis." Plaoul said much the same in 1406 (BdeC: 192).

64. *ALKG*, 6:219: "intulit . . . quod poterat procedi ad indifferenciam contra ipsum. Et hanc proposicionem fecit sine allegacionibus." For Alamant see in general A. Degert, "Alamand, Bernard," *Dictionnaire de biographie française*, 1 (Paris, 1933):1100 f. I find him described as "baccalarius legum, civis Mimatensis, legens in studio Montispessulani" (ASV, *Reg. sup*. 36, fol. 106r, 23 November 1362) and as "decretorum doctor" getting a parish church from the pope (ASV, *Reg. sup*. 45, fol. 26v, 19 December 1365); he got his bishopric of Condom in 1371.

65. *ALKG*, 6:221; cf. Haller, *PKR*: 359 ff., and Martin, *Origines du Gallicanisme*, 1:280 ff.

66. Thus in AN, J 518, fol. 403r, the vote of the abbot of St. Jean en Vallée, near Chartres: "Jasoit ce que en l'autre conseil derrenier fut mis en deliberaction d'aucune substraccion partiale; et en ce present conseil ait este propose et mis en deliberacion sur la substraccion de toute obeissance"; and fol. 368v, the vote of the theology professor Guillaume du Jardin: "oultre la substraccion particuliere concluse en l'autre concille par l'universite ma mere . . . , c'est assavoir que la collacion des benefices et la recepcion des pecunes audit pape Benedic . . . lui soit ostee. Et que les ordinaires donnent les benefices, ainsi comme les anciennes sanccions canoniques le tesmoignent. . . ." See also Pierre Plaoul's remark to this effect, BdeC: 64. Cf. also the anonymous "Iste sunt conclusiones ponende Parisius," ASV, *Arm*. 54, t. 22, fol. 26v, datable to his time by its reference to the contemporary mission to Paris of the bishop of Bazas (see Valois, 3:98; Ehrle, *ALKG*, 6:260); it mentions two such conclusions, one a subtraction of collations, the other of finances. See also Pierre d'Ailly's ballot, discussed below.

what would have happened had the latter been pushed; one theologian's vote known to us by mere chance may have expressed the views of many impatient professors: "The king should and can throw out the two contenders for the papacy without delay, as soon as can well be done, and cause both groups of cardinals to assemble in a certain place and elect a third, universally recognized pope of the whole holy church, with the two others punished as schismatics."[67]

Passing over the substance of the debate, which is only barely known to us and which would hardly have been different from later subtractionist-papalist controversies, we note how expeditiously Louis of Orléans handled the whole thing. The debate which began on 29 August was finished by 1 September, thanks to the duke's insistence on strict time limits, no digressions, and no real discussions of the points at issue. On 4 September the voting began, each prelate and professor delivering his opinion in writing, a process complete by 7 September and resulting in ballots from at least forty-three bishops and archbishops, perhaps an equal number of chapters, thirty-three abbots, five universities, and an unguessable number of professors. The texts filled three sacks, which Louis of Orléans collected and removed; when the prelates were finally allowed to go home on 15 September, they had no idea which side had prevailed, nor did they ever find out for sure— although two years later, Arnaud de Corbie would tell the Third Paris Council that while many at the Second had voted for subtraction, a majority had favored first asking the pope once more to accept cession. Valois believed him, Haller did not,[68] and the present writer would be surprised if anyone had ever counted the ballots at all. Everything said above about the course of the council suggests its phoniness, as a program to be run through because French diplomacy required it. As for the alleged majority opinion in favor of an option which the official opening speech had not even mentioned, it was obviously the only acceptable choice regardless of how many actually voted it: France's policy at this time was directed towards putting together the English-French-Castilian coalition that would indeed demand of both popes that

---

67. In his vote at the Third Paris Council the master of theology Pierre Fleurie referred to his vote at the Second (AN, J 518, fol. 370r): "La second proposicion que je di de present, et baillay en l'autre conseil, est que . . . le roy . . . doit et peut . . . les deux contendans du papat bouter hors sanz delay, le plus tost que bonnement faire se pourra; et faire que les cardinaulx des deux contendans qui seront de ceste opinion, assemblez en certain lieu, eslisent un tiers pape universel de toute sainct eglise, et punir les autres comme scismatiques." He had been one of the university's official representatives at the Second Council (ALKG, 6:219).

68. See PKR: 223 n. 5; Haller's argument was that Orléans was then dominant, that he wanted a vote against immediate subtraction, and that he would not have kept the ballots secret unless they had contradicted his wish.

they accept cession.[69] The contents of the three bags have not survived and one is tempted to guess that they were dumped.

So ended the university's effort to make its Gallican program the official policy of the French crown; we can guess that its failure resulted in a corresponding rally of the oppositional forces that had been pushed aside but not liquidated by the cessionist surge of the past two years. Already Jean Gerson's treatise, *De schismate vel de papatu contendentibus* of May or June 1396, had advanced nothing less than a categorical refutation of the whole basis of university policy up to this time: Benedict's repeated declarations of his readiness to act for union had to be at least provisionally accepted; he was therefore not obviously a schismatic; those who declared otherwise had no competence to do so; and there were no grounds for subtraction of obedience; at the same time, the *via cessionis* was useless without prior agreement from the other side, and it was both unwise and dishonorable to the University of Paris that its original three ways had been brought down to cession alone, with the others defamed as inept—a general council at least would be necessary in any case for the election of a new pope.[70] Pierre d'Ailly had argued in the same sense in his ballot at the Second Paris Council, defying the prohibition against any discussion of the policy of cession, urging that all possible ways be considered so as to facilitate an eventual agreement of both sides, and going on to demand a review of the First Paris Council itself, to begin with a true account of its deliberations—"and it is not inadvertently that I say a *true* account!"[71] Hitherto that council had had its public entity in the form of Simon's report of its work; d'Ailly now challenged this image by stating that the prelates had not then wished to present Benedict with only one way, as an ultimatum. Indeed he went still further and challenged the whole juridical structure of the Paris councils, for he said it was wrong for the French clergy to deal with the pope through the crown rather than in a general council of the Avignon obedience. In another *cedula* supplementary to his ballot,[72] he pursued his

---

69. Thus in February 1397 Raoul d'Oulmont could argue against partial subtraction because of the planned English-French demarche: "It was evidently the intention of both kings that no obedience be subtracted at least until these requests [to the popes] had been made" (BN, *ms. lat.* 1475, fol. 79v; the Latin is quoted by Harvey, "Letter of Oxford University": 122).

70. Gerson, *Oeuvres*, 6:24–28.

71. The text of his ballot in Ehrle, *Alpartil*: 476–480; see above, Ch. IV.

72. The text in Ehrle, *Alpartil*: 482–489. While the first *cedula* can hardly be understood except as a ballot ("Circa materiam . . . pro qua ex mandato regis prelatorum et cleri Francie congregacio extitit convocata, . . . ista michi videntur esse dicenda et . . . consulenda"), especially since d'Ailly did not figure among the speakers mentioned in the *ALKG* report, the second *cedula* gives the impression of supplementing the first, by spelling out the details of a *via* that d'Ailly's ballot had referred to but explicitly refused to set forth in detail (pp. 476, 482).

critique of the *via cessionis*, advocated Benedict's *via convencionis*, and broached the possibility of a general council even in case of a double cession, in order to elect a new pope. On the other hand he took care to accept the crown's policy of presenting the popes with a deadline for action (as would be provided in the English-French treaty of 5 November) and outbid the other side by declaring that if the contenders refused to accept any way at all, "they should be coerced not only by a general subtraction of obedience but indeed by real persecution directed against their lives." Whatever may be said about this last, it is clear that Gerson and d'Ailly—and one supposes others, apart from Benedict's curial apologists—were moving towards a counter-attack against Cramaud and the leaders of the politicized university.

We recall that the latter had already raised the question of partial subtraction before the royal council in August 1395 and that its leaders had again brought the issue to the fore in connection with the planning and transactions of the Second Paris Council. Direct results were nil, but the publicity had no doubt won ground for the future. In any case, the university returned to the charge in autumn 1396, voting for partial subtraction with virtual unanimity and taking strong steps to bring its decision before a royal government that was evidently felt to be rather unsympathetic.[73] It was probably because of conflicting viewpoints within the royal council that this body responded by scheduling a formal debate for February 1397. One of the pro-Benedict participants, Raoul d'Oulmont, read out a commissioned treatise that fortunately survives and informs us explicitly that the issue had been defined by the university's request to the crown: whether the king legitimately can and should subtract obedience from Benedict XIII "particularly in the two points under discussion, collation to benefices and collection of the accustomed revenues."[74] A treatise by Petrus de Muris which seems to fall in this period puts the question similarly: "Whether the papal contenders justly can and should be forced to abdicate the papacy, . . . so that if they refuse to do so subtraction can be made from them and obedience denied"; and he clearly means *partial* subtraction, "of all fruits and

---

73. Valois, 3:139 n. 1.
74. The "Allegaciones domini Radulphi de Ulmonte," BN, *ms. lat.* 1475, fols. 69r–80v, defines the issue on fol. 72v: "Quod rex non potest nec debet nec sibi licitum est domino Benedicto pape XIII° obedienciam substrahere vel tollere in aliquo de presenti, presertim quo ad duo de quibus tractatur: scilicet quantum ad collaciones beneficiorum etc., et quantum ad percepciones pecuniarias consuetas." In its final paragraph (fol. 80v; quoted by Valois, 3:139 n. 4) Oulmont, a graduate in laws, says he had written to refute a request for subtraction that had been made to the king, that he had done so on commission from the king, princes, prelates, and royal council, and that he had won. See Swanson: 116–119.

emoluments."[75] What it all added up to is not clear: Oulmont claimed to have carried the day, but the Monk of St. Denis's notice of the debate says that the subtractionists won, and his list of participants does not include either Oulmont or Petrus de Muris.[76] Perhaps the most significant thing was that neither of them felt any hesitation about attacking the *via cessionis* itself, which they said had been illicitly chosen (one recalls d'Ailly's statement to this effect in August 1396) and was in any case "irregular," "lamentable," and "miserable."[77]

Recalling in contrast the tremendous solemnity of the First Paris Council and its consequences, also Duke Louis of Orléans's prohibition of any discussion of the merits of the *via cessionis* at the Second Paris Council, we can sense how the university Gallicans' single-minded pursuit of partial subtraction in late 1396 was running counter to the force lines of a political situation now dominated by plans for diplomatic initiatives and by the consequent possibility of a revision of policy; Oulmont indeed made exactly this connection in his commissioned treatise.[78] It is at least interesting against this background to see that in January 1397, when the ambassadors of Henry III of Castile arrived in Paris after talks with Benedict XIII in Avignon, they denied that their master had ever fallen in with the French program of cession. Simon de Cramaud had to defend his honor by showing the sealed letters he had brought back from Spain, which proved that his report of his success had been correct.[79] We sense a gathering of anti-cessionist forces in Paris reinforced by an upsurge of papal initiative in Avignon. Benedict had of course been pursuing his own diplomacy for a *via iusticie,* the exact opposite of the *via cessionis,* and his circle of intellectuals now began to review the facts and legalities of the events of 1378. We know, for example, that

---

75. The "Tractatus sive allegaciones domini Petri de Muris," the author identified in the table of contents as a doctor of laws, is in BN, *ms. lat.* 1475, fols. 81r–88v. On fol. 81r the question is defined, "Utrum scismate ut prochdolor nunc vigente, iuste possint et debeant contendentes de papatu cogi ad cessionem papatus seu iuris quod habent vel habere credunt aut pretendunt, sic quod si renuant cedere, possit eis fieri substraccio et obediencia denegari"; cf. fol. 83v for the specification: "omnium fructuum et emolumentorum percepcio substracta."

76. *RSD,* 2:524–526 ("hii omnes . . . tandem subtractionem racionabilem concluserunt").

77. Thus Petrus de Muris wrote, "Quis ergo bonus vir . . . arbitraretur a via cessionis flebili, miserabili, infelicissima . . . inchoandum? Certe nullus" (BN, *ms. lat.* 1475, fol. 88r). And Raoul d'Oulmont wrote, "Si dicatur quod via cessionis est electa et contra illam non licet arguere, ut alii dicunt, . . . potest dici: a quibus est electa? Pluribus forsan videretur quod a non habentibus potestatem, quia [nec] per papam nec concilium auctoritate ipsius congregatum" (fol. 76r).

78. See n. 69 above.

79. *RSD,* 2:524.

papal envoys to King Wenceslas IV were prepared in January 1397 by detailed discussions in Avignon about the origins of the Schism.[80] It is impossible to move firmly from these scattered indications to a reconstruction of the political conjunction during the period, and if we nevertheless indulge in some speculations to this effect, it is only because this was the time when Simon de Cramaud wrote his major treatise, *De substraccione obediencie*, which, as we shall see, owed its origin to precisely the critical interplay of forces that has just been adumbrated. The duke of Burgundy had returned to Paris on 6 September 1396; Berry had arrived by the eighth; and Simon himself got back from Spain at the end of the month.[81] The coalition was together again in the seat of power, with the Castilian success behind it and important new victories to come. French policy in Italy, for one thing, was radically changed when the Milanese alliance, hitherto the foundation of the Franco-Avignonese *via facti*, was replaced by an alliance with Florence, engineered by Queen Isabelle and approved by Berry and Burgundy; it was sealed on 29 September.[82] England had already been won over, as we have seen; and again it was Berry and Burgundy who figured in the events leading to the treaty of 5 November. We can recall in addition that while the embassy to Central Europe and the Western Empire had secured nothing of comparable solidity, it had still garnered important statements in favor of the *via cessionis*, statements that along with other gains allowed the cessionists to claim that practically everyone was in favor of their program.[83]

---

80. The matter is discussed in enormous glosses, which I identify by the handwriting as Pierre Ravat's, on Bernard Alamant's treatise of 1392 (see above, Ch. II); the writer mentions (Bib. Apost. Vat., *ms. Barberini lat.* 872, fol. 77v) that he made certain of his points "die quarta Januarii anno XCVII° in presencia dominorum meorum Pampilonensis et Sancti Angeli cardinalium, Avinionensis, Aniciensis, et Tirassonensis episcoporum, B. Gilberti et Bartholomei Lupi doctorum et sacri palacii auditorum, ad electum in regem Romanorum propter istud negocium mittendorum." (And see Valois, 3:126 n. 1.) The two cardinals were Martin de Salva and Pierre Blau; the three bishops were Gilles Bellèmere, Élie de Lestrange, and Fernando Perez Calvillo (of Avignon, Le Puy, and Tarazona); other texts of these same discussions are published in Mansi, 26:819–836.

81. Valois, 3:107, 109; Lehoux, 3:480.

82. Palmer, "English Foreign Policy": 105 f., sees the alliance as the result of English pressure; Jarry, *Vie politique:* 167, assigns the chief role to Queen Isabelle acting in the interests of the house of Bavaria (her grandfather, Bernabo Visconti, had been deposed and probably killed by Gian-Galeazzo). Heidrun Kimm, *Isabeau de Bavière, reine de France 1370–1435, Miscellanea Bavarica Monacensia*, 13 (Munich, 1969):53 ff., develops an interpretation based on a putative alliance between Isabelle and Philip of Burgundy, directed against Milan and Louis of Orléans. Lehoux, 2:357, follows Jarry's view, notes Berry's presence at the signing of the treaty, and adds some evidence showing the leading role of Queen Isabelle.

83. Thus, for example, the author of glosses on the Oxford letter (see n. 90 below) wrote of cession as "quasi a cuncto populo approbata" (Ouy, "Gerson et l'Angleterre":

Political victories of such depth and breadth are never cost-free, and we can suppose that Duke Louis of Orléans in particular did not observe them with equanimity. His own major action during this period, the negotiation of a treaty with Genoa, 25 October 1396, giving Charles VI lordship over that city, no doubt scored points for himself but was not otherwise to his advantage.[84] Son-in-law of Gian-Galeazzo of Milan, husband of Valentina Visconti whom Queen Isabelle had banished from court earlier in the year,[85] erstwhile and perhaps present cultivator of hopes of Italian conquests in the context of the *via facti*, the young duke could hardly have failed to see that the successes of Queen Isabelle and the dukes of Burgundy and Berry represented a construction of power that could only be developed at the expense of his position in the family concern. If we now suppose that the anti-cessionist forces emerging in 1396 to challenge the policy of Berry and Burgundy must have had a Paris patron of comparably high estate, we can guess who it must have been. Orléans still, to be sure, played his proper role as part of the government dominated by his uncles; he did not yet venture to oppose their policy head on; but it is not hard to imagine him encouraging debates in the royal council or extending his protection in various ways over those active on Benedict's behalf. Perhaps he was thinking of his future in terms of the *via facti*; perhaps he was merely moving along the lines of force generated by the whole political situation.

Considerations like these allow us to set Simon's treatise in a political context and to interpret his own account of how he had come to compose it, an account which comes down to us in three not entirely concordant versions. It was at the Third Paris Council on 30 May 1398 that he replied to Pierre Ravat's criticism of his treatise by saying:

As for the objection that in the book attributed to me I said that the lord pope was a schismatic and that he acted badly, etc.: My lords, when I returned from Spain the lord chancellor had ordered some members of the royal council, and me, that I write about subtraction, and so I did. I recited the punishments due to schismatics as given by Hostiensis in his *Summa,* nor did I choose any opinion but merely argued for both sides, as can be seen.[86]

---

76). Pierre d'Ailly's ballot refers more generally to "a new unity recently come into being, in that all princes and prelates of both sides seek the church's unity" (Ehrle, *Alpartil*: 476); this, too, must be read as a tribute to the success of France's cessionist propaganda and action in the past two years.

84. According to Nordberg: 76–110, Louis of Orléans was acting here on behalf of his brother Charles VI rather than pursuing—as the traditional view has it—a personal policy of Italian intervention opposed by Philip of Burgundy (cf. the related issue discussed above, n. 58). Heidrun Kimm, *Isabeau de Bavière:* 60, notes the apparently good relations between Orléans and Burgundy at this time.

85. Heidrun Kimm, *Isabeau de Bavière*: 58–60.

86. BN, *ms. lat.* 14,644, fol. 60r (in BdeC: 25): "Quod autem michi obicitur quod ego in libro qui michi attribuitur dixi dominum papam scismaticum, et quod male fecit

This is the report in Guillaume de Longueil's *acta* of the council; Pierre
Ravat recorded the same statement differently:

As for what the bishop of St. Pons [scil., Ravat] says about my book, where
he says I call the pope a schismatic, I reply that after I came back from
the king of Castile, I found that the king of France had ordained that certain
clerics should examine whether the *via cessionis* was juridical. Seeing
this I began to dispute a question, whether subtraction might be made from
the pope in case he would not accept the *via cessionis*. And I argued
pro and con for the sake of disputation; I did not argue for the sake of deciding the question but only disputed it. It is thus wrong, what has been
ascribed to me. And it is true that I said that if there were heresy the punishments are great, as Hostiensis notes. . . . It is also true that I said that
unless he accepted cession, it would seem that he could be called a schismatic,
and in consequence it follows that we are not bound to obey him; this is
confirmed by what Hostiensis notes on c. *Cum non liceat, De prescripcionibus*.[87]

Ravat then referred to this later on:

As for what the patriarch had said about his book, . . . where he writes that
the pope would seem to be a schismatic and a heretic, . . . the patriarch
replied that he had not said this as an assertion, etc., and that he had written
arguments about this pro and con when he came back from Spain, at the
chancellor's command on behalf of the king.[88]

Finally, the treatise itself contains a statement in its later redactions to
the effect that Simon wrote it at the command of the king of France;
also, in all redactions, there are some phrases to the effect that he has
"set forth some texts of laws for those wishing to see," "reserving to

---

etc.—Reverendi domini mei, cum regressus sum ab Hispania, per dominum cancellarium fuit iniunctum aliquibus de consilio et michi, ut scriberem super substraccione, et
ita feci; et recitavi penas debitas scismaticis quas recitat Hostiensis in Summa. Nec elegi
opinionem aliquam, sed solum pro utraque parte argui, ut apparet."

87. ASV, *Arm.* 54, t. 21, fol. 194r: "Item ad hoc quod dominus Sancti Poncii dicit
de libro per me facto, in quo assero, ut dicit, papam scismaticum: respondeo quod
postquam veni de rege Castelle, repperi quod rex Francie ordinaverat quod certi clerici
examinarent, an via cessionis iuridica esset. Quo viso incepi disputare unam questionem,
an posset fieri subtraccio pape, casu quo viam cessionis non acceptaret. Et argui [*ms.*:
arguo] pro et contra, causa disputacionis non causa decisionis, sed disputavi predictam
questionem. Quare malum est quod michi ascribitur. Et verum quod dixi quod si esset
heresis, pene sunt magne, de quibus notat Hostiensis. Et est verum quod me submisi
correpcioni sancte matris ecclesie. Verum est quod dixi, nisi ipse acceptaret cessionem,
videretur quod posset dici scismaticus et per consequens sequitur quod non tenemur ei
obedire. Et pro hoc faciunt notata per Hostiensem in c. *Cum non liceat, De prescripcionibus*
[*ms.*: rescriptis]."

88. Ibid., fol. 235v: "Ad illud quod dominus Patriarcha dixerat de libro suo . . . in
qua [parte] ponit quod papa videretur scismaticus et hereticus . . . , respondit dominus
Patriarcha quod non dixerat hoc asserendo, etc., et quod de mandato domini cancellarii
ex parte regis, cum venit de Yspania, super ista materia raciones pro et contra scripserat,
etc. . . . ."

everyone his free judgement," and that he "does not intend to rashly assert anything or stubbornly defend it."

Let us note first of all that the earliest known redaction of the treatise contains neither the Hostiensis passages nor the statement that Simon was writing at the king's command and also that *all* manuscripts show a work that is by no means just a dispute pro and con—there is a cessionist introduction; the arguments against subtraction are refuted in a final section, and the body of the work is a polemic for both cession and subtraction. Either deliberately or because of a faulty memory, Simon in 1398 telescoped what he had done in 1396/1397. If he had indeed begun his work as a mere disputation pro and con, he very quickly developed it into a determination pro; and we can guess that if he eventually obtained a "royal" mandate for his treatise—no hard task for someone in Simon's position—he probably began without one. Even the first report suggests that the chancellor's order had been given to others (the "and me, that I write" is syntactically disruptive), while the version in Ravat's primary report actually states this. For the same reason we may believe that what the chancellor in fact ordered was treatises about whether the *via cessionis* was "juridical." For as we have seen, this was the issue formulated by Benedict and his supporters: the Paris *via* calling for a double abdication without judgement was by definition non-juridical, and the pope insisted on precisely a *via iusticie* in which the question of legitimacy would be determined. Simon hit back, therefore, by developing an alternative structure of legal thought in which the "non-juridical" *via cessionis* was shown to be canonically obligatory, with total subtraction of obedience appearing as the legal remedy to enforce that obligation on a recalcitrant pope.

What Simon had found when he returned from Spain was an incipient revision of royal policy in a sense unfavorable to what had become his personal cause, and with implications potentially disastrous to the English-French entente that was by far the most important line of action at this time. If we ask how such a situation could have developed in a government otherwise well controlled by Berry and Burgundy, we need only note that the late-medieval "state" was still very much a matter of personages and their presence: with Orléans in Paris and Berry, Burgundy, and Simon away, even a policy as carefully established as the *via cessionis* would not have been immune. We can also reasonably suppose that the extraordinary boldness of that policy as a repudiation of a legitimate pope's legitimate authority made it permanently vulnerable to doubts and the counter-arguments of prestigious authorities that could prompt or justify changes of mind in high places. Such changes could have sabotaged even the projected Anglo-French-Castilian embassy, intended to present the *via cessionis* as a legally binding ultimatum to both

popes. Thus if Simon's account of how he came to write his treatise
suggests that it was a political act of major importance, we can surmise
what his political purpose was. The penetration of the royal government
by Benedict's agitation had to be contained; the triple embassy had to
proceed; cession had to be re-validated as the unique way out of the
Schism; and a canonistically legitimate deposition theory, in the form of
total subtraction, had to be made ready for use as soon as the anticipated
papal refusals should be pronounced.

   The essence of the political act carried through in the treatise lay in a
deliberate jump from the prospectus of partial subtraction to that of
total. The prevailing line of thought hitherto had been this: voluntary
cession is the best way to end the Schism; it is in fact the only feasible
way; it is therefore obligatory; and the recalcitrant popes can be justifi-
ably pressured into accepting it by partial subtraction—denial of their
fiscal and collationary rights. We see this line in such texts as the
University of Paris's proposals of 31 August 1395 and its letter of 26
August 1395; we see it even more in the many papalist treatises written
against it, refuting each of its points by references to the canon laws that
exalted papal plenitude of power, denied anyone the right to tell the
pope what to do, and forbade any interference with the exercise of papal
rights. These treatises are always convincing, and it is perhaps no accident that treatises on the other side are quite rare. But even at first there
was an alternate line of development in cessionist thinking, observable
in some of the texts produced for the First Paris Council, also in the
university's Nine Questions of August 1395 and in some passages of its
appeals in 1396; it corresponded to the non-theoretical realities of will
and power invoked, for example, by John of Gaunt as early as 1392. It
can be represented as picking up the point that cession is obligatory and
moving on thus: therefore a papal contender who refuses to accept it is
perpetuating the Schism, therefore he is schismatic; persistence in schism
is formal heresy, therefore he is a heretic, therefore he is legally incapable
of exercising the papal office; such a schismatic-heretical pseudo-pope
may not be recognized as pope, therefore total obedience must be subtracted, and this clears the way to harsher action: punishment, coercion, deposition. We do not know how many or which members of the
body of public opinion in France were thinking this way by the latter
part of 1396. We have seen the theologian Pierre Fleurie voting in this
sense at the Second Paris Council, and he must have had colleagues who
held the same views.[89] We can also point to a set of glosses on the Oxford
letter of 17 March 1396 which may date from this time or shortly after;
the anonymous author held that "even the true pope in the present case

---

89. See above, at n. 67.

who has refused to resign when duly requested holds his dignity to the damage, detriment and scandal of the church" and "is to be regarded as a schismatic"; "one can then proceed to a new election." And: "According to the deliberation of the University of Paris, obedience can be licitly subtracted from even a true pope who afterwards becomes schismatic or impedes the union of the church."[90] No one, however, had developed this line of thought on the basis of canon law in a programmatic treatise. Pierre Leroy's *Factum* went part of the way, providing the canonistics of obligatory cession and of royal action to enforce it, but he did not validate the latter by any discussion of the recalcitrant pope as schismatic and heretic; for one thing he seems not to have believed in this rather extreme position; for another, his ardent Gallicanism probably disposed him against a total subtraction that would solve the Schism at the expense of the constitutional reforms envisaged by partial subtraction.[91] It was thus up to Simon to grasp the nettle, with his politician's realism, his careerist's ruthlessness, his canonistic learning, and of course the authority of his prestige. The resulting treatise turned out to be not only an instrument of policy but something more as well: perhaps the first

---

90. The glosses are published by Ouy, "Gerson et l'Angleterre": 73–79; the items quoted here are in glosses 14, 16, 34. Ouy identifies the handwriting of the glosses as Jean Gerson's and infers that he was also the author, annotating the Oxford letter in early July in preparation for the Compiègne meeting with the English envoys (ibid.: 50). I cannot say anything about the handwriting, but the substance of the glosses is entirely irreconcilable with Gerson's views at this time, which opposed any but a voluntary cession, called for prior agreement by the other side before requiring Benedict to promise to resign, and opposed any coercion by subtraction of obedience. Ouy, ibid.: 52 ff. recognizes these traits of Gerson's thought but regards them as consistent with an espousal of the *via cessionis* in principle, hence with a defense of the Paris letter of 26 August 1395 against the Oxford attack. But even apart from the fact that Gerson had by now moved away from any solidarity with the cessionist program (see above, at n. 70), it would be impossible to see him as the author of the glosses, which show a cessionist-subtractionist orthodoxy alien in substance and tone from Gerson's habitually independent stance. The passages quoted above would suffice to make this point; see also gloss 10: "Do you not know that almost all the kings, princes, prelates, decent men of learning, virtuous religious, and even the ordinary commoners . . . are zealous for that so very perfect *via cessionis,* moved as it were by an act of God's will?" Note also that the "deliberation of the University of Paris" referred to with approval in gloss 16 (quoted above in the text) was probably something like the Nine Questions of August 1395, which Gerson had attacked (*Oeuvres,* 6:22–24). With Gerson's authorship excluded, there is no reason to date the glosses exactly in July 1396. In any case, they credit the anti-cessionist thrust of the Oxford letter with an urgency that it would largely lose after King Richard II committed his realm to the *via cessionis* 5 November 1396.

91. For Leroy's Gallicanism see Haller, *PKR*: 359 ff., and Martin, *Origines du Gallicanisme,* 1:280 ff. In the Paris Council of 1406, Guillaume Fillastre remarked that Leroy, in contrast to Simon de Cramaud, had not spoken of Benedict as schismatic or heretical, as he would have done had he been of that opinion (*BdeC*: 208 f.).

systematic, detailed, and technically legalistic exposition of the right of the body politic to remove its unsuitable head.

Reserving a consideration of its argument to the next chapter, we can now attend to its political dimension. At a time when the whole program of the First Paris Council was being called into question, Simon picked up what he had proposed on that earlier occasion and pushed it further. At a time, moreover, when France's union policy was on the verge of its greatest achievement, the projected English-French-Castilian embassy to both popes, he constructed the legal foundations for what he expected to come next: sanctions against the recalcitrant popes, to be applied by the universal church of both obediences, acting through its secular arm, the kings. Thus he defined his subject:

> My first question is whether the kings and realms of both obediences can canonically subtract or entirely deny obedience to Boniface and Benedict if these two refuse to renounce the papacy. My second question is this: Supposing that one of the obediences has been more diligent in seeking out the better *via*, and has solemnly requested its pastor to accept the *via cessionis*, and he has refused to accept it [even] on the condition that the other contender would be willing to—can it in this case also canonically subtract obedience?

The second question—answered of course with a yes—was in part perhaps a response to criticisms like Gerson's, that cession could not be required unilaterally; but it was certainly even more the product of the politician's realistic understanding that other kings and powers might go along with France, but only if France in fact went: that is, France had to create the public reality that others would then adhere to.[92] We have seen that in the negotiations of early November 1396 Richard II was probably asked to commit himself to future subtraction of obedience if Boniface rejected cession and that whatever the king said, it probably fell short of a clear commitment; Simon's treatise either anticipated this

---

92. It is obvious in retrospect that most of Europe would not have withdrawn from the obediences of the two popes at the time of the Council of Pisa unless France had blazed the trial. But it was not obvious in the mid-1390s, when men like Jean Gerson opposed the practical *via cessionis* by supporting *voluntary* cession, and it is therefore worth noting how Simon de Cramaud brought a politician's style of thought to the matter. We recall that when the news of Clement VII's death reached Paris in September 1394, it was Simon who urged that a new election be deferred, otherwise "one would have to deal with two contenders rather than only one" (above, Ch. IV); in his treatise he argued that while it would be best to work on both contenders by applying the sanction of subtraction, if that were not possible then at least work on one of them, "for if we get the consent of one, we will then have half of peace" (App. II, Pt. II, "One Side Should Subtract Even without the Other"). At the Third Paris Council he voted for total subtraction but added that if that were not agreed upon, then he was for partial because "it would be less evil to disobey Benedict in some matters than to obey him in all" (AN, J 518, fol. 365v).

experience or learned from it. On the other hand, the textual tradition of the work shows that, while the author did not find it necessary to change its substance or structure once he had produced the form which we know, he did remain constantly engaged with the work from its origins in the latter part of 1396 through into 1397 and kept on augmenting and in some places revising it—partly by adding more canonistic authorities as they occurred to him, also by changes designed to cultivate the University of Paris, to sharpen the legal case for harsh measures against the popes, and to give the whole work a more emphatically European quality as a demand for coercive action by a concert of kings of both obediences. Thus "king" was replaced by "kings," and Simon changed the original beginning, "Every kingdom divided against itself is brought to desolation" (Luke 11:17, in *Decretum* 25. q. 2, c. 4), to a quote from Psalm 2:10, "Be wise now therefore, O ye kings," followed by an argument that this applied to the Schism, that "Every kingdom divided" and so on, and that the kings should not be dissuaded by charges of persecution when they used power and coercion to enforce what was necessary to the salvation of souls.[93]

It is also noteworthy that the treatise was cast from the first onto a genuinely supra-partisan level, with only the most obligatory, formal, and non-structural declarations of its author's adherence to Avignon's legitimacy. Otherwise, and this was not common in Schism literature before the conciliar phase, Simon carried the Paris principle of non-judgement into his every argument, creating the image of a controversy whose substance was so out of reach as to be irrelevant. In fact the treatise, after the modifications just noted, was used not only in France but in France's whole diplomatic action, with French envoys bringing copies of it, probably throughout 1397, to England, Spain, Avignon, Germany, Bohemia, and—as Pierre Ravat would complain on 3 June 1398—"pretty much the whole world."[94] We shall return to the context of this diplomatic action in Chapter VII.

---

93. *DSO*, "Introduction."

94. BdeC: 53, "suum librum misit in Angliam, et Hispaniam, et Avenioni." ASV, *Arm.* 54, t. 21, fol. 235v: "cum enim liber missus sit in Almaniam, Yspaniam, et quasi per totum mundum."

CHAPTER SIX

De substraccione obediencie

A GRADUATE in laws of the University of Orléans, a sometime professor of canon law at the University of Paris, Simon de Cramaud must have composed at least the obligatory questions and commentaries of a student and teacher; no such work of his, however, is known to survive. If we consider his character as a careerist, a Berry client, a high official in church and state, a tireless accumulator of properties and honors for himself and his family, we can suppose that had it not been for his political commitment to manage France's union policy, he would never have done any theoretical work at all once his Paris professorship had been abandoned in favor of ducal service. The written work he did produce was political in a sense going beyond the merely tendentious aspect of ordinary publicistics, for Simon seems to have deliberately created canonistic theory for political purposes. Those purposes provided the questions that he raised, determined the answers he would propound, and consequently imposed the structures of argument that would lead from the one to the other. When he had decided to get Touffou Castle for his nephew Jean, he had calculated exactly how he could win with the means at his disposal and had used them systematically, single-mindedly, and ruthlessly until he got the castle. Just so in his treatise: he calculated what would be necessary to justify subtraction and other measures leading to the termination of both papacies; he searched his memory and manuals for appropriate legal texts; and then he put these together in the logical order that would lead to the desired end. Here too he was single-minded, ruthless, untroubled by any principles of intellectual purity beyond the strictly functional ones of self-consistency and the need to avoid a too-blatant and therefore readily detectable falsification of his authorities. It is not that Simon de Cramaud was the only man who ever strained to prove a thesis, nor that a late-medieval writer should be held to modern standards of textual fidelity, nor that his main lines of argument are false—only that the functionalism of his style of thought is the key to an understanding of his work. While his treatise De substraccione obediencie, "On Subtraction of Obedience"—the principal work to be studied here—certainly deserves a place in any intellectual history of the time, its ideas and arguments make sense as parts of a whole whose essential nature derived not from theoretical exploration but from political practice. At the same time, the treatise profits from these traits of its composition; for in comparison to other treatises of the time, it is remarkably clear and powerful, while elaborating ideas more original and indeed subversive than others were currently advocating.

These remarks about Simon and his work may suggest a parallel with his more famous predecessor Guillaume de Nogaret, another careerist and politician whose practical needs led him to generate ad hoc theories of remarkable force. One is even tempted to wonder about the extent to which the publicistics of Philip IV's "subtraction" from Boniface VIII (Simon's term) may have provided a paradigm for the Paris cessionists and subtractionists of the 1390s[1]—a possibility indicated not only by the large area of congruence in ideas but also by some overt references and data of manuscript tradition which show that the facts and words of ca. 1300 were still alive a century later. The main line of continuity was of course in the area of Gallicanism, focused on the problem of the proper relationship between the French church and the papacy; but as far as Simon was concerned, the important matter would have been the deposition of a heretical pope, a subject much in Nogaret's mind. For if "On Subtraction" ostensibly aimed to justify subtraction of obedience as a stage in implementing the *via cessionis,* its concept of *total* subtraction turned on the thesis that the pope who refused to end the Schism by resigning was ipso facto a schismatic, hence a heretic, hence not capable of holding the papal office. It was therefore up to the church to compel his resignation, and while one might imagine several ways to get "his consent even under coercion," simple deposition obviously marked the

---

1. Nogaret's ideas anticipated Simon's to a great extent. He validated Philip IV's defiance of Boniface VIII's jurisdiction over the French clergy by a canonistic argument that the pope was a heretic, that since his heresy was notorious he was *de iure* no longer a pope, hence deprived of all papal power and subject to deposition by a general council to be summoned by the king of France. His own act of violence against the pope at Anagni was justified by the canonistic argument that any Christian could use force against a heretic. He went still further: not only heresy but any extreme danger to the church might be opposed by such means. Later he proposed a more constructive concept of the "king and kingdom of France as a part of the universal church, . . . composing indeed a church in themselves, called the Gallican Church." See Richard Scholz, *Die Publizistik zur Zeit Philipps des Schönen und Bonifaz' VIII.* (Stuttgart, 1903): 363–375; cf. the less appreciative estimate by Jean Rivière, *Le problème de l'Église et de l'état au temps de Philippe le Bel* (Paris, 1926): 126. References to the earlier quarrel appear in the writings of both sides in the subtraction controversy, including Simon's, with the issues appearing in post-Avignon perspective. Thus in 1402 he wrote, against the Toulouse letter: "Nonne Philippus Pulcher contra Bonifacium, qui propter avariciam suam inordinatam ecclesias istius regni inhumaniter gravabat[!], eciam concilium prelatorum regni sui, invito Bonifacio, congregavit?" (AN, J 518, fol. 508v); and in 1406 he spoke of Philip IV's "subtraction" from Boniface (BdeC: 217'). See also above, Ch. V, n. 4.

end of that road.[2] But as radical as these ideas were, they did not have to come from radicals like Nogaret. On the contrary, the doctrine of a papal right limited by the church's corporate interest, which might even require the deposition of a criminal pope, was well known to all canonists and accepted by many, as we learn from Tierney's *Foundations of the Conciliar Theory*; and the canonistics of this doctrine were ready to hand in Simon's day. Tierney has shown how the conciliarists could crystallize their theories out of this matrix; we add merely that Simon de Cramaud had got there first and used the common fund for his own non-conciliar purposes. How his mind was opened to this perspective is another question, and it is here that conjectures about a Paris tradition of radicalism might be in order.

We have already seen that in the years 1392–1394, when the royal government was slowly moving toward unionism, a number of Paris theologians were pushing the cause with great force—while the canonists were more or less silent. We may recall some of the dicta of that time. One theologian had observed that "while the office of the papacy is a dignity concerning the common good, insofar as it concerns the person of the pope it is a private good" and that "anyone has to renounce his own good, if no guilt would ensue, for the sake of securing the common good."[3] John of Moravia, a student in theology, had preached that both popes should be killed.[4] Jean Gerson in December 1392 had argued that a pope who refused to resign for the common good was guilty of mortal sin.[5] The authors of the University of Paris's letter of 6 June 1394, defining the three ways to union, had not hesitated to assert that a pope who refused to adopt one of these ways was a schismatic and a heretic whose orders should not be obeyed and who should be driven out of the church and perhaps killed.[6] We can also recall the Nine Questions of August 1395, the University's second appeal of 3 August 1396, and the glosses on the Oxford letter. Simon de Cramaud was certainly aware of some of these pronouncements, probably of all and indeed many more; it would be reasonable to guess that they were in his mind when, after the

---

2. App. II, *passim*. One wonders if Simon had read John of Paris's *Tractatus de regia potestate et papali*, which also argues canonistically that a pope may be deposed, for crimes or acts against the church's estate, by the people, at the instigation of a secular prince, or at the request of the cardinals; the text in Fritz Bleienstein, ed., *Johannes Quidort von Paris* . . . (Stuttgart, 1969): 95, 138, 140. The discussion on pp. 197–211 of the pope's legal capacity to abdicate is also suggestive, since it is linked to the legality of deposition.

3. Gerson, *Oeuvres*, 6:11; see above, Ch. I, n. 29.

4. Above, Ch. II, n. 91.

5. Above, Ch. II, n. 92.

6. Above, Ch. II, at n. 106.

death of Clement VII, his turn came to be vocal while most of the prominent theologians distanced themselves from unionist policy. At the same time, the politician must have sensed how inconsequential such dicta were in spheres lower than that of the academy and its authority, and the canonist must have realized that the bridge from theological radicalism to practical policy lay in the canon law. A government guided by theologians was a dream of the theologians, but a government run by lawyers was a fact. While we cannot go further than this, we can say of the treatise that it used the canonistics of its time to create a legally validated deposition theory that gave political effect to ideas originally propounded by the radical theologians of unionism.

It would of course be good to know more. Had Simon's way been opened by anything he had learned at Orléans—perhaps the "glossa Aurelianensis quae destruit textum," as the University of Paris snidely put it in a different context?[7] Did he have bright young men on his staff? Did he use his memory, his current reading, and his canonistic manuals to build up his dossier of authorities serving his purpose? This last seems likely; for Simon was certainly *au courant* of Schism publicistics, and a number of the treatises he had read—above all perhaps Pierre Leroy's *Factum* of August 1395 and the writings of the French cardinals Pierre Flandrin and Pierre Ameilh in 1378/1379—would have given him good access to the canonistic texts relevant to his interest. What he did with them was something else, and whatever an expert might say about his treatise's technical quality,[8] its political importance was overwhelming.

A few paragraphs at the beginning of Part II of "On Subtraction of Obedience" lay out the main argument. First is the evident fact that there is a schism in the church "which subverts the status of the universal church and brings peril to innumerable souls."[9] Then—added in later redactions—there is the "strong presumption" that the two contenders have kept the church in schism for their own advantage in wealth and honor and that if these end, so will the schism. On this basis, Simon propounds his thesis in two parts:

Even a true and undoubted pope is not to be obeyed but rather resisted if he does anything that notoriously scandalizes the church or works to the peril and subversion of souls.

---

7. In its appeal of May 1396, Bulaeus, 4:817.

8. While Simon seems far inferior to, say, Zabarella in creative canonistic ecclesiology (see Tierney, *Foundations*: 220 ff.), he wrote as a publicist, not as a scholar, and subtlety could hardly have been either desired or useful.

9. In the analysis that follows, passages from Simon's treatise that can be readily located in the English translation in App. II are not footnoted; citation of *DSO* notes refer to the annotations of the text in that edition, which also shows the changes in the text.

Much more so, therefore, these two contenders who strive to keep the papacy to the very great scandal of the universal church, to the subversion and peril of innumerable souls—if they refuse to accept the way of cession which alone is deemed fully able to eradicate the Schism. [*He later adds:*] Each of them prefers to keep the church lacerated and truncated but his, rather than see it whole under the other; thereby they not only scandalize the church but utterly destroy it.[10]

The major premise is the basic theoretical statement; the minor asserts a special case under it. The two are fused toward the end of the treatise in an offhand but very suggestive image: "Many say that if St. Peter were living today and there was a division like this one in the church which could be resolved by his abdication, he ought to be forced to abdicate by subtraction of obedience and otherwise." With neither obedience prepared to admit that its pope was anything but the true successor to Peter, Simon's case for subtraction of obedience and coerced abdication could only rest on a fundamental definition of the limits of papal power even under an unquestionably true pope. Here he could draw on two and a half centuries of canonistic exploration of precisely this matter—the tradition to which Tierney's *Foundations* has directed our attention. The argument for resisting the two contenders in the Schism is that simply by maintaining their respective papacies they perpetuate schism, damage the church, and therefore infringe the limits of any pope's rightful power; the issues of legitimacy posed in 1378 become irrelevant, as the French program required.

The proof of the double thesis begins with three canons from the *Decretum* in which three early popes rhetorically declared how unworthy of office they would be if they were to commit sins instead of suppressing them or if they were to destroy the work of preceding popes or to fail to work for the church's welfare (2. q. 7, c. 41; 25. q. 2, c. 4; 24. q. 1, c. 10). But these texts are at once brought down to a context of positive judgement by a passage from Johannes Teutonicus's *glossa ordinaria* about the mode of condemning a pope whose acts tended to destroy the church. The same theme is then pursued more concretely with the help of the Decretalists—Innocent IV, Hostiensis, and Johannes Andreae—who were concerned to carry on the Decretist search for a rational definition of papal power vis-à-vis the church, specifically by considering not only papal sins and crimes but also the extent of the pope's power to dispense against decrees of his predecessors and decrees issued by general councils of the church. The pope cannot dispense against the articles of the faith, or for sin, or in a way that would

---

10. See Buisson: 125–165 for "scandal" in the canonistic tradition: the pope was bound to "caritas" (in Augustine's sense) and his power failed in acts that scandalized the church.

imperil souls—in other words, he cannot offend God.[11] But Simon then cites Pierre Bertrand to prove that neither may the pope do anything that would scandalize the church, like giving church property to his relatives. This points to the more general concept of the *status* of the universal church as the supreme interest against which the pope might not act. Already set forth in Decretist writings, in which "the necessity to preserve the *status ecclesiae* was always presented as imposing a limit on papal authority,"[12] the idea was further developed by even the normally papalist Decretalists of the thirteenth and fourteenth centuries. Simon can thus cite Innocent IV and Hostiensis as transmitted by Johannes Andreae for the far-reaching principle, "If the pope should command anything that would presumably disturb the status of the church, or that would give rise to other evils too, then he should not be obeyed."[13] The discussion is then pushed from disobedience to deposition by a reference to the famous *glossa ordinaria* of Teutonicus on *Si papa* (40. di., c. 6), which adds the dimension of criminal procedure: the canon itself had said that a pope was liable to judgement for the crime of deviating from the faith—namely, heresy—but the gloss added other crimes like simony and adultery, if they were evident ("notorious"), and went on to note that if a pope persisted in these after being warned to stop, he was contumacious, "and contumacy is heresy."[14] If Simon de Cramaud had been writing as a scholarly jurist, he might have made what would seem to be a natural distinction between the relatively exotic case of a pope deposed for crime and the more fundamental idea of a papal power limited by the welfare of the church; had he been a conciliarist he might indeed have featured the latter. But nothing of the sort was required by a work of publicistics devoted to justifying subtraction and deposition, and the point here would be that when Simon needed authorities for this purpose, he found many of them, varying in lines of attack but pointing in

---

11. Tierney, *Foundations*: 48 ff., 56 ff., 89 ff., for the background.

12. Ibid.: 51. Buisson: 125–215 parallels Tierney's discussion of the canonistic consensus but derives it from "caritas" and scandal, as noted; the more productive corporatist criterion of the church's "status" is neglected. Simon used both lines of thought.

13. Cf. Tierney, *Foundations*: 89 f., and *passim*; Yves Congar, "'Status Ecclesiae,'" *Studia Gratiana*, 15 (1972):23–31.

14. See *DSO*, n. 120. This concept of formal heresy was very important to Simon's argument (and to the Council of Pisa); it is the legalistic view that all crimes come down to disobedience. Heresy was officially declared by a legal sentence carrying excommunication, which was never pronounced against sin or crime per se, only against persistence in sin or crime after official admonition, hence against contumacy. Thus we find in, e.g., John Hus, *Super IV Sententiarum,* ed. V. Flajshans (Prague, 1904): 616, "maior excommunicacio propter solam contumaciam est ferenda," attributed there to the Archdeacon, Huguccio, and Innocent IV. If heresy is condemned only as contumacy, then that is what it is.

the same direction. Had he wanted more, he could have found them with ease.[15] Subtraction of obedience was rooted in the canonistic tradition of the previous centuries.

But the positions established thus far did not necessarily require the remedy of subtraction and coerced abdication. It was all very well to say, as Simon did, "obviously if we keep obeying ours as pope and the others keep obeying Boniface, the church is not only enormously scandalized but lacerated and wholly destroyed." The equally obvious response, asserted again and again by Benedict's apologists, was that the others were the ones making the schism, which could be ended soundly only by their submission. The Urbanists said the same. We have seen Benedict XIII beginning his pontificate with the warning that a non-juridical solution would lead to "something far worse than schism, namely to adore an idol on earth"; and years later, in 1407, we find him allegedly securing Gregory XII's agreement not to submit to an imposed abdication, because "it is more perilous to force the popes than for the church to remain as it is."[16] In terms of a papalist ecclesiology there could indeed be no greater disaster to the church than the termination of the true line of succession to Peter by means of a coerced abdication on the part of the true pope and a subsequent new election by pseudo-cardinals (possible even if the latter were mixed in with the "true" cardinals). The problem could be solved after a fashion by the "habilitation" of each side by the other's pope, with accompanying cancellations of anathemas and the like as provided in the *practica cessionis*;[17] but none of this would happen if both contenders were deposed, and *this* mode of executing the *via cessionis* was an eventuality that Simon had to keep in mind in developing his theory of total subtraction.

It was his canonistic doctrine—that the universal church and its welfare (*status*) were the absolute values to which papal rights and powers were subordinated—which allowed him to refute precisely the papalist

---

15. Simon's incessant addition of supplementary authorities to his treatise is shown in *DSO*, text and apparatus; it is obvious that he first contented himself with a merely adequate dossier, then improved it as new items came to his attention. Thus, e.g., the important canon *Anastasius* (19. di., c. 9; see Tierney, *Foundations*: 38, for its frequent citation) appears only in one ms., and the *gl. ord.* on 89. di., c. 2, which would have been ideal for Simon's purpose, is not cited at all, although the canon itself is (see *DSO*, n. 150; cf. Tierney, *Foundations*: 130). Many other examples can be given; see n. 69 below.

16. Pierre Ravat's glosses on the treatise (*DSO*, ms. *J*) refute many of Simon's arguments by merely insisting on the difference between a true pope and the schismatic contender (see below). For Benedict's position in 1394 see above, Ch. IV, at n. 17; for the agreements of 1407 see *Ampl. Coll.*, 7:768 f.

17. App. II, Pt. III; cf. *DSO*, n. 345.

stress on legitimacy; for the welfare of the church—its faith, its property, its unity, its governance—was the central matter, quite distinct from legitimacy, which once denied a central place, ceased to count for anything. Simon could therefore point to the situation of fact in which neither contender could be really sure of his right and in which "today it is more clear that both are schismatics than has ever been clear about one of them; . . . this is undoubtedly clearer to the universal church than which of them is the true pope and which the intruder."[18] There is much more argument to this effect, including a supra-partisan review of the events of 1378 and the conflict of opinions that had taken place then. Simon de Cramaud was perhaps the first major publicist in the Avignon camp to concede that the case for the cardinals' action in 1378 was matched by an opposing case that was not obviously less cogent: "Although our side does not lack the right, it lacks the ability to prove it."[19] This and other practical considerations were set forth at length to prove that no judicial solution, whether by arbitration or general council, would be possible. Underneath the practicalities, however, was the canonist's sense that by this time the issue of the Schism primarily concerned the welfare of the universal church comprising both obediences, whose *status* would not be impaired by ignorance of which papal line was the true one. As Simon put it in a later work, the important thing was not to know which side was schismatic but to end the Schism in such a way that "neither side would be schismatic."[20]

The argument was developed in legal terms by reference to a number of key canons and commentaries, in the first place the canon *Si duo forte contra fas* (79. di., c. 8; a rescript of the Emperor Honorius in the year 420):

If two men shall have been ordained [pope], perhaps irregularly, by the rashness of contending parties, we permit neither of these to be priest [i.e.,

---

18. Tierney, *Foundations*: 77, characterizing the Decretists and by implications at least some of the Decretalists, writes of "their underlying conviction that the maintenance of the *status ecclesiae* was more important than any other consideration whatsoever." This viewpoint probably lay behind Simon's invocation of the universal church to cut the knot of conflicting assertions of legitimacy by the two obediences.

19. App. II, Pt. II, "Theses." In later works Simon put the point even more strongly; e.g., in his glosses against the "Allegations" of Martin de Salva, BN, *ms. lat.* 1475, fol. 37r, he cited the cardinals' re-election of Urban after the tumult had died down, his coronation, the long period in which they treated him as pope, and their declaration in official letters to the rulers of Europe that they had made a canonical election. In his glosses of 1402 against the Toulouse letter, he emphasized the doubts which many in the Avignon obedience had felt from the first and still felt in 1402: see the texts in Ch. I, n. 79, above.

20. BN, *ms. lat.* 1475, fol. 48v ("et neutra pars erit scismatica").

pope]. But we deem that only he should remain in the apostolic see whom the divine judgement and the consent of the whole body shall have elected, by a new ordination, from among the clergy.

Inasmuch as the Great Schism had begun with everyone's refusal, in effect, to apply this canon, and since the *glossa ordinaria* on it seemed to require a preliminary judgement of irregularity by a general council before the canon could be applied, and since finally Gratian had noted that the canon did not apply when only one of the elections was irregular —it was not obvious that *Si duo* implied the *via cessionis* at all, let alone in 1396 when so much time had gone by. In fact it could be used in a contrary sense.[21] But Johannes Teutonicus had referred to *Si duo* as meaning that "if scandal be feared then both elections are to be quashed," and Huguccio—as Simon recalled in a later work—had explicitly noted that a contested papal election was irregular when "grave scandal" arose from it. This line was also confirmed by canons which decreed that to keep a benefice unjustly was equivalent to getting it unjustly.[22] Once again we see the direction imposed by the canonist's sense of *status ecclesie,* a line of thought itself imposed by France's political decision to end the Schism by giving up her insistence on the rights of Avignon; for Simon's exegesis of *Si duo* was a canonistic argument that the rights and wrongs of 1378 no longer mattered, the nineteen years of schism and scandal did, and the sense of the canon was that both contestants be removed. At the same time, this simple argument developed from one ancient canon had to be amplified by a canonistic elaboration of the legalities relevant to the fact of irregular election,. the import of scandal, and the remedy of coerced deposition.

These legalities, however, were not derived from the canons dealing with papal power and papal elections but rather from the massive corpus of jurisprudence dealing with the right to a benefice, in particular an episcopal one. Here Simon moved within the canonistic tradition which constructed law for the pope vis-à-vis "the church" on the analogy of the corporation law defining the relationship between the bishop and the canons of his cathedral, or indeed the bishop and his diocese in general.[23]

---

21. It is so cited in Pt. I of Simon's treatise (see *DSO*, n. 74) and in anti-cessionist treatises, e.g., the "Scripta cuiusdam doctoris Tolosani" (he was Aymeric Natalis) in ASV, *Arm.* 54, t. 20, fol. 187r, where the essential premise that *both* elections were *contra fas* is not admitted, so that *Si duo* is reduced to mean only that "ille solus debet permanere qui legitime fuerit electus."

22. *DSO,* n. 202. For Huguccio see Simon's glosses against Salva's "Allegations," BN, *ms. lat.* 1475, fol. 37r (quoted in Kaminsky, "Cession": 306).

23. For the canonistic tradition see Tierney, *Foundations*: 142–149, 184–190, and *passim*; the main figures are Hostiensis and Johannes Monachus. An example would be

It was, of course, more than just an analogy, rather an identity once the special quality of papal untouchability had been neutralized by the arguments already canvassed; and the issue of the Schism could be brought down to the relatively simple problem of how a dubious or contested claim to a benefice should be resolved in the interest of the universal church. Here Simon's big gun was a decretal of Pope Innocent III, *Nisi cum pridem* (X. 1. 9. 10), sections of which stated that a bishop might have to refuse an appointment if the people of the diocese were "maliciously" set against him and that he might be allowed to resign his see if necessary to avoid a grave scandal. A similar point had already been made by the pseudo-Isidorean decretal *Mutaciones* (7. q. 1, c. 34), "transfers of bishops may be made for the sake of the common utility and need" (which Simon also cited);[24] but *Nisi* applied the principle in great detail to the gritty cases of ordinary church life, and Innocent IV's comment on *Nisi* went even further: to avoid scandal a bishop might not only be allowed to resign but could be forced to do so if the welfare of the church in question could be preserved under another. His legal principle in general was the Roman-law maxim that Public Utility Is Preferred to Private.

The mentality that made such a maxim applicable has to be appreciated. A bishop was the successor to the apostles in bringing Christian doctrine and holiness to his people; he was indeed married to his see. How, then, could his tenure of that see be thought of as his private utility or property right? One answer would be that his see was understood by the canonists as a corporation, whose *status*—or "public utility" —was the supreme interest that its president or "procurator" (the bishop) had to serve above all; his own interest in being bishop was thus in contrast merely private.[25] But private and public did not then have the dichotomous meaning that they have today, for the modern notion of the public sphere as *sui generis* was not yet well developed. The private or individual good was, rather, part of the public or common good, and the difference could be expressed as one of quantity. As Simon put it, the common utility is to be preferred to the singular "just as the greater

---

the gloss quoted in *DSO*, n. 132, where a canon concerning papal elections (*Si duo*) is used to elucidate one about episcopal elections. Simon was of course aware of what he was doing; see, e.g., the passage in App. II, Pt. II, "Subtraction Is Fitting and Expedient," about proceeding "from like to like."

24. *Nisi* had been cited to the point in Simon's speech for the First Paris Council, ca. 1 February 1396, but only as corroboration for *Mutaciones*; here the order is reversed, with *Nisi* bearing a heavy weight of argument.

25. Tierney, *Foundations*: 96–131; cf. Simon's formulation (App. II, Pt. II, "Fraternal Correction") that the pope is the "dispenser" of church property, not its lord or possessor; in 1406 he used the more technical term *procurator* (BdeC: 120).

to the lesser," and as we read in another treatise of the time, "the private utility is included in the public."[26] Hence, to call a bishop's right to his office a "private utility" did not deny what we would consider its public import but only defined its quantitative value as less than that of his church's "estate." It was on the basis of such conceptualizations that benefices could be routinely treated as property for legal purposes, as we have seen.[27]

The terms used in "On Subtraction" for the relation between pope and papacy show a similar reification: occasional phrases representing the papal office as the headship of the corporate entity of the church—as in "a question only of the presidency of this or that person"—are far outnumbered by phrases like "to have a right to the papacy," "to possess" the papacy, "to keep that part of the papacy which he possesses," "the contenders try to keep the papacy because of greed and ambition." At one point, Simon wrote, "neither of the contenders has enjoyed *peaceful possession* up to now," the emphasized words being a technical term in the law of benefice rights.[28] What, after all, was the obedience to be subtracted if not a certain set of revenues and rights, both possessed as property? Even Benedict's spokesman Pierre Ravat thought in the same style, for example, when he replied to Cramaud's disingenuous claim that it was not a question of seizing the pope's property but only of subtracting obedience: "What property does the pope have in the realm of France *but* obedience—collations, provisions of benefices, procurations, vacancies, and the like?" He went on to note that this property was substantial, worth "ten or twenty thousand florins [a year]" (in fact it was more like 160,000!). (It is instructive that in two reports of Ravat's same discourse the words here translated as "What property" are given as "What goods" and "What right"—*que bona habet papa?* and *quod jus habet papa?*; thus, "goods" and "right" were evidently inter-

---

26. See above, Ch. I, n. 22. Mager, *Entstehung*: 13, observes that the common good was not the good of a collective but the good that the members shared among themselves. Ewart Lewis, "Organic Tendencies in Medieval Political Thought," *American Political Science Review*, 32 (1938):855, observes that "the good common to the individual members" is the only meaning of "common good" that she has ever found in the sources. For Simon's formulation see App. II, Pt. II, "Subtraction Is Fitting and Expedient," and for the quotation that follows see ASV, *Arm.* 54, t. 36, fol. 5v.

27. See the discussion of this matter in Ch. I, above, and Ch. VII, below. (The "private" property under discussion here was in the revenues of the benefice and enjoyment of its rights; the endowment and rights themselves belonged to the church.)

28. App. II, *passim*; for a similar reference to peaceful possession, see BN, *ms. lat.* 1475, fol. 15v: "neuter istorum fuit possessor pacificus papatus"; in canon law, three years of peaceful possession were required for a right in a benefice to be unquestionable— see Guillaume Mollat, "Bénéfices ecclésiastiques en occident," *Dictionnaire de droit canonique*, 2 (Paris, 1937):427 f.

changeable.)[29] We can thus understand how Simon could even include Augustine's *Quo iure* (8. di., c. 1) in his battery of arguments for royal action: the papal contenders may not say "What has the king to do with me?" for the answer would be "What does possession have to do with you? For possessions are possessed by the laws of kings." It was not the papacy as we would understand it that was so possessed but, rather, the "obedience" in which the papacy materially consisted; for the pope's rights in France (and elsewhere) came down to ecclesiastical property rights similar as such to the local ones that by this time were thought of as secured under royal protection, litigated over in the courts of the king.

One guesses that neither of the two Innocents mentioned above had ever dreamed that his assertion of papal power to enforce the public utility against mere bishops (in *Nisi cum pridem* and the gloss thereon) would or could be used to get rid of a pope. The pope had the right, by virtue of his plenitude of power, to dispense from the law—as Innocent III had put it.[30] But the *glossa ordinaria* of Bernard of Parma on this passage had noted exceptions to the pope's power to dispense; other commentators had pursued the matter in their glosses; and Bohic had put the whole tradition together in his manual for Simon to use. Thus we find that his use of *Nisi cum pridem* is followed by a careful explanation that its rationale is based on divine law, which binds the pope, for he cannot dispense from it. The authorities here are the glosses just mentioned, which refer to the canon *Sunt quidam* (25. q. 1, c. 6), cited here, too, by Simon.[31] Finally, long passages from St. Augustine establish

---

29. ASV, *Arm. 54*, t. 21, fol. 234v: "Quid enim vel que bona habet papa in nobis vel in regno Francie nisi obedienciam: collaciones, provisiones beneficiorum, procuraciones, vacancia, et similia, de quorum substraccione agitur de presenti? Et mirabile est dicere quod contra magis simplicem hominem regni Francie delatum de heresi, non fieret execucio in una vinea x. florenorum ante declaracionem criminis per iudicem ecclesiasticum, nec illius occupacio; et quod contra papam fiat in valore x. vel xx. milia flor." The version in BdeC: 53 reads, "Quod jus habet papa in regno, nisi obedientiam? . . . cum obedientia sit totum jus debitum superiori." Simon thought in the same terms, as in his response of 30 May 1398, BdeC: 26: "emolumenta illa seu obedientia," and in his reply to the Toulouse letter of 1402, AN, J 518, fol. 518r: "Obediencia quam rex noster cum regno et certis sue dominacioni subiectis fecit Clementi et Benedicto plus de multo ponderat quam omnium aliorum qui ipsis obediverunt. Maius enim emolumentum habuerunt Clemens et Benedictus et sui cardinales de terris predictis quam de omnibus aliis." For the sums actually drawn from France by the papacy before subtraction, see Favier, *Finances*: 475, 580, 687 f.

30. In c. *Proposuit* (X. 3. 8. 4): see the index and notes to *DSO*. Another important canon with its glosses was *Magne* (X. 3. 34. 7); see *DSO*, n. 117.

31. *DSO*, n. 116. Cf. Tierney, *Foundations*: 89 f., where the canonistic discussion of papal dispensing power is presented in reference to other decretals than those Simon cited; the substance is the same. See Buisson: 216–269.

that it is indeed a matter of divine law for a bishop to set the interest of his flock above his own and to avoid scandalizing them. In any case (and this sort of pleonasm is characteristic of the legal argumentation of the time), the pope must submit himself to the law he has decreed for others; the *glossa ordinaria* on 18. q. 2, c. 5 says so, citing the Roman law which discourages a guardian from building his house so high as to block light from reaching his ward's house: "Any act that he must *ex officio* prohibit another from doing, he himself should not commit." Public law for both state and church was in fact being developed from Roman laws about wardship, the rights of the trans-personal entities being assimilated to those of a minor;[32] and this whole development resonated with the reifying mentality that apprehended the "public" entities in terms of their property right, the *status* which they possessed just as did every other individual or corporate holder of privileges.

The full weight of *Nisi cum pridem* could be brought against the two papal contenders only on the premise that the *via cessionis* was in fact the sole feasible way to end the Schism and its attendant damage to the church. Simon established the premise in several different ways at various places in his treatise, most notably by the proofs already mentioned that neither a general council nor arbitration would be possible and by an argument based on France's action in approving the *via cessionis*. For this step had been taken by a council of the French clergy which, together with the clergy of Castile, who had subsequently approved that *via*, constituted much the larger part of the Avignon obedience. Hence these councils were equivalent to a general council of the church recognizing Benedict XIII and were therefore legally entitled to command him; for, according to the *glossa ordinaria* on 15. di., c. 2, "in matters of faith or matters which concern the status of the universal church, the pope is subject to a council." The gloss is misquoted and the whole argument is obviously forced,[33] although it deserves attention as a sign

---

32. Thus, for example, both *Quod omnes tangit* and the principle of inalienability, two of the most important elements in the conceptualization of a public sphere subject to public law, derived from the Roman law governing wardship; others were imprescriptibility and indefectibility. The assimilation had indeed been set forth in the late Roman Empire ("Res publica minorum iure uti solet," *Codex*, 2. 54. 4), but its creative force came in conjunction with real developments in government during the later Middle Ages. See Ernst Kantorowicz, *The King's Two Bodies* (Princeton, N.J., 1957): 374 ff.; Post, *Studies*: 169.

33. See *DSO*, n. 257, and, for the marginal note in ms. *C* at this point, *DSO*, App. II: the gloss did *not* mention the status of the universal church. Whether from ignorance or dishonesty, Simon kept using this incorrect formulation in his later works, e.g., the glosses against Salva's "Allegations," BN, *ms. lat.* 1475, fol. 35v (where the reading is "universalem statutum ecclesie"); also his glosses on the Toulouse letter of 1402, AN, J 518, fol. 514v; also his letter of 1401 to the archbishop of Canterbury, *Thes. nov.*, 2:1247. See Tierney, *Foundations*: 53 n. 1.

pointing to the future conciliar implementation of the *via cessionis*; but neither it nor the other arguments were intended to do more than indicate what had already been officially set as French policy and did not therefore have to be argued afresh. Both *Si duo forte contra fas* and *Nisi cum pridem,* with their attendant structures of canonistic elaboration, could therefore be taken as defining the two popes' canonical obligation to abdicate and, in consequence of their refusal, their status as violators of canon law. Simon had no difficulty finding condemnations of *that* and could push on to his big point: "Those moreover who seek to keep the papacy against the sacred canons are true schismatics." Glosses declaring that "there can be no schism without heresy" and "he who persists in schism thereby makes a heresy" were then applied to "those who say that they are not bound to resign for the peace and union of the church, and who thus keep the church divided in schism." Their heresy was notorious, which meant that it did not have to be proven, and it had been condemned in advance by the canons so that no further legal process was necessary: since the two contenders were already excommunicated by the canons, they had no more papal power—at least in regard to this matter. In the later redactions of the treatise the consequences of all this were spelled out; the contenders were subject to the penalties for heresy: "deposition, deprivation of all property, coercion by armed force, and delivery to the secular court, according to the canons; but according to divine law, fire and burning to death!"[34] We see here the true sense of subtraction as a stage on the way to something else, a prospect revealed again and again in little phrases: "subtraction or worse," "more effective measures," "proceed more harshly," "other measures will have to be taken."[35]

Taken by whom? We have reserved until now a line of argument that Simon introduced very early as a supposition, "that the kings are obliged . . . to put an end to this schism and bend all their forces to obtain peace in the church . . . obliged both as private men and as kings."[36] The thrust of this rather commonplace assertion was in fact radical, inasmuch as it was developed into the argument that a concert of kings should act to coerce the popes—should, in other words, exercise jurisdiction within the church, in defiance of the church's supreme head(s). It is instructive to see the most general justification of this point, in the statement that "the church militant is nothing but the congregation of the faithful here on earth"—that is, it includes the laity, not just the clergy. While this was the common view of the canonists, whose concept of the church as congregation of the faithful was integral to their

---

34. App. II, Pt. II, "Schism and Heresy."
35. See Buisson: 183–205 for this whole line of thought.
36. App. II, Pt. II, "Suppositions."

corporatist ecclesiology, it had been used politically in the time of Philip
IV to justify the king's action in curtailing clerical liberties, and this
was also its import in Simon's context.[37] In any case, the later redactions
of the treatise, with their beginning "Nunc reges intelligite!" taken from
Augustine's justification of royal power within the church to persecute
evildoers, show what Simon had in mind. The theme was pursued with
a number of passages from the *Decretum* reflecting the role of secular
power in the Christian Roman Empire and also with an invocation of the
"old laws" [i.e., in the *Decretum*] according to which "kings used to
judge delinquent clerics." But the prime text was Isidore of Seville's
"The princes of this world sometimes hold the highest offices of power
within the church in order to . . . command by the terror of discipline
what priests are unable to accomplish by the word of teaching. . . . Let
the princes of this world know that they must render an account to God
for the church whose protection they have taken over from Christ" (23.
q. 5, c. 20). Simon commented: "May the kings only hear how this
canon speaks to them!" Elsewhere he put it more clearly still: "O Christian princes who today 'hold the highest offices of power within the
church'—hurry and act!"[38]

Others more radical than Simon (Wyclif, the Hussites)[39] were using the
same canon to justify a regular integration of the church into the territorial polity, but here as always Simon had no interest in anything
beyond implementing the *via cessionis*; the remarkable thing is that the
totally non-doctrinaire politician shrank from no doctrinal extreme to
make his point. One wonders whether it was not perhaps Simon de
Cramaud who invented the form of the Paris Councils, in which a
secular-political assembly of the clerical estate under the crown acted as
though it were a synod capable of authoritative resolution of religious
issues. We have already looked ahead to see him at the Paris Council of
1406 pronouncing just this claim, that the king in council with the
prelates had judicial competence even in a religious matter like heresy.
While this almost casual repudiation of the past three centuries of the

---

37. Tierney, *Foundations*: 41 ff., 134–141 (esp. 136 f.), 202 ff., with a quotation of
Zabarella's definition, "ecclesia nihil aliud quam congregatio fidelium," which Tierney
says "only expressed the common opinion of his age" (p. 203). For the same thought in
Antequam essent clerici of ca. 1296, supporting Philip IV, see Pierre Dupuy, *Histoire du
différend d'entre le pape Boniface VIII et Philippes le Bel* (Paris, 1655): 21–23.

38. In a letter of 1402 to King Henry III of Castile, BN, *ms. lat.* 1573, fol. 33v:
"Eya ergo cristiani principes qui hodie intra ecclesiam potestatis adepte culmina tenetis,
confestim occurrite!"

39. For Wyclif see Howard Kaminsky, "Wyclifism as Ideology of Revolution,"
Church History, 32 (1963):63; for the Hussites see Howard Kaminsky, *A History of the
Hussite Revolution* (Berkeley, 1967): 153, 188.

church's drive for privileged autonomy presupposed the de facto Gallicanism that had taken shape in fourteenth-century France, as well as the peculiar development of the French church under the Avignon papacy, it also corresponded to the lessons of Simon's own experience as a careerist occupying multiple offices in church and state simultaneously and one might almost say indiscriminately—but always within the framework of the polity, the only structure that mattered.

It is clear, moreover, that the situation of royal power *within* the church by the arguments noted above was understood as something other than an alien intervention: the kings were to act as ecclesiastical judges, and the canons applying to the latter were now to apply to *them*. Thus the comments of Bernardus, Hostiensis, and Bohic (on X. 1. 29. 1; 5. 12. 6) to the effect that crass negligence in a judge is a grave sin, the context and apparatus showing that they were thinking of a bishop or other church magistrate, were taken as proving that the kings sinned mortally if they did not "compel both contenders to the way of peace." The canons carefully distinguishing between the secular and priestly powers—Gelasius I's *Duo sunt* (96. di., c. 10), Innocent III's figure of the sun and moon (X. 1. 33. 6)—were used in the opposite sense, of a dualism within the church that allowed the secular powers to act when the spiritual ones were not "well ordered." Also, while the standard canonistic doctrine held that the secular powers were to come into play only when the spiritual powers requested it, there were cases of exception noted by "the doctors": thus, "if a secular judge sees a cleric *in flagranti delicto,* he can arrest him without fear of excommunication, even if he has not been requested to do so by the bishop"; this was taken as a model for coercing the pope. As in the application of benefice law (above), this argument by analogy was developed quite consciously. Thus, citing the Roman law which provided that a judge could sequestrate the fruits of a contested property if the parties refused to submit to judicial settlement, Simon argued that this remedy could be applied by kings to the Schism, for "even if these laws do not speak formally of the papacy, . . . we have to proceed from like to like." There were indeed many such likenesses. Thus kings could use their power to subtract obedience on the analogy of canons ceasing their church services to bring an erring bishop to reason, or on the analogy of an interdict against a magnate from whom satisfaction could not otherwise be obtained, or on the analogy of the constraint imposed on the cardinals to force them to make a papal election.[40] A more direct argument was based on the decretal *Licet* (X. 1. 6. 6), which laid down special rules for papal elections—a two-thirds majority and automatic excommunication for

---

40. App. II, Pt. II, "Fraternal Correction."

violations—and explained the difference between these and ordinary episcopal elections by noting that only for the Roman see was there no superior to judge cases of doubt. Simon squeezed this in his lawyer's way to yield the conclusion that the kings could act even though the contenders had not been formally convicted, not only because the crime was notorious but "because in the present case there is no superior before whom a judicial action could be brought," and "while one may proceed judicially against one who has a superior, by going before his judge, one has to proceed by force [de facto] against those who seek to usurp the papacy against the sacred canons."[41]

The concert of powers called for in the treatise included not only the kings but all holders of de facto temporal sovereignty.[42] It also included the emperor, but only as one ruler among others; this appears from Simon's argument that a general council was not feasible because no one was generally recognized as competent to convoke it, not even the emperor:

Also, we would never attend at the will of the emperor—or rather the king of the Romans—for he has made himself a party to the dispute; history shows that when emperors convoked councils to settle schisms, they had not taken sides for one party so officially as now. In any case, the Empire today is fragmented and our kings regard themselves as emperors in their own realms, nor do they recognize a superior or defer to the king of the Romans, lest they diminish their dignity in any point.[43]

While these formulas of royal sovereignty were by this time old and rather commonplace (although still not universally accepted),[44] they had not usually been generalized as a picture of the actual political world of Europe. In fact everyone, including Simon here and elsewhere, recognized a certain degree of prestigious preeminence in the imperial title (the Emperor Sigismund's role at the Council of Constance proves it), but it was nothing to count on, and Simon's model for action was simply a realistic image of the loci of political authority within the congregation of the faithful. One guesses, however, that it was based more or less subconsciously on Simon's sense of France as the kingdom par excellence—the most powerful, the richest, the most prestigious in culture and religion, with her kings not merely "Christian" but "most Christian" and with a long history of a special relationship to the

---

41. App. II, Pt. II, "Theses," "Fraternal Correction."
42. Although Simon speaks almost only of kings, there is one reference (DSO, at n. 121, q.v.) to "reges et dominos temporales qui non recognoscunt superiorem."
43. App. II, Pt. III; and see DSO, n. 351.
44. See Walther Kienast, Deutschland und Frankreich in der Kaiserzeit, 2 (Stuttgart, 1975):309–311, and passim; cf. R. N. Swanson, "The University of Cologne and the Great Schism," Journal of Ecclesiastical History, 28 (1977):8.

SIMON DE CRAMAUD.

TOMBEAU *pres le Grand autel du costé de l'Evangile centre la clotûre du chœur de l'Eglise Cathedrale de St Pierre de Poitiers*

oxford collect? gaignieres.

ce dessein renferme a l'original

PLATE I

The tomb of Simon de Cramaud, originally at the choir of Poitiers cathedral. It originally had a statue of Simon *gisant* and another one standing against one of the pilasters; these were destroyed by the Huguenots in 1562. The painting and cornice were added after that, as replacements. The rest of the tomb was destroyed in the French Revolution; this is a drawing by Gaignières, ca. 1700. *Bibliothèque Nationale,* Paris.

PLATE II

Duke Jean of Berry, escorted by his dead kinsmen, arriving at the gate of heaven. From the *Grandes Heures* of the Duke of Berry, 1409, Paris, BN, *ms. lat.* 919. Jean's brother, Duke Philip the Bold of Burgundy (d. 1404), is in the rear wearing a high fur hat; his face and hat are identical to those in the portrait originally in the Charterhouse of Champmol, a copy of which is now in the Musée de Versailles. *Bibliothèque Nationale,* Paris.

PLATE III

Simon de Cramaud (?) at table with Duke Jean of Berry. The month of January in the *Très riches heures* of the duke of Berry; the picture was painted by the Limbourgs 1413/1414, and the hitherto unidentified prelate, in what seem to be the red robes of a cardinal, would most likely have been Simon de Cramaud, who became a cardinal in May 1413. By this date he was the only cardinal close to the duke. It is unfortunate that only the duke's face is individualized. *Bibliothèque Nationale, Paris.*

papacy.[45] "On Subtraction" was, in the first place, a justification for action by France and could hardly have been conceived of as such without this sense of French eminence; hence its extension to the other political powers of Europe inevitably bathed the latter in a French light—not always realistically, as a German commentator would observe.[46]

At any rate, Simon's combination of canonistic corporatist ecclesiology with an awareness of the French reality of royal lordship over the territorial church made him free to imagine a solution of the crisis of the universal church by means of action undertaken by a coalition of territorial powers—indeed by one or a few of them to begin with. Thus, for example, the Emperor Honorius's rescript, *Si duo forte contra fas,* which had been executed in the past by emperors, was now to be executed by the king of France in imitation of these models.[47] The general formula, lifted from the *Decretum,* was that "there are a thousand examples and decrees by which it is clearly seen that those making a schism in the holy church should be coerced by the public powers,"[48] and this homogenizing concept of "public power" which covered emperor, kings, princes, and cities indiscriminately, without regard for traditional notions about imperial or papal prerogatives, was evidently due to the mentality of the lawyer working as politician and publicist rather than as academic theoretician. Simon's world was the French polity, and when he had to generate a European prospectus, he universalized the special case of France.

The theoretical structure whose main lines have concerned us so far comes down to three basic positions: (1) a pope should not be obeyed when he tended to damage the *status* of the universal church in its faith, salvationary functions, or property; (2) a heretical pope ceased to be pope

---

45. See above, Ch. IV, n. 25.

46. Konrad of Soest's "Heidelberg Postil," *DRTA,* 6:406 f., notes that subtraction in Germany would mean the end of ecclesiastical discipline and the proliferation of heresies, "considering that every noble however petty is king in his territory, and every city exercises royal power within its walls"; also that the problem of handling dispensations, reserved cases, appeals, confirmations, and other matters under papal cognizance could not be solved in Germany, "where although *de jure* there is one head, the king of the Romans, in fact there are few or none on whom he can impose the kind of order in these matters that was imposed in the kingdom of France."

47. "Let your royal majesty manfully execute the decree of the Emperor Honorius, *Si duo forte,* just as on another occasion the Emperor Henry II [= III] is read to have done in the time of Pope Benedict IX" (glosses on the Toulouse letter of 1402, AN, J 518, fol. 502r).

48. Ibid.: fol. 549v; it is quoted from *Decretum,* 23. q. 5, c. 43, *De Liguribus,* a letter written by Pope Pelagius I (556–561) and hence reflecting the Roman-imperial political structure; its meaning ca. 1400 was something else.

and was subject to criminal process leading among other things to his deposition; (3) the universal church was the congregation of the faithful, laity and clergy, and when the clerical authorities could not act to preserve the church's *status* against a delinquent pope, the secular powers should do so. The first two points were canonistically impeccable, and Pierre Ravat even conceded them in his refutation of Simon's doctrine at the Third Paris Council,[49] although he of course rejected the program based on their application to Benedict: subtraction of total obedience leading to coerced abdication, alias deposition. For the consequences followed only from the point of view Simon had adopted, namely that of the universal church defined as the whole body of Western Christendom; only in this context could all papal claims to obedience be seen as damaging the church because perpetuating the Schism, and only so could the popes insisting on their rights be considered ipso facto schismatics, therefore heretics. To Benedict XIII, and of course to his rival Boniface IX, the church was defined as the body in solidarity with the true pope, whose insistence on his rights was the reverse of schismatic. As for the *via cessionis,* its unique and therefore obligatory quality as a remedy was obvious only from Simon's point of view; from the papal point of view it was if anything the worst of all possible remedies. Finally, once the first two points were neutralized, so was the third, inasmuch as the true pope was still very much in office and retained the prerogative of invoking the secular powers or not, as he saw fit. This point was anyway something of an artificial construction, based on "old laws" and analogies, and it fell away when the need to resort to such expedients was denied.

A closer look at the papal argumentation as set forth at the Third Paris Council—very largely in explicit opposition to Simon's treatise—will bring these remarks home and thereby throw light on the element of willfulness underlying the canonistics of the treatise. Thus, as noted above, Pierre Ravat's first thesis was not different from Simon's, except that here it was given a positive cast: "In those things that are not against the general estate of the church, or natural or divine law, the Roman pontiff is to be obeyed, even if his commands are opposed to positive law and burdensome to some."[50] The same may be said for the premise corresponding to Simon's second big point: "It is certain that the papacy is not lost except by infidelity alone [i.e., heresy], and this is

---

49. BdeC: 5 f.; ASV, *Arm.* 54, t. 21, fols. 220r, 221v (for these two reports of the Paris speeches, see Ch. VII, below). Simon noted this agreement in his own speech, BdeC: 22.

50. Ravat's speech of 29 May, BdeC: 5; ASV, *Arm.* 54, t. 21, fol. 220r has "contra . . . universalis ecclesie generalem statum."

the conclusion of Augustine of Ancona."[51] Not even considering Simon's play with the first point, presumably because from Ravat's point of view the Schism consisted not in the two rival papacies but only in the refusal of the Urbanists to obey Benedict, Ravat could go on rather effortlessly to show that Benedict was not in fact a heretic or a schismatic.[52] But even if he were, it would have to be proven. Here Ravat chose his own canons and authorities counter to Simon's and asserted that "the more common opinion of the doctors" was that even in cases of notoriety a judicial citation was required before sanctions might be applied. And who could judge the pope anyway? It was true, as Simon had said, that a pope could not infringe certain decrees of a general council, but these were only the ones pertaining to the faith or the sacraments; otherwise "he can be judged by no one"; "he has no superior and is not bound by the law." Hence the secular powers had no legal right to subtract obedience or otherwise act contrary to the pope's position.[53] In other words, the whole subtractionist argument developed as a solution to a crisis in the church was rejected. Ravat's underlying premise was set forth plainly in the beginning and repeated throughout: Clement VII had been the true pope; Benedict XIII was his legitimate successor; France recognized both as such, and the fact that the Urbanist schismatics did not hardly altered the case.[54]

Without dwelling on the other details of this confrontation—which included the issue of partial subtraction, the difficulties (*inconveniencia*) that would arise from the absence of papal functions within the French church, and also the important but rather uninteresting question, whether Benedict was a perjuror for refusing to fulfill the conclave oath which required him to abdicate at the cardinals' request[55]—we can usefully consider the underlying papalism of Ravat's doctrine as a counterposition to Simon's. Sometimes, as we have just seen, Ravat's critique consisted in an alternative choice of "doctors"; another example would be his rejection of the *glossa ordinaria* on *Si papa* which held that a pope

---

51. ASV, *Arm. 54*, t. 21, fol. 221v. The reference is to Augustine of Ancona's *Summa de potestate ecclesiastica*; for his doctrine, less narrowly papalist on this point than Ravat's words imply, see Michael Wilks, *The Problem of Sovereignty in the Later Middle Ages* (Cambridge, 1963): 469 ff., 500.

52. BdeC: 7: Benedict was not declared schismatic by those having the power to do so, nor had he been judged by a general council. In his speech of 3 June, BdeC: 52, Ravat argued that even if Benedict were a schismatic, he would not therefore be a heretic; the two are different vices; cf. *DSO*, n. 120.

53. BdeC: 54 f.

54. BdeC: 5, 51.

55. This last point was emphasized by all speakers at the Third Paris Council, but Simon merely mentioned it in his treatise, perhaps because it tended to bypass the more profound issues involved in subtraction.

might be accused not only of the crime of heresy (as set forth in the canon) but also of any notorious crime that scandalized the church. He claimed this gloss should not have been used because it had been rejected by "many"—specifically Augustine of Ancona, Pierre Bertrand, and Pierre de la Palu.[56] But there are other statements pointing to a more fundamental conception. Thus the prelates' oath as laid down in the canon *Ego N.* obligated the bishop to be faithful to St. Peter, the holy Roman church, and the pope, textually in that order; Ravat had charged that this oath inhibited the French prelates from subtracting obedience, but Simon argued in "On Subtraction" that the oath was to the church in the first place, to the pope only afterwards. This position was refuted by Ravat with the claim that the oath to the church *was* an oath to the pope, inasmuch as the head of a church represented its body: "the term 'Roman church' in the oath means the pope."[57] The framework of discourse on both sides is the corporatist ecclesiology of the canonists, but here we see it in its high-papalist version.[58] Again, in refuting the various justifications for partial subtraction—the Gallican Liberties—Ravat not only used more or less rational arguments (papal provisions were a better way of choosing fit personnel than collations by the ordinaries; papal financial exactions were the community's way of supporting its head)[59] but also struck at the very root of Gallicanism, with its doctrine of episcopal rights not derived from papal authority, by asserting, with Augustine of Ancona, that "the pope personally or by commission can do all the things in a bishop's diocese that the bishop can do, or a priest in his parish, and still more."[60] In general, Ravat's line of argument was to restrict as narrowly as possible the area of papal vulnerability to attack from the church,[61] to reject any supra-partisan play with the concept of

---

56. BdeC: 7; ASV, *Arm.* 54, t. 21, fol. 221v. Cf. Tierney: 213 f., Buisson: 187.

57. Ibid., fol. 232v: "dixi quod . . . nullum interesse ecclesie Romane est hic, cum pape tanquam capiti obeditur. Nam nomine ecclesie Romane in iuramento intelligitur papa, licet ad maiorem expressionem ipse eciam nominetur in textu." The passage in BdeC: 51 spells out the corporatist doctrine more clearly: "Ille qui jurat ecclesiae, episcopo principaliter tanquam capiti obligatur, et sic episcopi licet jurent ecclesiae, tamen principaliter jurant papae." See also BdeC: 6; *DSO*, nn. 22, 410; App. II, Pt. III.

58. Tierney, *Foundations*: 34 f.; Wilks, *Problem of Sovereignty*, index s.v. "Pope, as apex, = Ecclesia, = Roman Church"; Post, *Studies*: 352–354; *gl. ord.* on *Decretum*, 24. q. 1, c. 9, *in v.* "novitatibus" (the pope "is called the church").

59. BdeC: 9 f.

60. ASV, *Arm.* 54, t. 21, fol. 224r: "conclusio Augustini de Anchona, q. xix, articulo vi, quod papa per seipsum vel commissionem potest omnia facere que potest episcopus in diocesi vel presbyter in parrochia, et adhuc amplius." See Wilks, *Problem of Sovereignty*: 383 n. 4, for this passage and its implications.

61. Thus he not only rejected non-papalist glosses but interpreted non-papalist canons as narrowly as possible, e.g., BdeC: 55: "Papa potest contra concilia generalia. Jura

202 Simon de Cramaud

"the universal church," and—giving substance to both of these—to set forth a doctrine of papal sovereignty that was as close to absolutism as possible in that non-absolutist age.[62] It was only a corollary of all this that the kings were denied anything like the jurisdiction and lordship within the church that the subtractionists assigned them. Ravat rejected not only the arguments based on the crisis of the Schism but also the "old laws," which, he said, dealt with execution of the church's sentence on schismatics and heretics or reflected a weakness in the early church's position ("the primitive church was of small estate") that no longer existed.[63] The papalist conception of ecclesiastical liberty that runs throughout his Paris speeches refuting the subtractionists produces a strictly limited definition of the royal role in the church:

When it is said that the king on his own authority may act in this matter, I answer that this is not true—although I do not wish to detract from the king's power. . . . The proof is in the common laws [scil., of the *Decretum*] which say that ecclesiastical persons may not be judged by secular magistrates, and this applies a fortiori to the pope, for "he may be judged by none" (c. *Nemo*, 9. q. 3). . . . All the laws which speak about such lay judgement are to be understood as meaning "at the church's request." And when it is said that the Schism would then last forever, I reply that this is not true; and even if it were, the king can do nothing about it. If the king wants the pope to be judged or proceedings to be taken against him, let the king work to convoke a general council![64]

Comparing Ravat's doctrine with Cramaud's, one senses that the former flowed more effortlessly from the canons in their primary intention —with a few exceptions noted above. But canonists commonly used exquisitely constructive techniques to squeeze their ideas even out of contrary canons, and it is no criticism of "On Subtraction" to say that it was a tour de force of this method from beginning to end. On the other hand, if the strength of its component parts came honestly enough from

---

autem allegata in contrarium, loquuntur in illis quae sunt fidei aut sacramentorum" (cf. Tierney, *Foundations*: 50 ff., for broader and more normal views). Even if the pope were to disturb the status of the universal church, Ravat noted, he should be disobeyed only in that; obeyed otherwise (BdeC: 52).

62. Apart from the standard formulas of absolutism (above, at n. 53), Ravat even proposed a pseudo-historical foundation for papal reservations of benefices, against the Gallican complaint that this was a novelty introduced against the old laws and the uses of the primitive church; Ravat stated (BdeC: 9), "In primitiva ecclesia, solus papa conferebat episcopatus et alias dignitates; sed post . . . a papa data est potestas capitulis et conventibus eligendi."

63. BdeC: 11 f., 50: "Quae enim erat ratio quare imperatores interfuerant in electionibus? Certe ratio fuit, quod primitiva ecclesia erat in parvo statu. . . . Ideo intererant principes. . . . Nunc autem cessat illa causa, . . . cessat constitutio." Cf. Kaminsky, *Hussite Revolution*: 49 f., for other such views in this period.

64. Speech of 3 June 1398, BdeC: 54 (BN, *ms. lat.* 14,644, fol. 71r, compared).

the canonistic traditions of rationalization and corporatist ecclesiology on which it drew, Simon's arrangement of these parts into the justification for a political program that can only be called revolutionary[65] must be appreciated as a triumph of the will. When the Abbé Auber, Simon's first modern biographer, wrote of his hero's fervent unionism that "in these outpourings of a soul saddened by public evils one readily recognizes the language of a saint,"[66] he was thinking of Simon's exaltation of the *status* of the universal church as the supreme value. But his saintly language was a strictly functionalist technique; only so could Simon bring his authorities together and make them relevant to his program of renouncing obedience to the pope, subjecting the pope to physical coercion, and eventually deposing him, thus invoking a secular magistracy within the church that had not been seen on such a scale since the eleventh century. This was not *really* what his canons and canonists had been aiming at, and Ravat's sober exposition of the true sense of the law within a papalist framework serves to remind us of just how extreme Simon's doctrine was. "Proceed to subtraction of obedience and indeed to worse—the important thing is not what is done but why it is done" —Simon's principle comes richly enough from canon law, Roman law, and St. Augustine,[67] but all it means here is that the holy end justifies any means at all. One thinks of the extraordinary farrago of distortions and fantasies put together a century earlier to justify deposing Boniface VIII and the similar concoctions used against the Templars; one may also think of modern counterparts. Political power can create the facts and images that pass into thought as societal reality, and the intellectual servants of power can think dynamically rather than reflectively, looking to the future to make their thoughts true. When Jean Gerson complained in 1402 of the strategy of "bringing the present issue down to heresy or schism, charging such crimes against lord Benedict, and seeking thereby to depose him,"[68] he was obviously attacking this dynamic style as practiced by Simon de Cramaud, and one senses the academic intellectual's revulsion against the canonist-politician.

Something has already been said about the limitations of Simon's treatise from a scholarly point of view. Had Simon been working and thinking as the university professor he once had been, he would proba-

---

65. "Il nous faudra descendre dans nos annales jusqu'aux plus mauvais jours de la Révolution pour que la France revoie une crise semblable"—this is L. Salembier's rotund denunciation of subtraction of obedience, *Le Grand Schisme d'Occident*, 5th ed. (Paris, 1921): 169, and he was not even considering the deposition theory involved. See also F. Ehrle in *ALKG*, 7:42.
66. Auber: 281.
67. App. II, Pt. II, "Fraternal Correction." See Buisson: 17–73, 192.
68. The *Protestatio*, in Gerson, *Oeuvres*, 6:35.

bly have produced a much longer work, perhaps one as bloated as Pierre Leroy's cessionist *Factum* of August 1395. He would certainly not have omitted a whole series of apt canons or glosses that were widely known and which he could have found if he had taken the time.[69] Nor perhaps would he have resorted to a number of distortions, most of them more or less trivial, to bolster his argument.[70] But such criticisms are useful only to fix the publicistic character of the work in our mind, so that we do not pry it loose from its political matrix and hence from its historical import. The fact is that even a merely good mind, thinking to order and not floating about in academic speculations, could, if well trained, achieve a purposeful clarity that only the greatest academics were able to manage and could readily construct powerful and original chains of thought by the simple technique of freeing the intellect from traditional restraints in order to draw the straight lines leading to whatever goals seemed desirable. Ehrle's perception that "most of those views that came to the surface and were realized in . . . the whole conciliar movement" were rooted in the time of France's subtraction of obedience, 1395–1403,[71] suggests the extraordinary significance of Simon de Cramaud's treatise; for it helped bring about the Third Paris Council, set much of that council's program, and pointed out the way leading from subtraction to deposition, hence from Paris to Pisa and Constance.[72] In 1394, before Simon had begun his work as chief of France's union program,

---

69. See above, n. 15, to which I add a few more examples, with references to the pages in Tierney, *Foundations*, where the texts are mentioned: 24. q. 1, c. 9, with *gl. ord.* (p. 44; a distinction between the pope subject to error and the church, as congregation of the faithful, which is indefectible); 96. di., c. 4 (p. 49; maintenance of the true faith concerns laity as well as clergy); X. 3. 2. 10, and *gl. ord.* (p. 129 n. 4; *evidentia rei* is enough to justify avoiding a sinning prelate's offices—the gloss extends this to heresy, schism, notorious fornication); Hostiensis on X. 1. 6. 6 (p. 152; Simon has the canon and Innocent IV's gloss, but the gloss by Hostiensis implies a right of the whole community of the church to participate in remedying its defects); Bohic on X. 1. 6. 6 (p. 214; a reaffirmation of the crucial *gl. ord.* on *Si papa*). Note also that while *Cum non liceat* (X. 2. 26. 12) is cited in the treatise, the *gl. ord.* on it is not, although it has arguments supporting subtraction without a sentence; Simon did cite the gloss in his speech of 30 May 1398 (BdeC: 25), and one guesses that he just had not taken the time to look at it when writing his treatise.

70. For some of the cases of distortion or adaptation, see *DSO*, nn. 304, 306, 361 (with 289), 366, 394. There are others.

71. *ALKG*, 6:139.

72. For the movement from Paris to Pisa, see Ch. VIII. As for the Third Paris Council, the treatise contains much of the debate in its Pt. I as versus Pts. II and III. That Ravat used many of the canonistic texts in Pt. I may have been due to coincidence or to Simon's own borrowing from Ravat's sources; or it may have been Ravat's borrowing. The speech of Gilles Deschamps, on the other hand, seems obviously thrown together from Simon's treatise (see, e.g., the discussion of *Nisi cum pridem*, etc., BdeC: 40 f.). There are other echoes too, and of course Simon used his own treatise fully.

only a few voices spoke of a double deposition, and virtually no one in the Urbanist obedience was advocating even voluntary abdication; it was France's creation first of cessionist then of subtractionist reality, by her initially solitary commitment to both, that provided the point around which "public opinion" in Europe could crystallize.

This was in fact precisely what Simon had projected in his management of the First Paris Council, in his treatise, and then in his management of the Third Paris Council. Whether his treatise itself had any direct influence on the conciliarist writings connected with Pisa and Constance is a question that has never been raised, chiefly because the import of the French program has not been generally appreciated and the treatise had not been edited. We can only suggest that the European distribution of the treatise brought its powerful doctrine of disobedience and deposition to the attention of interested intellectuals and that this confrontation with a canonistically sound model of revolution may well have opened minds to hitherto unspeakable or disreputable lines of thought. Let us bear in mind that if the work refutes judicial conciliarism (a general council to judge between the papal contenders), it also propounds a doctrine of coercive conciliarism in its argument that the French and Castilian councils of 1395/1396 were together equivalent to a general council of the Avignon obedience and hence canonically empowered to command the pope to abdicate. The passage from this to a model for Pisa was rather easy; Simon made it himself at the Third Paris Council when he revised the *practica cessionis* to include a representative general council of the whole church in order to handle the double abdication or deposition and the new election.[73]

Finally, it may be suggested that just as Simon the non-conciliarist may have launched the intellectual movement that would lead to the Council of Pisa, so Simon the non-Gallican may have been the midwife of the "Gallicanism properly so called" born at the Third Paris Council.[74] We recall that the University of Paris had pushed for the Gallican Liberties, as partial subtraction, at the Second Paris Council, and had failed. Its leaders evidently recognized that they could get what they wanted only within the framework of the total subtraction advocated by Simon de Cramaud, and it was in fact a coalition of the partialists and totalists that carried the day in 1398. The *DSO* opened the way to this consummation by an explicit paragraph mentioning "the way advised by the University of Paris" as a possible alternative to immediate total subtraction, also by a few pages of Gallican arguments justifying the subtraction of papal revenues, and by a couple of additions to the treatise

---

73. See Ch. VII, below.
74. The phrase is in V. Martin, *Les origines du Gallicanisme,* I (Paris, 1939):243.

which suggest a desire to cultivate the university.[75] One should not make too much of this—Simon's suggestions for regulating church affairs during subtraction mixed Gallican and papalist points together with evidently no sense of commitment to the former,[76] and nothing in his career suggests anything but perfect adaptation to the papal system in which he would eventually become a cardinal—but what is there is enough. The entirely political character of "On Subtraction" opened it to its author's political calculations, including the need to get the university's support for total subtraction, and it was within this framework that the Gallican Liberties could find their way into the work and the political action that implemented its program. None of this bears very heavily on the treatise, whose central thrust was the program of coercion leading to deposition and whose major accomplishment was its corporatist deposition theory. It is only a speculation that this appearance of radical subversiveness as the quasi-official ideology of public power may have opened the way to other novelties of thought and action. The next few decades were full of them.

---

75. *DSO*, "Introduction," and text at nn. 221–234, and *passim*; also App. II, *passim*.
76. See the discussion in the following chapter, and cf. Ravat's comment on this inconsistency, BdeC: 53: "Patriarcha est sibi ipsi contrarius."

CHAPTER SEVEN

The Politics of Subtraction and the Third Paris Council

S I M O N de Cramaud had presented his treatise on subtraction as the answer to two questions, whether the kings and realms of both obediences might canonically deny obedience to their popes if these refused to abdicate, and then whether just one obedience might do it. The answer was yes in both cases. Of course, he conceded, it would be better if all the kings subtracted together, but that was not going to happen, and subtraction by one side would be a way of working toward the final goal. He was talking concretely about the Avignon side as led by France, and if he had ever had any hope of an easy ride down the *via cessionis*, he had certainly lost it by now. The decision to subtract would have to be carried through as a political act within the French government; the subtraction itself would have to be worked out in gritty detail with the collaboration of the French clerical estate; and only after this had been done could the French work to induce the rest of the Avignon obedience to fall in line. In fact many in the obedience would not. Only the king of Castile was enthusiastic; and even the College of Cardinals, won in advance to the project, had to be waited for and managed. As for winning over the rulers of the Roman obedience, France had indeed begun with her English partner but would have to keep working step by step until others would be drawn in; this would take ten years, during which the "way of cession" would reveal itself as a "way of ejection" (*via eieccionis*), with subtraction appearing as the preliminary to deposition. These were subversive novelties, and if most of Europe could undertake them rather painlessly as external actions for a few months in 1409, the French political community had to embark on a major constitutional reorganization capable of lasting for years. In any case, a fairly elaborate production of public reality had first to be brought off, to furnish the public mind with the requisite images of necessity and opportunity.

Simon's treatise was itself part of the process, in its conception as a political act within France and in its development as an instrument of propaganda for Europe. He sent a copy to Richard II of England some-

time in 1397 with a covering letter exhorting the king to act.[1] A letter
he wrote to be sent in the name of Charles VI to King Wenceslas IV of
Bohemia and the Empire set forth a compendium of the treatise's doctrine in its very words; a copy of the treatise itself was also delivered.[2]
Other copies went elsewhere (we have seen Pierre Ravat complaining
about them), and there is every reason to think that many more were
sent than we know about. Simon attended the Frankfurt Diet of July
1397 to try to win over the Western princes of the Empire, and it is
inconceivable that he did not take at least a few copies of De substraccione
obediencie with him.[3] Perhaps he then went on to Prague, in which case he
would have brought the copy mentioned above.[4] It is also unlikely that
the copy now in Pamplona and presumably sent to the king of Navarre
was not flanked by copies sent to Castile and Aragon; unlikely too that
copies were not sent to Italian powers like Florence. It was, to be sure, a
Latin treatise stuffed with canonistic authorities, but neither of these
traits would have limited its impact on the educated men who at that
time executed policy and often helped make it. Quite the contrary. Such
men all over Europe were now suddenly faced with a public statement in
due scholarly form which showed how the two popes were guilty of
criminal malfeasance and were therefore schismatics and heretics, how it
was the church's right to insist that they abdicate and to use force
against them if they refused, and how the kings and princes of both
obediences had every right even according to canon law to execute this
coercive action. Subtraction of total obedience was presented as the first
step in this direction. The arguments would hardly have convinced a
papalist, but that was not their purpose; they were now "published"
realities and therefore available to every decision maker who for whatever
reason would be inclined to go the French way.

Another production of subtractionist reality was the Anglo-French-
Castilian embassy to the two popes in the summer of 1397.[5] The French

1. AN, J 518, fols. 303r–304r; see DSO, App. V, n. 4.

2. DSO, App. V, no. 5. In about January 1399 the French envoy Honoré Bouvet
spoke before King Wenceslas IV and cited arguments "quas tetigit profundissime et
clarissime in suo libro, qui aput te est, dominus patriarcha Allexandrinus"—F. M.
Bartoš, ed., Autograf M. J. Husi (Prague, 1954): 55 (an edition of John Hus's autograph
copy of the speech); I suppose that the "book" had been brought in 1397.

3. DSO, App. V, no. 3.

4. In his speech of 22 May 1398 opening the Third Paris Council, Simon reviewed
France's diplomatic activity since 1395, including his own, and at the end remarked, "et
deinde ego fui iterato ad regem Romanorum" (Ampl. coll., 7:714), "Finally I too went to
the king of the Romans," the "iterato" referring to the 1396 embassy to Central Europe
by Leroy and others, and the "deinde" signifying in its sequence something later, hence
perhaps 1397.

5. Valois, 3:116–122.

delegation was headed by Gilles Deschamps. The plan was to demand of both popes that they accept the *via cessionis* and bring unity to the church by next Candlemas (2 February 1398), and while the English envoys did not lay this out to Boniface IX anywhere near as clearly as the French and Castilians did to Benedict XIII, the theatrical values were not much diminished thereby. Embassies were modes of royal action; ambassadors moved with deliberate ostentation; and their entries and withdrawals were as much public events as were the presentations of their messages. There was, moreover, other diplomatic activity going on at the same time: envoys from several princes of West Germany urged unionism on Boniface IX; French embassies were active again and again in Germany; both English and French envoys appeared in Prague for the same purpose.[6] One result was to pry Wenceslas IV out of his lethargy to the point where he actually travelled to the West, making an overdue appearance in the Empire and moving on in March 1398 to meet Duke Louis of Orléans and King Charles VI in Rheims, where the alliance between Wenceslas and Louis was consolidated and agreements about union policy were reached.[7] Although the agreements amounted to little, and the Schism was only one of the issues in play, the images of momentous movements and meetings at the highest level must have been retained by the political communities involved. In this sense, even the oppositional actions fed substance into the French machine. A sarcastic open letter to Wenceslas from Rupert II, Elector Palatine of the Rhine, warned him against falling into the clutches of the French, who sought their own good and not the Empire's, and urged that, in the matter of the Schism, France, which had made it, should not be allowed "to come out of it with impunity and without bearing the brand of error."[8] While the letter did Wenceslas no good, it drew the picture of massive French political action for union on cessionist principles and thus gave the image an extra charge of public entity. Similarly the counter-diplomacy of Benedict XIII and his ally and in-law King Martin of Aragon must have contributed to the public substance of unionism, not least when Avignon envoys went to Rome to draw Boniface IX into a common front of anti-cessionism—collusion, as the French charged.[9] It is true that both popes responded negatively to the embassy of the three kings, Boniface even refusing any sort of solution at all short of his own triumph; but

---

6. Valois, 3:125; F. M. Bartoš, *Čechy v. době Husově* (Prague, 1947): 151.

7. Valois, 3:126–135.

8. The text of the letter in *Thes. nov.*, 2:1172–1177, and *DRTA*, 3:51–58; cf. Valois, 3:127, for a review of scholarly opinions about the origin of the letter, and Bartoš, *Čechy v době Husově*: 153 n. 1, for evidence that it was genuine.

9. Valois, 3:120 f.

few could have been surprised. By the end of 1397 a new reality had been created, very much in line with the prospectus of Simon's treatise: "the kings" had joined to urge unionism on the popes; the *via cessionis* had been featured as the only acceptable way; and both popes had been informed that action was expected by 2 February 1398. Benedict had been told even more by representatives of both France and Castile: he was put on notice in due legal form that if there was no union by 2 February, the kings would "remove the causes of the Schism's prolongation," a by-now standard locution for partial subtraction, and "would also use all the other good means possible," a phrase perhaps meaning total.[10]

The man who uttered these threats in Avignon on behalf of the French crown was Colard de Calleville, who had also been chief lay member of Simon's 1396 embassy to Spain; it must be supposed that he had had his instructions and was carrying them out. In other words, the French government must already have decided on eventual subtraction, and only the passage of allotted time stood between that decision and its implementation: the embassy had to be put together; it had to go to Avignon and to Rome; and the deadline it set had to elapse. The debates before the royal council in February 1397 can best be related to this inferred decision, and the same can be said for Simon's revision of his treatise from the French form beginning "Every kingdom divided against itself" to the European "Be wise now therefore, O ye kings." Thus in his letter to King Richard II Simon said that he had not written his treatise with Richard in mind;[11] the decision to send him a copy must have come later, and such a decision would have been an official one of the government. It is indeed only in the revised text that we find Simon identifying himself as a royal councillor and declaring that he was writing at the king's command.

While nothing much could be done before 1398, the government did take some action designed to keep its union policy warm. On 12 September 1397 royal orders commanded the seneschals and *baillis* not to

---

10. According to the account of the embassy in AN, J 518, fol. 174v (*Processus nunciorum* . . .), Benedict was told that "rex requirebat et summabat eum una vice pro omnibus . . ." to bring about union by Candlemas; this is the vocabulary of a legal citation. Cf. Simon's discussion of the legal force of such a request in his treatise (App. II): "He who refuses after having been requested commits a crime that calls for his deposition." The threat stated here was that "transacto dicto termino rex intendebat providere taliter quod cause prolongacionis que fuerant date in hoc facto scismatis tollerentur, et eciam provideret omnibus aliis melioribus modis quibus posset." The Castilian envoy said "in substancia et effectu verba similia . . . et multo magis pungitiva."

11. AN, J 518, fol. 304r: "Dum in libello predicto contenta scribebam, ad eius [*sic*] sublimitatis vestre noticiam hec deducere non credebam."

allow anyone to write or agitate against the *via cessionis*.[12] On 28 October the government issued a letter to the pope, the cardinals, and church bodies in the realm stating that since Benedict had refused to accept cession and was using his powers of appointment to promote his sympathizers, henceforth the crown would recognize no prelate who had not been regularly elected or postulated and whose disposition in the matter of union was not such that the king himself would have recommended him. The letter was not sent out until January 1398 and even then was not enforced; it can best be considered a sort of rehearsal for the later, more substantial creation of a subtractionist entity.[13] Still earlier, "the king" had declared that he would not recognize any new cardinals Benedict might create,[14] and while this did not stop the pope from creating six in the course of 1397, including three from Aragon, the royal policy served to promote the full absorption of the College of Cardinals into the Paris machine, a construction begun by the duke of Berry during the ducal embassy to Avignon in 1395. By this time, indeed, almost all the "old" cardinals had withdrawn from Benedict's court and refused to rejoin him, and there must have been very lively contacts between the Paris leaders of cessionist policy and those cardinals whose history of loyalty and service to the Valois marked them out for leadership in this conjunction—above all, Pierre de Thury and Jean de Lagrange. Sometime around mid-January 1398 the knight Guillaume de Tigonville, a royal chamberlain and councillor, appeared in Avignon to declare that the king had taken the "old" cardinals into his protection and safeguard and that the king required the citizens of Avignon to act accordingly (even though Avignon was subject to the pope, not the king). He went on to say that these cardinals, at present away from Avignon, were about to return in order to attend to the business of church union and "accomplish" the conclave oath. We see here the result of an otherwise unknown agreement between the crown and the college to bring matters to a head. Benedict had already been told by the cardinals in 1395 that they thought he should accept the *via cessionis,* and this request would now, presumably, be repeated in a form official enough to activate the

---

12. Valois, 3:144 f.

13. Valois, 3:145 f. The text of the letter as received by the chapter of Notre Dame of Paris, 25 January 1398 (AN, LL 108B, p. 317), refers to the First Paris Council's deliberation in favor of the *via cessionis* and then goes on: "Et apres . . . nous meismes encore la chose en deliberacion en nostre presence, et presens aussi nos oncles et frere et plusieurs autres grans seigneurs de nostre sanc, et autres notables personnes de nostre conseil et de nostre royaulme," with the same result. This may refer to the debates of February 1397. See also the next note.

14. Valois, 3:143; cf. point 8 of Jean Canart's vote at the Third Paris Council, App. I.

conclave oath and face Benedict with the immediate obligation of promising to abdicate, inasmuch as the oath had empowered the cardinals
to make the decision in this matter.[15] No one thought the pope would
comply; on the contrary, he would henceforth be an evident perjurer and
schismatic, a perfect target for total subtraction.

Even before Candlemas of 1398 King Henry III of Castile had demanded that France stick to its plan of action, and sometime in February
the University of Paris requested Berry and the king to go ahead.[16] The
government's affirmative decision must have been made at once, for royal
letters were issued on 7 March to convoke the necessary council of the
clergy for 7 May. The bishops, abbots, cathedral chapters, and universities of the realm were reminded of the First Paris Council's decision in
favor of the *via cessionis* alone; of the subsequent adherence to this *via*
by the kings of Castile, England, Navarre, and Scotland and by all the
cardinals except one; and also of the Second Paris Council's alleged
recommendation to summon both popes one more time to accept cession.
Both had refused, and now it was up to the king, by virtue of his official
obligation to secure the welfare of the faith, to take the action necessary
to implement the *via cessionis*. In such a matter of public policy, the
clergy's attendance could be commanded "by the faith that you owe to
us" and on pain of incurring the royal displeasure.[17] Both the letter and
the course of action at the council show that here, as in the past two
cases, the clerical estate of the realm was being summoned by its lord
the king, exactly as the latter summoned meetings of regional estates to
provide him with aid and counsel. Thus the attendance and powers of
the proctors sent by chapters and others would be checked by royal officials; the meetings would take place in the royal palace and under the
presidency of the royal dukes acting in the name of the incapacitated
king; the subjects for discussion would be defined by a member of the
royal council, Simon de Cramaud, speaking on commission from the
government; and the whole order of procedure would be set by the
crown, with the proceedings to be in the vernacular for the benefit of the

---

15. Valois, 3:147; the text in *ALKG*, 6:245 f. The key passage reads that it is the
cardinals' intention to return to Avignon "pour besoigner du fait de l'eglise en ac-
complissant le serement contenu en une sedule, qui fu faicte a l'antier du conclave." No
further details are given. Although the cardinals' "declaration and requisition" for the *via
cessionis* in 1395 had not been signed, the text was regarded as official by the subtractionists in 1398 and was read out on 22 May (ASV, *Arm.* 54, t. 21, fol. 191v; cf. BdeC:
7, 17, 21, 26, 28, 57, for references to it); there is no evidence of a new declaration in
1398.

16. Valois, 3:137–141.

17. The text in *ALKG*, 6:274 f.; for the date of 7 May cf. Valois, 3:148; the account
in BdeC: 4 gives 1 May.

secular magnates.[18] Even the matter of subtraction that the council would deal with had a workaday secular dimension along with its import to the cause of union; for Benedict XIII had refused to renew the clerical aids that the crown had been receiving by papal permission for the past thirty years (the last ones were due to expire on 1 April 1398), and as the duke of Burgundy pointed out, "the prelates would not dare to grant the aids themselves if they were still subject to the pope—that is, if subtraction were not made."[19] The prelates at the Third Paris Council would indeed be asked for "aid" in this sense.

Bearing in mind what we have seen of Simon de Cramaud's methods at the First Paris Council, and anticipating what we shall see of his management of the Fourth (1406–1407) and of the Council of Pisa, we can imagine him planning this current production accordingly: a preliminary layout of the issues in a tightly controlled form allowing no room for the free play of controversy, a digest of the officially provided alternatives in the form of concise written "schedules" (cedule), and voting on these without further discussion. But this time it would not be just a question of managing the papalist opposition, for the weightiness of subtraction and its implications for the future evoked conflicting interests within the crown's coalition. The movement we have already seen among university men and some prelates in favor of the Gallican Liberties, alias partial subtraction, would press for novelties of this sort and would want to make them permanent, using the present crisis to create a new status for the French church in which the papal powers of taxation and appointment would be permanently curtailed. The cardinals, on the other hand, depended for most of their revenues on just those papal powers, for they shared in the income of the Apostolic Camera, including the annates and servicia paid in by clerics receiving benefices through papal provisions, and they enjoyed the revenues of a large number of benefices that they themselves had received by papal provision. Gallican Liberty would drastically reduce the Camera's revenues, would prevent future papal provisions to French benefices, and—as we shall see— would even prevent the cardinals from using papal provisions they already had. Submissive allies of the crown, the cardinals nevertheless wanted to preserve their estate through the storms of subtraction to come.

---

18. There are three surviving accounts of the council's proceedings: one composed by Guillaume de Longueil, in BdeC: 3–86; another, by the same anonymous author responsible for the account of the Second Paris Council, in ALKG, 6:273–287; the third, essentially a report of the speeches with some connecting material, composed apparently by Pierre Ravat, in ASV, Arm. 54, t. 21, fols. 190r–251r. See Kaminsky, "Politics": 374 ff., for more detailed references.

19. Douët-d'Arcq, 1:146–148; cf. Valois, 3:143 f.

Towards the end of May, therefore, two of them, probably Pierre de Thury and Jean de Lagrange, wrote their own proposals for subtraction to one of their contact men in the Paris government, who could hardly have been anyone but Simon de Cramaud.[20] Giving the same reasons used by Cramaud in his treatise, they concluded that Benedict XIII was a perjurer and schismatic, an active enemy of the *via cessionis,* and was therefore not to be obeyed as pope. Hence, they argued, there should be a *total* subtraction of obedience from him; "for particular subtraction would not sound right, as being subtraction from a man regarded in part as pope, in part as non-pope."[21] As for the form of total subtraction, it should affect only the pope, not the papacy. Thus, for example, the fiscal rights of the Camera were to be maintained, "collected by those to whom it pertains to do so," and either kept safe for the new pope of a united church or spent to prosecute the cause of union. The cardinals supporting subtraction were to be "fully assured of their rights, incomes, and the revenues of their benefices," and "rights" here certainly included the future use of papal provisions they already held, as well as the cardinals' share in the Camera's revenues. These would of course be temporarily diminished, for bishops and other prelates were to enjoy during subtraction the collationary rights normally reserved by the pope. The cardinals accepted this but otherwise sought the least possible change; they also demanded royal protection in their residences in France and in their continued work for union. All in all, this was a counter-model to the Gallican one.

Simon de Cramaud had referred in his treatise to both types of subtraction as possibilities in this or that case. Partial subtraction was laid out, along with its Gallican justification in "common law" or the "old laws" of the church, as "the mode favored by the University of Paris." We even read St. Bernard's formula, beloved of the Gallicans, that "the Roman church is the mother of other churches but not their mistress."[22] But Simon's own view favored a total subtraction conceived of in analogy to the way papal rights were treated *sede vacante,* when the papal see was vacant between popes. Thus "the papal camerary will administer what pertains to the Camera, as he can do in a vacancy," and "the grand penitentiary can exercise his office until we have an uncontested pope, for his power continues even during a vacancy."[23] His thinking here fitted

---

20. The text in *ALKG*, 6:256–271; for authorship and dating see pp. 253–256, and cf. Valois, 3:148 n. 4. See Kaminsky, "Politics": 373.

21. *ALKG,* 6:257, "nam particularis non bene sonaret, ut pro parte pape et pro parte non pape."

22. App. II, Pt. II, "Subtraction of Revenues," and Pt. II; at end.

23. App. II, Pt. III, "Reply to 'It Is not Expedient.'"

in perfectly with the ideas of the cardinals, and the probability that there was an actual understanding between Simon and them is reinforced by the speeches he would pronounce at the Third Paris Council, repeating much of what he had written to the point in his treatise, but with a clear preference for the *sede vacante* solutions over the Gallican ones. His own views are also evident in his vote, which called for total subtraction and gave only the most grudging approval to partial: "It would be less evil to disobey Benedict in some matters than to obey him in all."[24] At the same time, he must have realized what would in fact turn out to be the case, that the University of Paris and the French prelates in general could not be expected to give political and financial support to a kind of subtraction that would sacrifice their interests to those of the cardinals.

Simon's chief collaborators, here as before, were the theologian Gilles Deschamps and the canonist Pierre Leroy. Both were Gallicans, and although both were prepared to support total subtraction in their public statements, Deschamps personally preferred a simple imprisonment of the pope while partial subtraction was being implemented (that is how he voted),[25] and Leroy seems not to have believed in the juridical basis of total subtraction, namely the formal assimilation of schism to heresy. The furthest he would go in this direction, when speaking on behalf of his side, was to say that because of the notorious scandal of the Schism, the pope "should be separated from the body of the church," which in the rhetorical context of the time was downright anodyne.[26] It is striking to compare his speech of 31 May at the council with Simon's the day before. Simon had argued that subtraction was justified from a pope who was a schismatic and heretic because such a pope was no pope and that those subtracting did not have to fear Benedict's excommunications because as non-pope he had no power to pass such sentences.[27] Leroy, on the contrary, treated both issues on the basis of a concept of limited papal power even in normal circumstances: "Before anyone is obliged to obey the pope there has to be a salutary command, for the pope's power is limited to such." For the same reason, an unjust sentence of excommunication by the pope, like one against those subtracting, would have no validity.[28] Cramaud justified a temporary revolution on the basis of a

---

24. For his speech of 30 May see BdeC: 25: "Hoc casu, cum papa incidit in schisma, censetur sedes vacare. Et hoc solvit ad inconveniencia . . . quia tunc . . . potest provideri ac si papa esset defunctus"; and see p. 28. The quoted passage from Simon's vote is in AN, J 518, fol. 365v.

25. AN, J 518, fols. 390v–391v; the relevant passage in Valois, 3:175 n. 1.

26. BdeC: 58.

27. BdeC: 27.

28. BdeC: 30 f. See Buisson: 195 ff., 330 ff., for Leroy's antipapalism as deriving from the canonistic analysis of "scandal."

peculiar emergency, while Leroy argued for a permanent system of limited papal monarchy.

While these two concepts could and would come together on the practical point of total subtraction, the inner structure of this subtraction would be determined differently by the one or the other. The University of Paris recognized the issues in play within the coalition when it instructed its official speaker Pierre Plaoul to advocate total subtraction before the council but in its corporate vote declared that its support of total subtraction was not to be construed as contradicting its earlier agitation for partial; the new position "was added to the previous one, from which it did not intend to depart."[29] We shall see that this apparently fuzzy formulation was in fact realistic, destined for practical reasons to win the support of even those prelates—the majority—who had little interest in Gallicanism per se. A politician like Simon must have foreseen this probability and adjusted his own expectations to it, not least because he certainly knew that the government would ask the assembled clergy to grant financial aid. The constitutional principles governing the interplay between crown and estates on this basis had their own logic of mutual respect as the ground of consent, and this logic would determine the conditions under which total subtraction could become government policy.

The mechanics of the council had to be arranged accordingly. Here, too, the cardinals had offered their own suggestions.[30] They had urged that no agitation by Benedict's agents was to be permitted among the clergy in Paris; the subject of the council's deliberations was to be defined narrowly with no discussion of the via cessionis itself, only how to execute it; opposition to subtraction should not be allowed to take the form of a dispute; voting should be neither secret nor collective, but each member of the council should give his vote in person, alone before the dukes. Simon did not need to take lessons in such matters, and what we know of his directive practice before and after suggests that his plans in 1398 would have been similar to those of the cardinals; but he had to work through a royal council that included both oppositional elements associated with Duke Louis of Orléans and—one guesses—men of various affiliations whose tendency was to avoid taking final steps. Benedict XIII "had a lot of faith in some members of the royal council," and he tried to build up his party there and among the prelates by sending his agents to Paris armed with the usual repertory of papal favors and promises.[31] That one of these was the tactless and non-compliant Car-

---

29. For Plaoul's speech see BdeC: 64 ("mihi est injunctum, quod proponam pro totali"); the university's vote is on p. 76, and cf. p. 79.

30. ALKG, 6:267 f.

31. Ibid.: 267 (esp. "papa multum confidit de aliquibus de consilio regis").

dinal Martin de Salva, whose mission indeed the royal government refused to allow, suggests that the pope had gone beyond mere defensive thinking and hoped to create a real counter-force in his enemies' own capital.[32] He would fail; but meanwhile the prelates who arrived in Paris as summoned in early May found no royal leadership ready to take things in hand, only talk of prolonged delay. They eventually met by themselves on 14 May to beg the government to act and then had to wait still another week while the royal council "ordered the material"— a phrase that probably covered real dissension.[33] In the event the Berry-Burgundy junta came down in favor of radical action, Martin de Salva was refused permission to come to Paris, and the council opened on 22 May with Simon in control; the preliminary mass of the Holy Spirit was followed by an opening speech delivered "in the name of the king," laying out what must have been the royal council's final decisions.[34]

First he set forth the right and duty of "the Christian kings of this world" to bring peace to the church, noting that this had been the historical role of the French kings in particular; he gave as examples Pepin the Short, Charlemagne, "and many others," including Philip V and Philip VI. In the past, this had been done by force, but today the via facti was impossible; instead King Charles VI had acted to develop a union policy based on the via cessionis, whose origins and vicissitudes Simon reviewed. But Benedict had frustrated this policy, violating the oath he had sworn before and after the conclave that had elected him. Since the fulfillment of the oath had been converted into an immediate obligation by the cardinals' formal declaration to this effect, Benedict's refusal to comply had made him a perjurer. He was therefore not to be obeyed, inasmuch as such obedience "would tend to the destruction of the universal church." Simon then referred to the other requests for cession made by the kings of Spain (i.e., Castile), Aragon, Navarre, and even England, as well as the sentiment for cession of Genoa, Florence, Padua, and other Italian cities. He may also have added more or less extensive arguments in favor of subtraction, drawn chiefly from his treatise, including the prime argument for total subtraction ("A pope keeping the church in schism destroys the universal status of the church and is therefore deprived of administration over it") and the political basis

32. See in general the terms in ALKG, 6:247–253. It was the duke of Berry who took responsibility for denying Salva access to Paris.

33. ALKG, 6:275. For what follows about the course of the council, see in general Valois, 3:148 ff.

34. The text in Ampl. coll., 7:712–714; another copy is in ASV, Arm. 54, t. 21, fols. 190r–191v; much briefer reports are given in ALKG, 6:276 f., and RSD, 2:578–580. See n. 35 below.

of partial subtraction ("Princes are bound to preserve the church of their territory in its original liberty and to take care that it not be oppressed, especially by the pope who has no superior; . . . therefore a pope taking over collations, procurations, etc., is not to be obeyed.")[35] He then stated the official definition of the present council's function: "This is the cause of your convocation by the king, to advise whether the *via cessionis* should be practiced by means of subtraction or how. And although the king could do this on his own, he wants to deliberate with you; so for God's sake be diligent! For if you are negligent the king will ordain as he sees fit."[36] To this was added a formal limitation of the discussion to come: the king had already decided on the *via cessionis* and would pursue it to the end; no one should dare to dispute it, only to discuss ways of implementing it. Simon concluded with the flat statement that "the king" would convoke additional sessions of the council to declare what he had in mind, "so that the clergy might be dismissed as soon as possible."[37]

If all this reminds us of the tightly managed First Paris Council, it must have had the same effect on Benedict's supporters at the time. Their chief, Pierre Ravat, bishop of St. Pons, at once rose to demand that he be allowed to argue the pope's case.[38] Others no doubt supported

---

35. These passages come from a text published in *Ampl. coll.*, 7:714–717, entitled "Motivis sequentibus persuadetur subtractionem fore fiendam" and immediately following the report of the speech proper; the material seems to have been drawn from Simon's *De substraccione obediencie*. It is my surmise that he may have added some or all of this text to the main body of his speech; the report in *ALKG*, 6:276 f., although compressed, covers much more than that in *Ampl. coll.*, 7:712–714, and some of the extra material seems to correspond to the text in question.

36. *Ampl. coll.*, 7:714; ASV, *Arm.* 54, t. 21, fol. 191v, compared.

37. I conflate the following reports of Simon's concluding words: *Ampl. coll.*, 7:714: "Inhibetur tamen vobis ex parte regis et dominorum, quod nullus audeat disceptare super via cessionis disceptive, alias per ipsum electa. Rex mandabit, quando et quod sibi videbitur, et consultabit super materia." *ALKG*, 6:277: "Concludendo, quod rex istam habet pro conclusa, expresse reiecta via, quam papa nunc presentat. Et ista sunt, que rex, ut dicebat, sibi preceperat dicere, et quod breviter rex faceret dici alia, que proposuerat, sic quod brevius, quam fieri posset, clerum expediret." *RSD*, 2:580: "Tandem concludens intulit: 'Et quoniam via ista a tot et tantis electa fuit et conclusa, noverint universi quod rex intendit eam prosequi, et procedere ad unionem per illam. Attamen super modum procedendi alias evocabimini ad bene placitum eius.'"

38. The only source for this episode is *RSD*, 2:580, according to which Benedict had sent the bishop of Mâcon to the council, "qui, post verba domini patriarche, cancellario Francie instantissime requisivit ut fovendo causam domini pape audiretur." In fact there was no bishop of Mâcon at the council, but Pierre Ravat had held that see until 29 March 1398, when he was transferred to St. Pons; the chronicler must have ignored or forgotten the change. Ravat was not only Benedict's man but also, originally, a client of Gaston Phoebus, count of Foix, who in 1362 requested a canonry for him; see ASV, *Reg. Suppl.* 47, fol. 174v.

him, and the royal council had to meet, revise its plans, and provide for the sort of debate that would accommodate the opposition even while keeping it under control. The form would be that of the commissioned debates before the royal council when major issues came before that body, both sides acting under royal mandate; but this time the setup would be like that of the Second Paris Council and unlike that of the First—the spokesmen for each side would in fact be men who favored it.[39] The confrontation would thus be real, but it would be kept within the narrow limits defined by Simon; the papal spokesmen would not be allowed to develop Benedict's alternatives to the *via cessionis* but would have to attack subtraction solely as a means of implementing that way. Thus when Ravat felt that he could not make his point without calling into question the doctrine of the unique sufficiency of cession, the royal chancellor formally forbade him to do so,[40] and the papal side could be cheaply criticized for having failed to propose a way of implementing the cession that in principle they accepted.[41]

The original plan was for six speakers on each side, beginning 29 May, but it turned out that the dukes had had enough halfway through; after 4 June they allowed only one more speech, by the University of Paris's spokesman on 7 June. The two teams consisted of Simon de Cramaud, Gilles Deschamps, and Pierre Leroy versus Pierre Ravat, Jean de Lacoste, and Sancho Muler. Whatever the formalities, the listeners regarded them as representing the king's side and the pope's respectively.[42] It was indeed a major and perhaps unique confrontation between the territorial (alias Gallican) conception of the church and the papalist one, for the issue of subtraction's legitimacy cut very deep, and we have already seen in our discussion of Simon's treatise what the play of contradictions involved. Both Pierre Leroy and Gilles Deschamps, however, developed the Gallican themes far more consistently and fully than Simon had done, and the theoretically less interesting but more practical matter of subtraction's *inconveniencia* or difficulties was also carried beyond the level at which Simon had previously discussed them; both these matters require some attention here.

Ravat's papalist refutation of the Gallican positions has already been

<hr>

39. BdeC: 4; *ALKG*, 6:277 f.; see above, Ch. IV, n. 49.

40. ASV, *Arm.* 54, t. 21, fol. 239r: "Dominus cancellarius dixit michi in concilio publice, quod solum haberem impugnare viam subtraccionis, non justificare alias vias." Ravat adds that he nevertheless did say that other ways than cession had originally been held good by the University of Paris in 1394.

41. See above, Ch. IV, n. 51.

42. *ALKG*, 6:278; BdeC: 4; cf. the ballot of the abbot of Corveville, AN, J 518, fol. 428v: "veu les raisons . . . proposees . . . de la partie du roy. . . ." Several other examples could be given.

noted: The pope was "universal bishop" and could do anything in a
bishop's diocese that a bishop could do; indeed, he went on, the pope's
right to confer all benefices had originally been exercised by the popes
and had only later been granted by them to the ordinaries. There were
no grounds for legal objection if this right had been subsequently taken
back.[43] This false image of history was countered by Leroy's somewhat
truer one: The pope was *not* universal bishop; the rights of the ordinaries
had been decreed in the primitive church—indeed by Christ himself—
and this constitution had been observed for the first 1,200 (alias 1,300)
years of the church's history. It was only subsequently that the popes
had "usurped" the rights in question.[44] The result was a destruction of the
church's sacred hierarchy, a violation of the decrees of the general councils, an unwholesome involvement of the papacy in the petty business of
benefice titles rather than the major concerns that the papacy had been
instituted to deal with; it was a suppression of the church's "ancient
liberty," which should now be restored.[45] Deschamps spelled the point
out: such a restoration "would be legitimate even in a united church."[46] In
the matter of papal fiscal exactions, Ravat could not deny that the
demands for annates, *servicia,* and episcopal procuration fees had been
introduced by recent popes (John XXII, Innocent VI, Urban V), but he
argued that, like any ruler, the pope was entitled to support by his
subjects; in any case, it was sufficient to say that the pope had commanded the payments.[47] This principle took care of the Gallican arguments on points of detail, for example, Leroy's argument that since procurations were due to the bishops as payments for visitations of their
clergy, papal usurpation of such payments destroyed the practice of
visitation and the consequent correction of defects; Ravat simply said
that the pope had the right to take the procurations even if abuses
resulted.[48] On these points he was on fairly solid ground, and there is no
reason to think that the majority of the prelates did not agree with him,
no matter how much they begrudged the payments they had to make;
there are few signs of doctrinaire Gallicanism in the ballots of the
council, as we shall see. Whether the payments should be continued
even under total subtraction was another question, whose resolution

---

43. BdeC: 9; ASV, *Arm. 54,* t. 21, fol. 240r.

44. BdeC: 34 f.; ASV, *Arm.* 54, t. 21, fol. 198v (this version has 1,300 years).

45. BdeC: 35. For the Gallican background see above.

46. BdeC: 46.

47. BdeC: 10 f., 55; ASV, *Arm.* 54, t. 21, fols. 225r ("necessitas Romane ecclesie
est necessitas rei publice"), 225v ("habet communis conclusio quod princeps cui sua non
sufficiunt, pro utilitate rei publice potest a subditis subsidium exigere"), 226v, 239v,
240r.

48. BdeC: 35 f., 55.

would involve the Gallican positions set forth in the debates without being actually determined by them.

The *inconveniencia* alleged by Ravat and his fellows (neither of whom reached his level of solidity) were merely the obvious results of total subtraction. Papal absolutions in cases reserved to papal jurisdiction, papal dispensations for marriage within the prohibited degrees of relationship, dispensations to clerics from impediments to their promotion or provision, papal confirmation of bishops and abbots of exempt monasteries, papal jurisdiction in cases of appeal from bishops' courts—all these and more would not be available in a subtracted church. Simon de Cramaud, as we have seen, proposed various remedies including action by the ordinaries or by the cardinals, but his preferred general remedy was based on the *sede vacante* concept of subtraction: papal officials could continue to discharge their duties even in the absence of a pope.[49] It is instructive to see that Pierre Leroy's "general solution" was action by the ordinaries,[50] while Deschamps argued that the king and prelates, alias the king's council, could handle all problems,[51] and Pierre Plaoul held that all the *inconveniencia* could be resolved "by the necessity of making provision"—the same argument we have seen him making at the Second Paris Council.[52] Obviously the subtractionists would have to work out these contradictions among themselves, and we shall see them doing so at the end of the council; here too, the prelates in general would determine their positions on the basis of practical considerations and their own interests.

Meanwhile, however, the whole discussion of *inconveniencia* must have disturbed them, for Ravat and others not only had raised the questions just noted in regard to total subtraction but had also pointed to others consequent on partial: Would not the ordinaries and corporations be forced by the secular powers to grant benefices to clients of the latter? What would happen when holders of papal provisions tried to use them to get benefices against those chosen by the ordinaries? Would not the king follow the cardinals' program and collect papal revenues himself? What would prevent Benedict from excommunicating those who defied

---

49. Above, n. 24.

50. BdeC: 62. After discussing various *inconveniencia* which could be taken care of by the ordinaries, Leroy summed up: "ut generalis sit [*ms.* fuit] solutio, dico, quod nulla sunt allegata, quin possit [!] optime provideri" (BN, *ms. lat.* 14,644, fol. 74v, compared).

51. BdeC: 47: "Restat respondere ad inconvenientia allegata per D. S. Pontii [scil., Ravat] et alios, et pro solutione communi, dico quod nulla allegata sunt, quin possit [!] per regem et praelatos faciliter provideri." The version in ASV, *Arm.* 54, t. 21, fol. 209v, reads, "non video malum quin possit per concilium regis provideri."

52. BdeC: 74: "omnia alia argumenta solvuntur propter necessitatem provisionis."

him?[53] On 30 May Simon de Cramaud offered "the king's" assurance that, in case subtraction were approved, he would on the one hand force all the clergy to go along, on the other hand refrain from taking the church's property and converting it to his own use; "I have been ordered to tell you," Simon said, "that he intends to keep the church in peace and in its ancient liberty."[54] On 10 June, after a meeting of the royal council, the dukes ordered the royal chancellor Arnaud de Corbie to make the same promises in more formal style: first, if the clergy voted subtraction and the king accepted that counsel, the king and dukes would protect all from Benedict's reprisals; second, those acting against subtraction would be punished as schismatics; third, collations and elections to benefices would be free from pressure by the princes or nobles; fourth, the king would not take over the papal fiscal rights but would "keep the church of his realm in its ancient liberty."[55] We shall see these promises repeated and eventually guaranteed by royal ordinances at the prelates' insistence; it may not be too much to say that they owed these benefits in good part to the opposition manifested in the debates by both papalists and Gallicans to the program envisaged by Simon and the cardinals.

At the same time, however, the chancellor also prescribed the form of voting recommended by the cardinals: each member of the council would appear alone before the dukes and read out his written opinion, which would then be deposited. Begun on 11 June, the vote was interrupted once, on the 14th, by the University of Paris's public declaration of its adherence to both total and partial subtraction; this influenced a number of the clergy.[56] By 20 June the vote must have been complete, with a large majority voting for immediate and total subtraction. The majority was now swollen by eighty-one masters of the University of Paris, brought in for the purpose; and in early July the dukes cast their own ballots, all except Orléans voting for subtraction. Meanwhile the prelates had requested and were promised the first token of royal protection, a mandate forbidding the papal collectors to continue their exactions from

---

53. BdeC: 9 f.; see the next two notes, and at n. 27 above.

54. BdeC: 27: "Non obstat cum dicitur, praelati non obedient, etc. Dico quod . . . rex potest providere talibus inconvenientibus, et tenentur praelati obedire, et suum intellectum captivare, maxime habita conclusione per concilium. . . . Nec valet quod dicunt adversarii, quod rex capiet bona ecclesiae, fient in pensiones. Hoc est male dictum. . . ; intendit ecclesiam pacificare et eam tenere in antiqua libertate. Mihi est injunctum quod ego dicam vobis."

55. BdeC: 74 f. The report in *ALKG*, 6:282, is slightly different and gives five points instead of four, but the ballot of Jean Canart (App. I) shows that the official formula consisted of four points.

56. See the examples cited in Kaminsky, "Politics": 377 n. 55, and see Table 4 below.

the French clergy, whose long stay in Paris was costing them so much.[57]

One important addition to the subtractionist program was probably yet another response to criticisms by Benedict's party. Simon de Cramaud had not at first spelled out just how subtraction would lead to union; he had just talked of getting together with the English and Germans, that is, with Richard II and Wenceslas IV. Pierre Ravat had remarked on how vague this was.[58] When it came his turn to vote, Simon therefore proposed something more definite, a representative council of the whole church of both obediences. Each realm would send princes and prelates to meet together and act in conjunction with the cardinals of both colleges and in the presence of both popes, "willing or not." This council could demand that the papal contenders abdicate and, if they refused, depose them; election of a new pope could then follow at once. He went on to advise that the crown should appoint "certain clerics and notable persons" to implement this plan and meanwhile provide against the problems arising from Benedict's anticipated counter-measures.[59] On 20 June he presented the first part of this plan to the prelates, with the approval of the royal council and in a more elaborate form: the Gallican church would constitute as its representatives each archbishop and two bishops, two abbots, and two canons from each ecclesiastical province. We are told that the plan found favor with almost all, some even beginning to discuss who the representatives would be; if we also read that the meeting was forthwith adjourned and the matter was not taken up again as it should have been in the following week, we can suppose

---

57. The text of the royal letter in ASV, *Arm.* 54, t. 21, fol. 190r, dated 20 June and stating that it was requested by several bishops, abbots, and chapters currently in Paris for a council concerned with church union; the date fits only the Third. There is no evidence that the ordinance was in fact issued; this private copy in the *Libri de Schismate* is the only one known.

58. Simon's talk is known from Ravat's critical comments in his speech of 3 June, ASV, *Arm.* 54, t. 21, fol. 236r: "[Patriarcha] dixerat quod congregarentur prelati aliqui Francie, Anglie, et Almanie, ut reciperetur aliquid de qualibet via et ad alia procederetur, etc."; also fol. 240v: "dixit d. Patriarcha, postquam subtraxerimus ei obedienciam, conveniemus cum Anglicis et cum Almanis."

59. AN, J 518, fol. 366r: "Me semble que pour avoir un pape on devroit assembler de chascun royaume certaine quantite de princes et de prelaz ayans povoir de tous les autres en petit nombre, et adviser un lieu pour assembler avec le college des cardinaulx d'Avignon et ceulx de Rome, et les deux contendans vueillent ou non, et lors l'eglise toute ainsi assemblee par representacion pourroit faire un pape iuste et paisible, et faire renuncier ces deux contendans ou les punir comme scismatiques" (quoted in Valois, 3:163 n. 3). Simon went on, "Item est necessite, se le roy prent ceste conclusion, que lettres en soient faites par bonne deliberacion et bien tost, pour plusieurs causes, et aussi que le roy ordene, sur ce et autres choses touchant les provisions que on pourroit et devroit faire en ceste matiere contre sa male voulente, aucuns clers et notables personnes, des maintenant, qui advisent ce qui de droit et de raison pourra estre fait."

that the government wanted to take care of the business in its own time and way, as indeed we shall see in a moment.[60] Meanwhile we note how the political interplay at the council had forced the crystallization of Simon's program into its final form: a subversive, depositionary general council would consummate the *via cessionis*. It was the birth of what would become the councils of Pisa and Constance.

It was not until 27 July that the results of the voting were presented to the king and received his approval. The month's delay may have been due to the need to wait for him to emerge from insanity,[61] but more likely the dukes and royal councillors had to work out the line they would take in dealing with the clergy. The vote in any case had left little to be desired, and on 28 July Arnaud de Corbie could announce to the council that 247 had voted for immediate subtraction of total obedience until Benedict should accept the *via cessionis*; 18–20 had voted for subtraction with execution deferred until Benedict should have been summoned once more to accept; 16–18 had voted for another summation, to be followed if refused by a council of the Avignon obedience; a few votes (in fact 17) had been "singular." The king's acceptance of this "counsel" was declared, and the promise of royal protection of the clergy's "liberties and ancient franchises" was repeated, the duke of Berry adding the promise or threat that anyone going against the subtraction would be punished.[62]

But was the government's count truthful? The ballots survive, and Valois, the first historian to study them, has charged that these more or less long, often individualistic and qualified statements of opinion do not in fact fall into the above pattern; asking what each voter really thought about subtraction, he arrived at the conclusion that "the majority favorable to subtraction of total obedience was so feeble as to make one wonder if the result of the council would not have been quite different without the pressure exercised by the government from the very first day."[63] No doubt it would have been, but that is not the point; the pressure had in fact worked very well, and the majority was not

60. *ALKG*, 6:284. A copy of a list of "names of prelates who seem well-disposed for the council in question" survives in the *Libri de Schismate* and is published in *ALKG*, 6:195 f. (cf. Valois, 3:164 n. 1, for the date); it corresponds exactly to the scheme for provincial representation, but there is no evidence that it was ever used or given official status.

61. Valois, 3:166, 169; the sources he cites show that the king was lucid but still incapable of asserting a will of his own, and one wonders whether similar moments had not occurred earlier.

62. BdeC: 80–84; *ALKG*, 6:285 f.; Bulaeus, 4:847 f.

63. Valois, 3:172–182. The original ballots are collected in AN, J 517; codex J 518 has a contemporary copy of all of them, which I use for convenience—spot-checking of about two dozen shows the copy is faithful.

TABLE 1
The Vote According to Status

	Bishops	Chapters	Abbots	Totals
For	42	41	57	140
Against	27	25	16	68
Unclear	2	4		6
Totals	71	70	73	214

TABLE 2
The Vote by Benedict's Bishops

	Benedict's Appointees	Earlier Appointees
For	3	39
Against	7	20
Unclear	1	1

feeble at all. As Haller has argued, the government did not falsify the vote but, rather, quantified the ballots on the basis of its own question, whether the voter stood for or against the government's desired policy, with all qualifications disregarded that did not come down to rejection of subtraction.[64] My own study of the ballots on the basis of this criterion pretty much confirms the government's count, and I go on to ask other questions of historical interest. The results, omitting the ninety-three "for" votes cast by eighty-one masters of the University of Paris, each of the four universities of the realm, and the dukes and other notables, are shown in Tables 1–4.

It can be seen from the tables that the government's count was pretty much correct and that the Third Paris Council had fulfilled its purpose of securing massive and ostentatious support by the clerical estate for the crown's proposed action in the field of church policy. Subtraction could now be presented to the world as a "well-advised" action, taken "with the most mature deliberation"—key terms of public relations in the political world of estates.[65] The tables show something of how the result was obtained. In Table 1 we see a respectable vote for subtraction by the bishops and chapters boosted into an overwhelming majority by the abbots. Table 2 makes it clear what Simon and his associates had in mind when they accused Benedict of using his powers of appointment to put in men favoring his cause. Even Ithier de Martreuil, bishop of

---

64. Haller, *PKR*: 535–543.
65. See, for example, the formulation in Canart's vote cited below.

226   Simon de Cramaud

TABLE 3
The Vote by Regions (for:against)

	Bishops	Chapters	Abbots	Totals
North and central[a]	21:8	18:13	39:13	78:34
	(2 unclear)	(3 unclear)		
Normandy and Brittany[b]	12:1	11:1	15:1	38:3
Languedoc[c]	7:13	9:11	3:2	19:26
Aquitaine[d]	2:5	3:0		5:5
		(1 unclear)		

[a]The ecclesiastical provinces of Sens and Rheims, the northern parts of Bourges, Bordeaux, and Lyon-Vienne (which the record of the ballots lumps together), and the non-Breton parts of Tours. *Bishops for*: Sens, Orléans, Chartres, Meaux, Laon, Senlis, Arras, Soissons, Châlons, Angers, Bourges, Cahors, Poitiers, St. Flour, Luçon, Clermont, Saintes, Lyons, Chalon-sur-Saône, Grenoble, Angoulême. *Bishops against*: Troyes, Paris, Auxerre, Rheims, Beauvais, Thérouanne, Amiens, Autun. *Unclear*: Tours, Tulle.
[b]The church province of Rouen and the Breton part of Tours. *For*: Rouen, Séez, Evreux, Avranches, Bayeux, Lisieux, Quimper, Tréguier, St. Malo, St. Brieuc, Rennes, Dol. *Against*: Vannes.
[c]All of Narbonne, Toulouse east of the Garonne, the south of Bourges, the southeast of Auch, the south of Vienne. *For*: Mende, Carcassonne, Uzès, Béziers, Nîmes, Lavaur, Viviers. *Against*: Rodez, Albi, Castres, Vabres, Le Puy, St. Pons, Agde, Maguelone, Pamiers, Comminges, Toulouse, St. Papoul, Mirepoix. The last three voted by a proctor, Vital de Castel-Moron, who said only that he repeated his opinion in the Second Paris Council; I agree with Valois (3:177 n. 9) that the votes were almost certainly negative.
[d]Parts of Bordeaux and Auch. *For*: Condom, Lombes. *Against*: Auch, Couserans, Lectoure, Agen, Périgueux.

TABLE 4
The Vote for Subtraction

	Total	Total and Partial	(Including Strong Partial)
Bishops	23	19	(10)
Chapters	33	8	(2)
Abbots	44	13	(5)

Note: For examples of strong statements for partial subtraction, see Valois, 3:157 n. 2; Haller, *PKR*: 369; also the votes of Jean Montaigu and Jean Canart quoted below. Twelve votes among the abbots for "total" have phrases like "la voye de sustraccion par la maniere que nostre mere l'universite la propose, est assavoir, de sustraire l'obeissance totale" (AN, J 518, fol. 399v); I assume this was a formula and was not intended to invoke the university's official insistence on partial subtraction along with total (rather than as merely a consequence of total).

Poitiers and chancellor of the duke of Berry, also however one of Benedict's appointees, originally wrote a ballot against subtraction, asking
that Benedict be summoned one more time, then changed it to make
this conditional on the majority's approval; his hesitation was certainly
due to a conflict of loyalties.[66] The lesson of Table 3 is perhaps the most
interesting of all: subtraction was obviously a policy of the north imposed on the south, and in the north it was Normandy (with Brittany)
that gave the most decisive support to the crown—and let us recall that
both Pierre Leroy and Gilles Deschamps were Normans. We have seen in
an earlier chapter that the Avignon papacy had always been a southern-
French construction; the long tradition of Aragonese-Languedocian mu-
tuality found current embodiment in the pontificate of Benedict XIII,
whose inner circles were filled with southerners and Spaniards, and all of
whose spokesmen at the council were of this sort—a point illuminated
when we see Pierre Ravat excusing himself for speaking in his native
Tolosan because he did not know "Gallican."[67] Both Simon de Cramaud
and the duke of Berry had played roles in the direct exploitation of the
south; the Third Paris Council, which they dominated, marks a different
but no less effective sort of subjugation by the north.

Tables 1 and 4 raise other points, bearing on the practical issues still
to be worked out in the council. Both cathedral chapters and monasteries enjoyed extensive, often total, privileges of exemption from the
jurisdiction of their bishops; these had been granted by the popes, and it
was papal authority that stood behind the corporations in their frequent
conflicts over episcopal claims. But subtraction would remove papal
lordship and enhance episcopal power. Why, then, did the chapters
support subtraction in about the same ratio as the bishops, and why was
the abbots' majority so large? One answer would be that by the end of
the fourteenth century, royal protection of churches had become common; royal jurisdiction in ecclesiastical disputes had developed into what
has been called *Gallicanisme parlementaire*; and it was now the Parlement
of Paris along with the papacy that received complaints in cases involv-

---

66. The original ballot in AN, J 517, n. 56, written in Ithier's own hand, shows
that he first wrote, "Et videtur michi quod esset honestum quod execucio istius subtraccionis suspenderetur, quousque iterato fuisset [Benedictus] requisitus per clerum pre-
sentem, et assignaretur certa dies," then changed it to "Et videtur michi quod in casu
quod maior pars condescenderet, quod per clerum requireretur, et debet ei assignari
certa dies."

67. "Et primo excusavi me de vulgari, quia nesciebam Gallicum, sed Tholosanum"—
ASV, *Arm.* 54, t. 21, fol. 230r. Whether the dukes and other northerners understood
him may be doubted; cf. Ch. VIII, n. 70, below, for the different tactic of the Lan-
guedocians in 1406.

ing ecclesiastical privileges and jurisdictions.[68] Table 4 underlines the point. The cleric who entered the presence of the dukes and voted for total and immediate subtraction was voting "right" and had no reason of prudence to say anything more. If he went on to say that he also supported partial subtraction and perhaps added a few words about recovering the Gallican Liberties, that was an extra, hardly explainable except on the basis of prior conviction or of a realization that, in the event of subtraction, the Liberties would benefit him. Almost half the bishops added such extra clauses to their votes, and ten of these made strong statements. But the corresponding fractions of the chapters' and abbots' votes are so much smaller as to suggest that these groups were voting chiefly to support the crown in the political sort of total subtraction it was pressing for. The crown was their lord and entitled to their support; it could in return be expected to protect their rights and privileges.

The Gallican sentiments of some prelates and no doubt many university masters were destined to play an important role in the last week of the council, indeed as soon as Arnaud de Corbie had announced the vote. We have seen what total subtraction meant to the cardinals, to Simon de Cramaud, and no doubt to various other elements in the governing circles: papal rights to be preserved on a *sede vacante* basis, with only that minimum of temporary Gallican Liberty required by the temporary absence of a pope. The complicated work of running the new ecclesiastical structure and guiding it through vicissitudes would presumably be left to the small group of "certain clerics and notable persons" that Simon had called for in his vote; these would be vested with the authority of the Gallican church by a procuration that the prelates and proctors would make in due legal form.[69] They would also vote a financial aid to the crown. All this would be done in the week following 28 July; and on 4 August, according to Arnaud de Corbie's announce-

---

68. Guillaume Mollat, "Conflits entre archidiacres et évêques aux XIVe et XVe siècles," *Revue historique de droit français et étranger,* 4th series, 35 (1957):549–560; idem, in *Histoire des institutions françaises au moyen âge,* 3 (Paris, 1962):342 ff., 362 ff.; J. Gaudemet, ibid.: 245; Guillaume Mollat, "Les origines du Gallicanisme parlementaire aux XIVe et XVe siècles," *Revue d'histoire ecclésiastique,* 43 (1948):90–147; Jean-Pierre Royer, *L'Église et le royaume de France au XIVe siècle* (Paris, 1969): 227–312.

69. The draft of a procuration in which the king and the Gallican church empower unnamed proctors to do everything necessary at the future representative general council survives in a copy in the *Libri de Schismate,* ASV, Arm. 54, t. 26, fol. 150rv (see Valois, 3:164 n. 1). It allows the king to increase or reduce the number of proctors and allows the latter to add "whatever of substance or solemnity might be necessary to pursuit of the present business." There is no evidence that it was officially promulgated, constituted, or used, but its existence suggests the terms in which the government was thinking. See also the discussion of the procuration below.

ment, the council would formally end with a thanksgiving procession to the church of St. Genevieve and—one supposes—the publication of the subtraction ordinance.[70]

But even the duke of Burgundy had foreseen that the clergy would not want to vote an aid in defiance of papal authority until the subtraction had in fact been made, and that meant not just a promise but actual promulgation in royal ordinances. And what precisely would be the legal status of clerical persons, corporations, and privileges in the church headed by the king rather than the pope? What guarantees would they have that their exercise of collationary rights and their non-payment of papal charges would not be accounted illicit in some future time of restoration? There were many questions of this sort, corresponding to the extreme complexity of the papal system that was now being suspended, and all of them had to be answered by something more definite than Simon's little steering committee and vague assurances of royal goodwill and ducal protection. The financial aid itself could not just be voted without ado; there had to be safeguards for the future and recognition of the principle of clerical liberty—otherwise the clergy would soon find themselves taxed at will by their royal master. Thus, even though there is no reason to think that the doctrines of Gallican Liberty had been cultivated by more than a minority, the new situation created on 28 July made those doctrines peculiarly appropriate to the clergy's needs. It was not Gallicanism but simply the logic of the lord–subject relationship that had led the great majority of the clergy to consent to the crown's desire for total subtraction, but it was Gallicanism now that provided the clergy with the only practical model for preservation of their *status* in the subtracted church.

The most fully developed Gallican programs in the ballots of the council appear in those cast by Bishop Jean Canart of Arras and Bishop Jean Montaigu of Chartres, respectively the chancellor of the duke of Burgundy and a member of a family attached to the duke of Orléans. Both were important men, apt to have been leaders of the clergy in the present conjunction. Montaigu had voted for total subtraction but had also requested that the king, with the council, decree "that the church of this realm be free"—no papal exactions ("unless from the greater benefices") and the ordinaries to have the collation of benefices; this decree should be promulgated "right now, along with the total subtraction."[71]

---

70. This report of Arnaud de Corbie's speech, in French, concludes the main account of the council by Guillaume de Longueil (BN, *ms. lat.* 14,644, fols. 81v–82v; published in Bulaeus, 4:847 f.).

71. AN, J 518, fol. 395rv; see Kaminsky, "Politics": 385, for a fuller excerpt and quotation of the French original.

This corresponded to the university's formula of total subtraction added to partial, and it reflected the same set of ideas going far beyond the merely political matter of how to end the Schism. Jean Canart's ballot expressed the same views, but in a detailed eight-point program that applied the ideals of Gallicanism to the issues of political action that remained before the council. We shall see that his project seems to have guided the prelates in their subsequent negotiations with the crown; it is an important text, given in full in Appendix I.

First of all, he voted for total subtraction until Benedict should have accepted the *via cessionis* and begun to implement it. Second, however, he asked that "the king should restore the church of his realm to its due and ancient liberty, simply and absolutely, without any time limit," and he spelled out this liberty in its Gallican sense. Collations and elections and confirmations to benefices were to be made by those ordinarily entitled thereto, and there should be an end to "exactions imposed on churches against the provisions of the law and against the *status* of the universal church." These included annates, pensions imposed by the pope on certain benefices,[72] the papal *ius spolii* (confiscation of a dead prelate's movable property), and papal claims to the bishops' procuration fees. All these were usurpations and could not be validated by "prescription"—their long-standing practice.[73] Third, while "particular subtraction"—the cutting back of these papal abuses—had to be implemented as a distinct program, for otherwise "the Gallican church would remain under the yoke of perpetual servitude," total subtraction had also to be implemented along with particular, so that the pope might not be able to take reprisals against the clergy of the realm. The fourth point was a call for working out in detail of the scheme advanced by Simon de Cramaud for a representative general council of both obediences, including the cardinals, and its serious promotion by the French crown among the princes and prelates of both obediences. Canart then passed in point 5 to the *inconveniencia* described by the "negative" side in the debates, particularly in the matter of still-outstanding papal provisions to benefices, for some of which legal actions had already been begun—all these should be quashed, for the sake of union and "the public good."

It would be very useful, he noted in his sixth point, to get the consent of the cardinals and the chief barons of the realm to the imminent subtraction, to give the act more solemnity and a better chance of

---

72. See Favier, *Finances*, index, s.v. "pensions," for the popes' use of this practice to benefit cardinals and lay personages.

73. Canart here refutes the assertion of Pierre Ravat at the council: "et vix est memoria de contrario quin papa contulerit beneficia, receperit annatas et procuraciones" (ASV, *Arm.* 54, t. 21, fol. 240r).

acceptance, but the subtraction should not be delayed for this reason. In the future, moreover (point 8), the royal ordinances previously issued against recognition of Benedict's newly created cardinals and of his collations of unacceptable candidates to benefices in the realm should be enforced more diligently than in the past, to ensure the government's credibility in its similar ordinances to come.

Canart's seventh point may be quoted in full: "With regard to the four points publicly stated by the chancellor on the king's behalf in a meeting of the council, royal letters should be prepared on these and given to everyone requesting a copy, for the better preservation of the liberty of prelates and churches." We shall see this point taken up earnestly by the prelates after the vote had been announced; it carried profound constitutional implications and also represented the common sense of a political expert who knew how little trust one could put in royal or ducal promises that were not embodied in official, legally usable decrees.

A crucial point in this Gallican line of thought was that, while the total subtraction should be directed against Benedict, the partial subtraction (i.e., the Gallican Liberties) should be from the papacy itself. Hence the provision in Canart's vote and many others that the total subtraction would last only until Benedict accepted cession; Simon de Cramaud wanted no such possibility of a restoration (and managed to get his views into the royal ordinance).[74] Hence too, the insistence on a separate royal establishment of Gallican Liberty apart from the total subtraction and without reference to any time limit or conditions relating to the Schism. The same concern appears in a request by Bernard Alamant speaking "in the name of most of the prelates" right after Arnaud de Corbie's address on 28 July: he asked that the subtraction be put under the legal protection of an appeal to a future uncontested pope. This went against the legal basis of total subtraction as set forth by Simon and the cardinals: the notoriety of Benedict's schism and heresy sufficed to justify withdrawing from his obedience, and the public declaration of subtraction would also declare him to be a schismatic; hence "he would have no power to sentence anyone, but would be lower than any Christian."[75] No appeal was needed. Alamant's request must therefore be understood

---

74. The majority vote as announced by Arnaud de Corbie was for total substraction until Benedict should have accepted the *via cessionis*; the royal ordinance of subtraction, 27 July, dropped the condition; see the discussion in Valois, 3:183. Haller's view that the condition remained nevertheless, *PKR*: 242, seems baseless; in any case, the *Avisamenta* discussed below outdates both Valois and Haller on this point.

75. For Alamant's requests see BdeC: 83; *ALKG*, 6:286; for Simon's speech of 30 May, BdeC: 27.

as one more sign of resistance: total subtraction was not to be excluded by partial but added to it, as the university had said; and the Liberties involved in partial subtraction would have to remain in force even after Benedict had been replaced. Indeed the appeal itself implied that the pope appealed from was a legally competent public person rather than the civilly dead schismatic-heretic of the totalists, so that the Liberties were being instituted in his face, not outside his position. Arnaud de Corbie's reply to Alamant was that "sufficient provision had been made for this," and it was generally understood that the prelates and proctors would make a procuration constituting their representatives to lodge the appeal;[76] what all this meant on the government's side was something else, as we shall see.

Exactly what argument took place on 28 July is unknown, but the confrontation of the two positions we have delineated must have produced its effect. For we find that the government's scenario had to be replaced by one conforming precisely to the prospectus laid out by Jean Canart. Arnaud de Corbie had to advance the date of the procession from 4 August to 1 August, on which date the subtraction ordinance would be published—the sine qua non, in the prelates' view, of any further action on their part—and he had to promise that the prelates' counsel about the nature of the subtraction regime could be duly given; royal secretaries would indeed be provided to take down "the points concerning this matter," which would then be "ordered and defined, point by point."[77] The process of ordering and defining took place between 28 and 31 July, producing a list of points known to us in one surviving copy, written in French and subsequently labelled *Avisamenta,* which also bears its quondam possessor's Latin notes indicating the disposition of each article in the discussions that ensued, beginning on 2 August and ending by the 8th.[78] Another text, *Sur les inconveniens qui pourroient advenir a cause*

---

76. Arnaud's words in BdeC: 83; *ALKG,* 6:286; *Sur les inconveniens* (see n. 79 below) has, "on pourra provoquer ou appeller, en tant comme besoing en est." The procuration is discussed just below.

77. The date of 4 August is given in the French report of Arnaud's speech cited above, n. 70; the date of 1 August along with the other information I summarize here appears in the Latin report of the speech in BdeC: 79–84. See Kaminsky, "Politics": 386, where I give my reasons for thinking that the discrepancy represents the difference between a first speech and a revision of it to take account of the prelates' demands; the Latin report would have embodied the second version.

78. The "Avisamenta necessaria pro ecclesiasticis, tam prelatis quam aliis, quomodo se regent post substraccionem" (a descriptive title in the hand of the Latin notes, for which, see below) was discovered in an unrelated papal codex by Geoffrey Barraclough, who edited it in "Un document inédit sur la soustraction d'obédience de 1398," *Revue d'histoire ecclésiastique,* 30 (1934):101–115, the text on pp. 113–115. Barraclough identifies the hand of the French articles as that of the royal chancery, the hand of the Latin

de la substraccion, corresponds roughly to §§ 11–17 of the *Avisamenta* and also records the discussions on these points; it can be used in conjunction with the *Avisamenta.*[79] We shall follow the latter's order more or less closely in the following analysis.

Point 1 requested the royal ordinance of subtraction and its executory letters; the Latin note, evidently added after 1 August, says that this has been done. Point 3 mentions that a "good counsel" about the *inconveniencia* was said to be available and requests copies; this seems to refer to the headings of *Sur les inconveniens,* and the Latin note accordingly refers to §§ 11–17 below. Points 2 and 4, however, are more complex, asking for:

[2]   A notarized instrument of the procuration mentioned on Sunday, 28 July. And if it has not been officially published, then let it be. And a letter promulgating it for the use of the prelates, if need be, as adherents.

and:

[4]   A letter or copy of the procuration ordered to be made by the prelates to certain persons; and the names of these persons who are to pursue the principal matter, of union.

The prelates were evidently asking about two distinct procurations, one to pursue the appeal and a second to constitute representatives of the Gallican church to work for union—as in Jean Canart's fourth point. But while the Latin note to § 2 reads, "It has been drawn up and adhered to by all, notarized as a public instrument," the note to § 4 says, "This is contained in the procuration mentioned above."[80] It is impossible to avoid the inference that Simon de Cramaud and others running affairs from the government's end had deliberately combined

---

notes as that of the papal chancery. It is an original document, not a copy, written on paper whose watermark is like no. 8477 of C. M. Briquet, *Les Filigranes,* new ed. (Amsterdam, 1968), attested for Paris 1398 in a register of Parlement. The text was written after the meeting of 28 July, which it refers to as past (§ 2), and before the publication of the subtraction ordinance on 1 August, which it refers to as not yet written (§ 1). I have consulted the original but cite Barraclough's edition; for more details and quotations of the text on each point, see Kaminsky, "Politics": 386 ff.

79. The text, "Sur les inconveniens qui pourroient advenir a cause de la substraccion de obeissance totale, ont este advisez les provisions et remedes qui s'ensuivent," has been edited from BN, *ms. lat.* 14,643, fol. 335rv, by Bulaeus, 4:851 f., and BdeC: 291 f. I use my own collation of this ms. with the text in *ms. lat.* 12,544, fols. 28v–29v. Although the division is less formal than in the *Avisamenta,* this document also consists of points for discussion plus a record of what was said.

80. *Ad* § 2, "Facta fuit et per omnes passata, notata manu publica." *Ad* § 4, "Istud continetur in procuracione de qua superius fit mencio." See Kaminsky, "Politics": 388 n. 123, for my disagreement with Barraclough's interpretation of the note to § 2; cf. Charles Ducange's *Glossarium* for "passare" as "pactionem facere."

the two procurations in order, first, to frustrate or downplay the appeal and, second, to get a small inside group empowered by the Gallican church rather than an elaborately representative group as mentioned on 20 June. In fact, the single procuration that the clergy made did *not* mention the names of those empowered thereby,[81] and we can be sure that the omission was intentional.

Point 5 of the *Avisamenta* shows the prelates pursuing the Gallican demands formulated by Jean Canart and Jean Montaigu:

Inasmuch as it has been said that before the general subtraction the king would ordain, for the liberty of the church, that all charges customarily levied by the popes on the church or the clergy would cease; and also that the prelates will be able to grant out the benefices in their collation—that the prelates have letters on this to show for their permanent excusation, even when a pope should be well ordained.

Both this mention of an earlier promise and a corresponding passage in *Sur les inconveniens* imply that at some point, perhaps at the meeting of 28 July, the government's promises of protection during subtraction had been teased into a more permanent commitment, the protection to be prior to the subtraction and hence capable of surviving it. If so, the promise was not honored, for the Latin note to § 5 reads, "This has not so far been provided for," and in fact the royal ordinance reserving collations to the French clergy and ending papal fiscal exactions was issued with a predating only to 27 July, the date given to the subtraction ordinance itself, and it established the Liberties only as a consequence of the subtraction. Hence there was nothing to allow the prelates to "excuse" themselves from allowing collations and finances to a future uncontested pope.[82] On the other hand, the ordinance did at least provide that, on these matters, the subtraction would be arranged in the prelates' interest and not on a *sede vacante* basis, nor with the crown collecting papal revenues or interfering with collations.[83] For most of the prelates, one suspects, this was the crucial point: the Gallican Liberties had served to formulate the model of a subtraction in which the burdens of the papal system would not have to be borne in the absence of its benefits, and had a majority of the prelates wanted more they would have fought harder. Their main interest seems to have been to protect their *status* during the subtraction. This can also be seen from a different angle in the points concerning the grant of a financial aid (§§ 6–9); for

---

81. See n. 69 above.

82. For "excuse" see *Dictionnaire de droit canonique,* 5 (Paris, 1953):628, "toute cause qui justifie l'inexécution d'une obligation . . . légale."

83. The text in *Ordonnances,* 8:270 f.

while the Latin note reads that "aids from the clergy were granted for a
three-year period, just as the pope had customarily granted them to the
king," the articles show that the prelates demanded and got all the usual
securities: a royal stipulation that the grant would be "without prejudice
to the church," a royal promise that no more money would be requested
from the clergy during the period of the aid, and royal agreement that
the agencies of collection would be set up by the clergy, with no secular
coercion unless requested.[84]

Point 10 of the *Avisamenta* takes us deeper still into the dialectic
between crown and clergy. It was a request for royal letters confirming
"the privileges, ordinances, and good customs of the churches, and those
granted to them by the kings." The prelates presented the request with
some diffidence as a counsel that the dukes be asked to procure the grant
by persons in whom they had confidence; at the same time, the tone of
the article conveys a sense of urgency: "It would be . . . a great honor to
our lords if they would provide aid and relief to the church in her need."
What the prelates wanted, apparently, was a set of comprehensive royal
letters confirming every right and privilege currently possessed by every
church, whether of royal or other origin—in short, a new legal establishment of the church to carry it through the uncharted waters into
which the crown was leading it.[85] Who could foresee the future? Valuable
in any event, the desired royal privilege could, if the emergency lasted,
become the foundation charter of a distinct Gallican church. Needless to
say, the request was not granted. Royal privileges were sold, not given
away; and neither the clergy's vote for subtraction nor their grant of
financial aid entitled them to anything so vastly transcending the immediate issue.[86] But once again we may remark that if a majority had
really been intent on Gallicanism for its own sake, there would have
been some evidence of a struggle on this point; in fact, there was none.

When it came time to discuss the *inconveniencia,* there was an effort,
most likely by the Cramaud group, to win support for a *sede vacante*

---

84. See Valois, 3:187, for the nature of the aid and other texts relating to it; the aids
were sales taxes on all merchandise, with special rates for salt and beverages. See in
general Maurice Rey, *Le domaine du roi et les finances extraordinaires sous Charles VI,
1388–1413* (Paris, 1965): 228–262; on p. 341 he writes that a tenth (10 percent of half
the assessed value of benefices) was also voted at this council, but he gives no sources.

85. This is my interpretation of the language in the text: "Item, advisent nosseigneurs les prelas de faire adviser a part nosseigneurs, que ilz veulent octroyer que le
roy conferme les privilieges, les ordonnances, et bons usages des eglises et a eulz octroyez
par les roys. . . ."

86. For the principle relating aid to privileges, I follow R. Cazelles, "La réglementa-
tion royale de la guerre privée de Saint Louis à Charles V et la précarité des ordonnances," *Revue historique de droit français et étranger,* 4th series, 38 (1960):547.

solution in such matters as absolutions[87] and dispensations[88] in cases reserved to the pope, cases of first instance pending in the papal court,[89]
and perhaps also the status of debts to the Apostolic Camera. On all
these points the prelates rejected such a solution in favor of the rights
and powers of the ordinaries—that is, the bishops in their respective
dioceses. But here we find no trace of a Gallican desire to make the
chosen solution permanent; rather, an explicit recognition that sooner or
later the re-establishment of papal authority would resolve matters that
had been settled provisionally or left pending. Thus, previously incurred
debts to the Camera were only suspended, not cancelled.[90] When the

---

87. "Absolutions in cases reserved to the pope, which are many," forms § 11 of the
Avisamenta; and the Latin note reads, "Deliberatum est quod prelati absolvent": on the
basis of four canons: X. 5. 39, Chs. 11, 26, 58, and *Sext*, 5, 11. 22. These provide for a
conditional absolution until such time as the one absolved could have access to the pope.
Cramaud had explored this way in his treatise and had cited X. 5. 39. 11; at the same
time, he had also considered treatment of such cases by the grand penitentiary or by the
cardinals (see above, at n. 23); *Sur les inconveniens* records all these proposals as having
been made in the discussions.

88. The Latin note to § 12 of the *Avisamenta* dealing with "dispensations pertaining
to the pope alone" reads, "Consilium dixit quod prelati faciant." *Sur les inconveniens*
reports this view but also the suggestion that the College of Cardinals, if unanimous,
could grant dispensations in major cases like marriage within the forbidden degrees.
Simon's reference to the powers of the grand penitentiary would have applied here as
well.

89. Here there is no explicit evidence of a *sede vacante* proposal, but there was
discussion of different possibilities. The Latin note to *Avisamenta*, § 15, reads, "Fuit
dictum quod ordinarii cognoscent, aliis reiectis," and the *Sur les inconveniens* text in BN,
ms. lat. 14,643, fol. 335v, has, exceptionally, a Latin statement to the same effect: "De
litibus pendentibus in curia romana, veniant litigantes coram ordinariis." But the text in
BN, *ms. lat.* 12,544, fol. 29v, has a more complex statement, in French: "Item, des
pletz pendants en court de Rome, il a este ordonne que eulx demeurront en suspens en
l'estat en quoy ilz sont aujourduy, jusques a ce qu'il soit pourveu a l'eglise d'un seul
pape; se non de commun consentement des partis litigans en la dit court de Rome,
icelles parties vousissent que les diz pletz et litiges prinssent fin devant les ordinaires. Et
donc en ce cas, que les proces fussent apportez de Avignon et renvoiez devant les
ordinaires, qui y peussent proceder et administrer justice, etc." Note that this reports a
decision, not merely a discussion.

90. *Avisamenta* is silent on this point, which, however, must have come up in the
discussion of § 5 (see above). *Sur les inconveniens* shows that there was indeed a discussion
about "those who are under sworn obligation to the pope, to pay on pain of excommunication" and reports that "it was said that by virtue of the subtraction this obligation
was suspended." This was in fact the decision, for it appears in the ordinance covering
collations and exactions, which guarantees that the clergy will remain "quictes et paisi-
bles" vis-à-vis Benedict and his collectors (*Ordonnances*, 8:270 f.; cf. at n. 57 above).
Both Simon and the cardinals had suggested that papal revenues should still be collected
during the subtraction (above), and this may have been the sense of the government's
promises of 10 June, as reported in *ALKG*, 6:282, that the king would not collect the
Camera's moneys but these "would be kept intact" (*conservabuntur integre*). This was not

question was raised of how to supply certain standard papal privileges to clerics—licenses to make wills, to say mass in interdicted territory, and so forth—nothing at all was done.[91] In the matter of appeals, instead of setting up a Gallican structure involving provincial councils, the prelates preferred not to make any provision, in the hope that an uncontested pope would soon be provided.[92] The problems posed by the exempt status of monasteries and other corporations were somewhat more complex, but they were treated in the same spirit. The papacy had been the guarantor of these privileges, had served as a court of appeals in cases concerning them, and had directly confirmed the newly chosen heads of exempt monasteries; now papal power was removed, and it was up to the ordinaries to do all this.[93] It would be the ordinaries too who would "compel" the exempt to pay their share of the clerical aids, using excommunication and recourse to the secular arm. On this last point we happen to know that the council as a body had not treated the question but had left it to the government's leaders of the Gallican church, in this case, Nicholas de Bosc, bishop of Bayeux, and Simon de Cramaud.[94] But insofar as the council did address itself to the particular problems of the new situation, in the matter of how to confirm new abbots, it showed much restraint: the ordinaries would do it but would also provide the new abbots with letters declaring the Gallican church's decision that such practices would not prejudice the exempt status in the future.[95] All in

---

what the council wanted, and in 1399 the cardinals would repeat their request, with equal futility: *ALKG*, 6:297–300; 7:43.

91. *Avisamenta*, § 13: "Item des graces qu'il peut faire, comme de reconcilier, d'absoulte a jour, de faire testament, etc., chanter devant le jour, devant entredis, etc. *Nichil fuit dictum.*"

92. *Sur les inconveniens* records two proposed solutions, leaving the appeals to "the common law, as when the papacy is vacant by death, inasmuch as the church . . . will soon have a pope," or letting the appeals run from bishop to archbishop and from archbishop to the provincial council—to be held once a year. But *Avisamenta*, § 16, shows that there were objections to holding such councils "so often" and that "No decision was taken."

93. *Avisamenta*, § 17: "Item, a qui l'en appellera des exemps? Ou ilz appelleront si sont grevez, ou seront confirmez, ou auront recours? *Fuit dictum quod ad ordinarios.*"

94. Two strips of paper at present glued to the *Avisamenta* contain notes by Bernard Alamant, bishop of Condom, to an unknown bishop who had written to ask how the exempt would be "compelled" under the new regime; Alamant, still in Paris, asked Nicholas de Bosc, bishop of Bayeux, a court prelate, who told him that it was to be done by the ordinaries, using ecclesiastical censure if necessary, with final resort to the secular arm; the next day, Simon de Cramaud confirmed this. "Compel" in context obviously referred to the collection of the clerical aids. See Kaminsky, "Politics": 391 f., for more details.

95. All this is spelled out in *Sur les inconveniens*, and it corresponds exactly to the notarized instrument of the decision preserved in *RSD*, 2:592–596.

all, then, we see a readiness to revive the pre-papalist powers of the bishops and of the Gallican church only as devices for dealing with sub-traction's *inconveniencia* on a provisional basis; there was no desire to make these particular faculties permanent, but rather the reverse. What-ever may be said about the Gallican aspect of the prelates' desire to cut back papal collations and fiscal exactions, it is clear that they appreciated the benefits of papal authority in other respects and wanted to keep them in a united church.

Of all the *inconveniencia,* the problem raised by papal provisions still outstanding caused the greatest concern, both to Gallicans like Jean Canart, who regarded them as infringing the principle of Gallican Liberty, and to the less ideological clerics who thought in simpler terms of who would get what during the subtraction. The point was put in the *Avisamenta* in these terms:

> Although the ordinaries will ordain concerning benefices that become vacant in the future, there should be deliberation about those whose vacancy dates from the past, where no right has been acquired *in re* [i.e., *in the* property], even though it may have been acquired *ad rem* [i.e., *to the* property].[96]

The actual discussion on 8 August issued in a notarized instrument that the prelates caused to be drawn up to record their decision; here the question was phrased somewhat differently:

> Whether in the light of the decision to subtract obedience, and of the tenor of the [royal] letters on the matter, expectative graces should take effect— those over which legal actions have ensued, as well as other graces through which however no right *in re* has yet been acquired by anyone.[97]

This seems to call into question not only rights acquired *ad rem,* as in the *Avisamenta*'s formulation,[98] but even rights *in re*; for such rights were acquired in some cases as soon as the legal actions were taken. Canon law concerning benefices recognized three grades of property right: *ius ad rem,* or a right *to* the benefice; *ius in re,* or a right *in* the benefice; and real possession. The first posed no problems, inasmuch as it came down to nothing more than the right of a provision holder to get a legal

---

96. *Avisamenta,* § 14: "Item, combien que des benefices vacans pour le temps a venir, les ordinaires ordonneront, toutesfois soit advise de ceulz du temps passe vacans, ou n'est droit acquis *in re, licet ad rem.*" Cf. Boniface VIII's revocation of his predecessors' grants of expectancies in cases "in quibus ius non esset quaesitum in re, licet ad rem" (*Sext,* 3. 7. 8).

97. AN, J 518, fol. 291r: "Fuit quesitum an, conclusione predicte denegacionis obediencie et tenore litterarum super ipsam confectarum attentis, gracie expectative, tam ille super quibus processus secuti sunt, quam alie per quas tamen nondum est alicui ius quesitum in re, suum effectum deberent sortiri."

98. It is instructive that Simon de Cramaud had also presupposed as a matter of course that only rights *ad rem* would suffer from subtraction: App. II, Pt. III, at end.

judgement of whether his claim to a particular benefice coming under the provision was good.[99] Since no property had yet been acquired, this right could be regarded as ipso facto annulled by the subtraction. *Ius in re*, however, was a real property right, acquired by a judge's collation or institution of the claimant in the benefice, and giving the holder the right to draw the benefice's revenues.[100] "Real possession" was then acquired after three years of uncontested exercise of *ius in re*.[101]

The problem consisted in the fact that some papal provisions to future vacancies gave more than just *ius ad rem*: these privileged graces were made "on the pope's own initiative" (*motu proprio*) and carried "automatic execution" (*execucio parata*); they went to the upper clergy and above all to the cardinals.[102] The graces were accompanied by bulls naming the judges-executors and instructing them to proceed *without* actual judgement to collate the providee to the benefice he claimed under the provision and then to install him; all the claimant had to do was "publish his bulls," or "take his legal actions," and he would secure *ius in re* to the exclusion of any other claimant.[103] A cardinal would have acquired many such benefices and would have provisions to still others whose vacancy he was waiting for, and many such unactivated provisions would have been granted by Clement VII, about whose papality there was no question.

---

99. Carl Gross, *Das Recht an der Pfründe* (Graz, 1887): 170—the full form was *ius ad rem petendam*, entitling the holder only to "imploratio officii judicis"; see Geoffrey Barraclough, *Papal Provisions* (Oxford, 1935): 93 ff. The great majority of papal provisions conferred only this (ibid.: 91).

100. Gross, *Recht an der Pfründe*: 187, quotes Johannes Andreae: "Licet in aliis rebus vel juribus non quaeratur dominium vel quasi nisi per traditionem vel quasi. . . , in beneficiis ecclesiasticis secus, quia in eis jus quaeritur sine traditione vel praesentia rei, ita quod per collationem quis statim jus habet etiam in re." See also ibid.: 174; Barraclough, *Papal Provisions*: 93; Guillaume Mollat, "Bénéfices ecclésiastiques en Occident," *Dictionnaire de droit canonique*, 2 (1937):416, 424. Collection of a benefice's revenues was legal proof that *ius in re* had been acquired: Guillaume Mollat, "L'application en France de la soustraction d'obédience à Benoît XIII jusqu'au Concile de Pise," *Revue du moyen âge latin*, 1 (1945):152.

101. Mollat, "Bénéfices ecclésiastiques en Occident": 427 f.; Gross, *Recht an der Pfründe*: 187.

102. Barraclough, *Papal Provisions*: 92.

103. Both the vocabulary and the procedures in question, as well as the issues raised by the subtraction, are shown in the following passages. In February 1397 Raoul d'Oulmont argued against partial subtraction: "Impetrantes apostolici frustrabuntur expectacionibus suis contra racionem, presertim quia plures *iam bullas suas fieri fecerunt et processus, et eciam publicari*. Isti *processus aut sentencie* ligabunt episcopos" (BN, *ms. lat.* 1475, fol. 80r; my emphasis). The archbishop of Bourges wrote in his ballot that the king could subtract collations from the pope, "dumtamen expectantes qui fecerunt bullas sint provisi, et qui eas intimarunt" (AN, J 518, fol. 449rv). See also Jean Canart's ballot, App. I.

The prelates wanted to annul these provisions and even the *ius in re* titles that had not yet been perfected into real possession. Their decision in answer to the question posed on 8 August was this:

From the day of subtraction there should be no further obedience given to the executors . . . deputed . . . by . . . Benedict over such graces, nor to their legal actions taken or to be taken, through which legal actions meanwhile a right *in re* may nevertheless have been acquired by someone.[104]

This seems to be the very decision reported by the *Avisamenta* and *Sur les inconveniens*, respectively:

The council said that all papal graces are to be null, whether legal actions have been taken or not.

As for the claimants who have taken their legal actions, it was concluded that they will not profit from their graces in any way if these graces had not fully taken effect by the day of the subtraction.[105]

While the decision was justified by the argument that any obedience to the judges-executors appointed by Benedict would violate the subtraction, it was also obviously a defense of the interests of the French clergy against the cardinals, who here as elsewhere relied on the crown's favor. There is plenty of evidence to show the cardinals working closely with Berry, Burgundy, and Simon at this time; and in a letter pre-dated to 27 July and probably written only a few days later, the royal government had assured the College of Cardinals that, if they joined in the subtraction, their "honors, liberties, and benefices" would be defended by the crown—they "would lose nothing by the subtraction."[106] The cardinals' role in subtractionist strategy was crucial, as we have noted; and while the government could expect them to continue to be as submissive as ever, lordship, here as always, carried the reciprocal duty of protection. Hence, the royal ordinance establishing the Liberties during subtraction, and following the instrument of 8 August point by point,

---

104. AN, J 518, fol. 291v: "A die facte denegacionis predicte, executoribus . . . a domino . . . Benedicto super huiusmodi graciis deputatis. . . , ac processibus eorundem factis et faciendis, per quos tamen interdum sit alicui ius quesitum in re, non obediatur de cetero." The language is awkward, and one's impulse is to suppose that "interdum" is a mistake for "nondum" or some other such negative (no other copy is known, but cf. the text quoted in n. 112 below); but the reports quoted just below seem to substantiate the actual reading, and there remains the fact that in 1399 the cardinals had to complain that *ius in re* titles were *not* being respected (*ALKG*, 6:298).

105. *Avisamenta*, note to § 14: "Fuit dictum per consilium quod omnes gracie papales sint nulle, sive sint facti processus sive non." *Sur les inconveniens*: "Item, quant aux impetrans qui ont fait leurs proces, a este conclus qu'il ne jouiront en quelque maniere de leurs graces, se elles n'avoient a plain, au jour de la substraccion totale, sorti leur effect."

106. *ALKG*, 7:178.

deviated in the crucial passage in order to move towards the original construction of the issue:

From the day of subtraction there should be no further obedience given to the executors . . . deputed . . . by . . . Benedict over such graces, nor to their legal actions taken or to be taken, through which legal actions no right *in re* had meanwhile been acquired by provision and collation.[107]

Thus actual collation, presumably after publication of one's bulls, would be taken as conveying *ius in re* for practical purposes. The effect of this ordinance is less clear than its tendency, for a half-year later we find the cardinals forced to urge that *ius in re* titles should indeed be recognized.[108] Perhaps Parlement judged cases according to the prelates' intent after all; certainly the as-yet-unused provisions granted to the cardinals by both Benedict and Clement were not honored.[109] We can note merely that *ius in re* was indeed a real property right and that it was extremely unwholesome in the medieval view ever to deprive any right-holder of what was his. Jean Canart had alleged the *bonum commune,* the "common good," as the principle under which such individual rights might be overridden; but as we have seen, the Gallican Liberties had not yet been given that status. They were still the ideology of a party, not part of the public law of France.

They passed into public law later, however, as a result of the next and much smaller Paris Council of February–March 1399, which here, as in some other respects, perfected the work of the preceding one. Once more it was a question of finance, the crown requesting more clerical aid in spite of the promises it had made on 2 August 1398. The cardinals, taught by experience to foresee what the dialectic of crown and estates would lead to, sent emissaries to Paris to propose that this time the crown not ask the prelates for a tax but, rather, enforce the fiscal rights of the Camera instead. The crown would get more money this way, the cardinals said, and with less trouble.[110] Of course the cardinals could then expect to have their own revenues, provisions, and *ius in re* titles protected in spite of the clergy's opposition.[111] But in fact the prelates were asked to grant a tenth of their revenues and could therefore proceed to

---

107. *Ordonnances,* 8:291 (AN, J 518, fol. 299rv compared; also *Thes. nov.,* 2:1153 f.): "Depuis le jour dudit departement, aux juges executeurs . . . deputez . . . de par ledit Benedit sur les dictes graces, a leurs proces faiz ou a faire par lesquieux aucun droit n'estoit lors acquis en la chose par provision et collation, ne sera doresenavant obey."

108. *ALKG,* 6:298.

109. Mollat, "L'application": 152 ff.

110. *ALKG,* 6:299; *RSD,* 2:680.

111. The cardinals' instructions on these points to their envoys to Paris are published in *ALKG,* 6:297–300. See also *RSD,* 2:676–680, and *ALKG,* 7:43 f., for the course of events at the council.

reject the cardinals' fiscal demands, invalidate even Clement's expectative graces still extant, and go on to insist that the treatment of the whole matter of papal provisions be based this time on the principle of Gallican Liberty. The resulting royal ordinance gave them what they wanted on this important point; for while it repeated that *ius in re* titles acquired before the subtraction were still valid, it declared Clement's graces null and noted that one purpose of the previous ordinance (of 8 August) had been that "the Gallican church might remain then and for the future in the liberty which it had been used to have from the time of its foundation, according to the sacred canons."[112] While as much may have been promised during the Third Paris Council, we have seen that the ordinances emerging from that consultation had *not* embodied the Liberties as a principle in their own right; now the promise was fulfilled, and we know that Parlement in fact judged case after case against the cardinals.[113] A guess here would be that the subtraction status of the church had already acquired substance by simple duration and that the prelates' consent to extra taxation at this time therefore implied similar consent in the future, thus a renunciation of the traditional limits imposed by the papacy on secular taxation of the clergy. Henceforth just one estate of the realm among others, the clergy could expect a permanent protection of its liberties in exchange.

All we know of Simon de Cramaud's role in these transactions is that the Monk of St. Denis sourly accused him and his associates of causing the royal demands for more clerical taxes in order to finance their expensive and fruitless embassies.[114] We must suppose that the expert politician saw that such taxes would have to be paid for by privileges in return, and perhaps he recognized the intrinsic justice of the French clergy's insistence on not submitting to papal burdens without papal

---

112. *Ordonnances*, 8:325–328, 7 May 1399. The decision of the Third Paris Council is represented as "quod habentes gracias expectativas per quas nondum fuerat eis jus in re quesitum post conclusionem . . . denegationis obediencie, . . . nec uterentur dictis graciis, nec eciam ipsorum executoribus obediretur"; and the ordinance of 8 August 1398 was said to have aimed, "primo, ut ecclesia Gallicana in libertate quam a sua fundacione secundum sacros canones habere consuevit, ab illo [tempore] tunc in futurum remaneret" and, second, that Benedict's judges not be obeyed. See Valois, 3:312–315, for the background.

113. Mollat, "L'application," *passim*; cf. the statement of a cleric who successfully defended his right to a benefice against Cardinal Pierre de Thury's efforts to get it by virtue of provisions dating from the time of Clement VII—he is speaking of the Paris Council of 1399: "Cardinales, qui quasi omnes similes gracias dicebantur habere, nisi fuerant tantum facere quod predicte substraccio et declaracio quoad dictas Clementis gracias eisdem non preiudicarent; quod tamen non potuerant obtinere" (AN, X 1A 47, fol. 121r, an *arrêt* of 3 April 1400).

114. *RSD*, 2:688.

benefits; we can go on to visualize the shrug with which he would have told his allies in the College of Cardinals that their rights were the ones to be sacrificed; they may, however, have received some revenues in compensation.[115] In any case, he had gotten what he wanted. Benedict had been officially declared a schismatic and heretic; obedience had been totally subtracted from him; the authority of the Gallican church had been given by procuration to the inner circle of government prelates in which he figured as chief; the diplomacy of unionism could now be pursued in both obediences, as he had planned. The road that would lead from Paris to Pisa had been opened, and he could begin the new task of organizing France's efforts to induce the rest of Europe to take it. The internal politics of subtraction which we have analyzed here, and which have a substantial historical interest of their own, were the medium within which he had to work in order to pursue his macropolitical goals.

---

115. *ALKG*, 7:152—a statement in 1400 that the cardinals in France were receiving "some of the revenues" pertaining to the Camera. Exactly what the cardinals got and under what title is unclear; Haller, *PKR*: 244, refers to a yearly pension for each cardinal, but the only source seems to be the one just cited.

CHAPTER EIGHT

From Paris to Pisa with Simon de Cramaud

F R A N C E ' S total subtraction of obedience was intended as only the first step towards a European subtraction that would lead to a representative general council of both obediences, including princes, prelates, and both colleges of cardinals. The two papal contenders would also be there, "willing or not," as Simon had put it in his ballot, and after their schismatic-heretical guilt had been declared, they would be forced to abdicate or else be "punished as schismatics." A single new pope would then be chosen for the reunited church. If the half-year's time officially set by the French government for the implementation of this scheme[1] seems ludicrously short, the more than ten years that would in fact elapse before the French scenario could be produced into reality at the Council of Pisa (without the two popes, to be sure) may seem unduly long. The miracle, however, is that it happened at all in a Europe of hatreds, wars, depositions, and disintegrative novelties, with a French government whose commitment to the subtractionist program was spasmodically interrupted or even reversed by conflicts among the Valois dukes. Indeed the subtractionist program itself was no Rock of Gibraltar, for if Simon had succeeded in putting together an alliance between those supporting total subtraction in his sense and those whose chief interest lay in Gallican Liberty, the story told in the preceding chapter has suggested something of the alliance's inner contradictions and how they might have been expected to break out. It is remarkable, for example, that Simon's opposite number in the Burgundian affinity, Bishop Jean Canart of Arras, wrote a ballot of overwhelmingly Gallican inspiration, hence in favor of partial subtraction; that he added support for total subtraction only until Benedict XIII should have accepted the *via cessionis,* and only for the practical purpose of removing the pope's power to take reprisals against the unionists; and that he included not a word of Simon's theory of total subtraction from a schismatic-heretical pope or of the canonical obligation to depose him. Supporters of Benedict, and men like the theologians Pierre d'Ailly and Jean Gerson who

---

1. Valois, 3:292.

refused Simon's canonistic theory in principle, had only to bide their
time until changes in Paris or Avignon would allow them to demand an
end to the totalist program—and in the case of d'Ailly and Gerson, to
try to replace it with a conciliarism harnessed to the doctrines of Gallican Liberty.[2] And yet the Council of Pisa would take place after all;
Simon would preside; and he would have the satisfaction of officially
declaring the contenders deposed on the basis of precisely his arguments.
The road from Paris to Pisa was neither straight nor smooth, but no
other medieval roads were either; and if Simon could find his way to the
end, it was because at every step his politician's flexibility showed him
how best to use the resources he had: the objective ineluctability of his
program; the weight of his own high estate; and above all, the power
radiated by his patron, Duke Jean of Berry.

The First Push and Its Failure (1398–1401)

Even before the end of the Third Paris Council, we can see the duke of
Berry appearing as the leading personage in subtractionist policy at the
princely level—energetic, unyielding, and harsh to the point of brutality.[3] His brother of Burgundy seems never to have given anything less
than full support, but the difference in role between the two was so
marked that Benedict's partisans, including King Martin of Aragon,
looked to Burgundy as one who might perhaps help them.[4] As for Duke
Louis of Orléans, he had argued against the decision to subtract obedience, and he only made his own subtraction, on 19 October 1398
(with Simon de Cramaud there to represent the Gallican church),[5] because that was now the crown's official policy. But it was at just this
time, in the latter part of 1398, that he began to move openly and
decisively to aggrandize his own position at the expense of the duke of
Burgundy; his aims were to put his clients into positions of control in
the royal government, to enlarge his appanage, to get a much greater

---

2. Below, at n. 56.

3. So, e.g., F. Ehrle's judgement of Berry's leading role, *ALKG*, 6:248, 293; Lehoux,
2:376 ff., 403 f., 412, 415 f., 429; Benedict's complaints of 9 June 1398 and Berry's
harsh reply, *ALKG*, 6:249–253. See also Ch. IV above: it was Berry who led the ducal
embassy of 1395 that presented the *via cessionis* to Benedict as an ultimatum, he who
refused discussion, forced the cardinals into line, and in the end threatened Benedict
with subtraction.

4. In the text cited in n. 21 below, Martin instructs his ambassador to seek out the
duke of Burgundy first of all and to be guided by his will. For similar reliance on
Burgundy in Benedict's circle, see the texts in *ALKG*, 7:66, 106.

5. The text in E. Jarry, *La vie politique de Louis de France, duc d'Orléans*, 1372–
1407 (Paris, 1889): 439–443.

share of royal revenues for himself, to build up his own network of allies among the princes of the Western lands of the Empire where Burgundy's main interests lay, and to pursue a generally aggressive foreign policy in all directions, including Italy.[6] Naturally, then, he became the champion of Benedict XIII's cause and indeed of the *via facti*. It would take a few years for these lines of action to produce significant results, and these few years were what Simon had to work with. As Berry's client, as patriarch of Alexandria—the most distinguished titulary in the Gallican church—and of course as political leader of France's unionism from the first, Simon joined Cardinal Pierre de Thury, who led the subtractionists in the College of Cardinals, in a Berry team that acted under the duke's patronage but in the name of the royal government, using the royal seal, and issuing royal orders in implementation of their union policy.[7] It would be reasonable to suppose that all acts of the government in this sense were in fact their acts.

The first move, immediately after the Third Paris Council, was to send an embassy to King Richard II of England to urge him to subtract obedience from Boniface IX as the essential preliminary to the general council that would end the Schism. The instructions for the ambassadors show that the council was to be presented as conforming to the position taken by the Oxford letter of 1396 ("our views are now one").[8] A royal letter to Florence of 2 January 1399, evidently written by Simon de Cramaud, made the same request and advanced the same conciliar project;[9] and in this period similar letters and embassies went out to King Wenceslas of Bohemia and the Empire, King Sigismund of Hungary, and the kings of the Avignon obedience: Scotland, Castile, Aragon, Navarre.[10] The embassy to Richard had set Lent of 1399 (thus February/March) as the date for the council, and a comparably early date was probably proposed to the other powers as well, perhaps merely as an indicator of desirable speed. The immediate results, however, were meager. Henry III of Castile subtracted obedience from Benedict on 12 December 1398; Wenceslas vaguely declared his intention of attending an imperial diet

---

6. Nordberg: 65 f., 120, 156–169, 177; see above, Ch. V, n. 58.

7. So a report by one of Benedict's supporters in Paris, *ALKG*, 7:69: "The patriarch and Thury's secretary wrote many orders to Avignon under the name of the royal council and sent advice to the cardinals," and (p. 96) Thury reputedly held the royal signet and used it to authenticate letters to the cardinals; see also pp. 67, 71, and see Valois, 3:190 n. 4. For other evidence see Kaminsky, "Politics": 370.

8. The embassy's instructions in Perroy, *L'Angleterre*: 416–418, and (abridged) in Valois, 3:292.

9. AN, J 518, fols. 304r–305v; published in *Ampl. coll.*, 7:627–629; cf. Valois, 3:289 f. The phrasing, style, and content seem unmistakably Simon's.

10. So it is said in the just-cited letter to Florence; see also Valois, 3:261 f., 295; also Ch. VII, n. 2, above.

in Frankfurt in May 1400; and Richard II arranged a meeting of Oxford professors and selected prelates in late January 1399 to formulate a new position responsive to the French requests although still eschewing any coercion.[11]

The Lenten season of 1399 came and went without action; the Valois dukes, who had been destined to play leading diplomatic roles, were replaced in early 1399 by less exalted embassies;[12] and Simon had to wait until the Frankfurt Diet of May 1400 before he could even attempt one of his grand productions. Here he led a huge Franco-Castilian embassy, prepared to present France's program to the German princes; but Wenceslas did not show up, and nothing concrete came out of the episode.[13] Meanwhile Richard II had been deposed on 29 September 1399, and the West German princes had made their plans to depose Wenceslas; they did so on 20 July 1400 and elected the Count Palatine Rupert III as king of the Romans. Although Wenceslas was still king of Bohemia and still enjoyed imperial recognition among the German princes of the East, he was now all but useless for Simon's purpose. In fact, little remained of the diplomatic infrastructure that Simon had counted upon, and the prospect of a European council seemed hopeless.

Failures of equal moment attended his policy vis-à-vis Avignon. It was essential that Benedict be first isolated, then taken into custody; on 1 September 1398 royal officials appeared in Avignon to proclaim the crown's ordinance of subtraction and to summon all French personnel of the Curia to abandon the pope.[14] All but five of the cardinals moved across the Rhone to Villeneuve, at the same time claiming the governance of Avignon; and Benedict withdrew into the papal palace, prepared for a siege and counting on help from King Martin of Aragon.[15] A

---

11. Richard sent the French proposals to Oxford and Cambridge on 20 November 1398 (having waited until a concordat with Boniface IX about control of appointments to English benefices had been assured)—Perroy, *L'Angleterre*: 348–350, 386. Cambridge's reply made only slight concessions—Walter Ullmann, "The University of Cambridge and the Great Schism," *Journal of Theological Studies*, n.s., 9 (1958):53–77. For Oxford's response and its qualifications see Margaret Harvey, "The Letters of the University of Oxford on Withdrawal of Obedience from Pope Boniface IX," *Studies in Church History*, 11 (1975):187–198; idem, "The Letter of Oxford University on the Schism," 5 February 1399," *Annuarium historiae conciliorum*, 6 (1974):121–134. See in general Swanson: 135 f.

12. *ALKG*, 7:45.

13. Valois, 3:295 f. This would have been the likely occasion for Simon to have sent his treatise *Ad ostendendum clare* to the Rhineland; it was composed largely of passages from his "On Subtraction of Obedience." See *DSO*, App. V, no. 10.

14. Valois, 3:189 ff.

15. Valois, 3:197 f.; see Favier, *Finances*: 657 ff., for Benedict's dependence on funds from Aragon (whose king was married to Maria de Luna, the pope's kinswoman).

troop of soldiers led by Geoffrey Boucicaut, brother of Jean Boucicaut the marshal of France, was sent by the royal government to fight on behalf of the cardinals,[16] and hostilities began on 4 September; Avignon was taken in hand on the 15th; and the siege of the papal palace began a week later. Meanwhile on 17 September the cardinals sent the king, Berry, and Simon letters in which they signified their approval of the French subtraction and declared that they had done the same.[17] After this, however, they delayed for a long time in sending their delegates to Paris to work with the government (Simon had to write them a rather nervous letter of complaint on 28 October),[18] and it was not until January 1399, after a truce on 24 November had registered the siege's failure (it in fact became a blockade), that the delegates appeared: two former Berry chancellors, Pierre de Thury and Guy de Malesset, and the Valois kinsman Amadeo di Saluzzo. Dissatisfied with the Gallican structure of the subtraction regime, they asked that their papal provisions to future vacancies be honored and that the whole papal system of collations and fiscal impositions be preserved, mutatis mutandis; we have already seen why their proposals had to be rejected. At the same time, Pierre de Thury expressed their view that Benedict's status as partly pope, partly non-pope, should be ended by a council of the Avignon obedience, to be called by the cardinals, where he could be declared formally deposed.[19] If, at the same time, the cardinals supported the diplomatic efforts for a European council, and indeed offered themselves as ambassadors,[20] there could still be no mistaking the seriousness of the problem to which they had drawn attention. Benedict's heroic resistance to the siege had ended any hope of a quick disposition by force; as long as he was there, unsubjugated and enjoying the loyalty of many in France as well as the full obedience of the territories that had not subtracted (Aragon was the most important), the foundations of subtractionist policy were insecure.

---

16. Valois, 3:194 f.; cf. the inference above, at n. 7.

17. Valois, 3:192 f.

18. ALKG, 6:287 f.

19. The delegates' instructions in ALKG, 6:294–300. They included a request for deliberations with the royal council and others, "utrum . . . [Benedictus] iam esse desierit vel veraciter per sententiam seu ordinationem deiciendus"—this to be eventually determined by a council of the obedience preliminary to a general council that would act against both contenders, as Paris had written to Thury (295 f.). The wording sounds like Thury's *Factum* composed soon after the cardinals' subtraction on 17 September, which, e.g., includes the statement "quod consilium est necesse, quod declaretur utrum papa esse desierit vel a papatu veniat deiciendus vel non" (ASV, Arm. 54, t. 27, fol. 210v). Cf. Valois, 3:192 f., where Thury's *Factum* is distinguished—perhaps wrongly—from another *Factum* preceding it in several mss. A revised text of both items is in *Thes. nov.* 2:1177–1193; for the passage quoted see col. 1192.

20. ALKG, 6:296.

In fact even before the cardinals' delegates had come to Paris, an embassy from King Martin of Aragon was there to mediate between the pope and the royal government on the basis of Benedict's agreement to accept the *via cessionis,* dismiss his troops, and put himself under the royal safeguard.[21] It comes as an instructive shock to see that Simon de Cramaud, acting for the government with full powers to negotiate with the Aragonese, evidently felt obliged to accept conditions that left Benedict much freedom for the sort of procrastination, prevarication, and quibbling that Simon must have foreseen.[22] While the agreements were concluded in Avignon on 10 April 1399, Benedict did not confirm them until 30 March 1401; meanwhile he had secured many concessions, including the royal appointment of Louis of Orléans to exercise the royal safeguard; and his stated acceptance of the *via cessionis* provided his supporters and also the Gallicans with an argument against continued subtraction.

By early 1401 Simon seems to have made a politician's adjustment to reality. Pierre de Thury's proposed council of the Avignon obedience, which would formally depose Benedict, had not previously figured in Simon's thinking and indeed was unnecessary according to his theory, but it might be all that he could get; he therefore espoused it as at least a way of keeping the papalist reaction down.[23] At the same time, he could not resist making one last try for the European opening, taking advantage of King Rupert's desire for a French alliance to support his planned attack on Gian-Galeazzo Visconti of Milan. The project was supported by Queen Isabelle of France (Rupert's Wittelsbach kinswoman) and Duke Philip of Burgundy, but it was directed against not only the Visconti but also Duke Louis of Orléans, Gian-Galeazzo's son-in-law and a long-time ally of Wenceslas of Bohemia, on whose behalf Louis had warred against Rupert in 1400. As a token of rapprochement with the "France" of Burgundy and Berry, Rupert offered the chance to discuss

---

21. See Valois, 3:205–237, for the whole course of the negotiations. The instructions of King Martin of Aragon to his ambassador going to Avignon in October 1398 show the rough side of his mediation: Benedict was to be asked first to move the bishop of Tortosa to Valencia, under threat of Aragonese collaboration with Paris in subtraction; then he was to be required to promise to be guided in the present situation by the will of King Martin and the duke of Burgundy. The Aragonese text in S. Puig y Puig, *Pedro de Luna* (Barcelona, 1920): 457 f. (Valois, 3:206 n. 2, is to be corrected).

22. Simon's role and full powers are attested in Aragonese and papal memoranda, *ALKG,* 7:111, 118 f., which also refer to the criticism he had to face for accepting conditions that were too loose; see Valois, 3:216, 219 ff., for Benedict's bad faith and Paris's expectation of it.

23. In a letter of 6 June 1401 to a cardinal, *ALKG,* 7:157 f., Simon wrote that a council of the obedience would be useful, "ut novitates cessarent."

union at a diet to be held on St. John's Day (24 June) of 1401 in Metz.[24] Exactly how his envoys presented the idea is unknown, also how far they went in telling Simon de Cramaud what he wanted to hear; he at any rate either believed or pretended to believe that the Germans were ready to approve the *via cessionis* and subtraction of obedience and were inclined to get rid of Boniface IX, just as the French had gotten rid of Benedict XIII, and to proceed to the election of a new, single pope.[25] Royal letters went out on 2 April instructing each archbishop to send one or two bishops and other clerics from his province—obviously according to Simon's plan broached on 20 June 1398—and letters were sent to other kings of the obedience.[26] The subtraction ordinance of 1398 was renewed on 22 April; the dukes of Burgundy and Bourbon were chosen to attend the diet; and Simon received or more likely issued himself an order from the government to write letters to the archbishops of Canterbury and Dublin, informing them of the event and urging them to send a delegation—he even claimed that they had agreed.[27] The letters are particularly interesting inasmuch as they not only make the case for subtraction (with material taken from Simon's earlier treatise) but go on to offer a well-developed discussion of the church's right to depose even a legitimate pope who has lost his divinely conferred power because of his acts tending to damage the church.[28] If Simon really hoped to see such matters on the agenda of the Metz Diet, whose narrowly

---

24. For the alliance see Lehoux, 2:451 f.; Jean Schoos, *Der Machtkampf zwischen Burgund und Orléans* (Luxembourg, 1956): 137 f.; Valois, 3:298; Michel de Boüard, "L'empereur Robert et le Grand Schisme d'Occident," *Mélanges d'archéologie et d'histoire*, 48 (1931):218–225. See also Jarry, *Vie politique*: 193 ff.

25. See Simon's report of the German proposals in his letter of 6 June 1401 to a cardinal, *ALKG*, 7:156; the Germans had allegedly said of Benedict, "de nostro iam expeditum est," and had said the same could be done with Boniface.

26. Valois, 3:298–302. A royal letter of 9 August 1401 to the archbishop of Narbonne about reimbursement of his province's delegates, ASV, *Instr. misc.*, 5282, no. 5, can be added to Valois's documentation on p. 300.

27. In his letter of 6 June 1401, *ALKG*, 7:157, Simon said that he had written the two letters "at the will of the king and the dukes" and that he had heard that the English were going to send a delegation; Martin de Salva commented that this was a lie (ibid.). The letter to Canterbury carefully outlined the canonistic justification for the representative general council France was advocating, mentioned the Metz meeting in terms that related to this, then asked for a response about "carrying through the aforesaid meeting" (*Thes. nov.*, 2:1246 ff., 1249 f.). The other letter made the invitation clearer: "Let us assemble at Metz" ("Metis . . . conveniamus") and urged the addressee "to work as effectively as you can with your lord [scil., Henry IV] so that notable prelates and others will come from England" ("Vos ergo, pater, cum domino vestro . . . quantum efficacius poteritis laborare, ut ad predictam convencionem veniant de Anglia prelati notabiles et alii viri deum timentes, qui convenientibus nobis . . .") (ASV, *Arm. 54*, t. 21, fol. 258v.) See *DSO*, App. V, nos. 12, 13.

28. The discussion of deposition appears in the Canterbury letter in *Thes. nov.*, 2:1247 and also in the other, ASV, *Arm. 54*, t. 21, fol. 257v: "Sed quia de deposicione

political and partisan purpose could hardly have escaped his notice, he must have been a desperate man.

For Rupert's aims were not Simon's, and when he learned of what was going on in Paris, he sent word that the Metz meeting would not be a major assembly, only a preliminary meeting to prepare for a bigger one. Even so, Simon led a delegation there and did meet a German group, whose instructions were to propose first a general council presided over by Boniface, second a council to judge between the two contenders, and only third, a council to be called by Rupert, with the collaboration of the other kings, to prescribe a *via* obligatory for all. This was Simon's opening, and he seems to have carried on talks about the last two alternatives, also about deposing both popes and electing a third, with mention of a future meeting to work out the practical details. His new flexibility appears in his previously unthinkable agreement to the proposal that the projected council would include a preliminary discussion of the respective rights of each contender.[29] While the whole episode may be rated still another increment in the fitful preparation of the European

---

pape est superius facta mencio: Si denegata primitus obediencia, isti pertinaciter iuri quod se pretendunt habere in papatu renunciare refutarent, tunc ecclesia congregata ad istum finem posset ipsos ambos deponere. Nec valet ut videtur quod dicunt aliqui, quod potestas pape est a deo. Quia verum est, nullus potuit dare illam potestatem quam habet, viz. quod ligata et soluta per eum in terra sunt ligata et soluta in celo, nisi deus; sed quod ista potestas sic in Bonifacio vel in Benedicto a deo est ad edificacionem, non ad destruccionem, ut dictum est, si notorie turbet et destruat ecclesiam, per consensum ecclesie potest desinere esse in Bonifacio vel in Benedicto."

29. Valois, 3:302, notes the German instructions but abbreviates the last alternative and supposes that it left no chance for discussions of the French program; see Franz Bliemetzrieder, *Das Generalkonzil im grossen abendländischen Schisma* (Paderborn, 1904): 159, for a corrective—unfortunately not noticed by Boüard, "Empereur Robert": 221 f. A. Mercati, "Un' ignota missione francese nel 1401 presso Roberto de Palatino eletto re dei Romani," *Mélanges d'archéologie et d'histoire*, 61 (1949):209–224, has published a letter written by a member of another French mission which met Rupert in Mainz, 30 June to 5 July, then went to Metz to join Simon's group. The letter reports (pp. 222 f.) that the Metz discussions in July had developed the idea of a council of both obediences with a brief preliminary discussion of the rights of both popes, then—it was informally agreed—the deposition of both and the election of a third; the actual composition of the council and other practical matters would be negotiated at a later meeting. One wonders whether the author was reporting Simon's account or what he had himself found out. That a later meeting was scheduled for 1 September 1401, also in Metz, is a possible inference from the instructions to a French embassy going to Milan, 14 August 1401 (Doüet-d'Arcq, 1:207). Nothing more is known of this. But Simon seems to have held onto the Metz program well into 1402, when he wrote his glosses on the Toulouse letter; there he responded to the Toulouse insistence on Benedict's *via iusticie* by remarking, "Et in quantum sic confligere desiderant, ecce iam in ianuis habent quod petunt; nam domini cardinales, prelati Francie, et universitas Parisiensis requirimus concilium congregare ut ibidem cause merita parcium assercione pandantur" (AN, J 518, fol. 555r; Bonn University ms. S 594, fol. 70v, collated).

mind for acceptance of the French solution, nothing definite came of it at the time, a fact that Simon tried to conceal as long as possible, with some loss of authority as a result.[30] We may add that this was the one time that Simon may have left his patron behind; Berry did not approve of the Wittelsbach alliance or of the hostility to Milan.[31]

The council of the Avignon obedience was now the only expedient left, and Simon threw himself into the project, perhaps thinking to cover up his failure at Metz.[32] A meeting held at Senlis from 22 to 25 October saw "the cardinals, and with them the patriarch and a few other prelates, acting they said in the name of all the prelates," deliberating before the dukes of Berry, Burgundy, and Bourbon, as well as other magnates (but not Orléans), with all agreeing on a council of the obedience.[33] Whether the council would be stacked or composed of elected delegates, whether or not the pope would have any role in calling it, whether or not he would be required to submit to its decisions in advance—these points were not decided, chiefly because Orléans had made known his opposition to the more radical alternatives; but there was provision for teams from both sides to arrange the form the council would take.[34] Élie de Lestrange in Paris felt that the points could be

---

30. *RSD*, 2:766 (cf. Valois, 3:302, for the date), reports that when Simon returned, "he said that the Germans were well disposed to accept the way of the king and of the Gallican church" but that this "was found to be false"; Simon was therefore criticized by many for wasting money in vain embassies (cf. *RSD*, 2:688, for a similar charge *ad* early 1399), and the duke of Orléans banished Simon from the royal council, "stating that his 'ways' would go down in history as useless." Simon may have been pushed aside in 1402 (see below), but whether this is relevant to the *RSD* story cannot be guessed; cf. n. 32 below.

31. Lehoux, 2:437, 442–455.

32. According to Élie de Lestrange, writing from Paris 11 October 1401 (*ALKG*, 7:162): "It is only in these days that the hopes in connection with the Metz council, which had long kept us in suspense, have proven empty, although those working for it knew for a long time that they were acting in vain"—both the common people and many in the university were blaming them, and "they have been compelled by shame to take up the new enterprise of convoking a general council of this obedience, hoping that no one will dare to oppose this due, juridical, and holy way."

33. A letter of Élie de Lestrange from Paris, 18 November 1401 (*ALKG*, 7:255; cf. Valois, 3:251 n. 3, for the dating, p. 252 for more details).

34. The Lestrange letter of 11 October 1401 tells of a preliminary argument over the form of the proposed council, with Orléans rejecting the anti-papal provisions called for by the cardinals, and with the radicals proposing a new and better form (*"in forma iuris"*) on 4 October; Lestrange thought this would be accepted in the royal council on 12 October and that two teams of six each would be constituted to debate the issues at the projected council (*ALKG*, 7:163 f.). His letter of 18 November 1401, however, says that the issues still had not been settled at the time of the Senlis meeting, that Orléans would not accept even the *forma iuris*, and that the duke was apparently thinking of liberating the pope by force (*ALKG*, 7:255 f.).

resolved in Benedict's favor, and he wrote earnestly advising that the pope accept the council, that indeed he should have offered one long ago; a refusal now, he explained, would play into the hands of his enemies, who wanted nothing else in order to condemn him for contumacy and depose him.[35] But on 4 December 1401 Benedict refused because it seemed clear from what Simon de Cramaud and others had written[36] that it would be a council against him. Why otherwise would Simon want it?[37] The plan remained alive well into 1402, however, when Pierre d'Ailly and Jean Gerson wrote critical discussions of it,[38] and if it then faded away, that was because other factors appeared which led back from unionism to a restoration of obedience.

Restoration of Obedience (1402–1404)

The drive to assert and enlarge his estate that Duke Louis of Orléans had begun in the latter part of 1398 could only be pursued by unremitting aggression. His uncles had been getting royal rights, revenues, and lands for themselves over a period of many years, and what Louis demanded was that they recognize his equal rights as member of the family concern and not only deal him in for the future but share some of what they had taken in the past. Duke Philip of Burgundy was the chief sufferer, for various reasons, and at the end of 1401 he resorted to force, leading an army into Paris. Louis did the same, and if a civil war did not then ensue, it was because the duke of Berry and others of the royal family intervened and arranged peace on 6 January 1402. The peace,

---

35. *ALKG*, 7:163, 260.

36. Simon's letter of 6 June 1401 to a cardinal was circulated among the papal supporters with glosses by Martin de Salva to show the hostile source of the idea of a council of the obedience, and with reminders of how the enemies had manipulated the Third Paris Council against the pope. Thus, e.g. (ASV, *Arm.* 54, t. 25, fol. 209r): "Ista via concilii . . . est via machinata prius per illos qui ecclesiam dei turbare non cessant, et hoc potestis perpendere eciam ex copia litere Patriarche." Another little tractate (fols. 107r–122r, esp. 109rv) offers similar arguments, also the conjecture that the whole scheme was designed to elect a third pope, who would be French.

37. E.g., a letter from one of Benedict's men to another (ASV, *Arm.* 54, t. 25, fol. 209r): "Et rogo, attendatis si potestis presumere quod illi qui sunt notorii persecutores pape et inventores tocius mali et discordie nostre partis acceptent et procurent istam viam nisi mala intencione!" and fol. 209v: "Non possum credere quod ipsi vellent . . . concilium in forma iuris tenendum, quia non expediret eis." A copy of Simon's letter with the glosses was to be sent to Élie de Lestrange in Paris, no doubt to convert him from his approval of the council (fol. 210v).

38. Gerson, *Oeuvres,* 6, no. 260, *De concilio unius obedientiae,* written mid-April 1402. Pierre d'Ailly's *De materia concilii generalis* of August 1402/March 1403 uses much of Gerson's work—in Francis Oakley, *The Political Thought of Pierre d'Ailly* (New Haven, Conn., 1964): 252–342.

however, meant that Louis would be able to continue his push as before, and in this sense Berry's mediation was to the disadvantage of his brother.[39] We have seen a similar movement by Berry in mid-1401, in connection with the Wittelsbach alliance, and we may look ahead to the death of Duke Philip the Bold on 27 April 1404 and its sequel: an immediate strengthening of ties between Orléans and Berry, a common hostility to Philip's successor Duke John the Fearless, and in December 1405 an alliance between the two in opposition to Burgundy. That Simon de Cramaud became an Orléans councillor on 11 December 1405, with a stipend of 2,000 livres a year, was nothing but an implementation of this alliance.[40] While Berry remained undeviatingly faithful to the policy of the *via cessionis* and subtraction of obedience—and became quite angry when Louis of Orléans worked to reverse that policy—he evidently shrank from the predictable consequences of real opposition in this and other spheres; for had Berry stuck with Burgundy in an all-out effort to contain Orléans, a civil war could have broken out at once. Furthermore, Orléans was moving to establish feudal and family ties in the south that would join his interest very closely to Berry's, laying the foundations in fact for the Armagnac party that would include both families. While there was no one-for-one relationship between union policy and ducal rivalries, we can sum up the above considerations for our present purpose by observing: (1) that after he had struck forth in his own right as a full-fledged member of the Valois partnership, Louis of Orléans had no reason not to try to change a union policy dictated by his uncles and (2) that he could do so successfully because Berry at least was not prepared to risk civil war for the sake of his brother, still less for the *via cessionis*. We may add that in 1402 Orléans was only thirty years old, while Berry was sixty-two and Burgundy was sixty; also that insofar as Charles VI counted for anything in his more lucid moments (which is much to be doubted), his affection for his brother and lack of it for his uncles would have to be considered a factor in the balance of power.

The events leading to restoration of obedience can be sketched very quickly. After successfully blocking the movement towards a council of the obedience, Orléans introduced Benedict's spokesman Pierre Ravat to a royal audience on 4 March 1402, at which Ravat argued for restoration. Then, after sharp controversy with his uncles, Orléans had Parlement presented with a long anti-subtractionist letter that the University

39. The crisis is discussed in Nordberg: 65–70; it was probably provoked by the growth of Orléans's group of clients in the royal government as well as by Orléans's activities among the Western princes of the Empire.

40. Lehoux, 3:25 n. 6, 62, 69 n. 6.

of Toulòuse had issued several months earlier, and on 16 April he had this letter presented to the king as well. The death in 1399 of Pedro Tenorio, archbishop of Toledo, had removed the chief force behind King Henry III's enthusiasm for subtraction, and envoys of that king also appeared in Paris under Orléans's auspices to urge restoration. In the summer of 1402 the cardinals recognized Benedict's authority and so did Duke Louis II of Anjou and Provence. The tide was in full course, the Berry-Burgundy bloc evidently too weakened by political divergences to fight more than a rearguard action.[41]

Simon de Cramaud, the veteran politician, could hardly have misread the dark auspices and was still less likely to have had any illusions about the unaided power of the written word, but he could only use the weapons he had. As he put it, "right after the Toulouse letter was presented to our lord the king, I put my hand to the pen and within a month presented the text with my glosses on it to his majesty." The glosses were in fact an extremely forceful refutation of every point in the letter, based fundamentally on the doctrine of Simon's treatise on subtraction and arguing at one point that since the subtraction had been undertaken with the consent of a full council of the prelates, it might not be reversed without a similarly weighty consent. We can guess that Simon was thinking of the record for the future at least as much as of the present conjunction. He also sent a copy of the glossed text to King Henry III of Castile, with a covering letter urging the monarch to remember the wisdom of the Spaniard Seneca, the orthodoxy of the Spanish Visigoths, and the glories of Galician resistance to the Saracens. Reiterating the basic canonistic doctrine of total subtraction—"a pope who stubbornly fosters schism or lapses into heresy has ipso facto lost the

---

41. For all these events see Valois, 3:255–279, and the more analytical account in Haller, *PKR*: 247 ff. For Ravat's speech and its background, *ALKG*, 7:204–214; and for the Toulouse letter, Bulaeus, 5:4–24. Among those refuting the letter was Jean Gerson, who agreed with it but resented its attacks on the University of Paris (Gerson, *Oeuvres*, 6, no. 264); see Swanson: 140–144. My discussion of Simon's refutation, which follows, is based on the text in AN, J 518, fols. 500r–555v (it is the concluding item in this codex); the letter of transmission to Henry III is in BN, *ms. lat.* 1573, fols. 32r–37v; see *DSO*, App. V, nos. 15, 16. For the passage in the glosses on the theory of consent, see Kaminsky, "Cession": 317 (AN, J 518, fols. 541v, 543r). The historical references in the letter to Henry III appear on fols. 34r, 35v; the translated passages read: "Papa qui pertinaciter scisma fovet vel incidit in heresim, eo ipso ius quod habuit in papatu perdidit" (fol. 34rv); and "Unanimiter congregemur cum illis de obediencia Bonifacii qui hoc instanter requirunt, et faciamus nobis caput unum. . . . Vel ad reintegracionem canonicam partis nostre, et ad providendum super prosecucione unionis [ecclesie] universalis, conveniamus simul nos omnes de obediencia nostra. Et si fieri hoc non posset, saltim nos Gallici et Yspani" (fol. 36r).

right that he had in the papacy"—Simon went on to offer the king all
the fictive hopes and abortive possibilities of the last two years:

Let us together congregate with those of Boniface's obedience, who urgently
seek this [scil., the Germans], and let us make a single head for ourselves.
. . . Or let all of us of our own obedience convene, for the canonical rein-
tegration of our side and to provide for pursuing the union of the universal
church. And if this cannot be done, then at least we French and Spanish
should convene!

No one paid attention; and as for the dukes of Berry and Burgundy,
the most that they could get was agreement that the matter would be
taken up in a national council of the clergy and nobles. Letters went out
on 28 February 1403 convening the council for 15 May. Meanwhile
Benedict escaped from the Avignon palace and found freedom under the
protection of Louis of Anjou; the cardinals made peace with him on 29
March and promised a formal return to obedience; Castile restored obedience on 29 April. The stage was set for action in Paris. But nothing
could annihilate the material and mental effects of the subtraction years,
and Benedict was made to realize by agents of Orléans that he could
secure the allegiance of the French clergy only on certain conditions: he
would have to accept the *via cessionis* without his usual reservations; he
would have to renounce any punishment of what he considered injurious
or irregular acts consequent on the subtraction; and he would have to
promise to celebrate a council of the obedience within a year to deal both
with union and the liberties of the church, in particular with papal
financial exactions.[42] Armed with these promises in a formal memorandum, Louis secured Charles VI's personal declaration of obedience to
Benedict on 28 May and confronted Berry and Burgundy with the fait
accompli that evening. The council of prelates, which met only once, on
30 May, was merely asked to approve the king's decision, and the
meeting was dissolved when it appeared that only some would do so
forthwith. There was no debate and no vote, as Simon and others would
later recall.[43] Everyone moved at once to Notre Dame, where Charles VI's

---

42. Valois, 3:339; see *ALKG,* 7:280–282, for the memorandum containing these
promises (mentioned below). Haller's discussion, *PKR:* 252–256, is more exact than
Valois's.

43. Valois, 3:341. A brief account of the events tells how the memorandum of
Benedict's promises was read to the meeting of the prelates on 30 May, that they were
asked for comments about it (after having been told that the king had already decided to
restore obedience), and that some said they were ready to obey, while others said they
wanted to go home and confer with the bishops of their provinces; it was while this was
going on (*cumque sic agerentur negocia*) that the royal order came to command the dukes'
immediate presence in order to proceed to publish the restoration (*ALKG,* 7:280). On 8
December 1406 Simon de Cramaud recalled that there had been no regular vote for

restoration of his realm's obedience was publicly proclaimed, while the papal promises were read out as a supplement.

Simon de Cramaud seems to have left Paris after May of 1402 and to have been chiefly active elsewhere for several years.[44] We know that this was a period of intense activity in his own and his family's affairs in Poitou.[45] His feelings can only be guessed, but whatever chagrin he felt at having lost a round in the game may well have been balanced by a realization that Benedict XIII could be fully trusted to ruin his own cause. His promises secured by Louis of Orléans were clear, and he duly embodied them in bulls on 8 January 1404; but he had no intention of keeping them, and on the matters of closest concern to the French prelates, he had made no promises at all: the burden of papal exactions, the legitimacy of collations and elections made during the subtraction, and the large sums of money that the clergy had not had to pay to the Camera during the subtraction but which Benedict considered as owing to him. Orléans had merely assured the prelates that the king would ask that exactions be reduced and that it was understood that titles acquired during the subtraction would not be challenged on that account.[46] But

---

restoration but at best an alleged consensus (BdeC: 215). Cf. the statement by Jean Petit, 6 September 1406, that "n'y eut point de deliberation faicte ensemble a faire la dite restitution" (Valois, 3:338).

44. My log of Simon's Paris appearances in the royal council, etc., has thirteen entries for 1401, another on 14 January 1402, then nothing until May of 1403, in connection with the restoration of obedience; after that there are only occasional Paris appearances until 1406. The same impression of removal from the seat of power comes from the list of his works: after the two reactions to the Toulouse letter in early 1402, both of these clearly defensive, there is nothing until 1405 (*DSO*, App. V, no. 17), at which point, the old aggressive publicist returns to battle.

45. See below, Ch. IX, at nn. 53, 77, 78, 79. According to *RSD*, 2:766 (see n. 30 above), Simon retired from Paris to his commendatory see of Carcassonne; for a speculation supporting this, see Eugène Martin-Chabot, "L'affaire des quatre clercs pendus et dépendus à Carcassonne (1402–1411)," *Recueil de travaux offert à M. Clovis Brunel*, 2 (Paris, 1955):243. The evidence is not hard, however, and a decree of Parlement on 12 January 1404 (in an unrelated case) implies that Simon did not attend to Carcassonne's affairs on the spot ("attenta . . . longa absencia [eius]," AN, X 1A 51, fols. 127v–129v). It would seem more likely that when he was not pursuing his own affairs in Poitou and elsewhere, he was with the duke of Berry; see, e.g., Léopold Delisle, *Recherches sur la librairie de Charles V*, 2 (Paris, 1907; repr. 1967), the inventory of Berry's books, nos. 128, 67, for Simon's gifts of two books to the duke, on 13 February 1403 and 1 January 1404; on both occasions Berry was in Paris (his itinerary in Lehoux, 3:497–499), and Simon probably was too, pursuing lawsuits (Martin-Chabot, ibid., and the decree of Parlement cited above).

46. Haller, *PKR*: 254–256; cf. Élie de Lestrange's report of 11 October 1401 (*ALKG*, 7:165) that in this period the chief concern of the French prelates was that papal exactions should be reduced, rather than that future papal collations to benefices be eliminated ("today there is not much interest in the matter of collations").

Benedict made no concessions at all in principle and as few as possible in practice on all these points, and since Orléans could not be in Paris all the time, it was possible for his uncles to strike back. On 29 December 1403 they secured a royal ordinance confirming all benefice titles acquired during the subtraction, declaring their holders immune from papal financial claims in this connection, and prohibiting the collection of arrears of papal charges from those getting benefices after the restoration. The grounds given by the ordinance were that obedience had been restored on these conditions.[47] While Orléans was able to have the act revoked on 9 April, the true situation remained clear to all: the new obedience was not a simple return to the old system and was in any case a creation of political power at the moment. The pope's revenues, which depended on the clergy's sense of the inevitability of payment, had fallen by a third in spite of the restoration (from a yearly average of 180,000 florins gross before 1398, to 125,000 after 1403). His credit, which had already dropped from 1396 on, was never re-established; and the expedients to which he had to resort, like keeping bishoprics vacant for years in order to collect the revenue, neither made up his deficits nor endeared him to his subjects.[48]

The tensions over what we can call the Gallican issues were matched by disappointments in regard to the pursuit of union. Indeed they were related. Benedict did give Louis of Orléans a bull declaring acceptance of the principle of abdication, but it was not what had been promised—a readiness to abdicate if the other pope did, or died, or was deposed—but only what Benedict had professed from the first: he would abdicate when and if this seemed likely to lead to union, but he considered himself free to try any of the "juridical" ways that he might think promising.[49] As for the council of the obedience, he would convoke one in the near future but not necessarily within a year, nor did he promise to submit to it or to discuss a reduction of papal fiscal impositions. The truth was that he was still intent on the *via facti*, with Duke Louis of Orléans as the chosen instrument to invade Italy.

Louis at this time was maintaining a hostile posture vis-à-vis King Rupert in the north and Henry IV in Gascony, and early in 1403 he had

---

47. For Benedict's policies see Valois, 3:362–365; Haller, *PKR*: 264 ff.; Favier, *Finances*: 661–663; and see below. For the ordinance of 29 December see Valois, 3:366; Haller, *PKR*: 264, supposes that it prohibited annates, etc., even after the restoration of obedience, but in fact it only prohibited the collection of arrears—the crucial passage is obviously accurate in *Ordonnances*, 8:624, and inaccurate in Bulaeus, 5:69, which Haller must have used.

48. Favier, *Finances*: 475 ff., 549 (cf. 568), 664, 678, 688 ff.

49. Valois, 3:356; *ALKG*, 7:288. For the *"vie juris et justicie"* see the text of the bull in Jarry, *Vie politique*: 445–447.

decided to lead an army to Lombardy in order to bring Milan into the French orbit; he was in fact on the verge of doing so when he cancelled the expedition in December and went to confer with the pope instead. A result of these talks—along with the bulls of 8 January 1404—was a papal gift of 50,000 gold francs that would help finance a new Italian campaign; the money was cleverly assigned on the still-outstanding debts of the French clergy to the papacy.[50] The spring months of 1404 saw the beginnings of a massive Franco-papal diplomatic campaign to extend the Avignon obedience in evident coordination with Louis of Orléans's policy of war with England and his expansionist drives into Gascony, western Germany,[51] and above all northern Italy. The Genoese were actually converted (by October 1404); Milan became a French fief (15 April 1404); Florence was solicited; Pisa became an Orléans lordship (24 May); and other efforts were made elsewhere.[52]

Benedict's own first move was to send envoys to Boniface IX in July 1404 to urge union by a *via iusticie* that comprised a meeting of the two popes (*via convencionis*), a discussion of rights (*via iuris*), arbitration if necessary by a panel constituted by both (*via compromissi*), and an eventual abdication that was not the *via cessionis* at all,[53] but the defeat of the loser. Benedict's account of his envoys' proposals in Rome reveals under the obligatory veneer of fairness a core of Avignon arrogance that, together with the actual expansionism pursued at the same time, guaranteed failure and was no doubt meant to do so.[54] An Italian observer,

---

50. Valois, 3:354 n. 8; cf. Haller, *PKR*: 263.

51. Valois, 3:385–389; Lehoux, 3:15 ff.

52. Valois, 3:391–398.

53. Valois, 3:371–384; Benedict's objections noted on p. 374 n. 1 must have been to the mere phrase *"via cessionis,"* for what his envoys said they had offered in Rome under this heading would not have been the Paris program that the phrase had by now come to mean and that Benedict never accepted.

54. This is an account of the talks in Rome that Benedict sent to Charles VI from Genoa, 27 June 1405 (*Ampl. coll.,* 7:686–695), no doubt as propaganda for the *via facti* as a last resort. It shows how he had designed his proposals to be unacceptable. His envoys first said that if both popes met, the Schism could be ended. A week later (29 September 1404) they spelled this out: Benedict sent his admonition that Boniface should reflect on the circumstances of his and his predecessor's elections and should "recognize the way of truth," about which Benedict would fully inform him at the meeting—the "and vice versa" which they added was just an obligatory formality (col. 688C). Again, at the meeting, Boniface would, if moved by the Holy Spirit, "hear things that would not only induce him to agreement but would necessarily incline him thereto by reason and conscience" (col. 688E). There followed proposals for an arbitration as to "which of us two has the right to the papacy," with a declaration of Benedict's willingness to refuse no pains or perils for the sake of union "even if it should be expedient for us to abdicate the papal status or dignity and the undoubted right to it that we have, and ultimately even undergo bodily death" (col. 689). While these words

receiving information from a friendly Aragonese, reported that Benedict's envoys, under the color of unionism, "were working for the [Roman] pope's undoing."[55] For what Benedict had in mind was nothing less than a march on Rome to be effectuated by a grand army whose core would be French contingents under the duke of Bourbon and Duke Louis II of Anjou, who also pretended to the crown of Naples. Other units would come from King Martin of Sicily; his father, King Martin of Aragon; and troops recruited under the papal banner. The preparations were made during the first half of 1405. With proper force and on the basis of the previous year's more peaceful push, this last avatar of the *via facti* might have worked, but in August 1405 John the Fearless marched on Paris, Orléans was thereby paralyzed, and the campaign was cancelled. By the autumn of 1405 Benedict realized that his bubble had burst; meanwhile his fiscal exactions and inflexibility over the Gallican issues, both due in part to the costs of his *via facti,* had provoked a set of public opinion against him that would soon enough prove fatal.

The New Subtraction (1405–1406)

The public opinion just mentioned was centered in the University of Paris, where both subtractionists and anti-subtractionists came together on the common ground of Gallican Liberty. One of the advantages they expected from the restoration of obedience was that Benedict's extremely weak position would allow the restoration only of spiritual obedience, with temporal obedience remaining subtracted—and temporal obedience in this context meant those fiscal and collationary rights that the popes had usurped.[56] Another hope was that the pursuit of union might be more likely to succeed under papal leadership than without a pope. Benedict's policies and actions reviewed above frustrated both expectations, and various university figures began to call for a return to the status of sub-

---

certainly allowed for the abdication of either (but not both, as the French *via cessionis* required), it must have been obvious to Boniface how little Benedict really reckoned with the thought of his own defeat; moreover, the arbitrary and no doubt purposeful mention of possible death created the image of a trial by combat—war—rather than a peaceful judgement. See also Benedict's similar account in 1408, *ALKG,* 5:583.

55. Luigi Fumi & Eugenio Lazzareschi, eds., *Carteggio di Paolo Guinigi 1400–1430, Memorie e documenti della storia di Lucca,* 16 (Lucca, 1925):16, no. 27—a report of 7 July 1404; the key phrase is "vanno cercando lo disfacimento del papa."

56. This was the position of Gerson and d'Ailly in the treatises noted above, n. 38. Gerson was the more radical, even suggesting (*Oeuvres,* 6, no. 260, p. 55) that all jurisdiction in the church might perhaps be removed, according to the model of the primitive church; more seriously, he argued that retaining the subtraction of obedience in temporals even in a united church could be considered a good thing born of the evil of the Schism (p. 56). For d'Ailly's arguments, see Oakley, *Pierre d'Ailly:* 259–263.

traction inasmuch as the restoration had been conditional on certain commitments that Benedict had failed to meet. One does not get the sense, at this point, that either the duke of Berry or Simon de Cramaud was stirring up these sentiments, but they did respond to them. As for Louis of Orléans, his alliance with Berry and his increasingly bitter struggle against John the Fearless seem to have reduced his energy in Benedict's cause—and perhaps he too came to see how little chance the pope had of gaining any of his desires in Italy or France. At the same time, John the Fearless consistently pursued the unionist policies of his late father. The old Berry-Burgundy dynamo of unionism had passed away, but both the dispositions it had created and the new complex of ducal policies allowed the University of Paris to take the lead in generating new initiatives.

With John the Fearless appearing only spasmodically in the Paris government, the university worked chiefly in alliance with the duke of Berry, both in acting for union and trying to curtail papal power. A royal mandate of 16 December 1404, prohibiting collections of annates and *servicia* dating from the subtraction, effectively restored the ordinance of 29 December 1403; one guesses that it was Berry's work in response to a university request.[57] Two months later, when the university thought to take advantage of the new Roman pope Innocent VII's conclave oath to abdicate if necessary, Simon de Cramaud took part in its deliberations, and its embassy to Rome was joined by an envoy from the duke—carrying a letter composed by Simon (and containing a compendium of his doctrine of obligatory cession that Innocent did not much appreciate).[58] Subsequently it was Berry to whom the university particularly addressed its communications to the government—reports from its envoys in Rome and complaints (in May) about a new papal tax that did not respect the university's traditional exemption.[59] This issue, which remained unresolved during the Burgundian occupation of Paris in 1405, finally led to a suspension of lectures in November, with a settlement imposed by the royal government in the university's favor at

---

57. Valois, 3:421. The mandate would not have been issued without a request, and the university was the only permanent institution that would have represented the prelates' interest to the court; since Burgundy was not in Paris at the time, only Berry could have provided the necessary princely patronage.

58. For the letter see *DSO*, App. V, no. 17; the text in *Ampl. coll.*, 7:695–702; in 1406 Pierre d'Ailly referred (BdeC: 154) to "the instructions that had been drawn up when the embassy was sent to the 'intruder'" (evidently the mission in question here) and said that "good counsel had been taken then in this matter" and that Simon de Cramaud "les insera"—which I take to mean that Simon had drafted the instructions or seen to their inclusion.

59. Valois, 3:422–425.

the end of January 1406, by which time Orléans and Burgundy had
made a superficial peace, and the former had allied himself with Berry.
Indeed 1406 was destined to be a year of equilibrium among the
dukes[60] and a decisive step forward for the university; the two must have
been related, for the university's successes all required government support of a strength and continuity that had not been characteristic of what
Berry alone had been able to offer before. In mid-May the university
concluded from the reports its envoys had brought back from Rome that
Benedict XIII had not been seriously pursuing union in his embassy of
1404 to Boniface IX, that he was indeed a schismatic, and that the
subtraction decreed on 27 July 1398 should be regarded as legally still
in force inasmuch as the restoration of obedience in 1403 had been
conditional on the pope's fulfilling his promises. Master Jean Petit, who
had been delegated to present this request to the princes, was also
instructed to demand a condemnation of the University of Toulouse
letter of 1402, which was accordingly brought before the Parlement of
Paris on 27 May and attacked on 7 and 8 June by university spokesmen
joined by the royal procurator Jean Jouvenel. Berry associated himself
with the complaint; Simon de Cramaud represented the university in
asking the government to speed a decision; and eventually John the
Fearless joined his name to the roll of plaintiffs.[61] Their main theses, as
presented by Jean Petit—in French so that the princes might understand—were that the Toulouse letter's refutation of the principles underlying subtraction was canonistically and theologically wrong, also offen-
sive to the dignity of the crown, and that its more particular attacks on
the results of subtraction were without foundation. In addition, there
was argument to the effect that Benedict's nonpursuit of union, disre-
gard of the benefice rights acquired by prelates during the subtraction,
and oppressive taxation of the French church all constituted violations of
the promises in the memorandum read out at the time obedience was
restored, so that the restoration was thereby invalidated.[62] On 17 July
1406 Parlement issued its decree giving satisfaction to the University of
Paris. Meanwhile royal action in June had already suspended all papal
taxes and on 3 July confirmed the benefice titles acquired during the
subtraction.[63] Soon after, on 6 September, Jean Petit again appeared
before Parlement, this time to argue for a final decree of what he called
partial subtraction, understood as a cancellation of papal fiscal rights; on
11 September Parlement obliged in this matter too—all annates, *ser-*

---

60. Nordberg: 215 ff.; Lehoux, 3:64.
61. Valois, 3:431–441.
62. Ibid. More detail and quotations from Petit's speech are given by A. Coville,
Jean Petit: La question du tyrannicide au commencement du XVe siècle (Paris, 1932): 48–63.
63. Valois, 3:442–445; Lehoux, 3:81 n. 8 (evidence that the decrees were applied).

vicia, procurations, and other papal taxes were abolished as of the date of the original subtraction. Here too the duke of Berry had joined the complaint, and while the name of Simon de Cramaud does not appear in relation to the planning and execution of the action, the part he did play as noted above shows at least his involvement.[64] One guesses that there was more, since the next months would see him back in his old role as leader and manager.

Sometime in August it must have been decided that nothing short of another Paris Council, the Fourth, would be necessary to establish the new subtraction; letters went out summoning the prelates to meet on 1 November and provide "advice and counsel on how to work for the peace of the church and to have union"—a standard formula that covered the additional intention, to make "permanent provision" for the subtraction that was being currently pursued in the judicial forum.[65] One is reminded of the Second Paris Council of 1396: again it seems to have been the University of Paris's initiative, and now as then, the debates were concerned with a proposition put before the meeting by the university. Now, however, the university had evidently fallen under the control of its political extremists, and its demand was for *total* subtraction from a pope whom Jean Petit, its spokesman, branded as schismatic and vehemently suspect of heresy.[66] We guess that Simon de Cramaud was content to play along even if his own role would not be what it had been before. In any case, his new responsibility as a councillor of Louis of Orléans would soon take him out of Paris. Since April 1406 there had been preparations for war with the English in the northwest and in Guienne, Burgundy charged with the former and Orléans with the latter; and on about 20 September Simon left for the south in the company of his duke, probably not returning until after the council had begun in mid-November.[67] Since Orléans himself would not return until the end of January 1407, nor Burgundy until mid-December, and even

---

64. Valois, 3:445–448. Although the intervention by Simon mentioned here (pp. 445, 446 n. 1) took place much later (4 January 1407; see *Thes. nov.,* 2:1307–1310), it is not likely that the duke of Berry acted in such matters without Simon's advice or instigation.

65. The letters of convocation do not survive; in his speech of 11 December (BdeC: 150) d'Ailly said they had asked for "advice and counsel" (as in the text). On 20 December the royal procurator Jean Jouvenel told the prelates (BdeC: 233) that both he and the university were requesting "that what had been provisionally regulated when the university and royal procurator had made their complaint in Parlement should now be concluded and regulated by you, by way of a permanent decree or provision." The reference was obviously to the 11 September *arrêt* suppressing papal financial exactions.

66. BdeC: 113; the charge appears several times thereafter in the speeches of university spokesmen, e.g., Petit (BdeC: 224 ff.), Cramaud (pp. 121, 215), Plaoul (pp. 184 f.).

67. Lehoux, 3:86 f., cf. 87 n. 2; Nordberg: 127–130, 145 f.

Berry seems to have been out of town through the whole of November, the "solemnity" which had marked the earlier Cramaud productions was notably lacking; moreover, the prelates of the south seem to have boycotted the council, and attendance was in general not up to par.[68]

Arnaud de Corbie, the chancellor of France, provided what organization there was under the shifting presidency of the king, the ten-year-old dauphin, Duke Louis II of Anjou, Duke Louis de Bourbon, and other princely personnages including, later, Berry and Burgundy. But the organization was extemporaneous and flabby, taken from memories of 1398: after Pierre aux Boeufs and Jean Petit had presented the university's propositions, around mid-November, the chancellor told both sides—the university's and the pope's—to choose their speakers to debate the issues, under royal commission in both cases, as had been done on the former occasion. Now as then, Simon de Cramaud would have preferred a less neutral procedure, in this case wishing that the pope's men had gone first to say why they objected to the university's request for subtraction, with his own side coming on to support it; but perhaps he was not yet present.[69] One feature of the 1398 council was, however, changed: Benedict's own men commissioned to present his side were all southerners, and this time they saw how pointless it would be to use a language that the dukes and others would not understand. They therefore called on northern-French prelates—Guillaume Fillastre, the dean of Rheims; Ameilh du Breuil, the archbishop of Tours; and Pierre d'Ailly, the bishop of Cambrai—whom they provided with written briefs, relevant documents, and current information about Benedict's intentions.[70]

---

68. Lehoux, 3:88, 91 f., for Orléans and Burgundy; her silence about Berry's whereabouts in November 1406 (his itinerary on p. 502) suggests that he was outside of Paris; otherwise his name would have appeared in public acts. On the matter of the size of attendance, cf. Haller's critique of Valois, *PKR*: 280.

69. According to *RSD*, 3:466, the anti-papal leaders wanted to provide no formal occasions for the pope's side to be presented, but they agreed to the scheme of contradictory debate at the persuasion of the chancellor of France. But Simon de Cramaud in his speech of 27 November—the first in the debate—said in reference to this scheme, "As far as I and the others on this side are concerned, we would have preferred that those deputed for the pope's side should have 'opened the matter' by giving their reasons why my mother the university's request should not be heard and granted" (BdeC: 118). This would have given the university's request an official presumption of justice, with objections to it thus appearing as disruptive; Simon and his colleagues would then have appeared as defenders of the public interest.

70. Guillaume Fillastre said he had been requested to speak by "those deputed to support this side, because none of them knew French" and that he would "recite the memoir" that had been provided him (BdeC: 126; cf. Cramaud's remark, p. 216). Pierre d'Ailly used a similar phrase: "I will say nothing as assertion or conclusion but will only recite the memoir provided me" (BdeC: 151). Fillastre's detailed reproduction of Benedict's version of his envoys' actions in Rome, 1404 (cf. the text cited above, n. 54), as

On the other side Simon de Cramaud, Pierre Leroy, and Pierre Plaoul were teamed as they had been in 1398 but were joined now by the new young man Jean Petit and by the royal procurator Jean Jouvenel.

The debates, which ran from 27 November through 20 December, and which are known to us through a uniquely close report in the original French, were not kept to a single well-defined question; for if Jean Petit had formulated the university's request for total subtraction, Pierre Leroy devoted his whole speech to the case for partial, the Gallican Liberties, and kept notably silent about Benedict's alleged guilt of schismaticism and heresy.[71] Thus it was not clear whether the issue was emancipation of the Gallican church or how to proceed to union—for it could no longer be seriously argued that partial subtraction might cause Benedict to change his mind, nor would the Urbanist pope and cardinals, with whom both the government and the university were in very lively contact, have been favorably disposed by partial subtraction on the part of France.[72] Indeed a leading idea on both sides was that union by way of cession as well as other issues would be taken care of at a general council of both obediences, a prospect that evidently seemed far more substantial now than it had in 1398.[73] Benedict's men could do little more than provide the standard papalist refutations of partial and total subtraction, argue against the *via cessionis,* try to vindicate their principal's good faith and record, and urge that the whole complex of issues before the present council be deferred to a council of the Avignon obedience that Benedict was allegedly going to convoke for Pentecost of 1407 and to whose decisions he would submit.

---

well as other documents, suggests that his principals had given him a dossier; it seems that Benedict's intention to call a council by Pentecost and submit to its decisions was revealed for the first time by Fillastre, Ameilh du Breuil, and d'Ailly (BdeC: 141, 148, 158 ff.; 220′ ff.; cf. 226′).

71. For the character of the stenographic report see Valois, 3:458 n. 1; Haller *PKR*: 279. That Leroy's speech was something of a surprise appears from Fillastre's complaint in reply: the original question had been whether Benedict was a schismatic-heretic, but now "une autre question toute nouvelle" had been put, about collations to benefices (BdeC: 199 f.). Fillastre also commented that Leroy's total silence about Benedict's alleged schismaticism-heresy showed disagreement within the university's party (pp. 208 f.).

72. See the discussion below of the evolution of attitudes among the Urbanist cardinals from 1404 on.

73. BdeC: 124 (Cramaud), 146 (Breuil), 203 (Fillastre), 218 (Cramaud), 153 (d'Ailly), 220 (Breuil), 228 (Petit). While d'Ailly and the others on his side proposed a council of the obedience as substitute for subtraction and a preliminary to the general council that would bring both union and reform, Cramaud and Petit presented subtraction as the preliminary—the council of the obedience was passé. Thus Petit (p. 228): "Leissons ce conseil, leissons, et nous en allons au beau conseil general de l'une et de l'autre obeissance, et là se Dieu plest, sera l'église reformée."

The university's spokesmen seem to have been chiefly intent on re-creating the former political action community of king and Gallican church, negatively by declaring the pope to be a schismatic and suspect of heresy, positively by establishing the Gallican Liberties through royal enactment and under royal protection, subject only to the future disposi-tion of a general council. That the Liberties were apt to be attractive to most of the upper clergy for reasons of interest or idealism was impor-tant but not perhaps crucial.[74] The *inconveniencia* of subtraction, which had figured so large in 1398, were treated with little anxiety; the arrange-ments of 1398 could be reinstated, and indeed amplified by instituting regular meetings of diocesan and provincial councils, a point that found wide agreement.[75] For the rest, the most striking feature in the discourses on the university's side was an utter coldness toward Benedict, whose sabotage of the *via cessionis,* refusal to offer it to Boniface IX, indifference to any work for union that could have succeeded, extreme fiscalism in recent years, and systematic mendacity were cited again and again as sufficient reasons for breaking off with his papacy. Plaoul and Petit even moved towards a supra-obedience view of the issues of 1378, much as Simon de Cramaud had done in his treatise ten years earlier.[76]

The formal debate ended on 20 December; the next day the prelates were to begin casting their votes by reading out their written ballots one by one—not in the presence of the dukes, as in 1398, but in full assembly under a president of their own. When we read that Simon de Cramaud now took on this presidency, in the face of some outspoken resentment from his colleagues of archiepiscopal rank,[77] we can assume that here, as in 1395 and 1398, it was the royal government that had in effect appointed him, and we can guess the reason. Without resorting to the more blatant forms of manipulation he had practiced in 1395, he could still use his function of reporting the vote as a way of bringing the congeries of personal and often diffuse pronouncements down to a polit-

---

74. Lestrange's report that the issue of collations had lost much of its interest for the prelates (above, n. 46), is confirmed by the university's concentration on finances rather than collations in 1406. The university was in fact better off sending *rotuli* to the pope than trying to get its graduates placed within the Gallican framework. Leroy seems to have been the only spokesman at this time (Gilles Deschamps was in Italy) to have emphasized collations. As for finances, the speeches in 1406 attacked above all the excesses of Benedict's fiscalism rather than the question of principle raised in 1398, when one after another prelate complained that the French church bore heavier burdens than others.

75. BdeC: 117 (Petit), 174 (Leroy, with much emphasis), 155 (d'Ailly), 233' (Jou-venel). It is instructive to find that the provisions made for subtraction status in 1398 had already, less than a decade later, begun to pass into manuscript oblivion; see the remarks of Jean Petit quoted above, Ch. IV, n. 5.

76. BdeC: 183, 188, 223'.

77. *RSD*, 3:470–472.

ically usable division; at the same time, he could use his presidency to crystallize action out of moods and opinions.[78] His technique seems to have been the same as in 1395: after the balloting had revealed an allegedly tenfold majority in favor of partial subtraction, he caused a memorandum (*cedula*) to be written on each point of consensus, and then he submitted these to a vote in a full session on 3 January under ducal presidency. As far as the abolition of papal fiscal exactions was concerned, this had already been decreed in Parlement's *arrêt* of 11 September 1406, and the prelates merely requested that the *arrêt* with its provisional quality ("until otherwise ordained") be replaced by a royal ordinance of permanent validity and that the levy of tenths and taking of *spolia* be added to the list of suppressed exactions: annates, vacancies, procurations.[79] Another *cedula* covered the suppression of papal collations and provisions in favor of elections by the corporations, collations by the ordinaries, and presentations by the regular patrons; this was carefully declared to be not a novelty but a restoration of the church's ancient liberty, and it too was to be permanent, "even after the Schism," pending final determination by a general council.[80]

It was probably in reaction to these conclusions that, on the same day, the University of Paris asserted its own desire for total subtraction by in fact subtracting itself "to the extent of its power" from Benedict XIII ("a schismatic and vehemently suspect of heresy") and urging the king to do likewise for the realm;[81] its appeal from Benedict to a future general council and future single pope was also published.[82] It is remarkable that the government this time—in contrast to 1398—did not want total subtraction, but partial, and that Simon de Cramaud urged this too (or accordingly);[83] the reason was probably that the experience of the last few years, as we shall see, had made deposition of the popes by a concert of

---

78. One ballot happens to survive, quoted by Valois, 3:472 n. 3; it is clear enough in gist but conditional in form (e.g., "if there was reason to make total subtraction before [i.e., in 1398], then there is still more reason to do it now") and rambling in its points. See below for Simon's use of *cedule* to crystallize opinion.

79. See the summary quoted by Valois, 3:474 n. 2; cf. the text of the *arrêt* of 11 September in Bulaeus, 5:132.

80. *Thes. nov.*, 2:1307–1310; benefices vacant *in curia* were excepted. This text is a notarized instrument of the action of 4 January which includes an account of the proceedings the day before. A revision was made on 12 January to eliminate the original phrasing that had made the Liberties seem to derive from the requested royal mandate (ibid.: 1310 f.).

81. Bulaeus, 5:134–137.

82. *Thes. nov.*, 2:1295–1307; the university also published its list of charges against Benedict (Bulaeus, 5:137) and a historical summary of the evidence for his bad faith, beginning with his actions in Paris 1393/1394 (*Thes. nov.*, 2:1340–1344).

83. *RSD*, 3:472–474; Jouvenel's concluding speech had also been for partial subtraction (BdeC: 232 f.).

princes—the thrust of total subtraction—seem less likely than action by the two colleges of cardinals, with or without their popes, to impose abdication or decree deposition—with French initiative to move things along. To have dissolved France's formal ties to Benedict now would have been premature, especially since new openings were promised by the death of Innocent VII (6 November 1406), news of which had reached Paris by the end of December.

On 4 January 1407 Simon formally reported the council's conclusions at a full meeting in the presence of the princes and members of the royal council, with the *cedula* on collations read out again, to be ratified by the prelates.[84] Then on 7 January the council approved another *cedula* that Simon had composed, requesting the king to forbid all attacks of word or deed on the *via cessionis* (which had been attacked in some speeches at the council) or on the subtraction status and regime ordained in 1398, which were thus to be reinstated as the mode of running the Gallican church under royal rather than papal lordship; royal letters of 14 January complied with this request.[85] About this time, however, more news arrived from Rome: Gregory XII had been elected on 30 November, and he had not only sworn to achieve union by the *via cessionis* but had ardently demanded it as soon as possible.[86] Paris rejoiced, officially on 16 January in a solemn procession with a sermon by Jean Gerson; the prelates of course took part. Then on 21 January the council took note of the Urbanist conversion to cession by concluding that union was to come from a double abdication, with Benedict either going along (and thereby redeeming himself from the guilt of his past obstructionism) or being bypassed; the Avignon cardinals would join their Roman counterparts and provide for a single pope, or if all else failed, the Gallican church would send its delegates to Rome for the purpose.[87] Finally, on 22 January, the council—still led by Simon—voted to annul all Benedict's bulls since restitution of obedience which had cancelled collations and elections made during the subtraction.[88]

The council was over, its conclusions well considered and clearly defined but also rendered less opportune by the course of events. Gregory XII's initiative had changed things, and by early February Paris learned that Benedict had accepted his rival's proposals; the actions voted by the prelates could easily interfere with the hoped-for meeting and abdication.[89] It was therefore decided to hold these actions in abeyance.

84. *Thes. nov.*, 2:1307–1310.
85. Bulaeus, 5:137–141.
86. Valois, 3:479 f., 486–489.
87. *Thes. nov.*, 2:1312 f.
88. Valois, 3:481; *Ordonnances*, 9:191.
89. On 31 January 1407 the Avignon cardinals wrote letters to this effect to the duke of Berry, complaining of the *novitates* being carried through against Benedict, and

Two royal ordinances of 18 February did embody the provisions for partial subtraction in respect to collations and finances, and a third threatened total subtraction if Benedict did not keep his promises; but the first two were not promulgated, and the third was kept more or less secret. On this basis even Orléans could approve the ordinances—he had done his best to hold them up, but he was no longer disposed to support Benedict in any other *via* than that of cession.[90] At the same time, the government decided to implement the council's conclusions of 21 January by constituting a massive embassy representing all factions among the prelates and the dukes and headed by Simon de Cramaud, to go to both popes and see to it that their hoped-for abdications, whether at a distance by procurations or at a meeting of the two, were not impeded by inertia, material difficulties, or Benedict's bad faith. A half-tenth voted by the prelates would finance this action. The ultimatums voted on 21 January and officially ordained on 18 February were to be published if necessary. The Schism had entered its last phase.

Before moving on to consider the negotiations leading to the Council of Pisa, in which Simon de Cramaud's leading role was as marked as ever, we may pause to take note of those changed dispositions on the Urbanist side of the Schism that made the eventual success of the *via cessionis* possible.[91] The same modern tendency to analyze political action on the basis of interests rather than abstractions which has led to our presentation of the Avignon enterprise after 1378 as essentially the *via facti* has caused Arnold Esch to characterize the other side as "the

---

noting that the Roman pope was not being treated thus by his subjects (*Thes. nov.*, 2:1293–1295).

90. The texts of the first two ordinances in *Ordonnances*, 9:180–184; the third in Bulaeus, 5:141–143; cf. Valois, 3:495. Orléans's cold-eyed attitude to Benedict is spelled out in his letter of 2 March 1407 telling the pope that the old game was over and nothing remained but to abdicate; see Lehoux, 3:100, also 3:79, where Orléans's change of attitude is related to his alliance with Berry.

·91. What follows has to do with the attitudes of the Urbanist cardinals; public opinion in general on both sides has never been systematically studied and cannot be considered here. Perhaps the most interesting scholarly consensus lies in the impression that by and large the common people and most of the propertied laity were unaffected by the Schism, unconcerned about its duration, and inclined to look with equanimity on the prospect of a Europe permanently divided into two or even more papacies. See, e.g., the remarks of Jean Favier, "Le Grand Schisme dans l'histoire de France," *GDGSO*: 15 f.; Peter Herde, "Politische Verhaltensweisen der Florentiner Oligarchie 1382–1402," *Geschichte und Verfassungsgefüge*, Walter Schlesinger Festschrift (Wiesbaden, 1973): 190, 192; Harvey, "Letter of Oxford University": 124; the 17 July 1394 letter of the University of Paris in *CUP*, 3:633; Arnold Esch, "Das Papsttum unter der Herrschaft der Neapolitaner," *Festschrift für Hermann Heimpel*, 2 (Göttingen, 1972):754–756. One can imagine a history of the Great Schism in which the movement for union would be seen as stemming not from a general religious torment but from the common interest of certain elites in preserving the structures of their hegemony and legitimation.

papacy under the domination of the Neapolitans"[92]—or more particularly, the absorption of the papacy by those clans of the Neapolitan nobility, the Brancacci, Caraccioli, Tomacelli, Cossa, and others, whom Urban VI (his mother was a Brancacci) had perforce brought in to staff a papal government virtually emptied by the French defection.[93] In 1387 the successes of the party of Louis II of Anjou deprived this group of their Naples base; henceforth they would have nothing but the papacy, and they along with lesser families filled the cardinalcies, curial offices, and governmental functions in the papal states. The death of Urban in 1389 marked another stage, for the Perrino Tomacelli who succeeded him, as Boniface IX, belonged to the younger generation who had no memories of the old papacy to interfere with their systematic appropriation of the new. Insofar as Boniface's stonewall rejection of every unionist overture from the other side requires a special explanation, this may well be found in the compact solidity of his Neapolitan group; at his death in 1404 there were only ten cardinals, eight of whom were from the kingdom of Naples, and five of these were related to him.[94] The ensuing conclave, however, led to the election of a pope unfavorable to the Tomacelli, Innocent VII; for whatever reason, this election was preceded by a con-clave oath that each cardinal swore, namely that if elected he would do everything possible, even abdicate, in order to reunite the church.[95] We have already noted the Paris response to this oath and the even more enthusiastic Paris response to the stronger one sworn in the conclave of 1406 that elected Innocent's successor, Gregory XII, a Venetian, whose first act was to offer the *via cessionis,* simply and without conditions.[96] While neither of these oaths would have been sworn or even contem-plated if the French program launched in 1395 had not made union and cession into European watchwords, their emergence in this period and then their consequences, including the Council of Pisa, have to be understood from the other side as well.

Here we are reduced to speculations on the basis of Esch's material, for the political history of the Schism and the councils that ended it has received little modern attention. The obvious beginning would be the

92. Esch, "Papsttum": 713–800; see also idem, "Simonie-Geschäft in Rom 1400," *Vierteljahrschrift für Sozial- und Wirtschaftsgeschichte,* 61 (1974):433–457.

93. Esch, "Papsttum": 714–732; cf. Favier, *Finances:* 136 ff.

94. Esch, "Papsttum": 734–745.

95. Valois, 3:381 f., explains the oath as an emulation of the Avignon conclave oath of 1394; I do not know that any real explanation has ever been attempted. Innocent VII was from the kingdom of Naples but not from Naples itself; Valois regards him as a continuator of Boniface IX's policies, but Esch, "Papsttum": 746, emphasizes his efforts to reduce the Tomacelli's offices and influence.

96. Valois, 3:479, 485 f.

assumption that the Neapolitan clans dominating the Urbanist papacy had come to the conclusion that they had little more to gain from a continuation of the Schism, or that they had more to gain from ending it. The Urbanist popes in fact had nothing like the apparatus of collectories enjoyed by their Avignon rivals and probably drew little or no net revenue from the papal states; their chief financial expedients were the sale of benefices and of spiritual privileges (dispensations, indulgences, and the like) and the exploitation of the temporalities of such Italian churches as they controlled.[97] The reunited papacy after Pisa, however, and also after Constance, would turn out to be Italian after all; no papal official or cardinal on either side would lose his job; and although the revenues of the new papacy were to be much less than those before the Schism, they were undoubtedly much more than those of the Urbanist popes during the Schism. Union would have only advantages, from the Italian point of view, and this result could have been foreseen, inasmuch as the French program by its very nature signified an abandonment of French claims on the papacy.[98]

Following Esch, we may note the exceptional importance, under these conditions, of the Brancacci clan, which had its members in both colleges of cardinals and in both papal services; they played major roles in contacts between the two papacies during the Schism, then in the activity leading to the union of the two colleges in 1408, and finally in the Council of Pisa.[99] At the same time, the figure of Baldassare Cossa emerges, first as a Tomacelli protégé, then as a cardinal (from 1402), and from 1403 on, as a virtually autonomous papal legate in control of Bologna. Extracting large sums of money from his offices and from the papacy, he regularly deposited them with the Medici—as did other papal Neapolitans, creating an enduring tie between their cause and the Florentine banking house.[100] When we learn that three days before the opening of the Council of Pisa, Cossa withdrew 42,000 florins from his Medici account and that he later claimed credit for having supported the

97. Favier, Finances: 155 ff., 590–610; Esch's critical notes, Göttingische Gelehrte Anzeigen, 221 (1969):152–154, suggest that even Favier's summary of Urbanist financial resources is too favorable. Simon de Cramaud was probably right when he wrote in 1402, in his glosses on the Toulouse letter (AN, J 518, fol. 527r), that the Urbanist pope had already lost much of his authority: "Sibi obediunt si de spiritualibus ad nutum ipsorum disponat, et tunc perfunctorie sibi obediunt, et magis verbo quam facto."

98. The matter is discussed below, towards the end of this chapter.

99. Esch, "Papsttum": 746–754; see the articles by Dieter Girgensohn, "Niccolò Brancaccio," "Rinaldo Brancaccio," "Tommaso Brancaccio," in Dizionario biografico degli Italiani, 13 (Rome, 1971):3–10.

100. Esch, "Papsttum": 771–777; also idem, "Simonie-Geschäft in Rom," passim; Favier, Finances: 680 f.

council at his own expense,[101] we are not surprised to find all the Neapolitans involved in that enterprise, whose eventual fruition from their point of view would be the election of Cossa as Pope John XXIII in the Pisan line.[102] While the French program projected onto Europe since 1395 had not created all these lines of action, it had evoked them by creating the framework in which their motivations could emerge and their goals could seem feasible. The policy of the *via cessionis* was the main factor; the French-Florentine alliance of 29 September 1396 was another. In any case, the events we have just previewed in general outline represent the success, shaped by the Italian medium, of the new Parisian initiative launched in 1407.

Simon's Embassy and the Road to Pisa (1407–1408)

The thirty-six ambassadors who left Paris after Easter 1407—the end of March—included all the speakers on both sides at the recent Paris Council, as well as clients of the Berry-Orléans coalition, with the University of Paris's leaders representing both the academy and the policy of John the Fearless, who had made himself its patron. It was in fact a delegation of "the realm and church of France,"[103] led by Simon de Cramaud in an extension of the official leadership he had assumed in the last phase of the Paris Council; the Orléans client Pierre Fresnel, bishop of Meaux, was his associate.[104] Its instructions, drafted no doubt by Simon, also reflected the dominant mentality at that council.[105] Gregory's already declared disposition to abdicate purely and simply, with no discussion of rights or any other complication, was assumed; Benedict's was evidently doubted inasmuch as he had never, not even in his recent response to Gregory, used the sort of clear language about the *via cessionis* that would have precluded resort to one of his "rational" ways.[106] One key point

---

101. Esch, "Papsttum": 785; Favier, *Finances*: 682 (with a comment, "Cossa had worked for the council [of Pisa] by robbing Boniface IX and his successors").

102. Esch, "Papsttum": 758, 796 (Cossa "drew the whole Neapolitan group onto the side of the Council of Pisa").

103. Bulaeus, 5:142; the formula appears regularly in the sources.

104. Valois, 3:499; although decisions not covered in the embassy's instructions were to be made by majority vote (*Thes. nov.*, 2:1362 f.), Simon's leadership is evident from his role as chief speaker and decision maker. For Fresnel's Orléanist affinity see Nordberg: 217, 139 (where Fresnel and Cramaud were teamed in March 1405, evidently representing Orléans and Berry respectively, in a secular matter of government policy).

105. *Thes. nov.*, 2:1358–1363, with a memorandum of diverse opinions about practical points on cols. 1363–1366.

106. Benedict's letter of 31 January 1407 to Gregory XII (see the texts cited by Valois, 3:494 n. 1) made a point of declaring his preference for a *via discussionis* at the same time that he accepted the other's offer of a double abdication. Even Louis of

of the instructions was that bulls committing himself to the *via cessionis* "plainly, unconditionally, and without ambiguity" be obtained from him. For the same reason of distrust, it was advised that the best way would be for each pope to abdicate in the hands of his college or of an irrevocable procurator, with the preliminary habilitations, cancellations, and confirmations that the original *practica cessionis* had called for. Only if *both* popes insisted on abdicating at a meeting between them would Benedict be allowed to do it that way; in any case, he would have only twenty days from the arrival of the embassy at his court to accept its plan plainly and without tricky language; otherwise he would be told of the subtraction ordinances of 18 February, advised that the king and church of France were withdrawing from him as from a schismatic, and told that the embassy was proceeding to Rome to work with Gregory anyway.

But by early May when the embassy had reached Aix-en-Provence, the last stop before the papal court at Marseilles, Benedict had already concluded an agreement with Gregory's envoys, led by the papal nephew Antonio Correr, that both popes would meet at Savona on the edge of the Avignon obedience by 29 September or at the latest 1 November; the compact had been made on 21 April and Gregory was to ratify it before July.[107] Cardinal Pierre de Thury and Antonio Correr came to Aix to discuss the news, the latter urging that the ambassadors not irritate Benedict or try to use the threat of subtraction against him, for that would have a bad effect on Gregory's dispositions also; meanwhile Simon and Pierre Fresnel were asked to get galleys from Genoa to go to Rome and fetch Gregory to Savona.[108] Fresnel was detached to do so, while Simon and the rest went on to Marseilles for the confrontation with Benedict on 9 May—Simon's first personal meeting with his antagonist since the latter's election.

First in public audience on the following day, then in a secret meeting with the pope and cardinals, Simon and his colleagues asked for the bulls about the *via cessionis,* also one or two other concessions; and as they had no doubt foreseen Benedict refused the bulls—for a hodgepodge of ad hoc reasons that he later expounded to those of the ambassadors he deemed sympathetic to his cause. One of the other requests, that he at once habilitate the other side's cardinals for the future elec-

Orléans felt obliged to write Benedict that this letter had not been greeted in Paris as favorably as Gregory's because "some complained that you were still offering and openly preferring ways of justice and discusson of rights" (quoted by Valois, 3:497 n. 2).

107. For the events covered here and in the following pages, see Valois, 3:502 ff.

108. *Thes. nov.,* 2:1347–1357—an anonymous memorandum covering the embassy's actions up to 10 November 1407; see col. 1347 for Cramaud and Fresnel at Aix.

tion, was referred to discussions between the ambassadors and ten of the Avignon cardinals, who naturally did not want their counterparts to be habilitated before Gregory did the same for them.[109] At a final audience on 18 May, Benedict repeated his intention to put the *via cessionis* first, "but no other rational ways were to be excluded"; here as before, Simon simply declared that this response was unsatisfactory. Benedict later that day complained about all the bad things Simon had said about him in the past when he had called him a schismatic and heretic, and the pope suggested that only his imminent abdication would spare Simon a due punishment. One report has it that Simon now broke down in tears and implored forgiveness prostrate before the holy old man, but another and more likely account has Simon rather coldly responding that such had been the role assigned to him in the various commissioned debates before the royal council.[110] In any case, there was neither a meeting of the minds nor a reconciliation, and only a sense of opportunity made the ambassadors decide, two days later in Aix, that it would not be a good idea to pronounce the subtraction threat at this time.[111] Two members of the embassy were sent to Paris to report; another group was left behind with Benedict; and the main body moved along the coast to Genoa, arriving at the beginning of June. Here Simon and Fresnel borrowed money to outfit the promised galleys,[112] and other preparations were no doubt made for the hoped-for meeting. Then one contingent went on to Rome overland, arriving on 4 July, with Simon's group following by sea and arriving on 16 July, at which point a new set of negotiations had to begin.

For it turned out that Gregory now was unhappy about meeting at Savona, in his rival's obedience, and that he had begun to lose his early

---

109. Valois's account of the Marseilles talks must be supplemented and corrected by the report published by André Bossuat, "Une relation inédite de l'ambassade française au pape Benoît XIII en 1407," *Le moyen âge*, 55 (1949):77–101, the text on pp. 92–100. Whereas Valois follows the Monk of St. Denis, who no doubt got his information from his abbot Philippe de Villette, sent to Paris to report after the Marseilles meetings, the Bossuat text gives information probably supplied by the dean of Rouen Hugh Lenvoisié, one of the University of Paris's delegates, who had been sent back to Paris with Philippe. The two held quite different views, Philippe favoring Benedict, Hugh opposing him.

110. The first report is in *RSD*, 3:602, the second in Bossuat, "Relation inédite": 99.

111. *Thes. nov.*, 2:1363. It may be that they had just received news of the bull of excommunication of all subtracters that Benedict had drawn up on 19 May as a secret weapon (see below): Valois, 3:515 f.

112. Valois, 3:602 n. 3; cf. Simon's deposition at Pisa, in J. Vincke, ed., "Acta Concilii Pisani," *Römische Quartalschrift*, 46 (1938):246: "We armed two galleys at the king's expense and hired them for three months." See AN, X 1C 107B, no. 162 (9 May 1414), for the final settlement of the debts Simon et al. had incurred in this matter.

enthusiasm for the *via cessionis* itself, referring to it much as Benedict had been wont to do and declaring that a contradictory discussion of rights would be better after all.[113] Reasons for his change of heart can be guessed all too easily: his relatives certainly were not enthusiastic about his abdication; King Ladislas of Naples was not in favor of it either and was in any case threatening the papal dominions and Rome itself; while in Rome there had been turbulence and even a Colonna putsch, unsuccessful, the month before. Gregory also complained about the conduct of the French ambassadors, especially Simon, whom he accused of trying to intimidate him by stirring up the Romans and of alienating his cardinals from him. In fact Simon had addressed the Roman magistrates on the Capitoline hill, to declare the benefits that cession and union would bring to the city, and he had indeed been working on the cardinals to persuade them to go through with the Savona meeting in case Gregory should fail to keep his word—in other words, to join in deposing him. It may also be true that Simon's own discourse before Gregory was more minatory than the old man would have liked, especially after the latter had resorted to the non-cessionist gambit of declaring that he was after all the true pope—to which Simon replied, "That's exactly what we disagree about."[114]

But without excluding any of these grounds for the pope's distaste or fear, we must also make room for collusion between Benedict and Gregory about which many charges were made, especially at the Council of Pisa; for they carry an intrinsic probability that balances the inevitable lack of direct evidence. The chief agent would have been Benedict's envoy Simon Salvador, who enjoyed constant access to Gregory's chambers at all hours and was frequently observed on his way to and from

---

113. Valois, 3:542 n. 1; Gregory's anti-cessionist remarks began as early as 8 July.

114. Valois, 3:538 ff.; *Thes. nov.,* 2:1351 f. The text refers to the dealings with the cardinals: "The ambassadors frequently asked the Roman cardinals to induce Gregory to fulfill the treaty, . . . and they replied that they would, but in case he did not, at least they would fulfill their promise. . . . The ambassadors praised this resolve and said that if, similarly, Benedict failed to keep his promises, then other Christians would have to proceed to union in despite of them." Haller, *PKR:* 295 n. 4, supposes that the French ambassadors had begun very early to detach the cardinals from Gregory in pursuit of the result finally achieved, the union of the two colleges against their respective popes. Simon, who knew of Gregory's recalcitrance already before leaving Genoa for Rome (*Thes. nov.,* 2:1348F), was certainly capable of concluding that his own mission's success could now come only from such quiet intrigue. Unfortunately the sources tell us much about the public statements presuming the pope's goodwill, little about the intrigues. For Gregory's complaints that the ambassadors were stirring up mutiny against him and that Simon's speech had been insolent, see *Ampl. coll.,* 7:767 f.; *Thes. nov.,* 2:1355; Valois, 3:539. During his stay in Rome Simon lodged at the house of Cardinal Giordano Orsini (*Thes. nov.,* 2:1337).

them.[115] A member of the French embassy who was in Rome at the time
has left a report dated 13 August of what he heard about this matter
from men whom he called trustworthy, and in fact the statements have a
sort of prima facie substantiality that makes them hard simply to
dismiss. Their gist is that the two contenders have promised each other
"to deal with the issue of union by themselves and their own men, not by
the counsel of princes," or by other parties who have not been requested
to intervene; also that when they do meet, they intend to discuss several
ways "that they deem to be juridical" before they resort to abdication,
namely, trying to convince one another, or submitting to arbitration,
or—Benedict's alleged favorite—agreeing each to habilitate the other as
his vicar, with the survivor becoming sole pope. It was also reported to
the same writer that the contenders both regarded the efforts of the king
of France and University of Paris as more hindrance than help and that
in any case they intended to choose a place of meeting from which they
could freely withdraw in case of non-agreement, "for it would be more
dangerous for them to be coerced than for the church to remain as it is
in schism." Along with this went an agreement that they could change
the time and place of meeting as they saw fit.[116] One consideration in favor
of this evidence is that its substance does correspond to a truly papal
view of the matter, Benedict's view in fact, according to which the true
pope was the supreme director of Christendom, in whose hands alone the
weighty business of union might rightly be dispatched, not a mere
puppet of the princes, politicians, and professors who were presuming to
tell him what to do. It is hard to imagine Benedict *not* conveying these
views to Gregory, perhaps quite sincerely; and it is easy to imagine the
latter, moved by any or all of the practical considerations noted above,
seeing their virtue.

It is true that Benedict played his cards more cleverly than his rival,
who failed to ratify the Savona rendezvous in time, made endless difficulties about the galleys provided for his transport, and after he did
leave Rome by land on 9 August got only as far as Siena on 4 September, where he stayed until 22 January 1408. Benedict, on the contrary,
was at Savona on 24 September, five days before the first deadline; and
then after the second one had elapsed, he offered another scheme—he
would go to Portovenere and Gregory to Pietrasanta—and again showed

---

115. Valois, 3:536 ff., 576 f.; cf. Simon's deposition at Pisa, 1 June 1409, in
Vincke, "Acta Concilii Pisani": 256. Haller, *PKR*: 294, calls these charges a "fairy-
story"—here he is swayed by his desire to vindicate Benedict XIII, even though the
latter's alleged efforts to influence Gregory would not have been discreditable from
Benedict's own point of view.

116. *Ampl. coll.*, 7:768 f.

his good faith by going to Portovenere on 3 January and staying there until 15 June, while Gregory moved only to Lucca on 28 January and stayed there until 19 July. At the same time, Benedict refused to go to Italian places in Gregory's obedience or of Gregory's choice but would consider only those towns on the Ligurian coast that were under French lordship. Not only that, when a chance came to go to Rome under French military auspices (Paolo Orsini had offered the lordship of the city to the king of France), Benedict seized it with all his old ardor; only the capture of the city by Ladislas of Naples on 25 April spoiled this prospect of a real Avignon solution.[117]

Meanwhile, however, a crisis was coming to a head in Benedict's relationship to France. While no one in the government supported him, the participation of Louis of Orléans in the current French enterprise worked to moderate the savage anti-papalism of the University of Paris and its chief ally John the Fearless of Burgundy. Louis's assassination by John's hirelings on 23 November 1407 changed the picture, and after the month or so in which John's confessed guilt kept him out of the government, he returned more powerful than ever. Henceforth French policy towards Benedict became much more peremptory.[118] The subtraction ordinances of 18 February 1407 had not been published nor, as noted above, had they been revealed publicly to Benedict by Simon's embassy; at the same time, the pope knew about them and had prepared his riposte in the form of an unpublished bull dated 19 May 1407, imposing the church's ban on all who infringed papal rights, no matter what their estate, even if they were kings, with all the religious and political consequences spelled out. On 12 January 1408 the royal government, irked by the lack of results, decreed that if the two popes had not given the church union by Pentecost (24 May), France would be neutral; and on 4 March the University of Paris was given the subtraction ordinances of 18 February a year before, so that these too would be published by the same deadline. When Benedict learned of the neutrality threat, sometime in mid-April 1408, he warned Paris not to try it and enclosed a copy of his bull of 19 May 1407 as a sign of his earnest. Deliberately taken as an actual thrust against his Most Christian Majesty, this communication from Benedict became the signal for all the measures the pope had tried to prevent: the subtraction ordinances were published on

---

117. Valois, 3:581–584.
118. Valois, 4:41. The university had gone on strike in protest against the embassy's failure to publish the subtraction ordinances after the unsatisfactory talks with Benedict in Marseilles (Valois, 3:517); cf. Bossuat, "Relation inédite": 100: "Universitas cessat ex eo quia Rex non sibi tradere [*sic*] litteram substractionis beneficiorum," i.e., the university itself now wanted to publish it. Burgundy would see that she could.

15 May; a massive popular demonstration under royal auspices in Paris on 21 May declared Benedict's crime one of lèse majesté; and on 25 May 1408 France was officially proclaimed neutral in the papal Schism.

Meanwhile Gregory's camp had also been losing loyalties, and his cardinals above all were being urged to take matters into their own hands and follow the French example. Simon de Cramaud was the prime mover. Refusing, unlike his fellow ambassadors Pierre d'Ailly and Jean Gerson, to break off negotiations with Gregory about galleys and rendezvous as long as there was the slightest chance of success,[119] he left Rome only on 10 August 1407 along with Pierre Fresnel and others and joined Benedict at Lérins in early September. From there or perhaps from Savona, where Benedict moved at the end of the month, Simon seems to have gone to Avignon in order to fetch the cardinals still there and bring them to Savona, by early November. While Fresnel joined Benedict's envoys sent to Gregory in Sienna in late November, Simon remained with Benedict through the latter's move to Portovenere in January. Simon then made his way back to Gregory's court, now in Lucca, perhaps to urge the new scheme that Benedict go to Livorno, Gregory to Pisa; but certainly to work on Gregory's cardinals with arguments and no doubt promises of money.[120] By early May Gregory had decided to break off negotiations for union by the *via cessionis*, which he would formally repudiate on 12 May, after creating on 9 May four new cardinals in violation of his conclave oath. He also ordered his cardinals to stop all contact with the French envoys in Lucca, who were now forced to leave for Pisa.[121]

----

119. Valois, 3:542 n. 5; I suppose Gerson and d'Ailly were in fact opposing Simon's tactic of working subversively with the cardinals even after Gregory had proven hopeless.

120. For Fresnel's activity see *ALKG,* 5:628, and Valois, 3:563. Simon left Rome soon after Gregory's departure on 9 August and was in Genoa by 21 August (*RSD,* 3:698), Nice by the 27th (Valois, 3:546 n. 4), and at Lérins with Benedict by 2 September (*ALKG,* 5:609; Valois, 3:547). The trip to Avignon seems indicated by the text in *Thes. nov.,* 2:1346 (cf. *ALKG,* 5:610; Valois, 3:547 n. 1); for Simon in Savona on 4 November see *Thes. nov.,* 2:1356, and cf. Valois, 3:559, 562. Lack of contrary evidence suggests that Simon moved with Benedict to Genoa, 23 December, and Portovenere, 3 January 1408. His appearance in Lucca is attested on 19 March (*ALKG,* 5:631), but he must have been there earlier; he was still there in the first weeks of May (n. 121 below). In his deposition at Pisa Simon referred to his continued presence in Lucca during the last set of offers to Gregory (Vincke, "Acta Concilii Pisani": 250). At the same time, the Paris government had taken care to send the Roman cardinals its neutrality ordinance of 12 January and a request that they take counsel with the French ambassadors (Valois, 3:604 n. 2).

121. Valois, 3:587 f.; H. Heimpel, *Dietrich von Niem* (Münster, 1932): 42. The cardinals at Pisa later fixed 3 May 1408 as the date when Gregory had ceased to have papal power (*Ampl. coll.,* 7:1101). Cramaud's Pisa deposition mentioned Gregory's having prohibited his cardinals in Lucca from meeting together, or with Benedict's

On 11 May most of Gregory's cardinals defied his orders and fled from Lucca to Pisa, where they were joined by others and by most of the papal court; they put their action under the protection of appeals to Christ, a general council, and a future pope. Benedict, still in Portovenere, was led to believe that he could work with these cardinals and perhaps become sole pope himself; on about 20 May he sent four of his own to Livorno, which was under French lordship, to deal with them in preparation for his advent. Exactly what went on there is not known, but it is probably enough to say that Simon de Cramaud was at Pisa with the main body of Gregory's cardinals; then at the end of May moved to Livorno, where a group of these were dealing with the four Avignon cardinals; and that the upshot was an agreement that the two colleges would pursue union through the *via cessionis* and a general council by their own efforts.[122] Benedict himself felt increasingly threatened by the French government's intentions and sought to carry on what he still thought were the Livorno negotiations by a group of his representatives while he himself withdrew to safety; but Simon de Cramaud blocked the necessary safe-conducts for the representatives, and on 15 June Benedict left Portovenere for, eventually, a safe residence under Aragonese lordship in Perpignan. On 19 July Gregory left Lucca for safer quarters in Siena.

Meanwhile, on 29 June, the bulk of the two colleges of cardinals had met in Livorno to declare their union in the steps to come: "We promise each other . . . by irrevocable oath to pursue the union of the church . . . by the way of abdication of both papal contenders, . . . and if they refuse or are contumacious we will take other measures by deliberation of a general council; we will then provide the church with a single, true, and indubitable pastor by a canonical election to be made by both our colleges meeting as one." This agreement was made publicly in the presence of Simon de Cramaud, Pierre Fresnel, Pierre Plaoul, and one or two other members of the French embassy.[123] The actual letters convoking the general council to Pisa—here, too, French influence was necessary to secure the permission of Florence, Pisa's lord—were issued in succeeding

---

envoys, or with the French ambassadors, and it went on, "he ordered me to leave Lucca" (Vincke, "Acta Concilii Pisani": 279).

122. Simon at Pisa (Vincke, "Acta Concilii Pisani": 279): "I know that the Italian cardinals . . . withdrew from him and came here to Pisa. . . . And I came to them soon after they had arrived, working for a meeting between them and the cardinals of our college." See the full account in Valois, 4:3 ff. Simon's role in preventing the safe-conducts (below) is explicitly attested along with his trip for that purpose to Sarzana in early June, where Boucicaut was staying (*ALKG*, 5:650).

123. *Ampl. coll.*, 7:798–803.

months, variously predated, and ultimately set the date of the council
for 25 March 1409.[124]

Here, finally, Simon de Cramaud had promoted the political construction that would fulfill his program of 1395. Staying with the
cardinals until some time in September, he then returned to Paris by the
middle of the month, in time to take over the presidency of another
national council of the church, which had been meeting since mid-
August. Its purpose was to give constitutional solemnity to the measures
of subtraction and neutrality already taken, to impose sanctions on adherents of Benedict XIII, and to set up the constitution of the Gallican
church removed from papal government.[125] This last was done more or less
on the model of the 1398 provisions, but with more detail and solidity;
as in the deliberations of the 1406 Paris Council, great importance was
attached to the regular meetings of provincial church councils to handle
dispensations, appeals, and other matters that would normally have gone
to Rome. As for the collations of benefices, the successive specifications
that had been introduced after the 1398 decisions in order to take care of
university graduates and others with some special claim to preferment
were consolidated into a new system that set up a committee of leading
prelates (Simon was of course a member) to take the pope's place in
approving benefice rolls that the ordinary collators would have to honor.[126]
But apart from all this, the council had to provide the support to the
cardinals that Simon had no doubt promised: he it was who had its
members swear the same oath the cardinals had sworn on 29 June, who
secured the approval of a half-tenth to support the expenses of his
embassy and of the future participation in the Council of Pisa, and who
saw to it that the official delegates for Pisa would be chosen now in Paris
rather than freely later at provincial councils.[127] This last step was taken on
6 November, the day after the formal closing of the Paris Council.
Simon's duties were of course not over. Apart from acting as the cardinals' "ambassador" in Paris,[128] and doing all the things that were necessary

---

124. Florence's permission was granted 23 August, after Simon and Cardinal Giordano
Orsini had gone there in July to obtain this and other Florentine concessions for the
cardinals (Valois, 4:18). For the predating of the letters of convocation to Pisa, see
Valois, 4:19 f., but cf. J. Vincke, *Briefe zum Pisaner Konzil* (Bonn, 1940): 12–15.

125. Valois, 4:21–43; Haller, *PKR*: 303–306, offers some additional appreciations
of the final, "revolutionary" form of the liberated Gallican church set up at the Paris
Council. Simon's presidency had been ordered by "the king" (Mansi, 26:1030).

126. Valois, 4:34 f. Simon's grandnephew Guy de Pressac was one of those taken
care of by the new committee (AN, X 1A 61, fol. 143rv).

127. Valois, 4:39 f.; cf. Lehoux, 3:149 f., on the prelates' oath of 31 October to
pursue union by the *via cessionis* and a general council; she mistakenly regards the two as
incompatible.

128. Bulaeus, 5:168; *Ampl. coll.*, 7:888 f.; DRTA, 6:307; Mansi, 27:46.

to make everything happen as it should, he had one more German embassy in store—to the Frankfurt Diet of early February 1409—which probably accomplished little;[129] then on his return he was perhaps kept busy by other political efforts to expedite the Pisan project.[130] He himself arrived at Pisa on 24 April, a month late.

The Pisan Solution

Simon's first session was the council's sixth, on 30 April, and here he assumed the presidency, a role for which he was qualified by his rank as patriarch, his position as chief of the French clergy in its political aspect, his unique status as the most widely known prelate among the political elites of Europe, and—it may be guessed—his proven talent for running a council smoothly.[131] It would be foolish to suppose that the striking unanimity displayed at Pisa and duly noticed by the council's modern historians had not been carefully prepared by caucuses and conversations hidden beneath the glassy-smooth surface of the official *acta,* and while there is no proof that all this was the work of Simon de Cramaud, we can suppose that at least much of it was. The *acta* themselves reveal his characteristic mode of procedure, the reading out for uncontroverted approval of written statements (*cedule*) obviously worked out in advance on each of the main points of decision in the council's agenda.[132] On one

---

129. Valois, 4:73; *DRTA,* 6:357, 362.

130. A text published by Herbert Immenkötter, "Ein avignonesischer Bericht zur Unionspolitik Benedikts XIII.," *Annuarium historiae conciliorum,* 8 (1976):245, reports that many French clerics trying to attend Benedict's Perpignan council, which opened on 21 November 1408, were intercepted "by agents of Simon de Cramaud." Much activity of this practical sort must be imagined as occupying Simon in the winter of 1408/1409.

131. Valois, 4:78 n. 3, suggests that Simon's presidency was an honor paid him as head of the French embassy. But it was much more weighty than that. For one thing, if the president was to be an embodiment of the European hierarchy vis-à-vis the cardinals, a patriarch would have been called for; on several occasions in fact, Simon appeared on the presidium with the two other patriarchs at the council. At the same time his role was that of an organizer and leader, not just of a titular eminence; he had, after all, been the author and director of the French scenario that the Council of Pisa produced into reality. The last point was noted by Job Vener in the "Heidelberg Postil" at the time (*DRTA,* 6:399 ff., nos. 59, 62, 90, 118, 122, 125, 148) and in his own way by Haller, *PKR:* 312–316, against Valois's thesis that France acted disinterestedly (on which see below, n. 143).

132. Valois, 4:77 f., comments on the appearance of unanimity, and the connoisseur of Simon's ways will smile knowingly when he reads Leclercq's comments on the remarkable "bonne entente" at the council, the reduction of the sessions to mere registration of decisions taken by the directors, the way opinions were expressed "d'après un programme arrêté d'avance"—in C. J. Hefele, *Histoire des conciles,* trans. H. Leclercq, 7(i) (Paris, 1916):6. Simon's work with his various *cedule* appears in the *acta* in *Ampl. coll.,* 7:1087, 1088, 1093, 1095, 1100, 1101.

issue, however, we get a lot more, when the *acta* suddenly crack open to show an underside of conflict and intrigue. This was the issue of how to elect the new pope after the two contenders had been deposed (by decree on 5 June, for which see below). On 10 June, we are told, a meeting of the French delegates discussed this matter, some evidently favoring a special mode of election that would prevent the French cardinals from being numerically outweighed (only ten out of twenty-four would be Avignon cardinals, only five or six of them French),[133] but the University of Paris and Simon de Cramaud urged a proposal by the latter that the two colleges simply be fused and that their election should be regarded if necessary as having the authority of the whole council.[134] We are even told by the compiler of the *acta* that many of the French complained that Simon's group had been making propaganda for their proposal by inciting the other nations to accuse the French of trying to get a French pope. But when the time came at the seventeenth session, 13 June, Simon rose to read his *cedula*, which was somehow approved without discussion and without even a count of votes, much to the scandal of many.[135] Without trying to penetrate more deeply into the interests at stake here, we can see how a problem that could well have developed into a disaster was smoothly suppressed by exactly the directive techniques that Simon had used at the First Paris Council in 1395 and the Fourth in 1406/1407. We can guess that it was not the only time.

The same impression of Simon's dominating role is given by the council's decree of 5 June deposing the two contenders. It is not just that Simon was the one who read it out but that the doctrine of the decree is literally identical to that of his treatise "On Subtraction of Obedience":

The holy synod representing the universal church, sitting as a tribunal in the present case against Pedro de Luna and Angelo Correr, formerly known as Benedict XIII and Gregory XII, decrees that all their crimes are notorious, and that they have been and are schismatics, fosterers of schism, notorious heretics deviating from the faith, ensnared in notorious crimes of perjury and violation of their oaths, and notorious scandalizers of the church; and that they have been notoriously incorrigible, contumacious, and stubborn in these respects. For these and other reasons they have rendered themselves unworthy of every honor and dignity, even the papal; and the synod decrees that they

---

133. Valois, 4:104; see the lists in A. Franzen & W. Müller, eds., *Das Konzil von Konstanz* (Freiburg, 1964): 36 ff.

134. *Ampl. coll.*, 7:1099.

135. *Ampl. coll.*, 7:1100: "Et ista est cedula, quam ipse patriarcha fecerat, cui multipliciter alias fuerat contradictum, et sic transivit contra deliberationem omnium provinciarum regni Franciae, etiam non scrutatis votis in concilio, secundum quod erat in aliis consuetum fieri" (the French delegates acted at Pisa in their church-provincial groupings). The tone of outrage here is striking and unique in these *acta*.

are ipso facto deposed [*abjectos*] and deprived of all right to rule or preside, by God and the sacred canons. At the same time the synod, by this definitive sentence, deprives, deposes, and cuts off the aforesaid Pedro and Angelo, prohibiting them from acting as supreme pontiff. And the synod decrees that the Roman Church is vacant.[136]

By this time of course there were many to write similar things, and if now the more luminous lawyers of Italy—Antonio of Butrio, Pietro of Ancorano, the faculty of Bologna—came forward to say the same,[137] overshadowing their French forerunner, that can be taken as merely evidence that the fifteen years of political action in which Simon evoked the Council of Pisa included a work of propaganda that stimulated the appropriate turns of thought among the learned. Nor was Simon any less the publicist now than before: we can guess that he had brought copies of his treatise with him in his work with the cardinals during 1408; we know that now at Pisa he pronounced a canonistic discourse validating the council's legitimacy[138] and that he had his own documentary collection with him for opportune use.[139] No doubt he had also had much to do with legally establishing the above-mentioned papal crimes, by helping to construct the dossier of accusations against the two popes which occupied most of May. The core consisted of sound testimony including his own about the obstruction of union by the contenders. Some weird charges against Benedict—sorcery, recourse to Jewish and Saracen books— remind us of what French ruthlessness could do when it had wanted to get rid of Boniface VIII and the Templars, but we can hardly guess who was responsible for including them.[140]

At the end of his discourse of May, Simon added that his government had instructed him to declare that the king of France would adhere to whatever decision the Council of Pisa made about union and to whatever pope it elected; the king did not seek a French pope, nor did he particularly want the papacy to reside in Avignon. He offered as expla-

---

136. *Ampl. coll.*, 7:1095–1098; see Vincke, "Acta Concilii Pisani": 295 ff. My translation sharply compresses the decree but is otherwise literal.

137. See, e.g., the various formal opinions given for the benefit of the Roman cardinals and published by J. Vincke, *Schriftstücke zum Pisaner Konzil* (Bonn, 1942): nos. 3 (the Bolognese Bartolomeo of Saliceto); 4, 5, 16, 17 (anonymous); 18, 19 (Pietro of Ancorano). See Valois, 4:57, for Bologna's views and the treatise of Antonio of Butrio.

138. Vincke, *Schriftstücke*: 165–177.

139. Thus, e.g., in his depositions at the council (Vincke, "Acta Concilii Pisani"), he mentioned documents that he had with him: the conclave oath of 1394 (p. 220: "et habeo penes me de presenti") and an instrument of Benedict's original rejection of the *via cessionis* (p. 221: "quod eciam habeo penes me"). He must have had a whole collection, and perhaps even the reference books he would have needed to produce works like the one mentioned just above.

140. See Valois, 4:92–97.

nation a point he had made two years earlier to Gregory XII: the French
royal house had gotten more from the popes when they were in Rome
than when they were in Avignon, namely Charlemagne's empire and
Charles of Anjou's investment with the kingdom of Sicily.[141] Simon had
indeed always disclaimed French interest in having a French pope, his
rhetoric over the years producing a whole gallery of exotic alternatives:
Let it be a good German! An African, an Arab, an Indian! A Tartar! A
Turk!—as long as he is orthodox![142] Many in France did not feel this way,
but Simon's union policy, as we have noted, was based precisely on the
reification of church and papacy that made benefices and their revenues
the supreme objects of the secular powers' ecclesiastical interests, and the
Schism itself had guaranteed that the royal share in the disposition of
such things would be satisfactory no matter who was pope. The fact that
the France of a century before which had appropriated the papacy had
now become a complex of princely conglomerates poised to tear the
country apart—1408–1410 happened to be a period of uneasy balance—
certainly fitted in with this way of looking at the matter.[143] It is thus
instructive to recall that with all the political and financial help that
France gave to the cessionist-depositionary side of the Pisan enterprise, it
was the Roman cardinal Baldassare Cossa whose financial resources would
prove decisive in the reconstitution of a united papacy; they made him
the real power in the conclave that on 26 June elected his candidate
Peter Philarges, cardinal of Milan, as Pope Alexander V.[144] France had her
own interest in this, to be sure, but as we have seen, it was Simon de
Cramaud who had formulated the voting procedure that signalled the
removal of French directive power from this stage of the council's work.

Greek by origin, Italian by career, the new pope would soon die and
be succeeded by Cossa himself as John XXIII on 17 May 1410, but
meanwhile he served well enough to create the image of a reunited
church to which most of Europe adhered: France, the Burgundian complex, England, Wenceslas of Bohemia and most of eastern Germany,

---

141. Vincke, *Schriftstücke*: 177; cf. the report of Simon's speech before Gregory XII
in Rome, 18 July 1407: "Dixit regem non tendere ne curia hinc abstracta Avinione
resideat, solam unionem pocius expetere, plura beneficia a papa consecutum dum Rome
resideret, quam dum Avinione maneret": in Noël Valois, "Jacques de Nouvion et le
Religieux de Saint-Denis," *Bibliothèque de l'École des Chartes,* 63 (1902):249.

142. Haller, *PKR*: 311, has collected the passages.

143. When Valois wrote (4:106) that "la France avait tout sacrifié au besoin de
l'union"—her interests, her *amour-propre,* even the traditional principles of her rulers—he
was indeed indulging in what Haller (*PKR*: 312–316) labelled "patriotic fantasies that
have nothing to do with history." But Haller's own assumption that France strove to
control the Pisan papacy was equally nationalistic and probably wrong in point of fact.

144. See above, at n. 101.

Poland, Florence, Milan, Venice, and others. It is true that the two deposed contenders still had their obediences—Benedict enjoying the support of Aragon, Castile, Scotland, and some principalities of southern France; Gregory supported by Ladislas of Naples, Rupert and other western German princes, and Carlo Malatesta of Rimini and some other north Italian powers. But the Pisan line would soon attract a number of these, and in any case the Schism was over as far as France was concerned; she was with the majority on precisely the basis of non-discrimination between the two obediences that had been the sine qua non of her union policy, the *via cessionis*. Much still had to be done, chiefly in the Council of Constance, but France would henceforth be among the problem solvers, not the problems; in this sense—Simon de Cramaud's—the Council of Pisa was a total success. It was also a success for Simon personally, not only in his eminence as president and chief director but also in his ecclesiastical career, stymied ever since he had taken up the leadership of the struggle against Benedict. The day after Alexander V's election, Simon was among those who supplicated for promotion, asking for the archbishopric of Rheims and getting it by an appointment dated 2 July 1409. In 1413 John XXIII would make him a cardinal.[145]

The two contenders deposed at Pisa did not, as we have seen, accept their fate. Both indeed had called their own councils, Gregory's at Cividale from 6 June to 27 August 1409, and Benedict's at Perpignan from 21 November 1408 to 12 February 1409. Neither was successful even in consolidating what obedience he had. Gregory would eventually come to terms with the Council of Constance, abdicating on condition that he first "convoke" the council that had already assembled—a step that legitimized it not only in his eyes but in those of the Italianized papacy that Constance turned out to inaugurate. Benedict held out to the end, losing his allegiances one by one through conquest or attrition (Avignon was conquered from his nephew; most of his Languedocian support eventually faded away) until only Aragon, Scotland, and Armagnac were left; the king of Aragon finally subtracted his obedience on 6 January 1416, Scotland following in 1418.[146] Benedict himself resided in Perpignan at first, then finally moved into the castle perched on the rocky tip of Peñiscola, a spur jutting out into the Mediterranean, where he died in his nineties, in 1422 or 1423, leaving behind a few cardinals who kept his papacy going, although not without making a new schism among themselves. It was not until 1430 that the count of Armagnac

---

145. For the supplication see *Ampl. coll.*, 7:116; for the rest see the next chapter.
146. Valois, 4:146–174, 437–478; see R. N. Swanson, "The University of St. Andrews and the Great Schism, 1410–1419," *Journal of Ecclesiastical History*, 26 (1975): 223–245.

turned to the Roman pope, but by this time there was nothing left of the old obedience anyway but personal affections here and there. Perhaps the deepest meaning of the whole story would be that a certain conception of the papacy that had justified Benedict in every one of his actions to the very end of his long life had found its tomb in the rock of Peñiscola, its refutation in the choices made by all those, including almost all of Benedict's most ardent supporters along with the Thurys and the Cramauds, who at one point or another decided that it did not *matter* who had been the "true" pope.

CHAPTER NINE

The Last Chapter

THE FIFTEEN years of Simon's union activity that we have traced in the preceding chapters form a coherent story ending with the crescendo that took its hero to the heights of prestige and success that he achieved at Pisa. He was then about sixty-four. The sequel that would take him to his death at seventy-eight, on 19 January 1423, began with a few good years and then slid into a decline, the contracting horizons of old age resonating with the disintegration of Valois France into regional factionalism, civil war, and dismemberment by Lancastrian England. The great work for union in the church had brought its rewards, but these did not include grateful recognition of Simon's merits; indeed the Italianized papacy that he, more than anyone else, had brought into being was determined to break with everything that linked it to the world of Schism, Gallicanism, and the councils. The Cramaud family, whose "estate" Simon had amplified at great expense and which should have formed a massive pyramid under him, turned out to be, at best, reliable receivers of favor; his nephew Jean turned out worse, as we shall see. With a bit of luck, Simon could have ended his life as the venerable sage of a stable political society, his last years cheered by the rising fortunes of nephews and nieces, brightened by the chatter of little Cramauds, and adorned by the trappings of wealth and power that befitted the man he had been. The picture we get instead is of a has-been, isolated in the remnants of his grandeur—too big for the "kingdom of Bourges" that now confined him, but at the same time weakened by the ailments of old age and tormented by the greedy importunity of a nephew who should have been his chief support. While it may be aesthetically fitting that the last stage of Simon's personal life should have been of a piece with the rest of it—a rather grimy hustle, with nothing coming easily or with grace—sentiment would prefer something happier. But perhaps Simon saw things differently, for his life had not been lived in a world of happy endings.

Archbishop of Rheims

Simon's request at Pisa that he be made archbishop of Rheims had been coupled with a request that Alexander V also move Archbishop Pierre

Aimery of Bourges into Simon's now-vacant patriarchate of Alexandria with the administration of Carcassonne and that Bourges be given to Guillaume Boisratier, who had just become the duke of Berry's chancellor—Bourges being of course the ideal see for that functionary.[1] There is no reason to think that any of this was not determined by the duke's policy, and as far as Simon was concerned we can say only that while Rheims was certainly a promotion in terms of importance, power, and rank within the polity (its archbishop anointed the kings and was himself a peer of France) and possibly in terms of revenue,[2] Simon's chief function in his new dignity was to stay in Paris as the duke's man in the royal government. He may have made a trip to Rheims after returning from Pisa—we do not know; the only evidence shows him resident in Paris from 9 September on, and his formal "joyeuse entrée" into his new see was not until 15 December, soon after which he returned to the capital.[3] This period, until mid-August 1411, was perhaps the most narrowly political one of his whole career, partly because his secular political action was no longer overshadowed by his engagement in union policy, partly because of the crisis in the French polity and Berry's own stance within it.

We have already seen that even in the lifetime of Philip of Burgundy, the duke of Berry had refused to give his brother whole-hearted support against Louis of Orléans and that after Philip died, Berry and Orléans made an alliance (which absorbed Simon de Cramaud as well). Underlying all this was a combination of familial and geopolitical interests that

---

1. *Ampl. coll.*, 7:1116; cf. Lehoux, 3:222 n. 6.

2. Carcassonne was rated by the Apostolic Camera at 6,000 florins, Rheims at only 4,000 (Hermannus Hoberg, *Taxae pro communibus servitiis ex libris obligationum ab an. 1295 usque ad an. 1455, Studi e testi,* 144 (1949), s.v.), and while in principle the gross values would have been three times as much, in fact the real values could have been quite unrelated to the ratings at this time—see the discussion above, Ch. III, nn. 48, 59. In his lawsuit with Cardinal Amadeo di Saluzzo (below), Simon claimed his see was poor, yielding only 3,000 livres gross in temporal revenues, 1,000 net, and 2,000 net in spiritual revenues (AN, X 1A 4789, fol. 55r; X 1A 59, fol. 117r), but Saluzzo countered that the temporals were worth 4,000 livres a year; the spirituals, 5,000; and that Simon would not have given up his prestigious patriarchate and profitable Carcassonne for a less profitable dignity (AN, X 1A 59, fol. 119v; cf. X 1A 4789, fol. 58v).

3. The first evidence of Simon's presence in France after returning from Pisa shows him sitting in the Great Council on 9 September 1409 (*Ordonnances,* 9:463). On 24 September he made an accord in Paris with the heirs of Guy de Roye (AN, X 1C 98B, no. 216), and he appeared in Parlement on 12 November—P. Anselme, *Histoire généalogique et chronologique de la maison royale de France,* 3d ed., 2 (Paris, 1726):43, also the source for the formal entry into Rheims on 15 December. He was back attending the Great Council on 9 and 15 January 1410 (Valois, 4:128 n. 1; BN, *ms. fr.* 20,883, no. 35) and no doubt thereafter—for his presence in the *Requêtes* sometime in March 1410, see *AHP,* 26:183.

attached Berry to the south, along with his sense that it was up to him to keep the factions in balance so that the Valois enterprise would not founder. When John the Fearless of Burgundy had Louis of Orléans assassinated, on 23 November 1407 and then admitted it to Berry, the old duke wept but chose eventually to swallow the scandal so that John could still participate in the royal government.[4] On 8 March 1408 Berry and the rest of the royal family had to listen to Master Jean Petit's vindication of Burgundy's crime as a case of virtuous tyrannicide, and no one dared to protest; nor was the defense of Orléans, arranged by his widow Valentina Visconti on 11 September, sufficient to undermine Burgundy's position. The Peace of Chartres, 9 March 1409, consummated this line of appeasement: Valentina Visconti had died a few months before; Berry was the "curator" of her three sons (the eldest, Charles, was fourteen); and it was on his counsel that they declared their willingness to forget the past and be reconciled with Burgundy. "Peace, Peace, and there is no peace" was the comment of one observer, and Berry's modern biographer has remarked that the Peace of Chartres was not only a guarantee of civil war but also "one of the most iniquitous actions in which Berry ever took part."[5] One can agree, and one can also accept Lehoux's generally unflattering judgements of Berry's qualities— "pusillanimity," "absolute lack of character," "as devoid of judgement as of character"[6]—and yet suspect that the old duke may have known or at least sensed what he was doing: playing for time and allowing Burgundy's excesses to consolidate the opposition.

Thus when Jean de Montaigu, grand master of the *hôtel du roi* and chief member of a family prominent in the service of both Orléans and Berry, was arrested on factitious charges of malfeasance and then beheaded on 17 October 1409, all on the insistence of Burgundy, neither Berry nor Queen Isabelle had been able to halt the process; but the reaction in the political community was decisive. A week and a half later, Charles of Orléans renewed his father's old alliance with Count Bernard of Armagnac, Berry's son-in-law, and in early 1410 Berry and Armagnac met to lay the foundations of what would become the Armagnac party. Charles of Orléans would marry Armagnac's daughter (the contract was made on 18 April), and the princes of the faction would enter a formal alliance. This was done on 15 April 1410 in the League of Gien, which united the dukes of Berry, Orléans, and Brittany, the counts of Alençon,

---

4. Lehoux, 3:108–115; Richard Vaughan, *John the Fearless* (New York, 1966): 47 f., 67 ff. The summary of political history in this and the next paragraph is based chiefly on Lehoux's account, the most detailed available.

5. Lehoux, 3:144–146.

6. Ibid., 3:167, 216, 222.

Armagnac, and Clermont (another Berry son-in-law).[7] The pact provided for the formation of a joint army, the precondition obviously of any realistic effort to roll back the gains scored by Burgundy. The object of contention was control of the royal government, which of course meant mastery of Paris; and while the conflict generated conflicting political ideas—Burgundy making himself the patron of the university and of the Parisians in attacking the crown's by-now-traditional incompetence and extravagance—there is no reason to suppose that the ideas were more than the decent drapery of a struggle for power.

Meanwhile the duke of Berry's policy still tried to preserve the formality of peace within the family, and while neither he nor other princes of his party had much say in the Paris government after the end of 1409,[8] some of their clients still sat in the royal council. One of these was the new archbishop of Rheims, Simon de Cramaud.[9] Later in the year, after the mobilization of Orléans-Armagnac troops had threatened to precipitate civil war, Simon was among the envoys sent by Paris to the duke of Berry and his allies (mid-September 1410), with the eventual result that war was avoided by the Peace of Bicêtre on 2 November, constituting a supposedly non-partisan but in fact bipartisan government in which none of the princes would take a direct part. Simon was one of the members of this government, and we find him in Paris more or less continuously until the summer of 1411.[10] These fragile arrangements, almost certainly due to Berry's policy of appeasement, were doomed when Charles of Orléans and Bernard of Armagnac took over the reins of their faction's control and demanded a showdown; at the end of May, Orléans named ten royal councillors as in fact Burgundian, and on 7 June Burgundy replied by saying that eleven were Orléanist—Simon de Cramaud of course among these.[11] His Orléanist affinity did not to be sure prevent Simon from trying in July to lead an assembly of prelates into voting funds to strengthen the royal government; it was Jean Gerson on this occasion who spoke for the University of Paris and blocked the move with a speech about the tyranny of unjust exactions.[12] But this was the

---

7. Ibid., 3:154–170.

8. Ibid., 3:163 f.; Vaughn, *John the Fearless*: 80 f.

9. See n. 3 above.

10. *RSD*, 4:358; Lehoux, 3:192–201; Valois, 4:185 n. 2. Simon attended the Great Council on 8 October 1410 and 4 February, 28 February, 19 April, and 12 June 1411—*Ordonnances*, 9:546, 573, 575, 581, 611. In mid-July he was chief of the prelates assembled in Paris (n. 12 below); on 21 July he attended the royal council (Douët-d'Arcq, 1:343); on 29 July in Paris he received 4,800 francs of the Guy de Roye legacy (below); on 12 August 1411 he sat again in the royal council, the last time known until years later.

11. Lehoux, 3:224 f.

12. *RSD*, 4:414–418; Lehoux, 3:228; cf. *Ordonnances*, 9:643. Valois 4:183 ff., discusses papal fiscality and papal grants of clerical taxes to the crown in these years and

last moment of the Bicêtre regime. Further attempts at mediation by Berry failed, and on 14 July Charles of Orléans issued his Manifesto of Jargeau demanding that John the Fearless be punished for the assassination of Charles's father; Charles then issued a formal challenge, which John took up on 13 August.[13]

At this point the duke of Berry had to recognize that his posture of pacification was useless and that he had to become overtly what in fact he had been for some time, the formal head of the Armagnac-Orléans faction. All of which meant that Simon de Cramaud's position in Paris was both pointless and untenable, the latter inasmuch as Burgundy now dominated the city; sooner or later—and Simon must have been thinking in these terms along with his patron Berry—the archbishopric of Rheims itself would become untenable. It had given him a northern and national stature during the period when Berry's policy called for him to have this, but he and his patron would now be much better off if Simon could, so to speak, come home. This would take some managing, as we shall see. It was not until mid-1412 that Simon could begin to arrange the actions that would lead, on 14 April 1413, to his elevation to the cardinalate with a simultaneous exchange of Rheims for Poitiers; meanwhile he probably took up residence in Rheims.[14]

While his tenure of his see lasted less than four years, much of it, as we have seen, spent in Paris, Simon did not neglect its affairs. "He reigned laudably" was how a Rheims necrology put it, and there is also less conventional testimony from one of his successors as late as 1472 who remembered with approval his defense of the church's rights.[15] Simon himself remarked that he had a special affection for Rheims because he

---

shows how the University of Paris took the lead in resisting both—sometimes in open opposition to Simon de Cramaud. On p. 193, Valois writes that Gerson's opposition in July 1411 failed, but it is not clear why he thinks so.

13. Lehoux, 3:228–232; Vaughn, *John the Fearless:* 87–90.

14. Lehoux, 3:235 n. 6, following Noël Valois, *Le conseil du roi au XIVe, XVe, et XVIe siècles* (Paris, 1888): 125 f.; no evidence is given for Rheims as the place of Simon's withdrawal, but it would be likely. Cf. the data in n. 10 above.

15. Pierre Varin, ed., *Archives législatives de la ville de Reims*, 2, *Statuts*, 1 (Paris, 1844):107 f., gives the text of a Rheims necrology composed ca. mid-1414 which remarks, "tribus annis cum dimidio huic ecclesie remensi laudabiliter prefuit" and goes on to list his benevolences. The testament (1472) of Jean Juvenal des Ursins, archbishop of Rheims, reviewing his legal actions of recovery on behalf of his see, remarks in one case, "Reperi quod Simon Cramaudi quondam Remensis archiepiscopus contentus de his quae petebam fuerat" (*Gallia christiana*, 10, *Instrumenta:* 81). Evidence of Simon's concern to define his rights vis-à-vis the chapter, and of his good relations with the latter, appears in Pierre Varin, ed., *Archives administratives et législatives de la ville de Reims*, 1 (Paris, 1839):663, a reference to an act of 1411 in which Simon recognized that the chapter had the right to elect the *scholasticus* and dean, while he also claimed that he had rights of collation to eight canonries.

had been a canon there in his youth,[16] and he found an additional tie in the fact that a Guillaume de Cramaud had been among the canons in the 1240s (Guillaume, he declared, had been of Simon's own house and family).[17] There is in fact much evidence of litigation in which Simon defended or extended archiepiscopal rights—for example, his right as secular lord of Rheims to name salt measurers there, or his visitation rights over churches in the diocese, or his rights over jurisdictions, properties, and revenues claimed by monasteries or other churches.[18] Much of this would no doubt have been semi-automatic, carried on by the archiepiscopal legal staff and officialty with the approval or at the request of the archbishop but without his direct intervention. A few matters, however, rise above the rest in interest or importance, with Simon clearly playing a key role, and they can help fill out our picture of the public man and of the late-medieval world of rights, revenues, and estate in which he moved.

One case which yielded a rich crop of litigation put Simon in conflict with Cardinal Amadeo di Saluzzo, who held the major archdiaconate of Rheims.[19] Originally an important jurisdictional official within the archbishop's staff, the archdeacon like the other canons had developed an autonomous status focused on the enjoyment of property rights (which included jurisdictions) held as part of the benefice. This was the usual situation in cathedral churches by the thirteenth century. The next stage of reification lay in converting these rights into cash: thus in 1392 Amadeo and Simon's predecessor Guy de Roye agreed that the former would give up all his jurisdiction plus the twenty-two advowsons he held and would get in exchange a yearly pension of 1,115 gold francs

---

16. In pleas before Parlement in the Guy de Roye case (below), AN, X 1A 4790, fol. 292r (19 July 1415), Simon's lawyer said his principal was well disposed to Rheims, "car des sa iuenesse fu chanoine de Reims, puiz fu arcevesque."

17. See above, Ch. III, n. 10.

18. I cite only the references for some examples: AN, X 1A 59, fols. 87rv, 152v–154v, *arrêts* of 28 November 1411 and 18 June 1412; X 1C 102, no. 32 (10 July 1411); X 1C 105B, no. 260 (17 April 1413); X 1C 102, no. 160 (19 September 1411); X 1C 103B, no. 207 (28 April 1412); X 1C 100A, no. 148, an accord of 27 August 1410; X 1C 103B, no. 192, an accord of 22 April 1412; X 1A 4790, fol. 9v (27 November 1413). Varin, *Archives administratives*, 2 (Paris, 1843):82, mentions an *arrêt* of 18 July 1413 referring to Simon's refusal to pay a *muid* of wheat a year to the monastery of St. Denis of Rheims.

19. The case has been summarized by Guillaume Mollat, "Démêlés des archevêques de Reims avec le grand archidiacre, du XIIIe au XVe siècle," *Revue du Nord*, 38 (1956):161–166. I follow this along with the records of the pleas, AN, X 1A 4789, fols. 55r–56v, 58v–60r, 339r, 340rv, 349r, 355v (19 February 1411–29 November 1412), and the *arrêt* of 30 March 1412, AN, X 1A 59, fols. 115v–121v, which summarizes the pleas up to then.

payable in two installments on 1 January and 1 July, the amount to be doubled if payment was not made in four weeks from the due date. In addition the archdeacon was exempted from archiepiscopal jurisdiction and taken under direct papal lordship. Pope Clement VII confirmed the pact on 25 December 1392, and in August 1393 the Parlement of Paris registered it. All of which meant that the archdeacon henceforth would be getting a very large sum of money each year for doing nothing, and the archbishops would see no obvious reason why they ought to pay. So it was, even with Guy de Roye, at least once.[20]

When Simon took over, one of his first acts was to lay the legal groundwork for a flat refusal ever to pay: perhaps in August 1409 he or his procurator demanded that all the dignitaries of the chapter (the dean, cantor, treasurer, *scholasticus,* and so on, including the archdeacons) swear an oath of fealty and homage to him, and sometime in September his bailiff confiscated the benefices of those not swearing, among whom was the major archdeacon.[21] Amadeo thus had nothing to be paid for. This of course was not his view, and after Simon had missed his first two deadlines (1 January 1410 and 1 July), Amadeo sued him in Parlement for non-payment—a simple property case—to be met not only by the above argument but a whole battery of others as well. The most interesting of these was that the pope had no right to impose a burden destructive of the temporal estate of the archbishop—who was a vassal of the king for his temporalities and also a peer of France. For while in fact the archdeacon's jurisdiction was "spiritual" and figured as such now in the archbishop's hands, the pension that the latter had to pay was simply a portion of his total revenue and had to be considered as also a burden on

---

20. ˙Saluzzo alleged that Guy de Roye had met his payments (AN, X 1A 59, fol. 116rv), and Mollat, "Démêlés": 164, repeats this, but in fact Saluzzo had to sue him at least once: AN, X 1A 49, fol. 11v (a letter of 12 January 1402). Suits continued under Simon's successors: e.g., AN, X 1C 107A, no. 26, and 107B, no. 148 (22 January, 3 April 1414)—Pierre Trousseau; X 1A 4791, fol. 141r, etc. (3 September 1416)—Regnault de Chartres.

21. AN, X 1A 59, fol. 117rv; the principle alleged was "quod prepositura, duo archidiaconatus, et alie predicte ecclesie Remensis dignitates in fide et homagio ac fidelitatis juramento tenebantur, easque et presertim dictum magnum archidiaconatum possidentes et tenentes ad faciendum suum erga ipsum archiepiscopum debitum in suo adventu jocundo maxime requisiti astringebantur." Simon later added that the oaths he demanded had been sworn by the dean, cantor, treasurer, and *scholasticus,* with Saluzzo and some others not doing so, and therefore he had instructed his bailiff to confiscate the non-swearers' benefices in September 1409—or at least he had approved his bailiff's action (fols. 120v–121r). Saluzzo's response (fol. 119v) was that his office was subject only to the pope: "Idem archidiaconatus nulli in aliquo subiciebatur preterquam Romane curie." He also claimed (fol. 120r) that Simon had not taken over the archidiaconal revenues until 11 October 1410, after Saluzzo had begun his lawsuit in July 1410.

his temporalities;[22] indeed these were what the cardinal had to sue to attach, in a secular court like Parlement. Simon's lawyer could therefore urge the above argument, and the royal attorney joined him on this point.[23] The concept of "estate" thus worked in conjunction with the quantifying effect of money to fudge the traditionally crucial distinction between temporal and spiritual powers, which were in fact less and less distinguishable to the extent that they were thought of as property and revenues. Parlement however refused to accept any of these arguments and issued its decree in Amadeo's favor on 30 March 1412.[24]

One can sympathize with Simon, whose imagination and intellectual's taste for theory had turned a perfectly common conflict over money into a daring adventure in political thought and who now had to face the consequences of his failure. It was a huge debt. At the date of Parlement's decree he would have owed two and a half years of arrears, doubled because of the penalty for non-payment, hence 5,576 francs (1,115 × 2.5 × 2); the half-payment coming up on 1 July 1412 would bring the total to 6,134 francs. Since Parlement's decree was final, he naturally turned to the "court of Rome" for some sort of relief, but to no avail; his next recourse was to the University of Paris, where as a former professor he could profit from its privileges and secure a three-year moratorium.[25]

---

22. AN, X 1A 4789, fol. 55v: "Le pape ne puet charchier le temporel dudit arceveschie de paier ladite pension; car ce seroit entreprendre l'une iuridiccion sur l'autre." In this context Simon noted his status as peer, as anointer of the kings of France, etc.: AN, X 1A 59, fol. 117r. It was all the worse, then, that the temporalities, held as a fief from the king, would be destroyed by the burden of such a pension (fol. 117v).

23. AN, X 1A 4789, fol. 56r: "Le procureur du roy propose et dict que ladicte cause heurte fort la couronne, pour laquelle appoier furent ordonnez pairs, desquels est l'arcevesque de Reims, comme en l'empire Cologne, Mayence, et autres sont pairs de l'empire, pour le aider a soustenir. . . . Les pairs de cette couronne . . . doivent avoir bon et vaillant temporel pour maintenir leur estat, qui est pour aider a soustenir ladicte couronne; si ne doibt point le pape inconsulto rege le diminuer."

24. This is the arrêt already cited, AN, X 1A 59, fols. 115v–121v; as usual, no reasons are given for the decision. One result of Saluzzo's initial action was to have the temporalities of Rheims taken into the king's hand; this hand was now to be lifted in Saluzzo's favor.

25. AN, X 1A 4789, fol. 340r (15 September 1412): "dit Salusces que . . . Reims est ale en l'universite et en la nation de France pour empescher plus a plain la dicte execucion, et ce qu'elle se adiognist avec lui, et si a empetre une triennelle selon la provision contenue es ordonnance, par laquelle a fait arrester tout." Simon's reply, ibid.: "Et a ce que dit Salusces, qu'il empesche l'arrest et l'execucion d'icelluy, non fait; et suppose qu'il a este en l'universite, c'est au regart du grief qu'a l'eglise de Reims en l'accort passe en court de Rome sur quoy avoit obtenu liens appliques; mais il n'en puet venir a bout, car en court de Rome a este dit que contra cardinalem non licet cardinali contraire, et pour ce a requis l'universite, dont est ancien docteur, et ses suffragans et bourgeois, qui tous ont este d'accort de . . . assister avecques lui." See n. 40 below for "contra cardinalem. . . ."

Then, summoned by "the king" to take part in the royal council at
Auxerre in July and August of 1412 (at which the Peace of Auxerre was
concluded between the ducal factions),[26] Simon put his case before the
royal council and got ordinances granting him interim enjoyment of the
contested property.[27] At the same time, however, he had been negotiating
through agents at the papal court for over a year to reduce the total sum
he owed. The details remain unknown, but we have Simon's account of
the results: after spending at least 4,800 francs (diverted, as we shall see,
from another enterprise), he got the consent of Amadeo and the pope to
a composition that left only 400 francs of his debt still outstanding.[28] But
the pension itself remained intact, to plague his successors and generate
new lawsuits.[29]

Simon's own troubles were not over. The 4,800 francs deployed in
Rome for the final composition, and no doubt for commissions and
sweeteners, had come from a legacy left by former archbishop Guy de
Roye for a quite different purpose: to endow a Paris college for Rheims
students at the university. No bishop could simply leave money free and
clear for anything: apart from the miscellaneous claims of creditors, both
the cathedral chapter and the next bishop would often allege damages,
missing inventory, unhonored promises, and neglected repairs, while
questions could always be raised about how much of a bishop's wealth
was his personal property. Guy's will provided two things that would
satisfy the chapter—the Paris Collège de Reims and a cathedral library—
and his heirs were ready to satisfy Simon as well. An accord of 24
September 1409 made in Paris among Guy's heirs, the Rheims clergy in
Paris (at the university), and Simon, divided up the legacy so: 5,000
francs were to go to set up the college; 1,000 and 4,500 were to go to
Simon to pay for deficient inventories and neglected repairs; 2,000 livres
tournois were to go to Simon as his share; 1,200 écus were to finance the
library; 2,000 livres tournois were to go to Guy's chief heir, Mathieu de
Roye. Simon promised, out of "liberality, benignity, love, grace, and
courtesy" to contribute 1,000 livres and some of his books to the col-

---

26. Lehoux, 3:272–280.

27. AN, X 1A 4789, fol. 340r; Simon's plea was that Saluzzo's attachment of his
temporalities left him nothing and that he had offered several modes of settlement, in
vain: "Mais il n'est raisonnable offre qu'il vueille recevoir, et pour ce a expose son cas au
grant conseil a Aucerre ou a este mande par le roy, qui lui a grandement couste; si a
obtenu la dite provision selon les ordonnances qu'a executee le bailly de Vitry."

28. See n. 31 below. In spite of the language there quoted, Simon's composition
relieved only himself, not "the church of Rheims." In any case, he did not pay the 400
francs either—see AN, X 1C 107B (30 April 1414) for Saluzzo's intention to keep suing
him.

29. See n. 20 above; also AN, X 1C 107A, no. 26 (22 January 1414) for the
amount.

lege. Evidently too busy to take up the matter now, Simon deposited 4,800 francs (in lieu of the 5,000) in Notre Dame of Paris, whence he withdrew them on 29 July 1411 with a formal promise to use the money to get the pope to assign benefices to the college that would bring in 200 livres tournois a year.[30] This last date was quite close to the end of Simon's period in Paris as Berry's man in the royal council, and it would seem that the political troubles described above made it the opportune time for Simon to follow through on the Rheims obligation. He turned the money over to the "Lombard" Bartolomeo Ruffino for transfer to the Roman Curia, where two "gentlemen" took about nine months to arrange (as we have noted) not the originally intended endowment of the

---

30. The facts come from various accords and pleas. An accord of 9 August 1409 between the chapter of Rheims and Guy's heirs led by Mathieu de Roye dealt with the disposition of Guy's movables, but Simon de Cramaud first opposed it, then agreed to take part in it provided the archbishop's rights in the matter were recognized. The new accord was dated 23 January 1410 (AN, X 1C 99A, nos. 58–60). One effect of the original opposition was to involve Simon as an executor of Guy's estate and to make possible the accords of 24 September 1409: AN, X 1C 98B, nos. 214, 216, preceded by the procuratory of the Rheims scholars at the University of Paris, 23 September (no. 215). The Paris locale is given in no. 215 and inferrable from AN, X 1A 56, fol. 189v, a letter of 24 September 1409 in which we see Simon as executor appearing personally in Parlement to have surrogates appointed. In AN, X 1C 98B, no. 214 we read that there had been argument over the validity of Guy's will and that the accord was made to avoid lawsuits. Guy's whole estate was said to be worth 50,000–56,000 francs including some possibly uncollectable debts, while the repairs due to archiepiscopal castles, houses, mills, ponds, etc., would cost at least 40,000; furthermore, Guy had left a project for a perpetual chantry in the cathedral, and an amortized *rente* had to be provided for this. It is here that we read of Simon's promise to contribute, "de sa liberalite, benignite, amour, grace, et courtoisie." Item no. 216 is the accord between Simon and Mathieu et al., and here we read of Guy's having left 5,000 francs to be converted into *rentes* for "the chaplains of the chapel of the archbishop of Rheims" (cf. AN, X 1A 61, fol. 96r, for a similar designation in Latin) and of Simon's commitment to take this sum and convert it "es usages"; all this about the chapel must refer to the Collège de Reims in Paris. Later on, the foundation is described so (ibid.): "in sustentacionem quorundam scolarium qui essent pro tempore de terris temporalitatis ecclesie Remensis." It is from the later lawsuits and the resulting *arrêt* that we learn of what happened after: AN, X 1A 4790, fols. 190r, 195rv, 231v–232r, 292rv, 310rv (17 January–2 August 1415); X 1A 61, fols. 95r–96v, *arrêt* of 15 February 1416. That Simon himself deposited the 4,800 francs appears in AN, X 1A 4790, fol. 301v. His obligation in withdrawing the money later was put so: "qu'il feroit que l'en pranroit 200 livres sur certains patronnages qu'il empetreroit du pape" (fol. 190r); alternatively, he was to arrange with a certain (unnamed) prelate "qu'il devoit resigner iii de ses benefices et il auroit l'arcediacre de Reims, et si feroit unir iii patronnages au College de Reims, et en devoit faire bailler et envoier les bulles pour ce que ladite finance estoit laissee au profit du College de Reims, et ce devoit faire dedans l'an 1412" (fol. 195rv; cf. AN, X 1A 61, fol. 95r for the date— Simon was to fulfill his promise by Christmas of 1411). The reference to the "arcediacre," etc., suggests a link with the Saluzzo case.

Collège de Reims but the reduction of Simon's debt to the archdeacon.[31] Exactly what Simon did do for the college has to be inferred very tentatively from the conflicting pleas in the lawsuits that Mathieu de Roye brought against him for fraud (after having his temporalities attached, 9 August 1412): admitting that he had used the 4,800 francs for a different purpose, Simon insisted that he had nevertheless provided 200 livres tournois worth of ecclesiastical revenues for the college by other means—buying a *rente* here, building water mills there, buying property—and he also claimed that he had turned over half or all of his own share of the legacy for the college's benefit. Or rather—this is characteristic of Simon's dealings—he had turned over the *equivalent* in yearly *rentes* (valued at 10 percent of the principal). Mathieu de Roye claimed that it was all a fake and that no solid revenues had been provided.[32] The truth may lie between, for although the college may have started off with a shoddy and problematical endowment instead of the honorable benefices Guy de Roye had planned, it did in fact start off and acquired a house in Paris and a corporate entity.[33] In his testament of 11 March 1422 Simon made his own gesture and left the college his Paris

---

31. Simon himself said (AN, X 1A 4790, fol. 292r): "Fu ostee ladite somme pour les debas qui estoient en ce royaume entre les seigneurs." He went on to describe what he had done: "Puiz pour descharger l'eglise de Reims d'une grosse pension deue au cardinal de Salusces, fu bailliee a Barthelemi Ruffin ladite somme, et il s'obliga pour bailler les bulles; et fu la chose accordee par le pape, tant que l'eglise de Reims fu deschargee de tant qu'il ne demouroit que 400. Et si devoit faire finance de 200 livres tur. admortie. Et a ladite descharge faire se consenti le pape et Salusces, et pour ce poursuir envoia ii gentilizhommes a Rome qui y furent viii ou x mois." His version summarized in the *arrêt* reads (AN, X 1A 61, fol. 96r): "financiam huiusmodi in Romana curia liberandam et solvendam certis mercatoribus . . . , ut ecclesia Remensis . . . excessiva quadam pensione archidiacono Remensi debita, aut certa porcione ipsius, exoneraretur, tradendo." Elsewhere these merchants are called "Lombards" (AN, X 1A 4790, fol. 195r).

32. For the royal letter of 9 August 1412 ordering the attachment of Simon's temporalities, see AN, X 1A 61, fol. 95v. Simon tried to delay proceedings by shifting the case from Parlement to the *Requêtes,* but on 3 May 1415 Parlement ordered pleas to begin. The details of financing which Simon alleged and Mathieu de Roye called fake (e.g., "un tripot"—AN, X 1A 4790, fol. 301r) are too complex and fragmentary to be laid out here; I quote only Simon's summary of his work as given in the *arrêt* right after the "tradendo" of the passage quoted in n. 31 above: "Ac dictis scolaribus in collegio de Remis Parisius fundato studentibus, ut in eodem collegio aut eius oratorio iidem scolares facerent in missis ibidem celebrandis certas oraciones dici quas dictus Guido archiepiscopus ordinaverat fieri per cappellanos successorum suorum, 200 francs renduales aut pro ipsis duo milia francorum donando, et donum huiusmodi per summum pontificem ratificari . . . faciendo." Cf. his plea, "Et si ly devoit le feu arcevesque 2,000 francs, qu'il [scil., Simon] a donne au College de Reims et a l'augmentacion d'icellui" (fol. 292v).

33. Bulaeus, 5:202, notes the foundation of the Collège de Reims according to the agreements of 23 and 24 September 1409, and the college's acquisition of the "domus Burgundica" in Paris, 12 May 1412, from Count Philip of Nevers for 1,000 livres

house—which the Cramauds could not enjoy anyway, in Anglo-Burgundian Paris; as it turned out, however, the college never got it and the Cramaud heirs did, in spite of Simon's will.[34]

If the story thus far seems to have revealed to us the manipulative traits of the Simon we already know, it must be said that the man had in his own way moved towards meeting his obligations. In the matter of the cathedral library he seems to have done more. Those immediately involved had nothing but good to say of his fulfillment of Guy's project, which he amplified with more than 200 écus of his own and a five-volume *Bartholus super Digestum* that he commissioned, also by providing a separate building for the library instead of housing it, as originally planned, in part of the archiepiscopal palace.[35] He also benefited his church in other ways. In the last months of his tenure Simon instituted and endowed a chantry in conjunction with one founded by his putative thirteenth-century kinsman Guillaume de Cramaud in celebration of the Conception of the Virgin Mary. Simon's foundation provided for masses to be said the day after that—eventually on behalf of his soul and the souls of his kin and benefactors. The endowment must have cost him at least 80 livres. He also made important gifts of vestments, jewels, and other ornaments and declared his intention of augmenting another one of Guillaume de Cramaud's foundations, masses in honor of St. Martial, whose cult was important in Simon's native territory (he was the patron of Limoges and of the Rochechouarts).[36] Putting all these acts together,

---

tournois (Gerson was among those involved). The event presumably fitted in with John the Fearless's wooing of the University of Paris. Cf. AN, M 187, nos. 1, 2, for original documents of 20 February and 8 March 1415 connected with this matter; also AN, X 1A 4791, fol. 159r, 10 December 1416, for the continuation of Mathieu de Roye's lawsuit against Simon.

34. In his will Simon wrote [AN, X 1A 8604, fol. 91(bis)v]: "Item do et lego hospicium meum Parisius quod fuit domini Petri de Setigny, scolaribus fundatis et fundandis per executores et heredes defuncti domini Guidonis de Roya . . . in domo Burgundie Parisius." But notes of 17 May and 3 August 1420 in the registers of the Paris Parlement in the Burgundian years (AN, X 1A 4792, fols. 218r, 239v) refer to public notices of attachment for sale ("criees") being made in Paris by Mathieu de Roye on this and another house belonging to Simon, who was powerless then to defend his property. The data in A. Berty & L.-M. Tisserand, *Topographie historique du vieux Paris: Région occidentale de l'université* (Paris, 1887): 450–454, show that the house was confiscated by Henry V in 1423 and given to Me. Jacques Braulart, a royal councillor in Parlement, but that at some later time it came back to the Cramaud heritage, for heirs of Jean de Cramaud sold it in 1486. Thus it had never passed to the Collège de Reims.

35. Jacqueline Le Braz, "La bibliothèque de Guy de Roye, archevêque de Reims (1390–1409)," *Bulletin d'information de l'Institut de recherche et d'histoire des textes*, 6 (1957): 67–100. The necrology cited above, n. 15, includes an account of Simon's work for the library, noting the building and the *Bartholus*.

36. The same necrology details Simon's gifts of jewels, vestments, etc., as well as his endowment in December 1412 of the commemorative masses, with an annual revenue of 8 livres paris. See also above, Ch. III, n. 10.

and noting that there were others that showed a real concern for the see—as when, for example, Simon forced the abolition of royal notaries in Rheims in order to maintain the archbishop's monopoly[37]—we get not only the image of public action *comme il faut* but a clue to the corresponding mentality: that of a man who took pride in his high estate, which he built up by tight-fisted acquisition but validated by conventional acts of calculated magnanimity, and which he secured for the future along with the welfare of his soul by joining both in the endlessly repeated liturgical acts of the church. We shall see more of all this in the last decade of his life.

The Cardinal of Rheims

Pope John XXIII, successor to Alexander V in the Pisan line, had promoted three prominent French prelates to the cardinalate on 6 June 1411: Pierre d'Ailly, Gilles Deschamps, and Guillaume Fillastre. Simon's absence from the list, if not due to some odd factor beyond our grasp, can best be explained by supposing that he had not wanted to be promoted at that time because his quality as archbishop of Rheims was more suitable to his role in the Paris government during the period of uneasy balance. But it was just in mid-1411 that the balance was broken, as we have seen, with both sides moving to armed conflict and seeking English support—a phase that came to a precarious end with the Treaty of Auxerre, 22 August 1412. Meanwhile Burgundian forces had ravaged and indeed conquered most of Poitou; the Armagnac coalition had arranged for an English army to come and help them; and by the time they agreed at Auxerre to cancel these arrangements, the army was already under way; it too moved into Poitou and could be bought off only with difficulty.[38] Henceforth Paris would be Burgundian and the Armagnacs were out, until the reaction provoked by the Cabochien rising would allow the Orléans princes to enter the capital in triumph on 31 August 1413. Without imagining anything more precise than facts of this order would allow, we can suppose that by mid-1412 if not before, Simon and Berry had decided that a change was in order; the interests of both, personal and political, would be better served by moving Simon to the see of Poitiers. John XXIII was in the midst of the rather tenuous Council of Rome that had been opened on 14 April 1412, and Simon decided to attend it. He could wrap up his controversy

37. Varin, *Archives législatives*, 4, *Statuts*, 3 (Paris, 1852):512 f. The text here refers to a royal letter of 5 October 1412 in the archbishop's favor.

38. Lehoux, 3:257–289; René Lacour, *Une incursion anglaise en Poitou en Novembre 1412. Compte d'une aide de 10,000 écus accordée au duc de Berry pour résister à cette incursion* (Poitiers, 1934).

with Cardinal Amadeo di Saluzzo, could pursue the business of the
Collège de Reims, and could arrange his own translation by exchange
with the incumbent of Poitiers.[39] He left Rheims at the end of December
1412, took part in the last stage of the Council of Rome, which ended 3
March 1413, and on 14 April the pope made the exchange, simultaneously making Simon a cardinal. On 12 May he was formally named
Cardinal Priest of San Lorenzo in Lucina, his more familiar appellation
being "Cardinal of Rheims."[40] Poitiers was held as a commendatory see.
For the rest, we know only that he stayed on in Rome just long enough
to lose a number of his books and other belongings when he had to flee
before the city was taken by Ladislas of Naples on 8 June; he probably
went directly home to Poitou.[41]

---

39. When Simon requested that he be allowed to pay for his trip to Rome with
1,000 livres from his temporalities, which were in the royal hand because of the Saluzzo
lawsuit, the latter's lawyer objected, on 21 November 1412, that Simon was going to
Rome to pursue his case versus Saluzzo and to get a different bishopric ("qu'il va a
Rome, c'est pour plaidier contre lui"; "Salusces dit . . . que Reims se vuelt faire
translater"—AN, X 1A 4789, fol. 349r; Valois, 4:212 n. 4, quotes some more of this).
The exchange project must have been made known well before and conceived perhaps
even earlier. For the Council of Rome and French desires concerning it, see Valois,
4:199–217; Simon seems not to have had any interest in either beyond his personal ones.
His departure from Rheims right after Christmas 1412 is noted in the necrology cited
above, n. 15; cf. Valois, 4:205 n. 6, for his passage through Troyes on 2 January 1413.

40. K. Eubel, *Hierarchia catholica medii aevi*, 2d ed., 1 (Münster, 1913):399 (and cf.
p. 33) gives the date of 14 April for Simon's promotion to the cardinalate and provision
to Poitiers, the date of 16 April for getting the red hat in public consistory, and 12 May
for getting the title of San Lorenzo in Lucina. Valois, 4:212, gives 14 March as the date
for getting the hat. It may be that the matter is more complex still. In *Gallia christiana*,
9:134, we read that Simon was made a cardinal in 1412 and got the red hat in 1413.
RSD, 4:730 f., writes that the royal government's envoys to the Council of Rome in
1412 were told to pursue the "negocia regni" with the pope through the mediation of
Pierre d'Ailly and Simon de Cramaud, "recently the king's councillors whom the pope as
a favor to the king had recently taken into the cardinalate." Finally, in Simon's pleas of
15 September 1412 against Cardinal Amadeo di Saluzzo, we read the passage quoted in
n. 25 above, which would imply that as far as Rome was concerned, Simon was already a
cardinal in 1412. It is possible that the first two items are mistakes (Valois, 4:205 n. 7,
supposes *RSD* slipped and wrote Simon's name instead of Guillaume Fillastre's); the
third, either irrelevant or inexplicable. But it may also be imagined that John XXIII had
named Simon a cardinal well before the public ceremony of 1413, with the understanding that the cardinalcy would be activated when Simon was ready to leave Rheims for
Poitiers. The question requires more research; I note that the creation of cardinals "in
pectore" is supposed to go back to Martin V, John XXIII's successor.

41. For the loss of books see above, Ch. IV, n. 3. The time of Simon's departure for
home can also be inferred from a suit he brought against the estate of Pierre Trousseau,
his predecessor in Poitiers and successor in Rheims, claiming that Pierre had owed him
all the revenues of the Poitiers see "depuis le jour de leur translacion jusques a la feste
Saint Jehan ensuivant ou environ, qui se pouroit monter V.^C [500] frans ou environ"—
i.e., from 14 April to ca. 24 June 1413 (AN, X 1C 112, no. 58; 7 August 1416).

Now about sixty-eight years old, Simon was evidently one of those survivors whose story suggests that we ought not dwell too indiscriminately on the low life expectancy of medieval man. As far as the residues of the Schism were concerned, his action would be modest but vigorous and responsible. The French position and his own was that everyone should recognize John XXIII and join in liquidating the remaining obediences of Benedict XIII and Gregory XII,[42] but he had to put up with the fact that European opinion evidently demanded a new general council. The Emperor Sigismund was making this cause his own, prevailing upon John XXIII to convoke the council for 1 November 1414 in Constance, a city within the Empire, and working through his diplomacy to get attendance from adherents of all three papal claimants. In the case of France, this effort involved a political alliance between Sigismund and the Orléanist masters of the government on 25 June 1414, with the crucial question left open: would the council continue the work of Pisa, as the French wished, and try to secure universal recognition for John XXIII, or would it deal with all three papal claimants on an equal footing—Sigismund's intention?[43] It was in this context that Simon de Cramaud wrote his first work in five years, glosses on John Dominici's apologia for Gregory XII; addressed to Sigismund, the glosses urged him to accept the validity of the Council of Pisa, to reject the claims currently made for Gregory (and for Benedict XIII), and not to be put off by John XXIII's growing reputation for criminal immorality. The coming council was looked to as the theater of such a final settlement.[44] Exactly when these glosses were written is unclear—perhaps as late as the autumn of 1414 when Simon was in Paris taking part in various public actions. It was there in September that he received information and texts about John Hus's doctrines from Archbishop Conrad of Prague, turned the material over to Jean Gerson for expert examination, and wrote a short letter to Conrad urging him to be vigilant.[45] Soon after, one supposes, he took part in the assembly of the French clergy called by the government for 1 October to choose representatives for the Council of Constance and to vote funds for their expenses.[46] In January 1415 he

---

42. Valois, 4:233 f.

43. Valois, 4:232 ff.

44. The text, with legal etc. citations omitted, in H. Finke, *Acta Concilii Constanciensis,* 1 (Münster, 1896):277–289.

45. The text of Simon's letter and that of Gerson are in F. Palacký, ed., *Documenta Mag. Joannis Hus vitam . . . illustrantia* (Prague, 1869): 527–530.

46. Valois, 4:256 f.; Simon is not mentioned there, but his presence in Paris during October/November is attested in AN, X 1A 63, fol. 2r (a letter of Parlement, 23 December 1417): an opponent had gotten court orders in October 1414 citing Simon to appear at Anzay on 30 November, but Simon "estoit lors a Paris" and knew nothing of the orders.

assisted at memorial services for Louis of Orléans and sat for perhaps the last time in a meeting of the royal council.[47]

The Council of Constance had meanwhile opened in November 1414, and Simon planned to attend. Perhaps at the end of February 1415 he went from Paris to Poitiers to do his packing but left off and returned to the capital when he heard of John XXIII's flight from Constance on 20 March 1415.[48] The council, now, would obviously be quite different from the continuation of Pisa that Simon desired; its next two years in fact would be filled with the struggles over heresy, reform, and constitutional conciliarism that have made it a cynosure of modern historiography, but the seventy-year-old careerist would have foreseen only tedium therein. We shall see that he had plenty to occupy him back home anyway. But he dutifully went to Constance when the council was ready to get down to what he considered its real business of electing a pope—he arrived on 28 March 1417—and he contributed a short treatise urging that all accept the electoral scheme put forward by the French and agreed to by the cardinals: the latter would be joined by an equal number of other personnages chosen by the council, and the election would be made by a two-thirds majority in each group. By this time John XXIII had accepted his own deposition, Gregory XII had abdicated, and Simon could express his view of the council's current function in terms of the program he had developed over twenty years before and had pursued ever since: "This council is congregated here for two main purposes, to effectively depose Pedro de Luna and to unite the Spanish with the rest of us." He stayed to take part in the election of Martin V on 11 November 1417 and left for home in January.[49]

---

47. Valois, 4:250; H. Finke et al., eds., *Acta Concilii Constanciensis*, 4 (Münster, 1928):255.

48. In a plea of 11 April 1415 (AN, X 1A 4790, fols. 231v–232r), Simon's request for a delay in his lawsuit with Mathieu de Roye includes the argument: "Dit oultre qu'il est ale au conseil par Poitiers ad preparandum sarcinulas, et pose qu'il fust retourne puiz le pertement qu'a fait le pape du conseil, si ne seroit pas passe le mois apres le retour qu'il doit avoir." Nothing was said of such a trip in the pleas of 29 January 1415 (fol. 195rv); hence my conjectural dating. On 29 March 1417, after Simon had gone to Constance in fact, his lawyer referred to this as a return—"et est retourne au conseil general" (AN, X 1A 4791, fol. 217r); I suppose that the first trip, however abortive, counted as a real one for legal purposes, as indicated in the passage quoted above. If Simon had actually appeared at Constance the first time, his presence—as a cardinal if nothing else—would have been noted by someone.

49. Valois, 4:396 n. 1, for Simon's arrival; p. 398 f. for his treatise. The text is in Finke, *Acta Concilii Constanciensis*, 3 (Münster, 1926):653–661, the quoted passage on p. 659. See Valois, 4:402–405, for the election and Simon's participation in it; the January departure is mentioned without evidence by Guillaume Mollat, "Cramaud (Simon de)," *Dictionnaire d'histoire et de géographie ecclésiastique*, 13 (Paris, 1956):1012 f. Occasional

One can perhaps imagine Simon's role at the Council of Constance as that of a conscientious craftsman putting the finishing touches on his master work. By this time, at any rate, there was nothing else in it for him, and it is likely that affairs in Poitou claimed his major interest. A terse note in the register of the deliberations of the Poitiers town council on 24 January 1416 records a decision that "the mayor is to go to Paris, to the duke of Berry, in the company of the cardinal [scil., Simon]."[50] This alone tells us much about Simon's place in the political society of his *pays,* while at the same time reminding us that the seventy-year-old cardinal was still part of the duke's affinity and that the connection was sufficiently important to his own local interests to justify the winter journey. From here on, we can only guess that the trip had something to do with Berry's position in Paris as director of the Armagnac interest, with the new situation created by the death of the dauphin on 18 December 1415, with Bernard of Armagnac's entry into Paris on 29 December, and with the ensuing contest between him and John the Fearless of Burgundy for control of the capital. For the moment, Armagnac would be the winner.[51] When Duke Jean of Berry died on 15 June 1416, still another new situation arose: henceforth the Paris-Poitiers axis along which much of Simon's public life and personal interest had been structured would no longer exist. The final victory of John the Fearless, who occupied Paris in May 1418, only consolidated the fact, although the emergence of the Armagnac government in Bourges and Poitiers would give Simon an afterglow of eminence on his home ground. But personal, family, and episcopal concerns occupied almost all his energies. A commission by the crown in the summer of 1416 to resolve conflicts among the local magnates after Berry's death, and a notice of his presence at the Parlement of Poitiers on 24 April 1419, are about the only traces of anything more lofty.[52]

---

references in the modern literature to Simon's fulminations in Constance against the Hussites—e.g., H. Finke, *Forschungen und Quellen zur Geschichte des Konstanzer Konzils* (Paderborn, 1889): 15—are mistaken; they go back to L. Douët-d'Arcq, ed., *La chronique d'Enguerran de Monstrelet,* 2 (Paris, 1858):16, which mentions a sermon "Liber Deus Israel" preached at Pisa by "le cardinal de Poictiers" (Guy de Malesset). Pierre Frizon, *Gallia purpurata* (Paris, 1638): 468 f., thought this cardinal was Simon and mistakenly applied the account to Constance, and G. Eggs, *Purpura docta,* 3 (Munich, 1714):16, enriched Frizon's story by saying that the sermon was preached against the Hussites; Finke drew on Eggs.

50. Archive municipale de Poitiers, *Rég. délib.* 1, p. 87: "que Mons. le mayre aillet a Paris devers Mons. le duc en la compaignie de Mons. le Cardinal."

51. Lehoux, 3:394 ff.; Vaughan, *John the Fearless*: 209 ff.

52. Lehoux, 3:404–406, for the duke's death and obsequies; Simon's name does not appear among those at the funeral in Bourges, but he celebrated a mass for Berry in Poitiers cathedral—Abbé Auber, *Histoire générale . . . du Poitou,* 9 (Poitiers, 1893):213.

Simon naturally regarded the church of Poitiers as his home base: he had been its bishop before; his personal and family concerns centered in the region of the diocese; and it would obviously be the last church of his life. His use of episcopal jurisdiction and patronage in connection with his acquisition of properties during his first tenure of the see had created ties between it and his family that made his return as bishop a practical matter, probably one that he had been looking forward to for some time even though it entailed some reduction of income.[53] There had been much to keep him involved with the see meanwhile, for example the commemorative foundation of 1 February 1390, financed by an obligation of 100 livres a year from the bishop's jurisdictional revenues, and his papal commission of 1391/1392 "to reform what had to be reformed in the church of Poitiers"; and we have to imagine a number of unattested Poitevin trips and sojourns by the Paris-based prelate. We have already noted the relationship between his removal from Paris activity during the restoration of obedience, from mid-1402 through 1405, and his local activity in Poitiers and Limousin, including the endowment of choirboys in the cathedral in 1402 (described below) and the initial arrangements for his tomb there, which was completed by 1405 (see plate).[54] These actions and no doubt much more can be taken as the background to his return as bishop in 1413, which began his final and extremely intense period of devotion to the bishopric. Some of this took the form of new building: a sacristy was added to the cathedral, and an organ was built.[55] Already in his earlier tenure of Poitiers he had worked

---

The duke's titles in 'Berry and Poitou were taken up by the juvenile dauphin, for whose commission to Simon see *AHP,* 26 (1896):306–311. For the presence at the Poitiers Parlement, see AN, X 1A 9195, fol. 25v. For examples of Simon's many-faceted episcopal functions, including the exercise of jurisdiction over various churches in the diocese, see *AHP,* 37 (1908):332 f.; *AHP,* 53 (1942):98; ADV G 1345 (Ste. Rade-gonde, 1415).

53. Rheims yielded at least 3,000 livres of net revenue (n. 2 above), Poitiers at most about 2,500 (above, Ch. III, n. 59). Simon's pension of 1,000 livres a year as royal councillor (AN, KK 16, fol. 39r—1408) had presumably ceased after 1411, when he had stopped being active in the royal government.

54. For the tomb see Abbé Auber, "Découverte du tombeau et des restes du Cardinal Simon de Cramaud dans la cathédrale de Poitiers, le 14 Septembre 1858," *MSAO,* 24 (1857):371–399; *Gallia christiana,* 2:1196. Two stone tablets still in the choir of the cathedral and dated 1405 record the choirboy foundation and the erection of the tomb: "Fecit in isto choro fieri tumulum suum de marmore et alabastro." Damaged by the Huguenots in 1562, the tomb was described in an official report of such damages: Poitiers, Bibliothèque Municipale, *Coll. Fontenau,* 54, pp. 286 f.; a *gisant* lay on top of the tomb, and a life-sized stone statue of Simon dressed as a cardinal, his hands joined in prayer, stood against a nearby column. Cf. R. Crozet, "Textes et documents relatifs à l'histoire des arts en Poitou," *AHP,* 53 (1942):103.

55. For the sacristy, identified by Simon's arms and otherwise datable to his second tenure of Poitiers, see Crozet, "Textes et documents": 97. Jean de Cramaud in his

to assert the bishop's secular jurisdiction in Chauvigny against the competing claims of Louis d'Harcourt; this legal effort was taken up again when Simon caused a criminal to be hung there and then fought a legal battle vindicating this act against royal claims of monopoly. Less dramatic litigation of course abounded as well, including claims for neglected repairs against his predecessor; disputes with canons, abbeys, and other churches over patronage, jurisdiction, and fiscal rights; and efforts to maintain privilege of clergy in criminal matters.[56] Most or all of this was probably routine, nor in any case did Simon always win, and the main impression to be retained would be that of continuous, active, responsible work in the interests of the see.

Such involvement no doubt had a subjective dimension which can only be imagined but which must have lain under Simon's more personal benefactions to his church. These consisted of endowments benefiting chiefly the cathedral chapter, and of legacies of property to future bishops. The money involved would have come in principle from other sources than Simon's episcopal revenues, a distinction as rigorous in

---

lawsuit of 1426 with the then-bishop of Poitiers noted that his uncle "fist faire les orgres de l'eglise de Poictiers, ou y donna mil livres, et donna a l'euvre de l'edifice nouvel du chapitre" (AN, X 1A 9198, fol. 179v; 18 June 1426); his opponent did not deny these claims. Cf. R. Favreau, "Orgues et Psallettes à Poitiers à la fin du moyen âge," *BSAO*, 4th series, 12 (1973):47, for the remarkable vogue of organs and choirboy foundations in the fifteenth century; it would appear that in both respects Simon was a pioneer.

56. *Tables des manuscrits de D. Fontenau conservés à la Bibliothèque de Poitiers*, 1 (Poitiers and Paris, 1839):326, a letter of 23 June 1421 (also in AN, X 1A 9195, fol. 133v) issued by the Parlement of Poitiers on behalf of the Dauphin Charles, allowing Simon to exercise his right as bishop to high justice in Chauvigny *sub manu regia*, until the dispute was settled. This was extended until further notice on 13 November 1421 (AN, X 1A 9197, fol. 1r). Only then did Simon allow the corpse to be taken down from the gallows and buried. There was also other litigation against the government: e.g., AN, X 1A 9197, fol. 1v (20 November 1421), a protest against seizure of episcopal grain by the dauphin's officials. The ecclesiastical litigation was very intense; e.g.: *For repairs*: AN, X 1A 4790, fols. 173v, 312v (11 December 1414, 19 August 1415), Simon versus Pierre Trousseau; an accord was reached 7 August 1416 (AN, X 1C 112, no. 58), with Simon to get 1,500 francs; cf. nos. 84, 85, and see AN, X 1A 9197, fol. 105r (30 June 1422) re receipt of the money. *Disputes with church bodies*: With the nuns of Fontevraud over money, AN, X 1C 113, no. 111 (1 April 1417). With the hebdomadary canon of Poitiers over revenues, AN, X 1A 9195, fol. 109v (22 February 1421), and AN, X 1A 9190, fol. 149rv, an *arrêt* of 12 April 1421. With the chapter over forest rights, AN, X 1A 9199, fols. 72v, 163v, 211rv, 215rv (15 June 1428–9 January 1430); the canons recalled that Simon had sold off timber without their consent. Against an abbot over advowson to a parish church, AN, X 1A 9190, fols. 115v–117v, an *arrêt* of 13 July 1420. Against the chapter of St. Hilaire de Poitiers re criminal jurisdiction over a member of the chapter, AN, X 1A 9190, fol. 134r, an *arrêt* of 17 January 1421. *Privilege of clergy*: AN, X 1A 9197, fols. 73v, 136v (23 April, August 1422), shows Simon demanding jurisdiction; the same case was taken up by his successors: AN, X 1A 9198, fols. 131r, 133r, 183r (5 and 11 March, 25 June 1426).

concept as it was flabby in practice. In the past, Simon had received revenues from canonries, salaries for royal and ducal offices, and no doubt a great many more miscellaneous fees, gifts, and grants than we have been able to determine. Much of the money had already gone into the acquisition of property and the endowment of church foundations, as we have seen; how much if any was left over is quite unknown. But when Simon left Rome as a cardinal, "to enjoy his home country and his benefices,"[57] he took with him the usual cardinal's privilege of accumulating benefices for the sake of their revenues, up to the total value of 2,000 francs a year; and while the extraordinarily large number of lawsuits resulting from his implementation of the privilege suggest that "enjoy" was not quite the right word in his case,[58] they also give evidence of a massive push. One sympathizes with his victims in their complaints that it was wrong for one man to have so many benefices and that in Simon's case it was also unnecessary since "he spent no time at the Roman Curia but just stayed in his bishopric."[59] Simon's lawyer, whom

---

57. The comment of a Sienese at Pisa about another French cardinal, in W. Brandmüller, "Sieneser Korrespondenzen zum Konzil von Pisa," *Annuarium Historiae Conciliorum*, 7 (1975):182 f.; cf. Boniface Ferrer's similar comment on the plans of the French cardinals after Pisa, *Thes. nov.*, 2:1458 f.

58. The privilege figures in the lawsuits; one passage is quoted by Valois, 4:213 n. 2. It entitled him only to benefices worth 100 livres or more (AN, X 1A 4791, fol. 216v; 29 March 1417). In another case, AN, X 1A 4791, fol. 225rv (22 April 1417), Simon's lawyer noted that the privilege specified (or allowed) benefices up to a total of 1,000 livres in the church province of Bordeaux (which included Poitiers). I have found cases or references concerning nine priories (St. Hilaire de Melle, Pocey, Anzay, Coussay, St. André de Mirebeau, Moutiers de Maulxfaiz, Ligugé, La Roche, Rabasty) and the archpresbytery of Combrailles with the parish church of Hibersac, all claimed on the basis of this privilege. In pleas of 13 May 1417 (AN, X 1A 4791, fol. 236r) the opponent argued that Simon had already gotten La Roche, Rabasty, and St. André and should be content with them. In another case, AN, X 1A 4791, fol. 216v (29 March 1417), the opponent claimed that Simon had gotten more than twelve benefices ("Il en a accepte plus de xii"). If this last figure be taken as likely and compared with the evidence of litigation touching eight of the ten benefices listed above, it is apparent that few acquisitions were trouble-free; so, for example, in Simon's will [AN, X 1A 8604, fol. 91(bis)v] we find him bequeathing 160 moutons to a man who had paid him that sum as farm for the priory of Caunes (*Cauna*) but who had not been able to get hold of it and draw the revenues. I note the references without further specifications (omitting "AN, X 1A" and "fol."): 4790: 66v; 4791: 216v, 225rv; 63: 1v–2v, 201r; 62: 140v–141r; 4792: 57r; 9190: 28v–29r, 84rv, 138v–139r; 9195: 8v; 9197: 45v, 158v, 160r; 9199: 382r; also AN, X 1C 108, no. 104.

59. AN, X 1A 4791, fol. 216v (29 March 1417): "En disant que le Cardinal ne faisoit point de residence a court de Rome, et demouroit pardeca en son eveschie"; "Et si ne puet le pape dispenser contre les status et ordonnances des conciles generaux, de donner dispensacion a une personne de tant de benefices—c. *Memor sum*, 24. q. 1—s'il n'y a en la bulle 'de plenitudine potestatis.'" The privilege should be restricted because it was "ambicieuse et hayneuse."

he no doubt briefed, agreed that his principal would be better off with fewer benefices, provided only that the total worth reached 2,000 francs a year; for the rest, it was noted that the cardinal did after all attend the Council of Constance but that, even residing in Poitiers, "he still had to sustain his estate to the honor of the church and his dignity."[60] But the litigation went on to the end of his life and indeed beyond, with some cases won, others lost; and there is no reason to think he actually drew anything like 2,000 francs a year from these benefices. Since the salaries, pensions, and other emoluments of his active political career would now have ceased, his estate had to be sustained chiefly from the Poitiers bishopric—not rich, as we have seen—and from the income from his properties. But if by the time of his death his means were modest,[61] this was the result both of his reduced revenues and of the way he was now spending them. For the estate that he labored to sustain in these last years was not a matter of life-style but of the structures of honor and remembrance that his ecclesiastical benefactions would guarantee after his death.

The frame of mind in which such benefactions were made derived in part from his identification of himself with the church, particularly with the church of Poitiers, in part from his inability now to identify himself very strongly with his family. His family hopes had at first been high, leading to the arrangement he had made about 1385 with his brother Pierre and nephew Jean to buy property in their names for eventual incorporation into their heritage, with Simon enjoying the usufruct during his own life.[62] But some time before leaving for the Council of Constance, hence about 1414, he imposed a revision of the family compact on Jean (Pierre had died early, by 1388), so that all the properties bought with Simon's money returned to his full ownership and disposition. Jean was now reduced to the usufruct of those he had, and he probably had little else, for the Cramauds had "never bought a thing that was not paid for with Simon's money."[63] The new compact had to be

60. Ibid., fol. 217r: "Et jasoit ce qu'il ait este pardeca, toutesvoies il avoit a soustenir son estat a l'onneur de l'eglise et de sa dignite, et est retourne au conseil general." Cf. Valois, 4:217 n. 2.

61. AN, X 1A 9198, fol. 179v, Jean de Cramaud's pleas in his case with the bishop of Poitiers, 18 June 1426: "Dit que se le Cardinal ne avoit grant chevance en decessu suo, non est mirum. Il avoit fait de grans despenses."

62. See above, Ch. III.

63. A remark of the bishop of Poitiers in 1426, AN, X 1A 9198, fol. 185v; see Ch. III above. The revision of the compact is mentioned in Simon's will of 11 March 1422, AN, X 1A 8604, fol. 91(bis)r: "Que acquisita predictis nominibus existunt adhuc in mea disposicione tenore cuiusdam accordi alias inter me et dictum nepotem meum facti, et per curiam parlamenti solemniter confirmati." See nn. 64, 71, 82 below. I have searched in vain for this accord in Parlement's registers of such acts from 1410 to 1418 (AN, X 1C 99A through X 1C 116).

secured by a proceeding before the Parlement of Paris, evidently over
Jean's opposition, and we are told that it had been precisely Jean's
pretensions which had caused Simon's change of mind: Jean had behaved
as though the property acquired in his name was simply his and had put
his own arms on the Niort house acquired under the original compact.[64]
But it must have been far more important that Jean had failed to
produce children, so that by, say 1400 at the latest—sixteen years after
the wedding, with Jean at least thirty-five years old[65]—the future extinction of the Cramaud male line must have been regarded as very
probable.

Simon's sense of alienation from his nephew may have had another
dimension as well. The uncle had risen to the highest estate; the nephew
had been either unable or unwilling to use the advantages conferred on
him to rise higher than the estate of an ordinary nobleman in the
Poitiers orbit. Jean held the castle of Touffou and other feudal properties, but he also had his town house in Poitiers, from which he even sold
wine at retail, a privilege reserved to citizens. When the mayor seized
the profits and the remaining wine, Jean got them back by pleading that
he was a regular resident (*voisin*) of the town and that "if there were a
war there was no place in the realm where he would rather stay."[66]
Perhaps this is the clue to the proper understanding of what seems a
slanderous charge against him. Jean, we are told by a hostile voice, had
deserted the cause of his feudal lord, the duke of Berry, in order to
collaborate with the Burgundians who overran Poitou in 1412, and he
had actually become captain of Poitiers in the Burgundian interest,
rousing the *populares* against Berry and Orléans. The same source accused
him of having been in Paris as a Burgundian adherent at the time of

---

64. AN, X 1A 9198, fol. 185rv, the bishop's plea (27 June 1426): "Dit que
pretextu du nom Cramaut se vantoit etc. Et pour ce le cardinal l'en mist en proces en
parlement, sur quoy se fist accord passe par arrest narrans que l'acquest estoit des propres
deniers dudit feu cardinal, et en conclusion que ledit cardinal en jouyroit et pourroit
ordonner a sa mort, reserve 25 livres de rente a Cramaut, et oultre contient l'accord que
en cas que Cramault decederoit sine liberis, ce seroit a l'eveschie." "Dit que partie [scil.,
Jean] scet comment il despleut au cardinal de ce que la partie avoit mis ses armes a l'ostel
de Niort." See also n. 71 below. I have not found the *arrêt* either.

65. At the time of his betrothal in 1383 Jean had been fighting in Prussia; his
marriage was in 1384; and his first documented appearance in military service, 15
August 1386, was as a *chevalier* leading eleven squires (see Ch. III above). He could
hardly have been born much after, say 1365, more likely before. Since Jean's wife had
had two children by her first marriage, the sterility of her second would have been
deemed Jean's fault.

66. Archives de la ville de Poitiers, ms. 51, fol. 86r. See Robert Favreau, *La ville de
Poitiers à la fin du moyen âge, MSAO,* 4th series, 15 (Poitiers, 1978):248, 318, for a
summary of this case and for the general phenomenon of noble-bourgeois relationships
in the region.

John the Fearless's capture of the city on 29 May 1418.[67] The fact is that the bourgeois of Poitiers (like others elsewhere), no doubt the *populares* in question, had welcomed the Burgundians with open gates and had received various benefits from their new lords; then, when the Burgundians withdrew from Poitou, the Poitevins returned to their old Berry loyalty with neither shame nor pain. There was nothing either dishonorable or uncommon about such legal acceptance of power, and we can imagine how Jean de Cramaud, the *voisin,* might have gone along and perhaps indeed have been a leader.[68] But Simon's relation to Berry was of

---

67. Some of the charges were made in 1418 by Renaud II de Montléon to justify his 1417 seizure of Touffou; an *arrêt* of 1 February 1419, AN, X 1A 9190, fol. 2v, sums them up: "Preterea dicebant dicti defensores seu eorum procurator quod dictus Johannes de Cramaudo a tempore introitus seu eventus dictorum inimicorum [scil., the Burgundians], ipsis adherendo, Parisius fuerat et diu steterat, ac Magistrum Johannem Barbe procuratorem . . . defensorum . . . occidi facere nisus fuerat." Jean may have been in Paris to pursue his suit against Renaud—the presence of Jean Barbe there would suggest as much—before the transfer of the Orléans/Armagnac Parlement to Poitiers, 29 September 1418. He rejected the charges as a slur on his honor (ibid.). The final *arrêt,* 13 April 1429, sums up Renaud's later, more serious and particular charges of this sort (AN, X 1A 9191, fol. 127r): "Pendente processu, guerre et divisiones in nostro regno supervenerant, adeo quod circa annum domini 1417 [*sic pro* 1412] dux Burgundie plures villas et castra circumcirca . . . Touffou . . . occupaverat seu . . . occupari . . . fecerat; eidemque duci tempore predicto quamplures, et inter ceteros dictus de Cramaudo, parebant et adherebant. Qui de Cramaudo modicum ante tempus predictum plures gentes dicto duci faventes et que . . . ducis Biturie . . . et . . . ducis Aurelianensis partem tenentibus mortaliter inimicabantur . . . in dicto castro de Touffou tenuerat. . . . Et eciam tempore quo dominus de Hely, . . . duci Burgundie . . . favorisans, maiorem partem villarum et castrorum comitatus Pictavie . . . damnabiliter . . . occupabat, [illi] et suis sequacibus dictus Johannes de Cramaudo favorem, auxilium, et consilium prebuerat. Et una cum hoc, quamvis dictus Johannes de Cramaudo homo feudalis et vassallus dicti propatrui nostri [scil., the duke of Berry] fuisset et esset, et ab eo ambo, scil. ipse Johannes et Cardinalis, totum vel maiorem partem bonorum et honorum suorum recepissent et habuissent, nichilominus dictus de Cramaudo unus ex principalioribus popularium seductoribus ad ponendam villam Pictaviensem pluresque alias villas et castra dicti comitatus in obediencia dictorum ducis Burgundie et de Hely, et nomine ipsius de Hely dicte Pictaviensis ville capitaneus et gubernator exactorque plurium tailliarum pro dicto de Hely et suis sequacibus fuerat, pluraque . . . iniuriosa verba contra dictos propatruum et consanguineum nostros et sibi adherentes palam popularibus eos commovendo dixerat." For the Sire de Heilly's Burgundian invasion of Poitou in early 1412, see Lehoux, 3:257, 265; Poitiers was taken by mid-April, and by mid-May Heilly had left for Berry to besiege Bourges; see also Lacour, *Incursion anglaise en Poitou:* 11.

68. Lacour, *Incursion anglaise en Poitou:* 11, notes that the lord of Parthenay defected to the Burgundians at this time, and no doubt there were others. In the earlier struggles between the English and the Valois, from 1369 on, "the choice of side" for most of the lords of Poitou "was determined by the situation of their property," and those who later returned from English to French allegiance received full pardons and restitution of their confiscated property—Paul Guérin, in *AHP,* 19 (Poitou, 1888):xi–xii, and *passim.* For the behavior of Poitiers in 1412 see Favreau, *Ville de Poitiers:* 207.

quite a different order, requiring a steadfast reliability that in his case never failed. While he might have recognized the logic of Jean's behavior (supposing it was as stated), it could at the same time have forced him to realize that his hopes for a family "estate" smoothly integrated into his own were impossible. It could have been one more reason for revising the family compact in 1414.

At the same time, his sense of family had pointed him away from Jean even earlier, for Jean's lack of children led Simon to make an arrangement with a grandnephew, Pierre Tison, son of Jean's sister Jeanne by a first marriage. Pierre would change his name to Cramaud and bear the Cramaud arms after Jean's death, while Simon would provide the money and influence to get him well married and would give him enough property to support his new estate. But Pierre died soon after, and Simon could only pass part of the benevolence on to Pierre's daughter. For the rest, he financed and arranged a good marriage for Mathea de Pressac, daughter of Jeanne de Cramaud by a second marriage, and provided schooling and other advantages for several grandnephews.[69] Of these,

---

69. Simon described the arrangement in his will, in the context of his provision for Tison's daughter, AN, X 1A 8604, fol. 91(bis)v (I have compared an original copy in ADV, G 14, no. 1): "Item do et lego nepti mee filie domini Petri Tizonis mille francos in auro. Et ordino quod dominus Jacobus Beschade [or Vesthade, etc.] miles solvat sibi alios mille francos dumtaxat [mss., dum tamen] in castro et terra de Vevaco et in terra que fuit Guillelmi de Prun, quas ego acquisivi et dederam eas predicto nepoti meo Petro Tizonis, ut defferret nomen et arma de Cramaudo post mortem nepotis mei domini Johannis de Cramaudo. Et quia [sic] illud non potuit fieri neque potest sicut deo placuit, quia iam diu est, idem Petrus . . . mortuus fuit." The bishop of Poitiers referred to Simon's family provisions on 27 June 1426, AN, X 1A 9198, fol. 185r: "Dit que feu le cardinal despendi moult pour eulx. Il maria Messire Jehan de Cramaut; il maria Tison le filz de sa niepce; il tint ses nepveuz a l'escole." The economics of Mathea de Pressac's marriage are laid out in AN, X 1A 9197, fols. 34, 14r–15r (9 December 1421; 5 and 8 January 1422), and in the arrêt of 7 March 1422: AN, X 1A 9190, fols. 173r–174r. In 1402 Jean Le Brun, son of the Poitevin damoiseau Huet Le Brun, contracted to marry Mathea de Pressac, whose dowry, provided by Simon, consisted of 1,200 gold écus, part of which (1,000 livres) would be used to redeem a rente of 100 livres tournois that Huet had sold the year before. This rente was to be Mathea's property, passing to her children or, if she had none, to Simon and his heirs. But Huet did not pay her the 100 livres tournois a year, nor did he assign the rente on particular properties; indeed he was alienating even more property in his struggles to pay a ransom debt ("Huet pris des Anglois a vendu de son heritaige pour sa rancon," fol. 14r). In 1407 a deal was made giving Mathea the usufruct of the villa of Fourrier and the property of Charnay. But as time went on, with Huet selling off more and more ("si a ledit Huet beaucoup vendu de ou sur son heritage," fol. 14v), Simon and Mathea began to worry about ever getting the annuity established, and they decided to sue in order to have it done and to collect arrears (Jean Le Brun refused to join them). The case then turned on how much Mathea had collected since 1407 as well as on Huet's desire to prevent the annuity from escaping his right of retrait; the arrêt ordered him to make the assignment. Mathea and Jean Le

the most successful was Guy de Pressac, perhaps Mathea's brother, who followed a career in the church, received benefices and other favors at Simon's hands, and eventually became archdeacon of Poitiers when his uncle was bishop.[70] None of this however made up for the failure of the Cramaud line, which led Simon to take his properties back into his own disposition to ensure that a substantial number of them would go not to Jean but to the succeeding bishops of Poitiers; such a provision was included in the revised family compact imposed on Jean ca. 1414.[71]

The complex of ideas and feelings involved in late-medieval benefactions to institutions of charity or public welfare like the church was no doubt similar in many respects to the corresponding mentality today. One feels the satisfaction of virtue and takes pleasure in the thought that one's name will long be remembered for good. One difference would be that in the earlier period the family was far more apt to be the primary durative entity to which one attached one's mere contingent, individual existence; but we have seen the failure of this alternative in Simon's case. Another difference lay in the reality and concept of "estate" with its objective, legal, public character, in contrast to modern status or prestige. As we try to think our way into Simon de Cramaud's mind towards the end of his life, we find ourselves drawn ineluctably to his sense of his estate as something that embodied his societal being so objectively that

Brun turn up later, in 1434, among the heirs of Jean de Cramaud (AN, X 1A 9200, fol. 193v). Some other examples of Simon's particular benevolences appear in the records of Parlement. Thus pleas of 6 September 1423 (AN, X 1A 9197, fol. 252v) show that he had given the "land of Narbonne" to Jean de Pressac. One guesses that if Élie (Heliot) de Pressac was a bachelor *in decretis* and a canon of St. Hilaire-le-Grand of Poitiers (*AHP*, 32 (1903):131; a document of 1449), Simon had had much to do with it.

70. AN, X 1A 4790, fol. 301r (2 August 1415): Simon as archbishop of Rheims gave a 5-livre *rente* on the property of a local monastery to Guy de Pressac, who then sold it to the monastery for 100 écus. AN, X 1A 4791, fol. 71r (7 April 1416): Guy is called Simon's nephew and "serviteur commensal." AN, X 1A 9197, fols. 47v, 66r–67r (9 and 31 March 1422), and AN, X 1A 9190, fol. 240rv, an *arrêt* of 23 June 1423, show Simon as bishop using his power to confirm elections in order to override an election and appoint Pressac as prior of the almonry of Mirebeau. The religious of the priory claimed the right to elect and brought a property suit against Simon and Pressac. When later cited to appear before Simon at Chapelle-Bellouin, they refused to obey because of the evident collusion: "On ne doit avoir regart a telz hoquez ne a teles citacions ou lettres, car partie [scil., Pressac] a trop grand faveur chez l'evesque." Guy was named along with Jean de Cramaud as a chief executor of Simon's will.

71. See the texts quoted above, nn. 63, 64. There are other references in the bishop of Poitiers's pleas in 1426 (AN, X 1A 9198, fol. 184v): "Le Cardinal acquist pour lui et en son nom et de ses propres deniers, quocunque nomine les lettres feussent faictes, la Chapelle Bernoyn, Tillay, La Lande, La Roche, Chauray, Beau Regart, et l'ostel de Nyort; et . . . avant qu'il alast au concile a Constance il ordonna que feussent aux successeurs evesques de Poictiers in casu que Messire Jehan de Cramaut ne auroit enfants, etc. Et per testamentum factum l'an 1421 en fist lais, et en mars ensuite."

it could go on after he himself had passed away—something rather more than just trying to keep his name alive. If we turn to the picture of the duke of Berry arriving before St. Peter at the gate of heaven in all the splendor of his estate (see plate), we get an immediate intuition of how profoundly this societal conceptualization of the individual had penetrated even religious thought about the destiny of the soul.

In Simon's case we have not a picture but an equivalent testimony in the conventional phrases of his last will, which with all its conventionality is still the most personal document we have of his composition. He began with the standard formula: "First and foremost I humbly commend my soul to my Supreme Creator, to the Blessed and Glorious Virgin Mary his Mother, to the Apostles Saints Peter and Paul, and to the whole heavenly *curia*."[72] It is hard today to see anything humble in this unquestioning assumption by great men that God, Mary, and thousands of angels and saints would have nothing better to do than notice their arrivals and take an interest in the favorable reception of their souls. One's estate obviously outlasted one's mortal life. The same idea appears almost a fortiori when it is ostensibly rejected, again in Simon's will: "Even though the estate of my dignities would call for an extremely elaborate funeral by worldly standards, I . . . order that around my corpse as long as it is on earth there should stand only four wax tapers of any kind of wax, weighing twelve pounds, and four torches of any kind of material, weighing twenty-four pounds of wax and standing merely in four modest candlesticks." There follow provisions for distributing alms to the poor—200 livres in 10-penny lots (thus 48,000 gifts!)—and more substantial gifts to churches, and directions for clothing all of Simon's domestics in black, "each according to his estate," but only if this can be reasonably done, "for the price of cloth is too high."[73] The prayers that are commissioned in the same context "for the welfare of my soul" (*pro salute anime mee*) consist of nine-part vigils and a mass for the dead on the day of Simon's death or burial and presumably on the anniversaries forever, and they are to be said in each church of the four mendicant orders in Poitiers, Limoges, and St. Junien; each of the twelve is to get 40 livres except for the Poitiers Dominicans, who get 60.[74] All this is apart from

---

72. AN, X 1A 8604, fol. 91(bis)r; the phrase appears in all wills I have read. See Jacques Chiffoleau, *La comptabilité de l'au-delà* (Rome, 1980): 116, 141, 230 ff., 332 ff., for a discussion of contemporary testaments that illuminates some of the provisions of Simon's. Thus, for example, we learn that the black cloth mentioned below was much more expensive than the usual white and was reserved "for princes, kings, popes"; also that the foundation of chaplaincies was the rarest of luxuries.

73. Ibid.: "Item volo . . . quod me sublato de medio, omnes servitores mei et familiares domestici meis expensis panni nigri [*sic*] secundum cuiuslibet statum induantur, si videatur executoribus meis fieri posse, quia panni sunt nimis cari."

74. Ibid.: "Item volo . . . quod in qualibet ecclesia [of the four orders, etc.] . . . in die obitus seu sepulture mei corporis . . . vigilia novem leccionum et una missa de

the elaborate commemorations in Poitiers cathedral, which we will look at later on. In principle, of course, the endowment of such observances was a good work which, along with the liturgical acts themselves, helped to shorten the soul's sufferings in Purgatory; but in fact it was also an exhibition of estate in much the same sense that the candles, torches, alms, and black cloth were. There is nothing here of the feverish extremes of sensibility said to mark the late-medieval mind in its confrontation with death, only a thoroughgoing sense of *comme il faut* in terms of secular ideas of status, order, and proper behavior, to which religious thought was normally assimilated. Simon's whole life had been lived according to these ideas and he ended it accordingly.

He had indeed begun making commemorative foundations rather early, while still bishop of Poitiers the first time (1385–1391), with a gift of an annuity of 6 livres to the cathedral of Orléans, where he had earlier been *scholasticus*; as customary, the foundation called for masses of the Holy Spirit on his behalf during his lifetime, to become masses for the dead on the anniversaries of his death.[75] We have already noted his foundation of 1390 in Poitiers cathedral to be paid for by 100 livres a year from the bishop's judicial revenues: the beneficiaries were to be, eventually, the souls of Simon, his parents, the duke of Berry, and Pope Clement VII. We shall see Simon cold-bloodedly absorbing this into a foundation for himself and unspecified benefactors after Berry and Clement had passed from the scene and needed the benefits most. Then at some point during his tenure as patriarch of Alexandria (1391–1409), he saw to it that the anniversary of his death would be commemorated in the fashionable convent of the Chartreux de Vauvert in Paris; this was paid for by a gold chalice and "very many good things" that Simon had himself done for the convent and had influenced the duke of Berry to do.[76]

---

defunctis solemniter celebrentur, et cuilibet conventui do et lego ut . . . pro salute anime mee exorare habeant, . . . [the amounts follow]." A year after Simon's death, his goods were still attached by court order in favor of the archbishop of Rheims, suing presumably for repair money, and his executors had to petition, 31 January 1424 (AN, X 1A 9197, fol. 282r), "que la court leur fist provision des biens de l'execucion pour faire le service du bout de l'an de l'obit dudit defunt, non obstant les defenses que l'arcevesque de Reims leur a fait faire de non vendre ne aliener aucuns desdits biens."

75. Details of the service and endowment and of Simon's former position in the chapter are recorded in the *Livres de distribution* of Orléans cathedral, A. Vidier & L. Mirot, eds., *Obituaires de la province de Sens*, 3 (Paris, 1909):115.

76. A. Molinier & A. Longnon, eds., *Obituaires de la province de Sens*, 2 (Paris, 1902):700 f.: (*ad* 3 June) "eodem die obiit Symon de Cramaut, Patriarcha Alexandrinus, postea Cardinalis Remensis, qui dedit nobis unum calicem de auro, multaque alia bona nobis fecit et apud dominum ducem Biturie specialiter multa bona nobis fieri procuravit." The editors, p. 696, refer to this convent as "the object of the liberalities of the whole high society of Paris." See Lehoux, 2:273, for Berry's legacy to the convent of lands, a loaded reliquary, and the enormous sum of 20,000 francs.

On 10 October 1402 he expressed his identification with Poitiers cathedral in an important foundation endowed with a whole set of tithes, *rentes,* and lands: a music master and six choirboys were to become a permanent part of the chapter's structure, with revenues equal to a canonry, which the chapter agreed to contribute to; after Simon's death the songsters would have their own house near the church. Later on he transferred to them the 100 livres a year originally destined to pay for his 1390 foundation noted above, stipulating that they were to take part in the regular commemorative masses for his soul after his death.[77]

It is tempting to guess, as suggested above, that by this time Simon had come to terms with the realization that his family was going to die out in the male line; certainly these first years of the century saw him not only starting the marble and alabaster tomb, which was finished by 1405, but also embarking on a whole series of foundations continuing to his death and using up properties and revenues that would otherwise have passed into the Cramaud heritage. Thus in 1406 he endowed an elaborate set of four chaplaincies in the church of Biennac, where the Cramauds had been buried: each chaplain would take a one-week turn in a four-week cycle throughout the year so that every day forever a mass would be celebrated for the souls of Simon and his immediate family. The endowment consisted of the tithes of Biennac and a number of other revenues from local estates, all costing several hundred livres.[78] In the

---

77. The text of Simon's establishment "pro alimento perpetuo unius magistri cantoris et musici, et sex puerorum seu clericorum in arte cantoria et musica erudiendorum continue in eadem ecclesia deservientium" is printed by Jean Besly, *Evesques de Poictiers* (Paris, 1647): 200–202, also in the Fontenau manuscripts—BN, *ms. lat.* 18,377, pp. 195–198, cf. *Tables des manuscrits de D. Fontenau:* 317; and see n. 54 above. The endowment consisted of the "land" of Pouant, tithes due to his estate of Nouzilly, and other tithes and *rentes:* these were "amortized" by Charles VI to the value of 100 livres tournois in a letter of 6 December 1402, in *AHP,* 24 (1893):419–421. *Gallia christiana,* 2:1196, refers to both items. Benedict XIII confirmed the foundation on 23 January 1404 (BN, *ms. lat.* 18,378, p. 605). The later provisions appear in the foundation described below at n. 80. J. Salvini, *Le diocèse de Poitiers à la fin du moyen âge* (Fontenay-le-Comte, 1946): 67, writes that this was one of the first corps of choirboys established in France.

78. The provisions, described in Simon's will, are given more fully by a stone tablet of the time still set in the wall of the church of Biennac, with the Cramaud arms at each corner: "Reverendus . . . dominus Symon de Cramaudo, loco huius parochie, fundavit in ecclesia ista quatuor capellanias pro quatuor capellanis, quorum quilibet tenetur celebrare unam missam die qualibet de deffunctis pro animabus dicti reverendi patris et parentum suorum, perpetuo, alternis vicibus, videlicet quilibet capellanus in septimana, et revolutis quatuor septimanis debet reincipere ille qui in prima septimana mensis celebraverat. . . . Nec potest aliquis predictas capellanias obtinere, nisi personaliter resideat in loco isto de Bianaco. . . . Et pro sustentacione ipsorum acquisivit decimam huius burgi, et mansos de Royeria, et de Cramaudo, super quibus ante habebat XXXI sext. bladi; et pro residuo tradidit domino vicecomiti Rupiscavardi XLI libras in denariis rendualibus quas

same year, he joined his brother Pierre's widow, Almodis de Coux, to found masses in the church of St. Junien on the first day of each month for the souls of both and their kin; this too was in Cramaud territory, and the endowment consisted of local real estate as well as cash.[79] The last major foundation we know of was made on 2 July 1421 to provide monthly commemorations for himself at the high altar of Poitiers cathedral, plus responsories for the dead in front of his tomb in the choir, with the music master and choirboys taking part; the lavish endowment costing about 1,000 livres included the whole estate of Nouzilly, acquired in 1397, along with various other revenues picked up over the years.[80] Let us also not forget the already-noted Rheims commemorations and the one provided for in his will. No doubt there were others too—it is mere chance, for example, that informs us of prayers in the cathedral of Limoges which Simon expected to get in return for the gift of a missal, and commemorations by the Poitiers Dominicans in exchange for various benefits including a "dictionary."[81] All in all, it was a remarkably

---

dominus de Marollio habebat super habitantes Rupiscavardi ab antiquo, pro quibus solvit eidem de Marollio CCCC libras. Acquisivit eciam a Stephano Quadrigarii V sext. bladi, . . . super decimam bladi mansi de Chassanhas in territorio ville Rupiscavardi inter mansum Du Plantier ex una parte, et mansum de la Choussolie; et terciam partem decime vini dicti territorii; et aliqua alia, que ipsis perpetuo dedit; et per dei graciam alia dabit. Scripta sunt hec omnia M° CCCC° Sexto." Note the care taken to compose the endowment from immediately local, even familial sources, also the evident need to define each item of the endowment in terms of its past history. In Simon's will, it is stipulated that the chaplains will be instituted by the bishop of Limoges on presentation by the current lord of Cramaud.

79. BN, *Dossiers bleus* 222, no. 5649; Maurice Ardant, "Simon de Cramaud, Patriarche d'Alexandrie," *Bulletin de la Société archéologique et historique du Limousin,* 14 (Limoges, 1864):103–105 (the information taken from a copper plaque once in the church of St. Junien).

80. BN, *ms. lat.* 18,378, pp. 571–580; the amortization of Nouzilly for this purpose by Charles VII, 30 August 1434, in BN, *ms. lat.* 18,377, pp. 227–228; cf. *Tables des manuscrits de D. Fontenau:* 326, 332. Fontenau notes (p. 332) that Nouzilly's total value was probably about 70 livres a year; its capital value would have been ca. 700 livres. Simon had acquired it by purchase from Gerard de Maumont, lord of Tonnay-Boutonne, on 12 April 1397 (BN, *ms. lat.* 18,377, p. 189 f.); note that Simon had already given the chapter the tithes pertaining to this property, in his foundation of 1402 (n. 77 above), so that now everything was brought together. The endowment also included 150 livres; 12 *mine* of grain a year from La Talebastière near Chauvigny, which Simon acquired in 1409–1413; and the 100 livres from the bishop's judicial revenues that Simon had gotten papal permission to obligate in 1389/1390 and with which he had then endowed masses for himself, his family, Berry, and Clement VII (Ch. III, above). This earlier endowment was superseded by the present one, which merely named his "benefactors" along with himself and his kin. The regulations for liturgical service are extremely complicated as to choreography, millinery, and division of payments.

81. Ardant, "Simon de Cramaud," for the Limoges prayers; BN, *ms. lat.* 18,378, pp. 568–570, for the Poitiers Dominicans' decision on 4 July 1420 to give Simon a share in

extensive prayer-industry representing an investment of several thousands of francs acquired over a lifetime of officeholding, and while there is no reason to reject Simon's standard formula, that such things were done for the welfare of his soul, it is also obvious that in a purely objective and non-speculative sense, the product of the industry was "estate."

By the time Simon was ready to make his last will and testament on 11 March 1422, he had already disposed of much property in the endowments just mentioned, but he still had a good deal left, which it was now his task to divide between the family on the one hand, the future bishops of Poitiers on the other. Jean de Cramaud received full property in Touffou, along with the "lands" of Jardres, Bonneuil, Mathorre, Niort, and Mortemer; a debt to Simon of 1,400 livres was cancelled as well. While Jean lived, he could also hold most of Simon's remaining properties and the domestic furnishings in the *maison-forte* of Chapelle-Bellouin and the castle of Touffou; but when he should die without a legitimate heir of his body, the furnishings would go to Guy de Pressac and the properties to the bishop of Poitiers: Chapelle-Bellouin, La Lande, Tilly, Chauray, Rocherigaut, Beauregard, and appurtenances. In addition the bishop would immediately acquire a house in Niort and some land near Chauvigny.[82] Other family dispositions were few: Hermine de Pressac, a

---

their prayers and a yearly mass (but note the new benefactions in his testament, above). The two-volume "dictionary," "in libraria communi incathenatum," would have been a repertory of significant terms in the Bible, fathers, classics, etc.

82. AN, X 1A 8604, fol. 91(bis)rv: "Item quia temporibus retroactis quamplures acquisiciones nonnullarum terrarum et possessionum de meis pecuniis nomine quondam domini Petri de Cramaudo fratris mei primogeniti, et domini Johannis de Cramaudo filii sui nepotis mei, et eciam meo simplici nomine feci, que acquisita predictis nominibus existunt adhuc in mea disposicione tenore cuiusdam accordi alias inter me et dictum nepotem meum facti, et per curiam parlamenti solemniter confirmati: cum ex eodem domino Johanne de Cramaudo nepote meo sint nulli ipsius heredes ex sua carne procreati, de eisdem terris et domaniis sic acquisitis dispono et ordino prout infra. Volo enim et ordino quod omnes terre et domania sic ut predicitur acquisita, de quibus non disposui, sint et remaneant dicto domino Johanni de Cramaudo nepoti meo et heredibus suis legitimis de proprio corpore descendentibus. Si vero eum contingat mori sine heredibus de proprio corpore descendentibus, volo et ordino quod locus fortis de Capella Bernoyn, loca de Landa, de Tilleyo, de Claunayo [*recte,* Chaurayo ?], de Rupe Rigaudi, et de Bello Respectu, et alia ibidem circumcirca acquisita cum eorum pertinentibus, sint et remaneant perpetuo episcopo Pictavensi, cum de eodem episcopatu quamplurima bona habuerim et quotidie habeam. . . . Item volo, dispono, et ordino quod si locus de Touffou sit et remaneat dicto domino Johanni de Cramaudo nepoti meo una cum terris de Jadris, de Bonolio, Mathorre, de Nyorto, et de Mortuo Mari, possit disponere ad eius voluntatem. Excepto hospicio de Nyorto et aqua cum prato que acquisivi a Bruneto prope Calvigniacum, que lego episcopis Pictavensibus. Item remitto domino Johanni de Cramaudo, nepoti meo, summam mille quadringentarum librarum, in quibus michi

grandniece, was given 500 livres as a dowry so that she could get married; Pierre Tison's daughter was given 1,000 gold francs plus another thousand to come from the sale of the properties originally destined for Pierre.[83] There had of course been extensive family gifts in the past, but one is still struck by how few there were in the will. Other items, apart from the Paris house bequeathed to the Collège de Reims and other ecclesiastical endowments, do not add up to very much.[84] What the will shows is essentially the implementation of the revised compact imposed on Jean de Cramaud in 1414; more positively, since Simon's previous benevolences in the form of commemorative endowments had gone to benefit chiefly the chapter of Poitiers, he now undertook to benefit the bishops. Representatives of the chapter indeed asked him to give their corporation more, but he refused.[85]

Jean's reaction was to try to get his uncle to revoke the will just mentioned and restore at least the key properties to Jean's full ownership. A revised text to this effect was actually prepared at Jean's order, and it was produced after Simon's death as the true testament superseding the other one. It was challenged a few years later by the then-bishop of Poitiers, who in 1426 sued Jean de Cramaud before Parlement to have the original will declared valid and in addition to make Jean pay 20,000 écus for repairs to episcopal property that Simon allegedly should have made but did not.[86] Extraordinarily rich in detail, the pleas in the

---

legitime tenetur et est obligatus. . . . Et ultra hoc, do sibi lectos meos et alia domus utencilia que habeo in locis predictis de Capella Bernoyn et de Touffou, vita sua comite, et post eius mortem volo quod revertantur ad magistrum Guidonem de Pressaco archidiaconem Pictavensem. Heredem meum instituo dictum dominum Johannem de Cramaudo."

83. Ibid., fol. 91(bis)v: "Item do et lego Hermine filie domini Ademari de Pressaco pro ipsa coniuganda quingentas libras"; and see n. 69 above.

84. Ibid.: "Item volo quod . . . libri mei vendantur et vaissella mea argentea, et quod servitoribus meis solvantur summe de quibus infra fiet mencio."

85. According to the pleas of the bishop of Poitiers in 1426 (AN, X 1A 9898, fol. 184v): "Et toutesvoies il estoit fort induit par aucun de faire le lais a chapitre, et par autres que ce venist a ses heritiers, mais il respondi que on le laissast en pays . . . et persevera iusques a la mort"; and fol. 185r: "Dit qu'il y avoit deux chanoines qui vouloient y parler [in his last days], on leur dist qu'il ne y pourroit parler; ad idem au chapitre"; and fol. 185v, replying to Jean's argument that Simon had already done enough for the church: "Dit que il en fist a chapitre, mais encore est il plus tenu a l'eveschie quasi sibi ipsi. Et puisque gratis il avoit bien fait a chapitre, il est a presumer qu'il ne vouloit soy—i.e., son eglise—oublier, mais y laissier plus largement."

86. Ibid., fols. 150v–151r, the bishop's pleas: "Dit que en sa derreniere maladie et estant en article de mort et que la parole lui falloit, ledit Messire Jehan de Cramaut et autres en sa compagnie le requirent qu'il revocast ledit testament et le lais ou donacion dessusdit. A quoy il ne respondit riens et aussi ne avoit il voulente, sens, ne entendement, et neantmoins comme on dit fut faicte une escripture contenant qu'il revoquoit

case have already been used at a number of points in our account of Simon's life and works, and it remains now only to draw their picture of the dying cardinal's last days on earth. We see a man aged about seventy-eight, suffering from the pains of "the stone" and the weaknesses of an evidently sudden senility, to the point where he could not think or speak clearly, where his awareness of things blacked out from time to time, and where his loss of self-control led him, two days before his death, to exhibit himself naked to a visitor. The next day he attended mass unaware of the priest who was celebrating and was so debilitated in mind that he could barely speak. Jean de Cramaud nevertheless stood at his bedside demanding that he revoke his will of 1422, and he demanded it again and again in the face of his uncle's silence until finally the doctor said, "It's your nephew Jean," and Simon murmured "yes"— which answer Jean took as approval of his revised text.[87] Since Jean's defense turned not upon an alternate version of the circumstances but on arguments that the original will had been illegal or unfair, the ugly picture of his behavior can probably be believed; in any case, the version

---

ledit lais ou donacion; laquele escripture n'est pas vraie. Et ce venu a la cognoissance du demandeur, il a impetre mandement du roy contenant le cas lequel il ramaine a fait, iouxte lequel a este donne adiornement a Messire Jehan de Cramaut"; and, "Autre demande fait ledit evesque contre ledit Messire Jehan de Cramaut, et dit que ledit feu cardinal dont est heritier ledit Messire Jehan a este evesque de Poictiers bien xxv ans, onques n'y fist faire quelque reparacion, et toutesvoies les reparacions qu'il y convient de son temps montent bien a xx mil escuz. Pour ce est adiorne ledit Messire Jehan." Simon had in fact been bishop of Poitiers for a total of only fifteen years; he had certainly made some repairs; and it is possible that the figure of 20,000 écus was merely rotund speculation. Simon, as we have seen, had claimed the same amount (as francs) in his suit against his predecessor at Carcassonne, but experts assessed the actual cost of repairs due as less than half (above, Ch. III, n. 126).

87. The details come from the bishop's pleas, AN, X 1A 9198, fol. 185r: "Dit que le Cardinal morut le [mardi, le] xix jour de janvier, et le lundi precedent il estoit ja si debilite qu'il ne avoit sens ne discrecion. Dit que Cramaut le excita et fist exciter plusieurs foiz de revoquer ledit lais, riens ne y respondi quoi qu'il soit escript. Bien dit on que pour ce qu'il n'y vouloit respondre, Maistre Jaques son medicin lui dist que c'estoit Cramaut son nepveu, et que il respondi 'ouyl'—ce auroit este ut presumi potest car il vouloit complaire a son medicin dont il lui sambloit avoir a faire"; and, "Dit que des le dimanche devant sa mort un notable homme fut veoir le Cardinal apres disner et le trouva tout altere de sens; et ce le denote bien car le Cardinal se exhiba a lui tout nu. Et le lundi qu'il estoit a ouir la messe, le prestre aupres de lui, il demandoit ou estoit le prestre, et apparoit bien qu'il estoit ebete de veue et de sens. Dit que lui estant en tel estat que dit est, il n'eust peu faire testament; et par plus forte raison moins povoit il revoquer illud quod iustum et factum fuerat si long temps par avant. Et y avoit persevere sanz vouloir le revoquer pour personne qui lui en sceust parler. Dit que au temps de sa derreniere maladie il est tres vieil et fort passione de gravelle, qui sur autres trouble l'entendement, et ita propinquus morti quod varia cogitare non poterat, iuxta L. *Humana fragilitas,* nec loqui nec scribere, et sic pro mortuo habebatur. Dit que aucuns proudommes tabellions refuserent a faire instrument super revocacione pretensa, car ilz savoient l'estat et comment il en aloit."

of the will registered and then probated in Parlement was the original one of 11 March 1422.[88]

It did not, however, take effect. Simon's successor as bishop of Poitiers had to sue for his legacies, as we have seen, and there is no evidence that he won. The estate was further tied up by the current archbishop of Rheims's claim against Simon as a former archbishop who had neglected repairs, by the claims of a royal tax collector,[89] by leftovers from the old lawsuits about priories claimed under Simon's papal privilege, and no doubt by other objections as well.[90] Jean de Cramaud, named as *the* heir for legal purposes in the original will, chose to accept only "with benefit of inventory" in order to ensure that he would not be liable for debts in excess of his legacy, and a new lawsuit filed by the bishop of Poitiers against Jean's heirs after the latter's death in 1431 prompted them to make the same prudent choice.[91] But one way or another, the Cramaud

---

88. The copy of the original recorded in AN, X 1A 8604 is followed by a note, fol. 92r: "Collacio facta est cum originali testamento cuius execucio submissa fuit per executores dicti testamenti curie parlamenti prima die februarii A. D. M°. CCCC°. XXII°. [1423 our style]." Cf. AN, X 1A 9197, fol. 165v (1 February 1423) for the current notice of this action, at which time Bishop Pierre (below) was dead. Simon named as his executors Bishop Pierre of Gabulance; Jean de Vaily, a president of Parlement; Jean de Cramaud; the archdeacon Guy de Pressac; Ithier Marchon, dean of Thouars; and Master Jacques Perchet, who had been his doctor. Jean de Cramaud and Guy were the effective members of the group, and we find traces of their activity in the next several years in the registers of Parlement: e.g., in nn. 74 above, 91 below; AN, X 1A 9195, fol. 175v; X 1A 9197, fol. 328r sqq.

89. AN, X 1A 9197, fols. 330r, 337v (20 July, 11 August 1424).

90. AN, X 1A 9199, fol. 382r (22 March 1431)—the executors of Simon's will are suing the bishop of Maillezais over Simon's claim to the priory of Ligugé; cf. fols. 386v, 396v.

91. We read in the will [AN, X 1A 8604, fol. 91(bis)v]: "Heredem meum instituo dictum dominum Johannem de Cramaudo." In the lawsuit of 1426 Jean's lawyer noted, "Le defendeur est voirement son heritier, mais c'est cum beneficio inventarii"—this last was a Roman-law provision allowing an heir to avoid liability while determining whether claims against the estate exceeded its value. The first mention I know of Jean's death comes on 25 May 1431 (AN, X 1A 9199, fol. 396v), when the executors of the will of "feu Messire Jehan de Cramaud" appear in the Ligugé matter (n. 90 above). In AN, X 1A 9200, fol. 193v (21 January 1434) we read the list of Jean de Cramaud's possible heirs, as defendants in the lawsuit brought by the bishop of Poitiers for repairs and perhaps his other claims: Jean's widow, Orable de Montléon; Jean de Pressac (see n. 69 above), Simonne Tison (see n. 69 above) and her husband Regnaut de Velort; the knight Bertrand Rataut; Jacques Bechade (n. 69 above) and his wife Jeanne de Pruigny; Archdeacon Guy de Pressac; Heliot de Pressac (n. 69 above); Hermine de Pressac and her husband Pierre de Beauvolier (n. 83 above), Mathea de Pressac and her husband Jean Le Brun (n. 69 above). Orable refused to enter as heiress, and as for the others, "en tant que touche les reparacions . . . feu Messire Jehan de Cramaut ne se porta heritier de feu son oncle le cardinal que par benefice d'inventaire, et en ceste qualite les dessusdits . . . reprennent."

line managed to keep all or most of the properties Simon's will had refused them.[92]

The dark colors of Simon's last years were made more sombre still by a train of events that would eventually cause Jean and his wife to lose the castle of Touffou. Getting this for them had been one of Simon's great achievements in his first term as bishop of Poitiers, and we have noted the combination of expenditures, coercion, and chicanery by means of which the then-rising Cramauds pried the castle loose from the Montléons in 1387 and in the process disinherited the orphaned four-year-old Renaud II. But the latter had been brought up not to forget, and in 1403, as soon as he entered his twenty-first year, he demanded his castle back. When refused, he got royal letters allowing him to file suit even after so many years, and then after having to drop this action in 1404, he did the same thing in 1409. An *arrêt* of 29 April 1411 ordered an inquiry with Jean and his wife Orable left in possession meanwhile, and the matter rested there.[93] One guesses that quite apart from the duke of Berry's aegis and from Simon's own local and national influence, which must have been very great in such matters, Simon's resources of money and cunning were enough to frustrate the still rather juvenile Renaud II.[94] In December of 1417, however, with Berry dead and Simon probably not yet back from Constance, Renaud II put together a band of relatives and friends, some of whom entered Touffou under peaceful pretences; the others then showed up and were let in, and Renaud told Jean that he proposed to stay. Jean was expelled and walked in the evening to Chauvigny. His wife Orable left a month later. While obviously an inchoate *Fehde,* or "private war," fought to secure justice in default of other remedies, Renaud's action did take place in a kingdom whose institutions were supposed to ensure the orderly resolution of such issues, private wars being forbidden. He therefore justified his action in terms of the current civil war and alleged that Jean de Cramaud had been a Burgundian adherent and that Renaud merely wanted to make sure that his heritage of Touffou was held on behalf of the king and dauphin.

---

92. Thus Simon's Paris house remained in his family (n. 34 above), as did Chapelle-Bellouin—see André Lecler, *Dictionnaire historique et géographique de la Haute-Vienne* (Limoges, 1926): 87 f.; also Robert Favreau, "L'entretien du temporel épiscopal: L'exemple de Poitiers au XVe siècle," *BSAO,* 4th series, 9 (1967):446.

93. AN, X 1A 9191, fol. 122v, an *arrêt* of 13 April 1429, gives most of these details; for the rest see ibid., fols. 124r, 125r; X 1A 56, fols. 143v–144r; X 1A 4788, fols. 380v–382r, 398v–399r; X 1A 1479, fol. 157v; X 1A 9190, fols. 1v, 50v.

94. I suppose this explanation to be the basic one; Renaud II, however, argued later that the commissioners appointed in 1411 refused to make their inquiry because of the perils of the road and the disruption due to the wars within the realm (AN, X 1A 9191, fols. 126v–127r).

The Cramauds of course portrayed the whole thing as criminal, charging that Renaud and his band used Touffou as a center of brigandage in the region around it and destroyed property inside the castle.[95]

In any event, Simon must have arrived from Constance soon after and taken a hand in his characteristic style: royal letters were obtained ordering inquiries and provisional confiscation of the contested property; Renaud's defiance was met by new royal letters and citations; and by 1419 when the political situation of the realm had crystallized, with the effective royal institutions for the area now located in Poitiers and Bourges, the castle could be in fact regained. Renaud knew what he was doing, however, and as the price of his submission secured royal letters allowing him once again to sue for recovery of his hereditary right to the castle.[96] He filed his suit at once, in 1420, and was counter-sued by the Cramauds for damages committed during his occupation. Commissions of inquiry came and went; the rich resources of delay in the legal system were expertly exploited by the Cramauds' lawyers; and it was not until 1429, with Simon long dead, that a settlement was imposed. Touffou was restored to Renaud de Montléon; the accord of 1387 that had deprived him of it was declared null; and the Cramauds would have to pay over what they had drawn meanwhile, minus their expenditures for repairs and other improvements.[97] On the other hand the Cramauds could pursue their claims for damages and of course sue to get what they themselves and Orable de Montléon, Jean's wife, would have gotten in 1387 if there had been no accord. The lawsuits thus went on, at least until Jean's death in 1431,[98] but Renaud had won: married, blessed with sons, young enough to take part in the king's wars (he fought at Agincourt), part of an old and important family of the region, he could have

---

95. The details according to both sides are covered in the *arrêt* of 13 April 1429 deciding in the Cramauds' favor the suit for damages which they brought against Renaud et al. (AN, X 1A 9191, fols. 125r–128v). See also the *arrêt* of 1 February 1419, AN, X 1A 9190, fols. 1r–2v, and the miscellaneous information about efforts to make inquiries and put the royal hand on the castle, in AN, X 1A 9195, fols. 8v–9r, 24v–25v, 47r, 59r, 85rv, 106rv. See above, n. 67, for the charges of Burgundianism.

96. The *arrêt* of 4 October 1419, AN, X 1A 9190, fols. 50r–52r, notes that Touffou was "realiter et de facto" taken in the royal hand after royal letters had been issued on 17 April 1419 allowing Renaud to reopen the suit for his right to ownership of the castle. Jean de Cramaud and Orable were then put back into possession while the property case proceeded.

97. AN, X 1A 9191, fols. 121r–125r, an *arrêt* of 13 April 1429.

98. AN, X 1A 9191, fols. 125r–128v, another *arrêt* of 13 April 1429, condemned Renaud to pay damages, and the Cramauds pursued their claims in pleas of 1429–1430 (AN, X 1A 9199, fols. 189r sqq., 224r sqq). Royal letters implementing the various decisions in the property case were issued on 9 December 1429 and 30 January 1430 (AN, X 1A 8604, fols. 135r, 139r).

been kept out of the castle only if the Cramauds had achieved a comparable position. In 1387 Simon's power had been overwhelming, the
Cramaud prospects brilliant, and Parlement in Paris had sanctioned an
accord that disinherited an orphan; in 1429 everything was different,
and Parlement in Poitiers discovered that the earlier accord was legally
invalid.[99]

It is clear from phrasing in his will that Simon realized how shaky
Jean's hold on Touffou had become.[100] One guesses he did not much care.
The hopes he had formed thirty-five years before when he got the castle
for his nephew had all turned sour anyway; he had fixed all his own
aspirations for enduring estate on his benefactions to the church; and if
he felt anything at all about Touffou, it might have been a perverse
satisfaction that his nephew still could not get along without him. It is
one of the few mercies of old age that its human material is so shrunk
into the present that even the worst disappointments dissolve into a sort
of general discontent, and we can guess that the view from Simon's
deathbed was flat enough to be tolerable—apart from whatever may have
been the disturbances due to his kidney stones and mental lapses. It
would be pleasant and even realistic to imagine that his greatest pleasure
lay in contemplating his splendid tomb and the services to be performed
there every month till the end of time; this would be the reward of his
years of service to king and duke, of his political action for church
union, of his endless scheming and struggling for the estate of his family
and himself. The picture here is no doubt defective inasmuch as even the
most single-minded careerist must have other sources of delight than the
thought of his success, but with one obscure exception, there is no
evidence about Simon's private pleasures.[101] It is safer to stick to the public

---

99. The decrees of Parlement normally summarize both sets of pleas and then declare
the court's decisions; no reasons are given for the latter. In our case, one is of course free
to assume that the court was honest on both occasions, different judges coming honestly
to different conclusions; but the interpretation offered here seems less farfetched. For
Renaud's family and his public service, see André Du Chesne, *Histoire généalogique de la
maison des Chasteigners* (Paris, 1634): 241 f.

100. See the passage quoted above, n. 82: "ordino quod si locus de Touffou sit et
remaneat dicto domino Johanni de Cramaudo. . . ."

101. Boniface Ferrer in his treatise of 1411 in favor of Benedict XIII used figures of
heavy sarcasm to heap abuse on all those responsible for France's program of subtraction
and deposition. He included Simon (*Thes. nov.*, 2:1450 f.): "Habent etiam illam lucer-
nam sulphuream ardentem et fumigantem in medio nebulae Simonem de Cremaudo,
virum utique simplicem et rectum, omni divino timore respersum, residentem in omni
notitia in tantum, quod supra Job transit, imo totum librum Job et omnes sequentes
usque ad Canticum canticorum, et ibi resident, de quo habuit et habet tantam notitiam et
experientiam, quod totum exposuit et exponit ad litteram, quod beatus Gregorius non
potuit facere, ducens continue secum expositionem litteralem, ut semper aliquid addat,

ones and note that the paths of his glory had in fact led to something much more impressive than a mere grave. He had at least the luck not to know what would happen to it. The statues of his tomb were smashed by Huguenots in 1562, the rest was destroyed in the French Revolution, and it was only in 1858 that fragments were found and digging was done. Simon's first biographer, the Abbé Auber, removed the skeleton, measured it in both inches and centimeters (1.69 meters), and showed the rather large skull to a local artist. The latter judged that its original owner "must have been gifted with loftiness of character and energetic resolve."[102] By this time the Cramaud family had died out; the commemorative observances had been dropped or suppressed; and there was nothing to protect the dead bones stripped of their estate. But still: in 1849 the Abbé Auber testified that, by a custom lasting "almost today," the Poitiers choirboys sang prayers on Simon's behalf at a little altar by the site of the tomb, and when the prayers were done, they said, "Dieu fasse grâce à M. de Cramaud!"[103]

---

immo frequentissime totum divinum officium omittit contemplatione dicti libri absorptus." Valois, 3:34, recognizes what he calls the irony but seems to think the passage refers to an actual commentary on Job. If, however, we translate the sarcasm into positive terms, we get a picture of Simon as crooked, complex or *duplex*, lacking the fear of God and so arrogant in his assumed knowledge that he had no use for Job's humility or suffering but rather—figuratively—skimmed over such books until he reached the Song of Songs. There he stayed, living out the book's lessons in their literal, sensual and sexual sense, and indeed adding to them, to the point of neglecting his priestly duties. The testimony must be noted, but it need not be believed.

102. Auber: 371 ff.; Auber, "Découverte."

103. Auber, "Histoire de la cathédrale de Poitiers," *MSAO*, 16 (1849):161.

APPENDIXES

The Ballot of Jean Canart

BISHOP OF ARRAS AND CHANCELLOR OF
THE DUKE OF BURGUNDY, AT THE
THIRD PARIS COUNCIL

(AN, J 518, fols. 408r–409r)

HEC EST deliberacio mei episcopi Atrebatensis super execucione vie cessionis utriusque contendencium de papatu.

Primo, quod attentis causis et racionibus allegatis per illos qui materiam aperuerunt, michi videtur licitum et expediens quod rex, eius subditi, ac tota ecclesia gallicana denegent omnimodam obedienciam pape quousque viam predictam acceptaverit et eam diligenter fuerit prosecutus cum effectu, prout tam de iure quam virtute iuramenti per ipsum prestati et alias est astrictus.

Secundo, quod unacum hoc rex in regno suo simpliciter et absolute, sine prefixione temporis, ecclesiam regni sui reducat ad antiquam et debitam libertatem; videlicet, quod ordinarii beneficia conferant que ad eorum collaciones de iure, antiqua consuetudine, et per fundaciones ecclesiarum pertinere noscuntur, et quod capitula, collegia, et conventus eligant sibi prelatos, abbates, priores, et alios in dignitatibus electivis constitutos, confirmandos per illos ad quos de iure confirmacio pertinebunt; [et quod] cessent in futurum exacciones et onera importabilia, cum arreragiis temporis preteriti, super ecclesiis de facto contra iuris disposicionem et statum universalis [ecclesie] apposita—videlicet, annate prepositurarum, prelaturarum, et aliorum beneficiorum quorumcunque, pensiones imposite super beneficiis, levaciones bonorum mobilium per collectores apostolicos post obitum prelatorum vel aliarum personarum ecclesiasticarum, necnon percepciones procuracionum prelatis et aliquibus aliis in dignitatibus constitutis pertinencium. In quibus exaccionibus et oneribus, qui per modum perpetue servitutis imposita fuerunt, cadere non potest possessio neque prescripcio cuiuscunque temporis, eciam tanti de quo memoria non extaret. Quibus omnibus et servitutibus providere tenetur rex, et teneretur eciam scismate cessante, tanquam ecclesiarum gardiator et defensor principalis. Ad quam reduccionem debite libertatis inclinabuntur et ipsam sequentur cetere naciones, eciam obedientes intruso.

327

Tercio, quod non sufficit ad ecclesie pacem solidam totalem obedienciam ut supra denegare, nisi rescindantur abusiones et exacciones supradicte, que sunt nutritive scismatis, cause vel occasiones ambicionis dignitatis papatus adipiscende. Preterea, si per viam predictam cessionis vel alias scisma cessaret, nec esset provisum contra predictos abusus et extorciones, remaneret ecclesia Gallicana sub iugo perpetue servitutis. Non eciam sufficit rescindere predictos abusus, quod vocant aliqui substraccionem particularem, quoniam nisi unacum hoc denegaretur obediencia totalis, quousque papa viam cessionis acceptasset, ut supra, sibi remaneret exercicium sue potestatis, tam in iuridiccione quam aliis multis; per que, coloribus et viis obliquis exquisitis, pretextu criminum vel excessuum, gravare posset in immensum prelatos et alios viros ecclesiasticos regi subiectos, unionem ecclesie prosequentes; ex quibus infinita pericula et inconveniencia sequerentur.

Quarto, quod antequam prelati recedant, clarius practicetur modus per quem cristianitas unum verum summum pontificem solum et indubitatum habere poterit—scilicet, per modum tactum per dominum Patriarcham, deputando per regem et ecclesiam Gallicanam aliquos probos et litteratos viros, habentes per regem et ecclesiam Gallicanam plenam potestatem conveniendi cum aliis deputandis per principes et ecclesias ceterorum regnorum utriusque obediencie, sub equali numero, consimilem potestatem habituris, necnon duobus collegiis duorum contendencium, ad deliberandum, concludendum, et execucioni mandandum viam per huiusmodi deputandos et duo collegia determinandam ad habendum unicum summum pastorem, ut est dictum, ambobus contendentibus exclusis, nisi tamen ipsi contendentes in hac materia sic providerint, quod cristianitas habeat intentum—quod impossibile vel quasi reputandum videtur fieri posse per dictos contendentes aut alterum eorundem. Articulus autem iste plenius est pertractandus, et eius materia penes principes et prelatos utriusque obediencie per regem viriliter prosequenda; quoniam aliter supradicta parum prodessent.

Quinto, quod clarius advisetur et provideatur super inconvenienciis [sic] apertis per illos qui tenuerunt partem negativam. Scilicet, super perpetuis collacionibus iam factis, eleccionum et postulacionum beneficiorum reservacionibus, et in curia vacantibus, graciis infinitis per papam iam factis. Super quarum pluribus sunt publicati processus cum inhibicionibus, decretis, et sentenciis consuetis; licet videatur quod per ecclesie Gallicane reduccionem ad pristinam libertatem, tam propter acceleracionem unionis ecclesie quam propter bonum publicum, cessare debeant et cassa reputari omnia impedimenta que premissis obicem dare possent.

Sexto, quod in conclusione quam in hac materia rex acceptabit, multum expediret habere consensum dominorum cardinalium vel maioris partis eorundem, ac eciam principalium baronum huius regni, sic quod in futurum apparere posset regem in hac materia cum maturissima deliberacione processisse et ut conclusio firmiorem execucionem haberet—sine tamen dilacione conclusionis ex nunc per regem capiende.

Septimo, quod super quattuor punctis notabiliter ex parte regis per dominum cancellarium in audiencia publicatis, conficiantur littere regis tradende cuilibet postulanti, pro maiori libertate personarum et ecclesiarum conservanda.

Octavo, quod ordinaciones facte per regem super indebitis creacionibus novorum cardinalium, si tales nominari debeant, post obitum domini Clementis, et eciam de non recipiendis de novo promotis contra formam eleccionum vel postulacionum per capitula vel collegia factarum, diligencius solito firmiter observentur. Aliter enim vix creditur quod ordinaciones facte vel fiende per regem in hac materia debeant observari.

"On Subtraction of Obedience"

AN ENGLISH TRANSLATION

THIS IS an abridged translation with major omissions indicated; Part I is drastically condensed. References to the *Decretum* can be recognized by their form; the *Decretales* are indicated by "X"; other references are identified by name. Quotation marks indicate some of the more or less verbal quotations from the cited authorities. All headings and subdivisions are added; they correspond to those provided for the Latin text as edited in *DSO*, to which the reader is referred for detailed canonistic and historical commentary, as well as indices of proper names.

Apart from several independent references to St. Augustine (354–430) and St. Bernard of Clairvaux (1090–1153), most of the important sources and authorities cited (including biblical texts) are from the Roman law, the canon law, and their commentators. Gratian's *Decretum* of ca. 1141 became the standard collection of earlier papal decrees, acts of church councils, and passages from the fathers and the Bible—insofar as these were considered of interest to the canon law. Its *glossa ordinaria* ("ordinary gloss"—i.e., the standard commentary) was the work of Johannes Teutonicus in 1215–1217 and was revised by Bartholomeus Brixiensis ca. 1245. Other commentators on the *Decretum* cited here are Huguccio (d. 1210) and the Archdeacon (Guido de Baysio, d. 1313), whose work is called the *Rosarium*. The canon law after the *Decretum* was collected in the *Decretales* (or [*Liber*] *Extra*) of Pope Gregory IX (1234), the *Sext* (*Liber Sextus*, 1298), the *Clementines* (*Constituciones Clementine*, 1317), and two sets of *Extravagantes* which are not cited in this treatise. The *glossa ordinaria* on the *Decretales* was the work of Bernardus Parmensis (Bernard of Parma, d. 1266); that on the Sext was written by Johannes Andreas (or Andreae, d. 1348). The other chief commentaries cited here on the *Decretales* and subsequent collections were written by Innocent IV (d. 1254), Hostiensis (d. 1271), Johannes Andreas, Johannes Monachus (d. 1313), and Henricus de Bohic (d. 1350). The last-named was perhaps Simon's most-used author, for his work was a compilation of the commentaries of his chief predecessors.

The Roman law as codified under Justinian in the first part of the sixth century and, as studied in the medieval schools, consisted of the

Digest, the *Codex,* the *Institutes,* and the *Novels* (or *Authenticae*). The *glossa ordinaria* was by Accursius (ca. 1250).

Otherwise, the only important citations of authorities refer to the chronicle of Martin of Troppau (Martinus Oppaviensis), composed in the latter part of the thirteenth century and important as a compilation of much earlier work; the theological works of St. Thomas Aquinas (d. 1274); and the canonistic works of Pierre Bertrand (Petrus Bertrandi, d. 1349).

Introduction

"Be wise now therefore, O ye kings" (Psalms 2:10), which applies to the present case when the church is in such tribulation; for "every kingdom divided against itself is brought to desolation" (Luke 11:17). "And don't be put off by the prattle of men who say that" your royal power "persecutes when it represses bad actions or requires the salvation of souls. Persecution is coercion to evil; but it is evil that there be a schism, and men who make it ought to be oppressed by" your "powers" (23. q. 5, c. 42). For the "Crafty Enemy" has worked so that the church of God has been in schism for nineteen years: Italy, Hungary, Germany, England, and other nations hold that Boniface, now in Rome, is the true pope; while France, Scotland, Aragon, Navarre, Spain, and the original College of Cardinals adhere to lord Benedict who is now in Avignon. And there is so much doubt about this that the greatest clerics have been and still are of diverse opinions. . . . Thus the church militant "which is Christ's body and cannot be divided" (Augustine; 24. q. 1, c. 34) is lacerated so lamentably. "We must therefore check the Enemy's craft as far as we can, so that death not enter through our gates" (16. q. 2, c. 1), and this especially applies to kings, for as Isidore says (23. q. 5, c. 20), "He who has committed his church to their power will demand an accounting from them of whether peace in the church has been increased, namely by the faithful princes, or has been disrupted." . . .

With this in mind, the kings, especially the king of France, have assembled the leading men of their realms, interrogated them, and have found that the best and shortest way to eliminate the schism and unite the church is the way of cession or renunciation of both contenders for the papacy, with certain preliminary revocations of legal actions against each other and confirmations of promotions made by each—this to be followed at once by an election in due legal form of a future single and undoubted pastor. Since, however, one or both of the contenders have not accepted this way when formally requested to do so, there are many who now wonder how to proceed against the one or both not accepting, and one way proposed among others is that obedience be entirely subtracted from both contenders by both obediences, or by one obedience from the one who refuses cession. And since he betrays the truth who does not freely pronounce it, I, Simon de Cramaud, recently a Paris professor of canon law and now patriarch of Alexandria and administrator of the diocese of Carcassonne, have undertaken—at the command of the king of France, my natural lord in whose council I have long been retained—to set forth certain passages of law and dicta of the fathers which apply to the subject. I do not of course intend thereby to assert anything rashly or defend it stubbornly, nor to say anything injurious to lord Benedict; but I work only for the union of the lacerated church to which I and every Catholic am sworn in the first place, even before my oath to the pope (according to X. 2. 24. 4). Whatever I say, I submit to the correction of the holy Roman church and of my mother the University of Paris, and indeed of anyone who sees more clearly than I do.

I put the following questions. My first question is whether the kings and realms of both obediences can canonically subtract or entirely deny obedience to Boniface and lord Benedict if these two refuse to renounce the papacy. My second question is this: supposing that one of the obediences has been more diligent in seeking out the better *via* and has formally requested its pastor to accept the way of cession, and he has refused to accept it even on condition that the other contender would be willing to—can it in this case also canonically subtract obedience?

PART I: PROOF OF THE CONTRARY
That It Is Illicit to Subtract

(1) The pope is the head of the church militant, and the limbs cannot secede from the head. (2) The pope has his power and principate from God and not from men. Therefore whoever tries to take away the privilege granted to the Roman church by the supreme Head of all churches undoubtedly falls into heresy. A corollary would be that the way mentioned by some, namely that both contenders remain until one dies, with the survivor then elected as single pope, is the worst way; for there cannot be two heads in the church militant. (3) It is irrelevant to say that the pope keeps the papacy to the scandal and destruction of the church, for the law is that princes must be obeyed no matter what. (4) Even though it would be best to recognize a heavenly pope in case of notorious evil, obedience is not to be subtracted in a case that is merely doubtful, like this one. And compare the gloss of Innocent IV on X. 1. 6. 6, where he says that the pope must not be forced to renounce his rights. (5) A good part of Christendom says that the way of a general council is better and seems to reject the way of cession: see, for example, the letter of the University of Oxford. And many close to the pope say

that other ways should be tried before cession and that the conclave oath does not bind the pope to do otherwise. (6) An extraordinary remedy should not be applied as long as an ordinary one is available, and this is the case because Benedict has offered a way of arbitration—trustworthy men to be chosen by both parties to see who is rightful pope—and this would have the force of a general council, which is indeed *the* ordinary remedy; for as Johannes Teutonicus says in the ordinary gloss on the *Decretum* (79. di., c. 8; 15. di., c. 2), in those things which concern the faith and the status of the universal church, the pope is subject to a council. (7) How can we say that obedience should be subtracted from our lord the pope when he has publicly said that if he could only meet with his adversary, he would make peace in the church, even if he himself had to remain a poor priest without a benefice? (8) Since the inhabitants of the realm firmly believe that Benedict is true pope, the king should not order obedience to be subtracted from him, for he should not force his subjects to go against their consciences. (9) A forced renunciation would be as invalid as a forced election, which is what we objected to in 1378. (10) No one but God can judge the pope. (11) Not even partial subtraction may be made—that is, of collations and fiscal rights—because the pope has claimed these for himself and he is above all law to the contrary; he can do as he pleases. (12) Even if the king did command subtraction, if the pope commanded the contrary he would be the one to be obeyed. (13) In church matters the king must obey, not command. (14) A prelate must never be disobeyed as long as the church tolerates him.

That It Is not Fitting

(1a) If subtraction of obedience is illegal, then it is also not fitting for a king. (1b) The king should be constant in his opinion and his father's, that Clement and Benedict were and are legitimate popes. (2) People would say that the king wants to have a French pope, since he did not subtract obedience from the French Clement VII. (3) King Charles V did not subtract from Clement, and history indeed teaches that those popes supported by the kings of France always turned out to be the true ones.

That It Is not Expedient

(1) If obedience is subtracted, Benedict will excommunicate the king. (2) There will be no one to decide the cases reserved to papal dispensation and absolution. (3) The laity, ever hostile to the clergy, will more freely obstruct the church in her rights, will take over church property,

and heresies will proliferate. (4) Subtraction of obedience from the pope will lead to disobedience to the bishops and other prelates appointed by him; popular opinion will interpret subtraction as meaning that the pope was never legitimate. (5) Many graduates and others who look to the pope to provide benefices will not get them; prelates and perhaps princes will distribute benefices and will probably do it badly, also illegally. (6) There will be a lot of other unseemly consequences. (7) In any case, subtraction would not lead to union, for each contender would hole up in his strong places and keep the church in schism. (8) It is not expedient to proceed against the true pope in the same way as against the intruder.

PART II: FOR SUBTRACTION

Suppositions

On the contrary, subtraction of obedience from both contenders is allowed, fitting, and expedient. In support of this, I suppose first that the lamentable division now in the church, which subverts the status of the universal church and brings peril to innumerable souls, is so evident and manifest that nothing could be more so; furthermore that there is a strong presumption that both contenders have kept the church in this lamentable status for so long in order to serve themselves, not the church, seeking temporal benefits, riches, and human honors—and that when these come to an end, so will the schism and the contenders will more readily accept the way of peace. On the basis of this supposition I argue so: Even a true and undoubted pope is not to be obeyed but rather resisted if he does anything that notoriously scandalizes the church or works to the peril and subversion of souls. Much more so, therefore, these two contenders, each of whom would rather keep the church lacerated and truncated but his, than see it whole under the other. They thereby not only scandalize the church but utterly destroy it and in fact strive to keep the papacy to the very great scandal of the universal church, to the subversion and peril of innumerable souls. Much more are they to be resisted if they refuse to accept the way of cession which alone is deemed wholly apt to eradicate the schism.

The major premise is proven by dicta of popes Leo IV, Gregory I, and Sixtus II . . . (2. q. 7, c. 41; 25. q. 2, c. 4; 24. q. 1, c. 10). Hence it is that only two witnesses are needed to condemn the pope, although not so with other prelates; for when he does something tending to the destruction of the church, he is worse than all others "and is to be condemned like a devil, with no hope of pardon" (*De pen.*, di. 2, c. 45; ordinary gloss on 2. q. 4, c. 2). The doctors say therefore that in such matters the pope has no power against God, according to 25. q. 1, c. 6, as Hostiensis and Henricus de Bohic after him say, on X. 3. 8. 4, and also Hostiensis, Johannes Andreae, and Henricus after them, on X. 3. 34. 7. And it is proven by St. Paul, 2 Corinthians 10:8, where he says that the apostolic power is for edification, not destruction. The point is confirmed by Pierre Bertrand on *Clem.* 1. 3. 2, where he says that if a pope does anything that scandalizes the church—for example, if he should try to give all or a large part of the church's patrimony to his relatives—he should be resisted to his face, as Paul resisted Peter (Gal. 2:11; in 2. q. 7, c. 33). How much more in our case, for which see 12. q. 2, c. 20, and what Johannes says in the ordinary gloss on 40. di., c. 6—that a pope thus scandalizing the church and warned to stop, if he does not stop is to be regarded as a heretic, for contumacy is heresy (81. di., c. 15). Note that nothing in this should offend the kings and temporal lords who do not recognize a superior; for Christ said to the apostles (Matt. 20:25 f.): Kings exercise dominion, but not so among you! And St. Bernard to Pope Eugenius III: "The Roman church is the mother of all churches, not their mistress, and you should not consider yourself the lord of the bishops but rather one of them."

The minor premise is clear, for if this resistance is allowed in the case of an undoubted pope, much more in the case of these two contenders who strive to keep the papacy to the scandal of the universal church and the subversion of the status of the church and the peril of faithful souls. For obviously if we keep obeying ours as pope and the others keep obeying Boniface, the church is not only enormously scandalized but lacerated and wholly destroyed. Johannes Andreae is much to the point here when he writes (*Novella,* on X. 5. 39. 44) that if the pope should command anything that would presumably disturb the status of the church, or that would give rise to other evils too, then he should not be obeyed—indeed it would be a sin to do so; and he cites Innocent IV who was a pope and Hostiensis who was a cardinal, and they cite X. 3. 34. 7 and X. 5. 27. 8. . . . Note too that he about whose jurisdiction there is doubt should not attempt to exercise it, X. 1. 3. 24. And I infer that neither of the contenders should feel so secure about his rights that, the case being what it is, he would not have good reason to doubt. . . . For in our case, Christendom is divided and major clerics are of different opinions. And this is how we have to understand what Johannes Teutonicus writes in his ordinary gloss on 24. q. 1, § *Quod autem,* where he says that if two are elected to the papacy and each one of them thinks he has the church in himself, perhaps neither is a schismatic: he never meant it for a case like this one. This is clear from what he himself says on 63. di., c. 36: that when there are two elected and a notable scandal arises from their election, neither should remain. What Johannes had in mind was that when two are elected to the papacy and there is doubt at first about the election but each thinks he is in the right, then perhaps neither is a schismatic; but when they see that there is great scandal on account of their election, then such a belief may not excuse them.

I further suppose that the kings are obliged under pain of mortal sin to put an end to this schism and bend all their forces to obtain peace in the church—and that they are obliged both as private men and as kings. . . . Also: kings have the power by both canon and divine law to compel both contenders to the way of peace; therefore if they do not do so they sin mortally. The major premise is proved by Augustine, . . . "It pertains to the Christian kings of this world that they seek in their time to keep their mother the church in peace" (23. q. 4, c. 39). For just as God ordained the sun and the moon to establish the firmament, so to establish the church militant he ordained the sacerdotal dignity and the royal power (X. 1. 33. 6); and: there are two things by which the world is ruled, the sacred authority of the pontiffs and the royal power (96. di., c. 10). And while the royal power is the lesser in respect to the priestly power when that is well ordered, it nevertheless uses its sword within the church to exalt the good and punish the evil (1 Pet. 2:14). And rightly so, for the church militant is nothing but the congregation of the faithful here on earth, which is to be ruled, regulated, and disposed by the decrees of the holy fathers and the laws divinely promulgated by the mouths of the princes (8. di., c. 1). Furthermore, according to the old laws, kings used to judge delinquent clerics (11. q. 1, c. 45; 16. q. 7, c. 31; ordinary gloss on X. 2. 1. 17), and they can still do so today when ecclesiastical power fails, as Johannes Teutonicus notes in the ordinary gloss on 23. q. 5, c. 20. Saint Isidore proves it most clearly when he says (23. q. 5, c. 20): "The princes of this world sometimes hold the highest offices of power within the church in order to use it to reinforce ecclesiastical discipline. Powers indeed would not be needed within the church except to command by the terror of discipline what priests are unable to accomplish by the word of teaching. The heavenly kingdom often benefits from the earthly one, as when those within the church who act against faith and discipline are crushed by the rigor of princes. Let the princes of this world know that they must render an account to God for the church whose protection they have taken over from Christ!" May the kings only hear how this canon speaks to them! And Augustine says (23. q. 5, c. 42): "Many things have to be done by means of a benignly harsh coercion of the unwilling, whose benefit rather than desire is to be taken into account." The minor premise is proven by the comments of the doctors Bernardus and Hostiensis on X. 1. 29. 1, and Henricus de Bohic, dist. 2 on X. 5. 12. 6, where they say that crass negligence of a judge in providing when he is obliged to provide is a grave sin.

I infer as a corollary that even if the kings have not been requested to do so, they must work with all their force for the peace of the church; otherwise they are not excused from sin. This is supported by the doctors, including Bernardus in the ordinary gloss on the Decretals, Innocent, and Johannes Andreae (all cited by Henricus de Bohic on X. 2. 1. 10), saying that if a secular judge sees a cleric *in flagranti delicto,* he can arrest him without fear of excommunication, even if he has not been requested to do so by the bishop.

Theses

On the basis of these suppositions I argue that kings are bound and obliged to inquire diligently what should be done in this all-but-insoluble problem and to hold to the order laid down by canon law according to the commentaries of Huguccio and the Archdeacon on 20. di., c. 3: namely, "first to refer to the New and Old Testaments, second to the canons of the apostles or of the councils, third to the decretals of the Roman popes, next to the writings of the holy fathers of the Latin church, finally to the examples of the saints." I therefore argue so: according to the Old and New Testaments, the decrees of the councils and of the popes, kings cannot tolerate a schism without offending God; therefore they can and must subtract obedience from both contenders who do not accept the way of peace that has been offered to them duly and advisedly. The major premise is proven by the foregoing. The minor is proven by *Digest,* 2. 1. 2: he who has jurisdiction has whatever is necessary to it; also *Digest,* 3. 3. 56, 3. 3. 62, 23. 1. 16. There is excellent corroboration from the doctors cited by Bohic on X. 2. 1. 10, where they say that when a punishment is to be inflicted for contumacy, the first step should be suspension; then as malice increases, further steps should be taken.

Also, according to the New Testament and the decrees of the fathers, neither of the two should remain in the papacy; therefore the kings may subtract obedience from them. The major premise is proven by Matthew 20:26 f., and cf. Augustine in 19. di., c. 6. Furthermore, according to the decrees of the holy fathers, when two are elected to the papacy and the election is perhaps irregular—that is, when there is well-founded doubt about which election was canonical and which not (for the word "perhaps" denotes doubt about law and fact)—then neither should remain: in 79. di., c. 8 (*Si duo forte contra fas*). And especially so when a notable scandal arises from the doubt about the election, as Johannes Teutonicus expressly states in the ordinary gloss on 63. di., c. 36. The minor premise is apparent from what has been said, for the kings are bound to make provision, etc., by the duty of their office, and subtraction of obedience is a canonical provision, as has been said. This is so also because while one may proceed judicially against one who has a superior, by going before his judge, one has to proceed by force against those who seek to usurp the papacy against the sacred canons, as stated in 3. q. 1, § *Patet,* and cf. X. 1. 6. 6, at the end. Also, when it is essential that only one have the right, as in our case, and two struggle for it with so much uncertainty about their respective rights that it is unclear which of them in fact has the right, then they check each other by the struggle so that neither should have it: *Digest,* 34. 5. 10, 34. 5. 27, 26. 2. 30; compare Johannes Monachus on *Sext,* 1. 6. 2. These are rational provisions of the legislators, for it is better that neither have it than that one have it because of uncertainty who would otherwise not have the right. And that the church militant is itself uncertain which of the two contenders has the right is apparent from the diversity of opinions of those who have written on both sides.

Nor is there anyone to judge the matter. A council cannot do so, for the greater part of Christendom, especially of the bishops, holds with the one in Rome and almost all of them have been promoted by him; thus the question involves their own status and consequently they cannot be judges. This is even truer of them than of the original cardinals who took part in both elections of 1378, who however are excluded for this reason from judging in this case by Johannes Teutonicus's ordinary gloss on the *Decretum,* 79. di., c. 8, an opinion unshakably accepted by those who obey Boniface. And the same is to be said of those who obey Benedict, namely that they cannot judge. Thus neither a council nor the cardinals will judge in this case. And still less arbiters, for reasons to be given below. Furthermore, although our side does not lack the right, it lacks the ability to prove it, for the other side will not admit the testimony of the cardinals who were present at both elections. And for other reasons too, the doubt in this schism is so intricate, and there is so much uncertainty on the part of the church militant as a whole, that neither should remain. One can see from all this, moreover, that Gratian never meant his § *Hoc autem* after 79. di., c. 8, to apply to so dubious and controversial a case (although if it *were* clear that one of the two in a double election had been intruded by force and apostasy, the other canonically elected, then the chapter *Si quis pecunia,* 79. di., c. 9, would apply, along with what Gratian says there).

Supposing on the other hand that the election of one of the two was not irregular but just, holy, and canonical; even so, the true pope would be obligated to resign, according to canonical sanctions and the pronouncements of the holy doctors, because of the malicious ill will of the people or in order to allay a grave scandal; therefore if he does not resign it is allowed to subtract obedience. The major premise is proved by the chapter *Nisi cum pridem,* X. 1. 9. 10, § 5. *Propter maliciam,* and § 6. *Pro gravi quoque scandalo,* which is binding on the pope inasmuch as the argument of the chapter is based on divine law, which undoubtedly binds the pope, according to 25. q. 1, c. 6. As Augustine has said, we are not bishops for our own sake but for the sake of those to whom we administer the word and sacrament of the Lord. . . . The minor premise is proved by the first argument of this part, where it is said that even a true pope is not to be obeyed in those things by which the universal church is scandalized and which work to the subversion and peril of souls. Indeed in such matters the heavenly pope is to be recognized, as Bohic notes after others *ad* X. 3. 8. 4 and X. 3. 34. 7.

Furthermore, divine and canon law clearly show that a true pope is bound to resign to allay so great a scandal, for nothing is ever to be done which actively gives scandal, as the theologians say, especially St. Thomas Aquinas. And there are many who have no doubt that the present scandal was actively given, for did not the cardinals after electing Bartholomew, allegedly under intimidation, write to many that they had made a canonical election? Were they not with him for a long time; did they not show him reverence, supplicate for benefices, etc., as many say? And while these do not give a right in the papacy to someone elected by intimidation, nevertheless they give occasion of scandal. And to allay a scandal it is obligatory to avoid everything that can be avoided without mortal sin (X. 5. 32. 2); therefore the papacy is to be given up for this reason, for God knows it can well be given up without mortal sin—according to *Sext,* 1. 7. 1. Nor can it be said that this is a scandal only to the Pharisees—which was in matters of faith, in which it is better to let scandal arise than to abandon the truth. In our case, however, in which it is a question merely of the presidency of this or that person, a prelate can be forced to resign—not only because of likely or arguable scandal but even because of mere malice, as when men are strongly opposed to a prelate and the church's welfare can be secured under another (X. 1. 9. 10, §§ 5, 6, as cited above; also 7. q. 1, c. 34).
. . . A pope moreover who is bound to resign to allay scandal and who does not resign when requested violates canons founded on divine law and mortally offends God, according to 25. q. 1, c. 5, and this also seems to be the opinion of Innocent IV on X. 1. 4, the Archdeacon on 25. q. 1, c. 5, and Johannes Andreae and Johannes Monachus on *Sext,* 1. 6. 13. Especially so in the present case, where the scandal and peril to souls are so great; whatever may be said, it seems that the contenders who try to keep the papacy against the sacred canons do so because of greed and ambition, and this is the case covered by Innocent IV cited above. For confirmatory opinions see Johannes Teutonicus's ordinary gloss on 2. q. 7, c. 8, where he says that subjects can withdraw from the

obedience of a prelate who does not observe the canons; also Huguccio on 81. di., c. 15, and compare 16. q. 7, c. 15; also the Archdeacon on 23. q. 1, c. 4, where he says that subjects are not to obey one who seeks to keep official power uncanonically—which is to be understood as applying especially to those who seek to keep the papacy against the canons. Therefore they are not to be obeyed; indeed obedience is to be entirely subtracted from them by the kings, who otherwise would sin mortally just as the contenders do. . . .

Schism and Heresy

Those moreover who seek to keep the papacy against the sacred canons are true schismatics, as Innocent IV seems to say on X. 5. 39. 1, where he says that they are schismatics who do not observe the constitutions of the church and thereby divide the church. . . . Indeed by the same reason that one is called a schismatic when he intrudes himself into the papacy against the sacred canons, one is also called a schismatic who seeks to keep the papacy against the sacred canons, according to X. 2. 13. 18, where the text states that entering evilly and keeping evilly are the same; and see 12. q. 2, c. 21, which equates these three: to take a church unjustly, to possess it unjustly, or to try to stay in it by unjust defense. Therefore they are not to be obeyed but rather resisted by force, and indeed harsher measures are to be taken against them. . . . Some scholars go on to infer from the above, and perhaps correctly, that although Boniface and his adherents have always said that Benedict and his adherents are schismatics, and Benedict the same about Boniface, and it is true of one of them—nevertheless, today it is more clear that both are schismatics than has ever been clear about one of them. For both are bound to resign to allay the scandal, and if they do not, after being formally requested, they are true schismatics, as we have said. And this is undoubtedly clearer to the universal church than which of them is the true pope and which the intruder.

Not only are they schismatics, they are heretics; for "there can be no schism without heresy," as Johannes Teutonicus comments on 24. q. 1; compare Jerome in 24. q. 3, c. 26, with the Archdeacon's comments: "He who persists in schism makes a heresy" (cf. 7. q. 1, c. 9; 24. q. 1, c. 31). That is, the opinion of those who say that they are not bound to resign for the peace and union of the church, and who thus keep the church divided in schism, is heretical. . . . And many suppose that these two do incomparably more damage to the church by their stubborn opinion than would be done by one who held a heretical doctrine.

All of which leads clearly to the following: First, he who believes he is true pope but in fact is not, and by holding his belief for a long time keeps the church in this protracted schism, is not excused from schism or heresy because of his belief. . . . Second, if the two contenders persist in refuting the way of cession publicly or secretly, they are excommunicated as heretics by the canon *Ad abolendam* (X. 5. 7. 9) (this is the case noted by Johannes Teutonicus on 24. q. 1, c. 1, where the pope falls under a sentence already laid down in a canon) and consequently cannot excommunicate anyone or pronounce any other sentence (ordinary gloss on 24. q. 1). (And therefore many say that the University of Paris and others pursuing the way of cession do not have to worry about the legal actions taken by lord Benedict or by Boniface.) Some, furthermore, go on to infer something else: namely, that these two pertinaciously refusing the way of cession or delaying unduly to accept it incur or merit the following penalties: a sentence of excommunication ipso facto, as noted; then deposition, deprivation of all property, coercion by armed force, and delivery to the secular court, according to the canons; but according to divine law, fire and burning to death! (This last is proved by the words of the Lord, John 15:6, "If a man abide not in me, he will be cast forth and withered, and men will collect him and cast him into the fire," etc.) Hostiensis notes this in his *Summa,* "On Heretics," "Punishments," and Henricus de Bohic on X. 5. 7. 9. (Perhaps this is what Johannes de Moravia had in mind when he preached during the time of Clement VII that both should be killed.)

In any case, according to canonized law, it is permitted to subtract obedience because "those who refuse to serve in peace the Author of peace should not possess anything in the name of the church," nor can they say of the kings subtracting obedience in this case, "What has the king to do with me?"—Augustine in 8. di., c. 1. And again Augustine, to Pope Boniface I (23. q. 4, c. 24): "Let them not complain because they are coerced, but rather consider why they are coerced."

Subtract Revenues

It is permitted to subtract obedience from them also and especially in those things which they get from the church against the disposition of law, like the first annates of vacant benefices (which according to *Sext,* 1. 16. 9, should be applied to the utility of the benefice or reserved to a future successor to it) and the common rights to procurations (which are owed in return for visitations, according to X. 2. 26. 16) and similar things. As St. Bernard wrote to Pope Eugenius III, the Roman church is the mother of other churches but not their mistress. The Archdeacon, on 12. di., c. 1, quotes many authorities (St. Thomas, Innocent IV, Hostiensis) in this sense: thus, "although the property of the church is the pope's as principal dispenser, it is not his as lord or possessor." The

Archdeacon also cites Hostiensis and Innocent IV on X. 3. 49. 8, 1. 2. 7, to the effect that if any prince should issue a decree against natural law, for example, that one man's domains be transferred to another without just cause, such a decree is not to be observed in either the forum of the soul or the civil court; for the same principles and many other authorities, see Henricus de Bohic on X. 1. 29. 13. Perhaps indeed a pope imposing such exactions on the churches is held to make restitution twofold, so that "he may come under the law that he himself has made"—X. 3. 39. 23; compare 1. 2. 6, and Hostiensis on X. 3. 49. 8. Nor is a sentence given by him to be feared in such a matter, as Johannes Teutonicus notes on 11. q. 3, c. 1. Thus, while the pope has plenitude of power in respect to all ecclesiastical goods, both temporal and spiritual, he does not have it as lord but as minister and dispenser of the principal Lord, and his dispensing of such goods should be done only in those respects which would seem to be in accord with the will of the principal Lord (11. q. 3, c. 67). And if all this applies to an indubitable pope, how much more to these two contenders who are so dubious to the church militant and who, it seems likely, keep us so embroiled for the sake of such trivial things! Since they are against the peace of the church, they should be stripped of their office and also of their own property—according to 24. q. 1, c. 32. Therefore obedience can be subtracted from them in these matters according to the laws cited in the immediately preceding argument, which hold that those notoriously violating the canons are not to be obeyed.

Furthermore, if anyone who is excommunicated because of contumacy or otherwise stays under his sentence for a year, he is deemed suspect in faith, as Hostiensis says, and after him Henricus de Bohic and others, on X. 5. 7. 13, citing X. 5. 37. 13. How much more does this apply to those who have kept the church in this schism now for nineteen years, with the issues so controversial and dubious that the greatest clerics are of diverse opinions—one of them excommunicates the other, anathematizes him and his adherents, etc., and the sentences are ignored. It is therefore not only permissible to subtract obedience from such; it is necessary on pain of suspicion of heresy and favoring heresy: X. 5. 7. 16.

Fraternal Correction

Another reason why it is permitted to the kings to subtract obedience from both is that, according to Matthew 18:15–17, "If thy brother shall trespass against you, go and tell him his fault, . . . but if he will not hear thee, then take with thee one or two more, . . . and if he shall neglect to hear them, tell it unto the church; but if he will still not hear, let him be unto thee as an heathen man and a publican." According to Hostiensis as cited by Henricus de Bohic on X. 2. 20, 4, this authority is a precept not only for officials but for all, insofar as it refers to a caritative act (cf. 24. q. 3, c. 14). . . . Therefore if the kings and lords of both obediences have supplicated and requested their respective popes, humbly and mildly, to accept the way of cession or some other equally good one if such can be found ("if" here means no!); and seeing that this has done no good, if they then tell it to the church, that is the cardinals, who in this matter perhaps represent the church well enough (see Pierre Bertrand's *Apparatus* on the *Sext, prohemium,* where he says that in electing a pope the cardinals represent the universal church); and if the kings and princes have also told it to the prelates of their realms whose counsel they have taken on this—and if they still see that all this does not help: what is left? Evidently what is said at the end of the quoted authority, namely, that the kings and princes should regard the contenders as heathens and publicans, and therefore subtract obedience from them according to Ephesians 5:11: "Have no fellowship with the unfruitful works of darkness, but rather reprove them." And it does not invalidate this to say that the precept in question is an affirmative one that is binding only in place and time of necessity; where has there ever been a greater case of necessity of such correction than here?

Let us see now if the six conditions noted by the doctors [which make correction an affirmative precept with obligatory execution in time of necessity] are present in this respect in the persons of the kings. The doctors say that three things must be present in the one who corrects: certain knowledge of the sin, mildness in correction, and that no one else be more fitted for the task. Let anyone see if these three are not indeed present in the kings, princes, and major prelates! Then there are three things on the part of those to be corrected: hope of correction, that the sin be mortal and not venial, no hope of some other time more suited to correction. These three also are present today, most evidently. Is it not likely that the two contenders have kept us embroiled so long because of the obedience given to them, which gives them so abundantly the goods of the Crucified and lets them enrich themselves and their men? Subtract the obedience, and the desire and lust for lordship will cease, and they will thus be induced to abdicate for the peace and union of the church. As for the other two, the sin is obviously mortal from what has been proven above, . . . and when will there ever be a better opportunity than now, when the Holy Spirit has visited the hearts of men, so that all clamor for the church's peace and for the way of cession by both contenders. Hence it is quite clear that the kings, princes, and major prelates who have kept to the form of the evangelical precept in Matthew 18:15–17 are bound by precept to subtract obedience.

Nor may it be argued that this text does not apply in the case of a

subject vis-à-vis his superior: this is false, especially in regard to a pope
(2. q. 7, c. 33). And although Johannes Andreae says (on X. 3. 8. 4)
that this text does not apply to the pope, it does in our case when God is
so notoriously offended, for as he himself says at the end of his gloss, in
such a case, papal power ceases and the heavenly pope is to be recognized. . . . On the other hand, the text does not apply to kings, as some
say, opening the way to rebellion at will, for according to Matthew
20:25–26, "Kings exercise dominion, but not so among you." And, as
proven above, the pope is not the lord of the church but its dispenser.
Finally, if we say, as many believe, that it pertains to the kings' office to
reduce these contenders to peace and union (see 23. q. 5, c. 20), then it
is perfectly clear that Matthew 18:15–17 is a precept for them and that
they sin mortally if they do not observe it (see Innocent IV and Johannes
Monachus, as cited by Bohic on X. 2. 20. 4).

And if it be said that the kings cannot correct the papal contenders
unless the latter have been convicted, according to 2. q. 1, c. 1, and
they have not been, I say that, given the notoriety of the case in respect
to both law and fact, no other conviction is required, according to X. 5.
1. 9, with Bohic's and others' comments on it; also 2. q. 1, c. 17—and
especially because in the present case there is no superior before whom a
judicial action could be brought: X. 1. 6. 6. In any case, in this present
difficulty we should guide ourselves by the examples of the holy fathers
who issued the sacred canons and who introduced the remedy of cessation and interdict against magnates from whom one could not otherwise
obtain due satisfaction. Thus canons can use the remedy of cessation of
services against a prelate in order to bring him more readily to what is
right; also the lands of a prince can be interdicted because of his deeds;
also the cardinals who might keep the church embroiled without a
pastor are constrained to make an election by deprivation of victuals and
by being locked up in a strait place: Sext, 1. 6. 3. Thus kings, who have
canonical power against disturbers of the peace in the church, can proceed
to subtraction of obedience and indeed to worse—the important thing is
not what is done but why it is done (ordinary gloss, 23. q. 4, c. 24).

Benedict Must Obey a Council of His Obedience

Also, a council of the bishops who obey Benedict or of those obeying
Boniface constitutes a general council in respect to either. The point is
that if the bishops obeying Benedict, or the greater part of them,
canonically congregated in council, should decide that he is obligated to
resign, he would be bound to do so; for in this matter he is subject to a
general council as Johannes Teutonicus, glosser of the Decretum, says on
15. di., c. 2, where he writes that in matters of faith or matters which

concern the status of the universal church, the pope is subject to a council because the world's authority is greater than that of the City (as Jerome puts it in 93. di., c. 24). . . . Therefore, since the prelates of the realms of France and Spain, congregated by their kings—albeit separately—and undoubtedly composing the major part of lord Benedict's obedience, have indeed decreed that the pope is obligated to resign, their ordinance is that of his judge and it binds him; so that if, in case of his refusal, they say that obedience should be subtracted or that more rigorous measures should be taken against him, the kings should execute these decisions (according to *Digest,* 6. 1. 68; cf. 11. q. 3, c. 86). If indeed one considers how general councils have been celebrated previously, the council just mentioned [i.e., the First Paris Council, February 1395] should indeed be considered not only general but duly and formally so. Pope Benedict wrote the king of France asking for counsel on how to end the schism; the king decided to convoke and consult all the prelates of his realm and so informed Benedict, who wrote back that he approved of this and indeed ordered the prelates of the realm residing in Avignon to attend. And all but perhaps a very few agreed that the way of cession of both contenders was the only way to fully end the schism, that the king was to present this counsel to the pope, and that if Benedict refused, the king should put this way into effect by all possible canonical means. All but one of the Avignon cardinals were also of this view, and they so informed the king. And after the conclusion of this counsel-taking, the king of France informed the king of Castile of it so that the latter might join in, should he think this way to be reasonable; the French ambassadors indeed presented all the reasons for the way of cession in the presence of the king of Castile, of the pope's envoys, and of many weighty prelates, masters, doctors, and barons of the realm. The king of Castile then, after much deliberation, concluded in effect as the council of France had done. At the same time, the king of France informed those of Aragon and Navarre of his decision, which they publicly and officially heard, also the king of Scotland; and after they have refused to take up the canonical way of union in the church, all power in this matter remains with the two kings of France and Castile—one supposes, on analogy with the cardinals (in *Sext,* 1. 6. 3) or with the canons of a chapter in similar situations. In any case, the realms of France and Castile have most if not indeed two-thirds of the prelates of this obedience. Anyone can see, then, how the cause of union has been generally counseled in our obedience especially and how such a council can well be called general.

It is true, to be sure, that the prelates of the whole obedience have not met together, also that the pope has neither been summoned nor heard, nor has he given his authority to the conclusion just referred to. But these objections do not hold. First of all, there have been many valid general councils in the church of God where there were not as many participants as in the First Paris Council, where there were 110 persons plus the University of Paris; and this effect of a general council is not cancelled by the inability of those of Spain to meet with us on account of the great distance and the diversity of realms (today indeed there is no unified empire). . . . I add, moreover, that the king of England has adhered to our view and that the Electors of the Empire have formally requested Boniface to accept the way of peace (I have seen his response and can testify that it is bad, not that of a true pastor). It thus seems clear enough that if the Electors and other prelates of Germany join us in the way of cession, they and we are the greater part of both obediences and can therefore compel both contenders to resign by subtraction of obedience. And as for Benedict's not having been summoned, a summons is not necessary in a case of notoriety (X. 5. 1. 9, and the comments thereon by Bohic after others). Anyway both Benedict and Boniface have been requested and heard, Benedict refusing the way of cession and offering only the way of a conference of both contenders, to which he later added the way of arbitration, while Boniface neither accepted nor even proposed any way of union except that we be reduced to his obedience—and God knows that we will stay as we are until the end of the world before obeying him! Thus it is clear that neither has to be summoned any further. Nor is their authority necessary in this sort of council, because no one's authorization is required in a case concerning himself (*Institutes*, 1. 21, § *Si autem; Codex*, 6. 61. 8, § *Necessitate*). I know that 17. di., § *Hinc eciam* after c. 6, provides the contrary, but this is taken care of by the fact that Benedict approved the king's calling of a council and that the pope's envoys were present at the council called in Castile. In any case, the pope's authority is not necessary for a council in a matter concerning the faith, and although it is not a matter of faith to say that this one is pope and that one is not, nevertheless it is a matter of faith that we have one pope, as proven above. There have indeed been many councils called without papal authority (15. di., c. 1), especially when there have been two contenders. . . .

Subtraction Is Fitting and Expedient

It is not only allowed to subtract obedience; it is also fitting that the kings do so. For there is nothing that so adorns a prince as a peaceful people and a harmonious senate and a whole commonwealth marked by decent habits; nor is there anything so fitting for a prince as to take care for the true dogmas of God and the decency of the priests: see *Novels*, 6, 8, 114; also the dicta of Gregory, Cassiodorus, Augustine, Cicero; compare 2. q. 1, c. 21.

And it is also expedient to subtract obedience and provide otherwise for ending this lamentable schism, for the sake of the common utility which is always to be preferred, just as the greater utility to the lesser (this is the actual sense of the word *expedient* as noted by Hostiensis, Johannes Andreae, and Bohic after them on X. 3. 34. 7; see also X. 1. 5. 3)—if we consider the scandals, irreparable evils, the peril of subversion of the whole Christian faith, which have resulted from this schism in the past nineteen years. . . . It is expedient then—so that innumerable souls not perish, that Christ's faith not collapse, that the church not be totally destroyed—to seek out the peace of the church and pursue it by all ways; and the kings, who are bound to this by the duty of their office, have to consider diligently by what ways they can bring these two contenders to the way of peace that has been counseled. This is their judicial office in its fullest extent—*Digest,* 2. 1. 1. So too the Archdeacon notes on 11. q. 1, c. 50, that a judge should use a remedy by means of which the parties will be worn out and probably come more quickly to the way of peace. He goes on to say that when a judge sees the parties not trying to come to the way of peace but rather resorting to force, he can take the revenues of the contested property into his control or sequestrate them; he cites the *Digest,* 7. 1. 17, 22. 3. 20; also X. 1. 3. 24, and others. The Archdeacon believes that this holds indubitably in a case involving a benefice, as he sets it forth there. And how much more so in our case, in which it has been solemnly concluded that both contenders are bound to abdicate, so that they would seem to have a sentence passed against them; thus sequestration would apply, according to *Clem.* 2. 6. 1. It is indeed a fact that neither of the contenders has enjoyed peaceful possession up to now. In any case, even if these laws do not speak formally of the papacy, in this case which is so difficult and unprecedented we have to proceed from like to like: as indeed the Archdeacon implies on 11. q. 1, c. 50, where he says that when a judge cannot do what the law enjoins, he should make such provision as he can.

Another reason why it would seem to be most expedient to subtract obedience from both contenders is that as long as they are allowed to enjoy the livings they do, each of them will stubbornly regard himself as pope and use or abuse the papacy, as they have done for nineteen years. But if the fruits of the church are entirely withdrawn from them and obedience is denied them, they will come to the way of cession by which we will have peace now. . . . Obedience will likely lead to the total destruction of the church, but non-obedience to its restoration. And here there is one point that some have prudently raised, namely, that in order to avoid the evils that have come from obedience as well as the evils that might come from non-obedience, still harsher measures should be taken against them right now. And this would seem to be supported by some of the reasons set forth above, about their being schismatics and heretics. But in spite of this it seems more expedient first of all to subtract revenues; although I must confess that if subtraction of obedience does not lead them to correct themselves, then more effective measures would have to be taken without too much delay.

It would also seem most expedient to withdraw the collation of benefices from both of them, especially of the greater benefices, for that is clearly the fuel and food of the schism. They put men who favor them into the prelacies, and some who had sound views before their promotion change because of the benefice they have received. If indeed Pope Clement, who created almost all the prelates of his obedience, were still alive, many would perhaps not speak so pure-mindedly about the matter as they do; for we are only human and favor interferes with human judgement. Benefices and expectative graces are given out primarily in the intention that those who get them will not want obedience to be subtracted. What more is there to say? . . .

One Side Should Subtract Even without the Other

I infer as a corollary that whichever side has requested its man formally to accept the way of peace should subtract obedience from him if he refuses, even if the other side does not. For if, as argued above, both of them keep the church embroiled against the canons and damnably make a schism, the same applies to each of them. Another point is that he who refuses after having been requested commits a crime that calls for his deposition, for this is the penalty of going against the canons in so great a matter (§ *Hec etsi legibus,* after 4. di., c. 6). Thus no further admonition is necessary, as Johannes Teutonicus expressly notes in his gloss on the *Decretum,* 12. q. 2, c. 2, also the Archdeacon on 23. q. 4, c. 11, citing 81. di., c. 8. . . . Also, each side is more bound to work with its own man—it has better opportunities and is more apt to succeed. . . . Thus it is clear that one side is permitted to subtract obedience even if the other does not. I argue further that it is also fitting to do so and expedient. It is fitting that the kings who have been requested to subtract, wholly or in part, do so, for such a request imposes a deadline on them so that they would be responsible for the loss of faithful souls who perish and will perish because of the schism, unless God prevent it. . . . Here, too, the reasons applying to subtraction from both also prove it is fitting to subtract from one. And it is also expedient, for the following reasons. First, if we wait for the others and they wait for us, there will be no end, and we will drift into the prejudice or indeed total destruction of the church, a sort of vagueness and inaction that the laws prohibit in regard to even one single church or person

(*Sext,* 1. 5. 1; *Codex,* 7. 14. 5). Also, we can believe with some probability that after the kings of one obedience or even one of them begins to put his hand to the remedy of subtraction of obedience and other steps, the other kings will all do likewise for they will see that the proceedings are sound, just, and canonical. . . . In any case, since we are obligated to bring the two contenders to the way of peace, it is expedient to work without delay on the one and on the other, and if not with the one then at least with the other; for if we have the consent of one of them, we will have half of peace, and the whole burden of schism will then be on the shoulders of the one not accepting. And one can be reduced to acceptance easier than both, and the remedies would be easier.

There are some who object that "even though your reasons prove that obedience should be subtracted in order to secure union, what if ours agrees to resign on condition that the other do, too (for this way has been neither discussed nor counseled otherwise than so), but the other refuses: you will not have union. To subtract obedience from just one will then have no effect and therefore should not be done." The answer appears from what is said above, but I will add that to remain with such generalities is to perpetuate the schism; for if we say that we will not subtract because this will not bring union, so will the other side and we will stay as we are forever. Our man can say, "It is not my fault; go to the other one," and the other the same, so that their malice will keep us embroiled as we have been for nineteen years. Of course I concede that it would be better if God willed that all kings would proceed unanimously to subtraction of obedience and other canonical remedies; but this does not seem likely inasmuch as some of them are lukewarm about it, even though they have been formally and solemnly exhorted by the king of France.

There are also many who say, "The side which subtracted, without the other side doing so, would remain headless, and there would ensue the damages and difficulties that usually happen when the apostolic see is vacant (see *Sext,* 1. 6. 3, 1. 6. 6)." The answer is that it is a question of alternative sets of difficulties: one is that if no remedy be applied to the schism, it will last forever and the church will be totally destroyed; the other is that just mentioned. In such a case, the holy doctors have decreed that the lesser difficulty be chosen (13. di., c. 2). Which is the lesser: to remain as we are without a remedy, or to be without a pope for a while? Furthermore, if the one from whom obedience be subtracted comes to accept the way of cession, we will have what we want—half of peace—and as soon as he consents, his side will obey him until both resign, and it will be safe from any stain of schism. Or, he will not come to the way of peace after subtraction but will stick to his own opinion; in that case, many say that it would not be advisable to simply stay in subtraction of obedience but rather go on forcefully to other things until he gives his consent, even under coercion. In any case, it would perhaps be more expedient not to have anyone than to have two in such a schism. Note that there is a part of Christendom which has not obeyed either of the contenders for nineteen years, and yet they get on well.

If the above should seem inadequate, then the means advised by the University of Paris may be used: namely, first of all, that collations to benefices, exactions of procurations, the first annates of vacant benefices, etc.—which are against the disposition of common law—be subtracted from both of them, or one of them, and afterwards proceed further.

PART III: REPLY TO THE CONTRARY ARGUMENTS
Reply to "It Is not Allowed"

(1, 2) The first two arguments are taken care of by our proof that even a true and undoubted pope who does something that notoriously scandalizes the church should not be obeyed but rather resisted. As the ordinary gloss on the *Decretum* says, such a one can be accused if he refuse to correct himself after being warned; and this is to be understood in terms of legal action, namely, that if the crime be notorious, the pope can be punished without accusation (X. 5. 1. 9). The chronicles tell that this was done against a pope, John XII, and Ockham in his *Dialogus* cogently proves that it was done canonically. As for our case: either both contenders should not remain, according to *Si duo,* or he who has the right to the papacy should nevertheless resign to remove so great a scandal, according to God's will; and since it is not known which one that is, both are obliged to resign lest they seem to seek worldly pomp more than eternal glory. But they refuse. Whom to obey, them or God? Undoubtedly God.

(3) The argument that princes must be obeyed no matter what, is answered by Jerome citing Ephesians (11. q. 3, c. 93): Obey God rather than men. But God has ordained that there be only one pope, and when two are elected neither should remain, and that a true pastor is bound to resign if his people are evilly disposed to him and to end a grave scandal. These are indeed God's commands, promulgated through princes for the good of the church's governance: *Codex,* 7. 39. 9; 25. q. 1, c. 5. (4) As for the fourth reason—always obey in cases of doubt—there is nothing in human affairs so indubitable that doubt cannot be cast on it (Novella 44), and therefore the sacred canons and laws teach that in a dubious matter, the counsel of leading men should be taken, and what the majority decrees should be held without doubt (20. di., c. 3; 19. di., c. 6; *Digest,* 50. 1. 19). It follows that after the kings have assembled solemn councils in their realms and found the majority view to be that

the two contenders are obliged to accept the way of cession as the most beneficial and best, and that it is expedient to subtract obedience in order to obtain this, they ought to execute this decision without any doubt. . . .

(5) What is said about the University of Oxford's letter does not avail either. Mere cession, to be sure, would not be enough to end the schism, as they say (in response to the University of Paris's letter, which did not discuss how to put cession into practice); but when practiced in the manner advised by the prelates of France, it will end the schism better than any other. This is how the way of cession may be put into practice: Let both contenders meet in a central and safe place, say Genoa, and there, meeting together with their cardinals, let them both revoke the legal actions they have instituted against each other and their adherents, and let them absolve each other. Then let them confirm the collations of benefices and promotions made on both sides; and when there happen to be two bishops named for one church, he who possesses the city will remain as bishop, the other receiving a share of the revenues proportionate to how much he actually holds—this will keep him until a future pope provides for him otherwise. And if he holds nothing in the episcopate, then he will get nothing but, rather, wait for a future pope to provide. And the same in other benefices. As for the cardinals, there are fifty-one cardinal titles, according to the chronicle of Martinus Polonus, and there are not that many cardinals in both colleges; if there are two ordained to the same title, let the first to have been ordained to it remain in it, and let the other be assigned another title. In this way, the consciences of all Christians will be put at peace, for there is no doubt that the pope can resign the papacy or that the cardinals after the resignation can elect a new pope. I do not think the Oxford masters had heard of this plan when they wrote that letter. In any case, they confess in their own letter that a true pastor who sees that this scandal cannot be well settled otherwise should resign rather than stay in this scandal. And the king of England has decided to pursue church union by the way of cession, moved I think chiefly by this argument.

(6) Nor is the argument valid that one should not have recourse to an extraordinary remedy when an ordinary one applies. Even supposing that a general council ought to decide which of those two elections was canonical, this hardly seems possible. We would not assemble at Boniface's will; nor the others at Benedict's; thus it would not be a council but a conventicle (17. di., cc. 1, 4, 5). Or if both agree that a council be summoned, who will preside? Not both, for then there would be two heads; and there would never be agreement on one of them. Also, we would never attend at the will of the emperor—or rather the king of the Romans—for he has made himself a party to the dispute; history shows

that when emperors convoked councils to settle schisms, they had not taken sides for one party so officially as now. In any case, the Empire today is fragmented and our kings regard themselves as emperors in their own realms, nor do they recognize a superior or defer to the king of the Romans, lest they diminish their own dignity in any point. If it be said that the cardinals will summon the council, I ask, which cardinals? Ours, or the others? We would not attend at their call; nor the other side at ours. We say that they—and indeed all the prelates created by Urban and Boniface—are excommunicated, and they say the same of us. And if it be said that the kings will all ordain that the prelates congregate in one place, this would not be easy because of the disturbances today in Christendom, and how could there ever be agreement as to the place of meeting?

It is also impossible to see how such a council would proceed. Would not those favoring one side over the other be excluded from judgement? This would be the case certainly with all of us adhering to Benedict, especially the prelates promoted by him and his predecessor, and the doctors and masters who have gotten fat benefices from them; for we have a great stake in his legitimacy or illegitimacy. For example, if a general council should decide for Boniface, then certainly all the ordinations made by Benedict would be legally null; and vice versa; and even if a future pontiff would confirm all of them, the stain of infamy would remain. In general, what would be the point of assembling the two parties of kings, princes, and prelates for the purpose of giving judgement, after both sides, having heard all the contrary arguments at the beginning, have remained fixed in their opinions for almost nineteen years? It is no use saying that the majority would prevail, for in that case the matter is already decided—Boniface has the greater number of prelates (especially if you count the Italian *episcopelli*)—and what we regard as the just cause would lose. We would argue, moreover, that while our side is numerically in the minority, it is nevertheless the sounder one and therefore the greater one (40. di., c. 12, *gl. ord.*; X. 2. 20. 32, with Bohic's commentary). Nor is it valid to say that God would not permit a council to err; for while this is true in matters of faith, it is not a matter of faith to say that this man is pope and that one is not; in such things the church militant can be deceived (X. 5. 39. 28). This is particularly true about matters of fact, on which the arguments of both sides about the election of Urban turn. . . . And the same would apply to judgement by, say, a panel composed of one worthy man from each diocese: if they were drawn equally from both obediences, they would never reach a decision; and if they were unequal in number, neither side would agree that the other have the greater number.

It is not good, furthermore, to adopt a way that would not wholly eradicate the schism and settle the scandal. Now what would happen if a general council decided for Benedict? Either it would decree that all Boniface's ordinations are void (as always done in previous cases when a schism was settled by a discussion of rights)—and that would be a still greater scandal than the present one: I confess for my part that if such a sentence were to go against Benedict, I would resist it with all my power for this reason. Or the general council would decree that all ordinations were to be confirmed—but that would still be scandalous, for the losing side would incur indelible infamy, and its laity (ever hostile to the clergy) would say that their prelates had not in fact been prelates and had been deceiving them all these years. . . .

If it be said, let us adopt the way of arbitration offered by Benedict, that certainly would be no good. Only election by the cardinals can give a right to the papacy; the decision of arbiters would not give such a right to the one who did not already have it; such a decision does not give a new right but only declares an old one. Thus Innocent IV has said that arbitration cannot confer canonical institution in a benefice nor transfer one man's right to another (commentary on X. 3. 5. 21). And there would have to be an uneven number of arbiters, to reach a decision, and neither side would agree to have the lesser number. The same difficulties which we have seen attending a general council would also exist in case of arbitration.

As for the way of force [via facti], there is not much to say, for it seems entirely evil. Christ did not want his vicariate to be fought over by violence, burning, and killing (Matt. 20:25–26). Furthermore, as Augustine says (23. q. 1, c. 3), the purpose of waging war is to secure peace; but if we wage war on Boniface, those who obey him will probably wage war on us, and Christendom would be more embroiled than now.

It is thus clear that we are within the terms of Nisi cum pridem when we say that both contenders are required to resign to settle this scandal, for otherwise it cannot be settled.

(7) As for the argument that Benedict has virtually offered the way of cession by saying that if he could only meet with his adversary, he would make peace in the church even should he himself have to remain a poor priest without a benefice—would that he had said this to the king's uncles and brother when they came to him {scil., May–June 1395} and that he had issued a bull to that effect! But his true thoughts were shown more clearly when he offered the way of arbitration and repudiated the way of cession as non-juridical and as refuted by previous popes in similar cases. He also said at the end of one bull that should peace in the church not come from a meeting by way of arbitration, he would then provide other, juridical ways. Put all these together, and it

is clear that he is unwilling to accept the way of cession but wants only
to get by with general phrases and keep for the rest of his life that part
of the papacy which he possesses.

(8) It is not valid to argue that kings should not order obedience
subtracted because it might go against the consciences of inhabitants of
their realms, who would therefore not obey. It in fact pertains to the
kings in this great tribulation of the church to bring both contenders to
the way of peace, and it has been proven above that they can and ought
to coerce those refusing to accept it and make them do so. . . . They
have this power from God. Hence kings do not have to consider the
consciences of individuals, only that they themselves proceed with an
upright intention to the goal of peace; and their subjects have to obey
them in this—should they suffer pangs of conscience in so doing, let
them put their conscience aside or bring it into captivity and obey the
kings—according to 2 Corinthians 10:5, "bringing into captivity every
thought to the obedience of Christ." If they still want to follow their
erroneous conscience, the kings will compel them to obey nonetheless
(X. 5. 39. 44, 2. 13. 13; with glosses).

(9) The ninth argument is invalid because while papal and episcopal
elections must by their nature and by the law be free, the law also
provides that the cardinals are to be compelled to elect by depriving
them of food and shutting them up in conclave. Thus it is also the law
that a prelate can be forced to resign because of dissension between him
and his subjects, or a grave scandal—in *Nisi cum pridem,* with Innocent
IV's dictum, "that the public utility must take precedence over the
private." And I understand this in the present case to mean that the kings
can and must compel both contenders to resign, as proven above. . . .
Thus, while an election made under intimidation or compulsion is invalid, the abdication of these contenders under compulsion by royal
power will be just and canonical. . . .

(10) As for nobody being able to judge the pope, this is so unless he
does something which notoriously scandalizes the church and offends
God—in which case the heavenly pope is to be recognized and God
obeyed. Some indeed say that the laws which speak of obedience to the
pope always mean that the apostolic see is to be obeyed, and the Roman
church, that is, that the pope is to be obeyed when he guides himself by
the counsel of the cardinals in difficult matters (see Johannes Monachus
on *Sext,* 5. 2. 4). . . . Also, I have heard some theologians say openly
that canons like 9. q. 3, c. 13—"No one may judge the papal see"—
were made by the popes in their own cause [and that no great faith need
be put in them]. But a pope may in any case be judged for heresy, or
when he scandalizes the church, or causes subversion and peril of souls.
Or perhaps one might argue that no one may judge an undoubted pope

holding his see in peace; but when there are two contenders who refuse to resign, then if no one judged them, we would remain in schism forever. In such a case they are already judged by their predecessors, and it remains only to execute the judgement on them, which function pertains to the kings.

(11) The eleventh argument is taken care of by our arguments above. (12) The argument about obeying the pope rather than the kings does not apply in this case, when the kings are God's ministers in doing what is licit and expedient for the peace and union of the church; and who obeys them obeys God. (13) The same answer holds for this argument; (14) and as for the next, it is taken care of by what is said above, also by the fact that the kings can canonically command that obedience be withdrawn.

Reply to "It Is not Fitting"

(1b) Although the kings or their fathers did indeed obey Clement and Benedict, or Urban and Boniface, now that they see how long the schism has lasted and how the contenders are not trying to end it, they can fittingly subtract obedience. (2) Nor do they have to worry about people saying evil things about them if they act sincerely for peace; and if one has deferred correction until a more opportune time, that is a counsel of charity, not a case of greed. (3) As for the third argument, kings should guide themselves by laws rather than examples, for there has never been a schism like this one, nor in previous times did the popes use to grant prelacies as they do now. Now indeed almost all the prelates of both obediences have been created by the contenders and thus form a party for them, so that the schism is more deeply rooted than others have ever been. And while we do indeed read that sometimes when the church was in schism the ones obeyed by the king of France prevailed, I do not know that this has always been so, nor do I believe it has been.

Reply to "It Is not Expedient"

(1) The argument that the pope will excommunicate the king does not hold, because the kings subtracting obedience for the sake of peace and union do not have to fear him. And Johannes Teutonicus says in his gloss on 24. q. 1, c. 6, one whom the pope excommunicates without just cause is not excommunicated as far as God is concerned. And the Archdeacon notes on 2. q. 7, c. 45, that accusers are absolved from the judgement of the accused, for he is hostile. (2) As for cases reserved to the pope, they can be handled by the bishops, who can absolve in such

cases when necessity requires (X. 3. 46. 2; § *Sed* after 1. q. 1, c. 39). Or the grand penitentiary can exercise his office until we have a single uncontested pope, for his power continues even during a vacancy (*Clem.,* 1. 3. 2). And in major cases, the archbishops and provincial councils can provide. Or if there is some great peril, the cardinals can provide, for they have canonical power to do so (*Sext,* 1. 6. 3). As for providing to bishoprics and other major dignities, let the old laws be followed. Also, the papal camerary will administer what pertains to the Camera, as he can do in a vacancy (*Clem.,* 1. 3. 2). (3, 4) The third and fourth arguments, that if obedience be subtracted, the laity will take over church property and that bishops and other prelates created by the popes will also not be obeyed by an extension of the same principle: these arguments are also invalid. For there are regions of Christendom, for example, Hainault, which have not obeyed either contender for nineteen years or almost, and although I think they should have obeyed ours, nevertheless they live in greater freedom than those obeying one or the other; and while they do not obey either contender, they do obey their own bishops. Furthermore, the reason for requiring the pope to resign, to end scandal, does not apply to the bishops, each of whom is true and uncontested in his bishopric.

(5) The argument that subtraction will deprive many worthy men of their expectative graces, etc., is also invalid, since many are already so deprived even without a subtraction of obedience—for example, the University of Paris has refrained from submitting a benefice roll in order to avoid any occasion of tepidity in pursuit of union on the part of its members. If indeed obedience should be subtracted, then it would be expedient for the prelates, with the king's support, to devise a sound system of conferring benefices so that the worthiest clerics would have priority and others accordingly. Since with God's favor we will soon have a single true and undoubted pastor, and since for the public good someone may sometimes be deprived of his own property (*Digest,* 6. 1. 15; 21. 2. 11), how much more may someone be deprived for this reason of a right that he has *to* the property [i.e., a claim], not even *in* it [i.e., a title of ownership], as is the case with expectancies. (6) The argument about innumerable difficulties does not hold, since there would be far greater ones if the church remained torn apart. (7) As for subtraction not bringing union, it has been shown above that if subtraction does not bring the contenders to correct themselves, other measures will have to be taken. (8) It has no force to say that it is inexpedient to treat the true pope and the intruder equally; for many say that if St. Peter were living today and there was a division like this one in the church which could be resolved by his abdication, he ought to be forced to abdicate by subtraction of obedience and otherwise, as set forth above.

Simon's Properties and Expenditures

A PROVISIONAL list based on records of litigation, ecclesiastical endowments, and Simon's testament; estimates of expenditure are either given as stated in the sources or based on the assumption that a *rente* represented 10 percent of the capital value. T = Simon's testament, AN, X 1A 8604, fols. 91(bis)r–92r; items so marked were regarded by Simon as his own, even if held by his brother Pierre or his nephew Jean.

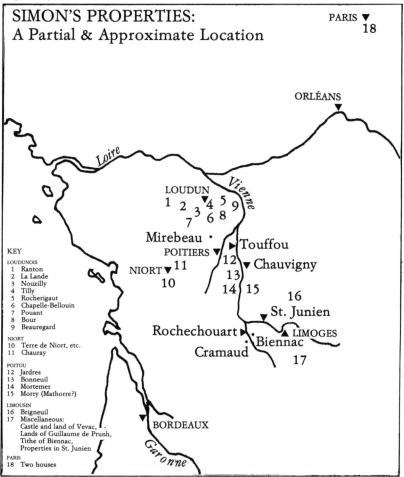

SIMON'S PROPERTIES:
A Partial & Approximate Location

PARIS ▼
18

ORLÉANS ▼

Loire

LOUDUN ▼
1 2 ▼4 5 9
3 6 8
7

Vienne

Mirebeau •
POITIERS ▼   ▶Touffou

KEY

LOUDUNOIS
1 Ranton
2 La Lande
3 Nouzilly
4 Tilly
5 Rocherigaut
6 Chapelle-Bellouin
7 Pouant
8 Bour
9 Beauregard

NIORT
10 Terre de Niort, etc.
11 Chauray

POITOU
12 Jardres
13 Bonneuil
14 Mortemer
15 Morry (Mathorre?)

LIMOUSIN
16 Brigneuil
17 Miscellaneous:
     Castle and land of Vevac,
     Lands of Guillaume de Prunh,
     Tithe of Biennac,
     Properties in St. Junien

PARIS
18 Two houses

NIORT ▼ 11
10

12 ▼ Chauvigny
13
14 15
            16
   ▼ St. Junien

Rochechouart ▶ • ▲ LIMOGES
            • Biennac
Cramaud   17

▼ BORDEAUX

Garonne

Properties

	Property	Acquired	Source
1	Touffou Castle	1385–1387	T; see text
2	Terre de Niort	1386	T; AN, X 1C 53, no. 21; AN, JJ 132, no. 56, fols. 33v–34r
3	Paris house, rue Poupée	1388	T; AN, X 1A 1475, fol. 234r; X 1A 38, fol. 233v; etc.
4	Jardres	ca. 1389	T; ADV, G 207 (a dependency of Touffou)
5	Morry village: lands	1392	T (? Mathorre); AN, X 1C 70B, no. 226
6	Rocherigaut Castle	1394	T; AN, JJ 147, no. 10, fols. 4v–5r
7	Ranton lordship	1394	T; AN, JJ 147, no. 10, fols. 4v–5r
8	Nouzilly lordship	1397	BN, *ms. lat.* 18,377, p. 189 f.
9	Brigneuil (one-third)	1398	AN, X 1A 50, fols. 169r–171v
10	A grain-*rente*, 12 *mine*	1409/1413	BN, *ms. lat.* 18,378, pp. 570–580
11	Bour: house and lands	?	AN, X 1A 51, fol. 122v
12	Properties in St. Junien	?	BN, *Dossiers bleus*, 221, no. 5649

Properties

	Property	Acquired	Source
13	Chapelle-Bellouin Castle	by 1389?	T; AN, X 1A 9198, fols. 179rv, etc.
14	La Lande	?	T; AN, X 1A 9198, fols. 184v sq.
15	*Rente* of 6 livres, Angle	?	BN, *ms. lat.* 18,377, pp. 195–198
16	Beau Regart ("locus")	?	T; AN, X 1A 9198, fols. 184v sq.
17	Claunay (Chauray?)	?	T; AN, X 1A 9198, fols. 184v sq.
18	Tilly	?	T; AN, JJ 158, no. 334, fol. 182v; AN, X 1A 9198, fol. 184v sq.
19	Tithes near Loudun	?	Besly, *Evesques de Poictiers*: 200–202
20	Pouant ("terra")	?	Ibid.
21.	Half tithes, Marigny	?	Ibid.; AN, JJ 158, no. 103, fol. 58v
22	Tithes, Biennac	?	T
23	Mortemer ("terra")	?	T
24	Bonneuil ("terra")	?	T
25	Vevac Castle	?	T
26	Lands of Guillaume Prunh	?	T

Items 1, 4, 5, 23, 24 were located in the region around Poitiers and Chauvigny; items 6, 7, 8, 11, 13, 14, 16, 18, 19, 20 were in Loudunois; item 17 was near Niort; items 9, 12, 22, 25, 26 were in Limousin.

Expenditures

Touffou	ca. 5,000	livres tournois (costs of Jean's marriage; purchase of *rentes*; costs of restoration and redemption)
Terre de Niort	1,300	livres tournois (or francs)
Paris house	4,500	
Rocherigaut and Ranton	450	
Nouzilly	700	
Brigneuil (one-third)	1,500	
Chapelle-Bellouin	1,200	
rente, Angle	60	
Jardres	300	
tithes, Biennac	400	
	15,410	

This figure of over 15,000 livres represents only a minimal order of magnitude for Simon's expenditures in the period of about fifteen years from 1385 to 1400. Much more must have been spent in the same period on properties I have not been able to date or evaluate, as well as properties not attested in the sources covered here. After about 1400 Simon spent thousands more on properties, chantries and other endowments, his tomb, and his testamentary dispositions. While some of his income would have come from the revenues of his properties, the huge sums attested above can only have been derived from his royal and ducal salaries, his episcopal revenues, and of course gifts.

THE CRAMAUD FAMILY

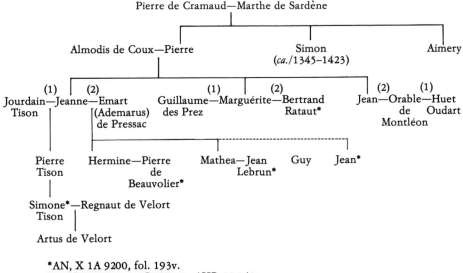

Pierre de Cramaud—Marthe de Sardène

Almodis de Coux—Pierre   Simon (*ca.*/1345–1423)   Aimery

(1) Jourdain—Jeanne—Emart Tison (Ademarus) de Pressac   (2)

(1) Guillaume—Marguérite—Bertrand des Prez Rataut*   (2)

(2) Jean—Orable—Huet de Oudart Montléon   (1)

Pierre Tison   Hermine—Pierre de Beauvolier*   Mathea—Jean Lebrun*   Guy   Jean*

Simone*—Regnaut de Velort Tison

Artus de Velort

*AN, X 1A 9200, fol. 193v.

For Marguérite see Guérin in *AHP,* 21:342.

For Jeanne ibid.; for Emart de Pressac, see AN, X 1A 8604, fol. 91(bis)v, and BN, *Pièces orig.* 925, nos. 20, 431.

For Mathea, see AN, X 1A 9190, fols. 173r–174r.

Dotted lines represent my conjectures, see AN, X 1A 56, fol. 53r, for Emart de Pressac as the son of a Guy—our Guy may be the grandfather's namesake.

Simone Tison evidently passed on the Cramaud titles; in 1471 she appeared as patroness of Simon's chapel in Biennac, and in 1483 Artus de Velort appeared as "lord of Chapelle-Bellouin and Cramaud." See A. Lecler, *Dictionnaire historique et géographique de la Haute-Vienne* (Limoges, 1926): 87 f.

Index